DARLINGHISSIMA

Hôtel Ritz
15, Place Vendôme
ADRESSE TELEGRAPHIQUE
RITZOTEL-PARIS-81
TELEPH.: 073 28-30
TELEX: 22262
RITZ PARIS
Monday August 28 - Paris 73
My darling One and only: what a Marathon you have run with the
Monday Night
Telephone:
HYDE PARK 0111
(10 Lines)
Darling kissima
Saturday

JANET FLANNER

Darlinghissima

LETTERS TO A FRIEND

EDITED AND WITH COMMENTARY BY

NATALIA DANESI MURRAY

A Harvest/HBJ Book

HARCOURT BRACE JOVANOVICH, PUBLISHERS

San Diego   New York   London

Requests for permission to make copies of any part of the work should be mailed to: Random House, Inc., 201 East 50th Street, New York, NY 10022.

Grateful acknowledgment is made for permission to reproduce the following photographs: No. 11, David Scherman, *Life* magazine © Time Inc.; no. 12, Tony Vaccaro; no. 13, Horst; no. 23, John Deakin; no. 34, Hugh Ford; nos. 39 and 40, Inge Morath. Arnold Weissberger's part-title photograph for the 1970s section is reproduced courtesy of Milton Goldman. Flanner family pictures are reproduced courtesy of Hildegard Flanner Monhoff. All other photographs, with the exception of those noted on the captions themselves, are from Flanner-Murray private albums.

Library of Congress Cataloging-in-Publication Data
Flanner, Janet, 1892-
    Darlinghissima : letters to a friend.
    "A Harvest/HBJ book."
    Includes index.
    1. Flanner, Janet, 1892-   —Correspondence.
2. Murray, Natalia Danesi. 3. Authors, American—
20th century—Correspondence. 4. Americans—France—
Paris. 5. Paris (France)—Intellectual life—20th
century. I. Murray, Natalia Danesi. II. Title.
PS3511.L285Z49   1986   814'.52 [B]   86-14813
ISBN 0-15-623937-X (pbk.)

Typography by J. K. Lambert

Printed in the United States of America

First Harvest/HBJ edition 1986

A B C D E F G H I J

EDITOR'S NOTE

In selecting and editing these letters of Janet Flanner, I have omitted some entirely and left out certain passages in others that would be of little interest to the general public. Her highly individual style—especially her punctuation, or lack of it—has, for the most part, been retained; her misspellings have, however, been corrected. I have also, in choosing these letters, kept in mind their unique value as personal testimony. Janet seldom dated her correspondence. The dates of almost all the letters are the ones on which they were mailed.

N. D. M.

ACKNOWLEDGMENTS

I would like to express my special thanks to Hildegarde Flanner Monhoff for her recollections of Janet's early years and for family photographs; to my agent, Helen Brann, whose collaboration in the selection of the letters encouraged me in the task; to my editor, Jonathan Galassi, for his appreciation and sensitive work; and above all to my son, Bill, without whose enthusiasm, support and invaluable editing this book could never have been completed.

I would also like to thank my two sisters, Lea and Franca, who helped me remember their World War II ordeals; my faithful housekeeper and friend, Maria Maver, for having stood by me; and the great photographers who have contributed their pictures to this book.

N. D. M.

CONTENTS

INTRODUCTION

Janet Flanner, under the pen name of Genêt, wrote her fortnightly "Letter from Paris" for *The New Yorker* magazine. Her first
"Letter" was published in October 1925, a few months after the
magazine was founded. The doyenne of the foreign press corps in
France and the most celebrated American in Paris, she has been read,
enjoyed and admired over all these years by countless readers, including the best and most famous writers of our time. "As a social historian,
there isn't anybody like Janet Flanner," wrote William Shawn, the
present editor of *The New Yorker*. "No one else over the decades has
consistently combined that kind of literary fire and dazzling style with
just good, solid, dependable reporting." Her "dazzling" style led one
critic to call her, with Edmund Wilson, "the supreme commander of
the English sentence in her time." Another remarked that "With her
superb gift of reporting, she emerges as one of the finest cultural
historians of our epoch."

"Often this old friend, in and out of her burrow, does seem an
owl-goddess, possessing preternatural wisdom, which in fact is sea-
soned common sense, the bird-lore of our species. She is also given
to prophecy . . ." wrote Mary McCarthy. "Her great quality is her
immediacy and candor of impression—a greatness that journalism is

inherently capable of . . . Thank heaven for such gratifications of the senses, external realities illuminated by pantheism, and for the peculiar excellence of Miss Flanner's prose . . . She excels in miniature portraiture, of a kind uniquely literary . . ." wrote Glenway Westcott.

Janet Flanner had wanted to be a writer ever since she was a girl of five in Indianapolis, where she was born in 1892. Writing was her passion, her devotion, her constant work. After a brief career on the Indianapolis *Star* as the first movie critic ever, in the early twenties she left America to go live in Paris, with the intention of becoming "another Edith Wharton on the spot," and joined the Left Bank American literary colony, where any one of its members (which included Hemingway, Pound, Dos Passos, MacLeish, e.e. cummings, Gertrude Stein, Kay Boyle, Hart Crane, Djuna Barnes and the Scott Fitzgeralds) could be found at Les Deux Magots, each, as she wrote in *Paris Was Yesterday*, "aspiring to become a famous writer as soon as possible."

It was shortly after, in 1925, that she began her own rise to fame under the pen name of Genêt. Her letters about Paris life to Jane Grant, wife of the *New Yorker* editor Harold Ross, attracted his admiration, and he asked her to write for the magazine under that name—perhaps his idea of "Janet" in French. Her assignment from *The New Yorker* was to report merely "what the French thought was going on in France," but she slowly added her own insight and taut analysis to what she saw, heard and read, giving birth to that special brand of essay-reporting that made her famous. Her gifts were not only confined to reporting events in the cultural, artistic and political fields; she also wrote marvelously about people. Her profiles of the personalities of her times form an enduring portrait gallery.

Except for the war period, when she returned to the United States, Janet Flanner lived in France for fifty years. "The idea that I've become French would be ludicrous and impertinent," she answered an interviewer. "I don't believe one shifts one's breed easily. The first twenty years of one's life stamp one, don't you think so?" "I write about what catches my eye, what catches my sense of what is true, important and dramatic," she said, in describing her work.

She had a great mop of bobbed silver hair, piercing brown eyes, a noble aquiline nose and a sensitive mouth that illuminated her face when she talked or smiled. She was always smartly dressed in Chanel or Molyneux tailored clothes or in a Saint Laurent black pants suit, with elegant French shoes—her particular pleasure—on her tiny feet, and the bright scarfs of which she was very fond. She smoked and read incessantly.

In later years she was not too enthusiastic about our times. "The lines have coarsened. The refinement of morality has been greatly lost. We are living in a society as corrupt as it is opulent. People are rich and dishonest."

She wrote her last "Letter from Paris" in September 1975.

Janet Flanner is the author of *The Cubical City*, a novel, published in 1926; *An American in Paris*, profile of an interlude between two wars, drawn mainly from her *New Yorker* writings, published in 1940; *Pétain: The Old Man of France*, published in 1944; a book of art monographs, *Men and Monuments* (1957); *Paris Journal: 1944–1965*, which won the 1965 National Book Award; *Paris Journal: 1965–1971* (1971); *Paris Was Yesterday: 1925–1939*, which drew on her *New Yorker* reportage from before the period of her *Journals* (1972); *London Was Yesterday: 1934–1939*, a selected collection of her London Letters which she alternated with her biweekly Paris Letters for a number of years (1975); and *Janet Flanner's World: Uncollected Writings, 1932–1975*, a selection of articles from other parts of the world (1979).

She has also translated books from the French, including Georgette Leblanc's *My Life with Maeterlinck* and two by Colette. A member of the National Institute of Arts and Letters, she received honorary degrees from Smith College and from Indiana University. In 1971 she received an honorary mention from the Department of Journalism of New York University and the Theta Sigma Phi in 1975, the arts award from the Indiana Arts Commission; in 1978 she received the Professional Achievement Award from the University of Chicago.

She has been decorated with the Legion of Honor and later promoted to the Order of the Legion of Honor.

In her last years she made her home in New York, where she died on November 7, 1978, at the age of eighty-six.

Janet entered my life unexpectedly on a lively New York afternoon in early January 1940, and there she remained until her death at dawn on that sad November day.

Our friendship—a passionate friendship—was nourished and flourished with World War II as its background. It was framed by two continents, North America and Europe, and took place against a panorama of events centered in the capital cities of Paris, Rome and New York.

Janet arrived at my house that day in January 1940 escorted by John Mosher, the *New Yorker* movie critic. The occasion was a cocktail party for my friends Tom Farrar (a well-known stage designer) and his wife, Beatrice, to celebrate their return to New York. Janet was returning too, in the wake of the Nazi invasion of France. I did not realize that this elegant friend of John's was the famous Genêt of the Paris Letters in *The New Yorker.*

What attracted us to each other? What special gifts, what blend of feelings, thoughts, beliefs, understanding did we give to each other? What longings? What needs of the heart and of the mind did we answer in each other?

In 1940, Janet was forty-eight years old; I was thirty-eight. She was an American who, in the twenties, had left her birthplace to live in France. At about the same time I had left Rome, where I was born, to come to America.

She had divorced her husband and made a life for herself in Paris. I had acquired one and made my life in New York, though by the time Janet and I met, Bill and I had gone our separate ways.

It was the combination of these elements—the Europeanized American and the Americanized European—that sparked our long and unique friendship.

In France, Janet found the tradition of beauty, art and culture she had so longed for during her Indiana days. I found in America a new climate of freedom, a new world with eyes turned toward the future, with every possibility open to a young woman who had seen the rise of fascism in her own land and hated it.

Janet became a writer and a famous journalist, interpreting European people and events to American readers. I was interpreting the American way of life, its spirit and freedom, by broadcasting daily to my people under fascism. Later I helped to establish a cultural bridge as the head of the first New York office of the publisher Arnoldo Mondadori of Milan, whom I represented for seventeen years. I then became the vice-president of Rizzoli Editore Corporation in New York, a position I held for eleven more years.

When we met we were two independent working women, passionately involved in the political and historical events of the day, as well as in the events of our private lives.

Janet's family was Quaker. Mine was Catholic, by tradition.

Neither of us was religious in an orthodox way, but we each retained certain basic characteristics of the religions we were brought
up in.

Janet had two sisters; so did I. But she had cut the umbilical cord
at an early stage in her life, while I had not. Only her youngest
sister, Hildegarde, married and had a son. Maria, the eldest, a pianist,
never married. My sisters and I all married and divorced. There were
four children among us, and an array of cousins and other relatives. We sisters had always been very close, though we lived far apart
at various periods of our lives, and in all areas of the world, because
our husbands were foreigners: one American, one Hungarian, one
Swiss.

This fact was partly the result of the education we had received
from our mother, Ester Traversari Danesi, a feminist and a journalist,
the first Italian female correspondent at the Italian front during World
War I and for years the editor in chief of *La Donna*, a leading literary
and fashion magazine. Our upbringing was modern, co-educational
and independent in the midst of a traditional, antique and Catholic
world. We adored our mother, who was widowed at thirty-five, and
so did Janet, who came to know her well when Mammina Ester, as
she was called, too anti-Fascist to survive in Rome as a journalist or
in any other activity during Mussolini's reign, joined me in New
York. Janet practically adopted my family, became very fond of my
son, Bill, today a writer and contributor to *The New Yorker*, and
she participated in our ups and downs with her own special intensity.
For one who had always lived in hotels, never wanted to own anything and hated domesticity, whose culinary expertise was confined
to knowing how to boil an egg, or what spices to use in whatever was
cooking, she took to my home and family like a duck to water.

I loved my home; I always had one. I had never wanted to escape
from my family, as Janet did. All she was really interested in, and
passionately so, was writing.

When Janet, the star reporter of *The New Yorker*, returned to
America in 1940, the war was not going well for the Allies, though
the Americans, of course, had not yet entered it. Hitler's armies were
running over Europe, England was under a shower of bombs, Rommel
was conquering North Africa, and very soon France would be invaded
and fall. Janet *had* to leave France. I was then broadcasting shortwave
to Italy from NBC, as I had been for two years.

I had not seen Janet after that cocktail party, but in June John

Mosher invited me to dine over the Fourth of July weekend at his house on Fire Island, where we both had summer homes.

Janet Flanner was to be his guest, he said. So we met again. We all went dancing at Duffy's dilapidated hotel, we toasted the end of dictators, we drank a lot and hailed our holiday. Something struck us, a *coup de foudre*. Janet and I knew that night that we were to become great friends.

Later, at the end of the summer, Janet, who had been staying at an inn up the Hudson, moved to New York and sublet the small independent suite in my house which had been freed with the departure of the Farrars. In those years, from 1940 to 1944, we shared our lives, our hopes and the war drama. We worked very hard and found comfort in each other, but we both wanted to get to Europe as soon as possible. Finally, in 1944, the war turned in our favor and we were permitted to go. In May 1944, I was given the rank of captain in Special Services in the Psychological Warfare Branch of the OWI (Office of War Information), and ordered to join the Army at a staging area in Delaware, where I remained incommunicado until my departure in a convoy carrying infantry and paratroopers for the invasion of the south of France and Arnhem. I first landed in North Africa. At the fall of Monte Cassino, I flew to Naples and arrived in Rome at the end of June, on the heels of the Fifth Liberation Army.

Janet received her accreditation as war correspondent shortly afterward; wearing a smart Army uniform, she left in September for London and, finally, Paris.

It is from this date that Janet's "other letters" began. They continued throughout our lives, during the long separations made necessary by our work. Janet often wrote me after she had finished her Paris Letters, or a Profile for *The New Yorker*. She discussed art shows, plays, books, people and, often, our families. Her observations and comments, even gossip, are for the most part more personal, more emotional, more natural and easy—sometimes violent, but never nasty or petty—than what she wrote for the magazine. The intimate Janet was witty, loving, caring and generous, a profound observer of life. Her letters also show how she worked and labored over her copy.

In rereading them, as I started putting my papers in order, I realized how unique our relationship was, worth sharing with the world not only for the value of the letters per se, but also as a demonstration of how two women surmounted obstacles, trying to lead their personal and professional lives with dignity and feeling. I hope that my grandchildren, and other young men and women like them, born in a freer, more liberated society, more knowledgeable about relationships between the sexes and without the inhibitions or taboos of an earlier era, will understand and value our experience and efforts to be, above all, decent human beings. That is the intention of this book. The letters speak for themselves.

NATALIA DANESI MURRAY

The Forties

1944

Janet's first letter was a photocopy made from a V-mail microfilm, reduced to a minuscule four-by-five inches, as was the practice of the day. It reached me at a military camp in Delaware, where I was to join the Army as a captain in Special Services attached to a press unit. From this staging area I would be shipped in a military convoy to Europe in utter secrecy.

It was the day I had been waiting for; Janet and I had applied to serve overseas as soon as women civilians were to be allowed into a theater of war. Janet would return to Paris as correspondent of *The New Yorker*, I would serve in whatever way my experience as a broadcaster could be of use.

Ever since 1938, when Hitler marched into Austria and annexed one-third of Czechoslovakia, NBC had had the foresight to start shortwave news programs beamed to Europe. When the United States entered the war, NBC became coordinated into the Office of War Information. By then we had attracted a large audience. But in 1938, alone in a small NBC studio in the RCA building in New York, I had faced a microphone without having the faintest idea whether anyone would be listening. Mine was a lonely Voice of America to Italy. By chance, radio hams on their sensitive shortwave radios would intercept my programs and hear an Italian voice announcing, *"Questa*

è la NBC che vi parla dalla Radio Città di Nuova York," followed by
the famous three-note chimes. They would spread the news around.
We eventually became well known to a large audience, and Roberto
Farinacci, secretary of the Italian Fascist Party, called me "the voice
of Italo-American anti-Fascism."

In those early war days, Janet would wait anxiously for the latest
news from my nightly broadcasts. Often the phone would ring. For
some mysterious reason our shortwave band beamed to Italy would
bounce back to the United States, having circled the world, and Maestro Arturo Toscanini would be on the line from his Riverdale home
on the Hudson. "Natalia, is it true what you just said on the air? Are
the Americans really getting ready?" he would ask. The insomniac
maestro was just as anxious as we were about the news; he was one of
my first radio fans. Every Sunday afternoon I broadcast his NBC
Symphony concerts to Italy.

What an excitement it was when my call came on that May day
of 1944! Though I was to leave before Janet, we tried to make plans.
How could we communicate? How could we meet? How would I
know when she would arrive in France? On the day of my departure,
Janet accompanied me to Washington. We both tried not to show our
emotions. In fact, we were very cool, very restrained. But once on the
train that was to take me to Delaware, reality struck in full force. I
became tense and, yes, frightened.

When I arrived in that vast military camp, I felt lost. I found myself
part of a huge anonymous mass of uniforms, awaiting instructions.
You could hardly talk to anyone. At the first inspection, a WAC
captain pointed at me. "Take them off," she ordered. "This is the
Army, not a ball." I had forgotten to remove my pearl earrings.

It was not easy to adjust to military life, to do everything in
unison, sleep with a dozen other people on hard camp beds under
the same tent, fall into line for toilets, showers, food. My companions
were mostly WACs and nurses, along with a group of second-rate
USO entertainers. But luckily there was also Elma Baccanelli, a
young woman who had been loaned to me by the OWI when I
arranged the weekly broadcasts by Mayor Fiorello La Guardia of
New York to Italy from NBC. As I was used to receiving the news
daily by teletype and to broadcasting twice a day, working under
pressure in which every minute, every second counted, it was doubly
difficult to stand the waiting.

Soldiers were arriving daily from all parts of the country, highly trained for dangerous missions and ready for action. They had to be worked to the point of exhaustion to keep them out of trouble. They were handsome boys, barely eighteen, who later were to be dropped over Arnhem in the Netherlands to help the British Second Army across the Rhine. How many would be returning? I thought of my son, Bill. He, too, would be called soon. When would I see him again? Would my mother, who was substituting for me at NBC, be able to see her other two daughters? We had heard only twice in two years, through the Vatican, that they were alive. And Janet—when would she and I be able to meet? Would we ever get back to the duplex we called our "chicken-coop," on top of the building on Fifty-eighth Street and Madison Avenue, to have breakfast in our roof garden, served by our faithful Harold? Would we ever see again the eccentric Mr. Sylvester we had inherited from our friend, the artist Pavlic Tchelitchew? Sylvester would suddenly appear up our fire escape with slips and flowers salvaged from the Brooklyn Botanic Garden, where he worked. The little maple tree he had planted with such care, and the long-necked sunflowers, Janet's favorites—would they still be there, swaying in the wind to the astonishment of passersby below and the secretaries at the office windows above?

We loved this rooftop duplex, to which we had moved from the Turtle Bay house when the latter had been sold in 1942. We had been very happy there. No friends or foreigners from overseas. No intrigues. No one but us, the family.

[May 11, 1944]

Darling N.

The iris in the garden are going to be blue in color and my spirits will match. Today is Thursday, May 11 and glorious with sun like Rome and haze like Paris, capitals precious to us both. . . . Sylvester appeared in a cloud of dust up the fire escape yesterday and brought some more red and blue verbena for the tub with the barren tree and also some dark blue petunias which I planted in the box by the maple tree. I watered the garden and also planted some more seeds. . . . It is absurd when I should be writing items of deep consequence to you that I am inscribing on this, my first V-mail letter I ever wrote, tenuous material idiocies devoted to a minute garden in the air of New York. . . . I went to the piano recital last night given by my sister Maria's ex-teacher, Mlle. Bert, and it was superb. Debussy, Fauré, and Chopin. After having deeply enjoyed the technique, playing and program, Maria, at the conclusion said, "Very fine. The piano is a half tone low." Afterwards Mlle. Bert mentioned it. Those musical ears. . . . I forgot to tell above that Sylvester persuaded Pavel T. to go to the Brooklyn Botanic with him to gaze on those cursed cherry trees, so he did get one fly in his spider web. . . . Harold has been a source of strength in the house; he wept over the first single breakfast he brought up; very touching. He is building a box for the garden and Louisa is coming to interview the moths. . . . Alice de la Mare had a note from a French friend, who had been to Paris and out; she saw Picasso at my café, who said, "Very good epoch for artists now as they must begin all over at zero," and that all there lead a double even triple life in resistance to cursed Nazis. Paris exciting as complicated resistance center, many friends in prison for aiding RAF to escape. . . . Darling find your likeness soon in some Renaissance portrait of a great Italian artist on any museum wall. Devotedly . . .

Janet's next letter (May 17, 1944) did not reach me in Delaware; by then, on May 18, I had left. I was on board the S.S. *James Parker*, flagship of a huge convoy of troopships escorted by destroyers, torpedo boats and minesweepers, crisscrossing the Atlantic on our way to North Africa. Elma, myself and Herbert Matthews, *The New York Times* correspondent, were the only civilians in uniform on board.

Time passed slowly. Every day Elma and I would look out of our portholes with eagle eyes; after days at sea, there was not even a seagull in sight, which would have meant land nearby. Once I called Elma excitedly, "Look, look, a buoy. We must be near the coast." I had crossed the Atlantic back and forth many times on our trips to Europe in those grand early days of steamship traveling, and I considered myself an expert. Suddenly, we heard an explosion and saw a gush of water. Depth charges had destroyed the floating mine I had mistaken for a buoy a few feet away.

We were, indeed, near our landing site. It was night, a deep African night without a star shining. May 29. We disembarked, loaded with gear, down a steep gangplank at Mers-El-Kebir, a resort near Oran, in Morocco, and were piled into trucks that sped along the coast toward what turned out to be Ein-El-Turk, our staging area, a rest camp for the military. We had arrived.

I slumped on a cot under a tent and fell asleep. The next morning

I could hardly make out where I was. A lot of activity was going on outside. I jumped up ready to fall in line, but nowhere could I find the WAC captain who had ordered us about on board ship. Instead, a bewildered Elma at my side was scanning the outdoors. It was a beautiful, sunny day, very warm. A few palm trees silhouetted against a clear sky were scattered among tents pitched on yellow, sandy ground. Elma pointed to a barracks where presumably we could wash up, and to an outdoor faucet around which quite a crowd had already gathered to fill their helmets with water. I decided to explore the barrack facilities first.

Nonchalantly, I took out a cigarette to help me face that ordeal. A WAC, pointing to a large NO SMOKING sign, warned me. "Careful," she said, "an absent-minded nurse blew up the chemicals by throwing a lighted cigarette down there and wounded her behind. She was given the Purple Heart."

On June 1 we moved to Algiers, where Army headquarters had been set up and where I found my colleagues of OWI already in their Operational PWB unit, among them Michael Bessie, head of news, later to become a well-known publisher and Janet's editor, with whom I established a long-lasting friendship.

That evening of May 17, just before my departure from Delaware, I had been allowed to telephone home. As soon as I could, I had called Janet. My head was full of things I wanted to say, but I couldn't utter a word; I stammered. I finally told her I'd be thinking of her, Billy, Ester. I was too emotional. . . . "*Addio*, Janet . . . farewell." And I could not go on. She had realized I was leaving. "Bless you," she said.

[May 17, 1944]
Wednesday

Darling,

It is ten minutes to 8 and after hearing your dear deep voice on the telephone I hurried to the garden—to mark this special conversation. There was a new iris, orchid pink, a novelty, blooming beneath the little maple tree—The others are blue: This is the precious exception —I did not mean to weep, tears being a form of contagion, but to hear is so moving—It is a remarkable new life you have quickly learned in which you, the individualist, are one in many and while it sounds as if you had turned into a laundress for your country's sake, the result must be handsome to the eye and of disciplinary value—You have become *la fille du* regimentation! Your mother is very well; seems to have the job in hand.

———

On May 30, Janet wrote a brief V-mail letter reporting on her first weekend at Fire Island. We were both very fond of that island, still so primitive though so near New York. I always opened the beach house on Memorial Day weekend, and she knew I would be pleased to have the local news. "Chatzie [Charlotte Seitlin] & I & Fire Island had our first weekend together this year. . . . Sunday was perfection of island's weather, soft breeze, blue sky, the first sailboat of the season visible across the bay, bombers overhead, the Farrar's porch gradually filling, with Burt, back from Alaska, brown, dear, disillusioned as to mentality of men of our dear democracy as exemplified by his post . . ."

Burt Martinson was one of our closest friends, and his return from the service had been greeted with proper fanfare. I was glad, too, that Janet had taken Chatzie with her for the weekend. Chatzie was then working for Simon and Schuster, and was handling the paperback edition—due, much to Janet's pleasure, to come out in June—of her four-part Profile of Pétain, "The Old Man of France," first published in *The New Yorker*. Marshal Philippe Pétain had surrendered two-thirds of France to the Nazis and established his autocratic government at Vichy, described by Janet as "a government of an old man at a Spa." He was later tried for treason and condemned to life in prison. He died of old age in July 1951. In the midst of the great events that were rapidly succeeding one another, these bits of personal news seemed to come from a different planet.

The news of the invasion of France, of the liberation of Rome, soon to be followed by that of Paris, our two beloved capitals, gave an added dimension to the general celebrations, personal and otherwise. I could easily imagine Janet's elation at the phone call she received from our friend Lucien Vogel, of the French section at OWI, giving her the first news. I don't recall what I did in Algiers that day, but I do remember the excitement all around us. I think I had a drink too many, and with good reason, on the terrace of our hotel. A lot of my colleagues would shortly be leaving for France too, and Janet would be anxiously awaiting her turn.

[June 6, 1944]

Darlingest,

This is the great day. Four years ago France trembled and began her fall, and it has taken the rest of us close to fifty months to arrange to pick her up, in the process of also saving ourselves. France has partially cost us all nearly four years; hers is a shocking debt, she can never wholly pay it and only history can eventually add up the cost. . . . I heard the invasion news at 5:15; I was by chance awake, some noise in the street had stirred me, my phone rang and I heard Lucien Vogel announcing that since two hours the invasion had started, near Le Havre; I was so stunned that I politely answered, *Merci* Lucien, *merci beaucoup* Lucien, *merci mille fois* Lucien, as if he had presented me with a bouquet of flowers. I hurried downstairs to tell your mother, but she was sleeping so profoundly (she had been troubled with a little cold) that I did not dare to rouse her after I called and she did not answer. I phoned Shawn at 5:30, went down again to tell Ester, still she slept, and five minutes later I heard her phone ring; it was the NBC and [Fred] Bate, giving the flash. So we had coffee. The Little Flower asked shops to close at one p.m., Lord & Taylor did not open at all in celebration, Mark Cross, Bonwit Teller closed, everyone went into any church or even synagogue he passed and prayed. . . .

June 7. It is the beginning of the end; we are all stunned that the German resistance was so weak, that we entered France's fringe so easily. Your first letters, darling, created almost as much pleasure in our house as General Eisenhower's order of the day. . . . On the heel of the V-mail came our special airmails, mine with the date cut off by censor's nail scissors, also one line which doubtless indicated your whereabouts in the Mediterranean. . . . FLASH! Billy has just raced upstairs to say that the OWI says you are in Algiers so thank heaven we have some geography to build up behind you now. Your mother especially was fretful at not knowing where to place you on the globe. I, my darling, was so delighted to know that you were safe on any kind of land that I didn't care what color it was on the printed map. When we read a dispatch from [Herbert] Matthews in *The Times* June 3, datelined Rome, I had one wild surmise you might be with him. The Fall of Rome and now the Fissure Into France has given all of New York, discouraged by Monte Cassino, the Germans there and the monk's crypt architecture, a new hope of speedier attainments. . . . The worst thing about the absence of a dear one is that it continues; if only there were one day a month when you were present, one quarter hour a week when your voice were audible; it is the consistency of the facts of absence which make one a little crazy. There is no question but what you were the centralizing element in our duplex; without you we become centrifugal—is that the whirling out motion? We operate on it. I have just re-informed Shawn that I wish to leave in October; the radio has been only a detour away from my real road, and it is useless for me to continue to plod along on it, sponsored or not. A new agent from Chicago came here to cook up other possible sponsors, neither as yet materialized but the agent is very intellectual, his wife by chance a former friend of mine from the University of Chicago so at least the quality of the dealings has been the opposite of the dreary vulgarity which attended the other negotiations. Your airmail letter was precious to me; there is also no privacy on this side of the ocean, my darling; we all must read aloud what we receive, and we all listen eagerly to the others' readings. . . . Fire Island is not the same at all, at all, without you. I find the Long Island Railroad more unattractive than ever this summer, indeed hardly worth its cinders. . . . The honeysuckle on the terrace is in bloom and rampant; Sylvester managed to have given us two small healthy vines of poison ivy, I discover. Honestly. The vines for which you strung the wires are clambering up, are now nearly two feet tall, of a lovely waxy green. The bamboo has revived, rather untidily; I have little interest in any of it, but the geranium tub, your hedge bushes, the little maple tree, indeed, that whole corner which I view this minute by raising my eyes, is sweet, green spotted and reminiscent of you. My letters to you seem very dull to me because so incoherent. I have nothing to say that I can say. The trivia of odds and ends seems too fragmentary to ask a boat or a plane to burden itself with, and carry for me, in these mortal times. I myself feel shapeless, patternless, somnambulistic, although heaven knows I sleep little enough at night. I now wake at seven daily, uncontrollably. I feel like an elderly grey butterfly, without flowers to feed on. I sag in the wind. I believe in your task ahead of you and that gives me, even at this distance, a direction. Bless you darling. All love. We all drank your health; on the Island your name is alive—

I hadn't meant to upset Janet with my description of postwar hardships. I was just warning her about what she'd find on her return to Paris. And it depressed her. She was also disappointed at the rating of her radio program, "Listen: The Women," a panel show Janet emceed that included two other prominent women: Virginia Gildersleeve, the dean of Barnard College, who later was to be the only woman member of the U.S. delegation at the San Francisco Conference in 1945, and Margaret Mead, the noted anthropologist, lecturer and writer. It was a brilliant program on various interesting subjects, which each week featured a special quest. "Esther Arthur was on the radio program Sunday night. She was wonderful!" wrote Janet. "I think that she can substitute for me as MC when I leave, thank God!" Esther Murphy, sister of the famous bon vivant and painter Gerald Murphy, had married Chester Arthur, son of the President of the United States, and was a specialist in American history. Of the noted co-panelist Fannie Hurst, another guest on her show, Janet would write: "Fannie Hurst was quite good and cross with a jade and diamond ring as big as the Ritz."

Janet had also been attentive to my interest in Fire Island, sending me constant news of what was happening there, with especially elaborate descriptions of a new house that my oysterman-landlord was floating over from the mainland "to be placed right on the bay for me," wrote Janet. "It is a plastered house, not mere board walls. Whether you want to rent it or buy it is all one to him, his devotion to you is as explicit as it is touching. When I asked the price either for renting or selling, he cast me an oysterman's-eye and said that he reckoned him and Miz Murray could figger that out between 'em as they'd allus had kind of fair dealings where business was concerned. . . ." Needless to say, I bought the house sight unseen.

In the meantime, in Algiers, I was in a hubbub of speculation. The general ferment was intense. Good news was finally arriving. The defenses at Monte Cassino had been broken, and the Allied Armies had entered Rome on June 4. On the sixth came the invasion of France. My eagerness to leave as soon as possible became an obsession. Everyone wanted to move, to share in the first victory for our side, *sur place* so to speak. I had, of course, an additional motive—finding my two sisters.

Toward the end of June, I decided to cut my own orders and try my luck. I collected my gear and at the suggestion of a kind corporal moved to the Casablanca airfield to wait for a chance at an empty bucket seat. I didn't wait long. A colonel failed to show up, so I took his seat and left for Naples on June 23.

[June 9, 1944]

DARLING,

I SHALL TRY WRITING TO YOU ON MACHINE AND IN CAPITAL LETTERS
IN MY NEXT V-MAIL LETTER (that was more practice in dexterity to
get my hand in) so that the reducing by photography to one-fourth of
the original size will not cost you your eyesight, as your welcome
V-mail letter of yesterday cost me. Your neat eccentric native Roman
script was reduced, really, to reductio ad absurdum, or nearly! It took
your mother, her magnifying glass, my steel Benjamin Franklin spectacles and some extraneous comments by your son, on the sidelines,
to decipher what you wrote. So be generous with your ink in the
subsequent letters, darling. . . . I have discovered that some people,
in loneliness or sadness, flower, become noble of speech, thought, and
are generally improved; I have become not a flower but a weed, have
become sour, bitter, cross and the wrong sort of garden growth of
late. I am shocked to discover that this is my nature; it had never
been demonstrated to me before, and I am trying, mentally—you
know me—to rectify it. I see nothing to do except try with one's brain
to change something, even character, when it is by the brain that one
discovers what is amiss. I think the loneliness which my sister Maria
has endured in her spinster life made her acid of speech and sometimes rancid of soul, poor woman. We look enough alike and really
are enough alike to alarm me at moments, heaven forgive me. . . . I
announce, in the way of flowers, some charming deep pink blossoms,
rather like wisteria, now in evidence on one of those strange sticks of
Sylvester's which he planted in our garden last autumn with the
promise that they were vines. They still are not vine, are still sticks
but at all events the flowers have come true. . . . I am impressed, sadly,
by your repeated warnings to me of the physical trials in being abroad
now; I had expected them, in my way, forgetting my white hair, yet
had not realized until you repeatedly pointed it out, that youth and
patience are essentials in enduring so large an administrative movement as modern war. When I look with distaste at myself in the
mirror (rarely more than once a day to see that I put powder on the
wrong way and my lipstick right) I now see myself as someone in
Europe might for the first time, on my appearance in the wake of
war: they would say, Mais quelle vieille femme, et quoi pense-t-elle
faire à son age ici?

Darling, I miss you simply terribly; that's the truth. I've been
knocked to one side, like a piece of furniture which has lost its place

in the home by your departure. There is no time sense left, no point in getting up, no fun in breakfast, no excitement at the end of the afternoon with your voice shouting up the stairs or demanding a cocktailino or my answering eccolino. . . . I am going to Washington for three days on Wednesday on the [Charles] Bedaux story; I shall miss you there too, but more bearably since I shall be disorientated at best. I shall probably have to sleep with Daphne and Geoff Hellman; no hotels. I am willing either to pay or be paid; philosopher. Sweetheart, all tenderness, boldness, love, patriotism and pride.

———

Janet's trip to Washington, D.C., to research an article she was writing for *The New Yorker* brought back the memory of our visit to the Jefferson Memorial, which had been the most touching moment of that last day there with Janet in May. I remember it clearly. We had held hands and looked up at that monument, paying homage to our favorite American in history. I can still see Janet's profile, which has often been described as being as American as that of the Indian head on the five-cent coin, with its fine bone structure, her white, short hair disheveled by the wind, her intense look as she turned around to have her photo snapped by a young man, a total stranger, who obliged.

In this letter she didn't describe herself as I last remembered her. She was depressed and it made me sad. I knew later, by experience, how hard it is for those left behind in the same surroundings and climate to stand the emptiness of a departure. It had been easier for me this time, because I had been the one to leave. I had been moving into another world under new circumstances, and had become absorbed by them. But the snapshot that had fixed our last moments together was a milestone on our path.

[June 20, 1944]

Darling,

I am almost out of pain for the first time since you left. My room here, high up, gives me a direct view over the White House Park onto the Jefferson Memorial where we stood and which I carry in duplicate with me: the photo of my preference now; you before his grand statue that last day here, is by my side now. I feel very close because I can identify you more here than at any time since you left. I don't know why it is true, but it is true. In a letter from you of June 13, received this morning just before I left at ten for the station to return to work here, you say, as if I hadn't written it already in all the ways I could to pass the censor whom you now tell me it doesn't exist for me, to tell you what is in my heart and mind. Apparently what I have already told you doesn't inform you, so I shall put it in physical terms as being more news-valuable: I weigh 114 pounds, look, so I am told, like death on horseback, rarely sleep more than five hours a night as can't get to sleep: each noise from the Avenue strikes my consciousness a blow, as if someone had hit my body, and I jump; I eat about three dinners a week: Chatz took me yesterday to a Hungarian photographer* for new pictures: he is young, very sensitive, intelligent, did that famous photo of Dali and of Landowska looking dead at her harpsichord: you saw it in *Life*. He uses the psychological method of contact with his subject before the lens. After he had taken twelve poses of me, of which he said I looked so sad, so suffering, so tired and tragic, he preferred to suspend the sitting.

Ross asked me yesterday when I would go to France. I said October. He was displeased I had signed the radio contract till October, though I had told Shawn twice. But was sweet and will send me at any time; he is so eager to please me and use me. I loathe the radio program; it is silly and futile, and I feel no responsibility farther than I have given: I gave three and one-half months on a gamble, lost $2000 at least, nearer $3000 in earning power and now I'm through. I'll finish my twenty-six weeks and go to Europe. My plan is the only thing that comforts me: to come to Rome first, then go up the Riviera to Paris.

I am paralyzed by pain most of the time by your absence. I hardly function. I can't write at all. All I do is bad. I miss you more than words can say. . . . There is no life in the house, nothing to come home to, to get up for, to look forward to. The days are like treadmill, my limbs ache. God bless you and keep you safe. I hope the Allies' leaders give more of hope and democracy in final practice than they seem to now in tentative. That is all I have to say. You know my suspicious fears and deep desires—also my Voltairean cynicism—Too few mortals are worth what many die to empower but could not know what to do with it—Liberty and Civilization—But we must never cease to fight. My hand is too tired to go on. I wrote three and one-half hours longhand in the Department of Justice this afternoon—It is suddenly cold here. It is ten p.m. I forgot to dine—I'll go see what food remains! A tender kiss.

––––––

* Philippe Halsman.

By the time Janet wrote this letter, I was on my way to Naples. I shall never forget that flight, or the emotional impact at the sight of my Mediterranean Sea—how blue it looked!—and at the contour of the long coastline as it started to appear, first dimly in the distance, then slowly revealing itself, clearly and well defined, as we flew above it. From the height of the plane, the land below looked peaceful. Patches of green and gold dotted the sunny plains on each side of the brown line of the Apennines, the chain of mountains, like a dorsal fin, stretching all the way to the heel of the Italian boot. It was difficult to imagine that a long and hard war had been fought right there, in cold, rain and mud, only a few months before.

As I looked at the landscape, incidents and episodes began to surface in a confusion of memories: my first trip to Naples and Capri in 1925. It had been not quite a honeymoon, but almost. We had been married, Bill and I, the December before in New York, and we had come to Rome to visit my mother and sisters that summer. We were young and in love. The beauty of Naples had enchanted us.

How many cheerful arrivals and sad departures had there been from that port! And then our first trip to Capri—the crossing on the *vaporetto* and the picturesque sight of the city from the bay, with Vesuvius and the gray pennant of smoke towering above it.

I had returned often to Capri. I even lived there for a while, after separating from my husband in 1929. Now I was returning, a divorced woman, in different circumstances. Another time, another period. Another stage of my life, in which Janet had become such an important part. Now, in my absence, she was holding forth in another favorite place, in another part of the world, where I had reconstructed my life with her.

The landing at Capodichino airport brought me back to reality. My God, here I was in my own land, a stranger in a foreign uniform, in the midst of the ravages of a war that had not spared much in its wake. Wherever your eyes turned, there were rubble and ruins—and people, lots of them, in rags, with large black eyes staring at this new set of military men treading their soil.

I do not remember how I reached my billet, a *villino* on the hills of Posillipo, where I was to spend my first night in Naples. I rushed onto the balcony overlooking the bay. By now it was dark. No lights flickered from the city below and around us, but the sky was lit by a phantasmagoric crisscross of flares from antiaircraft batteries scanning the heavens. The sight, odd and terrifying, could have been mistaken for a display of fireworks celebrating the feast of San Gennaro, Naples'

patron saint! Daylight dispelled that Felliniesque spectacle. Naples lay
there, half dead under the sun. Along the promenade of Santa Lucia
you could see a cemetery of ships crowding the bay, floating on their
sides like huge dead whales bobbing gently in the water. You could
have walked from hull to hull all the way to the end of the vast port
and beyond, if you had cared to. My first contact with the reality of
war took place there, in Naples. I had known about the suffering of the
city, the famous four-day resistance by *i guaglioni*, the heroic Neapolitan street urchins who dared battle the Nazis, but now I could see with
my own eyes their ruined streets and homes, the bombed-out buildings
and roofs, a sight which was to accompany me along the ancient Via
Appia all the way to Rome.

[June 23, 1944]

. . . Darling, darling some happinesses must have come to you already,
surely, for you have seen your two sisters by now. Recall how you
always said they, the poor slaves of war, circumstances and shortages,
would present themselves, from a battle-scarred impoverished land, in
chic coats, smart gowns and probably a background of slight mink or
ermine while you, from rich New York, would appear somewhat
dowdy if not even ersatz-shabby in their tolerant Roman eyes? Your
mother and I were laughing at the possible picture last night; tell us
the actual circumstances when they have taken place. I am going to
wire you today on general principles, just to send you a message. Yes,
one capital down, two to go. Paris should be next. One thinks one
knows what one wants in the way of victory until one sees pictures of
the result—the battered villages, the ruined Italian houses, the towns
by place and street which you especially once knew and which looked
intact on a map of Italy when you used to gaze at it, hopefully seeing
in your mind's eye that section of your native land finally freed from
Fascists and Nazi control. Victory, freedom. Yes. Then you see the
result, the result in our time, of victory. Destruction. The Nazis
destroyed the invisible, war is destroying, has destroyed the visible. The
houses, homes, churches, spires, the beauty of stone and brick, the
interior content of bed where love was made and the race carried on,
and portraits and proofs of genius held sacred and saved in museums.
By jove, no wonder women don't love war nor understand it, nor can
operate in it as a rule; it takes a man to suffer what other men have

invented, not only the *casus belli*, but the equipment. Only a male is competent to deal with a bazooka; he made it up. He made it up because another man invented a tank; he made that up because another earlier man invented machine guns. And so on back; we women have invented nothing in all that, except the men who were born as male babies and grew up to be men big enough to be killed, fighting. Your letter of philosophy and its sad tone is the correct tone, my dearest; an intelligent person's mind is in mourning these days and will so remain till our deaths. The next generation perhaps can be gayer because uninformed; more than roofs have given way in our time; an intelligence, the democratic intelligence, has been caught short in a period when sacrifice was not necessary; now it is saving itself in a wholesale loss of bodies to save ideas which could at least have been protected earlier, without blood. . . . There is nothing here in your absence BUT you, more even than when you were here. Everything that happens in the house or Island is a description of your absence because it is not the same as when you were here. Don't worry that I do not miss you. This place and my life and happiness are like properties with a large cruel sign, For Rent; Unoccupied; Owner Gone Away. . . . I am enclosing an excellent leader of Anne O'Hare McCormick's in *The Times*; we'll see if it is permitted to pass the censor; it would be a joke if it didn't; it is a splendid piece of writing and thinking. Oh, send news of your presence in Rome, your natal city, and where your mother's heart lies, ci gît, wherever you step. I embrace you with all my strength, darling, and miss you accordingly in that emptiness of now.

Worried about Janet, I wrote our friend Chatzie for news. Janet answered:

[June 26, 1944]

Your letter to Chatz was so much about me that I felt it was for me, and I swallowed every word. Yes, I have been restless, my pet, restless as a lioness. No, you have made no mistake, have not paid too high for your belief in liberty and freedom in leaving me; you know that, dearest. When I heard your mother sobbing, as I came up the stairs at midnight, I almost tore the door down entering; I was in terror she had

bad news from you. She called to me at once, "Do not fear. I cry of joy."
Poor lady *elle était déchirée, complètement.* Her cold is still bad; she
seems not to throw it off; but she looks very young and pretty with her
netless hairdo—without net and without center curl. She looks barely
fifty, younger than I. . . . My biggest sunflower plant is already visible
—if you know where to look—from 57th Street, and the jungle
arrangement can be seen from 59th Street; the willow tree is now
taller than the fence; it has grown, prodigiously. The vines have out-
grown the wires you stretched for them and are on a new series Harold
arranged. There are too few blossoms, but that I can't help; the geraniums you planted beneath your box tree by the straw matting flourish
with sparse but gay blooms and dozens of small buds to come, the
marigolds (yellow) on the shelf stuck against our clothes closet are
really very very good and fertile. But a colorful garden it isn't. Green.
Only chlorophyll. A basic principle, not a fancy development is all I
have been able to obtain. . . . Except for that brief period when I was
so sunken in a lethargy of despair that I didn't write you, I have written
constantly, darling, so don't complain to your mummy that I am not a
diligent correspondent. I AM. Oh, I wish I could see you and, above
all, hear your voice; that is what I miss most. The sound of you as you
come in at night or speak in the morning over coffee. Goodbye for this
moment. God bless you and keep you safe and sane and filled with
hopes. I said a prayer for you at St. Patrick's today. The central big
door was thrown open on invasion day and still remains so. The church
is often crowded with those who stop and pray. I had to place my glove
on my head as I lacked even a hankie to be respectful of God. I miss
you, darling Cherubino.

"Do you mind if I join you?" I had my orders to proceed to Rome,
and that commandeered jeep waiting outside our Naples headquarters
was just what I needed. There was only one other passenger, a Navy
officer. Without waiting for his reply, I jumped in and sat quietly at his
side. He didn't utter a word during the three-hour drive; retracing the
path of an army was devastating for me. Right and left, small ancient
towns crowned the hills, with pines and cypress trees lining their old
roads; villages huddled together along the way, once cheerful and noisy
with life, were now reduced to bombed-out ruins, disemboweled
homes, shattered altars, revealing to the stranger's eye the intimacy of
a life or place of worship and prayer, deserted and hollow.

You could see where the fighting had been more intense and bloody by the amount of damage caused. Everywhere people were rummaging through the ruins trying to salvage some personal belonging—small items that made up their riches. They looked like so many ants in a never-ending search for sustenance. Wherever I drove in later years along that same Route N. 6, as the military had named the Appian Way, especially if I veered onto the new parkway along the coast, I was reminded of how many soldiers had been lost in those heavy battles at Cassino, at Anzio, at the Volturno River, where they said the water had run red with blood. Our cemeteries—those long lines of white crosses—were stretched over the plain under the hot sun of a summer's holiday, all the way to the sea.

When we finally reached the Alban Hills, Rome lay in the distance before us, with its hundred cupolas and domes against the baroque sky. In between, on the Roman plain, as they had for centuries, stood the remains of those ancient aqueducts, like giant guardians to the approaches of the great city. Nothing here, as far as I could see, had been altered by the war. The lump in my throat became a cry of joy. My silent companion, utterly surprised, turned to me. "We did a thorough job of this!" he exclaimed. Later, that statement made the rounds and became a classic. . . .

I immediately found my way to the Hotel Ludovisi, where I was billeted, off the Via Veneto. Three weeks after the arrival of the Liberation Army the city looked like an armed camp. Soldiers were everywhere; jeeps scurried through the streets; tanks were parked in the gardens. Large crowds of Romans were milling around in a holiday mood. It was as if the city had reawakened from a nightmare and found itself alive!

It didn't take me long to find my friend Elma, because she was billeted at the same hotel and had just returned from the radio station when I called on her. She immediately became my mentor, with useful information as to my next moves, but I was too excited to sit down and talk shop and gossip. Here we were together again! "Let's go out. Let me look at Rome!" I said. I took Elma's arm, and we joined the crowds outside. I wanted to mix with the people of my city. I wanted to rejoice with them, to share their exhilaration! We walked along the Via Veneto up to the ancient walls of Belisario. Its arches led into the Borghese Gardens of my youth, but I took Elma's arm instead and turned right at the corner of the Hotel Flora. I didn't know why. We walked for a while in silence on that quiet street alongside the medieval walls, but it was getting late for our mess, said Elma, so we retraced our steps to the Excelsior, one of the two grandest hotels of Rome, evacuated by the Nazi high command just in time for our high officers to take their place. The streets were beginning to be empty. A curfew was being enforced, except for us, the military.

What inspired me to try to find a telephone directory, to frantically look up my sisters' numbers? It was utterly foolish of me to imagine that Akos, my Hungarian brother-in-law, who probably had been in hiding from the German SS, might have been listed, or that my sister Franca might have returned to Rome from the country, where she had been living since the outbreak of the war! I suspect that the fact that I found myself at the Excelsior, where phones had been restored, had given me that foolish idea. No civilian telephones were operating elsewhere as yet. Just the same, some mysterious force drove me on. I found the directory downstairs by the phone booths. No numbers were listed for my sisters' names, of course. Suddenly, I had a brainstorm. I looked for my cousin's number. He was a civil engineer, who was already working for the Rome area command. He was listed. The phone was working! The voice of Gabriella, his wife, answered timidly. *"Chi è?* Who is there?" she asked. "It's me . . . Natalia. . . ." "Natalia???" she repeated incredulously. *"Si, si.* . . . *Me* . . . Natalia from America!!" I heard a kind of thump. The line seemed dead. Had she fainted? I called: "Gabriella, Gabriella. . . ." The voice came back. "I can't believe it . . ." she whispered, and then, "Have you seen your sisters? They are both in Rome." "Where? Where?" She gave me the address. How could it possibly be true? It was the same street I had turned into earlier that afternoon with Elma, when we had gone strolling up the Via Veneto, as if I had been pulled by a magnet. I scrambled upstairs, grabbed Elma and ran out of the hotel like a lunatic.

It was dark by now. The streets were empty. The city was silent. Only a few M.P. jeeps were making the rounds. Luckily, we had our curfew passes and flashlights. At the corner we turned right a few steps and found the address. The large door and the shutters of the entire building were closed. A complete blackout. I banged on the *portone.* I banged and banged and called out to the *portiere,* the janitor. No answer. I kept on calling; Elma joined in. Someone had to be there, if only because of the curfew. . . . Finally, timidly, the head of a woman appeared behind a half-opened shutter. *"Signora, apra, sono la sorella della Signora Tolnay, sono Americana.* I am American, *signora. Apra,* please. Please open!" I begged her. A small middle-aged woman finally appeared at the *portone*, holding a flickering candle. She was terribly scared. I explained who we were, and our American uniforms reassured her. She opened the heavy door, unlocked a second glass one and pointed to a short flight of steps at the front of the entrance. My flashlight revealed a brass nameplate on a door. It read "Tolnay" and below, "Under the protection of the Swiss Consulate." What luck! When at last another scared face with a flickering candle came to answer, I pushed the poor maid aside and called out at the top of my lungs: "Lea! Lea! Lea! *Sono io* . . . Can't you tell? Me . . . Natalia???" Crash. Bang. A table overturned. Glasses smashed on the floor. In a minute, all hell broke loose, and we were in one another's arms. . . . Lea, Franca, who had just arrived that day, Akos, little Flavia, their daughter—the family, safe, together, celebrating the liberation. Sharing festivities were two American friends, correspondents from the States, who had called on them that evening, and looked just as astonished as everyone else at my sudden apparition. They were Daniel Lang of *The New Yorker* and Ed Morgan, who later became a well-known newscaster. They have never forgotten that night in Rome!

I had returned to my liberated city and found my sisters—all in one victorious day! How I wished Mammina Ester and Janet could have been there.

[July 7, 1944]

Darling,

Surely you must now be in Rome. We are still fairly certain that we don't know where you are; we are not positive we don't know, but inclined that way. Have you seen your sister Lea and your cadet sister Franca? What joy for you three. I hope you wear your uniform, your summer uniform, on your first meeting so they may be proud of you and of your liberty-loving land. Either liberty is a false ideal and men should stop dying for it, or the men who are against it in peacetimes should be assassinated before they may build up ripened wars. The trouble with the law is that it permits action only after a deed has been committed. Society would be well-advised to hang, to chop heads or to imprison upon suspicion, where rape of liberty is concerned. When one stops to think that in the middle of the 1920s the paper-hanging Hitler wrote a book called *Mein Kampf* and meant it, and those who read it only laughed, as if it were *Tender Buttons* by Gertrude Stein;

when one thinks and recalls that from 1933 on, he gave the most candid, truthful warning that any paranoiac ever spoke or wrote, or hired and bedazzled others to write and speak for him, and that nobody believed that he meant what he said; that we were governed—for we were, as if we were English and French—by Chamberlain, with his Adam's apple and an umbrella, the Adam's apple being his only bomb shape and the umbrella his idea of a parabellum and by [Georges] Bonnet the French Fox, whose very baldness described the vulturous hatching quality of a buzzard's egg—when we recall that the world of young men about to die, and older humans, about to grieve, allowed such crotty creatures to decide for us, to appease for us and themselves, to mismanage, to misread, misprophesy, mistake and misbeget the future as they did, I can only suppose we should decide to accept the worst in life, rather than the best as normal. Because we do not practice the best, we merely talk about it occasionally; between wars and during wars we bleed for and after armistices, we go back to practicing it too little again. Is the idea too high? How can we be sure we grow any closer? Is that your impression, returned to your native land where your grandfather or his brothers or cousins were willing to perish for Garibaldi, in order that Mussolini might swell his belly like a talking frog on the Piazza balcony? The world of men becomes more frivolous, even in its silly indifferences to dying itself, to counting the corpses of those others who were killed first because someone happened to cry, ô liberté chérie! Oops, the world cries, that's right, by Jove, I forgot all about it. Say, kid, let's get ready to die again. We haven't died in a long time, not since the last time someone shouted Liberty. It killed my father, too. Well, what's good enough for the old man is good enough for me. I sometimes think that whoever invented the idea did us a great disservice. The invention of the idea of God, who but little disturbs the world, was less harmful. The trouble with man is that a few of him are too good for most of him.

I came across Balzac's *Peau de Chagrin* the other day and reread the preface which precedes the English translation; I had forgotten what brilliance of paradox and scenery of words the old master was competent to toss into ink, then out to dry on the printed page. His basic idea in *The Wild Ass's Skin* was the beginning of modern society, and I doubt if he was thanked for the discovery—i.e., that excess is the natural reaction of a power-mad individualistic society with money the main goal. These things he says; they are still true. I suppose the politic of existence has taken the place of the philosophy of former centuries;

after all, it was no more idle for the medievalists to contemplate and try to decide on how many angels could stand on the point of a pin, than it is for us to consider and try to figure how many races can live on the point of the Balkans without fighting, or if *geopolitik* is the new kind of heaven on earth—for those who get there first.

I still don't know what makes the stars stay up in the heavens and am not only too ignorant but too limited mentally ever to be able to comprehend. Not only am I unable to comprehend the ideas of my own decade, but cannot grasp the essential physical truths of the universe. I suppose if I can't understand a comet, I'll never be able to grasp a Republican.

The heat is terrific; the *Times* prophesied ninety for today and if they call that news fit to print, it must be good news or nice news only to the iceman or the soda jerker.

I was woken this morning by a plane so low down and making so peculiar a drilling noise that I was startled, thinking: What must it be like in London? I see by a tiny little piece on the fourth page of the *Tribune* (where often facts of enormous importance are allowed to light, like a flyspeck) that the Germans have had to apologize to Sweden for the wild activities of two unpiloted gyroscope radio-controlled planes which the Nazis were experimenting with—over Sweden; not over dear Deutschland, of course, where they might kill another Hans or Gretchen. What new menace will that be, that plane? A bigger bloodier robot doubtless. We'll hear about it next month I dare say. I know we have them, in theory anyhow, but it's the Germans who make the practice, alas.

Please write to me. Your mother has had two letters lately, I none. They are more important to her than to any other human being, I suppose you figure, darling, because she is so trembling with home-sickness and patriotism combined. But I tremble with nostalgia and am homesick for you personally. Yours and with all my tender thoughts and noctambulisms of the spirit . . .

———

My first days in Rome were chaotic and heartrending. Apart from the painful specatcle of a capital city crawling slowly back to life under a new set of occupation forces, even if these jovial and friendly Americans were quite different from the Germans, we were still seeing a beaten city. Not so much physically, for Rome had been spared the heavy bombings of Milan or Naples, but morally, psychologically and practically. For one thing, nothing was working, not yet, anyhow. Neither electricity nor water were available except for a few hours a day. No coal or gas to cook the scanty meals, no food in the shops, no easy transportation to go foraging in the outskirts of the city or further out in the countryside. No facilities or drugs for the sick and the elderly, no cloth or woolens to protect oneself. Nothing really had been left for the people to use for their own survival. You could read their ordeal on their faces, you could listen to their tales of hardship, you could only wonder at how people had survived. The ingenuity and cunning of an old civilization had helped. In a short time, bicycles by the hundreds started to reappear from walled-up closets, attics, cellars, where they had been hidden from the Gestapo, who seized them as soon as they realized that they were the means of communication for the underground. The *camionettes*, rickety small trucks equipped with plain wooden benches and unsteady steps, began carrying passengers about and were practically assaulted by would-be riders at every stop. And around the corners from the main arteries, as if by magic, sprouted carts full of blackmarket goods of every kind, including, of course, chewing gum from our PXs.

Moral values, the backbone of a society, had been so distorted by twenty-three years of Fascist rule under a weak, ineffectual king followed by a long war that now, free, people seemed confused, at a loss to understand such a defeat. Now everyone had to reassess and restore new sets of values and beliefs. Citizens had to learn how to be responsible for their own actions. They had to understand the working and meaning of democratic rule. They had, above all, to find a new source of pride in themselves. To have been beaten so badly as a nation had left them severely hurt psychologically. No wonder Janet felt incensed at the criticisms of our democracy by foreign refugees, mostly French, which prompted her outburst . . .

[July 10, 1944]

Sweetheart,

I suppose that, were I to have any grandchildren who might read my diary when I had become dust, today's entry could thrill them. Today I am to meet a rebel, a hero within his limits and at all events a tall strange man—General de Gaulle. I am to meet him as private individuals do so often in the diary manner; I shall be in the same room with him at the Waldorf press conference—see him, hear his voice and rush home and note the small report I have to give. The day is hot and republican in climate; it was a hot day when the Bastille fell, and it had been hot before when we declared our July independence.

I am fed up with the Europeans AND the American intellectuals who constantly criticize our ill practice of democracy; that we are able to practice it at all, considering that a majority of humans are not noble enough to comprehend or use any fine theory of life whether personal or public, is already a miracle in mankind. And especially those Europeans who nag at us, pointing with derision at our non-demos in life, here, there, in the Poll Tax, in discrimination against Negroes, in our lust for money, our stupid legal backing of free speech by Bundists and traitors in words such as the seditionists now being tried in Washington and given more benefit of law than a sincere radical mind would be—those refugees here who sneer at our maladministration, or non-practice in details of our fundamental great whole—how dare they carp? They have sprung from the body politic of regions where men were content to use the womb as a prison, to say Thus you were born of a certain man and woman and thus are you sentenced to jail for a life in their class; or where the breeding principle, the womb restriction works upward as well as horizontally among the middleclass or downward among the serfs, where kings, if you please, are bred at night, by Hapsburg jaws and hemophiliac wives, inert, respectful and as ignorant as dairymaids, on their backs, and from such a bed-untidiness Europe has bred royalty. If kings were given the realism by courtiers which a farmer gives to his bull, the royal cows and sires would have been beef long since or at any rate driven from the pasture lands where they fatten upon taxes like animals on grass. At any rate, democracy had an IDEA quite frankly more intelligent, scientific, rational, logical and essential than any of Europe's ideas until the French killed a herd of nobles, dukes and pinched off the heads of a couple of royalty as you would step on an unimportant if rather decorative caterpillar or beetle. When I consider how the European mind, including the British, can still have so diseased an eye that it can still SEE the idea of a king, I feel that their whole organism is abnormal. They are like degenerates who are color blind, except that they see something which is NOT there, instead of failing to see something which is. Democracy has worked no worse than any other political form, and its idea was so far superior than all others that it can support the low level of performance, proportionate to its great splendid height; as half democrats we are nobler and more exalted than a king at his peak or the populace which in acclaiming it is lower than the belly of a pig, wallowing in muddy sour mash, self-fouled and thus familiar, precious, even comforting because not strange.

. . . Do for heaven's sake write me and personally; your mother and I have done the best we could and can with all things; my heart writhes for you for I know that your maternity is taking more of your thoughts, at long distance, than it ever did probably, from New York to Exeter. But what you are doing is more important than the lapses or even the confusion and losses you leave behind. Remember that, my darling in uniform; be a fine talking soldier, use the air for freedom, for air is free. And God love you as I do.

[July 17 and 25, 1944]

CARISSIMA MASSIMA,

How's that? Still no word from you, though your mother had two more over the weekend from Rome and how delightful, how nourishing to read from you of the reunion of the three Roman sisters! I see by your report that the characters of the two younger have remained intact through civil strife, political upheaval and war. Reading Tolstoi's *War and Peace* showed me as it had first showed him how little character is changed by changing events; the revolutionary is changed because society becomes his second nature, but the rest of humanity merely weathers events as trees weather storms but still putting forth the same leafage; it is their green pattern formed in the acorn or maple seed as the first fell to the earth and was missed by the swine or as the second fluttered down to the soil on its little *hélice* which later men, stealing its unpatented invention, use in the front of planes today to promote speed that is new, to us, and war that is old. . . .

———

I spent long evening hours on those first days of our reunion listening to my sisters' tales of endurance and hope: Lea and Akos in Rome; Franca and Fred in the village of Anticoli Corrado. It was because of their characters, reminiscent of our mother's courage and strength, that they had been able to endure "civil strife, political upheaval and war."

Lea and Akos had been living in Paris. At the arrival of the Germans they were in the south of France, so with little Flavia they fled into

Italy. The idea was to try to sail for the States. At that time it was hoped that the efforts of President Roosevelt to keep Mussolini out of the war might succeed. Lea, a graduate from Barnard College, had worked for many years at the Frick Art Reference Library. She felt she could find a job at the Frick again, and Akos, a movie writer and a journalist, might have found work in Hollywood. Besides, we were there, Mother and I. But their efforts failed. Akos could not get a visa, so they had settled in Rome instead.

As a Hungarian, Akos should have answered the call for service in the German Army. Once in Rome, however, he asked the Swiss Consulate for protection and tried to lead a carefully guarded life. Mussolini entered the war shortly afterward, and, when the Americans landed in Sicily, the Germans occupied the country. The hated Gestapo of Colonel Kappler ruled Rome. Everyone lived in mortal dread of the daily roundups that snatched men off the streets to be sent to work camps or, if Jewish, to the extermination camps.

Akos was picked up in one of those roundups. Lea became desperate. How to find him? One evening, she heard an unexpected knock at the door. Terrified, because one never knew who it might be—the Fascist police, the Gestapo—Lea, trembling, opened the door. "I can't tell you my name," whispered a young man, as he quickly stepped inside. "I am a partisan and bring you news of your husband." Akos was being held at Regina Coeli, the dreaded prison with the celestial name "Queen of the Heavens," he told her. "I need money and cigarettes, not for me, for him," and vanished into the night. The underground had been at work. Now that she knew where her husband was, Lea had to try to get him out. To whom could she turn for help? Then she had a sudden flash; she remembered a young Hungarian who, for a few thousand lire, had hauled valises full of food Akos's mother had been sending from Budapest. This young man had been most useful. He had disappeared when the Brenner Pass closed down all but military traffic. Once, however, he had come to see them. Unrecognizable and all dressed up in new clothes, he looked smart and prosperous. He was working for the Germans, he said, without explaining in what capacity. "I've become very important. If you need me, call me." He had given them his telephone number. Not quite certain if he could help, Lea rang him up just the same. "Don't worry," he said, "I'll phone you as soon as he's released." A few days later, Akos returned home.

Franca and Fred had been summering in Anticoli Corrado, a picturesque village north of Rome, perched on a hill in the Sabine mountains where the natives were known for their good looks, especially the women. Many were blond, full-bosomed, with blue eyes, long shapely legs, slender ankles and narrow waists.

The men were also tall, slim, with flashing black eyes and dark, curly hair. They tended their flocks of sheep on the upper slopes in summer and down in the valleys below in winter.

The village had always attracted foreign visitors, especially painters, who found there by far the best models for the pastoral landscapes characteristic of the late-nineteenth-century paintings. Large studios soon appeared all over Anticoli. Franca and Fred, with their little son, Fritzy, had settled into a comfortable villa. Fred worked for United Artists in Rome and commuted. The war, however, changed their plans. It would be safer to remain in Anticoli, they thought. In fact, most of the artists there optimistically believed Italy would not be dragged into a war. As time went on, however, and the war became a reality, life became more difficult. When the Allies landed in Sicily and Mussolini fell from power, everyone once again thought the war was over. But after a brief respite, during which the prisoner-of-war camps were opened and men began trying to reach the Allies in the south, Italy became an occupied country. German troops had poured down from the north and organized a formidable resistance at Cassino and at Salerno and Anzio, where our troops had established invasion beachheads. British Spitfires and American bombers began to strafe and bomb German positions, communication centers and military headquarters around Rome, which had been declared an open city. The Germans had established one of their command posts at beautiful Tivoli in the valley below Anticoli, so that Allied planes made an appearance over the entire zone every day. "We experienced hunger and fear," Franca told me simply, as if it was an everyday occurrence, as it was. And then the escaped Allied prisoners began to show up. They had found themselves stranded in the middle of the countryside, without shelter or food and afraid of being recaptured. They would arrive surreptitiously, late at night, tired and hungry. Many of them stopped by my sister's home because they had been told they would be helped. They were hidden in caves above the town and provided by the local people with clothing and food, and were kept informed of events by my sister's radio, until finally it went dead. A bombing had damaged the local power station, and the whole village was plunged into darkness. The men were of all nationalities—South African, New

Zealand, English, American—and only fourteen of them were s
there, in hiding, when Anticoli was finally liberated by turban-weari\
soldiers—Indians from the English troops moving up from the souti-
west. These liberators began systematically to loot the town, astonishing the local people, until the prisoners out of hiding helped put a stop
to it.

And so my sisters' stories continued; even the joy of being free could
not obscure the grim daily facts of life. "The struggle between contemporary aspirations and primitive necessities continued. . . . Danger
and drama had touched every Roman life that was worth living," I
wrote then in my first article from Rome, published in *Harper's Bazaar*
in 1944. "The laughter and songs were things of the past. A quietness,
heavy with grief, began settling in. In a popular section of the city, in
Trastevere, some hand had scrawled in large letters on a wall, '*Anná-
tevene via tutti. Lassátece piange soli*. Go away, all of you. Leave us to
weep alone.' "

[July 17 and 25, 1944]

Sweetheart,

A lovely tender-hearted letter from you to me, from Rome, once
capital of the world and still capital of the Danesi ladies, came to me
this last week. What joy. Bless the inventor of writing, be he Chaldean,
Arab or stone-cutter from prehistoric, shapeless scribes without known
geography. By words we can write thoughts, we can write loves, hates,
hopes, angers, memories, hungers of soul and senses and make plans
for a future. I have sent you two letters the last week and hope you
know how oftener even than I can write, my thoughts telegraph via
heartbeats my tender concentration.

I enclose an excellent review of my *Pétain*. I am told that old Per-
shing, to whom Ross sent a copy, snorted angrily, "Good God, on this
principle I am guilty of Pearl Harbor!"

Oh, darling, I do miss you terrifically.

———

"News of your flat sounds fantastic," wrote Janet on August 10. "Is
there space for me?"

I had taken a flat in Rome that had been occupied by someone who
had fled when the Allies arrived, and who must have lived in fear,
because I had never seen so much hardware on any door: double

locks, chains, bolts. The flat was high up, on the top floor, overlooking a convent of red-robed priests, a Hungarian order of Jesuits, who would take their constitutional on the rooftop at sundown, reading their breviaries under the Roman swallows flitting over their heads. Many civilians had hidden out, disguised under those robes, during the German occupation. Every convent and nunnery had had its quota of anti-Fascists or Jewish refugees within its walls.

Pierina had been another lucky find. She cooked miraculous meals over a coal stove set inside the large fireplace in the living room, when gas, water, electricity were scarce or nonexistent. In fact, almost everything was unavailable during those first months of liberation, with the exception of flowers on sale at corner stands. The Germans had emptied every shop as they fled before our soldiers. Even our Army rations became coveted delicacies. I began writing home asking for foodstuffs, medicines, vitamins, coffee, sugar and clothing.

"Your mother has purchased all the items you desire," wrote Janet. "She thinks of everything; she is wonderful; her energy which is her trademark, coupled with her spiritual generosity which is the climate of her soul, plus what I always call her nineteenth-century Tolstoian idealism, make her ready to give, give of body and soul and of woolen."

Our household in New York had become a kind of shipping center, as I started to send requests for all sorts of things for family and friends. My trips to the APO eventually required a jeep to transport all the packages that arrived, and I was often regarded with suspicion by the MPs on guard there.

On August 16, Janet gave me important news: my son, Bill, had been called up. I was touched as well as surprised, given Janet's nature, so resistant to domesticity, to see how she had also been watching over him, she of all people, so little inclined toward motherhood, disliking on principle all youths, with their aggressive appetites, lack of discipline and ignorance. Here she was, with an eighteen-year-old impetuous colt, ready to leap into life, who had nearly driven her out of her mind while waiting to be called and having himself a generally good time:

"Bill left for the Army day before yesterday; he laughed and was gay, referred to his coffee and toast—which, as Harold pointed out, he was unable to eat, poor lad—as 'the warrior's last breakfast at dawn.' His train left at nine, and he was warned to arrive a half hour earlier to identify his contingent and section. As he said, 'Ridiculous. They act as if there were a war on. Fancy asking me to make a railway station at eight-thirty of a Monday in Manhattan!' Ester and I hung over my terrace and shouted to him on the street below. He looked up with a flash of white teeth and laughter; he walks gracefully, handles his body well now, is a man, a young man physically."

. . . I thought of Bill now in the service. I knew that his boyhood had ended, that on my return I would find a man in his place. The experience of Army life, if not actually of war, would mature him faster and help him develop. I felt I had lost a part of me. A sadness, a nostalgia for time past, coupled with what I was then experiencing of the losses and suffering around me, weighed on my heart. I walked slowly through Villa Borghese. I recognized the paths and alleys where I had played and explored as a child, the statues and fountains I used to climb. I could smell the pine cones we used to pick from the ground. When I came out into Piazzale Flaminio I was retracing my school steps from our home just outside the great door cut through the Aurelian walls and out across the Piazza del Popolo, with its famous ancient obelisk. We used to cross the piazza every day during our teens to go to our high school, the Liceo-Ginnasio Visconti, at the end of the Corso. Through the door that had been opened to usher Queen Christina of Sweden into Rome, just inside the wall, stood the lovely old church of my youth, Santa Maria del Popolo. I now entered it timidly for the first time in many years. I knelt under the "stars of the firmament," the mosiacs designed by Raphael, and prayed. I prayed for the safety of my son, of my beloved ones and for sanity to return to men's minds.

August, September and October were months occupied with prepa- rations for Janet's departure. The three-part article on the French embezzler Bedaux for *The New Yorker* had been delivered. Her con- tract with NBC Blue Network (later ABC) was ending. Her thoughts were turning entirely to France, and she felt confused, sad at cutting the last tie to our lives together in New York. She felt restless, slept badly. She complained of being somnambulistic, of looking like "a battered old eagle." She wondered where we would meet and when. She felt cut in pieces by geography—New York, Paris, Rome. The network had offered her a regular broadcast from Paris, fifty dollars for ten minutes weekly, which she thought would be very good school- ing for her, but with only a three-month contract, which disappointed her.

"My disillusion through the Blue of Big Business has been another lesson," she wrote. "Luce will become dominant—Luce of *Life*—if the government allows him (anti-trust or something law) to buy as much more as he wants of his stock; he has only twelve percent now of Blue stock. But the new men look like buccaneers to me, like a lot of hard-boiled Christopher Columbuses setting out in boats for a gold coast where they will murder the natives; that a Columbus set sail for a different reason would depass their comprehension. They are not hurting for the invisible party; they think they know where they are going. I fear they do, too."

She also resented having received only a number four rating as a correspondent, which had mainly to do with travel priorities abroad. At the end of September, Bill Shawn, Janet's editor, and Cecille, his wife, gave a *New Yorker* office party for Janet. She wrote:

"I wore my uniform to get the shock over with, and it was approved, even declared becoming. Oddly enough I look thinner *à la militaire* than in my civilian suit: my jacket fits tighter around my ribs. I shall buy a proper WAC top coat since I shall probably go by boat as flying seems too slow, ironically. The delay in getting a better priority than the N. 4 I now have, also the bottlenecks, the being laid off at Lisbon, which from there on into London is British Airways while generals Plushbottom AND their lady loves fly back for Downing Street tea, makes flying take a week, at least. Also, friends who have just returned say that civilian planes have been so stripped that vibration is really agonizing; two men I know spent four days in bed in London after arrival. . . . With half of France declared unoccupied, in theory, and England now open to travel, the surge of bystanders to return to Europe has begun. I must have a French visa to get in now. . . . Lang, the *New Yorker* writer, has also influenced Ross and Shawn against my flying, says boats are better and faster though Ross insists I may do as I choose. . . . I must decide by Monday as I have the possibility of a ship. Jane Grant [Ross's wife] is worth ALL the men in the office as a fixer, I've discovered; if I ship, it will be via her efforts, done in one afternoon of phoning all over the country. . . . Shawn took photos of me yesterday while everyone lined the room and made cracks; I was never so embarrassed. Then we went to Bleecks for dinner; there was the usual table of inebriated journalists and wives, singing college songs. I have no news. Nothing inside my head but work, worry, dull confusion. . . . A poor way to start forth toward cold, discomfort, uncertainty and surely no joy."

Dan Lang had brought back some letters from Rome.

"Lang gave us the letters," Janet wrote. "I wished too that he were you and so bringing the comfort of an embrace, not letters, mostly for others. Being a man, he could tell me none of the things about you I wanted to know and asked, all the small personal questions: how is your flat arranged, is it charming or dull, what do you eat at your mess, are you always in uniform, etc. He didn't know."

In subsequent letters she asked: "Are you growing fat or thin and can you stand not liking the American mess food when your eyes must tell you others would yearn to have it? What a predicament. . . ."

I had been giving reports of what I was doing and what the war had done to people's lives, because on October 24 she wrote:

"Your long letter gave a horrifying and illuminating picture of what history calls modern war does to the old human values of people: Sauve qui peut though must seem the only natural physical reaction left. I don't know what to think even about what you think there, because I have no concrete experience of my own; I read your words, know them to be true—and stop there. Because (and this is the tragedy) even for a knowledgeable person like me, general past information is not enough for the rethinking needed; it takes one's own eyes, ears, nose, as you have used all three, on the place visited itself—I go to Paris with great confusion for my work, knowing all that has been already written, and what is left for me? . . ."

During this time I had begun organizing my Press Reading Bureau. My job consisted of preparing regular reports on the Italian Press mushrooming from all shades of Left, Center and Right. A number of partisans, young men who had been fighting with us and for us, had gathered around our Intelligence Unit. Some were operating across the Gothic Line, which had cut Italy in two, with the north still under the Fascist puppet government disparagingly called the Repubblichina of Salò, or Little Republic. Those who were in Rome or had followed our armies from the south were ready to be of use to us. They were mostly college students or young graduates, well educated, reliable and anti-Fascist. From this group I drew my staff of readers. They were to become well known in their fields: columnists, professors, jurists, writers, journalists, but at that time they were young, eager, hungry and poor. Our PX provided most of their wardrobe, and our mess most of their food.

My British colleagues had set up our own mess at the requisitioned Villa Blanc in Via Po, destined to become famous later. We used to invite to share our rations—made palatable by our local cook with vegetables gathered in the countryside by Tonino, the film extra turned waiter—Italian anti-Fascists: politicians and diplomats, artists and writers. On any given day the Demo-Christian leader Alcide de Gasperi could be found sitting next to communist leader Palmiro Togliatti, or Count Carlo Sforza—ex-foreign minister in pre-Mussolini days—next to Alberto Tarchiani, ex-Italian ambassador to Washington; Alberto Moravia and Giorgio Bassani; Leonor Fini; Carlo Levi, Luigi Barzini. Italian partisans came in and out of the Gothic Line with the latest news and information. Even officers of the High Command and Allied diplomats finally wanted to be invited too. We excluded them. But before my own mess I took my meals at the Excelsior.

The food consisted of our military rations, of course. Not the customary elegant food of prewar times, to be sure, but plentiful, and certainly "others were yearning to have it." Soon I discovered, to my dismay, that what those "others" were hoping to have were our leftovers. They couldn't believe that our strict hygienic military rules forbade the use of leftovers. Everything had to be destroyed. Our fear of germs overruled all sentiments of Christian charity. Not long afterward two old friends came to see me, Marchesa Maria Theodoli and her sister, Isabella di Rende. "Could you get permission from the area command to pick up your leftover food for starving children from the war zones? Can you give us your garbage?" they pleaded. "Please help us!" The Italian Red Cross was in a shambles. It was from this outcry over the plight of so many children orphaned by the war that the Foster Parents Committee for Italian War Orphans was born. Once I had obtained the appropriate permission, the military were the first to help. They responded because they knew; they had children, too, back home, safe and healthy and sheltered.

When our newspaper, *The Stars and Stripes*, announced formation of the committee, requests began to arrive, then actually to pour in. On their furlough, the GIs came up the hill to look at the children, each to select his own foster child by paying a monthly due of five dollars, "enough to keep one child for a month," said the sturdy, heroic, middle-aged mother superior, who had barred the door to the Germans when they had wanted to occupy the orphanage during the battles at the Anzio and Nettuno beachheads. Although it was hard to tell one kid from another, sometimes the requests were very specific. "I want an orphan from Sardinia," said a bombardier, who had flown bombing missions over that island. "I want an orphan from Sicily," said another, who had fought his way from the end of the boot to Rome. On furlough days the road up the hill to that shelter was a constant coming and going of jeeps.

In New York, the ladies of the Italian Welfare League, stirred into action by my mother and Signora Carla Toscanini, began organizing the Italian-American communities and the word spread. In no time, cases of all kinds of merchandise and medicine began to arrive through the Vatican channels, whose permission had been secured for us by Ambassador Myron Taylor, President Roosevelt's representative to the Holy See. Later, after the war, this initial Committee of Two spread its wings and became a national organization.

"I, too, want to adopt an orphan, a boy . . ." wrote Janet.

Janet had arrived in London. The following letter was her first one from Europe. Her depressed moods and worries of the last months in New York had changed. She sounded elated and eager. Pleased to have found old friends and admirers, like the great gardener Russell Page, on his way to Egypt, with whom she had a good time going around the city, and Eric Sevareid of CBS, as well as her *New Yorker* colleagues John Whittaker and William Duel, with whom she talked admiringly of A. J. Liebling's articles in the magazine, and of Anne O'Hare McCormick's brilliant columns in *The New York Times*. She was again on her home ground. I had expected that, and was relieved.

[November 9, 1944]

. . . I wrote your darling mother today; am now giving you my first moment alone in my room, except to fall exhausted from fatigue at after midnight, since my arrival this week. To make the city seem natural, Russell has just arrived, is soon leaving with his Cleopatra* sketches for an even more ancient distant civilization. I expect SHAEF [Supreme Headquarters, Allied Expeditionary Forces] to have my final papers for my last voyage this week; shall purchase extra uniform; we are encouraged to wear nothing but, for safety as foreign ladies on the boulevard of that once gay city. My journey was splendid, as much a cruise as yours, darling, if high enough to demand oxygen, superb weather, except from Scotland down; had we continued our island hopping, I should have been in line to see you, in your flat! Eric Sevareid said he'd seen you, that you were intelligent, handsome, discouraged. You still seem the first two to me. The desperation of Europe and even this island's plight in physical destruction has already affected me, as it has you, with so much more experience and sadness,

_____
* Janet's code word for Egypt.

and my heart seems deadened with so much talk of politics, plans, what Churchill said in public, in private, which country has bled most, which will have the most children in the next twenty-five years, so the largest army. I miss you, your warmth, laughter as I knew it, the intimacy of friendly American life and safety, of lights and no fear and no cold. I have gained two pounds here, food portions seem so large, in reaction to what they have not had to eat in the past four years, I suppose; I have had to lunch out since arriving to see people make necessary connections; constant trotting about, taxis hideously dear, bus queues endless but our Public Relations officer and the Air Transport Command men of such memory, thoughtfulness, kindness and personal politeness as to make me find them angels in uniform. I miss you darling, more than I dare say. The last days of packing up in the flat were tragic for me. I did not hear from you the last days at all, but your mother read me her letters from you; papers here so small that there is NO Italian news, so far. I miss not knowing what goes on in your beloved Rome, in your heart and mind. Jane Grant wangled a number two priority for me after the magazine had achieved only a number four; came over with *Life, Reader's Digest*, etc.; everyone is wonderful to me here, certainly our magazine has a superb following and reputation; saw John Whittaker and W. Duel by chance in Claridges, good talk, both feel reporting from Paris has been silly, Liebling and McCormick excepted. I am calm as a bird in flight, no fear. I was calmer than all the men! Love and love!

Janet was now in Paris. She was billeted at the Hôtel Scribe, which was now the headquarters of the foreign press, opposite the Opéra. Our direct communications had not yet been established. The first news of her arrival came in brief messages from "carrier pigeons" in the guise of correspondents coming my way from Paris. By the end of November our V-mails began to arrive directly, bringing more details and impressions of Janet's first days in her favorite city. On November 24 she wrote: "Europe is indeed like a picture of something now fallen to the bottom of a well, with water clouding the image and mud despoiling the color. The city still is lovely as Rome is and equally unharmed, I dare say. But a people has been partly destroyed, less than in your land for which my heart bleeds even though I have not seen with my eyes what I see here, where the disintegration has been certainly less because briefer. The few French friends I have seen are all completely deteriorated by the war and inflation of money which the Germans scientifically constructed as part of the ruin of the country."

Janet went immediately to see her dear old friend Noël Murphy, Esther Arthur's sister-in-law, at Orgeval on the outskirts of Paris, where before the war she had been spending weekends in a lovely farmhouse. When the war came, Noël had chosen not to leave France; Janet had been worried about her.

[November 26, 1944]

Darling,

. . . I am returned from three days with Noël where I went immediately on arriving in this familiar city. Emotions of the heart and sentiments are, as you have long known, rare; rare here, too. Rain, poverty, cold, little hope and absolutely no soap; what a picture of this still beautiful city. N is *courbée de son travail*, like any peasant after four years' labor in mud and wind; the hands are nearly unrecognizable; the soul is perfectly happy at the expression of devotion to this land; the health superb for first time, owing to dairy diet and regular hours—and work. Work, that organizer of fate. N devoid of hate, irritation; with a flash of old violence and bright blond laughter said, "How can one hate anyone; everyone is so awful." House still in perfect condition, charming, my room intact, all untouched though Germans encamped for two years on farm nearby; battle was fought over N's house in air, bombings on both sides, a fort was made of neighbor's barn; by chance at last moment, our men decided not to wipe out N's village where they thought enemy was hiding, or so a colonel at dinner told later. He could not have known he was eating labor of N's hands, back and flesh—ham from pig cabined next to Main B's* limousine in barn, potatoes dug as well as planted under N's window, and sour cream from cow named Salomé; white ducks to make me laugh, five geese, chickens and now another piglet, two cats; the Caucasian maid very changed, bitter, secretive. My hotel sordid, dirty, unkempt, am happy am billeted near Manon and Louise, room with bath, *placie*, excellent mess; prices fantastic. Men are unbelievably charming to me: received personal invitation today to go back to the front, from two darling fellows, returned today. Have bicycle, also *réchaud* and small electric

* The couturier Mainbocher, a great friend of Janet's.

radiator, purchased in London and will need. Not yet bitter, only damp, chill, sad, sad, sad, ah, *la tristesse.* My nostalgia for New York is destroying all my concentration on my job. Doubt if I can go to Italy at all; am aligned to SHAEF, have no idea why this restricts but it does; any sortie from this theatre must have been made in New York. Last night read Liebling's stuff sent before my arrival; it is so wonderfully good that it alarms me, to try to follow in footsteps. It is impossible to write what I feel, Cherubino. Please write directly, darling. A toi . . .

———

On November 27 came a letter so in tune with my feelings, as if we had both communicated orally our distress—distress at our separation, difficult to endure after seven long months away, and distress about our experiences in Europe. We were both working hard, with little relaxation and few comforts. It was bitter cold in Rome, too. Homes and offices were unheated. I used to keep my gloves on in the office and for the first time since childhood, I had chilblains. When visiting friends, we sat wrapped up in blankets, as if squatting on a drafty, cold deck in the middle of a stormy transatlantic crossing. Our blankets were coveted by everyone in Rome; they made very warm coats. I started to drink good martinis at the Excelsior bar at the end of the day. They became my needed relaxation. Though I had many friends in Rome and, of course, the family, I missed Janet, and was starting to feel restless and doubtful about our being able to meet soon.

[November 27, 1944]

My darling,

If the summer heated me to explosion, the chill of this early winter which I have now known in three different countries and latitudes has frozen my mind and body. If I could only frankly fall ill, I should enjoy a relief which my burdensome endurance denies me. I suppose I am suffering my version of a nervous prostration, from fatigue, the shocks to soul and serenity, the weariness of unhappiness. But my terrible physical strength keeps me going; my mind is however faltering; my memory betrays me; men walk up whom I know and have known for years, I cannot remember their names; the confusion I feel at seeing here a face which I saw there, the last time, robs me of any sense of connection. I don't know who other people are; often I don't know me. Only occasionally, in patches in talking, do I know what I am talking about. I seem to make a general sort of sense, but it is as if she, a she, some other person, a he, another man, anybody, were talking, and I listening, not very interested. Nor informed. I reread your mother's enclosure, from Rome, dated October 2, and even the clarification of drama and disaster was like a river of words, with debris flowing upon it; I felt more as if I were drowning than reading. After two days, I knew the communication by heart and well enough to recite it, *mot à mot*, yet only in brief periods could my brain listen, my eyes actually see the words which make a language, which carry thoughts, news, belated sorrows, truth. . . . Are you better? Your strength and health and relief, in—darling, you must stop it, you must—pulse-ruining drinking are the only words which keep coming to my mind. For heaven's sake, don't add a created disorder to that which already exists, angel. Use your endurance; I used mine. I have nearly perished of it, true. But I shall have no peace if you are wrecking your entity, ever, ever. I continue to feel I shall fall awake soon, as one falls asleep, a process of nature, and when I fall awake, nothing which has happened will be true. So must the people of Europe feel, and they have had to hope to awake for five years. How true your letters about the sadness of this Continent and how it set up the prototype in misery which private lives, in their smaller complete sadness, have duplicated. I wish I could hear your voice speaking Italian; it was always such a delight. Are you thin, are you sober, are you chill, are you warm, are you more Mediterranean than ever? Why did that anger you? It is a classic to the world. No one from Europe ever loves an American long, either as a race or as an individual; we fail them, and they do not forgive. Their failure seems part of their fascination for us. We are on the same side of the ocean, darling.

[December 14, 1944]

Darling,

For your birthday which is today you gave me the present I most desired, a letter direct from you in your capital city. True it had been opened, but whoever read it could have enjoyed it far less that I . . .

I do not see how the upper class minds, the anti-democrat brains which have shown such stupidity in the decades just past, have enough intelligence to force onto the world what they want today, yet such seems the case. Everywhere the true democrat forces seem pushed down as if they were dogs and the stupid class *patronale* with its selfish habit of privilege, its contempt for all those beneath and for the intellectual who sits, too often fawning to one side. Judging by Italy, Athens,

Belgium, I don't know who has won the war so far except that it seems merely not to have been the Germans. Outside of that fact, I should say that several other enemies have won, as usual. France seems in a state of complete paralysis because there is no coal to open factories on, too few workmen to work, and little desire to work either, I must say. The black market is the only commerce which is operating, and it in a disorganized fashion since the peasant, fearing devaluation of the franc, prefers to keep his cow rather than sell for bifsteak. So what one could purchase before the liberation if one had money, one can no longer buy. Paradox.

I miss you more than I can say. Happy birthday, darling.

1945

Nineteen forty-four closed with a note of optimism. We celebrated its demise soberly, but joyfully drank to the New Year with family and friends.

My seven months in Rome had been crammed with experiences. I felt like a veteran compared to Janet, who had just arrived in Paris.

Looking back, I could say that I had enjoyed my work. I had met most of the Italian press and members of the Committee of National Liberation, who had come out of hiding and were giving new voice to the six political parties they represented. Among them were Alcide de Gasperi, who became the premier of Italy's first Christian Democratic government, and Sandro Pertini, a hero of the resistance, today—1985 —Italy's president. The exiles, too, had been coming back. The Communists held their first large public rally, with Palmiro Togliatti, back from Russia, at their head. It was held in the ancient grounds of the Palatine Hill, the residence of the Roman Caesars. I went with Margaret Bourke-White of *Life* magazine. Peggy, as she was called, was photographing that historical event, and I helped her with her equipment. I even met face to face with one of my radio listeners; Count Carlo Sforza introduced me to him. "I listened to you every evening from my villa in Piedmont," he said. "You kept our hopes alive. I want to thank you." He was Professor Luigi Einaudi, who would soon become president of the Italian Republic.

These eminent political figures would often come to our PWB mess in Via Po, as it became known to the Italians, to express their opinions and keep us informed about the political scene. There were also pleasant evenings with writers and literary friends, who had started a monthly magazine on the arts, politics and sciences, called *Mercurio*. It was directed by my old friend, the novelist Alba de Céspedes, and the first issue had appeared in September.

"We are surfacing from underwater life. An obtuse, menacing silence had surrounded us. No voices reached our ears. Today we can talk. Italy has no bread, nor coal or arms, but it has a new voice . . ." the introduction to the first issue declared in part. That issue did indeed have new voices—from Hemingway to Joseph Kessel, from Ilya Ehrenburg to Franz Kafka. These famous writers had been banned by the Fascist regime. *Mercurio* was followed by other quarterlies of prose and poetry. It was like an explosion of voices, a chorus singing a hymn to liberty.

On our time off, the thing to do in Rome was to go to the nearby mineral springs of the Acque Albule, where we could bathe al fresco. Whenever I was lucky enough to find an officer friend with a jeep I would take the road to Anticoli to visit my sister Franca. But there was no way I could get to Paris and Janet. I had to be patient and hope that she would finally be able to come to Rome some day, when the war ended. This was my secret wish for 1945.

The winter of 1945 was bitter cold. To add to life's discomforts, snow fell copiously in Paris, while a *"tramontana,"* a nasty northern wind from the Carpathian Mountains, blew all the way down to Rome, making it impossible for the population of either city to keep warm. We were still without enough electricity, coal or oil for furnaces and stoves. In fact on January 11 Janet wrote:

"We have six inches of snow on our Paris landscape. Beauty. Prettiness. Murderous prettiness, enemy-aiding beauty: our soldiers perish in it, in the north . . ." Her first Paris Letter had appeared in *The New Yorker*, which drew cables of praise from both Ross and Bill Shawn, which, of course, pleased her, but, "I failed to send second as was so upset by disillusion here I tore up second and sent only a Christmas fragment, which was printed. I am sending third letter next Monday. You can judge if I am devoid of hope here, for first time in fifteen years never had I missed sending off my job of work before . . ."

In this same letter, Janet mentions the actress Margalo Gillmore:

"Margalo Gillmore gave me your sweet messages at Versailles, where I went to see the show in Louis XV theater . . ." Margalo was an old friend; in fact, she was the first American woman I had met when my future husband Bill introduced me to her in Rome in the summer of 1923 (or 1924). Margalo and *The Barretts of Wimpole Street* touring company, starring Katharine Cornell, had just arrived in Rome to perform for our GIs. I had recently been in touch with my old friends in the theater, so that when producer Remigio Paone asked me to arrange a performance of the play for an Italian audience I willingly obliged. No Italian had seen an American company before. Fascism considered anything Anglo-Saxon perverse, decadent, therefore forbidden. The show was a triumph, Margalo reported to Janet; she later collaborated with Patricia Collinge to write about it in *The B. O. W. S.* (*The Barretts of Wimpole Street*) published by Harcourt, Brace and Co. in 1945.

For the first time since her arrival in Paris, Janet wrote me a long, three-part letter, giving details of her life and feelings. We were growing restless from being so near and still so far apart, from having our letters opened and read, from not being able to meet, imprisoned by the rules and helpless to do anything about them.

[January 21, 1945]

Darling, two letters from you, like two warm, friendly messages in the midst of the snow, two letters sent like a two-part story. Yes, I, too, feel the unreality, dream and nightmare quality of existence, but not that you lack reality. Our flat and garden are the only real landscapes I know, more real than the streets here that I look out upon, and you more real than those journalists in our eternal green uniforms whom I see eating around me at mess. I think more real than I do, because they go to the front and that gives them some vital touch with WHY we are all here, why the world is as it is; my lack of touch with the blood elements of this war—and it is made on blood, either flowing out of men because they are wounded, or being poured into them by a medic, for the same reason—give me doubtless an animal mental noctambulistic quality, even to me . . .

My first *New Yorker* letter has just arrived in a pony edition, slightly rewritten so often as to make me ill; its sharp anger softened, an "I think" inserted; I have never used the first person pronoun in my entire career; it is utterly discouraging, especially as they had cabled, both Ross and Shawn, how splendid they thought the first letter; Ross was so impressed that he decided it was "a historical moment in journalism" to have me back at my job, as Genêt, which title he wished to continue for that reason. . . . I can understand that you sought strangers on your birthday and Christmas nights. The strain of hiding the heart is more anguishing before the family than before unfamiliar faces who know nothing of us and anyhow, being not of our blood, do not make us ashamed of passion. Incest is so revolting a sentiment that we do not want to be intimate enough with our family even to think of passion, for another, in their presence; it seems indecent. That is why, in longing, one can long freely only away from them and best among strangers, darling.

How wise you are in saying we are all now provincials in our capital cities because cut off from communication from each other. I feel like a woman in Balzac. Shall send two more letters with this, darling.

[January 23, 1945]

Darling,

My V-mail letters are incoherent, dull, meaningless. I cannot learn the habit of writing publicly, of inditing a letter to you, or even to my family, which is read by eyes that have never seen anything of me but my thoughts and those without interest. What strange intimacy. I feel like a prescription in a drug store when I write to you, filling out first the initials, then the numbers, which indicate me, and you, as if we were a certain quantity of quinine or grams of aconite or this or that, reduced to doctor's shorthand. . . . A letter from Russell [Page] yesterday, from London; curious. Perhaps he has finished his task in Ceylon. What secrecy we all live in. Only when we are killed is it admitted where we are—or when we are published. Your chilblains horrify me, darling, what on? Your toes or your poor fingers? Tell me. Where on God's globe do you suppose your trunk is? Ester must be frantic; she packed and sent it in summer heat. . . . Paris would be beautiful if each snowflake were not a frozen tear for the cruelty of suffering it adds to civilian life here, even not to speak of men at the front. Little food for average, modest French families, no heat, no light between eight-thirty and five; coiffeurs closed until five, then open till eleven. [Robert] Capa, *Life* photographer, is here in my hotel; shall ask him to photo me tomorrow, in my new officer's pink pants, to send you; Jimmy Sheean off to front. SHAEF frankly informing correspondents they are too numerous in Paris, war news is what they are here for, so get on with it; is sending fifty back home, I hear. No, I don't know the men in my hotel, and I am so dull and workaday, I don't frequent the few new orchids among us such as Capa, who amuses me, whom I have known for years, or Lee Miller.* I must. I sit in my room alone, mostly. I wish I could dream at night; I never do. So I always know the truth, that you are there, I here. If I could dream, I could be removed from the truth, happier in fancy for a fleeting night. Miss you, darling, more than I can say. More than I can add up, more than distance can mark off in miles. My Lord, I am homesick, house-sick, Manhattan-sick, Murray-sick. Why do my letters to you never reach you? Yours reach me. Who is getting my letters to you? Your letters always come unphotographed and opened. How can one write in public like this? Indecent.

[January 23, 1945]

This is probably the best way to communicate, in a series. Outside it is night; I can hear our soldiers at their Paris version of war, snowballing the French girls. How different men are than women. The instinct to attack, to fight, to throw, to torture, if only for a little, if only with snow on a blonde's face, if only fright and the fun from it as is achieved by one man on a Paris boulevard corner with a handful of snow in his hand and a strange, foreign woman passing, then running, then crying out with her small terror, part in mockery, part in the true fear the female feels for the male, who is stronger than she, crueler, equipped with muscles and reflexes which enjoy battle. Which enjoy. I shall never understand them. . . . I have two superb big photos of Radio City on my dressing table, both taken from top story of *Life* building; you know my passion for that architectural group; my pride that you worked in finest edifice in land. These pictures are my PORTRAITS, as of the beloved. Whenever I passed RCA, mist or sun or night or day, I gave it my eyes, my memory, my admiration impersonally, my love individually. (The Blue has cabled their man here to ask if I am in town and a weekly broadcast seems perhaps possible, providing they will properly pay me. As they offered me fifty dollars in New York, I supposed it was not a very polite way of saying they did not want me then. In New York, money is a scale of desire.)

* Also a *Life* photographer. She later married British art critic Sir Roland Penrose.

I walked into Notre Dame last Sunday—and out. It meant nothing to me. I have never liked its nave, which I find hard, its columns of a too late Gothic; it was a period of my past which I was no longer interested in and on which I walked out. I seem to have no aesthetic interest left at all; it alarms me. It was my chief intellectual passion. I never read, never have; I was all eyes and for beauty. If I no longer care for that, I might as well be blind, if I only use my eyes to see what I eat. . . .

I have met no one who interests me as a companion, except for an hour's bar talk, contact with brandy. I have become able to drink it again, having learned with you to love whiskey and loathe Cognac. So can one's palate turn in a circle. I am a little fatter than in New York; I have no scale as in our bathroom, but fancy I weigh perhaps one hundred and fifteen; I am lonely, emptied; today five people said I looked tired, and truly. Not from work. From lack of emotional nourishment. Ernest Hemingway here again; he talks such Hemingwese as to be almost incomprehensible now. I miss your voice, your leetl' occent. Send me a snapshot of you in Rome, please, darling. By a carved door or fountain or ruin. Some scene. Mimosa on the street corners makes me think of your city; the first time I ever saw mimosa, I saw it as a chrome large Roman tree. I could not believe my eyes, thought they were deceiving me with delight. Nothing delights me now. I am not enough awake. My mind and senses seem asleep, like an animal in winter. I have to force myself to try to think, to work, to answer letters, to phone—a lengthy complication at best—darling. Sleep well. I am thinking of you and missing you and our Manhattan scenes. I miss your mother extremely. I miss my captain's room. And yours. And breakfast. Before and after. Yours . . .

In this three-part letter, Janet, in answer to my queries, mentioned some of the press colleagues she had met at the Scribe, because, despite her complaints of feeling lonely and depressed, she was much sought after. Everyone enjoyed her company, her conversation, her wit. By nature she was sociable, she liked people, if they were intelligent and amusing. She detested them if boring, pompous or pretentious. She was often surrounded by people fascinated and entertained by her conversation and observations. She later became the doyenne of the correspondents in Paris, a center of reference for visitors, literary or political, from the States. If, during your first days in Paris, you were asked, "Have you seen Janet?" the reference could only be to Janet Flanner. She was like a major monument, not to be missed.

Breakfast at the Scribe, then, was always lively. You met everyone in the large press corps, exchanged news and gossip, made plans for the day, already set up by the military in their briefings and, if you arrived in time, you could also enjoy an egg, a rare delicacy coveted by many. Most of the time you missed it, because you wanted to catch the hot water for your bath, which was briefly available during the breakfast hour. It was a question of either/or, but one morning Janet decided to have both. She rushed in to breakfast, had her egg and rushed back up to her room for her bath. She looked at her watch: "By Jove," she exclaimed, "I've made it for once!" Her victory was short-lived. Inside her tub, enjoying the hot water, lolled a bearded fellow—her pal Hemingway. Several colleagues who later encountered the wet, half-naked Hemingway in the corridor could never quite make out what had happened until Janet recounted the event, half annoyed but also amused.

"Venomous [Charles] Maurras, who for nearly half a century had been the chief of French royalism, anti-republicanism and anti-Semitism, and the editor of *L'Action Française*—the daily paper which spoke for all three and was published in Lyon instead of Paris during the occupation—was tried primarily on the charge of intelligence with the enemy," wrote Janet in her Paris Letter. She had attended the trial, which she mentions in her letter below. But, of course, the great news of the day was the tightening of the noose around Germany.

[February 2, 1945]

Darling,

I am just finishing my *New Yorker* Letter; they asked me to delay it one week, heaven knows why. I shall not have earned a penny this year, what with journeys, delays, etc. Monday I am sending Bedaux, checked here by his private secretary whom I have chanced to meet, shall send it by bomber packet which is almost as quick as V-mail and nearly as cheap. I have done the *New Yorker* Letter as a Letter from Lyon where I attended the Maurras trial, or did I tell you? I cannot remember anything anymore, whether I say it or write it or if someone else does. . . . The snow has melted in a roaring, dribbling thaw with some sun but the weather prognostication is for another terrific cold snap later in February. Isn't the Russian news exciting to body, mem-

ory and mind? Russians in Frankfurt, near the suburbs of Berlin;
Russians in Germany to the east and we to the south, in little villages
where the memory does not jolt with recollections as in thoughts of
Berlin or Frankfurt, but in the enemy land, tout de même. My
revenge, my hatred for the Germans is having its holiday. Curse them,
may God curse them and hell arrive to burn them in their own
towns, in their own great cities, in their own great pride. That the
DNB [the official German news agency] has just warned Berliners
"not to lose their heads in panic when they see the first enemy tanks"
fills me with gloating delight. I am not ashamed that I have these
evil joys in me; they are their fault. Now the Berliners will know
how the Poles, the Greeks, the Belgians, French, Dutch, Italians lost
their heads when the tanks, which seemed like picnic wagons to
Berliners then, spread terror and havoc and captivity over those other
lands and bodies of people. *Tu me manques sans cesse et sans cesse.*

––––––––

By the end of February, the Russians had begun their assault on
Berlin. It was wildly exciting, especially considering what they had
suffered when Hitler turned against them the entire weight of his
armies—one hundred and eighty-five divisions—to fight a terrible war
on their soil, destroying great cities, scorching the earth and killing
twenty million of their people. Russia's suffering was the weight that
Stalin threw into the scales at Yalta, demanding, as his price, all of
Eastern Europe and half of Berlin.

Hope, then, for peace in the spring was high in our hearts.

March 13 was Janet's birthday, and I asked Margaret Bourke-
White, who was just then going to Paris, if she could take some
little presents to her. Meanwhile, Janet had begun visiting places and
towns where there were still some pockets of German resistance, or
which had just been taken by our First Army in Germany proper. In
fact when Peggy arrived Janet was on the verge of leaving for Cologne.
Hence the following letters, that reached me after weeks of little
communication between us.

[March 24, 1945]

Darling,

No word from you on my return from Cologne. Only a letter from
me to you, returned. I had given it to someone who knew someone
who was going to Rome; I don't know who he was. He did not go,

I suppose. It was the letter in which I thanked you for my birthday presents, which Peggy brought. They are PERFECT; what a joy. I opened all except the superb silver pendant before March thirteenth; I think the little mosaic pin is almost my favorite, though it may be the delicate silver cross, which I wore for salvation to Cologne, to avoid German mortars constantly coming in; the adorable heart-shaped leather box for the treasures, AND the Moroccan slippers which we will wear together. I showed everyone the mosaic especially; today, Colette, the daughter of Colette the writer, left me a little gift so appropriate as to take my breath away; a small paperweight of black stone, with five mosaic medallion scenes of ROME! St. Peter's, Sta. Maria Maggiore, the Temple of the Bocca, Trajan's Column and the Forum. I identified them all, easily. I adore it; she does not know how she pleased me. She is the amie of someone here in our hotel; is a nice, stout, intelligent campagnarde. . . . Darling, I long to see you and Rome so, I am perishing of it. I dislike my malaise in Paris less, am growing more used to it; but I can never be happy again here surely. . . . Will you be a major with your promotion???? I received a letter the other day, a *première de la couture*, addressed to General Flanner. Oh, my darling Major Natalia, I do long to come to Rome to have a holiday, and salute you. I am sick of our communications consisting of intelligent comments on political affairs. . . . Please write to me, darling. Long since I've heard from you. La tua . . .

Janet, who hated flying, was hopping about the war zones like a bird, on small, scary planes with hard, uncomfortable bucket seats, and behaving like a trooper.

[April 10, 1945]

Darling,

I hope to heaven there is word from you when I return to Paris. It has been two weeks since I had a note and then three weeks before that since I received news from Rome. . . . The little snapshot you sent of yourself and your adoptive children is such an excellent likeness of you as to be an amazing refresher of the memory. Some people have a physical vividness which transmits itself easily in photography; yours does; the black hair, its orderly shape, your white teeth. I usually look like a cross between an old pope and a whale seen from an angle in a snapshot. . . . I am at Luxembourg where I did not mean to be and have been for five days with great profit and an unbelievable amount of relaxing pleasure. I flew from Paris toward what I thought was Nemours, but owing to stupidity in my orders which read Trier, FRANCE, and the fact that the plane never did or had gone to Nemours, I landed near Verdun, was flown across to the air strip here in a cub with my luggage to follow in another. It took four days to arrive; I slept in my coat lining, was given a new toothbrush and fine food. While waiting, I flew up to Coblenz the second day as a plane for the press was going to facilitate the meeting of the twenty-three generals at Ehrenbreitstein, across from Coblenz, and the flag-raising there. Day before yesterday, I drove back into Germany as far as Trier; tried to get to Piesport, a famous Moselle wine town, but the bridges were out. Spring has arrived here; it looks peaceful in fields, though the cities look destroyed; only villages have escaped, if devoid of the modern improvement of railway stations. I do not understand why the war does not end; defeat of Germany seems not the definition of peace. Please, darling, write to me . . . Do write.

With the occupation of Germany the terrible, incredible atrocity stories of the concentration camps came to light.

[April 24, 1945]

Dearling,

I am in Wiesbaden where I have been for five days, writing an atrocity story on Ravensbrück, the women's camp, near Stettin still held by the Germans. . . . I fly to Weimar tomorrow to do Buchenwald if I can stand it as a form of further knowledge about these dreadful Huns, and will try to jeep to Nordhausen for an atrocity story for *The New Yorker*. . . . Germany is like a big male that has been finally knocked down, his ugly face bleeding while he whines. Can you believe it? They are toting up lists of bombing damage to present a bill to the Allies? I met three such beautiful Italian displaced girls in the staircase of the spa hotel the other day; kids who had been sent to slave labor here, one a true Italian beauty. You know my appreciation of the type! I patted her arm and wanted to touch her, in memory. Your last letter I brought with me; such relief and delight to hear from you; who brought it? It came in TWO DAYS, a miracle of closeness. I go to Paris by plane Sunday; a cable will be there from Shawn, answering my inquiry about going to Rome. I can NOT wait longer. I have told him I am tired. Tired of not relaxing as I wish, where and how. . . .

Now that the war is nearly over—isn't it, the re-doubt worries me—I have finally got proper clothes for flying, khaki woolen pants and a short khaki jacket, very smart. My radio broadcast engineer here lives at Bay Shore. We talked Fire Island lengthily. How I miss it. I am tired after my long piece and radio speech; it didn't get through, I fear. I broadcast from a caravan Mackay outfit, on a grassy hill beneath apple trees in bloom! You'd not know me. I fly around like an elderly white crow; I have a fine Nazi pistol; I stand journeys which slay the younger women. I am trying to watch, learn, think, decide as to what will happen to this wicked Europe. I long for New York and the roof garden and Sunday breakfast with *caffè latte* and Harold and you. And your dearest mother's energy and voice and her cigarette in the center of her generous, wise mouth. How fine she is. She was a great friend to me. I shall reread your letter. I shall visit you in your great viewed new apartment. I shall be a shabby officer with a chic civilian. I have no civilian clothes. I shall love Rome and its cherubs. I long for heat and the classics.

———

The Nazi occupation of Italy collapsed in April 1945. German troops had been occupying the peninsula since 1943 in an attempt to resist the Allied landings in Sicily, Salerno and Anzio. In July of that year, Mussolini's own Grand Council forced him to resign. Arrested by the king and imprisoned on top of the Gran Sasso, he had been rescued by German paratroopers and, in September—only forty-five days after his escape—the Repubblichina of Salò had been set up in the north. Marshal Pietro Badoglio, the new temporary head of government, had been forced to declare that "the war continues."

But two years later, as the Allied liberation army was moving north, Mussolini fled from Salò. He had been seized by Italian partisans at Dongo, only five miles from the Swiss border, where, disguised in civilian clothes, he had been attempting to escape with his mistress, Claretta Petacci. He had been shot on the spot, with Claretta at his side; she had heroically chosen to die with him. Their bodies were hanged by their feet in a public square, Milan's Piazzale Loreto, for everyone to see, sneer at and ponder about.

On April 30, just a few days later, Hitler lay dead in his bunker in Berlin, a suicide. The Allied saturation bombings had destroyed his industrial towns and ports. The Battle of the Bulge had been lost, and his armies had been defeated on every front. On April 25, the combined Allied armies had met at the Elbe River, cutting Germany in two.

[May 1, 1945]

My darling, my darling,

Death to tyrants. They are dead, now both are dead. How have the mighty fallen. What rejoicing. How feeble the mere headlines, Mussolini Dead, Hitler Dead; type size gives them their only magnitude. The Bible alone with its terrible paeans of praise for the dead enemy are suited to the hearts now light with joy because of death. The enemy and the avenger. It is wonderful news to you, to me, and to your mother. . . . I returned from Germany last evening after a flight from Weimar which left me as dizzy as an insect from circling and being battered in the air. I had not heard the full news of the due and disgraceful death of your tyrant until I reached Paris. How suitably he died, crushed by those he desired to crush. The terror he had inspired was his own justice, spat on and lying in an indecent public embrace with his paramour. Thank God for the violence of the Italian heart and hand, he died proper to his own works and not in bed, ill and gravely like a statesman. And now his twin, his Austrian counterpart from over the mountains, is fallen to death. Curse them both. There was no news from you to me, waiting me here, but there was the death of your enemy and mine, and that was news from your ardent eyes and republican heart. God bless spirits like yours and keep them lighted. I embrace you in this moment. I recall Fire Island and your dazed moments when your mind could hardly believe that Il Duce had at last fallen from power. Now it is completed. *Bacio, bacio.*

On May 7, Germany surrendered at Rheims, in France. The Nazi state was no more, and the Germans were prisoners in their own land! It seemed incredible.

On May 2, Janet wrote:

"The peace means the end of war. That alone is clear—of what else is the beginning? The French were dazed: (all except youth, which shouted and marched) Europe will be Russian Europe if it's anything. French Europe is dead, doubtless died at Waterloo."

In Rome, the peace was greeted calmly. Here, too, people were dazed. No shouting in the streets, no extra bells ringing from the three hundred and fifty churches, but a sigh of relief could be heard through the entire peninsula. Although Italy was considered a defeated country, many citizens took pride in the resistance of the partisans, who had battled the Germans in the north and had gotten rid of Mussolini. But the mood, as a whole, was a sober one.

On May 16, Janet wrote:

"Nothing but public history has been happening, the victory at last. Physically war stops; mentally it now begins. I wish we could talk. I am tired of writing, writing like a pair of scribes. I wish the heard voice. The one to listen to . . ."

After V-E Day, Janet made another attempt to come to Rome, but without success. Frustrated, angry, disappointed, on May 17 she wrote:

"I am frantic. I am willing to go to the Ambassador, anybody, anywhere, anything. It is now over a year since you left and I saw you last, weeping in the station. Cherubino, help me; go see General MacChrystal if you know him, or at any rate, for Christ's sake, know the truth—that I am going mad with effort, to see you."

On May 29, Janet, back from Buchenwald, sent me the following note:

"Buchenwald was a horrible shock; the news from the concentration camps seemed to me the most important news of all the years of war. Hitherto, the struggle had been mainly military. But with the concentration camp emergences of dead and dying, what lay behind the war, vaguely perceived but not so important as the military figure of Nazi might, suddenly became the great, horrible, shocking protagonist. It must never be forgotten . . ."

[June 17, 1945]

My darling,

Note new address. SHAEF went to Frankfurt and took our APO number with it. It was like someone moving your house, but leaving the street still in place. Two letters, one of May 22, came to me ten days ago just before I went to the First Army*; none on my return, as our mail STILL goes to Frankfurt. But those two letters were such a joy, such nourishment, such pleasure, that rereading them is almost as

* The First French Army of Occupation were stationed at Lindau on an island on Lake Constance, under the command of General Jean de Lattre de Tassigny.

agreeable as having new ones. I sent you a hasty note by Allen Grover of *Fortune* this noon at Ritz; I felt dashed when he said, Oh, I have a letter to her already from Bill Murray. Husband number one. Allen says he can go to Rome—tomorrow at eight, if only I were in his plane—because he is a non-filing civilian visitor. My heavens, I am willing to turn into the pope or a salamander or a white crow, if only the transmutation will get me to the holy city. Phoned again Saturday to ask if Rome is unfrozen; still frozen. It sounds like ice; it feels like it to my impatience. [Edmund] Wilson's airy statement that he can go where he pleases is one-half false, the other half inaccurate, so far as liberty is concerned; he CAN'T go where he pleased because it would please him to come to Paris; yet he cannot come—as yet—he is indeed free to go wherever he can as *The New Yorker* doesn't care where he goes since he is a roving correspondent and any place is fine for his talent and fermenting mind. My job is, alas, France, and as SHAEF in France included Germany, as a traveling spot or other near lands, I could go to them, but Italy is not in the same SHAEF zone, hence my difficulties. Since the peace, the army here is becoming as penurious and cranky as an old curé; nearly no transportation, quarrelings about the two taxis we have for one hundred journalists. We are allowed one guest a week and next week none—no hardship as food has become vile. None of these items count, darling, but the slow spread of stupidity, of mass confusion and an instinct only to choose to do the wrong thing, never the right, to complicate all issues under red tape, masculine vanities, jealousies, so that what was meant to be done is lost, stifled, under men's army uniforms, their moustaches, their ridiculous arm patches, like football teams, their drinks, their mistresses, their ambitions, their misconceptions of Europe—and its misunderstandings of them—this is the condition, now growing darker and uglier, like a hard, hot storm in summer, with no coolness coming afterwards. I shall laugh or slap the next man I ever hear mention women being jealous. The evidence of rank cruel active jealousy, stiffened by ambition, that I see in the army is as much more fierce and active and general as a man's strength is greater than a woman's, that any woman's jealousies I ever saw or heard of. After all, theirs is usually sexual or domestic; men's is big-time, as they say with relish about all they touch. I am tired of talking on the male level. I am tired of their levels, which are indeed all flat, some being higher than others, but all platitudinous. The only man I really like is Eisenhower. Honestly. He's good. He's honest. He has some sense of values in his work and is personal. He might help save Europe and Europe in us. The rest will wreck it, because they will try to act like adults when they are not. They seem not to know there are things called values. Darling, I am desperate for Rome. Yours . . .

Janet arrived at Ciampino airport at the end of June, on a golden Roman summer day. Not since my arrival, about a year before, had I felt so excited, so full of expectations, so anxious, so happy. Only when her elegant figure appeared, framed by the doorway, did I really believe that she had finally come to Rome. It had been a long time since we had seen each other, and we were overwhelmed by the intensity of our emotions. Here we were, two serious women, behaving like schoolgirls, giggling and chattering, with tears of joy streaming down our cheeks, in each other's arms. We had so much to tell, to ask, to hear, to know. Our first days were spent doing just that, over Pierina's special *risotto con funghi* or her delicate *gnocchi di spinaci con ricotta*, accompanied by glasses of cool white Frascati wine from the Alban Hills. Or we would go out to eat at Cesaretto's friendly, inexpensive trattoria—a gathering place for artists—for a tasty minestrone or a dish of spaghetti, or at Alfredo's, which had again started serving his famous *fettuccine alla crema*.

Food was still scarce in Rome, but the warm weather brought into the open markets fresh vegetables and fruit from the nearby farms. Pierina was sent at dawn that first day to pick out the best, while I decorated the flat with bunches of carnations, daisies and roses to welcome Janet to my Roman home at the top of the house. Luckily, the old elevator, most of the time out of order, functioned for once without stopping in midair. I also made sure my neighbors were not stealing water from my tank on the roof, as they usually did, so that Janet could take her bath in my exotic black-tiled bathroom and tub, in more than the two inches of water usually left for my own use.

As we had promised each other, no politics, no complaints, no shop talk; just fun and relaxation, like two proper tourist ladies enjoying their first vacation abroad.

At the Caffè Greco, where Mark Twain had sipped his aperitif in the company of the other artists of his time, we usually met our friends for cocktails. At the Caffè Rosati, on Via Veneto, we read the morning papers over a *caffè espresso* or a *cappuccino*, sprinkled with finely grated chocolate. One day I borrowed an American officer's jeep and took Janet to Anticoli to visit my sister Franca, still isolated on her hilltop, her marriage a casualty of the war. We saw Lea and Akos often. Akos was involved in the making of *Rome—Open City*, directed by Roberto Rossellini and starring Anna Magnani, the first so-called neo-realist film to come out of Italy after the war.

No museums were open yet, but the squares, the fountains, the palaces, the columns, the ancient sights were there to please Janet's eager, appreciative eyes. The narrow streets were bursting with people, and the shops were making the first efforts at showing new fashions out of whatever materials could be found, mostly in the black market. Pottery and glass from the provinces appeared in a variety of colors, shapes and forms. There was a vibrant feeling in the air, and, keenly aware of our limited time, we were enjoying every moment of our holiday together.

Even our rushed trip to Naples had its unexpected surprises. The city was still a shambles, but the San Carlo Opera House had re-opened its doors; that night there was going to be a gala performance of Puccini's *Turandot*. "Let's go," I said to Janet, who was an opera fan, though I had no idea what kind of performance we would hear! Neapolitan ladies in their best evening gowns, escorted by their men in white evening jackets, smilingly made their entrance. United States naval officers, in their dress uniforms, appeared with their lady friends, and in the *"barcaccia,"* the loge box reserved for members of selected clubs, single men peered through their opera glasses at the women, to whom they would also bow politely, in salutation. The scene seemed familiar, but there was a new electricity in the air.

The San Carlo Opera House was beautiful, all white and gold and rococo. The scene had a dreamlike quality. And then *that* voice —its range, its volume, its freshness, its high notes, all the way up to high C's! A revelation! Who was this young, fat soprano who sang like a goddess? Her name, we discovered, was Maria Callas. We had witnessed the beginning of her meteoric career!

Capri was another surprise. It had been selected as a rest camp for our airmen, so, as we were both in uniform, we had no trouble getting there.

The island teemed with tourists, but this time of a very different kind. American GIs were everywhere, living it up in the best hotels at a dollar a day, driving their jeeps at full speed through winding cobblestoned roads where no cars had ever entered before, or climbing up Via Castiglione to the villa of Edda Ciano, Mussolini's daughter who had escaped to Switzerland. The house was now reserved for our honeymooning couples.

Janet and I were staying at the Quisisana, the deluxe hotel in the middle of town that had been requisitioned for officers. It hadn't changed much from the old times, I was pleased to notice. When a chambermaid entered the room, we stared at each other and screamed, "Maria!" "Signora!"—in unison. When we regained our breath, Maria said, staring at my uniform, "My goodness, Signora, aren't you here for good?" She touched me to make sure I was real. We exchanged family news, as ten years had elapsed since we had seen each other. "Now I am working for the Americans, here, in this hotel." She smiled proudly.

The island had not been touched by the war or the Germans. It seemed a miracle.

Our first holiday was over. Next day, we returned to Rome, and Janet went back to Paris.

[August 27, 1945]

Darling,

The voyage of return was not the same. The blue sea, the islands of Napoleon's birth and ambition's death were naturally there, the fields of France, but there was a heat haze which blurred beauty, as also there was no animation acute in my mind or heart, so all was changed. The difference between going out and coming in, which is what soldiers said about shellfire. It's all the difference in the world. It's just after midnight, and I shall obey you and try to sleep early, for me. Paris is hot, noisy—the noise is American, not Parisian; you will believe me when I tell you that my Breton waiter, chagrined at dinner, said, "Oh, poor madame, this is the first time we have had pork for dinner since you left." I ate potatoes and one lemon, the latter upstairs. I had been given a banana by our pilot as we flew over Corsica. He said that Tuesday was his mother's birthday, that he hoped she had received the gifts he had sent her, and would I accept the gift of a banana, due (I gather) to my white if unmaternal hair. Americans are sweet, as we insist, and like boys, as we cannot deny. Everyone says I look remade-brown, fattish, devoid of circles around my eyes. Ross writes that he will give me ninety dollars weekly for expenses which I did not dream he would reach as he is so bitter about the Blue giving me nothing toward expenses. . . . It is not yet a dream; it is part of memory and facts, you, the oleanders, the figs, the ochre of Rome, the blue water of Capri. The meetings had the civilized extra excitement of the great new setting, of strangeness. Tanti bacci, tanti amore.

────────

My visit to Paris was not as successful as Janet's visit to Rome. For one thing, the weather was bad—the usual gray skies and intermittent light rain that you get often in that city. It was chilly, too. There was a kind of melancholia in the air; people looked sad. The treason trial of Marshal Pétain was in its last days. Janet was covering it for the magazine and took me there. That spectacle alone was depressing enough. I could feel no elation at the sight of this very old man, who had once reached the height of power; a soldier who had sold out his country to the enemy and turned against his own kind. He sat like a marble statue, expressionless, unperturbed, unrepenting, in the dimly lighted courtroom. It was a tragic sight, never to be forgotten.

Then there were all the questions about our future life together.

I had extracted permission for a trip to Paris from my boss, Professor Rufus Morey of Princeton, the cultural attaché at the head of our United States Information Service (USIS). The agency had only lately been transformed from a wartime function under PWB into a peacetime operation, and I was to visit the Paris branch. We had several projects in the planning stage, and an exchange of views could be helpful.

I hadn't realized how hard it was going to be for Janet and me to come face to face with our situation: Janet back at her job in Paris, and I torn between my desire to live near her and to be close to my own work in Rome, which I felt too important to be cast aside. Last but not least, my son would soon be released from the service, and I knew I would eventually return to New York. Paris was Janet's city; she had spent most of her adult life there. Rome was my native place, but New York was now my home, the place where I felt I eventually belonged. I sensed that Janet and I faced the difficulty of long separations, and I didn't know if I could bear them. We were sitting on a bench in a solitary Paris street when the question stuck in my throat. "Will we ever? . . ."

[September 4, 1945]

Darling,

One week ago today you phoned me with your dark voice to ask to hear mine. That is always such a touching compliment, to ask to hear again that communicating breath, the voice, the sound of a dear human, his particular little noise. I suppose birds who, each according to their species, sound alike to us do not to each other, or there would be domestic confusion in the nests which there never is. One robin doesn't mix up the voice of his Mrs. R with that of Miss R, two nests down the orchard. . . . I miss you. I am still baffled as to why we were so unhappy here when we had been happy in Rome. Even in the midst of the unhappiness, I felt sorrier for your unhappiness than mine, because you were a stranger, a visitor; you were homeless and helpless. It seemed so unfair that you should suffer in strange streets and under an alien sky. Your having often been here had nothing to do with your lack of protection this time. I passed the street bench where you cried that night; it is a terrible and sad little monument to me. Twice I have passed it; the second time I sat down, privately patting it, to comfort you, really. It was curious that both of us, like the same organisms, automatically were less sad the day before you left. I had been happier, too, in the days that have followed. I still feel transitory; in my work and soul, always jerking from one job to another, always in flight from some sense of guilt, for this, for that, for giving you suffering, for giving me suffering, too, by God. It is not reasonable for anyone to plant suffering instead of flowers in another's heart; what a harvest. . . . I have not heard from you, but that does not make any difference, for once. I have enough in memory. I identify you with every headline on Italy in any newspaper. Riots in Milan, I read, and think of you, your country. A piece about the Italian peasants being determined to obtain a share of land from their noble owners; I think of you and Capri and the terrace and the *mezzadria* system you explained, and I probably spell wrongly. . . . I miss you and wish I could see you to be gay again. You have no idea how I suffer when I am so silent and so inert. It is like a death for a day or so. Most of all that is ever wrong is always my fault. Perhaps part of what is right can be, too, but I rarely get around to thinking of that. . . . Write to me, too, my carissima. Are the oleanders blooming on your street? And the swallows singing and circling at sunset? I am thinking of you, darling.

When I returned to Rome, I felt better, more positive about my own life. After all, everything else was so precarious; how preposterous to pretend I could solve my problems all at once. So I went back to work with renewed energy. I had regained my confidence and my trust in Janet. She had resumed her travels and had found a good companion in the journalist Monica Stirling, a British writer covering Europe for the *Atlantic Monthly*, with whom we established a long-lasting friendship. This time Janet went to Denmark, and wrote from Copenhagen:

[September 15, 1945]

My Roman darling,

I am in a country of blondes—here your dark hair and antique soul would be anomalies, highly appreciated. It is a charming city of decent, handsome, yellow-haired people: they have taste and good manners; they lack the chic frivolity and vicious charm of the French. I feel a consolation here: mankind still seems competent to be honest in this land, flowing with milk, cream, honey, schnapps, excellent beer and more magnificent food than anyone else in Europe, except Sweden, can put in its stomach. It's time the Danes will now steal tobacco or chocolate, because they have nearly none for six years, But they do not rob on principle. . . .

———

Upon returning to Paris, Janet added more impressions of Denmark:

[September 24, 1945]

Wednesday, after lunch, darling. I returned from Copenhagen Tuesday afternoon. It was a delight to be in a normal city, where blond-haired children and youths do not mean enemies, where food abounded, eggs were fresh, cream was sweet and schnapps flowed over the bar like water over a dam. . . .

I bought the Osbert Sitwell book, *Left Hand, Right Hand*, in Copenhagen. It's exquisitely written; as Monica says, the Sitwells' snobbery can be excused on the grounds that they've a right to it; they are aristocrats, talented, eccentric and important. They discourage a mere commonborn American like me; the snobbery of the uterus is so cruel. . . . We had had a very cold flight and, thank God, I had my Texas boots on with wool socks inside. We had to fly seven thousand feet high above the cumulus, and in the cold, high sunshine, for three hours to avoid the lower winds. I am always a little ill at ease so high. What is man doing a mile and a half above the earth, he who has no wings, no feathers, no business, really, except by his inventive mechanical sense, to be up there? Man with his artificial things he keeps inventing; false birds which are our airplanes, false whales that are our submarines, and now a false end of the world that is the atomic bomb. I miss you and wish I were you yourself, sometimes, so I could undertsand you, thus understanding me and could finally find peace. Please write to me, though only when you wish, darling, and with words to say. It is a lonely life in this hotel, at best. Yours . . .

On October 12, Janet announced that she was trying to come to Rome at the end of November.

It would be our last meeting before my leaving for New York. I had received my orders and notification; I was going to sail from Naples on December 15.

[October 12, 1945]

My darling,

The autumn is my best time in the year. I love nature most then, and feel most fertile with love. Why I don't bud in the spring, I don't know; perhaps having been born old, I love better the aged and melancholy season. I have not heard from you since Sam [Ratenski] brought the last letter. I do indeed write you once a week and wish you might write so often to me. I go down the steps in a treadmill looking for word from you in our little post office on the second floor, and too rarely am given the gift of discovering your handwriting on an envelope. Nothing happens to me except work. I sit at my desk, as you have seen me, whether here or in New York, except that here I sit more. Monica runs in to say goodnight or to borrow a book and to forget something; she always leaves something behind her, like a snail leaves its trail. . . . I went to Versailles alone and walked in the garden the day before yesterday; I had to go to see about a paper in the town and, with a feeling of excitement, like an escaped child, decided to be a tourist, to be a walker, to be out of doors for my job for an hour. The gardens were beautiful, French, old, in perfect condition and stiff, with French form. I do not admire Louis XV's taste except in women; they sound lively, up to Maintenon, and she must have been a bigoted bore. Louis XIV is my favorite, including Pompadour . . . My Bedaux piece is finally out, with considerable comment. I disike everything I have written for *The New Yorker* since in Paris. I like only one piece as an exception, the Cologne piece. Everything else is heavy, complex, dull. Ross says it is the best work I ever did. He is mad. I think Monica has much more talent than I have, though she gives far less information. I suppose I could never do that book [on the 1850 period] either; I haven't the concentration for a long job. But my imagination is kindled by the idea where my knowledge fails . . . I shall go to Marburg for a piece, to Sam, then to see Katie Hume [author of *The Nun's Story*] and do an UNRA piece and two days in Berlin for a broadcast with a new colonel I have unearthed, very intelligent and head of our propaganda for the Germans. I miss you, my Cherubino. I have read your letter brought by Sam until it is tearing like old silk. Send me another, fresh, so I may wear it to dear shreds, too.

———

Janet arrived in Rome the first week of December, so that we had a chance to spend a few days together before my departure.

Our visit was brief but easy, even gay, utterly successful. Janet promised to join me after the New Year, and I was glad to get back to New York, to my son now out of the Air Force, and to Ester, who had nobly and generously substituted for me in my absence, perishing of nostalgia.

On December 9 Janet wrote the following letter from Munich, the last I received in Rome:

[December 9, 1945]

Darling,

I have just finished re-reading Conrad's "Heart of Darkness," that phantasmagoric, brief epic of African ambition and horror, a story of intercontinental hot greed and salvationism, something like [Charles] Bedaux's vision of his Sahara railway, Peanuts in a grateful world lapping up his peanut oil thereafter as a form of gratitude to him. As I look out my window at midnight, I see snow, the ruin which is the wall across the court from my bed, and I am back, not in a book which I had first read thirty years ago when moved by, but in a wicked, male, cold world, also filled with more real ambition and horror and results. It has been a curious psychic shock, this emergence from this book and its African power on my imagination and memory, and my emergence at midnight into the cold, snow-lined, ruined

Bavarian capital. Munich was the first city in Europe I ever was fascinated by. I feared it as unknown, strange, beyond me but, as I sat in the train leaving it (I was nineteen years old) with my parents, I recall staring at the two copper domes of the Frauenkirche Cathedral, murmuring as you'd say dramatically to my inner self, "I shall be back and live here." It is one of the few vivid recollections of my early life which my memory retains. I have never since wanted to live here, but it symbolized Europe, and there I did live. The city is ruined, a mass of blackened, broken buildings, and the white outline of snow. I am here after seeing dear Sam in Frankfurt, on my *Monument* job, a terrific one. I shall do a Munich Letter for *The New Yorker* and motor to Nuremberg on Thursday, only three hours distant, and get a day at the trial over with so as not to return after Christmas—I had hoped for some message from you from Naples (departure for New York), darling, before leaving, but none came. I wrote you once from Paris. I was never so rushed and quite ill: two days after arriving from Rome, I came down with a vile cold from fatigue, and that last night at Ciampino with the soldiers stewing by the fire asleep, and me awake on the fringe of the cold room and in a stiff chair. I ran a fever and felt quite ill and still stiff like a hippopotamus. Darling, your sense of life was so strong over me after leaving you. I felt so conscious of you constantly, of your voice and spirit and soul and love. I felt animated and nearly young. I kept wondering what you were doing in Naples, what street you were walking or driving on, what day of blue sky you would sail away in, for New York and your mother, and the flat and Billy. Please write when you have a moment for your hours will be taken there at first with tears of joy with Ester, I know. God bless you, my darling. Kiss New York for me for now, and kiss yourself for me, darling, darling.

Janet was in Munich while I had been tossing on the high seas for two days. She had just returned from Nuremberg, where she had attended the war crime trials of twenty-two high officers of the Nazi regime, surely the most spectacular and awful trial of our time.

[December 17, 1945]

My very darling Natalia,

My very darling human, this is to tell you how I see you, how I hear you, and how I think of you, if one can give an active verb as clearly to the brain as one does to the memories of the ear and of the eyes. I see you in a cocktail gown, with long skirt—that red and white hooded gown which I so loved you in. I see you walking with the greatest weight of dignity in steps I ever saw a woman have. The voice I remember as the dark vocal accompaniment and, behind it, your active mental spirit. Your instinct to speak up and decide which is part of your nature and not part of mine. It's no good pretending that parents can do more than restrict children: not develop them. The character is in the cradle, already made. I long to see you again, and I will either come to New York soon, as you and I pre-visaged, or in the summer if you return to Europe. Oh, good God how I long to be *happy*, to be free, to be still strong enough, young enough to hold happiness, to see you again as a strong vision of happiness for us both. I so deeply respect your sense of responsibility toward one, darling. Do, *do* believe my great sense of strong and deep responsibility also.

At the Nuremberg trial where I went for an afternoon and next morning session, I thought of you and the Pétain trial. This trial is also important, and is also weakened by the tiresome egotism of individual professional men, so far among the Americans, who want to drag out their time in court and make personal, cheap history by their talkativeness. But the principle is *rigid*. It may be one hundred years from now that the accumulated effort, on paper, of this trial will become a new precedent for controlling ambitious men and the blood of men who only follow and fight. Goering looks like a middle-aged soprano woman. . . .

The giant ship assigned to bring us home—literally thousands of troops from the Mediterranean theater—was the aircraft carrier *Roosevelt*, sent from the Pacific theater and stripped of its planes and pilots. She was an impressive sight, towering over the waters, with a row of rising suns—each representing a downed kamikaze plane— painted on her side.

The crossing had been delayed by very stormy weather and took ten long days. When at last we entered the harbor and came up on deck, we were pale, green and exhausted, but thoroughly happy. Tugboats surrounded the ship as she made her way slowly to her dock at Ellis Island. Fire hoses let loose their gushes of water high into the air in salutation, and cabs and cars stopped along the coastal parkway to blow their horns to greet us. The Statue of Liberty was there, against New York's skyline, noble and solemn. She seemed to smile, pleased that we were home. It was Christmas Day.

I could hardly get down the gangplank with all my gear—helmet, duffel bag, canteen. A handsome young soldier came forward to help me. "Bill!" I cried. He saluted and grabbed me in his arms. "Welcome home, General," he said finally. We both burst into hysterical laughter.

The drive home dazzled me. The whole of New York looked like a Christmas tree. So many lights, so much gaiety, everything looked so normal.

Breathless, I climbed the stairs to our house on the rooftop. Mammina Ester, with her luminous smile, was there. Inside, a tree all dressed up in tinsel and garlands, a bottle of champagne, a cable from Janet, were waiting for me, welcoming me home. I was happy. I broke down and wept.

1946

After the holidays were over, enhanced by the excitement of my return—the parties and dinners in my honor, the usual characteristic New Yorkers' outgoing joviality and friendliness—the impact of finding myself in such an atmosphere finally hit me. The city seemed untouched, whole, its major concern the day's sports results, and I found myself in the comfort of a home well heated and lit, with all the food and drink one could have wished for. The experience left me speechless, numb. The one real joy in this feeling of strangeness was to have found Ester, now nearing seventy, youthful in looks, spirits and health, with her usual understanding and warmth. And Bill, too, was home—safe, tall, handsome, a young man. To be with them, heart to heart, was my relief and satisfaction.

The only personal note of chagrin was the absence of Janet from our rooftop.

[January 15, 1946]

Darlingest,

Your first letter, dated December 29 from New York, has just arrived, to move me with its picture, which I can see as if watching, of your tears at entering the living-room door. Hooray for darling Ester and her bottle of champagne, in itself a form of liquid wisdom at the moment. Did she receive from me a letter with, among other small items, a ten-dollar bill, asking her to be so sweet as to find a bottle of that delicious drink to serve to you all on Christmas Day?

It has turned bitterly cold here, according to the French thermometer which becomes hysterical at freezing; as nearly no one is heated in the home, the hypersensitivity is founded. We have heat in our hotel, far more now that it is derequisitioned and filled with Belgian travel-ingmen than when it was strictly American last winter, though no Frenchman would believe that, of course. Italy is much on the front pages here; I enclose some clippings.

I saw the Giraudoux play, *La Folle de Chaillot* [The Madwoman of Chaillot]; it took three weeks to get places. It is two acts of a strange, intelligently fantasy piece against crooked money, against company stock sellers who sell what the British call "pie in the sky"— nothing. The solution by a quartet of old lady lunatics, to shut these wicked money men in the sewers of Paris and there let them rot is most satisfying—yet hardly practical, after all. However, as nothing which is done rationally to control such immoral men in all walks of life seems to bring peace to society, and as government seems in-capable of performing by logic, what should best serve its people, may be the sewers, lunatics, Giraudoux (whose plays were constantly per-formed before the Germans under Occupation here) and costumes by Christian Bérard are a relief anyhow . . .

. . . I have tried by reading the history of the last century in France to arrive at a balance for today. Unfortunately, I went so far back that I reread the history of the French Revolution and became utterly hor-rified at the bloodshed, the cruelty, the screaming delight of old harridans and young men to see other compatriots' heads cut off in public. I don't know which is worse, the French killing each other for a political ideal in their Revolution, or the Germans killing every-body else in camps for a political ideology. Man is so wicked and cruel, so strong of arm in torture, so violent of mind in his notions of im-proving the world that he scatters blood like a fish leaping from a lake, merely in pleasure and strength. I used to see the good things which men hoped for or wrote, and now I see more clearly their evil and even in the good writings I see the evil in ink, like a typographical error. I haven't the wisdom to know the real truth about anything, and my half-minded, half-hearted sorties into facts, and then my insolently sure-sounding reports on them are beginning to terrify me. Who dares tell the truth, even the little he knows? We all cheer the French Revolution, even today; read about it. We all cheer our ally Russia; read about their Revolution. We all curse Germany; read how much sense they mixed with their insanity, sense which we do not show in our knowledge either of Europe or men. I am sick and disgusted and long for you.

With deep devotion, yours . . .

While I was slowly adjusting myself to New York, Janet was reorganizing her life in Paris:

"In February we are tossed out of uniform and become civilians, without PX, without anything left but our Embassy rations which permit us to have six thousand francs per month at a private journalists' mess across the street in a rented room at the Grand Hotel," she wrote, and added: "I moved all my last possessions from my old little Left Bank hotel. These are years of pulling up roots and breaking off branches and of new flowers of hope . . ."

Janet had lived in the small Hôtel Bonaparte on the Left Bank for many years, ever since she had started writing for *The New Yorker* in 1925. She had never wanted the responsibility of an apartment. Since the Hôtel Bonaparte didn't have a room with a bath of its own, she had built one for herself. Her possessions were minimal. She felt that possessions restricted her movements, her feeling of freedom; they trapped her. Her ideal would have been to put all she owned in a suitcase. She was a great admirer of the snail, with its house on its back. She had been staying at the Hôtel Scribe, but it had become evident that soon she would have to move to a more conveniently located place, more comfortable than the old Bonaparte of prewar days. Meanwhile, her broadcasting, which she was going to drop in a month, and her writing were taking up most of her time.

"I am so slowed down in my work, I have such difficulty *thinking* anything new or fresh, that tomorrow's broadcast has taken two days to write. I probably have made a mistake to start the work again. I fear so. I can't possibly keep up with *The New Yorker* regular Letters, and do the two double Reporter pieces I am supposed to do and have done all the data collecting. This year has taken more out of me, of us, out of the world, God knows, than any I have ever yet lived and worked through. I suppose you are in Washington. Have been, are there, or are going. I await with acute impatience your decisions, and whether they seem good to *you*. If they don't serve *you*, too, and Ester, they must not be made. Or they must be made differently. Maybe you feel discouraged and disgusted with Europe and your hopes you once had in it, that your disgust with Americans seems more easily managed than that you have for the Old World. Maybe you feel that in New York one can avoid the worst of the New World, by selection of friends, while here there is no way of avoiding the worst in humanity because all people are desperate . . ."

Janet was a great admirer of General de Gaulle. He resigned because, as Janet wrote, he could not and would not carry on with the Chamber of Deputies as elected, thus weakening all hope of a stable government.

In a letter of February 9, she elaborated on the same subject:

"The Communists and Socialists here, thrown into what should be accepted as power by the departure of De Gaulle who really abandoned la belle France the way a man leaves a woman and with damned little in the house to eat and no money either—the Coms and Socs are now acting like any conservative majority; they are 'waiting for the elections in May' and after, before putting any of their reforms into practice. Just like Tories, always promising; only the minority ever hollers for reforms; when it becomes a majority, it acts, just like the previous majority which it displaces, or nearly, as stuffing."

I had been discouraged by the political attitude of the Allies in Italy. The Americans, largely ignorant of Europe and its history, were backing the conservative elements, including the monarchists and the reactionary right, and leaving the astounded new democratic forces wondering what they were doing. Amid such confusion it was not surprising to see the Communists gain strength while the ex-Fascists were pushing for an alliance with the monarchists. Certainly it wouldn't have been for this that we had fought such a deadly war and made such a propaganda effort for the democratic cause. And all this at a time when the country was painfully trying to get back on its feet, needing not only material help, but moral and political guidance.

[February 1, 1946]

My dearest one,

Your letter of January fourth reached me two days ago. The ocean seems to grow larger; it demands more time to cross. This note of yours was a job and a sadness that I was not at your side to make writing unnecessary. Only a touch of hand, without the pencil or the pretty blue paper. I hope you are not angry that I've ceased broadcasting. The moment I again began the broadcasts after the month of December off, in Germany, I knew I could not stand the burden mentally. I'm too tired in my head; I have too few thoughts. . . .

I am happy you find such happiness in companionship with Billy, my darling; you are a curious mother, less maternal than most; far less than your mother. It is a final reward for your purely physical maternity that finally you have some spiritual companionship with your child at last. Does he still look merely like your best beau when you go out together? . . .

Monica has written a short story which culminates in Italy and is a sort of art rhapsody of its paintings and sculpture and of you. I love to see your name and to see the fountains of Rome mentioned even on typewriting paper, but I did not think the story one of her best, unfortunately; too hastily done perhaps. I seem to have read so little, of late, that my mind is like a desert, devoid of roses and leaves. . . .

Please think of me when you hear a song called "Symphonie": I adore it and think of you. Is it silly to be childish like that? Think of me with love, be so kind—

———

I had been listening to Janet's broadcasts most attentively, because they were the only reliable news for me, and she had been almost offended by my not having clearly understood her meaning. Just to confirm my own feeling of disillusionment, I had queried Janet on a statement of hers about democracy.

"I was sorry my enquiry in my broadcast as to why democracy was not to be feared didn't seem as clear, ironic and devoted to you, as to me; what I meant was that if democracy is as good as it should be, it would be so attractive to all men that no one would find attractive any other form of political life, and thus we would not have to fear Communism's popularity, but the Russians would have to fear ours. . . ."

For the first time in over a year Janet was wearing a civilian suit. In a coquettish mood, she ended her letter with a penciled footnote:

"I wore my De Jez black suit (recent here to fit) and my bracelet as a civilian last night, my pearls and my Russian fur hat and fur coat, and was cheered by the men at my mess as I walked in. . . ."

[February 14, 1946. St. Valentine's Day]

. . . For the first time in my recollection, Paris shopkeepers have mentioned this saint. Florists have signs about him out front, among the tulips, explaining that you should buy a pot of blooms (at three hundred francs) to send to your beloved. So business has grasped the value of hagiography here, finally, as connected with this particular saint; God knows the Church has made money on its relics for centuries, and why Valentine, of whom I know nothing at all, was overlooked on the Continent, I don't know. When I was a child, the American valentines were prettier, more formal, made of paper lace like ladies' panties or frilled petticoats, and with hearts and flowers of colored cardboard stuck on, here and there, among the rudimentary lingeries setting. Sentiment and the sartorial, combined . . .

———

Janet had been trying to telephone me and had had to wait two hours and a quarter while some American official, who had priority, was talking. "I said he could not be talking intelligently because such men never did, and even a human intelligence couldn't talk well for that length of time, so he must be reading the dictionary aloud. . . ." She announced that she was going again to the Nuremberg trials. She was traveling with Madeleine Jacob, an excellent Paris reporter and comrade.

Just before flying to Nuremberg, Janet wrote me the following letter, on very special paper—an astonishing missive to receive out of the blue, on which she had written in pencil at the top of the page, "I stole this from Hitler's office in Nuremberg." (The letterhead, under the Nazi emblem in a corner, read "Zentral—Personalamt der Reichsleitung der NSDAP.")

On her way to the airfield at Orly, she scribbled:

"There were police officers and cars at the entry of the Fort de Châtillon—Jean Luchaire is being shot this morning, a traitor to his country and our profession. He was press chief for the Nazis, and [Otto] Abetz in prison here testified in his favor at his trial. Death to tyrants!"

[February 21, 1946]

My darling one,

This morning, the weather was spring, animating and affecting us all—all us human beings—like a drug, a pleasant poison of annual mortal gaiety. A divine hasheesh, of flowers in the air, soon to come. I felt *happy*. Now tonight I still feel happy, but it is winter. Snowflakes are as large as white carnations. The Place Vendôme, where I met you as you stepped from the airfield skies, was beautiful.

Your statement that Bill looked at you as if you were swearing (when you said you cared more for ideal than money) is very adorable. So characteristic of you both! Then your note added after we had talked as Valentine greetings to each other: "Wasn't it wonderful to hear each other's voice?" I was trembling, as you, as I told you, darling. I shall be in Nuremberg two weeks at least, at Shawn's special request. He wants at least three Nuremberg pieces which I think a mistake. . . .

. . . Ross just wrote and said you said I'd taken an awful beating over here! I think he thought physically, too, which is not true, but mentally yes—oh, yes—like you. . . .

I loved you and Billy being taken as husband and wife! Incest is all that family lacks so far. This is a dull letter. I am very tired from packing, etc. . . .

[March 12, 1946]

My darling,

. . . I shall think of you tomorrow; I shall be fifty-four years old, my darling. I shan't comment! So life goes full of joy and sorrow, joy and tenderness, and your youth. I never dreamed when young that I would live so long and creatively and richly.

I shall go upstairs and take my morning look at Goering, the strongest personality in the room. The real battle will focus on him as it would have on Hitler. As the crimes were graded, so will the punishment be and, as the brainier men rose high, so they will too be brought lowest, as being the guiltiest.

The trial has had long hours and days of monotony, though to me there is always speculation to revive me when I look at those men in the prisoners' dock. On the whole, the American prosecution has been important, effective and brutal! No finesse, no elegance of phrase or body. [Robert] Jackson, when cross-examining, sticks his hands under his coattail, shows his bottom off, and is vulgar of speech and attitude, BUT the Germans fear him, which is important. The English have the greatest national power in Court: the law, the tribunal, and the bench are their natural climate. I wish you were here for two reasons: for me, and for the Court. There is, however, *no* room in our villa where we women live, two or three in a room, one bathroom for thirty females, and with the Russian ladies and wenches piling into the bathroom a half-dozen at a time, all evening long, leaving it like a pigsty. We Democrats have no chance against them: we want to go in one by one and be alone. The Russians seem to *love* functioning even with plumbing in community groups. I have been taking massage here: a German masseuse from Carlsbad is in the village (five miles from Nuremberg), and all the ladies use her. She has helped my sciatica somewhat. I am a little fatter. Weighed one hundred and fourteen with my clothes on at the ATC before flying here. My God, I wish we had some whiskey here. Nothing to drink but foul Spanish brandy.

This letter was written in pencil on an official paper entitled "Proposal for Supplementation for the Defendant Hermann Goering (Defense Counsel Dr. Otto Stahmer)." It pertained to the mass shooting of Polish war prisoners in the forest of Katyn, for which, according to the Russian prosecution, a German military formation had been responsible. The German defense maintained that the depositions upon which the prosecuting authorities based this assertion were untrue. Janet added, in the margin:

"This will obviously be a bitterly fought and declaimed quarrel between the German defense and the Russian prosecution. The Poles say it was really the Russians who did it, but we can't go into that here and now!"

One of the things I had been trying to do during my first three months in New York was track down *Rome—Open City,* the film that had been completed just as Janet arrived in Rome in November of 1945. Roberto Rossellini, its director, had screened the film for us, and Janet wrote in *The New Yorker* that it was the first great resistance film to come out of Italy. I wanted to preview it in the United States for the benefit of the Foster Parents Committee. I needed to make money for my little orphans. I had immediately cabled my mother in New York, and ladies of the Italian Welfare League were ready for the task. I had, of course, to find the film. I had forgotten the name of the sergeant who had brought it to New York. But I did remember that he had arrived with his military sack full of film, to the astonishment of his mother, without knowing what to do with it. He went to Joe Burstyn, then known as the best distributor of foreign films in New York. Joe took a look at the footage and knew instantly that he had something special on his hands, but how to handle it? This was the first film out of Italy, a new type of neo-realist movie, and from a country which had been in the enemy camp—a difficult task of distribution, to say the least. At that particular moment, I showed up with my request for permission to put on a preview for the benefit of my orphans. Never was a request accepted so quickly. Joe saw it as a perfect way to make the film known, to receive the right kind of publicity and then distribute it commercially. He did just that —and made a pile of money. So did we, for our orphans. The film made history, made an international star of Anna Magnani, and made the reputation of Roberto Rossellini as a brilliant innovator in film-making.

My coming into contact with Joe opened up other possibilities in a new field—the movies. While waiting for clearance from the State Department, I was exploring every avenue that could bring me back to Rome. I was ready for anything. Now that Akos was shooting *Teheran* with his Hungarian compatriots at London Films, Alexander Korda, Steven Pallos and his recently formed production and distribution company, we thought we could do some useful business together.

George Davis, the editor of *Mademoiselle* and a good friend, had already published an article of mine on Italian women. He would probably give me other assignments, but how many pieces could he publish from Italy?

So I concentrated on the film business, since Italy was beginning to turn out movies that were stirring up much talk and excitement in the motion-picture world.

[March 26, 1946]

My carissima,

. . . Darling, what ARE you going to do in business? I thought you were so horrified by those movie men's minds that you found in them the dregs worse even than in the rest of humanity. Isn't it curious how the so-called entertainment world usually attracts the roughest, toughest characters to manage it. (I am not referring to Bill Murray, so excuse my reflection!) There is little difference between the mentality of a bordello keeper, a prize fight manager, the Shubert brothers and the Beverly Hills Millionaires from Warner's studio. Yet there is a great deal of difference between Ernest Hemingway and Kay Boyle and Anne McCormick and Phil Hamburger. Did you like his Belgrade piece? I thought it a beauty. . . .

Shawn sent me almost the most enthusiastic cables about my Nuremberg pieces that I ever received, even from that flattering and emotional office. But now that I see them in print, they appear to me to be good, informing, but ordinary enough. No real pleasure for me to read. Kovener* says I'm the poorest judge of my work of any writer she knows, and she thinks us all inadequate; perhaps I am. But I used to know when I was good. Now, even when it seems rather special as I send it off, there's always a slight cutting here or there that mars the final appearance when printed. I thought of how angry Ester would be that I called Goering intelligent. But he is; he was formidable on the stand in his own right and seemed even more dangerous because of the stupidity of our Jackson. How can we explain the men whom our dear president chose at the last and left to us like bad debts after death? Truman, Jackson and Bob Murphy, so favored and such a friend to all that was wrong even during FDR's life.

Perhaps you did not like the new house at Fire Island at all, or very little. I would be very sad if so, darling. It will be much more comfortable (must I apologize for sounding like an Amurrican?) than the other. I can see you on the beach, on our terrace. God keep you safe. I'll hear your beloved, beautiful voice Saturday. Yours with anguished feelings and hopes . . .

———

On April 5 Ester sailed for Italy on the *Vulcania*. It seemed as if all the Italo-Americans wanted to visit their relatives in Italy! But nothing could have marred Mother's excitement at rejoining her two daughters in Rome after years of separation and worries over them.

On the same date, Janet wrote that she was going to Cracow, Poland, for one week, "if my promised invitation comes through. I would go as a guest of the Polish Art Commission which is returning a great altar to the Lady's Church there, which the Germans stole in 1940. I have also nearly completed Part I of my Monuments Arts piece.

* Lola Kovener, of *The New Yorker*, secretary to William Shawn; she later worked in the "Goings On" section of the magazine.

It is a terrific job, almost as heavy as the Pétain in notes and not nearly so worthwhile, except that I am turning it into an analysis of the Germans. I wish to God you could have been to Nuremberg with me. I can see your black head there and your angry, dark, Republican eyes."

And then on April 27:

[April 27, 1946]

My darling,

I have little notion that you will come to Rome so, illogic being today's laws, you will doubtless fly over. But the news from Italy is so bad and sad that, as you so truthfully said, you will no longer lend your voice and brain to the dissemination of promises to your compatriots which our government means not to fulfill, thus arousing first hopes then bitterness in the souls and bodies of your listeners or readers. I thought that your last letters have constituted an amazingly impressive and wise criticism of our government and our times. The best I have yet seen. With passion in the heart and clarity in your mind, you described the ruin in your nature of what had once been your constructed pride and belief, partly in Europe, mostly in America. I have not yet met one intelligent human being, at work in either a job like yours or mine, who does not feel as we.

It is raining. The land needs it. Paris has suddenly been beautiful of late, clean, clear, breast-white. More lovely than since I had come. Less sordid and shabby. I don't know what the exact change is due to; perhaps spring only. The green of the trees hides the shabbiness of the works of man. I keep thinking of Ester and her first tears and speeches of joy, with her fine, shining eyes with tears. She has eyes which actually do shine, a rare endowment of nature . . .

I received Carson McCuller's book.* It terrifies me. To think that such disorder, physical and mental, resides within her perpetual juvenility is an alarming sight to see in print. I am stricken with wonder as to what on earth I can write to her about her book. I am moved by its record of accuracy in juvenile female suffering, but aghast at the sordidness of so young a nature and body, with such free grossness—so like the young, lacking conscience or experience—as to leave one bereft of comment. Puberty is the worst period even in one's

* *The Member of the Wedding.*

memory, and to have to participate in someone else's puberty, in print, now, at this time of the world, seems unbearable. I prefer the adult agonies and cruelties, if one must have them. . . .

———

The event which prompted Janet's cable and letter of May 3 and 4 was my experience in Washington, D.C., where, after the first euphoric days of liberation, I was to get my first taste of postwar disillusionment.

After serving for eighteen months overseas, I had returned to the States on furlough on Christmas Day 1945. At the end of my furlough I was expected to go to Washington to report to the State Department. By that time the Psychological Warfare Branch (PWB) of the Office of War Information had been transformed into the peace operations of the United States Information Service (USIS) and we had come under the jurisdiction of the State Department. I was placed in charge of a Special Projects Division under Professor Rufus Morey, who was the new cultural attaché at the heart of our organization. It did not take long to find out that the Italians wanted to know everything from and about America. The fall of fascism had opened windows and doors to the free world. The younger Italian generation, born under fascism, had been forbidden foreign journals, books, jazz, movies, theaters, radio—in general, all the arts that were not manufactured by the regime. The task before us was exciting, if overpowering, but also opened up a vast opportunity for us. We soon started bombarding the State Department with our requests.

Despite the difficulties we encountered from the cumbersome bureaucracy in Washington, we did succeed in organizing some events of importance. Italy needed to reconstruct its devastated lands, so we had mounted an exhibit on land rehabilitation, reforestation, new methods of planting and harvesting, the latest machinery and technology, illustrated with photographs, films, posters and lectures. The entire Italian cabinet, headed by Premier Ferruccio Parri, had come to the opening.

Italy's public libraries were devoid of up-to-date scientific publications, but the Library of Congress sent over cases of books that had been placed aside for that very purpose, which we delivered to the Ministry of Education. We arranged lectures, roundtable discussions and other cultural and educational events, so that when I arrived in Washington at the end of my furlough to report to the State Department, I was very proud of our initial successes, and full of enthusiasm in presenting plans for the future. I expected to receive help from the government. We needed fresh material, documentaries, films, lecturers. . . . But, to my surprise, all our inquiries and requests received no response. For days I went from one office to another, uselessly. I kept going despite my frustrations, hoping that one day I would find someone interested in what we were doing, what we were trying to accomplish. Now that we had won the war, had we lost heart and interest in the peace? It didn't seem possible. And yet . . .

The final shock was still to come. One day I was summoned to an office; something was going to happen at last. But as I looked at the stern face of the man waiting for me, I became uneasy. I sensed trouble. He leaned over politely, and handed me an official-looking document. It was a letter of resignation for me to sign. To my astonishment, the man had no explanations. He bowed politely and left. Even today, after so many years, I can feel the embarrassment, the grief, the disillusionment of that incredible situation. Why had I been so brutally dismissed?

In retrospect, recalling those early postwar days, I have tried to find a reason for my dismissal. Had I been too aggressive? So enthusiastic at my task that I had aroused suspicions of being too pro-Italian, too anti-Fascist? Or had I been too successful, as a woman, in my job? Or, now that the war effort was over, had the time come to curtail our peace operations? Cut down expenses overseas? Limit our activities merely to establishing the USIS libraries? I still don't know the answer. But I do know that at that time, when we could have done our best work, we were failing. I was left downhearted, dejected and hurt.

At that moment, Janet's words, her understanding and strength, arrived to console me. . . .

[May 3, 1946]

My darling thinker,

Your letter announcing our government's abandonment of you just arrived. I can only congratulate you—sincerely.

We are now going into the desert, a few of us, and we will learn to support the loneliness and heat—I am with you—I love you and respect you and admire you—I spit on government as a function, which betrays the genius of man for hope, poetry, faith and *doing*. You were one who did, who worked, who performed—So now you are ranked as undeserving, because you served—what poor satisfaction, from government's viewpoint, but how much better than having been born a Jew and becoming a Catholic as a means of finding a climate of belief. *I* believe in you—I know you—I no longer believe in my government nor any, except Moscow's which I dislike. *Good* for you —You have been martyrized on East 58th Street. I am your witness—I love you. Take your pain slowly, darling. Slowly—your heart is quick.

[May 4, 1946]

YOUR INTELLIGENT INTEGRITY IS STRONGER THAN ANY GOVERNMENT DECISION STOP WE FEW OF FORMER HOPES ARE ALL UNITED NOW LIKE THE ONLY TREES ON A DESERT AND WILL QUIETLY GROW IN PRIVATE STOP CABLE ME DARLING IF AND WHEN YOU LEAVE OTHERWISE EYE SHALL RETURN THIS SUMMER YOUR ADMIRING =

JANET FLANNER

The problems of our lives, mine and Janet's, had begun to take a dramatic turn. In addition to her regular "Letters" for *The New Yorker,* Janet was still working on a three-part article, "Men and Monuments," about the looting of art by the Nazis in France. I didn't want to worry her with my problems. Her distress at my news would turn into her customary habit of introspection, so she could find a way to blame herself for what was happening to me. I couldn't confide in Ester, my mother, who could have given me good counsel with her wisdom and understanding, because she had sailed for Italy in April. Bill was at Harvard. "I must try to get back to Rome," was my main preoccupation.

The first task was to find a job in which my experience would be valuable: Writing assignments? Film representation? Publisher's agent? After all, *Harper's Bazaar* and *Mademoiselle* had already published my first articles from Rome, after the liberation, so why not more pieces? Given the success of *Rome—Open City,* why not ask Joe Burstyn, the U.S. distributor, to find other Italian neo-realist films, then shooting in Italy, for distribution in the States?

In 1945 I had brought back two novels, Vasco Pratolini's *Chronicles of Poor Lovers,* and a new book by Alberto Moravia, *Agostino,* for publication in translation, so why not continue along that line? I began to make rounds. I even proposed writing a biography of the

House of Savoy, for which I was promised a contract. Various assignments for articles started to materialize. I had little money; my future jobs would not earn me much, but I was on my own, not dominated by an overpowering bureaucracy. I had confidence in myself, in my ability to work hard and in my usual optimism. I could now write to Janet with renewed energy, telling her that I would be able to return to Italy soon, happy in the thought that she would be relieved not to have to face troubling decisions about her own work and our lives. . . .

[May 11, 1946]

Darlingest Natalia,

No word again this week which means you are still living in the limbo of uncertainty—I would say for God's sake, let's stop trying to fix Europe for us this summer and use New York, except that now you have your business of films and of writing to consider, and they must be exploited in Rome, to start with. My mind keeps whirling in a vortex whenever I lie down to sleep at night, and there are three circles of different directions almost: one is the present truth of uncertainty, and I try to move out of its suction and fall into the stream of current. Number two, which is mere hope, of mere daydreams, dreamed before sleeping at night, daydreams of perfect happiness, of perfect accomplishment, of perfect luck and joy in relations without pain or difficulties—Circle number three is the past, as against the future—the known thing and things we have had, the things which can be repeated to the mind and heart, the things that have already happened and exist in memory to be borrowed again and relived in the middle of the night. On the number three circle I can finally sleep. Number one is childish, like believing in Beauty and the Beast, or makebelieve, but a sweet lie until it becomes the truth, if and when. Number two can become insanity. So I sleep with number three . . .

Settle for you now, and your work. No longer try to fit in with my work. *Act for yourself.* I'll do the fixing on my side. YES, I'll come to Rome, my beloved idiot!! *Yes*—

Word from *The New Yorker* is that I've alarmed them and that Ross feared I was suicidal, on the verge of chronic melancholia.

If other planets are like this, why do not the stars fall with the weight of man's folly—or the folly of whomever inhabits the outer spaces? *Stop worrying*—I'll come to New York—or I'll come to Rome. Now take your decisions calmly. My daily new colleague and writer—

I think it absolutely marvelous you have those writing jobs offered you—and you can do them splendidly. The Italian royal family idea seems excellent, *with* the political background of Italy since the Risorgimento. A popular idea, and it will sell. The value of the book would lie in your ability to give an historical slant *behind* the royal figures and use them almost as effigies, dead and in the way, even while still alive. The abdication of the King is joyful news, but will the Prince step up to cause one's hopes to droop again? At least so far he dare not claim that either God *or* the Italian people want him!! That made me laugh with real triumph—

[Walter] Lippmann's last three articles are superb—He needed long since to come over here. Now he can tell the world what he felt and heard here. It is warm, dull, and a storm is coming.

I wish to Christ we were on the island, and time had not happened, nor space—

Yours with tender true love . . .

———

Kept apart by circumstances, events, work, habit and preferences, with our personal relationship strained because of it, we often wrote trying to disentangle our inner feelings from those concerned with the beliefs, political or otherwise, that had invested our attention, our work, our hopes. We both had been suffering from our separation, Janet even more deeply than I.

[May 29, 1946]

. . . Yes, I shall return. I must see you and be with you again to find some path for our emotions and our labors. You say you dreamed you were dead; yes, surely on that horrible Paris bench which is my painful monument; I feel dead but do not dream. I see now why when I was flying toward some small and safe end of the war that I felt more alive and expectant; I was leaving myself on the earth at the flying field. . . .

I have not yet finished Part II of my Arts piece. I have almost had a mental breakdown and might as well admit it to you. As you have noticed, I did no Paris Letter since returning from Nuremberg in March until last week—a poor one, too—the first time in twenty years that I failed to carry out my commitments to *The New Yorker*—thinking to relieve myself and finish the job as indeed I have, two-thirds. But I go through long days of inattention and sleepless nights. I MUST go to Berlin to check on Part III before returning. I WILL finish it, within a fortnight, go to Berlin, then plan to return at once to New York, the Island, and you . . .

I hate the world being so large, because there is room for its space to agonize us both; I hate the pattern of work and the necessity of it, after all these years, because my habit of it now means another root torn away as I move; I am tired, tired of suffering, of making suffer, or not having joy and freedom. We have been in our concentration camp, you and I, and we have suffered until we are worn and thin and frail and starved, too. The world is too large, and my life seems like a vine, tendrilling over its countries. When I make believe—I, too, as you clearly wrote, find that it has become the only reality that is bearable—when I think that I can find quiet and peace on the Island with you and pretend that I am already there, on it, in the house (for I know the house by sight; that is one advantage of my imagination), then I wonder if I really can rest. I realize that I have never stopped in twenty-five years of work. Even the so-called holidays I took here, motoring here or there, produced work; I wrote articles. I am sick of them, too, sick of this spatter of writing, like a small, worked-up storm that falls out of a silly, dramatic-looking very small cloud every fortnight or so. I feel as if my life had consisted of taking in and letting out short breaths, that I would have to take a long breath or perish.

This is a violent sounding letter; it would seem to have no joy or tenderness in it because my violence has been boiling up in me for so long, I have had no practice of tenderness since you left. . . . I am so short-tempered sometimes that I am horrified; I am so easily irritated as to be rough and rude. So be patient a little, please, I beg you darling. The agnosticism which was my natural shape, mixed with idealism which is always the ironical component part in disbelief has now become real misanthropy, directed at me more even than to mankind. Loneliness has not sweetened me either; I feel the loneliness of living. I think the position of the little artists, the high-class artisan, if you choose, the person like me with intimations of and appreciations of great talent and yet not having it—the little nature and mind like mine, somewhat talented but essentially lazy, ignorant and poorly read because lacking that true spark of superb energy which marks the genial high fire—I think that now, with the world of hope and truth failing about us, as we look back, we petty creators feel a loneliness that is terrible; we know that only the great mind can have served, only the great mind will rise to a slight enough height over these years to make a bridge over chaos for thinking, to the next more stable era of life—if it is allowed to mature.

I am not sure maturity will be permitted; Russia is one kind of atomic bomb, and the atomic bomb is another. I see Europe slowly moving into the political color of Russia, as printed on whatever map, for the Russians are in no hurry; they count almost as a reflex on time ahead of them as the Church has, in reference both to life on earth or in heaven. I have been in love with democracy. The words of some men, like Lincoln, have been like love letters to me. But it is not a good lover any more; it is somewhat senile, very rich, and its mood is Saturday night, not a long arcadian perspective. This is the century of Saturday night, in America at least. . . . I wish to Christ I had the power of magic; I would close my eyes, with great risk, and wish myself transported physically (with great danger, almost like dying or taking an anaesthetic) across space to the Island, and I would emerge in the fog in the living room and in the wind and storm we could be alone and real at last. I feel weakened but solidified by this letter. No human can guarantee their future, but we will manage our past. . . .

─────

With this letter, Janet enclosed a check as her share of commitments on the Island until her arrival in July. She did not return that summer, because I went back to Rome, but the house that came across the bay on a barge in the summer of 1945 sits there still; it is where I am assembling these letters, and where Janet happily spent the summer during the last years of her life.

Janet began to worry about whether I would be able to return to Italy. Any change, any new decision, any possibility of having to give up Paris, her work, her friends, to return to America because of me, threw her into utter confusion, made her feel physically ill. In her heart, she knew, of course, that I would not allow anything like that to happen, though sometimes our efforts to be together despite space, time and work demanded such will power, such physical struggles, such need for inventions, excuses, defenses, that at times it all seemed too overwhelming for our limited strength. Yet our feelings and need for each other had grown even stronger and deeper. Nothing could break the solid, indestructible bonds cemented during the four years we had shared in New York. Without realizing it, we had become dependent on each other for counsel and consolation, for understanding and affection. For fun, too.

In New York, facing my new situation and new decisions, I felt out on a limb and full of doubts about my future. My son had suddenly left Harvard, where he had returned for a second term upon his discharge from the Air Force. He couldn't take it, he said, after fifteen months in the Army. He was fretting to be on his own, and despite his father's fury had disappeared into the Village, where he was sharing a cold-water walk-up with George de Kay, his old pal from Dalton days. I was alone. Ester had already sailed, and now Bill had spread his wings toward his as yet unknown horizons. The chicken-coop on the rooftop of Fifty-eighth Street and Madison Avenue looked empty and sad.

[May 31, 1946]

. . . I feel stronger, more alive and less weak for work since I wrote you day before yesterday. The lack of focus on my nature, when faced with a *physical* decision which means physical movement—actually deplacement—produced a sort of mental paralysis; until I had written you, I couldn't work and my mind was so stagnant and slowed down, I couldn't even lift my hand to write. I don't know . . . whether my physical condition has been the result of the mental or whether a weary brain lost its whip-hand over my body; in any case, I believe I can start to work, now, to finish Part II, without which and its checking in Berlin I cannot leave in July as I plan. I don't know anyone, more than you, whose *character* is more a part of her love; your love has the same shape as your character. It seems to me my love is better than my character; that my love has finer shape than I.

Yes, as you say, and as I have commented to you, you have indeed matured in these pained last years; you were always more adult than I, in many ways, because you are not divided against yourself any more than a tree or a flower is, because you were a part of your people's past, as a beach plum in bloom is part of the system of the million-year-old plum stone itself whose rhythm of life, though it alternates, repeats. It is a blessing, Natalia, to be a European by birth, no matter how great their physical misery now, because they have the practice of living, with thinking and pattern part of their inheritance, like beautiful buildings. It is we Americans who, each one as we are born and mature, try to make for ourselves a pattern which our country fails to give us—it is we who are the silly elderly battle-faced children of the world, playing with slogans of morality and ideals, like children reciting senseless nursery rhymes but whatever our mouths say, our hands constantly occupied with our real game—business, money making, which we roll like marbles or like hoops over the world, because our concentration is only really physical, that is all we have learned yet as children always learn it first. . . . Surely when I arrive in New York my mind will find more strength in rest; I have difficulty in talking straight, and cannot always find my words so my letters are incoherent and stupid, but I believe that with relaxation and cessation of worrying about my lack of strength, the strength will return. . . . My only entanglement here (as you call it) is what it has always been: my work and my conscience! And my pain at giving pain. I must have had the wrong picture of me all my life; I saw me as good and only lately I see me as bad.

Other people must suffer less at giving pain than I and by accepting their consequences, seeing themselves clearly, function naturally and are less bad than the moralist, like me, who has failed in goodness since, oh my God, one should handle the life of another, one's beloved, one's former beloved, one's friend, one's soul like me, my own soul, my own peace, my own strength and ease of mind, my right to sleep quietly or indeed sleep at all—one should have moved through life with gentleness, with sweetness, with kindness, with charity and protection offered like a hand on the head or underneath the shoulders of the loved object, to save it from pain my darling. The only happiness I have had in two years was in Rome with you. I suppose in analyses (my ideas keep turning in my head constantly but do not fall into place) it is the three main elements in the life of man which have all seated themselves in my lap at once, and I have not been able to seat myself, instead, at their side; the elements are time itself, and space itself, and the employment of the human faculties themselves, and they are in two parts, love and creation of work. Time itself means age in my case; space itself means living again in a New World, and my faculties are my love for you and my hope still of loving the creation of thoughts with my brain, as a writer. All must be placed again in relation to each other, and I must be at their side, part of their line, not the holder of them, in my arms, or in my head, till they become too heavy, simply because I am not using them but keeping them in suspense . . .

I don't know if I make sense darling; I try to so deeply. My feeling time so strongly, my being tired, it seems to me, has prevented my thinking and formulating and feeling quickly and richly. Have you any ideas what I could write about, for work, when I arrive? The struggle to write little, in size and shape and utility, when the imagination had meant to write large, makes one akin to a farmer or a factory worker; we are all merely workers after all. . . . It would only be a temporary readjustment, if you came to Italy, and I think Americans are always cooking plans that they either burn or leave raw and unfinished, so probably the *Digest* idea of sending you to Italy will not mature. It is anguish to see what is happening or to read what is happening to Italy; a new king. For God's sake, why should that family which breeds itself and exists only because it can make fertile love in bed and produce a son—why should it be endowed falsely with the notion it has had any other ability of late? Monarchy is a form of phallic worship which sickens the mind and eye when one sees it in its clear shape. . . . I must dress and go see the Foire de Paris, my darling.

Oh, my fine, intelligent, good, darling friend, my true and sweet generous friend, I send you over the ocean like a cloud moving from this continent to you, on whatever pavement you are standing or in whatever address with its particular chair where you are sitting, I send you my heart beat, my head beat, my beating of my soul against time; I send you my message of attachment. I sent it with frantic effort, as if pushing it forward and out to you. Touch it, take it; you have touched me with your words; they touch me like your thoughts, as if they had form one could feel with one's skin or hands. I shall prove the truth of the Phoenix and move upward and be a proof of legend. Your sanity and simple strong truthfulness are my strength. Goodbye for now, beloved. I must try not to be incoherent.

On the second and third of June, Italy held a referendum on whether to keep the monarchy or vote for a republic. It was obvious that the people had to be heard and decide; after all, it was they who had been betrayed. There was no other way to bring order out of the political chaos that followed the war—the end of the Fascist regime, the flight to safety of the king, his subsequent abdication in favor of his son, Umberto, and then total defeat. The referendum had been the first order of business of the government of Ferruccio Parri and the Committee of National Liberation. The people voted overwhelmingly for a republican form of government, with a new constitution providing for and reinstituting a Chamber of Deputies, a senate, and a president elected for a seven-year term. It was a great victory.

My family had always been both democratic and republican. My grandfather, Augusto Traversari, had fought in his youth with Garibaldi; the Danesis, on my father's side, had been political prisoners of the Papal State for their known liberal political, anti-papist views, and, of course, my mother had been a rabid anti-Fascist from the very beginning. It was natural for us to rejoice at the outcome of the referendum. Janet shared my feeling.

[June 6, 1946]

. . . I cheered when I read that the king had been dismissed by the people's voice. As we two cried that night at the Island when you heard Mussolini had fled. "Death to tyrants," I shouted, alone in my room, "down with kings." His disappearance is little enough satisfaction, and yet he leaves a healthy void which will be filled with something at least, not with a crown on its head instead of a hat, or no hat at all, like you with your magnificent curly scented black stiff hair, like a cock's feathers, or my white sheep wool.

France is healthier, too, than it was; a great change in the feeling of notions and people here. Vitality is picking up, decisions are being made, more clothes to wear on the body while its naked mind goes on trying to clarify and to function. The choice which the future offers is limited indeed; we destroyed physical Germany which desired to englobe the world like putting a snail's shell on it. Now what shall we do with the Communists who sincerely and earnestly desire the same captivity for us? One of the great comforts between you and me is our identical belief in the life shapes, our both being in love with democracy. You have been a source of strength to me when my cynicism and disillusion made me ill like any malady; you can be my cure.

Forgive my strained and dour letters. I have been really not normal; I have looked so ill and strange that I have tried to remain in my room and not go out. . . . I feel stronger now, able to feel stimulated rather than stricken by change. I still worry about being able to work enough to earn sufficiently in New York; I passed lean years there and, if I could have had another year here in Europe where my function is automatic and fatter, it would indeed have better served me, now, at my time, my darling, so each time you have a new hope of coming over, I share it, believe me! Also, I am less sick at heart than I was here; the

French bloodstream is less decadent than it was six months ago, so one's slow, sad sense of depression is less. I could have felt almost—not quite—as alive here in Paris as I did in Rome where the vitality seemed to me to be in each façade and gleam of the sun. . . . The abdication of the King is made as the finale for your book on the Piedmont family. He has just given you your last chapter. I think the idea of that book is really valid; it could be a history, too. It would have to be; your description of your plan of handling it seemed to me excellent, just, illuminating. I feel sure the book could be a best seller if you were able to obtain enough inside material to upholster your central, passionate, skeletal theme—democracy. . . .

Janet had been wondering what to do if she had to return to the States because of me, and had come up with an idea for a book on a period in history that fascinated her, to be called *One Hundred and a Half: 1800 to 1950*. She had suggested it to an American publisher and received an enthusiastic response. This somewhat relieved her anxiety about what her earning powers would be should she come back home—which she really didn't want to do. That is why she sounded so enthusiastic about my own book project on the Savoy family. . . . I had spoken to Frank Taylor, editor in chief of Reynal and Hitchcock, about it:

"I am in a fever of impatience to know Frank's decision on your book: a whole new element of life work and medium is opening for you," she wrote, and added: "God bless your Italy, curse her king, and set her free—for the Communists, doubtless. Free, free—not what from but what for—Liberty is one's great physical and spiritual love. Good night and good day—"

Janet resumed her correspondence after a few hour's sleep, at nine a.m. She was expecting a cable announcing that I had signed a contract, which I had not yet done. But a letter of mine *had* arrived, prompting this reply:

"Many phases in your today's letter, again, referring to Italy, could be used in your book. I have enormous faith in it, darling. As Monica said, how *débrouillard* you are, rushing to Boston to see Salvemini*

---

* Professor Gaetano Salvemini, historian and exiled anti-Fascist, who was teaching at Harvard University, which has one of the best modern Italian history libraries.

and knowing that the best Risorgimento sources are there. Your book must be a *history*, too, so that indeed the royal family is only a gilded herring dragged across history's trail as if to put off the Republican sentiment from following its destiny. God bless you, if he exists. . . . How *horribly* interesting life is: what is the true history of any life and body and its organs and its mind and how they conspired or cooperate? Surely all pressure from Society is to teach us to lie, one way or another for the good of all. Know thy self, Jesus said.* I think you know thy self, my sweet. I know part of me; my evils seem facts I'm familiar with, but I truly find no good, literally: talent but no good; an occasional flower, but no forest of growth, no plantation of strength to sail ships on, from thin timbers, or house one's heart and head. Darling, my tenderest salvo of embraces, like a loud noise across the Atlantic. Thanks, thanks your letters.

Janet was always full of delightful surprises. In a brief letter, hailing the impending news of my flight on July 30 to Paris, she wrote: "Bless Mrs. [Ogden] Reid** and even the *Herald Tribune* and Salvemini and even the black record of the Italian royal family." She also enclosed a postcard:

"My darling Italian,

"This is borrowed documentation from the land whose plan, if successful, will make writing a communication between individuals, like us democrats, so dangerous that a postcard, signed, will be like a death sentence. A journalist friend of mine spent two weeks in Moscow, guest of the new Ambassador. I asked for a postal card and stamps. Observe how this stamp has the iconography of Christianity but transposed to our uglier century. Lenin rising from history and via photography and in pants and jacket enroute to the heights of the heaven his followers sensibly deny. Jesus in flowing robes, and also elevated by faith, looks more credible and artistic."

Then, a few days later, incensed that Frank Taylor was still undecided about my book and had told her on the telephone that he was waiting for my *theme*, she advised me.

---

* She may have meant Protagoras.
** Owner of *The New York Herald Tribune*.

[July 2, 1946]

... Tell Frank, if you have not already given him your outline when this letter arrives, that you can't be expected to say more than this: you plan to use the Royal Family like a gold useless frame around the modern Republican movement of Italy: this will make a double history. First the history of the individual King and what he hoped and then did (like good King Emanuel II with the background of the Risorgimento, etc.) then the next King (and wife, family, kids, etc.) and the anecdotes about them AND what was happening politically to democracy in Italy. Stage by stage, King by King, with the political and economical events of Italy. Plus the background of what happened to other European kings as they fell from their thrones. The book begins with the Emanuel II who gave Italy its unity, proceeds to Mussolini, and the king who helped through Fascism to lose democracy and ends with current events picture of Italy since liberation (with the Northern Resistance and the exile of the recent royal father and son). I see it very clearly. I tried to give a few words in it to Frank on the phone today—"history of modern Italian republicanism, related within a royal tarnished gold frame," but he could not hear me.

I'll be here, *of course*, for your arrival. Yes, I believe I can go down to Rome with you. Ross will certainly take two Italian Letters I'm sure. *Anyhow, don't worry.* For God's sake, the USA sounds so appalling, I don't see how either of us can desire to live there. Maybe we prefer Europe which is real, if cynical, not unreal and brutal like America. Maybe the Russians are barbarians and partly still in the eighteenth century, but we are adolescents, a teenage empire of forty-eight states governed by a consistory of ruler or citizen men and women who are playing with the mechanism of the twentieth century like children playing with toy engines on the floor of civilization or exploding atomic bombs like firecrackers on July Fourth—a new kind of "hot-foot" gag to make the world jump while we laugh haw-haw like louts. The first pictures of a movie star on the atomic bomb, flown by a plane called Dave's Dream, makes me want to vomit. . . .

This is an incoherent letter. It is *blazing* hot, beautiful sun. I hope it lives in the sky for your arrival, darling, darling.

———

At midnight on the Fourth of July Janet wrote a short letter.

"Darling and independent one,

"To you dates in history only mean calendar events in which men gained liberty or a man, a tyrant, dissolved liberties. We continue to wave the flag in 1946 in memory of 1776. I just received (in a package from Bloomingdale's) some mint-orange pekoe tea, mixed. Was mint tea the cause of the American Revolution—an ersatz nobody wanted to drink but on which men could make more money faster? I begin to think so. It casts a new description on the founding of our dear land.

"This is only a note and you must be like a bird with three wings flying in all directions. Bless you for all your efforts. No more now except *bacio tenerezze*."

On July 19, just before I left, I received one last note from Janet, announcing that she had reserved a room for me at a picturesque old hotel in the center of Paris. It had once been a convent, and still looked it.

Those final months in New York had been full of chores; apart from buying the Fire Island house and subletting the New York penthouse, Bill had provided some worries. He had fallen in love with a pretty girl, and wanted to become an opera singer. The whole picture was pretty dismal. Luckily, the singing prevailed, though attempting to become a tenor without Caruso's basic equipment seemed rather foolish to me. Although Bill eventually became a writer, he did keep up his singing, and together we often sang Roman and Tuscan *stornelli* (folksongs), with Janet accompanying us on her harmonica.

When I arrived in Paris that August, I was immediately revitalized by Janet's understanding of the motions of a wounded being, by her uncanny comprehension of things unsaid, of worries not expressed, and, of couse, by her welcome.

Paris, too, looked different, in better shape. The Parisians were enjoying their first holiday since 1940. Tourists had begun to reappear. But this time there had been an influx of foreigners who had nothing to do with tourists. They were diplomats, translators, journalists, correspondents. The Peace Conference was taking place at the Palais du Luxembourg, the seat of the Council of the French Republic. Italy's cause would be pleaded that day by her new premier, the anti-Fascist Christian Democrat, Alcide de Gasperi, on the afternoon of August 10.

Janet had secured a press pass for me, too. We wanted to secure a front-row seat in the reserved press balcony. The sound of softly spoken Italian all around me revealed the presence of numerous Italian journalists. I recognized some of their faces, particularly serious that day, and perhaps worried. The last row of empty seats bore a large placard that read "ITALIE" in bold black letters; it was there that the Italian delegation would be seated.

A British delegate was the first to appear, followed by the Chinese, Ethiopian and Indian delegations. The Yugoslavs came as a group. James Byrnes, the U.S. secretary of state, entered, fanning himself with his gray stetson, and took an aisle seat in the front row. Vyacheslav Molotov, the Soviet foreign minister, with his lieutenant, Andrei Vishinsky, came in last. Aneurin Bevan, the British foreign minister, was nowhere to be seen. Georges Bidault, the French foreign minister, arrived promptly at four p.m. and sat in the center of the tribune. He asked the secretary general to introduce the Italian delegation. As all eyes turned to the rear of the hall, the door opened and in came the ten-man delegation, headed by de Gasperi, a tall, thin man, dressed severely in black, his face pale, his countenance dignified. He slowly made his way to the podium, bowed to Bidault and, facing the stern audience, began:

"Speaking in this world assembly, I feel that everything, with the exception of your personal courtesy, is against me, and above all my qualifications of ex-enemy presents me as the culprit and has summoned me here, where the most influential of you have already formulated your conclusions. But before the conscience of my country and to defend the vitality of my people, I have the duty to speak as an Italian and the right to speak as a democratic anti-Fascist and the representative of the new republic. . . ."

In asking that Italy be permitted to join the United Nations, de Gasperi noted the absence in the treaty of any consideration for Italy's contribution to the fall of fascism and for her cobelligerency with the Allies. He enumerated the Italian losses: one hundred thousand men dead or missing, in addition to military and civilian victims in Nazi concentration camps and estimated partisan casualties of fifty thousand. . . . "During eighteen months, the Germans, in their slow retreat to the north, pillaged, devastated and destroyed what the aerial bombings had spared." His final words were an appeal for justice and peace. A deadly silence greeted the speech, which had lasted thirty-four minutes. De Gasperi descended the podium and started up the aisle. Only Mr. Byrnes, the U.S. secretary of state, grasped de Gasperi's hand and shook it. No one else made a gesture. I turned to the Italian journalists. They looked moved, as I was. Janet, too, had been moved. We all felt that de Gasperi had stated Italy's case soberly and effectively.

Then, arm in arm, we walked silently to the Ritz Bar and had a good strong martini. It had been an historical day for me.

Rome looked radiant in an early autumn light when we arrived in September. Janet had planned to write a number of Letters from Italy for *The New Yorker*. After greeting Ester and the family in Rome, we decided to go north to visit a part of the country we had not seen yet.

One of the large northern cities, which for centuries had been a bone of contention between Italy and her Austrian neighbor, was the port of Trieste, at the top of the Adriatic Sea. It had become part of the Austro-Hungarian empire, its only great port in fact to the Mediterranean. Not until after World War I had it been returned to Italy. Trieste had been very much on de Gasperi's mind at the peace conference, because the Yugoslavs were expecting, and would later receive as compensation for their own partisan resistance against the Germans, certain Italian territories in addition to Pola, Fiume and the Istrian Peninsula, which they already owned. It was quite rightly suspected that they had their eyes on Trieste.

On March 25, 1946, a group of Italian youths suddenly began gathering in the streets, waving the Italian tricolor and chanting, "*Italia! Italia!*" That handful of excited youths became an avalanche. In a flash parades filled the town, flags appeared at every balcony and eventually a mass of people crowded into the city-hall square, summoned as if by magic to the greatest manifestation ever held in the spirit of the Risorgimento. "Trieste had displayed her Italian soul," wrote Giani Stuparich, reporting on those two historic days—March 25 and 27. Trieste had always aroused passionately patriotic sentiments in all Italians.

When we arrived that fall, the city looked regal, orderly and clean, busily trying to reorganize its life and business. Trieste had once been very prosperous, and still retained the old-fashioned look of the elegant *fin-de-siècle* days characteristic of the epoch of the emperor Franz Josef. It had also been the city beloved of James Joyce, who had been befriended there by the novelist Italo Svevo, with whom he maintained a long relationship.

I didn't want to leave Trieste without visiting the Podgora, a mountain in the Carnic region of the Alps, near the Brenner Pass into Austria. Bloody battles had been fought in this part of the country during World War I. In fact it was there that my mother had served as a visiting war correspondent for *Il Messaggero*, the Rome daily. A

photograph from a family album depicts her standing on a ridge overlooking a group of soldiers in a trench, a couple of officers at her side.
She is wearing an ankle-length white trench coat, laced boots, white
gloves, a light scarf blowing in the wind. How pretty she looks! She is
smiling and the men are looking up at her in astonishment. At that
time she was in her thirties, and in those days activities such as hers
were considered extremely daring. But then, Mother had always been
exceptional. We children adored her. We used to hover around when
she was dressing or making up to go out, fascinated just like those
soldiers in the picture. Janet often referred to Mother's "luminous
smile and her golden, sparkling eyes."

The Podgora looked majestic and quiet. Its sides, all the way to the
top, had been carved into a series of giant stone steps, with the word
"present" sculpted on each and every one of them, a strange pyramid
dedicated to the war dead. "There, there," I said to Janet, taking hold
of her arm. "There Ester visited the front!" But my vision of her had
been blotted out, leaving only that word "present," repeated endlessly
up the mountainside . . .

We left the rugged mountain road to head for Gorizia, the new
Yugoslavian border town. In fact, Yugoslavia was now at the doorstep
of a friend's villa; we had to enter it by the back door, which was on
Italian soil.

Until recently it was quite normal for Italians to cross over into
"Yugo" to buy cheaper vegetables, strong *grappa* or gasoline, while the
"Yugos" came into Italy to buy household appliances, fridges and
elegant boutique clothes. The town had been actually cut in two by
a line drawn on a map by some so-called experts at the peace treaty.
Here was the tangible result of decisions taken without consideration
for the practical human side. That situation was eventually changed.

From Gorizia, we proceeded to Venice, where the limited dimen-
sions were more in tune with our human size. You feel immediately
at home in Venice, because you see only people—no cars—in the
narrow alleys and tiny squares, the so-called *calli* and *campielli*; you
hear only voices, steps echoing over the bridges, the swishing sound
of gondolas below, occasional church bells, and silence. The film
festival was over, the crowds had gone. Venice was there, with all its
riches, for our pleasure alone. This time we found, *mirabile dictu*, an
extra surprise to treasure: the Tintorettos of the Scuola di San Rocco,
which had been removed from their walls for safety during the war,
had now been returned. They were on display at floor level, to be seen
for the first time well lit, in all their splendor. Here we were face to

face with the greatest romantic genius of his period, and the experience proved to be unexpectedly overwhelming.

In that particular season of the year, late fall, the mist drops its veil of mystery over the lagoon, the air is still soft and silence is everywhere; you never want to leave. "This is heaven, Janet!" I remember saying. "Let's stay!" But of course we couldn't. Good-bye, dreams. . . .

On our way back, we stopped at nearby Padua to see the famous panels by Andrea Mantegna in the Church of the Eremitani, depicting the martyrdom of St. Christopher. The Gothic edifice had been directly hit by a bomb, which had been intended for the railway station not far away, and its dome had become the open sky. The floor was still littered with stones and plaster, which workers had been busy selecting and removing. Four of the six beautiful frescoes had been destroyed. Janet described them "according to art experts, one of the two greatest aesthetic single losses" inflicted by aerial bombings, the other being the frescoes by Benozzo Gozzoli in the Campo Santo of Pisa, totally burned. We were able to see the two surviving Mantegna panels, on display in the Church of Sant' Antonio. They had been saved simply because they had been previously removed for repairs—a real piece of luck. How dramatic they looked, those celebrated paintings by Mantegna, a native of the city, and how colorful his scenes, with those handsome youths in the foreground, their long limbs in colored stockings, dressed in short velvet jackets, their faces framed by curls and looking at us as if at the artist, whose weakness for lovely youths he had so admiringly emphasized!

The Chapel of the Scrovegni next door was comforting. The fascinating earlier frescoes, pure and graceful scenes depicting the life of Christ, by Giotto, had suffered only a single large crack, slashed across one fresco like a deep wound. The rest were intact, faded slightly from the ravages of time, but still enchanting.

This trip had been an entirely new experience for us, a special kind of diversion. Even though our impending separation loomed at the end of the year, we had been strengthened, and felt that we could look at our future with more confidence.

This feeling was not just a private one, not ours alone, but one that seemed to prevail all around us. Despite the political squabbles that had begun to divide the new governments between Left and Right— economic problems, riots and strikes by the unemployed, troubles common to all of Europe after the turmoil of war—reconstruction, both individual and public, had begun in earnest.

Italy, despite terrible losses, had, by the end of 1946, rebuilt half its three thousand bridges, over four thousand kilometers of highways and tunnels, fifty percent of its ports, two-thirds of its railroads and railway stocks, and one million of the four million rooms destroyed by bombing and shelling.

Artists and writers had resumed their creative work. Literary prizes had been reinstituted. A new wave of films, having discarded the so-called white-telephone era of bland comedies, was depicting life as it really was. For the first time, Italian high fashion made its appearance, executed by a new breed of designers who were challenging what had been till then the exclusive domain of the French. These so-called *princesses*—some titled women of the aristocracy, others from the upper middle class—had rolled up their sleeves and gone to work in their elegant ateliers. The De Robilants, Viscontis, Galitizins, the Laurettas and Colettes of those days, were the forerunners of today's Valentinos, Missonis and Armanis. Their clothes were inventive and glamorous. And a new group of architects and decorators appeared, to replace the Piacentinis of the redundant Fascist style; they were to pave the way and create a vogue for the modern, the daring, the new. Everyone was busy at something.

It was not surprising, as Janet often remarked, that for reasons of work or personal interest, we should both be continually involved with the people and the events of our time. More often than not we found ourselves thinking and feeling as one, which made our lives richer and closer.

1947

I do not have any letters from Janet in 1947; in that year, we saw each other often. Janet had not been too well. She had begun to suffer from sciatica, which plagued her off and on in later years. I frequently went to see her, one of the privileges of my independence.

That winter Carson and Reeves McCullers arrived in Paris. Carson's *Reflections in a Golden Eye* and her book of short stories, *The Ballad of the Sad Café*, were out on the stands in the French translations. "They seemed to go very well," Janet wrote, adding that she [Carson] had been invited "in two different automobiles" to go to Italy and that she would almost surely be coming.

Janet was critical of Carson's "perpetual juvenility" while I, knowing Carson better—her internal turmoil, her turn of mind and background —admired her talent with more compassion. In fact, I was very fond of her. I had met her when *The Heart Is a Lonely Hunter* came out in 1940, and she was staying at George Davis's brownstone, his haven for writers in Brooklyn. She had come to see us in Turtle Bay, where she had sat at the piano and began playing soft, lovely music. I hadn't known that she had been trained as a concert pianist. She was then in her early twenties, but looked like a schoolgirl as always—partly because she was very shy.

I was pleased to meet her in Rome, where her arrival became the important literary event of the year. She and Truman Capote were considered the brilliant young inheritors of the southern literary world of William Faulkner. *Reflections* had been published in Italian as well, and everyone wanted to meet her. She had already been lionized in Paris, and now Rome! Carson, who spoke only English, was frightened by all the attention and arrived quite tipsy at the party I gave in her honor, which startled and shook the literary pundits and admirers gathered to meet her. Her looks also put people off. She was wearing one of her girlish outfits: a blue coat with a martingale, knee socks, a schoolgirl shirt and skirt, moccasins, and her husband's military fatigue beret. All in all, a very unusual sight. When she came with me to Ciro, my Roman tailor, to order a suit like mine, the receptionist, who mistook her for a beggar trailing behind me, shooed her away. But not Ciro, who made for her a most elegant suit, transforming Carson, who was tall and thin, into a veritable fashion model. As a token of her appreciation, she presented him with a copy of the Italian edition of *Reflections*, inscribed "from one artist to another."

Despite shortages and outbreaks of hiccup strikes, so-called because they periodically and unpredictably paralyzed services of one kind or another, usually for only an hour or two, but just long enough to create chaos, many foreigners started coming to Rome. Even Francophiles seemed to have found the Italians more sympathetic and life pleasanter there than in Paris or London. The British resented the fact that life, and especially food, was better in defeated Italy than in their own victorious island, and most Americans disliked General de Gaulle for his critical attitude toward their own country. They also were put off by the irritability of the French in general. The Italians laughed a lot, were happy, worked hard. This was the impression many of our friends received, visiting Italy for the first time since the war.

In numerous letters written during this period, and later on in 1948 and 1949, Janet refers to friends reporting on Italy. One of them had sent her a postcard from a recent trip to Venice. "She is, as everybody, wildly enthusiastic at revisiting Italy," Janet wrote. "The card said I have fallen in love again with this country and its people. . . . The phrase is so often used these days by so many different individuals as to seem like a loving, contagious fever, and several high temperatures caused by Italian sun and beauty. Mina Curtiss (she is Lincoln Kirstein's sister) drove down from Mentone to Alassio and up to Cuneo: She has never been to Venice or Rome. I dined tonight with her and she is 'so in love with Italy' (her phrase!) that she lands in Naples on her next visit to Europe. She compared the French so unfavorably with the Italians in kindness and charm and good nature as to make it painful to hear for me: I was never sentimental about the French. I think they are acting well now. My God, I've known them ten times more irritable than they are now."

Janet admired the French for their culture, their logic—what she called *"la suite dans les idées"*—their critical faculty, their gift for conversation. She also admired General Charles de Gaulle, for whom she had a soft spot in her heart, mostly I think because he was so literate and such a superb speaker. And, of course, she loved the country as a whole, but she was always pleased to report what people had to say or felt about my native land.

In June, Bill, who had been totally involved in his musical studies, came to spend the summer with me. "Well, I shall return to Italy as a man. What a strange feeling this will be—the return of the native son, so to speak. I can hardly wait," he wrote. He was now just twenty-one, and had been only eight when we left Italy to return to the States.

That summer of 1947 with my son in Italy was delightful. His renewed contacts with his childhood, with the country itself and its people, stimulated him. The language he had cast aside in his anxiety to identify himself with America had come back easily; he was soon completely bilingual, something that Janet herself, with her near-perfect French, never quite achieved, to her constant regret. Even the Caprese dialect came back to him during the days we spent in Capri, his old playground and mine. This time, however, it was not to go down to the Piccola Marina accompanied by his Italian nurse, but to disappear into a night of pleasure, with his toothbrush tucked into his pocket, a shouted *"Ciao, ciao,"* and a wave of the hand.

In September we sailed back to New York—Bill to return to the Manhattan School of Music, I to attend to my own business. On our way to board the S.S. *America* in Cherbourg, we stopped off in Paris.

Janet was very happy to see Bill for the first time in three years, more mature now than when he had left for the service. I was glad, too, that he would be with me, a needed balance for my emotional nature. Having him with me in New York, I would not feel so alone, so nostalgic.

1948

"When and when and when do you come back? Advise me my darling, of our motion across the earth . . ." Janet kept asking. It was October 1948.

Months had gone by since my arrival in the States, months full of time-consuming chores. Janet's life was slowly getting organized. Not mine. I was preoccupied with earning enough money to live abroad, and I was worried not to be able to devote enough time to writing my book about the Savoy family. The small advance I had received for the contract was not sufficient to keep me going during the necessary research period, let alone the actual writing. I needed to earn extra money.

That winter in New York a new magazine had been announced by Fleur Cowles, the dynamic young ex-advertising executive wife of the publisher of *Look*, who aspired to have a slick periodical of her own, (to be called *Flair*), on the lines of the old, elegant *Vanity Fair*. Backed by the resources of the Cowles empire, she lured our friend George Davis away from *Mademoiselle* to be its editor-in-chief, a brilliant move on her part, for George was the best editor to be had. He had been my mentor at *Mademoiselle*, so I knew he would use me as soon as the occasion arose. I suggested a number of stories, which he promised he would consider, and then he introduced me to Mrs. Cowles.

By spring, Bill had sailed back to Italy. He had decided to pursue his singing career in Rome, where, with his GI Bill of Rights money and with a job that Mammina Ester had immediately secured for him as a staff editor on a new bilingual encyclopedia, he was certain he could support himself better than in New York. Ester had been hired to direct this elaborate project, for which she was surely better qualified than almost anyone else, given her love and understanding of both the United States and her own country.

It was a touching surprise upon my return to find grandmother and grandson working together—Mother sitting at a desk, smart hat perched on her head European style, and Bill, an eager young American type, at her side.

Having re-sublet my New York chicken-coop and my summer house on Fire Island, I was finally ready to sail, but, alas, a dock strike on both sides of the Atlantic detained me in New York. Janet commented:

[November 19, 1948]

. . . Nobody but the communists wants to go sufficiently far ahead in a prophecy as to where strikes and the labor and union power may take society. In a capitalistic society they can take us as small citizens into not only inflation, as today, but constant worry about how to earn enough to pay enough to live—providing, that is, that the owners of business keep passing on higher wages WITHOUT cutting their high profits. Until capitalism realizes that each side of labor and capital is entitled to a wage AND a share of the profits, we won't have peace. Money is a muscle in our society like that of a leg or arm of a man with a shovel, and both muscles must have a wage; but profit has become something different than it was. It is not a privilege but an interest in the state of society; if strikers can continue to get wage boosts by striking, they will strike. Only when lack of production caused by strikes cut into their profit would they cease. I think profit sharing as a form of socialism is the only honorable answer today, not just to stave off communism, but because it is an honorable, just answer anyhow. All these plans to stave off communism are silly and dishonorable; only sharing has in it social dignity. What a world. . . .

I hope I can be more energetic when you arrive, stirred by your vigor, my darling one. I have never known inertia before. The grey dull winter days do not make the blood leap, either!

I hope the good weather will hold in Rome so we may scamper about on its old stones. I already greet you tenderly.

In early December, Janet wrote:

"My darling: Your stars have crossed with the State Department, shipping unions, capital and labor and the Communist Party, not to speak of the White Star Line. As of tonight's papers there is no news of any settlement of the dockers' strike, but I have a notion that it will be settled within a day or two, simply because the government cannot afford to have it continue—the cost being too great to Democratic fifth-term prestige, to the Marshall Plan and to Big Business and Little Business generally. . . ."

And added a comment on Monica Stirling, who had said that all she was interested in writing about was love:

"We were talking of Elizabeth Bowen and her *Heart of a Child*, and M[onica] said that Bowen was interested in social relations, as was Turgenev (whom I am now rereading). Yet what varieties of love in Turgenev's stories, 'Spring Freshet,' *Smoke, Fathers and Sons*! I have never realized how strong was the middle class in his work; an occasional aristo crops up but always with an explanation of him or her as a phenomenon. For the rest, it is the bourgeois, his wife, child, neighbor, the cook, the fusty intellectuals always going to Germany—not France—to live in exile to avoid old Mother Russia as a place and backward state of mind. Many of his landowners have already freed their serfs, are already suffering from the money loss which they do not mind and in philosophy accepting the fact that the freed ones are impudent and work badly which is very discouraging as a prophecy of today.

". . . I must think about the Russian necessity of Turgenev's time to go to Germany, Dresden, Heidelberg, the spas; there is something of interest to consider, in their deformed national, anti-national mind; always the extreme and in theory which they apply as a practice as simple and direct as if all Christians walked up and down the streets carrying a large cross, too big to get into the metro with certainty."

My impending arrival after a long separation made Janet think of our reunion and of my eagerness to know what friends or events she had seen or participated in. It was my way of sharing part of her life, of bridging the gap of our separate worlds:

"I think constantly of your arrival and our relation in the future. You must help me and also help yourself so that my faults of character, in these last years of my life, can be weakened, not strengthened. I loathe lying. I only lie out of timidity—because I fear your reproaches and anger—or to protect—to spare you something I think you would rather not hear. I want you to know that I entertain the hope and wish in the future never to lie to you so much as about a lost postage stamp, and I beg of you to help. It is too degrading to lie, and it nearly kills me; it murders me . . .

"I want to write a piece, for my pleasure, about why women have been left out of man's civilization. This will be a relief to my imagination, for usually I report only the result, not the cause.

"My darling, when and when. I tense with the thought of our meeting."

Unfortunately, Janet never did write such a piece, but at any rate kept her word about lying: an interesting resolution for the approaching New Year.

1949

Darlingest:

I think of you and Rome when I am looking at people in Paris or Paris itself. I have never enjoyed your society and company more, nor felt more eased by happiness than this time with you. It was special for me and that is of value, whether or not it doubled to include you. The single contribution is also important. You were so gentle and understanding, and I did not make your handsome features turn the wrong way. Here it is grey, chilly with a wind. The hotel greeted me with smiles and handshakes of joy—very kindly. I have my old room tomorrow. We shall, if needed, poison the gent in it. I am next door in waiting till he leaves. Monica burst into tears when I phoned her a few minutes ago, sobbing in full tempo, poor dear, weeping for gladness and murmuring your name with mine . . . I wired you from here and sent a note from Modane. I expected to send a wire from there, too, but we were late and did not stop long enough. It would have explained a little about Jerry Mayers' pajamas! He left them in room 145, hanging in the bathroom. Save them if you can and if it's no bother, he implores. We had a pleasant voyage. He is gentle, well bred and entertaining, and a devoted friend to you. I hope for a letter tomorrow. Bless you and thank you.

A new breed of artists had surfaced in Italy and were becoming known to the world. Born or raised under fascism, they had had little or no chance to be influenced by the modern painters who had made art history in France. They had suddenly blossomed on their own, in new abstract forms, attracting both the interest of the art merchants and early buyers.

Janet, with her keen interest in art, always alert to its movements and expressions, wrote about them in her Rome Letters and stirred up the first curiosity about them. The Basaldella brothers—Mirko, a sculptor, and Afro, a painter—became good friends, as did Corrado Cagli and Umberto Capogrossi, Carlo Levi and Mimmo Spadini. We spent many pleasant evenings with them in their studios in Via Margutta or at Cesaretto, the small trattoria on Via della Croce that served homemade minestrone and lots of good Frascati wine, and was the scene of argumentative talks lasting late into the night. Most of these were about art as a form of political propaganda, and how it had muted their creativeness under fascism. Quite a few were sympathetic to the Communist party, and some had become members, mostly as an idealistic reaction to fascism. The Communists were beginning to impose similar restrictions on them, and later, with the exception of Renato Guttuso, most of the artists left the party.

Mirko had forged the impressive iron gates at the entrance to the Ardeatine Caves, a tragic monument to three hundred and thirty-five victims of wartime Nazi brutality. They had been chosen at random and slaughtered there by the Germans for a partisan attack that had killed thirty-five German soldiers as they marched down Via Rasella, in the center of Rome. Many of the innocent victims had been left to die, half buried under the rubble, when the Germans had blown up and sealed the entrance to the caves, which lie just outside the city gates. They were found after the Germans left Rome in their hasty retreat before our advancing liberation army, and the discovery horrified the city. Mirko's gates, with their intricate, symbolic design of spiked weapons and tortured arms, interpreted that horror in an unforgettable memorial.

[March 25, 1949]

Darling,

I wanted merely to hear your voice and so telephoned. I heard it, but not the tone I longed for, for you were in your office, surrounded, and, by the time the phone call came through, a young man on *The New Yorker*, here for some long piece on provincial Quaker camps in France, was in my room, so I could neither be intimate enough, nor could I explain why I had asked Shawn to let me do another Rome Letter. It contained exactly thirty-one deletions, changes or errors by the checkers; phenomenal. The main disgrace was a reference to "a man who works under the name of Mirko." Also, they referred in print to his bronze gates being of "barbed wire" instead of briar. The Naples Letter also contained several gaffes and, above all, my critiques of ECA and the Marshall Plan were all either softpedalled or cut out. I am asking for permission to do another Rome Letter (in which I can apologize for Mirko reference which I could not in a Paris Letter). I told Shawn I was displeased and was sending a detailed report on my last Rome and my Naples Letter; he has just cabled back that he awaits it "gloomily." He also said checkers declared that both Mirko and Afro worked "under pseudonyms." Considering that errors like this, about friends, are far worse than errors about unknown people, I am really sick at heart. In Paris, no one ever helped me; in Italy, people did help me. Thus, this clumsy misprinting and misediting really made me feel ill—especially in relation to you and me, and your sweet, high hopes and pleasures in my work . . .

[March 1949—no date is given]

Darling one,

. . . I had a long letter from Ross about my Rome Letter, complaints, and a long cable from Shawn, and now all is well. Ross says my criticisms of ECA were cut because they sounded oracular, sounded like a damned columnist, he says, of which we have enough in the newspapers, and ours is a magazine founded for REPORTING. He is right. He says I am given more leeway than anybody, except in Comment (E. B. White or [Wolcott] Gibbs, too, now), because I am considered to be doing interpretative writing, but I had gone too far. He also said, "you seem to be pretty far gone in socialism. Oh my, oh my, and I am still contented to be a Democrat!" Shawn says that with my kind of

writing, I should ordinarily see my proofs except that, of course, distance makes it impossible, that he has cut badly, that apparently the
checkers were wrong (I have not heard from them as to their excuses
yet), and we will all do better and my complaints served to help us
all and clear the air . . . So . . .

In March, my ex-husband died in New York. Despite the years of
separation and our divorce, we had remained on good terms. The
affectionate ties that bound us through our son had remained alive.
The finality of death was a sad blow.

[March 15, 1949]

Darling, darling Natalia,

Your voice is always its own joy to me, even in sadness as you spoke
tonight. The largest events of life—and they are birth and death—
always provoke the identical comments in man in all ages: birth is
always the great miracle, and death is always the irrevocable. All man
can do is to add the finality of his emotions to these familiar unchang-
ing events and the quality of your letter to me concerning Bill's death
was fine, lifted above all that was small in the person or of memories
and utterly without selfishness, both you and Bill. That I shall not
forget. I feel respectful of you and of your superior, terrible comprehension of detachment from Bill Sr.'s mistakes in life. Both your letters,
even the sad one, gave me pleasure because both reflected you in your
inner state. I copied in my diary what you said of the heart—that it
does not grow older like the other organs. . . .

A few days later Janet wrote:

"As for the American man who brought you to New York and
America and eventually to me, among other Americans who love your
Roman's face and spirit, I can only say that Bill displeases and dis-
appoints me, dead, as much as he did in the little I knew him in life.
He forbade to others, like his son, the intellectuality amidst which he
posed when old and which had given him pleasure and strength when
young; and on the money side, to which he had sacrificed his mentality,
he did not even function with efficient fidelity to Mammon; he left
neither life insurance, like a good American tycoon, nor did he remember his firstborn son, if only as a form of snobbery among his millionaire
class of friends who usually imitate that aristocratic consideration for

primogeniture. . . . I am glad that Ilka [Chase], at least, had a mind warm enough to write to Billy and present the last picture. . . . I miss you, and my heart is soft, tender and sad for you, darling.

je t'embrasse."

In April, our friend Cheryl Crawford, the theater producer and co-founder of the Group Theatre and of the Actors Studio in the thirties and forties, arrived in Rome from London, where she had attended the opening of *Brigadoon*, her musical hit on Broadway. She came by way of Paris and Janet, on the last leg of her European trip. She was eager to see what was going on in Rome's theaters, but there was not much to see, because most activities stop by spring; special summer productions of the classics take place in Greek or Roman amphitheaters. I did manage to introduce her to Paolo Stoppa and Rina Morelli, the acting duo who later starred in many Tennessee Williams and Arthur Miller plays. That season they were appearing in *Life With Father*, the Howard Lindsay–Russel Crouse comedy, directed by Vittorio De Sica. The play had been a hit. It was the first of many others to follow that I handled for the Italian theater. After the war, De Sica had become the brilliant director of such movies as *Shoeshine* and *Bicycle Thieves*.

Janet had been the first to write about Rossellini's *Rome—Open City*, and had followed very closely the new wave of Italian film directors who, as she wrote from Rome in January of 1949, "began to experiment with a new naturalistic type of film, based on a special blend of disorganization, penury, realism, and imagination. For plots, they took the unusual dramas that postwar history was writing around their own people's lives. . . . These men have founded a literary-celluloid Italian style of realistic story telling. The latest example has just made its appearance here—De Sica's *Ladri di Biciclette*, or *Bicycle Thieves*. Even the commercial cinema people regard it as *capalovoro* [masterpiece]."

One of Rome's treats for Cheryl was a popular nightclub in the old underground crypt of a Roman basilica, near the Trajan Forum. From the look of its labyrinthine caves, thick brick walls, low vaults separated by arches, stone floors and seats, the place could easily have served as hiding places, catacombs for persecuted Christians. Anna Magnani would drop in in the small hours, after the theater and the place would become bedlam.

Cheryl's visit brought me a breath of Broadway and a glimpse of its brilliant lights—a taste of the exciting theatrical life I had lived through and enjoyed so much. She was a tangible manifestation of the friendships I had left behind, and which I had always appreciated from my very first day in America—the day I had arrived escorted by the unforgettable Mr. and Mrs. Otis Skinner, real Broadway troupers, to whom I had been entrusted, alone and scared, to join my then-fiancé in New York, William Murray.

[April 21, 1949]

Darlingest:

I went today to the opening of the Peace Partisans (Communists) Congress. The French government cut down the delegates from visa countries to eight each, but as no visa is exchanged now between France and Italy, there are *three hundred* Italian delegates. It was wonderful to hear your language so constantly spoken. [Frédéric] Joliot-Curie is president and made a fine spring address: part of it was an intelligent appeal to women to organize against war. He said that as civilians they suffered more and bore more burdens than male civilians and suffered more than any other bystander at the worst destruction of war: their sons. The Congress is a brilliant propaganda answer to the Atlantic Pact, but so many delegates from different countries lack the loud disciplined "spontaneous" enthusiasm of the regular Party meetings here. The applause was mostly perfunctory, except when really intelligent statements were made when anybody would have applauded. Nenni spoke, in French, this afternoon. It was much more a straight hack party speech than Joliot-C: down with Yankee Imperialism, etc., but his concluding demand for peace brought big applause; it would no matter WHO had said it, even Tom Dewey, I suppose. I took Monica [Stirling] with me; she had a very good time, said "Hasn't this been fun, like old times."

Janet was starting work on a Profile of Léon Blum, "the leader of modern French socialism, as he was known the world over," whom she admired deeply.

Léon Blum embodied the qualities that Janet most admired in man —especially in a political man—because he was a liberty-loving, erudite, patriotic pacifist, with ideals and international visions, as well as a man of action. He had been the socialist political leader, at the head of his party, and he greatly influenced France's modern political life.

Finally, in May, I had good news to send Janet. I had been engaged to handle the publicity for a film to be shot on location on the Italian Riviera, near Bordighera and Ventimiglia at the French border. Sheer luck!

The film was a co-production deal—a mixture of Italian and British crews, American and British actors, with a Russian director, Gregory Ratoff, and an American star, Edward G. Robinson—under the banner of Alexander Korda. It was called *My Daughter Joy*, and starred Peggy Cummins and Richard Greene.

The prospects seemed good and the timing right. The film was to begin in the summer, just when Janet was planning to come to Italy. She could work at her Blum profile in Bordighera, where we would be living.

That May, I was in Florence on a writing job. A group of art restorers had set up their unique headquarters in the Boboli Gardens, inside a *limonaia*, a conservatory that in winter sheltered potted lemon trees. The restorers had erected a strange construction made of hollow metal tubes—it looked like some huge toy—and on it they had rested precious canvases in need of work. Armed with delicate tweezers, brushes, powdered gold leaf and palettes of all colors, young students of many nationalities, dressed in white coveralls, were painstakingly performing small miracles on priceless works of art that had been damaged by bombings and other wartime disasters. The sight of this remarkable hospital was as impressive as it was touching.

Later, when Janet and I went to Florence, this astonishing place had been dismantled, and the *limonaia* was again serving its customary function.

[May 24, 1949]

My darling one,

I have saved on my desk and put beneath a bouquet of lilies your card of beauty and male statues sent from Florence. Yes, they still present a spectacle of beauty left for your eyes, my eyes, and a few thousand other pairs of blue or brown eyes, somewhat console for mental and political ugliness. Beauty gives the artist more importance than he socially deserves, perhaps, but lack of beauty brutalizes society in general. I have taken two interviews on Blum this morning, one beginning at ten, took a third at lunch with Suzanne Blum, sister of his secretary, and am going to a party tonight given by Sartre and Mlle de Beauvoir.

. . . I am working exhaustingly and am not exhausted though ill last week from overeating with these crowds of visitors. Five more arrived this week . . .

[May 30, 1949]

Your postcards are as handsome as flesh, those marble males and females, this sensuous replica of beauty, idealized, so that perfection is the rule of the hip, thigh, bosom and head—meaning that perfection was the rule inside the head of the artist which created them. I am literally nearly mad with overwork, interviews, firemen, no clothes, and a certain fatigue, but will be in the best form when I see you. Florence sounded for you as it had been for the Medicis. They made it for themselves and for individuals like you. . . . All that is sure is beauty as a resource for satisfaction now; I feel as you feel. It is a less form of faith than religion, a more visual actuality than belief in gods which give beauty to the spirit; but carnate beauty is the only surety left to me in this age. What a comment. Thank you for your heart. Please hold mine in your hands.

———

Janet was received by Léon Blum and arrived, as planned, on June 9, and in July we left for Bordighera.

The filming at Bordighera was quite an experience. The place had been a fashionable resort at the beginning of the century, frequented by royalty, especially British and Russian. It had grand old houses, gardens and promenades, and had once even boasted a gambling casino, now abandoned. Many of the palatial villas, some of which had been converted into pensions and inns during and after the war, were desolate and empty.

That summer the place had again become popular with tourists, and had regained some of the sparkle that had once made it famous, particularly after the arrival of our troupe, which was lodged everywhere along the coast. Janet immediately and comfortably settled down to work, her desk overlooking a splendid blue sea.

The actual film was shot in a villa perched dangerously on the rocky coast. Everyone was in a jolly mood when we arrived, with the exception of Gregory Ratoff, whom I never once saw smile and who grumbled like a bear all the time. The location fed the gambling fever of the actors, who, more often than not, had to be rescued from the roulette tables at the San Remo Casino in the early morning hours, while the crew had a lot of trouble positioning the generators on that uneven, difficult terrain. The mixed crew created its own difficulties, too, when the Italian workmen moved cameras, booms or anything else supposed to be manned exclusively by British union members, delaying the shooting. Then there was the unlucky British sound engineer who crashed through the glass door, cutting himself severely.

"*Mamma mia!* We told you not to start the film on Friday the seventeenth!" exclaimed the frightened servants, who had pleaded with the Italian crew. "*Dio mio*, it's bad luck . . ."*

However, nothing was going to dampen our spirits during those first days along that sunny Riviera.

Those summer months were very special for me; Janet's presence made all the difference. At the end of the day we would be together, sharing our daily experiences, enjoying the peaceful surroundings and each other's company.

But film work is hard and tiring; I was glad when it was over. Janet was right to have doubted Ratoff's ability. The film was not a box-office success, and nobody had enjoyed working with him.

In Paris, Janet couldn't get back to her room at the Scribe and moved to the Hôtel Vendôme:

[October 1, 1949]

Darling,

. . . My first view of France from the train window was so character-istic as to make me laugh out loud, alone; fog on the fields and skirting the trees, the sky an exquisite grey-like silk and sun of pallid solid silver. The gold of Rome was gone. . . . I have not been out of town, have been readying for my Paris Letter; a Gauguin exposition of consequence but art is always dull to write about, only good to see . . .

I thought Winston Churchill's attack on the Labourites, as reported in the London *Times*, was one of the wittiest, most bloody attacks in parliamentary history, today at least, and roared in applause and laughter. I have already bought seven books and eighteen copies of Blum's *Populaire* for the Profile and have finished reading one book already.

* In Italy, Friday the 17th is considered a much more unlucky day than Friday the 13th.

Oh, Gladys [Robinson] has a job for you; I saw her at lunch, slightly over-cocktailed, but very funny, of course. Had to witness a fitting at Marcel Rochas after lunch at Maxim's and heard the gossip. This is that Ratoff has trained nurses now, in a complete nervous breakdown. Anyhow, the picture is to be finished and Eddy [Edward G. Robinson] says he plans to have a white Christmas at home in California when it finally finishes. I think she has a job in mind for you to do publicity for twenty-six expositions of her present show in twenty-six American cities, to get money for some French village which needs aid. I say no more because I know no more; it will be a lonely job, and I will believe it pays well when I see your contract! She is generous though when alone, bless her. Kisses and embraces even to the Pope whom I can almost love because he inhabits your capital city of orange and gold.

Worried about the higher hotel rates, Janet had written Harold Ross for an increase on her allowance. She reported:

[undated, 1949]

Darling,

Ross has definitely refused my request. I expect he was merely cross the morning he wrote me, cross at his own income tax. I cast up my earnings last night in a general way (I can't tell exactly, because one letter runs long, another short and I'm paid by the word), and after all, ONE-THIRD of my annual income comes from that ninety dollars weekly, so it would be madness to quarrel about it, and it is extremely generous. In the long run, I have cost the magazine surely less than its other main contributors, not only in salary-cum-expenses, until since 1944, but in the saving of those expenses over all the years for breakdowns, delirium tremens, divorce courts, falling downstairs and other physical items of mistaken pleasures. I wrote Hawley [Truax], making the point that all I stated was that the power of the ninety dollars had decreased by half over the last year in hotel rooms purchase alone; that if Ross doesn't want to increase, say so, but don't insult me because I pay no income tax and save my pay. He might as well insult me because I have no stomach ulcer from excessive drinking . . .

Shortly afterward, Janet again noted Ross's refusal of her request for a bigger allowance in "quite a snarly letter." She had written him back at once:

"I spent two thousand of my earnings last year (true) on my living; that living had gone up six times since I arrived with the same allowance in '44," and enclosed a letter from the Hôtel Scribe saying that her room, which had been seven hundred francs, would be nine hundred francs; that it was sixteen hundred francs in June and would be eighteen hundred in the current month, and asked to forget the whole thing, adding that Ross had said that "I seemed to have developed a frantic financial ambition and I answered that I probably had, at my age; women were always more frightened (recalling their past history) of being dependent in old age than men. I also said I had thought my allowance had to do with lesser amount of comfort in Europe—electricity cuts, no taxis at noon or day if one was working on a story, etc. His letter was quite upsetting to me, the first I have ever had which was rather angry. As he talked to everybody else like that for twenty years, I shall not worry. I recall the tarot cards prophesy that I might worry more than the case warranted . . ."

This was the first and last real squabble Janet had with Ross. Later, the allowance *was* increased.

On October 22, 1949 Janet announced a new move—from the Vendôme to the Hôtel Continental, rue de Castiglione.

[October 22, 1949]

My darling,

Believe it or not, a chimney sweep is just coming in to clear the chimney of my room in this very quaint hotel. I hope he will wear a top hat, carry a witch's broom and talk cockney as in the times of Charles Dickens.

I am moving. I am rapturously pleased. I cannot get the room I have retained at the Hôtel Continental till November 17. Tiny, in the roof, with a glorious view all over the horizon of Paris and the Tuileries gardens beneath, oh what a pleasure to have a vista of beauty; room newly painted, milk white, lovely new cherry-colored carpet, small elderly bathroom, only one big closet, two corner placards [armoires] with rounded mirrors (rounded at top, Gothic fashion), sloping roof, the whole utterly picturesque, with a tiny balcony of zinc, a railing of narrow iron bars which must date from the Second Empire in style and with the mansard roof bulging up at either side. I fancy I could perhaps squeeze a deck chair there if I kept my knees under my chin. The price is slightly less than the Scribe, but I shall be paying about $125 monthly for a room, a roof, a bath—but with beauty. I must work, my pet. Bless you, my treasure in any language.

———

By the middle of November, I had some more good news to give Janet. I was delighted, because no sooner had I returned to Rome from Bordighera than my family news became worrisome. Luckily my son Bill was doing all right. He was working for the Rome bureau of *Time* magazine, as a stringer, while still pursuing his singing career. But my sister Lea had suffered a nervous breakdown, probably brought on by the worry, fear and hardships she had suffered during the war years. Furthermore, Ester was in trouble with her passport. As a naturalized American, her permission to remain in her country of birth had expired. She had asked for an extension on emergency grounds, which the embassy had granted, but her American passport, which she had been asked to bring in, was never returned to her. This was a bad blow. Having at a mature age renounced her native citizenship and embraced with such enthusiasm the American citizenship of which she was so proud, she now had neither. Eventually, through the intercession of powerful friends in Washington, her passport was restored, but at that time we did not know how the affair would turn out. We were stunned and sad.

It was then, when I most needed the distraction of work, that George Davis asked for an article on Sicily for *Flair*, and assigned Karl Bissinger, the photographer, to travel with me.

When I returned to Rome from Sicily, I found Gina and Gigi Raccà, my best Italian friends in the United States, just arrived from Paris with a letter from Janet and a bottle of my favorite French perfume, Arpège, for my birthday. Janet was planning to come to Rome and asked me to reserve a room for her at our favorite old hotel, the Inghilterra, as a workshop and library for her Blum material, where she could continue to write away undisturbed.

In turn I asked Karl Bissinger, who was going to Paris, to take Janet a present I had found for her in Sicily.

[December 24, 1949]

Darlingest,

The Greek head is to be adored. It is exquisite. I have always *longed* for the profile of some small antique beauty, have stood by shop-windows staring at Etruscan heads, and now I may stare at my own. Thank you and thank you. The moment when Karl gave it to me, a flower seller came to the restaurant table, and he bought me some violets and these I put behind the head: its white profile and the purple flowers—a poem.

There has been sun for two days, the weatherman reports, but we cannot see it: the worst fog of the year. A fitting ending to it, with the exception of our town of Bordighera and the summer months where nature and the heart, our hearts, were happy. I shall see you soon, darling. I am working well and feverishly: I shall bring your Christmas present. Thank you for the beauty you gave me.

[December 28, 1949]

Darlingest,

Your letter of details, just received, is something I must thank you for. As one knows one's greatest happiness with another human being in the first moments of love, so one knows one's greatest use—a sensation of one's self bending, pushing, becoming as strong as possible—with the beloved in trouble. These two are part of the same emotion, part of the same utility, are part of the only two experiences we know, as emotional educations, in life. Happiness and trouble or pain, what else can we know? They are all that there is, and they have caused man to write poetry, to invent religions and gods and miracles to help him to bear what he cannot understand in pain (I note that he doesn't concoct a miracle to explain how he may be happy occasionally; that he accepts without question, poor bedeviled devil). I certainly don't see how you can work in these conditions of interruption, if only physical, to go to the clinic, to receive Akos, to listen to your darling mother, to worry about finances. The lugubriousness of hospitals in Europe and the meanness of the attention given by nurses, doctors, hospitals and the whole bureaucracy surrounding illness; the worst of all administration of society is there, as if charged with malevolence instead of kindness; hospitals are worse than a government, by jove.

A big piece on Giuliano* would be fun to do, just the same! You can include all the notions of his nonexistence which will make it gay; he has become the symbol of a series of Robin Hoods, of noble-hearted robbers who help the poor (somewhat) and annoy the rich. Ideal . . . If France's government doesn't fall this week, it might as well. It will go staggering, creeping along; first, the French heckle the U.S.A. for having given Marshall Aid and now they heckle America because it says it will cease giving it soon. Well, which? Society, its transitions, its hopes even, certainly its loss of values in money, the thing it constantly labors to collect and for which it cares more than for anything else, even in Russia (or what money represents as Soviet work there today—i.e., a better means of living and enjoying)—society is, as you say, in a morbid state. I myself would find life in the U.S.A. even worse because I can NOT stand the American juvenile mind or the juvenility of the adult mind, I should say, and its lack of any kind of cerebrality, mentation and knowledge of inherited values from minds of other men, centuries before. As against this, I naturally ask myself the question; and Europe and its excellent minds, its higher degree of mentality even in common men—where has its superior head led it? Look. Look around you, around them in Europe. Et voilà . . . It is bad either way, on either side of the Atlantic. Worse here, I suppose, because they should have done better, being more educated. I must work, darling. Am getting off a Paris Letter; they vary, some rather dull, some rather good. Sybille Bedford, back from London, spoke very kindly of the British admiration for my Letters; said they were one reason that the magazine sells as it does in London.

CAN I HELP YOU ON THE SICILIAN COPY! Send it.

I must work now. Thank God I have to work. What could I think up in idleness which would give me such discipline as work does, and sometimes even mental pleasure?

Bless you, a happier New Year to all.

---

* Salvatore Giuliano, famous Sicilian bandit.

The Fifties

1950

Janet arrived in Rome at the end of January—the beginning of the *Anno Santo*, or Holy Year, which, for the first time since the war, was to catapult thousands of pilgrims into the Holy City. The crowd of worshipers attending benediction in St. Peter's Square, bringing their faith and prayers, was an impressive sight.

Janet's arrival, as always, generated electricity and gaiety. Her presence was like a special tonic. At first there was a prolonged spree of good food, good talk, good drink—a renewal of friendship and warm affection. Then we settled down to work. Janet had brought lots of books and notes for her Léon Blum profile with her this time, and I had taken a small room at the top of our favorite Hotel Inghilterra, with a little balcony overlooking the neighboring rooftops from which we could just glimpse a slice of Trinità dei Monti, the church at the top of the Spanish Steps. Here Janet could work undisturbed.

Two events had a direct impact on our lives at this time—the first a loss, the other a gain.

At the end of March, Léon Blum died. His death was a sad blow to Janet. She had spent over a year researching her Profile of him, with the added intention of including a history of French socialism in her article. I remember our conversations on the subject of socialism in general, particularly in regard to France and Italy, both countries subject to periodical convulsions and then undergoing recurring government crises, with strikes and riots. Socialism of the Blum variety seemed to us at the time a possible alternative to the extremes of Left and Right. Immediately after the war, many had hoped for a United States of Europe—the creation in effect of a formidable, independent third force, with a demarcation line running from Stettin in the north to Trieste in the south. A promising beginning had been made with the Common Market and the formation of a European parliament. But it would be a long, hard road before the creation of an actual federation of states. At the time, Blum's brand of socialism seemed like a good compromise.

Janet knew that Harold Ross had not been too keen on a Blum Profile in the first place. He had said, "Oh, yes, another of those great historical pieces Flanner is always so crazy about." And, given *The New Yorker*'s policy against publishing posthumously, Janet's Profile was as dead as its protagonist.

The gain was Ingrid Bergman, whose arrival in Rome was a sensational event. She was abandoning glamorous Hollywood, a husband and child, to join Roberto Rossellini, an Italian director then barely known to the American public, which idolized her. The story scandalized conventional people, and would make front pages all over the world, especially with the birth of their child.

We had become friends with Roberto, so we met Ingrid soon after her arrival. Because, however, I was also a friend of Anna Magnani's, whose earlier relationship with Rossellini was well known in the movie world, I had a preconceived notion that I wouldn't like her.

But Ingrid immediately proved to be what she seemed to everyone who knew her—not only lovely to look at, but modest and straightforward, honest and devoted, and, above all, a dedicated actress. We liked her right away.

At first she felt lost in Rome, a city she did not know. I could sympathize with her, as I had had a similar experience when I first arrived in New York. At least she could speak English with me, and we soon became friends. Janet and I followed with resentment the vicissitudes that surrounded the birth of their son, Robertino: the siege of the clinic by the paparazzi competing to get a glimpse of the baby and devising stratagems to click the first snapshot to be flashed around the world, for a price; the clamor of the press in general; the callous infringement of privacy; the gossip. When the tumult subsided, Janet wrote her own report, soberly, in proper perspective, with detachment and fairness. Ingrid remained forever grateful.

By then Janet had returned to Paris, from where she wrote in April:

"Thank you for understanding about Blum. Today came an inquiry from Mike Bessie, now of *Harper*, asking to see the manuscript, either for the magazine or as a possible book. I shall think it over and answer him next week after I get my Letter off. It will be a terrific job, naturally, if I do the book for him and WHEN can I do it?—and for possible royalties of maybe a few hundred dollars. . . . I enclose [Walter] Winchell's inaccurate comment about my Bergman-Rossellini piece, not twelve pages and above all not gossip about the blessed event, but just the same sort of an attack on gossipmongers like him as our profile on him was . . ."

And again, on April 19:

". . . Still no word from Ross. I wrote him today, explaining my view, telling about the *Harper*'s offer, asking his explanation of why he now changed his mind about printing a posthumous Profile, pointing out that if *Harper* printed the work as an original book, I would be lucky to get three thousand in royalties. A very loving, kind letter, trying to help him. It is now clear that his slowness is part of his resistance to his instinct (wrong, I think) NOT to use the profile, and his instinct to try to protect me. I also wrote Blanche Knopf, asking if she would take Blum as an original book. I can't dawdle any longer; I'll forget all I read and stored in my memory on him. Ross is the best editor on earth; if he thinks the Blum is a dead article now, because he is a dead man, he must be right. I still do not think so . . .

"Carissima, I know you think of me, I know I think of you. I have done no work this afternoon and I feel melancholy and old and as if my machine has temporarily run down and my heart hurts me."

At the end of April, Janet announced the arrival in Paris of her favorite sister Hildegarde for a visit in May. What a relief from her recent disappointment! Hildegarde was an exquisitely sensitive poet, a dedicated and knowledgeable botanist in love with nature's treasures, an active conservationist; she was also the only one of the three Flanner sisters who had been happily married and had had a son. She made her home in California, where she also took care of their mother.

Though very different, the sisters had much in common. They admired and enjoyed each other's talent and company. Both were singularly witty and eccentric. But Hildegarde was reserved and introspective whereas Janet was outgoing.

Hildegarde was still a practicing Quaker, while Janet had no religious allegiances, though she admired the ethical ideal of Quakerism. Both had strong wills; both were in love with words and knew how to

use them. To me they embodied the best characteristics of the true
American spirit—democratic, liberty-loving and fair.

[April 27, 1950]

Anima vagula,

The photos and your brief enclosed note came yesterday by a miracle.
The sharp edge of the prints had entirely slit open the envelope, but
within it the photos were all nestling intact, and the note among them.
They will be framed at once by me in the manner we described. Today
is the day that Hildegarde should have arrived, or rather yesterday,
originally, all the boats having been delayed a day or more over the
past month schedule by storms. I am glad she is not landing and did
not land yesterday which was the most melancholy, even mildly alarming day I recall in years. There was no sudden rising peak to the storm
after which there can be relaxation in nature and a relative calm. It
was a continuous uninterrupted wind which bent the Tuileries trees
in jerking gestures that were as regular as a clock's wheels ticking and
the rain poured down as if from a sieve. There has been no danger in
any of it which has gone on now for five days and is still continuing;
no accidents, no dramatic disaster. It seems frightening because it
seems like a new kind of steady climate, like one which might arrive
if the world were very slowly going back into less light and more liquid,
toward a final, very distant end.

Esther [Arthur] was very sweet and utterly sober at our dinner,
took one martini while I sipped tomato juice like a vegetable connois-
seur, and failed even to finish her drink until I gently pointed it out
and the fact that we had to leave. She said nothing about her plans or
projects, did not even mention that her brother Gerald [Murphy] may
be coming over in May. She should try to see him to obtain money,
but if she doesn't catch him by the tail and nimbly, he is capable of
sneaking into town, hiding at the Ritz for two days, and wiggling out
again after having seen only in snobbish seclusion those persons here
he would wish to see, and she would not be one, poor sister. . . . Last
night I dined with Francis Rose, the painter, and though the suffering
from his painter's egotism during the first hour in his room in which he
first showed me, as if I were a schoolchild being forced to look at a
geography book's maps, every picture he had with him, then the
accompanying text of his press-clipping book—tho all this was bad and
was repeated while I waited for the benefit of another woman who

came late, still our dinner together, he and I, was very entertaining. He told very funny, fascinating stories and gave me lots of news. He has that English training of the snob, the aristocrat, the upper class once rich (now a poor and married painter), for gossip, for names, for incidents, for social values and balances which I utterly lack but which I appreciate in others at least.

I was reading the poesies of John Donne yesterday who wrote at the end of 1500 and into the early 1600. In one sonnet to his love, he spoke of his "naked thinking heart which little shows," and I thought it described my heart, too intellectual to give outward evidence and thus complete satisfaction. It is amazing how modern his tone was and how earthly of today's earth with the men upon it in modern mood, torn between science and recollected romanticisms. He mixes physical realism with inspiration and fantasies and wit and above all intellect and these, focused by his talent, give him a unique style of his own which seems pseudo-scientific and indeed was. The Scientific Society of England had been founded under Queen Elizabeth, I think, and its influences was readying for Darwin and Huxley under Queen Victoria, and now the traitor [Klaus] Fuchs under another Elizabeth Queen. . . . My god, there is a flash of sun on the gardens and so perhaps the dull storm and wet are moving back to heaven to remain. . . . A chap here whom I ran into from New York said that *Flair* had made relatively little impression because it had failed to do what it could have done to come out with a fine, well-chosen new make-up which her money could have assured and which would have made her book different from and superior to *Harper's* and *Vogue*. He is a man who used to be in the printing business and blamed Eude, her art editor, or blamed her for choosing him, formerly on *Town & Country* which he said *Flair* more resembled. Eude was the basis of Carmel's critique after she saw the first dummy. He had noted with interest your "Sky Over the Marshes"* piece, remarking on its pagination, writing and imaginative appeal, and is hoping soon to see the picture in New York, if and when. Anyhow, you sold him on it completely.

I am working today for my Paris Letter, seeing Baby Bérard's** retrospective posthumous exhibition at the Museum of Modern Art [Musée Nationale d'Art Moderne], seeing Chagall's show and the

---

* *Cielo sulla Palude*, a film directed by Augusto Genina, based on the murder of Maria Goretti, later sanctified. It was shot on location in the Pontine Marshes, near Rome.

** Christian Bérard, the artist and stage designer, was always known as "Bébé."

Vienna drawings at the Bibliothèque Nationale from the Albertina Museum, which should be a joy, and going to *La Beauté du Diable* this evening. Darling, you wanted to know what I am doing. This is and has been it!

[June 1, 1950]

My Sweet Natalia,

I have had hardly one moment to myself. People swarming in, taking my time, interrupting. June is always bad as May for visitors whom I I cannot in courtesy refuse to see, and get little from. Today came Bill Shawn's letter, finally, on Blum. The answer is No. Reason, "a multi-part profile, on a non-local dead Socialist, these elements combined make us cool." He had understood three parts not four. On receipt of manuscript will pay the full rates for Profile, not to be printed. Suggest to sell it to *Harper* instead, who I doubt would take it. Bill's last paragraph shocks me most because unexpected: They want me to return to New York for a visit of reorientation as mood of country has changed and I must not get too out of touch. I asked Bill to say frankly if my letters seem out of line and not what he wants. This is a bad year for me, too, my dear one. I told Bill I would return in October. Isn't that the best time for you, too, in relation to the flat of which you had spoken as making a necessity for your return then? Bill's letter was gentle, sweet, but firm—I wrote back with equal gentleness. So now I must get to work again on Blum.

Hildegarde gives me such delight, I can't tell you. So sweet, gentle, polite and quaint. She has spent two days in succession alone at Versailles, viewing the park! Trees and flowers are her art. I go to Prades alone tomorrow night for *New Yorker* (near Perpignan and Spanish border) for Pablo Casals' opening, Bach series, a big American-backed festival. I shall be back Sunday morning—two nights in train *without* sleeper. I'm glad Bill went to Florence and wrote you—Miracle! I bless you. I am tired and rather beaten by Bill's letter.

[June 10, 1950]

. . . The Bach festival was wonderful. I heard the opening night Friday of soli by Casals and two Brandenburg Concertos, and last night only his soli with piano. The concerts are played on the altar in the Cathedral, dark grey stone, spacious Gothic, with a faded blue ceiling of sky and stars and retable to the top vaults of Spanish ice cream, gilt, pink, blue and angels, trumpets *e tutti quanti.*

His playing of the cello is physical perfection though it excited me less than the orchestra. He plays Bach as if it were a love story, a sad story, a good story, a dance at a ball or a funeral march—he plays it *alive.* Orchestra is composed of one-half Europeans and one-half U.S. musicians, all young, all virtuosi, who came to *do* this festival to be with him and hear him play which few had. Sascha Schneider, violinist, dark, hairy, handsome, very Jewish, is concert master of Fête and really organized the affair. Peggy Bourke-White is here, asked after you, and is the Queen Bee of Prades, in bright orange shorts black sweater low-necked and sleeveless like evening gown and gay sandals. . . .

Janet had finally decided, intelligently, to drop the Blum Profile, which took a load off her mind:

"I cannot face the abnormality," she wrote, "of continuing to work on and write a complete opus on Léon Blum and French socialism so that *The New Yorker* will pay me much more for a long, intelligent piece NOT to print. It would be like working in a tunnel. I have been so depressed, dazed, confused. It was bad luck for me and, alas, fatal ill luck for poor Blum himself."

I was having trouble with my New York landlord, because I had not been living in the chicken-coop and had sublet it, in absentia, to friends. This was a good excuse to chase me out of it and raise the rent, which at that time was still blocked. My lawyer was handling the case, and I was waiting to hear what to do. I was also waiting to hear about my visa renewal, which was slow in coming. Despite having been a naturalized American since 1927, I still fell into the category of the recently "naturalized" citizen and could not reside in my country of birth for more than a few months at a time. I had lost my diplomatic status when I left the USIS, and my mother's troubles with her own renewal had made me uneasy. Luckily, it was finally granted.

[June 11, 1950]

. . . Thank God your visa seems assured. That is the best news in months. I can imagine your relief. It is so odd to think that one's shape of life now depends on a piece of stamped paper and that it declares you have changed the geography of your body long after your body was born. It becomes rather insane when one thinks of it lengthily. The world is becoming so illogical, so ordered by new abrupt *personal* laws, made not by many men deciding together but by ONE man, like Stalin now, Hitler and Mussolini yesterday. It makes us, the millions, feel like fools because we always feel inappropriate. We have an accumulated general past of centuries, of grouped anonymity and are gradually, indeed increasingly, being pried and separated from it. No good can come of all this.

As to Korea, first we back [Claire Lee] Chennault who had night club concessions in China which he had from Chiang Kai-shek and then we back a Communist in Indonesia after shooing the Dutch Colonists out, and now we back Syngman Rhee who sounds corrupt and a white capitalist puppet. One critique made by Europeans I do understand: they ask what *is* our State Department policy?

Le Monde tonight quotes an American journalist as saying that our soldiers say they have had not enough training. One wonders with anguish what is in Stalin's mind, that secret inside of his head which holds our lives and architecture, thoughts and hopes and habits in his brain power. The storms and heat here are like a background to our life this year. I will hear your voice at midnight Wednesday.

[July 8, 1950]

Precious,

I think I have never not written you for so long a time and space, and I apologize but without conviction for I know that anyone better organized could take the required few minutes for posting a note, but my disorganization has lately been at its most supreme, like a new sort of system in itself. Pressure, people, work, confusion in itself about the work, etc., and some worries, too, which shrink to nothing beside the size of yours, my courageous "bottered" one; you always say the word in so droll a way that smiles come with sympathy for the announcement of the ill. . . .

Is August first all right for you, for me to come? If you are not in Rome, I will find you wherever you are. Your newest job for *Flair* sounds *very interesting*; Gerald Murphy, E's brother, was in Italy and more impressed than with anywhere else, especially for work; spoke of a showroom in New York where Italian goods made by Italian craftsmen in old manner but in modern, saleable manner was being appreciated; himself had ordered leather merchandise in Italy which is unobtainable for work elsewhere; is this the same theme that she wants developed for *Flair?* . . .

Carson [McCullers] is here with Reeves, asks daily for you, her sweet affections are as much as expected of her as her physical debilities, both spiritual and organic. Her left hand has dried up into nearly a claw, her left foot drags as she walks; they are returning to Ireland for a few days where she passed a fortnight with Elizabeth Bowen, the only reward in the whole European tour this time which has been a failure. Carson cannot walk about; even to go out to eat a block away is a trial of strength. There are never any taxis at dinner hour; she feels ill so is returning to New York and then they are buying a house in Virginia, she says.

I am glad Pavel T. [Tchelitchew] liked my *New Yorker* note. I feared it would not satisfy him. Eugène Berman, here with wife Ona whom I liked, said of Pavel that if he were content to be a fine strange painter of this epoch, he would be all right, but he wishes to be hailed as a great metaphysical thinker of all ages. There is some truth in that.

Korea. And then what? If the United States moves forward diplomatically in any gesture these days, it is criticized; if it does not move forward, it is criticized, each with some justice. The inclusion of potato bugs into the diplomatic level is unbelievable, too comic to be believed except that it frightens more than makes to laugh. A French woman recently wrote here that peace protests from women had no more value than pieces of confetti. . . . That the South Korean army is inept, weak and clearly frightened; that its only activity is to flee is, of course, such a critique of the democracies as to make one silent with shame. In each coup d'état the people (pushed or not) rise to set up a communist revolution and government; no one ever makes a coup d'état to set up a democracy, and the idea is not so illogical as it sounds. We are not popular, democracy is not popular, except for those it profits. But yet it is beloved. I cannot believe its meaning of hope and ease for man's political soul has no meaning today. I have not lost my faith, Natalia, in being a democrat. Even when democracy becomes frightened and hysterical as ours is at home. It will find a new way of adopting the present (for it is old itself) to its uses. In the end, communism will have to become more democratic to survive; we will not live to see it, I suppose, but there one can prophecy. Political knowledges of the rare and great type do not die out so soon after their inventions, and man has not invented very many political prototypes. Democracy will have to include part of fascism and communism, too, for they were great political inventions. Yes, alas.

Natalia, forgive me for my disorders, my sweet and dark and handsome. I shall write again tomorrow and be calmer, more informative.
This has been a hellish year for us both, for you most. I shall try as I
do try to help you, not hinder you. Everything depends on *Flair*'s
decision.

I understand I am being asked back to New York for reorientation
to control my socialistic tendencies . . . Ah? We shall be together in
three weeks beloved.

———

Janet came to Rome at the end of August for a few weeks' vacation
before leaving for New York in the fall. Her trip to the States worried
her, and it was clear by then I could not go with her. I was utterly
disappointed. I had lost my New York home, I had little money and
work still remained to be done for *Flair*, which, it was rumored, would
soon fold. This had not been my lucky period. Everything I had
attempted to do since the end of the war seemed either to have failed,
or was going to, like *Flair*, on which I had based so much hope. Perhaps
I was going through the seven-bad-year cycle that astrologers had been
predicting for me. A true Roman, I had consulted my family's favorite
fortuneteller. "You are going through a difficult period," she confirmed,
pointing at her ominous tarot cards. "But it soon will be over," she
added, to cheer me up. The Korean situation did not help to the
general uneasiness.

We both managed to have a good vacation, despite our worries.
When we were together, difficulties seemed to disappear, because we
drew strength from each other's confidence and love. Between work and
play time flew, as Janet always wrote several Letters from Rome and
elsewhere in Italy during her trips. She was back in Paris only too soon.

"The trip to New York alarms me," she wrote in October. "I feel no
good will come of it. I grow more alert to a feeling of fear as the boat
day approaches. I hope to survive in New York, not to learn anything
much or to gain anything at all. . . ."

[November 1, Wednesday night—Toussaint Holiday, 1950]

Tesoro terrestre,

I am aboard, have dined and made an inspection of this British
Majesties Royal Mail Ship, Queen E. The portrait of his wife in the
grand salon is something he should have sued the painter about, had

the King any art sense which his family has usually lacked throughout history.

I sent a wire to you and an air letter from Cherbourg before going aboard. I am so numb from mere transportation of my body and mind and luggage and expectations that I am not intelligent as to anything but my own sense of lack of explanation. I always shrink at returning to my birth land and why: because I fled it with long pent-up desires for that flight. Always I return with a feeling of the ugliness of those surrounding hopes for greater beauty than I had known (except on my brief taste of Europe at seventeen in Germany whose picturesqueness only solaced yet made me suspicious as I loathed the people who so lived there). I think often of the dear calligrapher from Sorrento (whose name I no longer recollect, how bad) and my connection with the medieval which still seems *aesthetically* sound but only there. I adored Romanesque and afterwards Gothic, but I started on Archaic in Greece. So that connection is not quite clear to me. As for my morbid concentration on some sort of truth (this must make you laugh, you knowing how enforced a liar I have often been) the *kind* of intellectual truth in medieval minds has never at all interested me. I have never in *my* life been interested in any of the truths until the Reformation.

This is far from our reality, all this idle writing, but I am alive on a large ship, vacant of all connection except my mind and memories and my body, now putting out to sea. This seems to me a delayed dramatic point in our lives, this voyage, and I hope it can bring some positive proofs. My love for you is, as you know it to be, vital, tender and intense. My sense of destruction in your life through your generosity seems to be slowly killing my concentration. All you said in your letter is true: you think of me and I think of me. I must go to bed. I have not slept for seven nights. I am a sailor now. I embrace you.

[November 11, 1950]

Darlinghissima,

This enclosure will interest you. Why did Roberto never send over *La Voix Humaine* to show? Some equivocal reason doubtless, but it would have been more appreciated.

I had my first and only satisfactory talk with Ross last night at "21" at dinner. At least he was not cross as he had been with me and, indeed, everybody. He is again worried frantic like everybody, wondering how he can steer his business which is the magazine through another war if one comes. Our talk resulted in nothing new really: he asked what was going to happen in France, and I said coolly: How in God's name do I know? You tell me. If there is war, France will be caught and changed in a way only history can describe. I will drop everything and flee like all U.S. correspondents, for this will not be a reported war, not from Europe by Americans. He worries at me being a woman in danger, and I said, if you sent six men to take my place, you'd have to worry about getting six men out instead of me. He naturally accepts Italy and Letters as before. Mrs. White and Shawn and I have forced him to. Afterwards we joined two young *New Yorker* couples also dining at "21": the Brendan Gills and the Gardner Botsfords (R. Fleischman stepson), and I went on the town with them (Ross went to bed), and we ended up at the Stork Club with the tackiest, dreariest debutantes, all ugly and poor dancers. I was quite shocked! . . .

What a hideous year's end. Young men here all angry that Korean correspondents say men die there while others cavort at Stork Club: Botsford said last night, "I earned my Stork Club and damned dull it is. I was in the Battle of the Bulge and, if called, I'll have to go again and leave two children behind. I'll dance whenever I have the chance till then." I long to see you and shall soon. God save us all with the New Year.

The enclosure referred to in the previous letter concerned the film *Il Miracolo* (The Miracle), directed by Rossellini and starring Anna Magnani. It became a *cause célèbre* when Joe Burstyn, its distributor, fought in the courts against the municipal ruling that had banned it in New York, and won. It was a case of pure and simple censorship that had aroused the press and film world alike.

La Voix Humaine (The Human Voice) was the celebrated one-woman play by Jean Cocteau. Anna's role in the film version was one of the most magnificent and dramatic parts she ever undertook—that of a woman abandoned by her lover. For thirty minutes she pleads with him on the telephone to return to her, knowing that he never will. Both these performances were memorable, but the latter was not shown in the United States because of a complicated situation involving rights.

[November 15, 1950]

My darling, my friend,

One week ago yesterday I sailed. The sail fatigued me after my arrival Monday afternoon, and I went to *The New Yorker* office only Tuesday and Wednesday, each day all day. I think Ross's wanting me to come here is this: he is convinced Europe is "lost" as he calls it to "the commies." Odd that he, such a patron of good writing and editing, should nickname Bolshevism so it sounds like a baseball team. He is troubled by my defense of socialism and says if it fails to be as bad as communism, then Blum was only an idle dreamer who failed while dreaming and not applying it. All this came out in a gentle but intense short conversation at "21" restaurant where I had dined with Shawn and wife on Wednesday night. Ross, having dined upstairs with others and having come down for coffee with me, the Shawns having left, their twins being ill of bad colds. So far, that is the only meaning of my arrival, that and his almost helpless insistence that I've got to witness the turnover here, how fast things are changing, as if it were a spectacle he can't understand, and I, too, must look at it almost like somehing ugly which I must share as a penance.

Shawn spoke almost the same way, but with more youthful humor. Shawn looks very well, is a little fatter. Ross is thin but "mellower." That's the office word for it. All use it, meaning he is less violent. The payoff in my opinion was in my first accidental meeting with him in the office corridor (although he knew I had arrived), and he stuck out his cheek to be kissed and said, "Well, Goddamn it, we're so busy with the Christmas week on the magazine that I've been thinking it over and I guess you should have come *after* Christmas." I was staggered but laughed and said, "That's something you should have thought of sooner, say last summer, when you told me to come in August." Everyone is nice to me, sweet, kind. I've not seen Liebling. Mrs. White is having me to dine next week, an honor. I am to work at once on the Gulbenkian Profile, and then to do for March 30th issue a double letter on Blum alone (ten columns on my eighteen months' work as against twelve to fourteen columns for Prague, Berlin, etc., every three weeks) and then do a single-part Profile on Matisse. Berenson's Profile is included in a Profile of Joseph Duveen now in proof by Sam Behrman. No on Bassiano,* not important enough, maybe yes on Gulbenkian,

* Princess Marguerite Caetani di Bassiano, New England-born editor of *Le Commerce* in Paris and *Botteghe Oscure* in Rome.

but not enthusiastic. Everyone but Ross favors Rome Letters; he wants fewer of them, I'm told. We have not talked of it yet. I am very nervous here, as New York air is tense and the food, darling, is actually nause-ating. Dinner for three last night at Tony's Wife was $15.00—good prosciutto, very *bad* scalloppine al marsala, bad espresso, bottle red Chianti, rather sour. Prices are awful—$7.50 a day for bad, ugly little single room here.

I shall see Gibbs show Wednesday matinee (*Season in the Sun*) and write you. Office very happy at his success but no one understands jocularity of play as subject very bad, and only one good comedy character in it. There are no tickets available until after Christmas for *Gentlemen Prefer Blondes, South Pacific*, etc. I shall ask Terry* to ask for scalper's prices. *Call Me Madam* (Merman) sold out, of course, poorish music, not much fun, all say. There is a kind of *energy* that has seized things here and makes them turn the pleasure scenes to play like part in it. *The Lady's Not for Burning* [Christopher Fry] opened yesterday: I enclose notice.

I deeply apologize for this dry, grotesque letter. The shock of the energy, beauty and ugliness of the city have deflated me. I shall write lengthily about Fire Island. It is last boat of season, still warm, gentle and sunny here. I miss you and feel very strange.

The dogma in 1950 of Assumption Virgin which is idiotic but with lovely lights and flowers seemed more *normal* to me than New York does, darlingest one, honestly.

[November 22, 1950]

. . . Your reaction to the China news is something like mine. I feel that our part of the world is now being reduced like a melon rind. The Communists are eating us away like an old fruit. They have the appetite and we have the rich taste of a mango, but no sense of protection which fruits lack, and only animals and man have. Nobody here in the office takes it seriously that most of our colleagues were packed and ready to flee this last summer if war had come. I am con-sidered as dramatic and perhaps a little too tense in saying we all would prefer to be dead than to be captured, imprisoned, and shot. Ross, though, is deeply worried. He thinks the Europeans are finished, that they cannot resist. I cannot accept his worry as being a full picture, though, because his comprehension of WHY there is com-

* Daise E. Terry, office manager at *The New Yorker*.

munism is too simplified; it is a kind of anger, of competition, not a matter of understanding. Ross really has *no* comprehension of Europe at all, no more than a babe, no more than a soldier of World War I, which he still is, with Montmartre and Pig Alley [Pigalle] as his playgrounds.

I have spent ninety-five dollars in eight days, not counting hotel bill: lunch at Algonquin for two is seven dollars. I do not see how people live. It is terrifying the cost of life here. . . .

[November 28, 1950]

. . . The hurricane did not touch Fire Island. The wind in New York rose to one hundred miles an hour, glass from broken windows flew outside other windows still intact, women were blown across streets, *and* I saw men crawling on their hands and knees on the sidewalks at corners where the gale had an open path. The cornice which fell from *The New Yorker* building struck some parked cars, but no people, by a miracle. The cornice partly fell on a balcony by E. B. White's window, nicked the parapet, but did not even break the window glass. I was here in the building at noon on Saturday to fetch my typewriter but decided against it, in the storm. The cornice fell at three-thirty, scaring the wits out of the telephone operator, male, alone in the office, we being closed on Saturday. The devastation in New Jersey where also mosquitoes are largest is, as usual, worse than elsewhere. Long Island suffered less than in the hurricanes of 1938 and 1944.

I have been here nearly three weeks, and Ross still has not seen me except for twenty minutes at "21" the second night. But everything seems normal even at that. This is a note in haste as usual because I am constantly interrupted either by phone calls or drifters.

I shall be glad of four days alone on the train to California. No letter from you for nearly a week.

I am always paralyzed at first in this city. Like an old gray bird from the country that can find no perch. But beneath my feathers my heart beats for you, dear one.

Janet had been planning her next assignments with *The New Yorker* and was getting ready to leave for California to visit her mother and sister for two weeks. At the end of November, she wrote:

"I may not go to Washington for the Gulbenkian piece at least as what Ross wants on G, Shawn and I now think is unobtainable; a lot of personal, amusing and entertaining anecdotes. It took one woman one month even to trace the exterior pattern of his life. How trace his private conversations with other oily millionaires and over a life now in its eightieth year?

"If one could ever see anybody ALONE here. No: always bars, restaurants, with four or five others to dine, racket, clatter, MUSICA playing, etc.; I can't *think*, I tell you. . . ."

[On board the *Chief* en route to California,
December 4, 1950]

Carissima, nerissima,

This I shall mail in Albuquerque, New Mexico, in a few minutes. The landscape of red soil, blue hills and scant cottonwood leaves of yellow and grey is laid over by dust the color of pollen, which gives it an alchemistic air. It is beautiful. I still have headaches and shall be glad to see my Doctor Coke in Pasadena.

I shall be at the *Gladstone* again, until I sail January twentieth on the *Liberté*. So for once I shall not be apologizing for being later than I said. How untidy America looks with refuse, old paper, bottles, old outhouses everywhere in all suburbs. How poor it looks for one so rich . . . Je t'embrasse. We approach the station.

[December 19, 1950]

Darlinghissima,

I forgot your birthday, and I am as sorry as an early Christian who has forgotten a secret feast. I have always been on the outs with calendar as to feasts and anniversaries, and can no longer remember years in history except in a large way, such as Columbus discovered America in 1492.

I didn't write from California because my impressions varied so from day to day and each seemed final and therefore as they added up unjust AND confusing. Mostly Hildegarde seems to have been drowned once more in dishwater, a horrid semi-death for a poet. Money and a generous husband could have saved her long ago, and mother not having lingered so long as a frail burden and also what might have helped Hildegarde would have been to have been a good and easy housekeeper. She is a vague and earnest one, always at sixes and sevens in her routine in which disorder piles up like a local California mountain. Eric is slowly killing himself with overwork: is still the most intelligent American man I have talked to here, probably because he majored in philosophy at college so that his mind works in ideas not opinions and because he is a Californian and not a New Yorker.

Weather was divine and hot. I went barelegged in garden, roses in bloom and violets. Jan's eunuch cat was always asleep amid falling rose petals. I have already started work on the Matisse Profile, getting information here. My circulation in my right arm and leg are still bad, and Coke says nothing can be done. I don't know why. He says, "Exercise would help." That is always the advice given the aged. Coke says I had doubtless passed a blood clot in my right leg the night I sat up in hot train returning from Prades last summer. I still think life in New York is very difficult for soul—and life in Europe dangerous for body and mind.

I love you as I am, as you are. That is my testament for the grave end of a mid-century year. God bless you and yours and keep them safe, and keep Mr. Acheson safe, too!

[December 27, 1950]

My darlinghissima, my blessed Natalia, Buon Natale.

. . . I do not find it easy to discover what people are thinking here, because it is difficult to know what I think. America is like a gigantic row boat sliding in a dangerously stormy international sea, and we have neither the old-fashioned muscular simple strength to row ourselves to safety, nor have we the same kind of modern mechanics of thinking and practice which the Russians have and who are in another kind of boat, on the same sea, and are really causing this artificial storm which may sink us. There are no longer any media of communication or psychology, diplomacy, truthfulness, or foreign policy which today are practiced as they used to be practiced by Europeans and which, too late, we started to learn for now they would be useless even if we knew them well. We have no points in common for communication with the Soviets and Russians, and even translation at the United Nations does not succeed in making our ideas clear to them, since they can pretend miscomprehension which is a lie, but of constant use as a gesture of evasion to them.

I understood more of what is the American mind in California than here, I think, because Hildegarde has little money and her friends are in like situation, so are closer to reality. In trying to become the richest citizens on earth, we have merely become the people who spend the most to eat badly, overheat our homes, build motor cars too big to park or use, and goods which we throw away before they are worn out.

I keep looking for a letter from you that will give me further news of Bill, of whether you have started to write your D'Annunzio piece. The book which has most interested me is [Alistair Cooke's] *A Generation on Trial: U.S.A. vs Alger Hiss*, the report on the Hiss-Chambers trial; I shall bring it to you to read. Also, *Kon-Tiki* [Thor Heyerdahl], the story of the Norwegian ethnologists who sailed on a raft from Peru to the Malay Isles; it is exquisitely translated in a great bald vocabulary which makes it one of the greatest travel adventures ever recorded in the English language. . . .

I enclose the rapturous press agent blurbs on two films which we thought bad, *Bitter Rice* and the French *Manon*. The critics gave [*Ways of*] *Love* the best foreign film prize, partly to protest against the municipal ruling that the Rosselini film about the foolish shepherdess (who thought herself the virgin) had to be removed from the Paris movie theater here. And *Guys and Dolls*, a kind of tough new music show, runs on to rapturous giggles from an audience come to admire coarseness, bawdy innuendo, girls' bosoms, and men leering at them.

I am very low in imagination, hope and reaction. I shall be moved with joy to see you.

1951

Nineteen-fifty-one was the year I decided to return to the States. The combined efforts of Janet and several high-powered friends to help me find a permanent job had failed. I could not make a living as a free-lance writer. It was a hard decision to make, but, as it turned out, a wise one.

On my way to Paris I stopped in Milan to visit an old friend, the publisher Arnoldo Mondadori, for whom I had worked in my late teens, contributing poems and stories to a children's publication called *Girotondo*.

I had not seen Mondadori since his return from Switzerland, where he had spent the war years. His Verona printing plant had been badly damaged by the bombings in 1943, and his Milan offices left a shambles, but now, after eight years, they were operating at full capacity. "Thanks to Santo Giorgio," he said, "we have been able to rebuild the plant, the offices, everything. Thanks to Saint George. . . ." It was his way of expressing his gratitude to General George Marshall, whose *Memoirs* he later brought out in Italian. It was through the Marshall Plan that Mondadori had, like so many others in Europe, been able to rebuild his business. As an American, I embodied for him, at that moment, General Marshall himself.

My own name, under the insignia of the new Mondadori Publishing Company, would soon appear in gold lettering on the door of my New York office, in the Scribner Building on Fifth Avenue.

When we had met in Paris, I had told Janet of the possibility of a job with Mondadori in New York and, back in Rome, I wrote her that I needed her advice before giving my final answer. Nothing, of course, would change in our friendship, but crossing an ocean was not as easy as riding overnight in a comfortable sleeping car. We would be separated for the greater part of the year.

                                                    [April 2, 1951]
Natalia,

Your letter this morning saying that you are deciding your plans tomorrow makes tomorrow an execution day, and our hearts will be cut off. I feel as if my head were hanging low enough to be stretched forward for an axe. Yes, you are doing me justice when you say that the separation on your decision will be just as hard for me as for you. I shall suffer in my resources for sufferings which are different than yours and which to you have often seemed nonexistent, and you will suffer in your classic, richer manner and in those materials where you have inherited sensibilities like jewels as red as rubies and blood. I shall only bleed the way Indiana trees do, a sort of sap, a sort of bleeding of vegetation that could make something as fatal as opium if it came from a poppy. But I shall die of it, too, make no mistake, Natalia. I am too bitter and sad to write more. Thank you for writing all the details which have gone to help in making the decision on its periphery. Yes, the Mondadori work is more of your mind and level and would give you physical, spiritual independence. I am heartsick, darling. I am going to phone you tomorrow.

———

What would be waiting for me in New York? Luckily my son, Bill, had also decided to return to the States. By now he had realized that his voice was not big enough for the operatic stage; he would try musical comedy in New York. In fact, he had preceded me.

"I can't begin to tell you about New York," he wrote in his first letter, at the end of May. "I am in a mild state of shock. Prices are way up, and there is television everywhere, but everywhere. I can't get used to this necessity for noise, for something going on all the time. Even my friends, whom I hadn't seen in so long, either had to play the radio, or the jukebox, or watch television while we talked. . . ."

Yes, it would be difficult to readjust to American ways. Abroad, the Korean situation was still worrisome, and the McCarthy-style witch-hunt going on at home was alarming and distressing.

Janet had written me on the subject.

[April 4, 1951]

The witch-hunt against communists *is* alarming, but at least communists are people who had chosen to think something which describes them as individuals, making a choice in which they could be held responsible; but witch-hunting against an act of birth, a condition by birth, like being born a Jew or Negro . . . is terrible, more terrible, because those people have NOT selected to be what they are, it is not a matter of their thinking something which makes them an enemy of the people; it is a matter of condition by birth which all revolutions for democracy have always declared cannot be laid to the blame of man as a social stigma. This is a sad and cruel world in which fine men sincerely fight certain types of humans, being eaten alive but add the privilege of eating another variety of humanity, instead. I believe that all these hatreds are important; they are chemical, are instinctive, Jew-hating, American-hating, Negro-hating, homosexual-hating, Communist-hating, Republic and Conservative and New Deal-hating. People hate what they are not and do not like as dogs hate cats. The relation between cats and dogs seems insoluble and symbolic of society; they are the two rival domestic animals who are farthest developed socially in their psychology. Horses make no difference in the home and illustrate nothing except ambition on race tracks perhaps. But the hate between and the different natures of the feline and the canine remain something to ponder on, for us humans. I fancy that in idealism we are trying to declare what should not be true, is not true, because we wish it not to be true. Perhaps we ought always to include all in us, the bad and not just the good as our program for premise. Something is wrong in the way humanity operates and decides and reacts, that I am sure. Injustice is basic in us, that's why we pass so many laws to prevent it. We never pass laws about not doing things people *don't* want to do, only laws against their doing what they long to do, such as hate somebody else and to try to suppress him as a type.

I had hoped for a letter this morning. I am working feverishly to get my Matisse interviews done quickly, took two yesterday and got nearly nothing from one which took two hours. Peggy Bernier [Mrs. John Russell] is coming this afternoon. She has a lot of Matisse material she is giving me. Alice Toklas can give me some, but she is so inaccurate because she and Gertrude quarreled with Matisse, and so she warps events; how curious, it is as if I had quarreled with anyone you choose, say George Washington, and as a result denied that he even had wooden false teeth as a way of making him more unattractive and myself more superior. In my anguish and sadness, all the elements of everybody else's life and habits fall upon me as a way of adding to my burden because I am raw at this moment with my own wounds and so take on their mutual bruises, too.

My decision to accept the job offered by Mondadori had sealed my return to the States. The realization that I was leaving my life in Italy suddenly hit hard, and dampened the atmosphere of good feeling then permeating the air: in my personal life and in the country as a whole, which was enjoying the first two years of what would become known as "the Italian Miracle."

During this period, Hollywood established itself along the Tiber, with American producers making films in Italy. American movie stars appeared on the Via Veneto and at Cincecittà. Italy was *in*.

There was a feeling of renewal in the air, a feeling of spring inside the heart—and the desire to have some fun, too. Nothing could have been more suitable to the whim of the rich than Venice, the luscious Queen of the Adriatic, with her magnificent *palazzi* on the Grand Canal and her international film and art festivals. The younger generation of beautiful people, the so-called Jet Set, arrived from all corners of the world to re-create the splendor of the costume balls of their elders, the extravaganzas of the fashionable Paris of the nineteen-thirties. The gayest festival of all, the colorful Historical Regatta of the gondolas, took place in the first week in September, as it had since the year 900.

I was also heartsick, but I kept saying to myself that I, too, had received a kind of miracle, a chance at a new beginning. "Santo Arnoldo Mondadori," I murmured in my prayers, so I could stand the pain and be strong to face my future, mostly alone.

But only when I arrived in New York that summer did I fully realize the extent of the adjustments I would have to make. For one thing, the McCarthy witch-hunt had already begun to poison the atmosphere. It surfaced when I found myself face to face with the landlady of the new apartment I had rented through an agent. She looked at me suspiciously and said, "You are a foreigner, aren't you?" and slammed the door. For another, I found my son, temporarily installed in a small apartment loaned to him by Gilbert Seldes, lying in bed in a sea of perspiration. He had become sick and exhausted from daily subway trips to the race track, where, unable to find a job, he had been struggling to make a living. He proudly pointed to a cardboard shoebox on which, in bold letters, he had written, "Back to Italy Fund." He had saved two hundred and fifty dollars. I was shocked. "Money earned by gambling," I prophesied, "is never kept." A few days later the box was stolen, and Bill unknowingly passed the thief on the stairs.

"That Bill was robbed of his two hundred and fifty dollars seems the last straw. How horrid robbery is, and especially to meet the robber," sympathized Janet. Not long afterward, Bill accepted a temporary job to help me in my new office and moved into a flat next to mine.

My New York life had begun.

[September 5, 1951]

My darling,

What sweet, gentle letters of the patterned surface of your life have been the last two. They were like a report of the smaller physical events which have always made for correspondence between women over centuries and devoid as they were of that tiring intellectuality which stiffens my letters to you, were perfect models for me to use in writing to you from now on. As you said so truly, Basta to all my explanations out of the head.

I have stopped to send this in the midst of my Paris Letter writing which is coming easier than usual, being perhaps not very important in its topics. I nearly included the rumors precedent to the [Carlos] de Beistegui ball in the Palazzo Labia in Venice this week; facts would have been crazed enough but the rumors were really hypnotic. One was that he himself would receive his masked guests on a couple of elephants, mounted on special barges; another that Lopez was having his barge lined with mink, with a real diamond on each tail. These notions were being passed from mouth to ear all over Paris. Darling tough old Marie-Louise Bousquet put it most clearly of all; she went dressed as a giantess with Dior; she said those invited to the ball say as an excuse that it makes work for the dressmaking trade and those not invited say it is frivolous *merde*.

The rain never ceases.

I can almost see your office by your description, darling. The handsome huge Italian furniture will give you an ambiance of familiar line and volume that should aid your imagination and even resistance; like eating in an Italian or French restaurant in New York to pretend one is in Italy or France. Till the food comes and after it the check. Then one knows the difference. I am sorry Bill didn't get *The New Yorker* job, sorrier he didn't get the *Time* one as yet; for that is his special problem and he can work it out there better than elsewhere. That is where his first comprehensible revolt started, that is where he can best find out what revolt costs and also what it is worth. It can be worth everything. That he can work with you temporarily at Mondadori's expense is already a shelter for you both until he finds whatever he finds, maybe *Time* again. I am astounded how much more close to the points of decisions the young ones are today, he is for example, when at his age, until thirty or more, I drifted, events pushed me, people pushed me, a French civilization pushed me. I was like an eccentric young middle westerner in a foreign dream in which I lost my youth without noticing and all that energy for the best work which it could have brought. Then I became a journalist of our special kind and there was my beginning and end. I have had a good life. It was not what I had fancied. Even the best parts of it I would not have imagined nor the worst, in never having written to the extent of my talent, now so under time that I have to dig for it nor does it come up intact.

I feel happier today. I was in such a strain of depression last week as to be almost insane. I could not sleep nor think clearly. I frighten myself in such hours. There is an alter ego which manages me then, takes control and with violence, only subtly presented, terrifying. I shall do all I said to make our home. I shall come to New York over Christmas. Darling

[October 7, 1951]

My very darling,

I mailed my Matisse Part 2 yesterday morning and dressed and hurried to the opening of the United Nations; one had to be there at noon to have a seat in the theatre for the opening speeches at three. I spent seven hours there getting little information, lunched with Darina Silone, who has a job in the Press Liaison Section, sends you greetings, and fell into bed finally, so tired I could not sleep. These my reasons why I did not write you yesterday, especially at UNO where I had planned to send you cards with the new French stamps of the *poètes maudits* series, stamped by the UNO post office. It isn't yet open, nor is the Press Bar. Grave omissions! There was a beautiful moment just before the séance began; the morning had been foggy and rainy, suddenly the clouds had cleared, the sun emerged just before three o'clock, from the enormous salon which makes the lower base of the U-shape in which the building is constructed, which has its wall facing the Tour Eiffel entirely of glass windowing perhaps fifty feet high—suddenly, as I say, the fountains at my feet were turned on, a rare sight—great gushes of water shooting lengthwise in the basin from twenty cannons (they look like), and all the little jets on either side sprouted their fountains-jettes, too; with the sixty flags waving on either side of the basin, the fine view of the Tour, now accepted as a matter of beauty whether it is or not, and between its legs the view of the greensward running toward the Ecole Militaire at the far end of the prospect it was a sight so lovely, so refreshing to the spirit that I burst into tears of hope again. You see, I am an American hick, a provincial, always stirred anew with female provincial hope which European men are too experienced to believe in, especially when the hope rests on yokel Americans, so inexperienced with this elderly sacred Europe which the Europeans who do know all about it ruined.

I saw Anne McCormick later. She said she, too, had been moved for her few moments of American female hope, but also laughed with her fine diplomatic chuckle. Her pieces from London have been superb, as profound an interpretation as heavy with news on foreign affairs which seem suddenly taking a change in direction; the general new aim is dual now, to try to make a real European federation, if only in terms of the European army, and to find some way of paying the Europeans, I suppose, to arm themselves adequately which they cannot afford now, especially in France with the disgusting de luxe, spendthrift, non-taxpaying habit of the rich.

Yes, that Papal piece on the bed relations of Catholics; I was outraged. I yearned to write you a chapter on it; I was actually too tired in my hands after working from nine a.m. to eleven p.m., which is what I did for eleven days—to type more than I was already doing. En passant, it was extraordinary the vigor I felt during that work period and still do, a renewal of strength and health that is amazing. I was struck anew by the Papal advice to midwives with the odious sexuality of the basis of both the Jewish and Christian religions, in their primitive states of which among the Orthodox the law is still observed being thereon founded; the fact that Judaism was based on circumcision, and Christianity in having virginity intact for females, even if a mother in the case of Mary which I have always thought a very indelicate locality in which to set up the basic miracle on which faith is founded and which again as a locality provided the morality, the social pattern, which still influences Christianity, especially Catholicism; the Greek morality if they had any was purely social and intellectual as it should be, the Roman was civic, only the Christian remained like a prying new invention, the novel preoccupation with what lies between the legs as proof of one's good citizenship AND morality, both public activities usually being tended to in private with the door closed. . . . The miracle by which the Virgin was arranged last summer by the Pope to have assumted instead of assompted was the first of the Pope's innocuous egocentricities, and the vision of Fatima the second, both so malapropos to our century as to make one realize the church is not merely not helping fight against Communism, but is constantly, deliberately adding to Communism's good chances of becoming universal, not in our time, perhaps, but maybe in Bill's, as a very choleric old gent who, having done nothing but complain intellectually, and with justice, against democracy which is what men and women have made it, will find he will have no more of it to complain against. It will have disappeared. It will have run its course. . . . My darling, I was waiting for the real wooden-like anger you can be carved into and now report on in your last letter, which shapes you when you have no outlet for your imagination. If you do not come to Rome, I could spend a month there with you. Each time I see an airplane overhead, I rush out to look at it and force myself to think I am in it, as a moral training for my flight to come!

Is Bill singing nightly? If so, what fun for him. Has he a part, a role? Do tell me, please, for my interest never abates. Poor darling Bill, his hopes now must be turned merely to local pleasures as a songster. But if that is the physical truth about his vocal chords, only practical proof could have made him accept it. Not study nor lessons and, above all, not his mother's excellent, truthful technical, almost professional advice. I hope he helps with the dishes, tell him. . . . Stand fast till we meet soon.

[October 12, 1951]

Darling one,

What a charming animating letter is yours, the first written from your brownstone flat. The description is good, "even elegant in a modest way." That is the direction of descent which marks most of us these days, if cheerfully even; to be modest in an elegant way marked the direction of ascent for the rich arriviste intellectual bourgeois about the time of Stendhal; he was modest in an elegant way, was our Henri Beyle for in his hopes, ambitions and excuses for himself and failures he was always in ascension like a rocket that burned out his amour propre. I was last night reading his *Souvenirs d'Egoïsme*, in bed as pre-sleep reading, and I laughed so hard he woke me up. I cannot be sure if he meant to be funny especially at his own expense. "En 1821 j'avais beaucoup de peine à resister à la tentation de me brûler la cervelle. Je dessinais un pistolet à la marge d'un mauvais drame d'amour que je barbouillais alors." . . . Yes, a handmade picture of the pistol on the MS edge is sad fun. I am enjoying this brief book which I had read before without the same sympathy because I found it an irritant not an emollient; the oil of humor makes it slip gently now into this reader's consciousness where the private portrait of the writer, of any writer, must always reside if his image is worth saving or has had strength to form its own profile, aside from his talent which is something. . . . I was very interested in your meeting again with Borgese*; I was naturally gratified that he had approved what I disapproved and what I disproved even in Thomas Mann—the God-head, made of wood.** Glenway Wescott was the only literary friend who then stood by me, knew what I was doing and meant, as an aim in sincere destruction and thought it important. It even cost him a friendship or at least an adulation, that of a woman who was in the female ring of admiration and swooning that surrounded The Master and who screamed in shock at my blasphemy, which she herself had helped supply in an interview . . . Borgese's description of the differences in terms of borrowed similarities between USSR and USA is also valuable, a big bite to digest. It is of no value to remain on the smallest lowest plane of chronology, during a time of important dissatisfaction and deplore minute by minute and so hour by hour, even accumulating months of complaint at what is transpiring. For the record then is petty. It takes more time, it takes more slowness to base the complaint on what is heavier, larger and comes in slower accumulation, by the season or by the big thought and in

* Giuseppe Borgese, anti-Fascist writer and founder of the literary review *Hermes*; married Elizabeth Mann, fifth of Mann's six children.

** Janet's Profile of Mann, "Goethe in Hollywood," was published by *The New Yorker* in 1941.

this slowness comes the critical not the irrational faculty, which makes
for a real comment on the human affair which is being lived. I think
it is very difficult for us Americans, your kind or my kind, to locate
the large alarming thing or things behind the disillusioning minutes
that make a day of life in New York so irritating and upsetting and
alien—alien to what New York and America was a few years ago. It
isn't just the gasoline-filled Manhattan air or the fool in his car, radio
on full tilt, who screamed till you thought he was dying that the
Giants or whichever had won a homerun; the Manhattan air and he
are evidences but what is the real fault or change that lies behind?
Maybe it is so big we are afraid to find and name it. It is harder to
deal with now, whatever it is, because we have no other place philo-
sophically to go to; this may be what has happened to American
democracy but it still doesn't make what has happened to Russian
communism any less disillusioning as a place to send one's mind to
live. . . .

What worries me darling in the inquisitions of the last two years is
the lack of organization of the only defense material which will save
anyone or can CREATE THE PSYCHOLOGY, PRECEDENT AND APPARATUS
on which ALONE defense can now stand. I can no longer stand on
privilege of free speech, mostly because free speechers abused it by
saying I am free to preach the desired downfall of this country. In
cowardice we have given up free speech as both privilege and precedent. So what we have felt must be something new and it must be a
defense; as I see it it is dull-sounding, has no great blazing attractive
phrases and is tediously like law. But what else can it be? The defense
of anyone accused by Red Channels of having been pro-loyalist in
Spain in 1936 must be the following: (a) Should I have been pro-
Franco, do you think? Are you today? Being anti-Franco was not
necessarily pro communist as the loyalists were mixed democrats and
reds. (b) The date is of greatest historical importance; 1936 had its
own time sense; this MUST be considered as a basic description of the
issue at stake. That date carried many implications including being
anti-Hitler, anti-Mussolini, as well as anti-Franco. A date of thinking
has its own historical implication which cannot be dislodged; history
is made of dates, it is a calendar of events in terms of changes. (c)
There must be established the sense of disresponsibility of the donator,
who gave money or enthusiasm to an organization which advertised
itself as one thing—like a patent medicine advertising by mail to cure
everything you have of ills, from headache to snake bite—and which
later more or less openly let be known what it was really selling—i.e.,

Communism. There is a law against false presentation of products for sale; an extension of this will have to be made to include products of the political mind. I regret that all this sounds dull. Sounds legal. What duller? But after two years of McCarthy's smearing inquisition, I do not see any program of defense where people can turn for protection; there must be protection and it must be organized, alas, I who hate organization. When I think back I am sick to recall the agile jump of the Civil Liberties Union to protect any extreme leftist who said Up with Russia; he had his rights and his lawyer, for nothing. Where is the Civil Liberties Union lawyer for the man who merely said Down with Anti-Democracy? . . . The democrat is in a poor position today. He lacks extremes. Only extremes attract today; they attract either cowardice (the revival of fascism as a theory in a people like the Americans who have literally no idea what the full thing is either in theory or practice, and for whom it is a kind of import like sardines in bitter oil they have never tasted) or the other extreme which attracts toward the underground home of the martyred Leftist mind.

Excuse me. I am incensed.

Your flat sounds more charming to me than to you, but you will explore its pleasantness in these days and suffer less. That sounds cool, even callous of me, but it is a fact—it is one of the compensatory inevitabilities of domesticity—I am glad Bill is becoming his own good valet; he is too old to let important women work for him as maids, as your mother did when he was a boy. It is undignified. Who on earth is Victor Emmanuel besides an ex-King of Portugal?

Lunched with darling Marguerite Bassiano yesterday; she told Cass Canfield of Harper's when here that he must get in touch with you in New York to get better Italian books, to get HER authors, too! So give him a nudge. I don't think Irwin Shaw is here yet; I shall tell him your message, darling. Yes, I think that young Mondadori has called you a diavolo is a compliment, darling. A demon for work, maybe; anyhow, that you are amazing at your job I take for granted on absolute knowledge of you; that knowledge is empirical.

My Paris Letter of the week is so weak as to be the only bad one I ever wrote in my career—Mollie's* is importantly dull but importantly composed of heavy news; mine is trifling, composed of specks of the big news—also, it being cut here and there has added silliness—I did NOT see General IKE—Hq. is too busy to see anyone except other generals this week—General [Omar] Bradley and Suite were in my

* Mollie Panter-Downes.

hotel. An air lieutenant who flew my bicycle and electric cooker from London to Paris in 1944 is back on duty, in a brighter blue uniform. It is horrifying. I love you—I love you—

[November 26, 1951]

Darlinghissima,

. . . Do not think me despairing or frivolous, but do you really want to keep your American citizenship now? I should be astonished if you relegated it, even though the country itself represents to you—as to many of us—another country, less sure and comforting than it was formerly. But this seems to be a period in history when nothing is what one hoped or supposed in any nation; all peoples, except maybe the lesser sensitive-minded Russian masses, are disillusioned, bitter or bleakly disappointed. Nor does that mean that one would be helped by giving up whatever nationality one has; where go, on what other passport repose one's confidence? It seems that today all liberal movements and countries are paying for the steady abuse they previously suffered, against which they now erect rulings that are the very walls against the freedom they previously cherished as boundless but in which, as I say, abuses themselves conspired to lay the first stones. It is an age of papers, red tape, stamps, signatures, of life on a piece of paper itself, with the soul described in ink.

The anti-Americanism of the French is maddening here. Now when a Parisian almost erotically says, "Sûrement vous aimez bien la France, Mademoiselle," I coldly reply, "Et vous, aimez-vous l'Amérique?" This always scandalizes them, the idea never having occurred to them that they should do any loving!

Their idea of love is that they should receive it, not give it. I suspect from the tactful though informative dispatches from Russell Hill, from the Strasbourg Congress of Europe meeting, that the U.S.A. Senators and Congressmen there had a shock and probably gave several in meeting the attitudes of most west Europeans vis-à-vis America.

Certainly, France talks like a spoiled old beauty who still wants her hand kissed in admiration; de Gaulle's weekend speech about France's fate lying in the hands of a foreign general—i.e., Ike—is ridiculous really. France had her military fate completely in her own hands in 1939 and in June 1940, and it made lamentable history. I still find the Italian attitude the most civilized, because containing a sense of humor and history as well. At least they do not pretend to have been all-seeing and all-wise, do not blame others for what they themselves did and which failed. . . .

I find E. M. Forster's *Two Cheers for Democracy* one of the most stimulating, clear, delightfully strong collections of essays I have read in years; you would be enchanted by them. One can read with speed and joy, with profit, with nourishment. Bill would love them, too.

I saw a strange play* tonight, Jean-Louis Barrault playing Lazarus at the Marigny. Lazarus is, of course, furious with Jesus for dragging him back to life, though he doesn't mention the agony of having to die twice, which must be considered I should think. Then in act two—it has only two acts—Jesus, who talks against death as the great evil, makes him love life again as a second miracle, then himself goes out to die in a couple of weeks, he says. Very odd; the period of the play is medieval. No reference to the East, to Jerusalem of the period of Christ's birth. He and Judas who is the agnostic in a way and Matthew are dressed in sort of monks' clothes, the others in medieval garments. It was the second critics' night, great enthusiasm, about fifteen curtain calls.

No letter from you for days. Do not choke on Fleur Cowles' emeralds if eating her sandwiches at her parties. What wealth still exists there, which even we can touch by seeing on the outskirts. I am so completely cut off from fashionable or elegant life here that I probably don't know what French luxury is like. I only know that fortunes are being made and never spent prettily, in public at least.

Love . . .

Janet and I were very fond of our friends and we often gossiped about them. Janet had a special coterie from her earlier Parisian days, who hung about her like bees around a succulent flower. They were attracted by her personality, her notorious wit and intelligence, her perception and insights, and her brilliant, entertaining conversation, as humorous as it was illuminating. Newcomers into this exclusive company were considered intruders and snubbed. Not by Janet, who always disliked groups, clubs or cliques of any kind; she herself was the perennial rebel against any form of constriction.

Janet had been reading *The Fiery Fountains*, Margaret C. Anderson's second volume of memoirs, which had just been published. Anderson's name was linked with some interesting and daring events,

* *Lazare* by André Obey.

and I was intensely curious about her. In 1914 she and her friend, Jane Heap, had founded one of the most outstanding of the "little magazines," *The Little Review*, which had been the first to publish James Joyce's *Ulysses*—in excerpts over a period of three years. The event created a scandal, led to a famous obscenity trial and left her without a penny. It was then that she met, in New York, Georgette Leblanc, who had been the companion of Maurice Maeterlinck and had been on a concert tour of the States, "as a diseuse of exceptional fine sensibilities," wrote Janet in her Profile of Anderson, upon the latter's death in 1973. "From the first, they formed an attachment with all the signs of permanence."

I had finally met Margaret Anderson, preceded by her reputation and face, in 1942. I was indeed pleased to be able to have her as my guest when she first landed in New York from France. She, too, was escaping the Nazi occupation. When Janet took me upstairs to meet her, I was not overwhelmingly impressed. She had the dramatic manner of a grande dame of the theater and retained some vestige of her renowned good looks, but she was condescending and distant. She was lying on a sofa and hardly uttered a word, not even a polite acknowledgment of my hospitality.

She stayed only a few days. On board the boat that took her to New York she had met Dorothy Caruso, Enrico Caruso's widow, who introduced herself by saying, "I hear you published *The Little Review*." "By the time the boat docked," wrote Janet, only eight months after Georgette Leblanc's death "they had become friends—'the last great friendship of my life'—Margaret wrote, and they were domiciled together until Dorothy Caruso's death, in 1955." And when she left my home, she almost succeeded in taking with her, behind my back, my faithful couple, Louise and Harold, as her last gesture of gratitude. Yes, I was curious to read her memoirs. . . .

Nancy Cunard was another of those valiant women rebels whose reputations lay both in the world of letters and in their freedom of choices and action. I had met her in Paris with Janet, but briefly, in a local bistro. She, too, had been beautiful and had had an adventurous, stormy life. She was fifty-one when I first met her, and some of that fascination remained—I felt the charm myself. She was very tall and slim, wearing a typical British "tailor-made" with a kind of country look—stylish, but not "smart" in the French manner. Nevertheless, she did have chic. A cluster of tiny brownish curls peeped out from under the brim of her small felt hat and protruded over her forehead, rather as if she were wearing a wig. Her white skin was almost transparent, which made her large, penetrating green eyes—eyes that had a trace of madness in them—the major feature of her face. Enormous clattering bracelets of jade and ivory covered her forearms and announced her presence. She spoke very fast, a torrent of words intermingled with laughter. Janet was very fond of Nancy, who had broken all the traditional English laws of behavior and lived the life she had chosen for herself—unconventional, artistic, political and poetic. She managed to scandalize the fashionable British society to which her mother belonged, and was disinherited. She did not care, preferring her freedom, her Bohemian friends and lovers, and her poverty. She embraced causes, published some very good poetry, and ran her own presses. She was very special—egotistical, irresponsible and attractive.

Kay Boyle also arrived in Paris in the late twenties, but did not belong to that special clique, though she knew all its members. She was younger, for one thing. Janet admired her writings and her spirit, though sometimes she was critical of her fervent, missionary-like involvement in every cause that presented itself as worthy of her attention. Kay was as beautiful as she was opinionated. She had been married several times, had produced a cornucopia of beautiful children by different husbands, and managed to write, teach, proselytize, and help the brood whenever they needed it. I remember once going to see her in New York. It was in the early forties, and she was in bed. She always wrote in bed, her typewriter on her knees, pages strewn around and the children bouncing all over. She did not mind; she actually enjoyed it. I met her again in Rome, when she arrived there as a correspondent, and we have remained friends ever since. She later paid dearly for her strong liberal views. She was one of those intellectuals who were considered "premature anti-Fascists"—the stigma all of us who had fought fascism from the very beginning were to be labeled with and, therefore, suspected of. Those were the shameful days of McCarthyism. . . .

[December 6, 1951]

Wednesday night, my sweetheart,

Thank you for your cable of brief complete editorial news. I am well, I think of you. Your vocabulary has changed in America. You have new words you use with ease—antibiotics (I've no notion what they are) and poor Ariane Ross's logorrhea which is splendid, also a novelty to me and to all but the Greeks I dare say and lexicons today; but you do not use your old vocabulary of the simpler words of love and longing. Erotomania has a shocking, frigging kind of meaning for those who too much love love; we should create a nice new word for it which would dignify the madness. How about amorophile or venusienne for the ladies? Certainly Margaret Anderson was one; I thought her advice to lovers sounded a trifle frivolous as any program laid down so arbitrarily on home conduct between beloveds can sound, just as the Vatican program sounds the opposite of frivolous, a sort of sinister biological conduct program laid down by an institution which has fought biology every step of the way since the creation of the world, quite a long time. I have not yet read her whole book; how on earth did you happen to want to read it? Angry curiosity? I think it does indeed show editing, good editing, especially compared to her first book which was loose, irrational and megalomaniacal. I did, however, turn to read her account of Georgette's death which I found profoundly simple. Sincere, told in a tragic straight line that followed her observation of a tragic almost static event, the death of an old woman by cancer, confined to her bed over which her spirit still managed to make movements. . . . I had an extraordinary conversation from one to five with Nancy Cunard today, a lunch so-called which moved through several sets of bad bistro French coffee but not, thank heaven, through increasing bottles of bistro wine with which she sometimes floods and drowns her intelligence and in which invariably only her hates and irritations manage to continue to float. Never what she loves, only what she loathes. This lack of distinction between the two emotional or intellectual functions in the critical faculty have always given her her revolutionary destructive bias; she is always on some barricade, throwing stones, at first at her mother whom she completey lapidated (or at any rate their relation together), then at society, then at mere people whom she meets, sees, or watches, takes an instantaneous dislike to as complete as if she had investigated and added them up for years. She went on at length about Robert Sherwood whom she hardly knows, who is vaguely related through Irish ancestors and whom she described with relish as a stuffed shirt of a monster because he is too tall and had too high a position in BBC during the war, in her opinion. With all that she is absolutely fascinating, also crazed, also of a memorable memory which makes listening to her an irrational, uproarious pleasure, for she, too, laughs a great deal sometimes and did at our lunch. In a way she is something like darling K. Boyle; both "take a stand" about something, for or against, and develop a smouldering anger that it usually turns out not to be so black or so white as they had hoped for; both are social optimists, more embittered by their inaccuracies than their disillusions. Kay just wrote me; [her daughter] Katie has been accepted at the Conservatoire here, one of six out of three hundred contestants, fancy that; only other foreigner I believe was Monica [Sterling's] sister, how odd a coincidence; Kay wrote to ask if I knew a Shakespeare reader who could work with the child on English pronunciation, since obviously she wants possibility of playing eventually in both languages, and her English has a heavy accent, part Vail,* part Paris, part younger generation. . . .

. . . I am infuriated, my old hatred of lawyers as the vultures and gobbledygookers of society returns; they pick bones and squawk their meal in a language which they themselves have made so complex that nobody else in the field can comprehend it; we pay them for their insane translation of their crazed tongue they have built up and for telling us how and why they are robbing us and where we pay for their informative explanation while they fly away with one-fourth of the carcass. Poor Maria. Those music lessons she was paid small rates for cost her dearly indeed—over five thousand dollars. Nancy [Cunard] is having legal trouble with her mother's estate, too. Her mother managed to rush through a vast fortune at the last minute of her life as it were. Confined to her hotel rooms in London, she was a greater spendthrift than when entertaining King Edward, George Moore and the Asquiths at dinner table . . .

. . . Oh what disappointment; huge package from *New Yorker* just brought up, I thought it Matisse proof. It is *New Yorker's Cartoon Album*, kindly sent me by office as "A Memento of Our 25th Anniversary." I see on the cover lots of Saul Steinberg. I have just opened the book to take a peek; it has my completely favorite cartoon of lady on porch of colonial hut whose husband is obviously inside boa constrictor hanging from beam beside her, she saying, "Oh speak up, George, stop mumbling." Probably perfect example of our realism, sadism and also that state of improbability we put into drawings which takes truth out of the conception so that spectator cannot be really frightened; what we show looks possible and is funny because it is really impossible; if it were really possible, the drawing's message or subject matter would be unbearably frightening. . . .

---

* The American poet Laurence Vail was first married to Peggy Guggenheim, whom he divorced in the late twenties. He subsequently married Kay Boyle, in 1931, and divorced her in 1943. Vail died in Cannes, France, in 1968.

I sat next to him at a dinner party with my husband and his friends. It must have been soon after my wedding in New York, where I had arrived only a few months earlier, in the mid-twenties. He looked a bit peculiar, I thought. Perhaps because I was new to America or because I was accustomed to Italian men, always so careful about their looks, their dress, their appearance. But even later, after I knew him better, he continued to look peculiar and eccentric to me, as he did to many others who knew him well. Tall, lanky, with unruly brown hair and large, sparse front teeth, he was certainly neither elegant nor good-looking. He turned to ask me where I came from—France? Spain? Russia? Greece? With every negative answer, he kept on mentioning every place on earth, except, obviously, Africa or China. Proud as I was to be Italian, I became more and more irritated, wondering when he would finally remember Italy. He never did. When I asked him if he had ever heard of Roman Law, he stared at me in complete astonishment. "Noooo . . ." he exclaimed, "not Italian!!!!"

Was it because I could use a knife and fork properly, or because I spoke with an educated accent? I don't know, but I thought of our emigrants from the poor southern provinces, the bricklayers and subway workers, the vegetable vendors and the shoeshiners I'd seen around the corner from where I lived. Perhaps he thought that all of Italy was just one mass of poor, ignorant emigrants. I felt sad and offended . . .

This was my introduction to the formidable Harold Ross, who founded *The New Yorker* in 1925 and became a legend. His death was a blow to Janet; she had been so very fond of him.

[December 11, 1951]

Darlinghissima,

Thank you for your tender sympathetic cable on our loss, my loss, everybody's loss of Ross. I see by tonight's air edition of *The New York Times* in an editorial, he is also their loss as is indeed true. Thank heaven you gave me some warning, some advance news of his illness again so the shock was less; yet was it really? No. Death is the shock; recovery from illness after a warning leaves the warning forgotten; death after a warning is still death, the absolute shock, the final state of loss, the gravest question while we still live and think; our enquiry no longer is where has this human life gone or has the soul moved up to heaven, down to hell, or around the corner to purgatory; and shall we meet again? The question is not where do the dead disappear but how extraordinary the shock is, each time, that anyone CAN die;

friends look so immortal, we all feel so ageless, we look more aging, our friends' hair like mine grows white and few have the brutality that Ross once shocked me with when I said I thought Neysa McMein still looked handsome. "She's an old girl, so are you, so am I," he said harshly. He was right. Yet he too was struck as if by a blow when [Helen] Hokinson died, even when [Alexander] Woollcott died, as much as they had quarreled. I wrote to Jane Grant; Miss Grant; she was the first Mrs. Ross, I told her and a pity there were others to follow. I also wrote the last one to follow, poor Ariane; no pretty woman like that is to blame when an intelligent man, as ugly as he is brilliant like Ross, takes advantage of his appetite for prettiness and argues her into marrying him. Katharine White wrote me at once Friday, she having received my cable of sympathy already, saying only a few of them at the office knew he was being operated on; Shawn was down in Boston, I think Ross passed the operation to the surgeon's satisfaction then four hours later died—heart. Whether it was an embolism (and what difference can that make) she didn't know; his heart stopped. That is all one need know. That is the vital organ and whatever stops it, weakness or impediment or fatigue or long illness and slow exhaustion by overwork, which was his case, finally the motor stops. The carriage halts. Then a new carriage appears, that which takes the so recently animated lively moving swinging and breathing body away. That great magnificent machine, the body. The most astonishing ever invented. I am sick of the way men now repeat inventions nature patented first, birds that fly, fish under water, automobiles that can run as if they had legs like gazelles or pull in traction as if they had the bulldozer strength of elephants. I have just sent you a cable which represents my final decision; I now agree with your inference in your cable that perhaps it would be a good thing for me to come to New York; I don't know why I think so, for the best thing I could do for myself in terms of the magazine right now is go on and work at the two advance big jobs Shawn gave me with Ross's consent, which no one would now cancel. Actually, this might well be a time to remain out of sight and continue my job until I am told different. But I can feel how short the time will be in Rome and Milan, how much the family will cling to you with their love, how tired you would be; as much as I wished to make Ester happy, I think it is folly for our sakes, for some peace and quiet for us for me not to come to New York. I understand by your letter now that in your cable you meant to infer the question was I coming to the funeral, today. . . . Last night, always too late of course, I began thinking I should have flown for it; yet it is the truth it would have meant nothing to him or even to me; I remain very removed from that last experience to which others attach the great final importance. I would like to have in my will that no one come to my funeral. The grief when one does, if grief it causes, are the bouquets, the final adieu. . . . Also I could not have come, really; this will make you laugh angrily; I am waiting for my Matisse proofs; I cannot carry my library of books with me or could not in a plane; though why should I say that? I could have. One can carry anything.

I have really been so shaken with sadness that I could hardly write with a pen or pencil, my hand shook so. It was like a sickness, feeling so sad, feeling such a loss, as if the landscape had dropped away around me, all being now unfamiliar. . . .

If you do not cable to the contrary I shall try to get the material ready to bring with me for the story Shawn ordered. I don't want to be in New York with no work, it would make me feel so lonely during the day when you were at the office.

We will have happiness. We will be reunited again. Beloved.

1952

A new period in our lives had begun. From now on we would be following two separate roads: Janet remaining in Paris, now a fixture on the literary scene and the acclaimed duenna of the Paris correspondents; I re-establishing myself in New York at my new job.

Janet's realm would continue to be the mansard room on top of the Hôtel Continental, with her favorite view of the Tuileries and the profile of the Eiffel Tower against the silvery horizon; the spacious Oak Room bar downstairs would serve as her salon for friends and visitors at martini time.

I would settle in less de luxe style on the top floor of a brownstone on upper Madison Avenue, and into a small office in the old Scribner building in midtown Manhattan. The fact that I would be working in the building that housed the prestigious publisher of Hemingway, Fitzgerald and Wolfe—as well as the most attractive *Belle Epoque* bookstore on the avenue—was comforting and made me feel at home. So did the many friends who welcomed me back into the fold. So, of course, did the presence of my son next door.

The organization of my life took up so much time, attention and preoccupation that I did not realize at first what a drastic change it would be, compared with what I had been accustomed to for the last seven years.

The drama, too, had shifted from a general situation to a more personal one; from the intensity of the war and of the immediate post-war period to a more reflective and absorbing one, encompassing a somewhat nebulous and uneasy feeling about my private life. I was unsure of where and how to begin in my new job, but I had confidence in myself. I attacked it with fervor, knowing that, after all, it would be an extension of what I had been doing before and had hoped I could continue doing. The circumstances would be different, but the aim was the same—reopening the lines of communication for the flow of ideas, through books and writers. I started by re-connecting known authors with their Italian publisher, and securing new ones for Mondadori's prestigious "Medusa" series. I found everyone interested, ready to collaborate without prejudice or suspicion.

Furthermore, my job would take me to Milan once a year, and Janet would be coming—perhaps less reluctantly—to New York. During this period, our correspondence reflected the adjustments we had to make to the times, to our personal choices, to our work and personal independence. Our friendship would be strong enough to stand them; at least I ardently hoped it would.

[January 1, 1952]

And it is bright and clear, my darlinghissima. It is like a sign. It is the first day of sun and clarity in three weeks. In truth the solar presence is indeed welcome even to this country which esteems it less because it has it less than the Italians. The more one has of goodness, the more one is familiar with it. . . .

Thank you for your great generosity to me in saying that I must not come if I cannot find it easy; it *will* be easy, it must and can be because of its weighty importance, its vital strength and necessity, its demand, its promise of friendliness that binds us.

The appeal of the grey-blue pale sky, cleaned of mist, fog, rain and the action of wind which makes the air gleam is pagan today. The city landscape over the gardens have roared with winds for days and nights. . . .

I have taken vows today: to be no longer violent or angered, to arrange my life and work in a more unselfish pattern, to be a woman who grows in ripeness and finesse, if possible, like an old small tree or garden bush during the next twelve months. . . .

Happy New Year

Darlingest one,

I have ordered my passage for February 2. I had to take first class because there is no cabin alone with bath in tourist, and I will not share a cabin or go without a bath at my time of life for six days in doubtless very bad weather and with me a very bad sailor. Ah, the Captain Courageous on the *Enterprise*! He does not mind bad weather. What a man. But I am not a man; I do not want to arrive fagged and raggedish as you say to see you, but wish to arrive in the pink. I am having a new silk suit made, to wear under a fur coat for the theater and in summer or spring, black of course! I may go to Balenciaga or perhaps Lanvin who would certainly make it much cheaper, as Marie-Blanche de Polignac, Mme Lanvin's daughter, whom I know, would make me a little price d'amitié. Rain, more rain. Fog, more fog. . . . I just read a newly discovered manuscript by Benjamin Constant, very much like his *Adolphe*, called *Cécile*; it seems to be even clearer in its strange almost heartless analysis of himself as a vacillating character, torn between two women and tearing them. One was Madame de Staël who must have been a terror of a tyrant, threw objects at his head; they quarreled terrifically as lovers, yet as republicans, as theorists on the new political life after the Empire, as anti-Bonapartists they passed hours, many miles all over Europe and eventually fifteen years together. I also re-read *Les Liaisons Dangereuses* which I found at hand in preparation for Marguerite Jamois playing it soon; I don't see how she will dare; certainly the bedroom scenes are extremely lubricious, their words alone being such as could not be spoken on the stage, let alone the scenes enacted! But there the fact remains: it is a terrific first novel of Europe of the Eighteenth Century, along with Rousseau's *La Nouvelle Héloïse*; and how clearly, ruthlessly, [Choderlos de] Laclos shows that in the dangerous liaisons women's first inkling of liberty to come began, merely in bed for which they were so ill prepared by convent life and ignorance, till the night they were thrust into their husband's arms. The picture of the shocking deliberate sadistic scheme of humiliation for a lover you had had—you had to put him down so society would not think you had loved or slept with him, and if possible, you had to blackmail him so he would not dare give your name for if he did and you were a woman, a letter of complaint to the king, from your husband, and you would be sent BACK to the convent, even as a matron—all this absolute cruel callousness of a warring erotic society seems unbelivable today. It was a truly poisoned society; it was truly cruel and licentious. To love was considered appalling bad taste; to make love perfectly necessary, like a sporting exercise. After all, it was the same period as the lubricious philosophical writings of de Sade and, for the first time, I realized he represented an epoch, not merely his own special insanity.

. . . You can imagine with what eagerness I am now seized. Please write to me, mio tesoro.

———

Later, in January, Janet was delighted by the announcement that Bill Shawn had been named editor-in-chief of *The New Yorker*.

[January 23, 1952]

Just this minute received a cable from Raoul Fleischmann announcing with pleasure that Shawn had accepted to be editor-in-chief of *New Yorker*. I am so glad, so proud for him. I had taken it for granted. How nice of Raoul to wire me.

I feel the magazine's loss can be explained like this: We have lost Ross and there is nobody to take his place; Shawn will make a place for himself as he already has, and nobody can replace him either—or even aid him sufficiently. It is bad enough that we only had one Ross. In a way, it is more alarming that in twenty-seven years we have only found one Shawn. Bless him. I know how satisfied you will be also at this choice which is no less satisfying and pleasing because it was inevitable. Still, they might have tried to bring in some outsider which would have been fatal perhaps. There was a rumor in Bombay of all places that Fleur Cowles was buying *The New Yorker*!

Darling, if it is too difficult to meet me at pier—I always think it is a terrific corvée that takes the edge off the joy of more elegant private meeting—tell me frankly. Do whatever you prefer, and it is possible with your work. Nobody else is meeting me unless the magazine sends someone which it did not the last time. It is wonderful to see a darling face from the ship, but I shall see it two hours later anyhow. I am beginning to shake with nerves and expectations. I shall sleep and read and never move from my cabin.

———

Janet arrived on the *Ile de France* on February 13. It was a brilliant, sunny day. New York had never looked more stunning, with its towers and pinnacles piercing the sky. What a fantastic sight for the traveler arriving by boat! I soon spotted Janet waving her arms among the crowd on deck, as the gigantic ship slowly made her way along the side of the pier, her colored smokestacks puffing, her horns bellowing. Departing and arriving by ship were exciting events. So it was with Janet's arrival, a festivity that lasted the few weeks of her stay in New York. For the first time we were back together in the city where we had met and then left in 1944! We enjoyed every minute of it and made the most of it, too. We had never had a better time. We had never felt so free, so in tune, so liberated from the European nightmares. America had always given me a feeling of security, of wellbeing, no matter what the circumstances were. The rediscovery that the individual counted, that citizens cared, rekindled hopes that had been shattered by personal disillusionments and by the McCarthy witch-hunt we were then going through. Even Janet, so critical of the erosion in the fabric of our society, enjoyed her visit, her friends and colleagues, the city, even the food in some special bistros. Her presence made my own personal life seem just perfection; if only she could have stayed. But I knew that it was wishful thinking on my part, not to be indulged in. "Enjoy the moment," I kept saying to myself, "no regrets." I had been trying to be brave, to accept reality. It was hard. Now that I had returned to a fairly normal routine, I was more vividly aware of a void in my life, the desire to have someone nearby to share it with me. I realized, too, that, despite our mutual need for independence—especially Janet's—we had become too dependent on each other. There was no way to solve our problems but to accept them. With reluctance, I did.

At the end of March, Janet left again, this time for Covina, California, where Hildegarde and Eric had bought a ranch. A brief note of March 25 read:

"Darling one,

"I should be standing with you at your son's wedding day. Too many omissions are mine, and many are exterior to me. I am eager to fly to be with you if you will let me. I feel a personal connection with your events. I feel a vital personal connection with you because what touches you touches me."

On April 1, Bill married Doris Rogers in New York, the beautiful sister of an Exeter schoolmate. "Mother," Bill had told me a few months earier, "if I don't marry Doris, I'll never marry." He had gone to work for Italian Films Export, relegating his singing, as his emotional outlet, to Gilbert and Sullivan operettas. Suddenly, I had found myself a mother-in-law!

"From today," cabled Janet, "you are the most attractive mother-in-law on earth. Hope ceremony transpired beautifully and honeymoon endearing."

So it had been. I had acquired a lovely daughter—tall, slim, with large violet-blue eyes, dark hair, elegant in looks and manners, a graduate of Brearley and Barnard, young and in love. They made a startlingly good-looking couple. A few months later they both left for Rome, where Bill had been sent by IFE, and where he also began to write.

As soon as Janet returned to Paris, she found herself immersed in the biggest May season since the war, filled with events and people from all over the world. The first Congress of Cultural Freedom, an international festival of the arts, was taking place, with a succession of operas, ballets, art shows, and writers' conferences that kept Janet running all over town. She was always at her best when working hard, even when complaining of fatigue.

[May 16, 1952]

Your first letter has arrived, headed darling, darling, darling. Yes. That is the greeting proper from both to both. Thank you for it and for the letter of news, the clippings, the sense of your communication.

I have not quite had time to pick up after myself, on arriving; I still have one valise to unpack. I did the others pronto, but became drowned in work, appointments, the Congress activities, ballet for two nights in succession, a third tonight, a press meeting with the writers this noon, a cocktail with Fleischmann in an hour. Stravinsky had an ovation last night as he came out to conduct his *Orphée*, given its first audition in New York; the ballet followed, very stately slow ugliness of the new style of 1925 when la laideur était à la mode ici, with almost laughable costumes by Noguchi. Stravinsky himself did almost a danse, a sort of easy-toed, bear-like gallop off stage, after receiving plaudits for his music which was genial, agreeable, rather mystic and rich, and nothing like *Petrushka* of the old days. But Jerome Robbins's *Pied Piper*—a clarinet in an alley to whose playing (he sat on stage, merely a regular clarinetist on a stool, the part having been written for Benny Goodman) all the neighborhood youths came flocking in pairs to dance, finally ending up in a sort of boogie-woogie—that pulled down the house. Parisians went closer to violence of enthusiasm than ever I saw here before. The esprit du corps de ballet is astonishing, such perfection of training, far better than when I saw them in New York for some mysterious reason.

Nora Kaye terrific, also [Maria] Tallchief, the men very dainty and adequate, but not outstanding which the women are by physical height literally, and real grace and perfect technique and rehearsing. The ballet has, along with terrible chauvinistic cracks, the best critique of all the Congress events. Lots of sheer bitchery, some new, some inherited from other days of quarrels between Paris artists such as Chagall complaining about Balanchine not exactly following his sketches for décors and costumes, though in New York they had been used for years and he never peeped, so Balanchine simply cut out the *Firebird* of Stravinsky which featured the Chagall sets, a great loss in music to many, etc., etc.

I am grateful that nearly nothing—indeed nothing of importance is new or demanding of critique by me. All I have to report is what the French criticize, which is lots. I never knew Paris so full of events, films (*The Seven Deadly Sins*, scrap stories by [René] Clair, Rossellini, etc.).

———

Janet found the Writers' Conference very disappointing.

"Last night was the first of the writers' talk," she wrote, "and they talked much too much, from nine to twelve, and I nearly went to sleep. They did NOT say anything very fascinating." William Faulkner did arrive and received a big ovation from the public, at the final literary debate. "But," she added, "he merely said a few words about how American muscles and French brains could form the coming cultural world and then he sat down."

Of all the events she wrote about, the most popular were the New York City Ballet ("the greatest success since Diaghilev's days") and the Boston Symphony Orchestra. In the middle of the festival, the communists managed to stage a riot in connection with the arrival in town of General Matthew Ridgway, the commander of our armed forces in Korea.

[May 28, 1952]

. . . The bagarre called and put through by the Communists here last night must have been something pretty fierce in some neighborhoods; too intelligent to try to riot along the line of entry of Ridgway himself, they saved their shock troops maneuver for last night; one thousand attacked the police at the Gare du Nord, the papers say, and there was even a hollering group raising hob at the Odéon Métro Station. The only funny item in this very alarming illustration of their strength and organization is the fact that when the police arrested Duclos* in his car, they found beside his revolver and radio set for receiving and intercepting messages a box with two carrier pigeons in it! Funny, but sinister. They think of everything, including the fact that if he tried to talk on the phone, it could be tapped. But who can tap a carrier pigeon, except a falcon? I doubt if the Paris flics have falcons at hand.

Monica refused to take the pigeons seriously, said it was a blague, said the police put them in Duclos' car, took a generally sympathetic view of the rioters because they were fighting the Paris flics whom she hates so that anybody who fights them is her favorite. A very jejune attitude. I must talk to her. It occurs to me that the brutality, authority, personification of the law and trickery of the flic is merely a professional perfection of exactly the same psychology to be found, as amateurs, among the Commie rioters. . . .

The XX Siècle season ends this Sunday night, thank goodness, or we would all be in our graves from fatigue. The Britten opera, taken from Melville's story, "Billy Budd," quite homosexual, too, in the love of the frigate captain and also the ship's mate for the innocent sailor who yearns to establish the Rights of Man—it was queer to see and hear the Covent Garden singers singing their love for the sailor in English on a Paris stage—was the worst bore I ever sat through. Hundreds of us left before the last act because we honestly thought the opera had finally finished. The music was not bad; it was just bloody DULL, nothing like his *Peter Grimes* I heard in Berlin. Already I thought his last opera, its name escapes me now, was tiresome. He has grown in stature in that he has moved from the tedious to the boring, in monumental size. *Billy Budd* began at nine and ended at 12:45 . . .

Yesterday

I spent the day reading *Mémoires d'Hadrien* by a Frenchwoman who signs her name Yourcenar, an anagram of her own name, de Crayencourt, who teaches French at some girls' college near New York. A fabulous book in which she manages to *think like Hadrian*,

* Jacques Duclos, Secretary of the French Communist Party.

this thinking based on her profound Hellenism and familiarity with what culture he perused and used of his time, and the Greek past. It is a scholar's book, utterly unlike the emotional thoughts by herself which mark the Villa chapter* by Miss Clark, whom I don't at all recall. The Yourcenar chapters on Hadrien's grief at the death of Antinoüs are extraordinarily touching, so filled with detail of the founding of the Egyptian tomb city for his dear, drowned body, the minting of coins, the establishing of a temple, arrangements with the priests, etc., as to be a mountainous tribute to her scholarship, as well as to her emotions. Her book is written in the first person, purporting to be a life story he writes to the seventeen-year-old Marcus Aurelius. A strange idea. Stranger, too, that two women in the same years should have written on Hadrian, though Yourcenar's book was begun in 1929, and the manuscript was lost during the occupation, but enough notes were found by chance in a trunk in Switzerland after the war to start all over again, a gigantic task. One is never bored if one is serious while reading it; Miss Clark's hyper aesthesia and omission of FACTS in the Villa chapter—it is nothing but what she FEELS, exquisitely written, upon looking, gasping, swooning. A brilliant job. I wish I had done it myself, which shows how I admire it while appraising also its weak construction.

Tonight is Virgil Thomson's *Four Saints in Three Acts* premiere here. I am going tomorrow night, as I have to cover Faulkner and Malraux today until seven in the final literary debate. It better be better than the others.

The Communist riot of the night before last on Ridgway's arrival is the big news. It will probably always be recalled as the Two Pigeons' Riot. The police said that they were still warm at the time of the arrest. Mme. Duclos, in an interview in *Humanité*, says they were a gift of a farmer, and she was about to add fresh peas to them at home for next day's lunch. . . .

––––––––

Life in New York never relents; it rushes by. You barely notice the change from dawn to dusk unless nature intervenes, when you may pause and look with pleasure at the beauty of a white, silent day under snow, or at the blazing windows of buildings in a red sunset or at the myriads of sparkling eyes glittering from the tall towers in the dark of a night under a cold moon.

* In Eleanor Clark's *Rome and a Villa*.

It is then that you realize how citified you have become. "Pave-ment people," Janet used to call such types. Janet, too, was a city person, but she needed a city with trees, lots of trees, and parks, greenery, flowers, open spaces, views—Paris, for instance. At the end of a long winter and a brief, cold spring, I was ready to get away, to see Janet in Europe, and to visit the family. I returned to Italy in July. On my way back, I would visit Mondadori in Milan and the firm's printing plant in Verona.

I was looking forward to that. Verona was a favorite city of mine, the home of the Montagues and Capulets, of ancient ruins, of the arena—one of the most imposing Roman amphitheaters still operating as such in the summer months—Romanesque churches built from exquisite white and pink marble, elegant medieval and Renaissance buildings. At once intimate and majestic, Verona sits on the Adige River, in a rich valley of flowering peach trees. I loved Verona. I had looked forward to seeing it again some day with Janet.

She arrived in Rome in August, and we drove at once directly to Naples and Capri. The drive along the coast in my tiny Fiat, nick-named "Topo," was thrilling and gay. The sea came into sight im-mediately. From Terracina to the south we skirted the valley of Fondi rich with vineyards and fertile green fields. I noticed, however, that in many places the land was being developed. Everywhere the bulldozers were at work; small villas, sometimes entire villages, were springing up here and there. Most of the names were German, indi-cating that perhaps some of the soldiers, who had first seen this sight from the heights of the mountains in wartime, had returned to spend their summers there. The countryside looked prosperous, with crops growing everywhere; dozens of low sheds, covered with nylon sheets shimmering in the breeze, sheltered tomato and vegetable beds that ripened and were harvested twice a year. I would later become more familiar with that landscape and learn to love it, because I eventually came to be part of it.

Janet had been writing particularly well during this period, but she had been complaining of fatigue, which she ascribed to rich food, martinis and constant smoking. Typically, Janet would hold a cigarette between the third and fourth fingers of her left hand while talking, reading, writing and, it seemed, even sleeping. A martini at midnight was for years her usual nightcap. She always worked better under pressure, sometimes going whole days into the early morning hours at one stretch in order to meet a deadline or finish an article. She would rush around on her tiny feet to interview people for a Profile or to follow the latest political or artistic events before cabling her copy at the last minute, often without proper food or rest. ". . . I should have said I had fallen slightly ill from too much work now and too much play then, meaning before now. . . ."

"I have been quite ill for the last ten days. . . . I have not swallowed a drop of alcohol in cocktailini or wine for eleven days; I am smoking three or four cigarettes a day and not inhaling. I am glad my body is a mentor; what it does not want, what is bad for it, it counsels my brain not to take and above all my senses to dislike . . ." she wrote on June 28 and on July 7. Then, on July 28:

"Darlinghissima:

"Today a week you will be in Rome, having arrived like a bird, direct in flight across land and water. Your pink letter, as if gay by color in anticipation, announces the departure. Thank you for your offer of leeway to me on my arrival there for, in truth, I have been quite ill; I think I am nearly well now, though I have had setbacks of recurrence in the spasms. I shall have to eat in a dull way, not in a gay fashion such as you and I prefer. You will please forgive me. . . ."

Janet looked thin, but felt well when she arrived in August. At the Piccola Marina in Capri she perched undisturbed on top of a rock, like an albatross, uncomfortably seated under a parasol reading a book. It was the nearest she would ever get to the water, which she distrusted and disliked, like mountains, which she found "excessive."

One evening at a friend's party given in honor of the British comedienne Beatrice Lillie, we met an attractive, affable young congressman by the name of John Kennedy. He was on crutches from some accident he had incurred in Sicily, he told us, and laughed jovially, his hair all ruffled. He was with a dark young Sicilian girl, who looked awkward and out of place; we paid no attention to her. Years later, in 1958, this same attractive young man, now a senator from Massachusetts, would bestow an honorary degree upon Janet on graduation day at Smith College.

I came back home to New York in the middle of a presidential election campaign, which for the first time had been using television to bring us intimately into contact with the candidates—Eisenhower, the Republican hero, and Adlai Stevenson, the brilliant intellectual Democrat. For the first time, we had two *simpatico* candidates who, we hoped and prayed, would put a halt to the insolent behavior of Senator Joseph McCarthy.

In Rome that summer, people who had lived under dictatorships had been asking us how such preposterous allegations could be insinuated against loyal and respected citizens. It had been difficult to explain that this was how democracy worked; investigations by Senate committees were a safety valve against corruption or subversion. Guilt had to be proven beyond a reasonable doubt. McCarthy himself could not be dismissed as simply a lunatic fanatic, merely because he was endangering the welfare of innocent people and damaging the society as a whole. Personally I felt sorry and ashamed that a senator was providing a spectacle so unworthy of America.

The poisonous effect of McCarthy's campaign was brought home to us sooner than we expected when two of our best friends, Joseph von Franckenstein and his wife, Kay Boyle, became involved in it. Joseph had served in the U.S. Army during the war, first as a ski instructor-officer, then in the OSS (Office of Strategic Services), taking part in dangerous missions behind enemy lines. He spoke perfect German, having been born in Innsbruck in the Austrian Alps. He could be used to advantage, and was. During one of these missions, toward the end of the war, he was arrested by the Nazis, tortured, and—because he revealed nothing—sentenced to death. He succeeded in escaping just as the liberating Allied troops began to invade Germany, and was then repatriated and demobilized. He returned to Germany in 1947 as a foreign service officer for the State Department. He had been stationed in the small town of Bad Godesberg, in the American zone. His wife joined him with their two children and pursued her career as a writer and correspondent for *The New Yorker*.

Early in 1952, during the McCarthy period, the State Department had notified Joseph that charges had been brought against him and gave him the option to resign. But his conscience was clear, and he refused. A few months later the Consular Board called him to attend a loyalty security hearing. Kay herself was involved in the charges brought against him, so she would have to participate in the hearing as well.

The claim was that she had been a member of left-wing organizations.

[October 6, 1952]

Darling one,

It is ten past one in the morning, and surely you must have traversed the Atlantic by nine and now be landing in New York. We watched the plane out of sight; we all gave it a farewell wave of hands, and I kissed it on the air. It was our excitement of joy to see you at the field, the long wait for you to appear, the tense observation for the brief spasm of love while you were present, the running arrival, the field to find where your plane lay, then the wait to see you emerge, marching so gallant and firm, then the last intimate shouted words. Odette said your energy is such as to make you distinguished from all other people who may surround you.

Her car sprang a short circuit on the steering gear: one of the left-right arrows got stuck and turned the wires, so we had to stop to have it repaired in the Gobelins district, and I invited them to lunch in a little restaurant whose awning proudly said, "Le meilleur restaurant de Paris," and, by Jove, it really was! It was really large inside and packed with gluttonous, very middle class French businessmen who know good food. We all ate navarin de mouton of new autumn lamb and never ate one more tender. The little red wine we had never heard of was excellent, my BLUE muscat grapes luscious. Odette's Fontainebleau cheese looked like your favorite stracchino, and the bill was only 1450 francs. I tipped the waitress, and she said, "Oh, madame, you needn't. The service is on the bill." The old chap who owned it—he in white and his wife in respectable black silk— said to us, "Take the table of Louise, she will serve you well." She did. I longed to have you there eating Louise's navarin.

Kay phoned this evening: Joseph's *loyalty trial* comes up at Bonn the end of this month. She is now accused of having been a card-carrying Communist Party member from 1940 on. [General] Greenbaum of New York [Ernst's partner] is here now and representing them at Bonn. She had to see him this a.m. so could not come to Orly. She said the one thing that would do her good at Bonn would be to produce letters written by her to any friend over those years in which she denounced Communism. She can't remember ever having written one! Her usual denunciation was of fascism. The lawyers' fees, etc., etc., she said would run to five thousand dollars. I can hardly understand it. She is in real trouble because the red mud will stick—unless an extravagant vindication occurs in Bonn, with an apology, a rarissime occurrence anywhere. I am exhausted by the events and news of this day. You are a good democrat.

[October 12, 1952]

. . . Carson turned up yesterday with Reeves, both drinking multiple glasses of water from my bathroom. Their house is on an acre and a

half of garden in the ancienne presbytère of Bachvillers, town of two
hundred, in the Oise, about twenty miles east of Gisors. . . . Carson
constantly carries her paralyzed left hand in her right, like a headless
chicken, so distressing. Reeves says she has no lateral vision in the
left eye and thus balance is impaired. She used her left hand held
aloft like a sight on a run to aim where she is going. Tragic. . . .

The town is full of tourists. Mother of one chap in the embassy
ruined his reputation the other night by saying of the Louvre, "Well,
I declare, it's just the biggest bank building I ever did see." She also
said that the difference between Paris and New York was that in
New York you couldn't tell the difference between the rich and the
poor, but in Paris the rich drove big cars, and the poor drove the
little ones, so you could see the difference.

Hot, warm, balmy here. The owls in the garden and I, too, were
both up until two last night, working at our respective life tasks.

I love you, my beloved.

[October 11, 1952]

My darlingest one,
What relief to have your kiss and word from land after your having
been last seen by me in the skies. Intrepid is the word for humans who
act like birds. A much-publicitized English jet flew down the Champs-
Elysées this noon—there were actors in it—with wings more like a
shark than a falcon, and going nothing so fast, being a passenger plane,
as the three military jets which twice flew low by my window in a
deafening instantaneous visit during the July 14 army parade. It is
to be noted that where in the past history of millions of years of
nature creatures changed *themselves* to circumstances and necessities
of locomotion or defense, by obtaining tails when they had had none
before, or thicker skins, claws, teeth, etc. (or else simply grew so large
they couldn't manage themselves and perished), man is now too late
and too fixed to change his own body so he dreams up changes in his
brain which take the place of those physical changes he cannot make.

He flies though he only has arms. He swims beneath the sea though
he only has a motor to do it with, not fins. He even flies faster than
sound, which I understand should be forbidden to anybody except a
beetle which has the proper equipment in its carapace, at any rate,
for proceeding through the air at a tempo disproportionate to its size
and forbidden to soft-bodied affairs like men or butterflies.

Kay Boyle looked ghastly yesterday. She has lost fourteen pounds.

You can believe in my alarm when I say I even went shopping with her to hunt a blouse afterward for her five minute appearance at the Bonn October 26 hearing of Joseph's loyalty test. She can have no witness, only documents in which letters from us all figure, and I believe may speak for herself. She is really very encouraged though because the State Department men for whom he works and who have been unflinchingly loyal to them both, still stand firm for them and declare that so far ALL of such cases have been exonerated. With apologies? She says she does not want to go to live in the United States for Joseph's sake. He is forty (certainly fifteen years, if not more, her junior then) has made his only career in the Department, has no other training except to ski all year for which he is now old even at that junior age. She is much happier in the State Department people's company in Bonn than surrounded by the crass army group in the previous station. Sold her this summer's article of one hundred pages to *Satevepost** for six thousand dollars and has got an advance from them for her novel aimed utterly at the movies, with spies, a wicked USA Army sergeant who is charming but a blackmarketeer, etc. Oh, alas, alas, her need for money . . . She is now accused, or did I tell you, of being since 1940 a card-carrying Party member. It sounds so grim. She was terribly sorry not to see you, your strength, your clear sureties being part of what she missed, she said. A wonderful woman . . .

I love you darling, with such a sense of memory and lovingness and joy as has filled me anew, of eagerness to hear, see and enjoy your life qualities in ways which must be made closer and on a long path for us both. I miss you, heart and soul. All you gave me in Italy still remains within me. All, all, all, my darling one.

———

When witnesses were admitted to Kay's hearings, Kay asked Janet to testify on her behalf. Janet appeared before the Loyalty Board meeting held at Bad Godesberg, on October 26. The following is her report on it:

. . . Joseph's hearing was in Wing I, Second Floor. I was called for at my German inn on the Rhine in a car at three, brought to HICOG, waited in the stenographers' room until called as a witness in the room next door. Kay was trying to read in the stenographers' room, nervous,

* Janet's "cablese" for *The Saturday Evening Post.*

white, thin. Joseph's lawyer is a tiny little Hungarian Jew named Ferancz, and is permanently in Nuremburg on Jewish Restitution. Brilliant. Kind. Gentle. He introduced me to three judges, when I was taken in, and two assistants. There was a stenographer to take down the proceedings, and Joseph was sitting at my left, with a lawyer between us. I was sworn in, So Help Me, God, though I have no idea if I could be held on perjury, had I committed it unwittingly, or if the hearing was actually legal.

I was described as a *New Yorker* correspondent, a known anti-Communist. In all, I was questioned or talked for one hour and a half. One judge asked the regular questions; he seemed mostly wooden; legal chief of HICOG next to him (and most* important) seemed like cement. Third one could laugh and did, but was described as treacherous as water by Kay afterwards.

My intention, arrived at the night before, was to be quick, strong, and light as possible, to counteract the gloom, to give a shock of differentness from Joseph and Kay, who had been in the hearing all the day before and were in a state of paralyzed melancholy. I also determined to try to include the judges in any sweeping statement I made about our *all* being democrats and being against denunciations, etc. Both policies were good choices, I believe, but only the first really worked, I dare say. I opened (on the lawyer's advice) by sketching [the] expatriate literary Paris crowd whom Kay had known, she herself being someone I'd known "a quarter of a century" (also lawyer's advice). Having mentioned Hemingway, Joyce, Sylvia Beach, Dos Passos, etc., the judge asked, "You say these were all nonpolitical writers?" Eventually he wiggled around to asking if I thought Hemingway nonpolitical, when in Spain. I answered the judge had only to read *For Whom the Bell Tolls* to decide for himself. The legal judge, of cement, spoke only once, then very harshly. "You seem to speak of Spanish Left as if the Russian Communists weren't on that side." I answered, yes, and so were liberals, democrats and republicans from America, France, and England, etc., not JUST Communists alone but a mixture of democracies; whereas on Franco's side were ONLY Fascists and those we had all been against. "Weren't we, gentlemen?" I had described Kay as like a democratic light, in her life, and we could all see by her, when in trouble ourselves, that she had viability in her beliefs. (I had to explain word viability.)

I said maybe her maternity, six children, gave her even greater human belief in people than perhaps I had, having had no child. Asked if I thought her politically naive, I snorted, No, developed a lively attack on naivete of anyone who could think that. Was asked if I could imagine who might have denounced her. I said, you didn't have to know "who" nowadays, denunciations were like anonymous microbes in the air, a shame, a vicious, queasy atmosphere, which indeed had brought all of us Americans there, in that room in Germany, for that sad task that afternoon of defending a democrat, Kay.

I repeatedly stressed how Ross had admired her, how long he had known her; judges had never heard of Ross, judging by their empty faces. They were not ignorant men nor coarse, but were uninformed on literary circles certainly. I explained Ross as a roaring Colorado Republican. Much was made of Kay's name having appeared last year on the front page of *The New York Herald Tribune* as a "sponsor" for several subversive organizations on the attorney general's list. The witness previous to me had been Ed Hartrich, formerly on the *Herald Tribune* in Frankfort, and now on the *Wall Street Journal*. I had lunched with him. He said they had squeezed him to try and find why the *Times* hadn't printed it, too. He said because the *Times* printed only news fit to print. I said I had not seen this list which the judges could hardly believe till by deduction and inspiration I said it obviously had not appeared in the Paris edition. This, one judge then admitted, was true. The point of all this was why had Kay done nothing to protest her name on this list. What did we think of her having done nothing? What did *The New Yorker* think of her having done nothing, and of the list itself?

I answered that she should have done something, I thought now, but knew why she had not, from contempt, disdain, from inner knowledge of her own truth—that *The New Yorker* certainly had similar contempt for such slime and disregarded it. I was asked if I thought Joseph could have influenced her onto Communist path. I simply smiled at him lovingly and said, Oh, gentlemen, let's not be absurd. He's a Catholic and a Monarchist. I was finally asked if I thought Kay could possibly have led a "double political life." I laughed so loudly, with such relief at this idiotic question that all the judges but the cement one laughed too. I said I knew the Moscow art theater was famous on direction and training. It could perhaps train a male spy with false mustaches and a lady spy in sweeping robes (I imitated such spies with gestures), but Kay's talent didn't run that way. That it indeed must have been noted, even by the judges, how reckless it was to ask Kay what she thought and not run the risk of having her tell them, right out, bang.

I then went back to my thesis and redeveloped it. This was that

after thirty years of Europe, I now knew, we all knew who lived
here, as perhaps the judges did not know, that conviction of fascism
or communism so takes over a human's mind that in conversation,
let alone in writing, the convinced mind lets drop certain typical
symptomatic references, questions, connections, topics, something,
anything. But so symptomatic it is to be found, to be heard, to be
located by a trained listener just the way a doctor knows the symptom
of cancer when he hears it described.

I had never heard this in Kay. I had never heard anything but
Lincolnian democracy, of the sort she and I were brought up in, in the
middle west. On being dismissed, the judges rose, thanked me. I
thanked them for the privilege which still exists, of being able to come
from another land to speak in favor of my good friend, for whom I
had come to do good. That was my aim. That was my determination.
That was my hope, gentlemen. I came here to do good for my friend
whom I had known and believed in, to do only good. Thank you,
gentlemen.

The laughing judge then came out, said he had enjoyed meeting
me, had read me for years, was pleasant. Joseph said he heard him
say to the others, "Well, Miss Flanner's evidence cleared up several
things for me, at least." But he did not say what they were. A month
or more can pass before Joseph and Kay hear the judges' opinions.
Nearly all the men or women called for such loyalty clearings, as they
are called, ARE cleared. Once cleared, the case can be opened again
at any time, any number of times. This fact has utterly broken several
men's spirits. They have resigned.

I appeared only as a witness for Kay, not Joseph, and on Tuesday
afternoon. Joseph had been heard on Monday. The little Ferancz
lawyer (he refused to take any pay from Kay, a fine little man) had
created a surprise by bringing her in with him to the Monday hearing,
claiming he had a right to an assistant counsel, and she was it. This
put the judges into a huddle. Not knowing what to answer until they
had consulted the State Department in Washington, they let Kay
remain Monday. By Tuesday, they had phoned the State Department,
which said Kay could not function as an assistant counsel; thereafter,
she was called by Ferancz only once, and as her own witness, another
legal trick. She was not present when we four witnesses for her spoke,
each in turn. I was fourth. Joseph said Monday the judges asked him
—since he said he and Kay had a mutual bank account—what he
thought about her having given money to "subversive organizations"
such as probably Dot [Dorothy] Parker's for anti-fascist Spain. Poor

Jo, he must have looked a fool. Clearly though the male he had never even seen the family bank statement, finally mumbled that as a writer his wife earned money, and he had not paid much attention to what she did with what was hers, after all.

The fact is, Kay had given fifty dollars in twelve years to these subversive groups. "Treason" at the rate of four dollars a year, how ridiculous. Joseph was also questioned, he told me, about being employed for three weeks at $12.50 a week as a swimming instructor, just before going into the Army, at a nature camp in New York which, it was later known, was a Communist front sylvan affair. He said he also took the little boys on walks. "What did you talk about with them?" "Oh, I told them the names of trees. I told them about plant life." "How did you know the names of American trees?" A minute after, another judge said he didn't wish Joseph to think they did not think he spoke English very well indeed, for a foreigner. This is a perfect example of the insinuation if that is what it is or the naivete —if that is what it is—that makes such a hearing nerve racking. Jo, Kay and I are all semi-Europeanized, semi-Americanized. The judges were all utterly American. So perhaps we three were more suspicious-minded than they were.

I hope I helped Kay. Her first witness was Sonia Tamara, white Russian, bitter anti-communist journalist for the *Herald Tribune*, who lives in Frankfort with her new husband, Judge Bill Clarke, also a witness. Hartrich came third and I fourth. I hope we helped our friends to be cleared for the rest of their lives.

The charges against our friends were so preposterous that the Consular Board finally cleared them and formally apologized. They insisted on having Kay present, too, then asked Joseph, "Do you hold anything against the American government?" "No," he answered, "not against the government itself!"

Shortly afterward, McCarthy's henchmen, Cohn and Schine, were dispatched to look into the files of those State Department employees who had had loyalty hearings. Within twenty-four hours, all of them, including Joseph, were fired from their jobs.

When Kay and Joseph returned home, they began a fight to clear their names that lasted nine years. Kay was blacklisted and couldn't sell her writing anywhere. They found jobs as teachers in a small private school in Connecticut, where I often visited them. They looked to me like heroes. In the end, they were vindicated. Joseph was reinstated by the State Department and sent to Teheran as cultural attaché. Too late. He died [there] in 1963. Their wounds had been deep. They had been victimized by their anti-Fascist liberal views and by the hysterical fanaticism of the McCarthy era. I understood them well and could identify with them.

The sadness and anger we had felt at the dramatic experience of our friends had hardly abated when they were rekindled by the presidential election, which had also engaged our attention and hopes. I had been rooting for Adlai Stevenson and so had Janet, who, to my astonishment (knowing how restrained she usually was in such matters as political activism), wrote me, on October 31:

". . . I am wearing a Stevenson button which Ruth Flint of *The New Yorker* sent me and have distributed them to other Stevenson admirers. Now that Ike has said if elected he will go to Korea and— apparently—stop the war—he may easily win. Every man in the USA will vote for him to get our boys home. You'd think that no other women on earth ever bore one.

"We are waiting in suspension to know what McCarthy said at three a.m. our time this morning against Stevenson on the radio. . . ."

It didn't matter if all of Western Europe was for Stevenson. The odds were against us.

[November 6, 1952]

Darlinghissima,

I was too sore and stunned yesterday by the defeat of the man we placed our hopes upon to be articulate. I had never been partisan in an election before; Roosevelt won for me without my participation; he was dynastic to his death. Partisanship was a new experience, and I see how it involves the ego, the emotions, anger, the sense of owner-ship and loyalty, too, with both its sides and faces. This morning I feel differently because I think differently. I think that the colossal size of the victory reduces the pain of the loss and gives the loss a different value, and the victory too. As America is largely important in world affairs because of its largeness, so is the Republican victory; it removes us from our partisanship to a lost cause by its very volume. This is vox populi in a roar. So was the Ja vote for Hitler; so were the Si, Si repetitions to Mussolini on the balcony. I hope the analogy carries no conclusion. . . .

In Stevenson's last speech he revealed one of his civilized sensitivities which helped cost him the election; being over-scrupulous, he recounted to the entire United States where he might have been at fault. He has always showed the fractions of his self-criticism rather than that total of personality which men call and hail as a leader. I am glad only that the Republic victory has been utter. It is like a complete vaccination. How the public health will react over four years we cannot now see. But this is an injection into the public body politic of something so strong that if the public sickens, it will be the death of the Republican party as it now is, and hail to God if that should be so. We have seen already two versions of evil, of the embittering experience to the character of a man from long years in politics— Truman and now Taft.

Truman shocked me by much he said and more by the bitterness and hate he showed, real hate. That such a kindly, small man, in his original form, should have been so altered shows how venomous politics in the USA must be. But Truman at least had had open power and the success of being chief; Taft has always been the loser, now the three-time loser. His bitterness will be of even a worse, more nauseobondo brand, like a devil's concoction. I hope he does not poison the entire world with it, as a demonstration of what he now has the power to do, providing Eisenhower does not turn out to be a fine general, as president. A fine president he cannot be.

Mollie P*D from London is here. I am lunching with her. I like her enormously, a charming, civilized, quite handsome woman, handsome husband, lovely daughter here in school. Please write again, even if Music at Midnight is lost to us.

Mollie Panter-Downes, whom Janet had just seen in Paris, insisted that she should go to London for a few days "to get the climate." Janet had not been in London since 1944. She felt dispirited, she said, by having procrastinated over writing a profile of Sartre, which could have been finished and printed before Sartre turned Communist that October. Now, she wrote, it would never be published by the magazine, so at the end of November she decided to forget it all and give herself "an outing." On November 25, she went to London for a week.

She spent days, she wrote, touring the city by bus to look at the effect of the bombing, still evident everywhere, especially at St. Paul's and the remnants of the great Wren churches. All that remained of the Bow Church, whose bells were so famous that anyone born within sound of them considered himself a Cockney, was now merely a delicate white tower, burned and gutted. "The rebuilding in the rich West End where damage was less is greater but does not touch Milan. Actually, all the horror of fire in 1940 and Buzz Bombs and V-2s in 1944 and steady and occasional bombings in between, London (except for the City, its poor quarter) was far less wounded than even Cherbourg or Rouen, let alone Milan or Berlin or even Naples and Munich. . . ."

Besides surveying the city, Janet was having a grand time lunching with Rebecca West, having tea with John Strachey in the House of Commons, and going to the theater with Moura von Budberg, Gorki's long-time friend. Of our election results, she wrote:

"There is more optimism here about Eisenhower now that the British cannot get rid of him and have Stevenson than I would have thought possible . . ."

. . . "Do you realize it is only two months since we separated in Italy? It seems an ice age."

[December 4, 1952]

I had a devilish time getting off my Paris Letter for which I had to hustle up material like somebody running in haste through an antique shop to find something up-to-date. Papers a week old, a foot high, to compare and fathom. Your long green-blue letter, the color of your discouraged thoughts, my darling one, came with breakfast today, and I recalled what Bill had written me in his note the other day. "In letters from the General, she cheerfully prophesies the entire downfall of the USA democratic system under the Republicans." And you might be right . . . the only encouraging and comic new note is Ike's choice of AF of L Durkin as Labor Secretary, who voted for Stevenson and Taft's indignant scream, "It's an incredible choice"—after which it would seem Ike hurried off to Korea before Taft could say any more. Naturally, here in Paris there is among the people an almost hysterical hope, even belief, that Ike can stop the Korean war which would lead to their government having to stop their war in Indochina. But Le Monde recent report is bitterly cynical from Washington at least, saying nobody expects anything and omitting the emotional importance at least, which cannot be denied here, which has a value, if even no outcome. How stop wars? Who knows until too many are dead. Russia can afford to kill Koreans and Chinese indefinitely, a good plan for reducing the population and tightening her own authority.

By killing them, I mean she decided to let them be killed, by us. She does the planning, we drop the bombs and the napthalum [napalm] fire apparatus. This last seems to shock the French more than the reported microbe bomb in which only communists invariably believe —even Sartre told me he did not believe it, at least on the evidence as so far collected, but this fiendish, hellish fire weapon is constantly referred to with pride apparently in our own press. Men. Men. That is the explanation of the invention and the use of such weapons, and even of war, as you say. . . .

[December 9, 1952]

Your letters to me on what is to be felt and seen in London are better than mine to you, though I was the one who made the visit there. The truth is, as we know, seen from the longest vision in a time-telescope, that empires are kaput, as Marx prophesied. So England will one day be merely an island, without other holdings. Today it is not yet in that plight because of its invisible production of something which can neither be exported or imported: courage. That, with discipline, with democratic devotion and sharing of what they have not, instead of robbing each other of what we have which is what the rest of us do, is the moral commerce the island still lives on. I recall in 1939 in Perpignan where the Spaniards were fleeing in across the border after the fall of Madrid, hearing the correspondent for the London *Telegraph* say at this moment when he feared only that the Italian-German-Spanish Fascists would conquer the western democracies (the threats of Russia were not to be seen or heard then among liberals, and he was one), "If history continues like this," he said indignantly, "England will end up by being a horrid, unimportant little island—like Denmark."

Denmark is not quite an island, nor horrid, but it is small and dependent. He saw the future coming from the wrong side of the world, but he saw it . . . enough of politics.

I am tired of them. I have been reading Koestler's *Arrow in the Blue*, autobiographical, annoying, even maddening because he is an irritating male, as well as fascinating. But I am very grateful to read in a writing style of mostly clear exposition of talent. He has made himself a fine English style, actually, after having had one in Hungarian, German, then Yiddish, and French—the life history of a man of brilliant scientific mind (he was educated as an engineer and was a prodigy) who has lived all of the history which has happened in our time—all. You will be irritated and enjoy his book, too.

I am going to the trials today of the torturers of the Gestapo in the rue de la Pompe office where they held out during occupation. I must see it for work and experience. I shall tremble with hatred.

_____

Yes, it was true. It seemed an ice age since we had seen each other.

With the Christmas holidays coming up, I concocted a brief vacation in Paris. Announcement of it by cable to Janet prompted an immediate response.

[December 19, 1952]

Darling, your exciting telegram arrived with my dull French coffee for breakfast. I was at once over-animated and the room and the garden outside the window began falling into my imagination as new settings because serving a new character, you. There is a green sward, two small square lawn gardens in the Tuileries now highly visible because of winter grey and brown earth, and these two verdant islands I have often planned to walk to. I never have. But you and I will stroll to them on a bright day, and I can see you with my eyes on that garden grass. I have other plans, don't fear, darling, for gayer entertainment! *Les Indes Galantes*, Cuevas Ballet, the new night club called La Fontaine des Quatre Saisons to which I have invited our friend Drew Dudley to escort us, and I suggest we go to Chartres if you want. . . . I enclose a check, darlinghissima, and my heartfelt thanks run into unspecified millions that you have accepted the responsible energy encumbent for the voyage, which makes you the great donor of the journey. Oh, bless you, Natalissima.

_____

On December 23, I landed in Paris for a week of Sundays.

1953

After an ideal Christmas week in Paris, which Janet had set up for our enjoyment, I left her to her Malraux Profile. Not a cloud came between us; no recriminations from my side, and no politics—a true holiday.

In New York, I found Bill and Doris, just back from Rome after nine long months, busy installing themselves in a new apartment. Bill had decided to make a career of his writing. From now on, I would feel and be less alone.

I hadn't seen Carson and Reeves this time in Paris. Since their return to France, they had been living at Bachvillers, a village an hour and a half away. They were having their usual dramatic ups and downs, mainly because of their drinking. Once, when we had been together during one of their earlier visits, Janet and I had been invited to dine with them at their newly rented apartment in town. Carson assured us she was just drinking tea, but kept pouring a suspiciously brown liquid from a thermos into a teacup. We waited at least two hours for dinner to be served. Finally we were called downstairs. Carson, helped by an equally unsteady Reeves, could hardly manage the steps. The dining room was enshrouded in thick smoke emanating from the kitchen; the smell of burning was intense. As we reached the table, a maid came wavering out, obviously intoxicated, carrying in a

black, burned roast. She barely managed to set it down and disappeared, never to be seen again.

We ate nothing and left as soon as we could, sad at the pitifully
comic drunken scene we had just witnessed. Carson suffered a stroke
shortly afterward that partly paralyzed her long, thin body. It was in
this state of helplessness that she was now living, calling on Janet for
help.

[January 8, 1953]

My darling,

Your cable from New York and the sparrows nest came this morning,
Tuesday. By that time I had telephoned TWA and had been informed
that your plane arrived ten minutes early, though what you were doing
in Gander I did not inquire. Because it is the nature of man to imitate
by machinery or adaptation all the swift forms of transportation inapplicable to him himself, with only his two feet to run on, I accept
that it was inevitable that some day, today in fact, man should have
achieved his flying age. But it is more reckless than anything else
invented, except submarines. . . .

Colette* came to my room and drank some whiskey and talked till
nearly one o'clock. She saw me watching the clock and when it was
one o'clock said, "She is in Shannon now, and you must not worry."
She told me of the various passionate quarrels between her two
brothers, one Communist, one Fascist, neither of whom speaks to her
now at all—one because she is not a Communist, the other because
she insulted him for being a Fascist. She was very kind to keep me
company that night. I needed it. I finally slept at five. I missed you so.

It is cold. I am working on my Malraux questions. Carson phoned,
or rather Reeves opened the communication, and then she wandered
to the phone herself. They asked me to send a long redundant telegram
to Anne Frank's father in Switzerland, telling him that Cheryl says the
dramatization rights are free and that Carson has accepted to produce
the play version. She kept saying over the phone to me, "When I kept
reading her book and saw her po' (poor) li'l face and then Ah looked
at Cheryl's photo then Ah jus' thought mah heart would never forgive
me ef Ah did'n do thet play." So I said that if her heart had spoken,
she had made an emotional decision which freed her from any mental
calculation and that she had done right. She said she had finished a

* Colette de Jouvenel, daughter of the writer.

chapter of her new book, and she spoke of it with enthusiasm and promised to show it to me. I long to see it, of course.

My darling one, thank you, thank you, thank you. I shall sleep more easily for having written to you, communicated with you. Amatissima, mia.

Two old friends, the writer Bessie Breuer, and her husband, the artist Henry Varnum Poor, had arrived at the American Academy in Rome in 1950, he as resident artist.

Bessie was a middle-aged, small, plump, charming woman, with large, searching eyes, bobbed hair and a captivating laugh. She looked more like a good mother and housewife than the bohemian she really was.

Henry was a painter of note, a well-known ceramist, designer and builder—a modern Renaissance man of many talents and trades. He was big, stocky, with thick gray hair and a thin mustache; a reserved but friendly man.

Bessie had been planning to write an article on Ingrid Bergman's life in Italy. They had met Ingrid at home in New York, when she was playing in the theater, years before. Now in Rome, they met again in different circumstances, and became quite close. Ingrid was expecting Robertino, and Bessie became a consoling friend when all those awful letters started to arrive from the States.

Back in Rome that summer of 1952, we met again, and I offered to drive Bessie to Ingrid and Roberto's summer house in Santa Marinella, a seaside resort about forty miles north of Rome. When Janet, Bessie and I arrived one afternoon, we were received with their usual hospitality. The house was typical of its kind, a modern building with plenty of terraces, and a large garden with palms and pine trees. It was nothing like the sort of place you would expect to find in Hollywood. This house had no pretenses or luxuries, except, perhaps, for the number of sports cars and other automobiles—a great weakness of Roberto's—parked by the garage and entrance. Otherwise it looked like any well-to-do family home, which, in essence, was just what it was.

Ingrid looked her part, too. She was wearing a plain cotton dress, sandals, her short hair held back by a ribbon. She looked like a neat, young, efficient housewife—and, of course, was beautiful. She greeted us with her sweet, luminous smile, direct and straightforward.

Roberto was his flamboyant, noisy self, with a mischievous look and an impish smile. Casual in manner, intelligent in talk, he was not as

tall as Ingrid was, already a bit paunchy and partly bald. Not handsome, but with a great deal of charm; he was endearing.

He and Janet immediately started a conversation in a broken
English-Italian jargon, while Ingrid brought out a large tray and served
us tea.

"My new Swedish governess," announced Roberto, with masculine
pride.

Ingrid agreed to be interviewed by Bessie and Roberto concurred.
The visit had been a success and had gone very smoothly. "Why not
write a biography?" I asked Bessie, and explored the idea. They had
no objection. Back in New York, I was going to find a publisher for it.
What I found, instead, was that someone else had been writing one.
Had it been authorized? I wrote at once to Roberto for clarification
and, of course, to Janet.

[January 18, 1953]

Darling,

Your sturdy first letter from New York is still your last, so far.
Planes are grounded. Boats take weeks, but so do flyers now, perhaps.
Weather continues foggy by night, misty by day, with a continual
twilight. Even the French who are hardly pagan are already talking
eagerly of the advent of coming spring.

In your letter you made so eliptical a reference to the Bergman
memoirs that I can only infer, without being sure, that somebody
else has already written on her before Bessie had her chance. Is that
it? If so, alas, alas. Rebecca West passed through town enroute from
Rome. Odette [Arnaud, her French agent] gave a dinner party for her
at which I arrived at ten, having to finish my letter (it was a Tuesday).

Rebecca has become rather strange, at least to one knowing her only
now, and not formerly, when perhaps she was less determined to have
only her own view of individuals predominate. Rossellini and Ingrid,
for instance. She talked to me lengthily of them at Odette's and after
at the hotel when we got home, she being on the second floor in one
bed with her elderly husband! She said he always demanded a double
bed. He leered slightly at me as she said it, pleased to be considered so
sensual, doubtless.

Roberto or his lieutenant, named de Pappa or something like it, had
requested Rebecca to come to Rome to talk about writing the script for
Colette's *Duo* for Ingrid. Roberto kept Rebecca waiting three days in
Rome while he directed *Traviata* or maybe *Tosca* at the Naples opera

house. Actually. Dined with her, Ingrid and Rebecca's husband, Roberto being late by an hour, at midnight mentioned *Duo*, said of course would not stick to the story as Colette wrote it, then next day de Pappa phoned her quite disloyally I think and told her Colette's lawyer had already been there and made clear that NO deviation from the story would be permitted, which Roberto had not mentioned, although he had let Rebecca know he was not very interested in doing *Duo* at all.

They had one more dinner at which she insisted on talking business. He had invented some new story with English background—she said it is his property, so I may not tell you what it's about, but can only say it's of a vulgarity which is unbelievable and is not even English vulgarity. But when she protested at its unsuitability as a sympathetic vehicle for Ingrid, he disagreed as if that point were not important. (I am telling this to you as she told it to me.) When she asked what the denouement of his story would be, he said he had no idea, but the idea and the end would come as he worked on it with the camera. Scandalized, she returned to Paris. Anything she says, it seems to me, is open to a reinterpretation by anyone who likes Ingrid and Roberto, which she palpably does not. She spoke alternately well of Ingrid after having first said, "A nice, commonplace, Nordic girl, half-German, such as one would see selling ribbon in a shop and between sales taking care of children in the back room."

My loving defense of Ingrid led Rebecca to cross the room and say interim to Monica that perhaps Ingrid's Left sympathies—has she any? —might have roused my sympathies. This Monica hotly denied, saying I was violently anti-Communist. Then back came Rebecca with more, this time against Roberto whom she finds physically so revolting that there must be something wrong with Ingrid to love him! I pointed out that many women had, including Magnani, and all Rebecca said was, I wonder. I wonder if she really did.

This is all trash in a way and went on for an hour. This morning a letter from her, not worth enclosing to you. I had said that Ingrid told me she now felt freed of guilt toward Dr. Lindstrom, at last, for the shabby way he treated her with Pia in England last year. Rebecca now takes Lindstrom's side in this morning's letter! She said at Odette's she doubts if Roberto ever had talent, that she heard in Rome that Amidei had really written *Città Aperta* [*Rome—Open City*] and kept Roberto in line with the script. I simply advised Rebecca to forget the whole Rome incident, that she obviously was too organized to deal with an unorganized man like Roberto whose former works I had certainly found talented. She only spoke well of Ingrid in her eagerness to make what she calls his grossness clear, by saying (at Odette's) that he has no compunction about deliberately ruining Ingrid now with stories (like *Europa '51*, between you and me, with its child suicide, from non-love, like Pia), which can reflect on her private life as already led and as placing her before filmgoers as an insensate, sensual, greedy, selfish woman. Basta.

Monday morning. A letter from you, darling. What delight. So there was an Ingrid biography, but it has been refused and your project is now going forward. What good fortune. I congratulate you. That's splendid, darling. Now if only Ingrid won't be too tired, after one set of interviews, to undertake another. However, with Bessie she needs to talk little. Do suggest to Bessie that she employ a stenotypist, with one of those machines which takes down at great speed. I used one with Malraux in my interview which at least shows me how obscure if stimulating he was. I might not have been able to be sure of it had I tried to take notes while he talked at a mile a minute. Did I tell you that in one hour and a half he talked fifty-four typewritten pages? About fifteen thousand words.

No, darling, I have been too worried about Malraux to write that First Letter of our series. I'll try tomorrow. Yes, this is a bad life. Ours. I have influenced you. Now you influence me. I am frightened. For I love you.

[February 2, 1953]

Tuesday, my darling bambino,

Forgive this excessive hiatus. I worked seven days and half the nights in my usual excessive chronology, until two or four a.m., re-doing the political party piece for the magazine, then having asked and obtained of Shawn an extra two columns, nearly, had it to redo a third time. Delighted with more space to put it in.

I can only hope it won't be massacred, with dull facts left and gayer slants omitted. I have also been interviewing on Malraux for two nights during that push. Have finally found ONE French person, a woman naturally, Jennie Bradley the literary agent, who had kept a dossier on him, knows him, and will talk. Most of his humbler friends are in such a state of awe as to fear saying a human word.

Your postcards with Washington news convulsed me and depressed me, too, but made me laugh tenderly. When you are in as black a rage as that, you are like an angry little Italian rooster, with all feathers flying, chasing every stupid hen in sight. Je t'adore. . . .

I think Bill's UN Letter from Rome was very, very good. Talented writing, facts well assembled, very amusing, developed critical faculty, *bref*, very good indeed. Since *The New Yorker* developed this type of foreign letter (or actually I did), I took a modest pride in a second generation correspondent, like our Bill, stepping into the program. Please compliment him affectionately. I look forward to what will be his pointed, intelligent use of all of your cousin's Land Reform material. My omission to have read it first remains a mark of real failure in my career.

Just had a phone call to interrupt, but with good news. Jennie Bradley's niece, she knew Malraux's brother before the war, the one who was deported and died in Germany, also is bringing to dine with me a young RAF deputy who sees Malraux constantly. She knew him at Abbaye de Pontigny, a quiet intellectual retreat before the war for Gide, Pierre de Lanux, etc. So fate is starting to aid me in my work.

I have two pink hyacinths in bloom on my desk, fed on water for a week, and four little ones, still deep and green in bud for next week. I adore hyacinths, freesias, magnolias, camellias, gardenias, all white scented flowers, like the perfume of love in fresh sheets. I am wearing the green pyjamas this minute, under your scarlet quilted coat you gave me, with my red Turkish slippers from Milan. The yellow ones are always considered sensational. The pasha model, like yours. I meant to tell you—it sounds silly—that I was so ashamed I had my scarfs and stockings, etc., in such a muddle while you were here, in my chiffonier. It took me three hours to straighten out all my drawers, closets, etc. I now have my reference books on the second shelf in my left-hand closet by the window, like a private secret library. I am very tidy, beloved, at last. I love you, my feet are freezing, must bathe.

Had a thorough check-up with Monique Petin. She now has her doctor's office in her mother's hôtel particulier, very swell. Results are amazing for my health. I am normal only in one respect; my blood pressure is normal for my age. All other indications abnormal because that of a body twenty-five years old.

Feet now falling off from cold. Into hot bath. Kisses.

[February 10, 1953]

A pink sheet of paper to carry embraces of another grey day. One begins to be detached from the climate except when it mounts actually to disaster as in Holland. Today is the spring tide, the neap tide. In England the BBC is broadcasting each hour to warn its inhabitants on the east coast. Flares and bomb warnings and sirens and police loudspeaker cars are also in motion. God keep them all safe, even the policemen, the British bobby being the only kindly copper on earth. Perhaps because he does not carry a gun. It was to protect the unarmed bobby that the Home Secretary refused last week to grant reprieve to the young "cosh" or tough boys, aged eighteen, I think, who had shouted to his pal on the roof as the police approached, "Let him have it. Shoot."

He shot, the bobby died. The younger lad, of course, could not be hanged. Too young for such rough treatment as the rope, but the older one, major for death, hanged by the neck till he was dead, and dead while the English booed and prayed before the prison. A strange people, mixed of sentimentality, brutality, heartlessness, and a heart full of nobility. Human conduct still interests me more than history, I think. History is hardly a form of it, nor do I mean it is inhuman conduct only. But the individual is still of interest to contemplate. The mass in war or peace is less so.

Tatiana Tolstoi's *Journal* is running here in *La Table Ronde*, Mauriac's monthly literary magazine. Very charming. I should have written an obit of her when she died or a paragraph on her still alive, more to the point. My omissions stack up like a barricade around my memory, leaving me too little pleasure to look out on. I hope the Political Party Letter seems informing and not too dull. It had to be cut even though I was given seven full columns for THE FIRST TIME IN MY CAREER. I requested it by cable of Bill. You are such an enthusiastic darling where I am concerned, you think they will always run what I send, even if as long as a Domesday Book.

[March 4, 1953]

My precious one,

What has happened to our correspondence?—not that aimed at history but that between us as beloveds? I shall reapply myself to it like a small flood clearing a brook in spring. I was and still am so vexed and worried by my inability to obtain any interviews on Malraux of any consequence and utility that I have been made dumb, stupid and non-communicative. I am starting all over again with new people so that I can at least say to myself, I have done the best I could and all there was to do. . . .

And this morning's BBC announced as from Moscow the news that Stalin is dying, or is indeed perhaps dead, ill since Sunday. Now comes the time to hold our hats, my darling, and pray. Surely the afternoon papers will carry this news of terrifying vital importance to us all on earth. Now what? Let's not write each other politics for a while, my precious, dearest one. Let's just feel and think and communicate. I long for you.

As Janet wrote, we had been remiss in our personal correspondence.

Janet had been struggling with her interviews of André Malraux, which she disliked. "Each meeting was like one with a dentist for me. It costs me too much anguish," she wrote, and was baffled too by the "mythological attitude of his friends, partly adoration, partly terror of the myth itself."

Malraux was the most celebrated man of French letters. His exploits, his adventures, his famous novels and still more famous books on art and archaeology had created a halo of adoration and awe around him. He had been a hero of the *maquis* during the war, and had recently been named minister of culture by General de Gaulle's government. He was also a very private man, difficult, inaccessible.

Janet herself had been fascinated by the multifaceted acuteness of his mind, and eventually wrote a brilliant profile, the first ever written about him.

Many years later (he had just died), we were talking about Malraux in my New York living room; Janet was then staying with me.

"André Malraux was the most important verbal figure in France," she said. "Words cascaded from him in a plentitude of comments, especially those embracing history and politics, art and archaeology. These were subjects with which he was on terms of the utmost intimacy, he having in his life been an *haut aventurier* in revolutionary China and the Civil War in Spain. Art and archaeology were his dominant intellectual occupations. 'The life and works of Malraux suggest a man restricted to the heights of experience' was a comment once made about him."

At this time, however, Janet was unsatisfied and depressed by the poor result of her interviews.

My own work was demanding, too, leaving me little space in which to enjoy myself. My office had been developing into a center of information on Italy as well, a kind of cultural bureau taking up a great deal of time and patience.

. . . I was becoming doubtful that we could ever have a life of our own. A letter written at midnight on March 20 made me feel sad:

. . . A week ago I was sixty-one years old, to the day. As your letter clarifies with hunger and weariness, what am I doing with life? So far from you and how soon I will stop living in today's terms of work and start living in terms of what is the residue of love? We are not the only ones separated by work; I am not the only one who loves work more than domesticity. But I am the responsible one of us two for our lives as it is, so I am the only one of us two who has not made the sacrifice of self for tenderness. You know it and don't often say it. I know it and suffer from it and have not the strength nor plan to change it. Sometimes it seems (especially to you) that my protestantism (and it is indeed a shape of mind) consists of knowing, suffering and not doing, and I wish by God that I'd been born a roaring Irish Catholic from Indiana so as to be better equipped to have a natural place for the senses in my life which could dominate like you.

Furthermore, I am a "romantic," which largely means a selfish celibate and not a domestic. My address is public, anything to save me from the anguishes of domestic inheritance. Even before your letter came, I was undergoing a long period of frantic, really, actively violent melancholy. I still reread your letter in sections, here, there, put it away, bring it out again, like an inescapable document, like a will and testament I didn't make, giving one away, a legacy of what I have made of us and me which is bankrupted as the inheritor, which is you, make clear. Then I go back to if, if, if.

This has been a crushing spring session and solstice equinox for me, even more than you. Your cable of birthday greetings was the perfect loving summing up of your patience and loneliness. Love wasn't enough for me to give or even to inspire. *I am my captive.*

———

Knowing Janet's feelings and her sense of responsibility, I regretted causing her grief with my longings. Next day, upon receiving my letter telling her that I would with joy go with her to Ischia for her mud baths, she cheered up:

"Saturday

"Yes, my darlinghissima, the Hotel Lacco Ameno after two weeks at Capri from July 15 on. YES, for your TWA flight for June 24. I shall meet you wherever you land, here or in Rome, and stay with you or go with you (probably the latter, I should think) wherever you are going or staying. Oh, to see you soon. A date is a vision with a number and a month name to gaze forward to. Con tutto il cuore."

I was relieved. "Stop complaining," I said to myself.

[11 April, 1953]

Saturday, my beloved.

This paper just matches some cineraria blossoms blooming by my window. Today is the first sunny if misty day of kindly weather Paris has had since Holy Week which was like Gustave Doré's illustrations of the Crucifixion, everything that is but the Cross itself. . . . I feel unchristian myself. Carson is in the hotel since two days, expecting to go to Vienna. The trip with others fell through. Reeves was not going anyhow; he is hunting a job. He went out on the town last night with the woman she had intended to go to Vienna with and, instead, to Greece. Reeves has not yet turned up, and it is eleven o'clock. He phoned me at three a.m. I was so sleepy, I can't remember what he mumbled about.

Now Carson refuses to go to Greece with this woman (who struck me as vulgar, showy, boring, rich), and what is worse I have to go down to pack for Carson, to go back to her country place. A male friend is driving her out. But this is where I fail as a Christian. She asked me on the phone if I thought she could ask the maid of the hotel to bathe her—and pack her clothes. I said no, but of course said I would pack for her and did. I did not offer to bathe her. I felt I could not; the necessity is not that grave. She has a maid in her house who can bathe her tonight. Reeves always does this. . . . I am sick of their drinking and quarrels. They are so tragic and destructive. She is very calm, says she is simply going back to work and even after an hour in Paris, said she wanted to go back to the country. "I am homesick for my house." Touching. She was not drinking badly the other day in her room, but enough: four or five whiskies. She consumes about four bottles of bourbon a week plus a bottle or so of gin for before-luncheon consumption. . . .

I was interrupted by various incidents—packing for Carson, getting her downstairs (she can hardly move alone, with surety), ordering soup for her, waiting for the two fairy friends (very kind) to pick her up and take her back to the country where they will weekend, to keep her company. Just as we were walking toward the car, up popped Reeves, at three in the afternoon! I swear he seemed to have dropped from the ceiling of the corridor. He refused to return with her, wanted to talk "hard words" with her, said come back into the bar, let's settle things. And I said, "certainly not. You are not going to settle the remainder of your marital life in any bar, let alone mine." She murmured to him, "What is it you resent so?"

After she left, I begged him to STOP DRINKING. . . . I am so tired of arguments, people's voices and the pitiful spectacle of Carson and Reeves that I hope I see neither of them soon. What will happen to her alone with a French couple out in that godforsaken house and village? But what will happen to him if he does nothing all day long, for idleness (except when he is bathing and dressing her) is what drives him back to drink every so often. Oh, thank God you don't drink. Thank God for you.

———

Early in April, Irving Drutman, a journalist friend and leading publicity agent for important foreign films, telephoned me. "Could you help me in handling Anna Magnani's press interviews?" he inquired. She would be arriving, he said, for a promotional visit on behalf of the Italian Film Export group in connection with the première of her latest film, *Bellissima*, directed by Luchino Visconti which would be held in grand style at the Museum of Modern Art.

I hadn't seen Anna since my return to the States and had missed seeing *Bellissima* when it came out in 1951 in Italy.

Anna was a friend and a great admirer of Luchino Visconti's first two post-war films—*Ossessione* (Obsession, 1942) and *La Terra Trema* (The Earth Trembles, 1948)—and had often told him that one day she would like to work with him. Abandoned by Rossellini for La Bergman, and with the failure of *Vulcano* (the film she had made with William Dieterle to spite *Stromboli*, the first Rossellini–Bergman film, equally unsuccessful), she had turned to Visconti. "Luchi, when will we work together, eh?" she asked him. *Bellissima* is the story of a Roman woman infatuated with films, who decides to make a movie star of her little girl and enters her in a film contest at Rome's Cinecittà. Despite Anna's interpretation, praised by the press, the film had not been a box-office success. The prospect of a personal appearance in New York, therefore, cheered her up and gave her new hope of success.

To be with her on her first visit to New York intrigued me. I wanted it to be successful, for her sake. Luckily she spoke very little English and I could fend off the more tricky questions from the press. My answer to Irving was a resounding *yes*.

We met the S.S. *America* one April morning. Anna, her mane of raven-black hair, loose and untidy, framing her pale oval face and falling over her scintillating, inquisitive eyes, greeted us with her flashing smile as we made our way among the reporters to meet her on board. She was wearing her "uniform"—a black skirt and black turtle-neck sweater. No makeup, no glamour. A small black figure, dramatic in its simplicity. "Nat, it's you!" she exclaimed, as she saw me, and we embraced.

In those three weeks, I never left her side. She behaved like a lamb— or almost. She hardened only when the questions of the press became too personal. "My life as an actress belongs to the public, but my personal life belongs to me, gentlemen," she would say, stopping them cold. But in private she would burst out in her typical emotional style with colorful descriptions of her anguish. "Nat, I was so mad I could have bitten the furniture when I heard the news of *her* arrival in Rome, and Roberto went to meet her. . . . I could have bitten the furniture!" Even then, more than three years later, she could feel the pain.

Anna arrived with two escorts, two men friends eager to go on the town on their own, so that Anna, more often than not, was left to Irving and me. We planned her evenings and accompanied her around town. Her favorite spot was the Savoy, in Harlem, with its jitterbug dancing and Louis Armstrong's orchestra. We even went to Brooklyn to see an Italian acting company run by an old fan of hers from Italy, now the producer of a second-rate group of Italian actors playing melo-dramas of the old school to an audience of Italian-Americans that filled the Academy of Music every Sunday. When Anna was brought out in front of the curtain and presented to the audience, thunderous applause greeted her as she saluted them in Italian. She was moved; these were her people. An old man knelt in the aisle, as if to revere a madonna. It was touching, the perfect ending to her visit. A few days later she sailed back to Italy. That visit cemented our friendship. A few years later I would again be called to go with her to Hollywood.

[April 18, 1953]

Darlinghissima,

Del cuora tuo, I being your heart. Your silly letter as you called it gave me laughter and pleasure. Usually your letters are part of a correspondence to be saved for its merits, its gravities, conclusions, opinions—and deep sentiments. Yesterday's was like a debutante's. It must be fun to be so gay and public for a change, and with so dynamic a personality as the Magnani. You cannot have been so giddy and so public for years. Change is so refreshing; change to gaiety after solemnity or ill health, as you had, or even change after too much rollicking about to a more settled use of days and nights. . . . A tempest is blowing. It is the kind which smells of the sea and comes from the Atlantic. It is no day to be on a boat, going or coming.

The acres of tulips in the Bagatelle garden and above all in the newer fields near Gonsesse, ten miles out of town, will be wrecked.

Helen Kirkpatrick left me some gorgeous cerise perroquet tulips, shaggy as feathers, which had been given her, so I am having my tulip show in my room. . . .

[April 23, 1953]

Darling creature,

. . . I am going to *Boris* tonight with the newly discovered Bulgarian singer Boris Christoff, whose recordings, with other Russian-language singers, made such a hit in New York. Made here, of course, and the French never heard of it until by echo from New York. Five perform-ances at the Opéra, all the result—or so it looks—of Malenkov's new policy. That can't be quite true, yet no explanation is given, except that perhaps the Boris recording influenced the Opéra chief. It is an opera, *Boris* I mean, which when I hear it I have difficulty getting out of my head for several days after. I almost have musical pains in the head and memory. I can remember some and then not nearly all, and am not free at any time from not remembering some of it. By chance in the bar at nine p.m. I heard the opening strains of it in Russian the other night, and it was the great recording. The greatest *Boris* entirely I ever heard. It was given almost without interruption, except for a line or so of plot retelling and lasted three hours and a half. The entire opera was given in this record which I had never heard, it being usually cut and rightly as there is a great deal of musical repetition in the original score. How glorious was Moussorgsky's talent. Does Bill love

it? I only like three operas really, *Boris, Rosenkavalier* and *Don Juan*
[*Don Giovanni*]. I suppose I won't even be able to remember my own
name after hearing the opera tonight, after hearing the recording two
nights ago.

The chestnut trees are out . . . language certainly is what makes for
KINDS of singing, national singing. It is not singing methods that
make the different kinds of voices, I think. The Russian language
produces a kind of voice, especially in males, there being three great
voices in the *Boris* record of which two are almost as gorgeous in soft-
ness, ease, power, masculinity, rich tonality and breath control as
Christoff himself, and his is the finest I ever heard as a basso except
Chaliapin. An Italian voice is not merely bel canto training, it is the
singing of the Italian language, the same for the Wagnerian or lieder
voice, the French nasal tenor, the bland white British voice. . . .

. . . Please write a line of love, when you have time, when you feel
it, when you want to say it. Are you well? Has Magnani exhausted
you? The scandal of those McCarthy young men who came to Europe
for three weeks and "did" every bureau—they did Radio Free Europe
in thirty-five minutes, twelve hundred employees—has not died down.
The *Manchester Guardian* was savage with them and pursued them
all over the continent and London. They were so alarmed at what they
had stirred up in England that one arriving, on seeing the ambassador,
said nervously, "We won't say anything about having seen you. We'll
take the first plane out and keep quiet." He said rightly, "I am the
American ambassador. No citizen comes to see me secretly. You will
also give a press conference." The British roasted the skin off them,
including Schine's statement, I am an idealist, I am not paid for my
McCarthy work. As the *Guardian* added, he is also the son of a
millionaire hotel-chain owner of California. Here is the payoff: In
Paris they were allotted rooms by the Embassy at the Crillon. They
were not connecting rooms. They left the Crillon instantly (two at
night), went to Georges V, spent 36 hours there, with a bill of 45,000
francs. The press attaché of the embassy told me this. He is wild with
rage at them—is, I gather, a Democrat.

Helen Kirkpatrick is here with NATO. She sent you her best. She
certainly is a changed woman, has to speak very carefully now because
"COMPLETE loyalty" is demanded of State Department employees,
she said with a grim giggle. But the picture she gave of the department
in Washington and even before, during NATO, was bleak. I'll tell you
some of it later. NO ONE IS SAFE. For being outspoken, her head
can fly off like anybody's. And she has been outspoken. She says

nobody can resign now; the liberals and democrats have banded together to stick it out because if one resigns, for any reason, health,
discouragement, etc., McCarthy says "Another one I chased out." So
everybody has sworn to stay until the last ditch. It cannot happen
here, i.e., Fascism. How often you and I talked of it, you more dis-
cerningly than I.

Please write me beloved.

                                                       [May 19, 1953]

Darling beloved,
    . . . Your letter before last, in which you defined the situation in the
USA, was of exceptional strength and analytical acumen, darling . . .
    The Protestant curse of sin and redemption is a new danger, politi-
cally. I used to think the Reformation was the great necessary mental
step of the Renaissance in freeing the mind of European man from
the church chains and limitations: that was true, it *was*. But now the
Protestant mind wanders as in a desert waste; the chains are gone, but
so is the landscape of the mind. I have suffered humiliation and shame
at being an American lately. Then I thought of both the Italians under
Mussolini and the French under Defeat and realized that there are long
moments when one must be attached to the invisible land of Patrie; the
country when it was better, when it showed its better face, when it
offered its best parts, at least in part. You can't stop being French just
because France fell in six weeks, nor stop being a Roman just because
Mussolini marched on Rome and set up camp on a balcony. So I
cannot stop being an American because McCarthy has become an
odious foreign state without legal power. I feel more comforted since
I have come to this obvious decision. In one more way, America now
follows the European pattern and not the best either. We have been
temporarily conquered. One must remember the free days and hope
for them again. Like Italy, we have one man who makes our trouble
and corrupts our mind, what we have of a mind. Yours was assassinated.
I hope we soon have the same definite luck. . . .
    There has been a show here at the state museum of modern art of
twelve Americans including Betty Parsons, Pollock, also Ben Shahn,
Graves, etc. The Paris critics slammed them so that I could find
nothing reputable to use in my Letter so omitted it. Paris found them all
imitatively French, and guilty of having chosen the wrong things to
imitate. How anybody who has liked Mondrian, which many French

critics did, can object to Pollock is beyond me, although God knows they are different.

McCarthyism and French reaction to it has become a regular tornado of criticism. I had cocktails at Drew Dudleys the other day with the Walter Lippmanns. He said everywhere he had gone in Europe—Italy, Germany, France—the Europeans had begged him to explain what in God's name was happening to America. I cabled this to Shawn as the reason for my long piece in this week's Paris Letter, cabled today, on the reaction here against McCarthyism. Lippmann was very serious in saying that McCarthyism is now the greatest American problem in Europe.

Kay Boyle passed one day in Paris, Saturday. I saw her for forty minutes. She had motored one day to bring Kathe and husband from Bad Godesberg and was returning the next day. She looked absolutely ghastly, darling—thin, old, nerve-wracked. Joe was given a paper saying the Godesberg court had given them clearance on the disloyalty charge, but Kay said it was only a wicked dodge to get him to sign a paper saying he accepted being fired as a surplus which he refused to sign. For the Washington clearance which is the important one has not been given him and will not be, she says. Her story was so complex and bitter, I could not comprehend it. The law is so tricky and confusing. All I could understand was her statement and her brave little lawyer who defended her, that they had lost in all ways and that nothing remained now but to sit it out in their house until ejected, as a protest. *Time* is to do a story on them, she said. Will it really? They have no money or little; if the State Department chooses, she thinks, it may refuse to pay their way back to the States with their furniture because of their sitdown strike. Well, it sounds likely.

Professionally she is in a tragic position because the *Saturday Evening Post* has asked her to make changes in her serial or story for them, though they are including her in their anthology. As you know, she has had nothing printed in *The New Yorker* for more than two years. Now she is so frantic, she can hardly write her own name, poor darling Kay, so generous and free-spirited toward all. I am sadder and wiser than before I went to Godesberg. But make no mistake, darling, I shall never regret it.

Soon and soon, my beloved one, soon. I embrace you in advance, my carissima. Good night. It is two-thirty. I worked five days and three nights on my Paris Letter. They take more time than they used to. I must rise at eight to have my hair washed at nine, then catch the ten train to Versailles for my eleven o'clock appointment. A full day. How strange kings seem, even if one is in their palace today. Yet till my death and beyond if there must be anything to follow memory, is not that enough?

————

Tennessee Williams and his long-time friend and lover, Frank Merlo, were in Rome that summer. Tenn was beginning to think of Anna as the ideal Serafina for a possible movie version of *The Rose Tattoo*. He had often said that he had modeled his heroine on Anna, after seeing her in Rome in the winter of 1949. Irene Lee, story editor for producer Hal Wallis, had seen Anna in *Rome—Open City*, and, having advised Wallis to buy the motion-picture rights to the play, which had opened in New York in 1950, was now suggesting Anna for the role of Serafina delle Rose. Tenn mentioned the idea to Anna that year in Rome.

"But I don't know the language. How can I speak English lines?" was her first reaction. Yet she was flattered. The offer by a major American playwright to star in the movie version of his Broadway success made her feel good, and raised her spirits, especially after the box-office fiasco of *Bellissima*. Her own personal life was also a shambles. She needed love and affection but didn't know how to accept or give either. Her choice in men was often neither up to her intelligence nor to her talent. She was always disappointed in the end, left unsatisfied. Her one great love had been Rossellini, and now she was alone. Her temperamental outbursts, her suspiciousness, scared people away. Only toward animals was she outgoing and giving. Her home on top of Palazzo Altieri was a menagerie of birds, dogs and cats—stray or pedigree. She wouldn't hurt a fly. And there was her beloved son, Luca, then in his early teens. At this time he was having to undergo additional surgery on his legs, which had been paralyzed since infancy by polio. He lived in Switzerland, under constant medical care.

And yet, in the company of friends, Anna would become playful; she would burst out in glorious laughter, ready to have fun, to paint the town red. She loved to jump into her open sports car late at night and drive through the city, guarded by her ferocious black wolfhound, Micia, becoming part of the city itself, like those ancient columns and marble arches. There, among the ruins, she would crouch on a step and call to the city's famished cats, feeding them leftovers from a brown paper bag—the remains of a rich dinner at some favorite restaurant.

That summer Tennessee had given Anna the script of *The Rose Tattoo* to read, and she would let him know if, if, if . . .

When I returned to New York, I became the link between Anna and Tennessee's agent, Audrey Wood. Anna had the play translated and began taking English lessons. It took one year of intermittent correspondence and endless meetings before she made up her mind— provided that I would go along with her to Hollywood. I asked Mondadori for a three-month leave of absence, and was included in the contract as Anna's personal factotum. The film was to begin at the end of 1954.

1954-57

What induced me to take a three months' leave of absence from my job to follow Anna Magnani to Hollywood, to the set of *The Rose Tattoo*? Not money, certainly. My salary was only five hundred dollars a week, which, even for that time, considering motion-picture salaries, was little enough. It was my admiration for Anna, my unfulfilled love for the theater and acting that entranced me, and I couldn't have had a better opportunity to see movie life and work from the inside. I was still stagestruck.

I should have known, or at least suspected, that a three months' stint as Anna's interpreter, translator, comforter, peacemaker, confidante, good-will ambassador and victim would be no bargain. Hollywood could not have looked less glamorous than it did at six a.m. or at six p.m., inside those studios, cluttered with cables, with people shuffling about or hanging around in a multiplicity of chores, fussing and cursing. I would finally end up exhausted back at the hotel, gulp the tepid *potage au feu* that was served in the suite every single evening. We'd then go over the next day's schedule, rehearse the scenes, repeat the lines, get the rhythms right . . . oh, God, so hard. . . .

"How can anyone be ready to emote, to act a dramatic scene so early in the morning?" Anna would complain, accustomed as she was to start her working days at noon, as we'd drive to the studio in the company limousine at the crack of dawn, the air acid with pollution. You could taste it in your mouth; your eyes would be watering. She was restless, her nerves on edge.

"I couldn't sleep a wink, not a wink. That water again. . . ." In a week, we had changed accommodations several times. First from the bungalow, where she was afraid to be too isolated. "Tell the manager, Nat. I want a suite in the main building. . . ." That had to be changed, too; the next one was better, but she complained bitterly about a flushing toilet next to her bedroom that woke her up every morning. "Nat, go and tell the manager." When for the nth time I asked him if he wouldn't mind telling whoever it was next door that Miss Magnani couldn't sleep because of the water running, he looked at me oddly. "You tell her," he said. "Do you know who lives next door? Louella Parsons' right-hand spy for her gossip column. That's who lives there."

"You write the note, Nat," Anna told me, "and put it under the door." There was no way of dissuading her. Next day, the item appeared in Miss Parsons' column. "The cheek of these foreign stars . . ." Anna thought everyone was plotting against her.

On the set, she would look around as if hunted. "Go and hear what Burt [Lancaster] and Danny are talking about," she'd say. Burt was discussing his part with the director, I told Anna. "What? He doesn't know his part yet? He doesn't know what this truck driver thinks? What he has on his mind? Serafina, that's what he has on his mind! Serafina delle Rose . . . ecco!" She would be constantly thinking that people were lying to her or doublecrossing her or talking about her behind her back. Her character and temperament were a mixture of passion and hatred, abandonment and anger and constant suspicion.

When we first arrived, Danny Mann took me aside and asked me how he should handle Anna. I told him what Luchino Visconti had once said about it: "Just let her go. She is a thoroughbred, she always wins the race." She had studied hard, memorized her part, word for word. Utterly professional. She was Serafina, inside and out. Always ready when she stepped on the set. She knew how Serafina would look, what she would wear. She selected her own clothes. No star look for her. She knew her face, its best angle. "Take me on this side," she would direct Oscar-winning cameraman Jimmy (James Wong) Howe. "No, the lights this way," she would say to the electricians, with a certain familiarity, thinking of her latest lover, the electrician who had been on the set of Bellissima, applauding her. She liked younger men. Why not? "Look at me," she would say pitilessly in front of the mirror in her dressing room. "Look at those legs, like two sticks; this face, those bags under the eyes; these lines beginning to show. . . ." But she could look stunningly beautiful dressed up in evening clothes, her décolleté bejeweled like a madonna's, her diamond earrings shining as they framed her tragic face. She won the Oscar in 1956 for her Serafina, as I had told her she would, after watching her act. Especially that time on location in Key West, when the crew burst into applause after one of her dramatic scenes. How happy she was! That was real, true appreciation, but nonetheless she was utterly surprised when she was awakened early on that morning in 1956 by a phone call announcing her victory. "It's a joke," she thought and went back to sleep. The call came from Los Angeles, but not until more calls followed and familiar voices were heard did she finally believe she had won as best actress. It was a continuous champagne morning, with Anna radiant from her victory. But when she was on the set in those days, how she worried she would not be good! She would sit off to one side, mostly alone, sulking. She felt foreign, insecure. I felt sorry for her, but by then I yearned to get back to my own world, my job, my friends. Shooting ended in February 1955. I had been away three months and lost seven pounds. I had won Anna's trust and friendship, but I would never again be involved in that kind of Hollywood.

Janet considered me daring and heroic to have undertaken such a task, and followed my Hollywood vicissitudes with a certain apprehension, but she understood my need of a change of scene, the necessity to fill the loneliness of my life with outside excitement. I knew, too, the futility of dwelling upon our separation. It would have only saddened Janet and changed nothing. But it made me bitter sometimes. Depressed.

It was in one of these moods, more frequent since my return to the States, that I met Ernst Hammerschlag. I turned to him first as a doctor, later for consolation and company.

He was middle-aged, a bachelor, a distinguished internist turned psychoanalyst. He had been born in Austria and emigrated to the United States to escape Hitler's pogroms. His father had been Sigmund Freud's personal physician. Ernst was learned, cultured and witty. He was ten years older than I, and strongly built. He had curly hair and a sensitive face, but his most interesting feature was his piercing eyes, which seemed to understand what they saw and to be constantly smiling at the view. His nose was small, straight, aristocratic. His voice, with its very heavy German accent, was low, intimate, as if telling you some secret.

In the late thirties, with the advent of Hitler and the Anschluss, he had been helped by powerful American relatives to emigrate to the States, where he took up psychoanalysis. He was an extraordinarily good doctor. We became close and constant companions. He met my friends and family, and, eventually, Janet. He introduced me to the strange world of psychoanalysts, but I did not take to that world as he did to mine, even though he helped me to accept the realities of my situation.

It didn't take long for my mother, who was now back from Rome, to realize that Ernst had fallen in love with me. She never said a word, but I knew she didn't approve. Perhaps because he was Austrian, and the Austria of the Hapsburgs had been Italy's hated enemy during the Risorgimento and in World War I. . . .

One evening, after a pleasant dinner, we were sitting beside the fireplace, Ernst and I, when he looked at me intensely and in a whisper asked me to marry him. At our age! Utterly ridiculous. Besides, I didn't want to marry anyone. I laughed as if it were a joke, just to cover an embarrassing situation. His hands were trembling. He had tears in his eyes at my reaction to his loving offer, which must have been quite an effort for him to make—he had been a bachelor all his life. Ernst knew of my attachment to Janet; we often talked about her. I had confided my apprehensions to him; I considered his understanding and advice most helpful, but he hadn't taken my confidences seriously, and I wasn't prepared for our good relationship to turn into an emotional crisis. I had liked him as a friend, a special friend. He had filled the emotional gap that distance had brought into the life Janet and I had shared. I felt relaxed, at ease with him. He had been the only serious threat to my attachment to Janet, and I was afraid I was going to lose him now.

It was Janet who saved our friendship, because the moment Ernst met her he fell for her, fascinated by her mind and personality; nor did she resent him. On the contrary, she considered him an embellishment to our life and our circle of friends. A mutual admiration society evolved between them, and he understood me better, understood my reticences and doubts. I saved a soft spot in my heart for him until his death.

"Ernst was very funny and illuminating," Janet reported, after seeing him in Paris. "You know how his eyes crinkle when he is getting ready to be witty, in this case about Anna. Most terrible, true and serious was when he mentioned her grief that one of her big dogs had taken the other by the throat and killed him, 'chust vat she does to herself, she iss always killing herself by the throat, being strangled by vat she does to it . . . murder." He had also said she allowed no one to breathe around her—only to gasp.

Janet consulted Ernst about her health problems, which had been worrying both of us lately. She trusted him completely, whereas she was not so sure of her French doctors, particularly a cardiac specialist who took a "cardiac writing of my heart movements and says I must have medical treatments at once, for the veins, not the heart itself and perhaps all my life (not so long a life now as to merit that phrase). I am astounded to see how much too easily I took my superb health for granted in the past though surely I did thank God in my way, if only by boldly stating, 'I have *une santé de fer*' and abusing it. My view has considerably changed now! . . . I now concede they are right, that I have what I finally FORCED Monique [Dr. Cotlenko] to name, vascular thrombostene, or vascular *paresse* with perfect heart action and perfect blood tension. How can I have the first without any disturbance of the second too is a mystery. Why won't doctors tell you about yourself? I am today sending to Ernst the [medical] reports. . . . I consider him a doctor of extreme intelligence and wide experience, far wider than that of the cardiac specialist here."

Janet's physical resilience, aided by the medical treatments, restored her confidence and gave her the strength to continue her work without alarm, but not quite with the same trust in her health as before. "My recovery continues tremendously," she wrote. "I feel energetic, gay, lively, my old antique over-gay self." In a brief letter of December 1957, she reported:

"I'm going with Célia Bertin, Josette Lazar of *The New York Times*, a Rumanian girl awfully nice, and three chaps, one an Egyptian painter and the other two French artists to spend the weekend with Henri Cartier-Bresson and Eli his Javanese wife at his parents' house near Blois; it is a charming little place built as a folie by the Maréchal de Saxe to take his lovers to, away from the Loire château life and is said to be exquisite. Carson went there once, with ten bottles of whiskey over the weekend, and she and Reeves drank them all. . . ." Then, referring to the events of the day, she added, on December 13, 1957: "I see by today's *Herald Tribune*, in a tiny paragraph, that Jupiter failed to take off yesterday before the Congressional missiles committee and blew up within sight instead of seeking the vast interplanetary space. There is a certain angry satisfaction for you and me that American present group of millionaire gobbledy-gook talking rich industrialists have come to grief as leaders and managers; but the situation is now grave. Our top

1. Janet as a baby in Indianapolis. 2. Family photo of Francis and Mary Ellen Flanner with daughters Maria and Janet (*right*). 3. Janet as a girl. 4. Janet as a young woman.

7

5   6   8

5 and 6. My father and mother,
Giulio Danesi and Ester
Traversari Danesi. 7. My sister
Franca, with husband Fred
Muller. 8. Lea with husband
Akos Tolnay. 9. Myself with
husband Bill Murray and son,
Bill, Jr., Central Park,
about 1928.

9

10

10. Janet as photographed by the great Irving Penn in the forties. Note shoes.

11

12

11. Janet and Ernest Hemingway, Paris, 1945.   12. Genêt at her typewriter at the
Hôtel Scribe, Paris, April 1947.

13

14

15

16

13. Janet with the photographer
Horst at Noël Murphy's house
in Orgeval, outside Paris, and
(14) with my son, Bill, on Fire
Island. 15. Janet's favorite picture of me, taken on Fire Island
in the 1940s. 16. Together in my
Turtle Bay house soon after we
met. 17. With Poppy Cabot
Metcalf, Middleburg, Virginia,
in the forties.

17

18

19

18. With Anna Magnani at the Sherry Netherland Hotel, New York, in the fifties. 19. In Mondadori's first New York office, with my assistant, Maria di Sevo, 1951. 20. Janet being visited by her sister Hildegarde, brother-in-law Frederick Monhoff, and son, John, at the Hôtel Continental, Paris, 1955.

20

21. Broadcasting "The Italian Hour" for NBC during the war.
22. Janet receiving an honorary degree at Smith College, June 1955 (with Helen Kirkpatrick).

23. Our friend, *Vogue* photographer John Deakin, created this double portrait shot on the Palatine Hill, Rome, in the fifties.

25

26

27

28

29

24

24. My house on the bay at Cherry Grove, Fire Island, with some of the friends who visited us there: 25. Dr. Ernst Hammerschlag; 26. Irving Drutman (*left*) and Michael di Lisio; 27. Tennessee Williams and Frank Merlo; 28. Anna Magnani; 29. Ruth Norman (*left*) and Cheryl Crawford; 30. Ned Rorem.

30

31. Dinner at Monroe Wheeler's before Truman Capote's celebrated black-and-white ball, November 28, 1966. *Left to right:* Monica Stirling, Virgil Thomson, NDM, Glenway Wescott, JF, Anita Loos, Monroe Wheeler. 32. Janet at Orgeval with *(left to right)* Mary McCarthy, Noël Murphy, unidentified guest, James West, Josette Lazar. 33. Janet at her sister Hildegarde's, Calistoga, California, 1967.

34

34. Janet in Paris, July 1972: "I am looking out of my window at the Ritz—standing on the balcony—" 35. At Rizzoli's in the sixties.

35

36

37

38

36. Janet enjoying a laugh with
Glenway Wescott. 37. Janet's
eighteth birthday party, New
York, March 13, 1972, with
William, Cecille and Wallace
Shawn. 38. Janet's last public
appearance, at a conference on
"Women and the Arts in the
Twenties," Rutgers University,
April 8, 1978, with *(left to right)*
Berenice Abbott, Kay Boyle and
Lillian Hellman.

39

39 and 40. Visiting Arthur Miller and Inge Morath, Roxbury, Connecticut, in the seventies.

40

army and navy inventors and mechanicians seem very inferior in their
art and competence; they haven't yet designed the right models it
seems; as for the high school education in which future scientists must
be based, if you read the remarks of Mrs. Wheaton,* embattled by reporters after the President's 'chill,' you can see how IGNORANTLY
she talks; her plural subjects are followed by singular nouns and vice
versa; she repeats and stammers (granted, the men were all shouting at
her doubtless), but she showed basic lack of equation, in choosing her
words accurately and suitably. We are for too great a degree an
ignorant nation. The reporters naturally spoke like Churchillians compared to her. It will take twenty-five years to produce an educated new
generation. I hear we have what we call a new 'crash education program'; well, that gives you an idea of the vulgarity of our scope and
the mechanical pettiness of our rich-man's conception. 'Just get a good
crash program going, Butch, and we'll be turning out these here
scientists with the real old know-how and it'll all be jake.' I am so
ashamed and sad for my country; you had such high hopes in it as a
newcomer to our shore. I apologize with love and sympathy and real
shame."

On December 29, 1957, Janet announced a trip to the South of
France to visit the painter Bernard Buffet, then the most-talked-about,
successful young French painter of the new generation, who was
going to be the subject of her next Profile.

[December 1957]

Friday, my darlinghissima, carissima,
    ... My weekend with the Cartier-Bressons was absolutely delightful;
all the guests became so individual, like country people, not like
Parisians, but like people from Balzac, with their own individual
characters and tastes. It was a rare treat for me, as if I were seeing the
French as French, not as Parigots. . . . The River Loire flows just
behind their house, separated by a broad sand dune which is water-
covered in winter, they said, though not now, and the river itself is
shallow and blue as ice. The country richly varied, though surely not
rich in fertility of the field.

Blois is an enchanting town, where we got off the train, with the
irregular delightful roofs and façades of eighteenth-century manses
or even shopkeepers' dwellings. I am always more excited to visit a

* Mrs. Anne Wheaton was a press aide and later secretary to Eisenhower.

new small town in France than a big one, since modern life has so
minimized the qualities of those that are large that parts of Rouen might
as well be parts of Terre Haute, Indiana. . . .

President Eisenhower should be rolling into Paris in a few hours
today, unfortunate man. It seems almost fortunate that he suffers now
from aphasia. Perhaps this will prevent his saying some of the useless,
evangelical, uneducated and unadult statements which his administration has specialized in, especially in a crisis. In Nixon we clearly have
another illiterate in the semi-saddle; the specimens of his thinking,
expressed in his own language, as given for a whole pageful here in
the *Herald Tribune* alarmed me; he also cannot speak the King's
English accurately, uses words in slightly wrong or even totally mistaken contexts, the latter especially when he is trying to talk impres-
sively. Alas, our poor country. Belief in advertising has taken the form
of faith. Belief in getting rich quick has replaced the hope and
knowledge of democracy as a new politic by which men could improve
their lot. Belief in shortcuts has taken the place of belief in study and
education so that we are uneducated and cannot study.

As Jan [Hildegarde's son] answered me when I said, "What play of
Shakespeare's are you studying this year?" "Shakespeare! Why, we
wouldn't stand for that!" A man named Robbins who is apparently
Vice President of National Foods or whatever that corporation is called,
is here to give a look into all the USIS establishments in France, and
Freddy Pane* suggested he talk to me to have my opinion (I, knowing
nothing about any except one recently opened here in Paris where a
Negro man has been appointed as our representative, with a French
girl; a damn good idea). Robbins is nice, handsome and intelligent for
a millionaire, but his opening statement was, "Why should we have to
approach the French on what is called the cultural basis; everybody
knows we are cultured." I said, "I didn't know it and don't believe it,
either. That is the main cause of our unpopularity which you had
just inquired about."

He had told Marjorie Ferguson** that he had "done" the Louvre in
twenty minutes. His wife reproved him so he did not repeat that to
me. I was sorry as I was "laying" for him! My conclusion after seeing
Nixon's verbal style, after Ike's, is that one has to pass an illiteracy
test, and pass it with very high marks, too, to be allowed to vote the
Republican ticket. I will not, alas, have the chance to take advantage

* Pane was the American press attaché.
** Margie Ferguson was the U.S. Information Service chief in Paris.

of your excellent advice about Nixon coming here, since he is still with you and, anyhow, Shawn has sent [Richard H.] Rovere with the presidential party as an extension of the Washington Letter, an absolutely excellent editorial idea, I think, so he will cover NATO, not I.

I shall go Monday out of curiosity to see the opening at the Palais Chaillot, see Ike and the others. So my next Paris Letter is delayed a week. Then I will do two in succession. I have started collecting material on my Buffet profile to write in New York in our flat. I am going down to his château near Avignon (remember it, darling? Oh what fun we had, what pleasure in watching and hearing the *son et lumière* and that darling hotel) for three days between Christmas and New Year's. Marie-Louise Bousquet will be there, and it is a fine opportunity for me since she knows him well. Helena Rubinstein yesterday gave me a LOVELY ruby ring for my profile on her art collection in *L'Oeil*. That dear Patrick* engineered it when he heard I was not to be paid. (In the meantime, George did give me thirty thousand francs, how awful, for the first time.) It has nine cabochon rubies, like a great raspberry, with four diamonds about as big as matchheads stuck in the gold setting. It looks Indian and is as big as my other ring. I was absolutely overcome with joy and excitement; wasn't it generous of her? She likes me and knows I like her, so this made it possible, with her generous heart. . . .

Today the sun is shining for the first time. You have been snowed on and certainly are undergoing terrible inconvenience in your subway strike. The photos look maddening with cars tied in knots on the parkway roads.

My beloved, I shall see you soon. Yours ever, my darling one,
Kisses.

----

* Patrick O'Higgins, Helena Rubinstein's publicist. George Bernier and his wife, Peggy, were editors of the magazine *L'Oeil*.

1958

The seasons succeeded each other with regularity despite nature's capriciousness and violence. So did the political scene here and abroad, whose events kept repeating themselves: governments toppled and resurrected; unrest covered the globe; a parade of colonies demanded their freedom and began their hard road to independence; only France kept hanging on to a rebellious, cruel war in Algeria. For the first time, man was probing the infinite; Sputnik One went into orbit. The White House called it "a celestial bubble," using a poetical figure of speech, for once, and President Eisenhower congratulated the Russians. The fall of Senator Joseph McCarthy, hanged by his own rope of lies, reverberated throughout a country that, finally, could breathe with relief. Democracy has its own ways of being victorious.

I became the grandmother of a plump baby girl; Bill, by now on the staff of *The New Yorker*, had his first short story published in the magazine; his novel, *The Fugitive Romans*, about his experiences in the Rome of the movies, was also published. *Men and Monuments*, a collection of Janet's writings on art, came out, too, so that each in their own special way had contributed to our mutual heritage.

And I had acquired a modest property—two dilapidated peasant huts in a village halfway between Rome and Naples, along the ancient Via Flacca, the coast road once used by the Emperor Tiberius on his way to Capri. It was here, in a villa he had built, complete with its own marina and two swimming pools created inside a grotto surrounded by statues, that he and his retinue of slaves had stopped to rest on their journey. The village was hewn into a rocky promontory facing the Odyssean Circeo. Its whitewashed houses held on to one another linked by small archways made up mostly of steps going up or down, to and from the beaches, the coves, the main fishing port, the fountains of clear spring water where the villagers washed their clothes. I transported my Lares and Penates from Capri and built a small retreat, where Janet and I were to spend several summer vacations together. It was called Sperlonga.

[January 2, 1958]

My poor darling,

To have been ill, with Ester, and both to have missed the first Christmas of the grandchild was really a domestic tragedy in its doubly painful way. You were obviously tired to have caught the Asian flu and lucky as always to have had Ernst to aid and administer. As you say in your letter, the Angel Bug is only at an age to have her appreciation culminate in plucking everything apart and tossing it toward the floor but that, too, is appreciation, like a lamb eating a flower. I have come back to work and to the usual opening worry of how on earth a Profile can be made of this peculiar material, in this case too scant to see how anything at all can be written about Buffet who says nothing that counts, has not an idea in his head but painting, and won't talk of it—a parsimony of expression that leaves me as flabbergasted, as you say, as having had too much in the case of the other masters, the true ones.

It is so characteristic that in my moment of discovery at what seemed to me so felicitous a circumstance for a young painter—that Cézanne's Mont Sainte-Victoire mountain was that high peak I saw from my window and rushed to congratulate Bernard on his intimate connection with that great artist—that he merely smiled vaguely, and it was not until later that I discovered he loathes Cézanne's painting. I usually make several gaffes over any public meeting; this was my only one. It was his, of course, for not admiring Cézanne. Strangest of all of him is his face, divided into two opposed elements. The upper part, when he smiles, takes on the coy sweetness, perfectly sincere, the utterly purely concentrated allure of a feminine appeal, more than merely pretty because utterly perfected, and utterly natural—then the lower

half of the visage, with a horribly ugly, smiling, opened mouth, showing ugly pale gums and horrid teeth, a monstrous ugliness of line and
color and as pure in its way as shock, as an essence in unbeauty, in a
sort of male artistic perfection like something drawn or painted voluntarily by an *artiste dans la laideur* as his upper female face is exquisite—the two half faces together forming an alarming disparity.

As you can imagine, this is not something one can write of, publicly. But the ugliness of his mouth when smiling is so striking, is
such a "composition" for a painter, such a shock for its own physical
owner, that one can see the result—the dozens of horrid drawings he
makes of a man's face, with opened mouth, bad teeth and the tongue
showing, flattened as if speechless against such a fate. There was one
such drawing in my room, enough to give me nightmares were I susceptible. I have often noted to its various degrees the female in a young
man's face, but I never before saw a face that was literally half pretty
girl, of the Victorian era, and enchanting and alluring by its sweetness
of detail and appeal, and then what substitutes for the masculine
adjunct—the ugliness which stands for the curse of the artist, in his
case symbolizing, expressing his masculinity, his creative force.

This is about all I got as material in my two days and three nights
there—and a list like that for an auction sale of all the beautiful pieces
of furniture in his château. Monica says she saw him at Maxim's the
day Odette gave a fête there for Romain Gary some time ago. He was
lunching late with the Comtesse de Paris, wife of the Comte de Paris,
pretender to the throne, mother of his nine children, I think they are,
whose portrait he painted (hers, not theirs) and that Monica later
heard someone in that smart circle say, "Oh, yes, he's her lover you
know." The simplicity of the vice of those people's reactions is breathtaking; they have so little imagination and invention. They always
come to the same simplified, inapplicable conclusion about everything.

Marie Antoinette must have been tiresome and stupid in just this
limited way. The papers today announce the suicide of Dominguez,
the Spanish painter, who really was Marie-Laure de Noailles' lover, no
doubt of that. He was not even a pederast which must have lessened
her interest at first in the chase, as it is more difficult to capture them
in bed. He wasn't much to ruin as an artist, not as much as Bernard,
but she ruined him. He became a sort of drunkard and violent at a
[Carlos de] Beistegui dinner a few years ago—took off all his clothes
in the salon, for coffee, and danced, stark naked. The ladies merely
rose, left the salon, then left the house. He opened the veins in his

wrists and limbs, then probably lay down on the floor, being a dirty, untidy man, I always thought, and bled all over everything.

. . . I must get to work on my Paris Letter for Tuesday, must read Malraux's new art book and make a critique, no easy job for who can know as much as he, or even enough to criticize? A very small Profile of M appeared lately in the *Sunday Observer* of London. I laughed when I saw it since it was the *Observer* critic who said my book [*Men and Monuments*] had nothing new in it, nothing everybody did not know already, but their Profile of Malraux contained four main details in his life and development taken from my work, never having been mentioned before by others and in a quite long Profile of him in *L'Express* here in Paris—which preceded the new book, with four pages in color taken from it, quite a splurge—after the editress had had me rung up by her secretary, "as madame wishes to read your Malraux profile. Can't you send it to us?????" What cheek—I discovered that the *Express* article was almost ENTIRELY composed of my material. They are entitled to use it as a source material; we always use such sources ourselves. But it was the crude way the secretary said, "Oh, I don't know what she wants of your Profile, just to read it I suppose," and asking me to give my copy of it. That made the result so crude, as a steal. I, at any rate, need not have worried. *Express* would quote anything direct, which I specifically forbade them to do. Give any credit? Not on your life!

Tell Bill Mavis Gallant is here. We [*The New Yorker*] have taken a very long short-story of hers, Maxwell did, sending her a cable of congratulations and praise from Shawn himself that she carries in her purse and has reread until it is beginning to fall to bits.

Darling, now to work. This is gossip and love and chatter and tenderness. I HOPE you are now well, my beloved one. Take care.

[January 4, 1958]

Darlinghissima,

Am still worrying about your imported influenza. People who had it here say the convalescence is more tedious and takes longer than the illness itself, so be prepared perhaps to feel fatigued and try NOT to stay in your office until seven each night, overworking.

The *Reporter* piece you sent was, as always, first class in thinking, and I'd like to know why the best thinkers usually work as writers for the smallest periodicals (*The New Yorker* is in a way also an example, judging by its circulation), and why they must always be Left enough to rouse a certain suspicion among the pure Right. (All of us on the magazine, except Ross, are Democrats at least, and Rovere as a twenty-year-old was a Communist, he says and Shawn knows.) There is something about the extreme Right which is automatically as stupid as the Royalists here, as Marie Antoinette herself, poor creature, brave only about losing her head in the physical sense, with never an idea of changing what was inside it in time.

Have you read *Voss*, the new novel from London by [Patrick] White, an Australian? Its literary style is so marked by talent as to become a little tiring, like truffles in everything, until one is sick of them, but a large, powerful talent in characterization, in the big relations of 19th century men and women which one doesn't find today in books, Lord knows. The small inter-bed adulteries of Sagan's last book seem barely even to penetrate the female flesh, even enough to have made the sex act satisfactory. It is all on the surface, so nothing seems to have happened more important than that merely quick rub that the cock gives the hen in the barnyard; neither love nor passion nor the story of lives and certainly not a novel. *Voss* is a novel which makes it rare.

I enclose today's *Figaro* on Callas and Rome; it will entertain Ester perhaps because it gives citations from the Italian newspapers which I am sure *The New York Times* will not. The presence of poor Elsa M* as a kind of social garde-malade will not help cure public opinion against her, either. I hope to get my material on Buffet quickly so as to have the sufficiency to work on. There is a possibility I should do a Profile on the old Queen of Belgium, too, which would be much quicker and easier as Doda Conrad** wants it and would give it all to me, he being one of her close friends. He calls at the palace on his motor scooter.

[January 9, 1958]

Natalia,

I am appalled by your accident to your thumb which must have been agonizing to begin with and even more by the tripled agony of the surgical treatment without an anaesthetic, as Monica said, "There had better be an overpowering excuse for that." You didn't say in your letter what that could have been; that you should have been forced to be so Spartan.

---

* Elsa Maxwell, the famous hostess and socialite.
** A Polish singer and musician.

It seems only surface anger now to curse once again at those New York taxis which satisfied Detroit because being of a new design they brought in new money, at the expense of a public which at best only tears the pockets on its coats getting in and out and in your case has flesh torn. At moments one can so bitterly hate the prosperity of the U.S.A. as to wish it damned because it aims only to make money on something or anything which advertising pushes down the public throat, always as open as a whale's to let oceans of material flow in, anything that will make money no matter how harmful whether it's TV in the dark by the hour for school children, who thus don't study and lose what little mind they ever had, and crime comes for them no matter what delinquency they then learn, or canned foods that nourish only idleness in a wife who will warm up tinned fried potatoes rather than trouble to peel raw ones and fry them with her own hands, stove and effort.

Prosperity simply makes us dangerous to each other and lazy and, of course, so rich that all critical sense has long been discarded. Yes, we'll fly to Mexico. I plan by working without stop on the Buffet material to leave in a month for New York, darling. We can leave for elsewhere as soon as you desire.

I have just read Part I of the [Burton] Bernstein Profile [of his family]. Its flip manner makes me understand for the nth time why the British critics savaged my book's Profiles, for this on B is excessive enough to make all clear, in the undesirable realms of "hotting up" information in our house mag style until the serious work of the writer in research and the subject chosen, B himself, loses his seriousness in turn, at once. I envy the writer having had much material to choose from. So far, I still have NOTHING human about Buffet; am dining with Mme. Bousquet this evening for work on him. She certainly can help me, I hope, since she has frequently been in his château where some human incidents and anecdotes must have transpired, though none when I was there.

You will be glad I have discarded the idea of doing a Profile on old queen mother of Belgium; the moment Doda added that she hated publicity, I merely asked blankly, "Then what made you think I could do or wish to do any more than she could or would wish to have done, a Profile on her? Royalty doesn't change if it is really royal; it loathes publicity except that from the Foreign Office, in rare doses on its reign. Only royalty like the Duke of Windsor, no longer even slightly royal, covets publicity and aids it." So that is settled, I am glad to say.

. . . I finally received my copy of Andy W[hite]'s Christmas Carol to the personnel of the lovable magazine and was pleased to see a Murray and a Flanner as part of the list. Mrs. Packard wrote me that when Terry tacked up the carol on the bulletin board, it roused such an excitement and affection that the corridor was instantly packed with the nineteenth floor, and then twentieth and eighteenth floor people all trooped up to see, to read, to laugh with delight. She said nothing except Ross's death had so "united the people on the magazine." How strange.

[January 24, 1958]

Darlinghissima,

You are better served by Tenn's exciting new evening of playlets than were we by Sagan's ballet, *Le Rendez-vous manqué*. What excellent titles she always finds, her sense of the capsule, one almost containing a drug in its appeal to the reader, is amazing. Not being of *le monde chic*, I was not invited to the Monday opening where the true ballet must have been the women's personalities and clothes. As the London *Times* review said of it, there were more photos next day of Brigitte Bardot in the front row of loges, with Arletty and others, in décolleté than of the ballet dancers. Well, the ladies were prettier, better dressed and more entertaining than the dancing.

Buffet's décors were excellent and characteristic except we have never seen him paint a bathroom before, complete with *toilette*! I am told the bathroom scene—a backdrop only, high, top of staircase above artist's studio which is main set—contained a real bidet at Monte Carlo, on which the Vamp poised at least long enough to shock the audience. I must ask Marie-Louise Bousquet, for I don't believe it. The choreography, except for a delightful *pas de deux* of perhaps five minutes, was tedious, the jazz session and jitterbugging parts of the drunken friends was boring, colorless; the whole ballet with its mixture of romantic toe dancing and action music against jazz music and jittering, each music written by a different man, each dancing choreographed by a different choreographer,* produced confusion, not effect, and boredom, not stimulation.

I went Tuesday, the first public night. The orchestra was spotty with empty seats. There were exactly seven people in the front row. Françoise has now had her third piece of ill luck (*jamais deux sans trois*), so perhaps her *jettatura* period is finished; first her last book,

* John Taras and Don Lurio.

then the American film of *Bonjour Tristesse* and now her ballet, all failures even though the book has sold a million.

. . . Bill Bullitt* just phoned, will lunch with him tomorrow. Says he has been four months having his flat here redecorated, modernized; ceiling of salon fell in for FOURTH time yesterday (fortunately, not hitting him; unfortunately, not hitting any of the workmen), in the new bathroom, no water flowed, he called the architect and plumber who said impertinently, "You asked me to install plumbing. I've done it. You didn't say anything about my connecting it with any water." Furthermore, he had put the taps on backwards, etc.; this morning, heating system for the whole building broke down! Bill is going to Spain next week, disgusted. I don't blame him. Quality of workmanship here is a tragedy for France. I tell you, the working class is instinctively aiming to *destroy the bourgeoisie*. Part of it is the latter's fault, always conservative, selfish, avaricious, *démodée*, never wanting to share their profits with the workers in higher wages. Now they will pay in the ruin of their class eventually, I think, and of their country. I just came across a quotation from General de Gaulle: "The left is against the state and the right is against the nation. There is nothing which can be done." Alas. . . .

Finally I have an interview tomorrow at four with a stenotypist with Buffet and his friend. They leave Sunday. I feared they would not give me the time. His exhibition is very impressive if only by its size, one hundred pictures—a retrospective for a youth twenty-nine years old . . . unbelievable. The small canvases are moving, the huge ones—four yards square—of hanged men, of crucifixions, against war, bloated dead bodies, etc., are appalling when so huge. He is a very strange young man—gentle, timid, polite, speaks with a slight workman's accent, is thin, talkative in a pleasing way when his guests are talking nothings, but falls into complete silence if you try to talk art which he says he cannot discuss, knows nothing of it. (I received one or two exceptions to this, however. We did talk a little. He told me he thought Michelangelo was merely a *flou Signorelli* which was amazing.) He loves Carpaccio, but couldn't even remember his name—I had to supply it. An adolescent with a PASSION for work, for painting, for painting from two in the afternoon until two the next morning. Exception for occasional house guests at the château. He sees no one, no one, no one, lives like a millionaire young hermit. Reads children's books, laughs at comic records on gramophone. But his soul is old, angry, wounded by

---

* William Bullitt, U.S. envoy to France in 1957.

injustice of the world since time began, by man's cruelty, by war, by suffering, by poverty. He is rich but others remain poor. A strange, very pure youth in many ways. He loves animals more than people, yet has only a bitch dog, a pretty little female, a Doberman pinscher, and fantail white pigeons in his pigeon tower by the swimming pool. AND a white horse.

[February 3, 1958]

Darlingest,

. . . I am deep in my Paris Letter over this weekend, our German Nazi-fabricated Explorer satellite. How can the Americans not be susceptible to the shame of it, invented and worked over by captured Nazi brains from Peenemünde, the same brains that invented the V-2 which at the last agonized battered London? Yet the London *Times* of today, which just came at breakfast, fails to make the bitter connection of the sublimation of that ghastly weapon into one of blahblah rollicking Yankee pride, perhaps out of politeness or disgust passing words, for once.

It is a strange thing to see what we call "taste" today—I fancy it must be what the *honnête homme* of the eighteenth century understood as *la mesure* or proportion, now lost as the result of general ignorance of former standards and balances which kept conclusions within certain civilized shapes, and once those shapes are lost, they cannot be invoked as a criticism to the people who have lost it because it is a definition of something they do not understand, which has to be summed up by their own comprehension and this gone, they listen confused and without reaction, as if one were talking to savages about an invisible suppositional value which has nothing to do either with the belly or the gods or with wampum or whatever their primitive form of wealth. No definition defines for primitive people; definitions are class affairs, based on a level of understanding shared between the inquirer and the informer. If that connection is missing, communication will be vain. . . . All this you know.

What can I say you do not know, though? Always you put your white teeth into the center of an argument or problem, biting it firmly, masticating its meaning and by rapid digestion giving your report. I try to control my increasing impatience and worry about Americans and America, my confusion about the French, always with a theory to explain some folly of selfish action, knowing I know too little about the history and truth of either people to be susceptible to the deepest love, that it is the beauty of France that has always satisfied beyond questioning it, the education of the French people, not what they do with it in brains which perceive an idea per se but too often pervert it for gross, selfish reasons like avarice, which somehow makes them more refined (they think) than the open-mouthed, greedy, money-loving of our compatriots, which is, after all, stemming from the same golden calf—desire.

Jimmy O'Donnell of the *Satevpost*—he and his handsome wife Tony Howard have moved here to live—gave me a compliment the other night that rarely touched me; he said that in thinking over the years what has helped maintain the sense of French prestige in the U.S.A., he came to the conclusion it was my Paris Letters which had had a dominant influence, that along with being analytical, critical and informative, the result was that some essence of what France has had and still creates in part (like a special body odor of distinction, of attraction) had been felt and maintained by my work. If true, it has been a contribution that would baffle me to explain exactly. What a country right now! I swear to God, drowning the chamber and feeding the deputies to whatever fishes remain in the Seine seems the only answer to a base for reform—fear, stark terror, threat of death if selfishness does not cease which this time is really killing the Republic.

I must dress and interview the producer who put on that ludicrous Sagan ballet, to get the facts. I shall see Françoise herself later this week, though as she never talks either, what can she say about Buffet who doesn't talk to begin with? What to do about a painter of his celebrity—and he has something, if only the anguished and morbid, that people have been drawn to. It's not all a merchant's scheme any more than Picasso's early fame was. What to say about him when he has no translatable ideas on anything except his painting (which he can't explain), and for the rest is totally ignorant? After our interview the other day here at the Elysée Park Hotel, he was leaving to catch the plane back for Marseilles and I said, "Oh, Bernard, you have forgotten your Mickey book"—a huge Mickey Mouse. "Oh, I've read it," he said. "I'll get another when I come back to Paris next week." I suppose he did. Please don't tell this because it makes him sound arrière. He is, I suppose . . .

Darling one, please send a line to yours deeply, to one who loves.

[February 3, 1958]

Darlinghissima, my darling one,

Two important items of news. Trousers of those white Voltairean-jacketed pyjamas of which I have only the coat in our flat were discovered by Maria on my departure in March, are washed and readied for return to their upper partner. Second news: de Gaulle will most likely be called and will take power. Had long talk today at *France-Soir* with Charlie Gombault (great friend Johnnie White who has Fleur Cowles over Sunday to lunch in country, invited me. I can't go, thank heaven, am working and cabling piece), who was receiving long phone talk in my presence from their Algerian correspondent who said Algerians will not uphold Flimflam,* might uphold Guy Mollet because de Gaulle praised him in press conference speech; but truth is de Gaulle is expected to be offered big by Coty and obviously to accept it.

Talked lengthily also at *France-Soir* with Hélène Lazareff, far from a fool, of course, for explained better than the men did the amazing complications and paradoxes now operating in this struggle for power. This is first time Paris was not political head of France; city of Algiers is that now. Insurrection of extremist colons planned for weeks, works only too well, forced Salan and Massu to shift boats (symbolically), climbing aboard Algerians' plan, already launched, whereas military Putsch against weak republic was still being slowly readied. (Talked also today with Nora Belov of *Observer*, who finally said hesitantly, "Do you suppose we must face it that de Gaulle will come to power, for a time?" I said it looked like it, and she said, "Yes, it does rather look inevitable. Well, perhaps it won't last long.")

Colon insurrection openly posed question of secession from France; yesterday for the first time, Algerian events began eight days back, food, medicine, etc., were shipped by French government to troops there; tracts urging defection of troops, signed by French general, distributed to conscripts to be sent home to families in France were held up by ships being cancelled until three days back are now coming in. More serious is even *Le Monde*'s editorial last night which admits that de Gaulle can be best authority on mediation to end war, though ironically colons shout for him because they think he will be "strong" in supporting war against rebels, etc., etc. Am too tired to be able, darling, to collect all details have noted down in writing, but believe I have them fairly straight and authoritatively. Nora is checking for me and fur-

* Pierre Pflimlin.

nishing documents, background facts, etc. Already my memory is sickened by what I heard today; thank heaven I wrote it all down.

Ask Stanley on Monday to give you an idea of what I cabled Sunday afternoon; I think it will fulfill Shawn's hopes that my sudden flight is highly useful.

Exhausted. Love, darling, and thank you for your inspiration in suggesting my departure. All colleagues said to me, "Well, high time. We were sure you'd turn up!"

Blessings and embraces and kisses, too.

[February 15, 1958]

Darlinghissima mia,

Thank you for your two recent letters of tender welcome, one today. As I suspected, my letter of my sailing announcement must have been held up at the airport, closed by fog. I am now searching with my customary passion and weak sense of choice for a fine gift for you. I shop so rarely, even look into shop windows so occasionally, that I am always so surprised at what I see there that I can never make up my mind if it is desirable or is merely astonishing through my unfamiliarity.

Yes, I am deeply relieved that the Buffet Profile material has swelled amazingly through the interviews and information being collected for me by a chap on the *Express*; excellent reporter, knows the artist group here, knows the hermetic maneuvers of the art galleries, psychology of collectors, etc. Fascinating tangential material especially for the profile of a painter so young, so taciturn, so strange—and falsely presented in several ways. My chap has discovered Bernard never suffered from poverty, simply couldn't get along with his father who still adores him, is owner of a big mirror-cutting concern, was never rich but offered the boy everything, still piously keeps all his early school records and earliest paintings. Curious, now, that information starts pouring in. I receive one amazing item from one side and in a few days get the same information from another direction; in each case things never printed before, never mentioned, such as his marriage! It lasted three months; she was a painter; Lulu de Vilmorin (I interviewed her yesterday) said a ballet dancer friend of Bernard's not long ago pulled out a photo from the old days of himself, Bernard, and his wife. In a fury, Bernard seized it and tore it to bits.

I talked with Françoise Sagan yesterday for about fourteen minutes. She looks perilously thin, old, no lipstick, charming, well bred, sad, said muscles in right thigh still almost useless, though she does not limp from that accident in her car. She has just been found guilty of causing it. Question of insurance, I suppose, which will be bad for her on top of ballet, her last book, etc., poor girl. She said an interesting thing about Bernard: that his painting started so young had probably prevented his maturing. He still reads Mickey Mouse; had one on his night table at the hotel here.

I may fly down to Nice Monday or Tuesday evening to see [Jean] Giono, if he will come from Manosque, an old friend of Bernard's. Also, there is a ballet dancer there (or at Monte Carlo, maybe), who is considered most garrulous source on anecdotes which I still lack. Weather is like spring so flight should not be too alarming.

Truman [Capote] was here, dined with him Thursday night alone at Méditerranée. Flew yesterday to Prague in three hours, then two and a half hours by Russian jet plane, that miraculous new one, fastest in the world, from there to Moscow. Is going for *New Yorker*, to do piece on Teddy Boys there, also—not to be mentioned—on perhaps [Guy] Burgess and foreign colony. It sounds a dangerous assignment— for those he writes about. I must go out to lunch with Carmel. Haven't seen her yet. Is sober, lucid, in perfect condition now that it is too late. Poor Irish lady. How strange.

Au revoir, a rivedercci . . . bacio e bacio mille.

[February 22, 1958. This "letter" was written
on a series of picture postcards.]

Darlinghissima,

I am returning to Paris tomorrow. Buffet is here. I suppose the journey has been worth it, but am not sure. Weather warm and sunny. Today we motored to Villefranche to see Cocteau's Chapel, more imaginative and religious than that of Matisse which we revisited yesterday at Vence. I am surprised by Cocteau's poetic sublimation; it is a visual version of angelic apotheosis and most affecting. It is a heavenly decoration, far more pious than Matisse's . . . determination to produce some modern art. I had forgotten how lovely this Coast is. I have not revisited it to move about in since 1935 and not spent any time here since 1922, near Toulon. Nice in its backstreets still Victorian, is the least changed and prettiest. The rest is modern villas and hotels on the sea front and 18th century picturesque poverty in back streets.

The U.S.A. fleet is in harbor, five cruisers and two supply ships filled with Coca-Cola and contraceptives, gossip says. A horrid load for refreshment and health. So far I have seen no drunken sailors, but I have not frequented the darker streets. As you see (on postcards) Cocteau's theme on the façade which is delightfully gay and Italian is the Eye of the candlestick, then below it the nostrils and below that the mouth, all clear to see since they are appropriately colored. Inside the Chapel is tiny and lovely of pale grey shades and darker grey out-lines, mostly rather like mother of pearl in tone with occasionally dramatic touches of black like the ladder (which must symbolize that by the Cross later on Jesus' Crucifixion), on which the Cock stands, symbolizing France, I suppose, and also Peter's treachery!!! I dare say the best description of the affair is that it is a Lady's Chapel done by a famous pederast. I am told that the Pope has decided to accept it. I doubt He would descend so low on the mortal scale as to make a decision. I noticed that the altar, nicely trimmed in red, had not *hostie* in place. It is a little Comédie Française, but exquisite.

For Janet's arrival, I was able to secure an apartment opposite mine. She could use it whenever she came to New York, affording her both privacy, closeness and seclusion for her work. It turned out to be of great convenience—useful for visiting friends and family when Janet was away; easy to keep and to sublet.

My household had acquired an additional member in the person of Maria [Maver], who had been in the family since the birth of my sister's son in Rome, and had become a permanent beloved fixture of our life in New York. She appeared unexpectedly from a diplomatic household that had brought her to the States as a governess. Here she remained, and came to live with us. At different intervals she took care of my mother, of Bill's first and second daughters, of Janet, too, during her last years in New York. She also raised a daughter and made a life of her own here, until, after seventeen years of petitioning, she was granted permanent residency, went to live in her own flat, and became an expert on baseball. Janet used to call her the *"carabiniere"* for her forceful, efficient manner, and considered her "the best packer in the world." I call her my best friend. Her dinners had become quite famous and her presence would add comfort and pleasure to Janet's sojourn.

This year Janet suggested a trip to Mexico as part of our vacation. I enthusiastically agreed. Armed with *Sudden View*, our friend Sybille Bedford's delightful book on Mexico, as our Baedeker, we flew to

Mexico City, where we were met by our mentor, Rosa Covarrubias, the widow of the artist. She took us in hand and we joined a group of American friends, already settled in homes and hotels, for a stay of a few weeks.

Mexico was a great surprise. It was difficult to think of it as part of the North American continent, so different was it, so much closer to its Spanish roots. The country's characteristics were so diverse: the Spanish language for one thing, and its art and architecture, like its people, so Latin and Indian. It was a discovery for us, a delight. The only thing we didn't like was the Mexican cuisine—too coarse, too spicy, too strange for our French and Italian tastes. But we liked tequila and became addicted to margaritas.

Janet's amazing energy and strength held up during days of constant motion; she was indefatigable in her curiosity about the new scenery and culture. Rosa Covarrubias introduced us to her friends. With her we were able to penetrate, even if only on the surface, a little of the life of the Mexican people and the beauty of the country itself.

Janet returned to a France in turmoil. In Mexico, we had left behind pens and papers, as Janet suggested beforehand. The painful realities struck Janet especially, as the Algerian rebellion, with political implications and reactions, reached its climax.

[May 3, 1958]

Darlingest,

Will remain in my room all day today, working to read and digest all that has transpired, that I have seen, heard, been informed of. Each day I have been either to Chamber (Tuesday I attended three sessions which means nine flights of stairs up to the little visitors' gallery) and yesterday heard Chamber speaker [André] Le Troquer (Socialist) read aloud, while entire hemicycle of deputies stood at his request, the letter from President Coty proposing de Gaulle to found a government; mentioning "on either side men seem to be preparing a fratricidal struggle."

. . . Marquis Childs tells me that yesterday at three p.m. both American and British embassies regarded as very grave report they had from Algiers that yesterday afternoon was deadline in Algiers plans, for de Gaulle to be named to power. That if it did not occur the parachutists would take off for France, probably Marseilles first, but equally likely would ring Paris. Actually, all private airports around Paris, and secondary ones, are now closed. . . . Now we are waiting to see if the Socialists have decided to back de Gaulle, rather than stand against him which will prevent his getting Chamber majority and taking legal power. Then what? The parachutists apparently. If he does take power, what will the Communists do? Another version of civil war? I don't believe it. . . .

Probably it WILL be effective for twenty-four hours. I'll buy candles today, if I can find any, for my room, as I will have to work all tomorrow night. It isn't even sure de Gaulle will appear for investiture in Chamber, for fear of rousing the Communists to tumult which will be bad for public order, confidence, etc. Last night around ten and until three this morning, motorists began running up and down Champs and around Concorde tooting their horns, three short, two long, meaning de Gaulle au POU-VOIR, or L'Algérie FRAN-ÇAISE or maybe just three short and two long for Algiers radio station signal. Who knows? It was silly but gay, this tooting (nobody has been allowed to blow a horn for two years or more) and so far the ONLY pro-Gaullist public reaction, if it could be called that.

Things are very grave here, darling. De Gaulle can save most of the worst from happening, such as real civil war, parachutists and other events.

I can only hope for France he comes in tomorrow, because the worst that could happen in the long view is that if such a parliament, such deputies, such perpetual confusion of splintered power should continue, it is doomed to fail to govern France. Maybe French are ungovernable in fact; no unity which furnishes level for government to be based on.

If civil war or trouble breaks on Monday, I shall stay for one more letter, unless things become too dangerous. I have no desire to be popped into prison by my old friend Louis Aragon for being anti-Communist, that is one sure thing. Already there is talk the planes may not fly next week, but that's nonsense. Shawn admired my first letter, cabling me it was "masterly" which I did not think it was, but very informative and clear.

It's pouring rain again; chilly all the time except yesterday. I live in my two suits and at night my new grey coat.

You would be very excited were you here. I am. I try to sleep and eat, but don't do much of either—too wrought up. That whiskey bottle is going down rapidly! If I feel it my duty to work, to stay another week, I'll have Terry telegraph Smith College. If my degree honoris causa is because I was a good journalist, now is the time to prove it again, if I MUST. I HOPE TO FLY Wednesday. . . .

I kept thinking of you in the Chamber yesterday, with violence all around me.

Yours forever. . . .

———

With the drama of a possible parachutists' descent on Paris avoided by the return of General de Gaulle to power and the scare of a siege vanished, Janet could fly to New York in time to receive a degree *honoris causa* for journalism at Smith College in June.

Helen Kirkpatrick, a Smith alumna and a journalist friend, had arranged for me to be invited, which delighted me because, except for having participated in the graduation of my son at Exeter, I had never been to a graduation before.

On the platform were two other women in cap and gown to be honored along with Janet: Katherine Anne Porter, for literature, and Nadia Boulanger, for music. Below, on rows of chairs covering the great lawn of the college grounds, sat hundreds of young women graduates, who one by one filed past to receive their degrees. The commencement address, an impassioned speech for women's rights, was delivered by a young senator from Massachusetts, John F. Kennedy.

As I looked at Janet, smiling with pride and appreciation, my thoughts went back to a day in my mother's youth. She had been an honor student, I remember her telling us, and on graduation day, along with her degree, she would receive a special medal in recognition of excellence. She had studied hard, sometimes by candlelight, late at night and into the early morning hours. She had loved school, her studies; this was going to be her great day. At that time, young women were not allowed to go out alone, so her younger brother Carlo was summoned to escort her. He refused. He couldn't care less, he told his mother, who wouldn't have dreamed of forcing him. Esterina missed her graduation day, her prize, the one thing she had been working so hard for and had been looking forward to with such eagerness all year long. She took off her graduation dress, shut herself in her room and cried with rage. From that day on she became an ardent feminist, a pioneer for women's rights and for their independence. She campaigned for women's right to vote, she helped organize the first women's associations and later she headed the Italian chapter of the International Association of Business and Professional Women. Her graduation-day story remained impressed on my memory and influenced my life. At that moment, at Smith College, I was witnessing my mother's revenge! If only she could have been present. Later in the day I phoned her in New York. I wished to congratulate her!

In July, Janet flew to California to visit her family in Altadena and I went to Fire Island with my own family: Bill, Doris, Doodie and Maria. Before leaving, we had made plans for the rest of the summer. We decided to go to Denmark on our way to Italy. None of us had been there before, and this time I was taking Ester with us.

We found Denmark civilized, orderly, clean, quaint; its people dignified, blond, courteous, going around on bicycles, thousands of them, a sight to see. Copenhagen was a charming city; we didn't see poverty anywhere.

In about an hour from Copenhagen, we could reach the historic castles that dotted the countryside: the formidable medieval structure of Elsinore, Hamlet's castle, and then the most beautiful Renaissance one at Frederiksborg, on a lake with an exquisite little baroque church nearby. The trip had been a diversion.

Italy, with its chaotic traffic, a people so individualistic as to be almost impossible to rule—especially by a series of inept governments, and with so many poor, so much personal misery—was a shock after Denmark. Still as always on arrival, the impression was of a people enjoying life, glad to be alive, and smiling.

Janet returned to Paris from Italy at the end of August to cover the referendum on General de Gaulle. I left for Milan to discuss my contract renewal with Mondadori.

                                                    [Early September, 1958]

Beloved,

The train journey leaving Rome, leaving Italy, was of incredible beauty and filled with souvenirs shared with you. I recognized the gash in the mountain side that represented Carrara, red marble being the dominant quarry color; at following railroad stations slabs of red and also yellow, cut and polished for table tops, and white marble chips in villagers' sideyards, being crushed for a new path to the cow stable. The only country surely where a cow will walk on marble like a queen. By late afternoon the whole right side spectacle of the mountains and hills had become dark blue, of incredible intensity and loveliness, as true and old as when renaissance painters used it as their background. I tried to read during the less lovely sections but still could not keep

my eyes from what was better and fresher as information—merely
artistic beauty in which people LIVED.

A delightful dinner at Ester's pension . . . She seems perfectly
happy, delighted to spend October in her beloved country. I left the
hotel with plenty of money left over, forgot nothing, including my
jewels in a safety box, tipped everybody, shook hands with the great
concierge who gave me a coquettish semi-wink appropriately delayed
after the respectful bow for the 3,000 lire tip.

I find the Thurbers are in the Continental, a pleasure and a draw-
back, too, as Jamie has become more kingly than ever. There was a
whole page on him and Walter Mitty in *France-Soir* last night. A
four-page article by Sartre in the *Express*—read it if you can find it—a
real terror, showing that a mind once communized can in some cases
never be relied upon again for any republican comprehension, even
after a protested Budapest. . . .

[October 7, 1958]

Darlinghissima,

Well, I laughed out loud at your reported conversation with Il
Presidente as to why you were still there in Milan—and would remain
there until he signed your new contract. Only you, true enough, have
the native courage and candor to speak to him like that, to open his
mind by putting some truth and words of fearlessness in his ears. How
those tycoons of real psychological talent for mastery, for creation
through gifts including ambition, including their own type of genius
for construction, leave themselves deaf to criticism. This is what makes
their careers so cut off from any sense of continuity, of real foundation,
that as they grow old those about them wonder who can take their place
—know nobody can because their practices have kept everyone around
them *small*. It's the old H. G. Wells theory in his book on the civilizations of the world in which he talked of the Father Bull, who rides the
herd and seeks to gore all younger bulls, so he remains supreme; it is
the instinctive man not the democratic man.

Considering where the democratic man has now landed himself in
several civilized countries today—in a position of being so commonplace in his reduced mentality and originality that he is no different
than the common people who elected him—maybe the Bull Father
personality was indeed superior, if only through fighting and wear and
tear. That you won your points is another proof of your intelligence;
how could you have thought out all those details, possibilities and
balances? I am in respect and awe. You have really an extremely good

business sense, based on your high qualities of organization, memory and construction, and I know this yet it always surprises me to see you *apply* it with such shrewdness, such masculine particularity. . . .

There is still the void of our last meeting, manqué. I was so counting on it for mere *pleasure*, no confusions, no duties—I had at once firmly thanked Odette and refused her offer to meet you in her car at the air field, she and Monica. I said in that journey to the city you could give me all your Mondadori news and then we could feel free to eat, to drink and be merry, which could have included lunch with them. Odette is by nature energetic and greedy, so she wanted a dinner with you. Again, I said no. Monica is frightfully thin, with the most perfect mannequin silhouette, looks lovely in her simplest clothes, all remade to fit like her skin by an old White Russian, formerly a great dressmaker in St. Petersburg, now operating in a Paris attic; but she worries me. She is very nervous, seems so easily startled into what she called the other day "a panic."

[October 10, 1958]

My beloved,

It is seven p.m. Have worked here since Saturday morning really. Am shortly going out to dine alone so as not to disturb continuity of thoughts and work tonight on French political part of my letter for Tuesday. I wanted to write you to tell you I am thinking of you, tell you how much, how often I think of you, with what love, admiration, appreciation. Mexico was the most satisfying part of our summer. We must see to it that this coming meeting offers similar privacy, changes and stimulations.

I've just had bathroom water and Ballantine's Scotch which someone left me half a bottle of . . . oh, the Thurbers. We had lovable times for nearly two months in the hotel, excepting one evening at a dinner party when Jamie became violent and insulting about Ross and *The New Yorker*, but that too was as pathetic as it was revolting. His memory is the only organ he has left to guide him, and in his darkness his ego has developed like a fatal light. It is he, not Ross, who was the guiding lamp on the magazine in the early days. . . .

Yesterday, before I took Tchelichew's sister to Bernstein's concert, I stood on my balcony viewing the lovely chromes, in chromatic gammes (forgive pun) in the leaves of the Tuileries, not yet fallen from the trees. I had lunched with L* and his darling Felicia the day

* Leonard Bernstein, the conductor.

before at a charming fish restaurant directly opposite to the Tour Eiffel. We talked until four, then met again at Alice Toklas' rooms, where they met her and saw her pictures. (Doda Conrad brought them. Really, those Poles are pluperfect maître d'hotels; why didn't they ask me to take them? She is a thousand times more my intimate darling friend than he.) I wanted to take them after to Lee Miller's cocktail party in the Place Dauphine nearby, with her husband, Roland Penrose, whose new book on Picasso, after ten years' work, has just come out but they had to dine with Mlle. Boulanger.

Well, the vesper Pleyel concert of Bernstein yesterday was really riotous. He seems not to know, nor did I tell him afterwards in the green room, that Parisians applaud like pugilists, battering their hands, for anything foreign. He must have had perhaps thirty or forty curtain calls. It was as extravagant as his programme, direction and also solo piano playing of concertos by Bach, Mozart, Ravel then Gershwin's blues in which later he misses as many top notes, I said to a discreet male musical friend, as if he had been Rubinstein himself. In the green room he said he had never been so nervous before a concert. I had trembled as he began his Bach, took courage with his Mozart (exquisite, poetic, la seule réussite), was brave and too fast in his Ravel and banged right and left in the Gershwin of which Iturbi, it may please you to know my darling, is still considered here as having given the finest performance.

Leonard's reviews have been as phenomenal as he is. We talked of our supper table with you at Lillian's. I love you, I am hungry, going alone to dine, having not lunched, my hearing is *greatly* ameliorated, smoke not more than ten cigarettes a day (which affect arterial tension), and my heart is yours which affects its amorous tension, the only bloodstream of love which poets have yet traced. Forgive this awkward tender letter, which is ill-written by the brain, physically refined by the sentiment. Write me, darling, in a non-businessman's letter.

[October 21, 1958]

Darling one, Natalia,

. . . De Gaulle's triumph here is fabulous. His popularity at apogée, since the letter to [General] Salan and the military. This was what everyone—except the military and ultras—were waiting for. De Gaulle has won, is a new man with new aims, that is clear. I am happier for France as an entity, as a kind of personality, than at any time since the liberation. . . . *Tours de France*, the most conservative, pious, Catholic bourgeois weekly, bought that Papal doctor's most horrid photo and published it, Monica told me. I refused to look at it. It showed the doctor withdrawing the tubes from his [Pius XII's] nose and mouth, I believe, with blood flowing. That medico must be mad, as the little additional note in *Le Monde* which I enclose, insinuates. These small details, always in italics, are often what makes that newspaper so informing.

Everyone here is scandalized, even the mangia-preti; truly his acts and now his explanations can only be understood as aberrations. You will be interested in *Le Monde*'s quoting of *Il Giorno* and its criticism of the Pope's own good sense in having such a charlatan around him, without having identified his reckless, vulgar character.

I spent the weekend at Noël's for the first time since my return. Had only gone before for lunch and read all of Simone de Beauvoir's new book, nearly seven hundred pages which took me all day Sunday, Sunday night until two, all day Monday and Monday night until one. I read so much more slowly than I once did and than Monica does, lucky woman. I find it a fascinating over-long book. Her childhood portions up until the age of puberty are dull. It is called *Mémoires d'une Jeune Fille Rangée*,* a curious title for a book from her, but the truth. What a childhood of suffering from her strict coli monte parents, her father who was as "convinced of Dreyfus' guilt as her mother was of the existence of God" and worse even, Simone's own sense of obedience to them, trained into her psychology, so that she was aged seventeen before she had courage to ask her mother not to open her letters and read them aloud to her and aged twenty before she sneaked away, on a mensonge, to see the Russian ballet. My lord, she was farther behind the times in the intellectual early Twenties in Paris than I was, a Hoosier Quaker hick. It is a book which will fascinate the French, she being what she has become. It ends with several pages of exalted analyses of Sartre as a mind and a man, fascinating really. Her life for such it is reads like a novel, partly like the *Trials of Sophie* even. . . .

[November 28, 1958]

Darlinghissima,

I hope my election piece was as illuminating as I thought it was. It was like a second referendum for de Gaulle; now he will soon run for president so that will be a third election of him. Strange there should

* Published in English as *Memoirs of a Dutiful Daughter*.

be so many. We can only suppose he cannot rid himself of [Deputy Jacques] Soustelle any more than of the military power in Algiers; in other words, some of the worst prophecies are coming to pass, that he seems caught in their net, yet experts think he may prove so dominant in influence in the Chamber, as President of France with supreme powers, that all will be well. He is a changed man certainly, a humanist, highly senstive to improving the lot of the poor, of housing, etc. Though less of education. The two-day strike at the Sorbonne was significant—five hundred science students in each of the science halls with seats for two hundred, with students sitting on the floor, in the window sills, at the professors' feet on the rostrum or standing up, to take notes.

The minister of education asked for a bigger budget and it was refused by de Gaulle on advice from [Antoine] Pinay, a penny-pincher but an honest finance minister. How can one go on having hope in any country where intelligence does not reign as a practice, or where if an intelligent ruler appears, like de Gaulle, convinced that parliament was leading the land to ruin, as indeed it was, the greedy, ambitious men around him, scenting new power like blood, swarm like flies to suck and batten and swell their bellies and purses. Did you read the Montgomery memoirs as they came out in the London *Sunday Times?* His report of Ike's decisions that Berlin was no longer the goal of the war, as its end in capture, Berlin having become only "a geographical locality" as the war drew to its finish? Well, there's the explanation of the Berlin trouble right now. The Russians surround that geographical locality, as you well know, and by their devilish strategies and ruses have now once more put the stupid Allies in a pocket, the city itself. Strange how fiendishly brilliant all their inventions are when against the Allies, real inventions of the devil. They seem far less brilliant in creating strategies for their own people. The loss of the Communist party here in the election is almost unbelievable—a million and a half votes.

. . . I enclose the Wolfenden Report as discussed by the House of Commons reported by the London Times, also its editorial called "Vice." It's very fair-minded and the *Guardian's* editorial which I consider terrifying, like an inquisition. This is a very important public discussion of our private lives and I want you to read it. Then I want you to give it to Ernst to read. It is very important to have his opinion. Only ONE member of Parliament said anything intelligent on the subject. He is probably a pederast—and to think that every gentleman in the House who had gone to a graduate school had been steadily buggered from Eton through Oxford. . . .

[December 12, 1958]

Darlinghissima,

. . . De Gaulle looked more than ever like an elderly wax candle, often lit before, now partially burned down. It is natural that you, an Italian with the tragedy of Fascism-out-of-Socialism lying behind you, would be more alarmed than the French at the Gaullist-minded man who accepts the republican principles as part of his sober intellectuality, not that he believes much in it as a political form, I fancy. I should think what he believes in is humanism, shown in his Constantine* speech, and the strong Presidency on the complete American model which he will inaugurate January 5. I certainly fancy he believes little in the efficiency of a French parliament. Neither do I; neither do the French. We have all been too often disillusioned. I, too, bitterly regret the loss of Mendès [-France] from the Chamber, but I feel there is too emotional an attitude about him as a marvelous personality, and not enough accurate thoughtfulness on the harm he has done. His ambiguity on ECD is still a sore spot of political chicanery, an old-fashioned model of those practices which at least de Gaulle puts in a new form. He simply says *nothing* when the situation is not ripe enough to be discussed or shows hope of succeeding. Mendès ruined the remains of the old Radical Socialist party, the real middle left of political France, by trying to turn the whole group into farther leftist ground than many wished to be and its flexibility was part of its value, with the result that he sometimes had as few as only from seven to twelve followers in his own group. His attempt to discipline the whole party was as authoritative, toward the left, as much that Gaullists have done on the right, and both are regrettable.

In his last election, the radical-socialists emerged as a mere splinter of their former selves. For that, alas, the remarkable Mendès is to be blamed. Unwilling to be organized in his leftist disciplined cell, they began splitting in all directions. The truth is that the Left, all of it, from communists toward even the intellectual Left, passing through the Socialists, has proved a disillusion here as something that does not work, that at least has not worked politically probably because the

* "The Constantine Plan" was de Gaulle's economic new deal for Algeria.

average French like money too well. It is in the hope of getting better wages that a Frenchman is a socialist or communist. It is not to a theory that he turns, but to his possibly larger pay envelope, alas. All this, I think, is another version of the anti-Labour reaction in England after the Labour Party had been in power and heaven was still nowhere in sight, and its suburbs extremely costly for the taxpayer. France is taxed to death, next highest to England. There would be riots if the right to strike and to have labor unions and family allocations were destroyed. These are the real Left gains that are the functional part of society, but the political theory of socialism especially has dropped, drowned into a well with Mollet as Premier having been elected on a pacifist program and pursuing the Algerian war with a vigor which no Rightist government could have dared. He even dared run this month for re-election on the slogan, "Stop the Algerian war."

To me he is a harlot with moustache and spectacles. I believe this period right now is generally based on two confusions in the immediate past, now being better understood in their own truths. Communism applies at its best to underdeveloped, relatively little civilized countries, illiterate and unprosperous, to which it can offer autocracy that is useful. Democracy applies best only to literate, prosperous countries which do not need autocracy, having developed far beyond it. The democrats' silly, conceited error being that democracy is good for such simple peoples and capitalism, too, is good for lands where people cannot spell R-A-T and must have a picture of a rat on their ballot to vote for. Both political creations have their extreme limitations and as there are more underdeveloped lands of myriad populations than countries like France and the U.S.A., in the end the communists will have the globe developing the underdeveloped and holding a gun at our heads.

Forgive this long essay. I'll only add that the French communists' loss of a million and a half votes included largely lost votes from the French laboring class, obviously. As French, they have been unable over the years to swallow the communist autocracy, that of the purges, Budapest and recently Pasternak. Unfortunately for the party, the laborers here are not limited just to reading *Humanité* (as in Russia) but can read *Le Monde*, which has helped ruin the communist position.

My new version of Buffet fascinates me. I am mad about working on it and hope to finish it before Christmas. It is infinitely improved, an absolute new opening, changes, shifts, etc.

My beloved, these are state papers we write each other, not love letters, have you noticed? Perhaps we suffer from the times we live in. For my love is intense, still passionate, still tender and true.

My darling love,

Thank you for the most beautiful and complete love letter I have ever known in my life, larger and more illuminating on the meaning of the structure of love in a curiously lived life, as you lead and know yours, than any I have read, too, in poetry or memoirs. Stendhal's little volume on "Love," with its frequently trumpery incidents and, it is true, the flashes of his masculine losses which gave wisdom of comment, is poor fare compared to the analysis of emotion you gave to me. This is not merely complimentary, you know that. This is profoundly deep appreciation for your thoughts and their application on this great human subject on which, as I have often told you, each fortunate human talks privately in the early happiest love-period or experience of existence, but pitifully little has been *recorded of stated importance.* This you have achieved. I shall never forget this letter or lose it. It is the major apogee of the reception of the gift of emotion in my long life. I cannot in any way express my love for you in an equality of discovery and appreciation, except to tell you that I know that what you wrote is the *truth,* rarely approached, but seized by you in its significance as your own definition of your own significant deep nature.

With my thoughts I can only esteem yours and join them in an exalted admiration of what you were able to reach and express. In a way almost I do not count because what you say is of a truth which applies to the civilization of the heart and character which has emerged in these very supreme lines of verity, for all high enough to reach by appreciation, but placed there by you, in words, as communication of the power of love, within a heart and brain. I adore and love and appreciate you, the first two as since the day I first met you, the last in a fête of special identification. You are a superb, civilized woman of wisdom, gravity and grace. Always since I have known you I have said that the Italian civilization was maintained through the centuries not only by the art of their landscapes and of their artists' works, but by the perfecting of their knowledge of the education of passion, and how it has preserved and informed your race, since before the time of Christians back into the classic spirit of body and heart, in your land.

1959

This letter of Janet's, her appreciation of my devotion, which she applied as well to the civilization I represented in terms of my country of birth, just as she embodied for me all I had loved in her own country, which was mine too now, arrived with the New Year, which inaugurated our nineteenth year of attachment, as the best statement of the validity of our friendship, as a resolution for its continuity with a festive feeling of the heart.

We had attracted each other for so many years because we were, first of all, human beings, interested in the human spirit, its beliefs, its aims, its hopes; because we both loved life intensely. We complemented each other. We were so completely in unison in our way of thinking, of understanding, that we simply could not do without each other, despite distances, loneliness, difficulties.

I didn't go to Paris for the holidays, as Janet suggested, because I especially desired to spend Christmas with Doodie and my family. Christmas for a three-year-old child was a new experience to me, too. When Bill was three, we were in Italy. Christmas there is not celebrated with a decorated tree and presents. That celebration takes place on Epiphany, January 6, the date on which the three kings arrived at the manger with their gifts of gold, frankincense and myrrh. Italian children receive their presents in a stocking hanging from their bed railings, distributed not by Santa Claus but by a benevolent old witch called La Befana, who rides to her chores on a broomstick. On that night, Rome's Piazza Navona is filled with a noisy crowd swarming about the stands selling toys, sweets and crèches, a custom still observed today.

My decision to remain in New York proved to be right because, quite unexpectedly, Janet would be flying over for a ten-day visit; the best gift I could have received and an added pleasure to the season.

This year the Presidente, as the publisher Mondadori was called, was coming to visit New York and his American office for the first time. I was eager to show him our new premises, and to introduce him to the American publishers with whom I had established solid business ties—relationships which would flourish with even greater success when, later on, the new plant in Verona had been completed and the old offices had been moved from the center of Milan to the ultra-chic, modern Segrate building on the outskirts of the city.

My relationship with the Mondadoris had always been close and friendly. It dated from the time when, as a fledgling publisher, he had suggested Mammina Ester move to Milan to continue her directorship of *La Donna*, which he had just bought, as well as my own collaboration with his children's magazine, *Girotondo*. I was then given the responsibility of representing the complete works of the poet Gabriele d'Annunzio in the United States, and of heading Mondadori's new office in New York after the war.

[January 2, 1959]

Darlinghissima,

. . . I am MUCH, MUCH better, really feel well again and shall NOT overwork, but if you knew how I longed to be rid of Buffet. I met him by accident in Maxim's Thursday, where Mme. Rubinstein had invited me to lunch with Irene Brinn* and Gaspero and Patrick [O'Higgins]. Very jolly and he was in the next room, with his wife Annabel. She has a kind face, lovely long neck, is certainly not a handsome girl. He is far prettier than she. His show opens this week. All New York architectural drawings, I hear. Much of his future will depend on this show being popular or not. Gaspero thought it might

---

* Irene Brinn, the translator of Carson McCullers and a fashion writer, was the *Harper's Bazaar* Rome correspondent. Her husband, Gaspero dal Corso, was an art dealer, owner of the Obelisco Gallery in Rome.

not be. He was very helpful on Buffet. Told me he thinks I am right in having done him. He is worth it. (Others here so discouraged me, thought him not worth my time or *The New Yorker's*). Thinks my view of him absolutely justified, also my belief that his popularity is spontaneous, if also aided by merchant racket.

I MUST buy a new suit and frock. I am positively shabby. Nothing new since that heavy grey *tailleur* for a year. I think I'll order a grey flannel *tailleur*, very thin flannel, with a silk blouse of pattern and lining of jacket the same and perhaps a flannel topcoat to go with it all. I must rush to post this, darling.

I have just been elected a member of the American Institute of Arts and Letters. What is it? Isn't that Glenway's favorite organization? How little such idle honors mean. Only one's work can have counted and what one thinks of it. I think little because it has been ephemeral. I should have used my talent seriously for good books. Alas . . .

Your own and forever . . .

[March 3, 1959]

Sweetest heart,

I have some freesias on my table as I work to remind me that it is spring, as indeed it has looked to be over the past week of sunshine and abnormal warmth with the warmest Friday in the recorded temperature of Paris. With all the sunshine we wasted behind the two weeks of fog and this past week's solar joy, we now start to pay today with grey skies and chill air. Not a drop of rain here except one day for nearly a month.

Hildegarde writes me that their November rains failed to come, and, so far, February has been dry, an ominous warning which makes Californians recall their recent drought that lasted five years in its overall insufficiency. She says the foundations of the new house at Calistoga north of San Francisco have actually been dug, so I suppose I can believe her which I so wish to do. . . .

I was in the Fbrg. St. Honoré yesterday and saw a strange sight, though the papers have mentioned it as an occasional habit of de Gaulle's. Two mounted horse guards at his Elysée palace doorway which, of course, immediately attract crowds who wait to see him come out or go in and are shooed along by the police who indeed force you to cross the street to begin with. One cannot walk on the palace sidewalk. If he is going to imitate the guards at Whitehall in

London, at least let the tourists and citizens enjoy the sight and connect it with his high position as they do with the Queen's, rather than have their curiosity unsatisfied by being trundled along by policemen who keep treating them like chickens escaped from the barnyard.

I was very impressed by the Camus production of Dostoyevsky's *The Possessed*, though it intensified one's feeling that the main topic of the finest Russian nineteenth century novels are criminals, lunatics, sadists, anarchists or madmen. Or murderers. In this way, only Faulkner equals them among our Southerners whom I rank as our substitute Russians of genius. I have never read Thomas Wolfe, I regret to say. He is Southern, too, isn't he? I've never had the patience, but certainly crime alone was not his theme. Strange that degeneracy attacks the more cultured minds when accompanied by poverty and fear for survival, in a way it does not among the stupider poor, who though certainly not improved by a diet of corn pone and fat pork, or kasha and cabbage soup, do not decline in their intellects having had none from which to descend, perhaps.

I enclose some reports on the U.S.A. by young [Philip] Toynbee which seem to be alarmingly harsh even for an Anglican visiting our land, though often clearly accurate. I see by this Sunday's *New York Times*, published in Rotterdam, that Stevenson's warning that we may be licked this next time has been reprinted in the paper to give it again to the American readers, alarming as it is.

The Lippmanns are coming here next week. I am to dine with them twice, which will be an inspiration if only to look at him since he does not say much unless forced. His views on Berlin and why the Russians fear it may attract the Eastern behind the curtain countries seems to me false from what my few expatriate friends of those countries say. They all declare their compatriots still at home fear the Germans and hate them far more than they do the Russians EVEN WITH Communism. Nobody here in Europe, as you would well understand, thinks for an instant that Poland, for instance, would settle back, if it had a chance, even to its mild Pilsudski-like period of imitative democracy if freed from Russia tomorrow. These countries have all received elements of Communism which date them as part of the mid-twentieth century and will not drop it, though would if they had the chance, certainly, to put in operation their own version like Tito's, and with many admixtures of freed or more democratic procedures. But capitalism as a practice to replace the many nationalizations they will not return to. They have known too much poverty, too great inequalities, and I feel too keenly that the privacy, if I may say so, of any manifested democratic atmosphere or practice will be limited to shoptrade, some portion of farming most certainly, and things on that level, but that the state will continue to own and administer the overall managements and all that constitute the riches beneath the earth, coal, oil, metals, etc. Some private life will exist on top of the earth only. At least so I sense from what I read.

This is a dull letter of communications, my beloved. I will add more personally that at last I have ordered a grey flannel suit with a dark and light grey patterned silk blouse, at a small tailors in the Fbg. St. Honoré, the blouse costing $80, the whole three pieces coming to $200 instead of Lanvin's $450 if not $500 where I shall instead get a black silk afternoon dress as it is in a dress that the genius of the best dressmaking shows. I should think nearly anybody can cut and make a simple, short-jacketed suit such as I have worn for three years now. Anybody can and everybody does.

Restaurant prices have gone down a little for food, in fear of losing all clients. Shops nearly empty. The pinch has not yet started pinching the modest people on mere food prices at the market. Until it does, one cannot tell which way the Fifth Republic is going. It is in the grievances and reactions that its future will be shaped. I hope to God the general can win. I am sick of charlatanism in French politicians and parliament and hold them responsible for much of my saddened opinion of waning democracy. We will talk of these things and more tender ones at Fire Island. My joy, my jewel, my dark Roman.

As an unexpectedly wonderful treat, like blue skies and warmth in a chilly spring, came the news that Janet would be coming to New York for ten days around April 6.

The Overseas Press Club had planned a Paris Night Gala on April 10, and had asked Janet if she would come to make a short speech, along with Joe Liebling, Water Kerr and Tex Reilly, who would talk about their army experiences in France. Janet would provide topics "of broader interest," the cable specified. The invitation would give us the chance to see each other, to have a sweet drink together before our annual feast, when Janet would be returning to spend the summer at Fire Island.

Janet's arrival on April 8 coincided with Bill's thirty-third birthday party, and became an additional way to welcome her as part of our calendar. Except for the Overseas Press Club gala, no other engagements were made and no parties planned. We wanted to be together as much as possible, for the rumor of Janet's impending, unexpected arrival had spread like wildfire through the corridors of *The New Yorker*, where news is created and gossip is passed on—as my son, who was working there, could attest. I could see that she would be snatched up by greedy admirers and friends as soon as she set foot in New York. During Janet's absence I had sublet her flat, so I reserved a room for her at a nearby hotel.

The gala evening went off as well as expected. I do not recall the speeches, but I do remember the public's resounding and applause-filled welcome.

[April 1959, Friday, midnight]

Darling one,

Your wonderful letter of recollection and annotation of our miraculous reunion came in the late post tonight, speaking for your heart to mine, with the sentiments as equal as if weighed on a golden scale. Curious, our going to a new setting, in a new scene of privacy added romantically, one of the mysterious refreshments and stimulations of travel, of the new walls and ceilings, the new beds, the new view from the new windows. All these were perfect in that delicious, luxurious hostelry you chose, close to art, to quiet trees, to magnolias, to our pair of morning walks in sunshine down the avenue to work, across the cross streets close to your own dear apartment, your own darling Ester, whose presence is always a stimulation, example and pleasure. A profit too, by jove, with such a gift for saucing and cooking, the only good food I had in New York except our breakfasts. I wish I had taken BOTH orange juice and grapefruit now. I had a grappefroose as the French will call it when I ordered a pamplemousse last night, a miserable sour affair which I fear had Israelite blood.

The Floraleis has been an incredible pleasure and beauty. Russell Page's garden won the First Prize yesterday, or rather his patron's flowers with Russell's placing of them won it. The house of Vilmorin, three million francs—the pond alone cost a million and a half, he told me, as the cement had to be as well set as if in permanence, the entire electrical apparatus of the Palais de la Défense being set right beneath it and the danger of a short circuit something to be avoided. I never saw such a garden as he created. The London *Times* gave him the greatest praise, mentioned him only by name as the great creative gardener. I spent all Tuesday morning with him while he was putting on finishing touches, calling for him at nine, then spent all Wednesday afternoon with the garden by this time being complete—the only one that was, naturally.

André de Vilmorin* and wife were there, proud as punch at what he had done which, among other things, is to restore the prosperity of the business over the past two or three years, which those crazy money-spending Vilmorins, all of them slightly mad, had reduced over two or three generations to a dangerously low level.

The English orchid show in the hot house section was the richest plantation of those flowers I ever saw. You, who love them far more than I, would have been ecstatic. Literally DOZENS of sprays, including the Queen's from Windsor Castle, all pale into delicate purple splotches of color. Directly across from them was the Belgian Congo section, a kind of jungle they had flown up from the Congo, fantastically rich, dark plants with a jungle of rich, very dark colored orchids, some almost charcoal grey, nearly black in specks and spots, and close at hand another orchid display on a little French Gold Coast hut, with a tiny rope native bridge with three tiny stuffed grey monkeys pretending to be asleep rather than dead in it—touching but effective. I never saw ENOUGH flowers before in my life until I saw Russ's garden. It contained more than ten thousand potted blooming plants and probably another thousand or more bushes in bloom, plus birch trees, pines, red maples, etc.

The jet journey back was, it's true, sleepless, except from eleven-thirty until one-ten, by my watch New York time, because Ernst had told me not to take three sleeping pills. The next time I will as the two I took failed to induce slumber. The air was bumpy, too. Some people were a little airsick as well, as the plane rolled. I must say, it shook and shrieked so as we revved up for the take-off that I thought we were all going to blow up! But the trip was really fine because brief. The captain told us as we swung over the Atlantic it would take six hours, fifty minutes. Actually, it took seven hours and a quarter, but what is that? NOTHING, NOTHING. Oh yes, this experience has taught me to MOVE, an invaluable element of information for our time of life and for the time of the century.

I was fairly astonished that the Buffet seemed so rewarding by your report. I had become so sick of it, I suppose that its values, if positive, had grown stale and pale. I shall send Shawn the extra bits he wanted developed this week.

---

* Head of a noted Paris society family, who owned a flower business.

I can only say with deepest appreciation that I am grateful to Providence for the joy, delight, refreshment of love and the deep understanding of tenderness, of our value to each other, which we shared in our ten days, as preliminary for the fortnight to come and for the summer of heat and work you will have with Anna. We will live on that until I see you in September. You are not absent an instant from my heart and soul.

[May 25, 1959]

So the Puritan Dulles is dead. Judging by the first editorial reactions of this morning's Paris press, it is not a nation that forgets a man's life merely because he has moved on to the tomb. He trod on French toes even as he flew across the Atlantic, with his diplomatic powers, and once on earth, no matter where, continued to outrage their compendium of history and habits of dominant civilization which, though they have both lamentably changed in the last hundred years, they still lean against, like well-placed statues, when an incomer from the U.S.A., whose revolution turned out to enrich them, not to impoverish them as the French revolution did, with Napoleon's help, until very recently indeed.

I look forward to Lippmann's evaluation of Dulles, whom he admired as a character but could have given lessons to in diplomacy and foreign affairs and historical events. For there Dulles was just as entrenched in the past as the French, though in relation to a different revolution, the last, the Russian one. To ignore its solidity or accomplishment, its material, undeniable existence as a going concern, its power over something like a third of the world, now that communism possesses China, and to presume to decide, as if judging Right and Wrong, Good and Evil, that it was only a passing phase not worthy to be recognized, was the kind of folly of unreality that even the Catholic Church did not indulge in, once the Reformation really manifested its new hold on new men's minds. At least the Jesuits founded a Counter-Reformation, which was sensible and also built beautiful Baroque churches. . . .

This is a strange spring, my darling. One hot morning, then a cold afternoon, then a hot noon and then at night such chill that one needs a topcoat. It is a ludicrous mismanagement by nature, perhaps aided by scientific man. The papers report terrible rains in Rome, such cold weather with rain at Cannes that hotel keepers are weeping on their maîtres d'hotels' bosoms probably. Money. Well, nature was the first source of it. When one sees how elect is the idea of love for others, in the social scheme, how rare between individuals to carry in their hearts, as joy and a burden, too, because its laws are special, one is only amazed and touched that so few among the many, such an inexpert small percentage, led by even fewer geniuses of thought and conduct, have built the civilization of aspiration we have today and have had. I admire man because there is some good in him, an admiration which must be disproportionate to do human nature justice.

I saw Shaw's Joan of Arc the other evening with that Irish actress,* very plain and simple, as the Maid, and became so infuriated with the Catholic mind, the male mind, the folly even of her spiritual conceit and self-satisfactions that I developed a raging headache. I shall never sit through it again. All I enjoyed was the farcical last act.

Helen Kirkpatrick is coming this week sometime with her husband. It will recall our collegiate adventure and its pleasures and the young Kennedy on the rostrum, perhaps our future president one day. . . .

This is not a dull letter, really. It is what I would say were you in the room, what is in my mind of truth and intimacy, my beloved one.

Shortly after Janet returned to Paris, she decided to join her friend Noël Murphy for a fortnight of mud-bath treatments at Abano, an old Roman site in the middle of the picturesque Colli Euganei, the lovely green hills near Padua famous for their natural deposits of hot mud. The ancient Romans came here to treat their arthritis by bathing in the hot springs, as people still do today. Janet wrote that "she smelled like a match in that mud circle of Dante's conception," and that the chief doctor said, after taking a look at her, "I suppose, madame, you keep in such splendid form at your age partly by cocktails and cigarettes," to which she had laughed and answered, "Yes." He had laughed with her and added, "You have a remarkable health and energy. Give her the 'little' treatment," he told the nurse, so "I got only one bucket of mud whereas Noël got two!!"

Despite the success of the treatments, especially for her friend, who had a more serious arthritic condition than she did, and now feeling much rested, Janet became quite depressed when having to concentrate on her health, away from her usual life and working

* *Saint Joan*, with Siobhan McKenna.

routine. "I shall be in Paris Wednesday morning, thank heaven. I have had three or four days of such melancholy as to have been volcanic in their blackness. I must say frankly that Madame de Staël is the woman who helped pull me through. I had read nothing she ever wrote: I now meet her safely after her death to be fascinated and consoled and stimulated by her mind and its particularities in *Mistress of an Age*, by Christopher Herold, certainly the finest biography I have read for many years."

Back in the forties, when we had lived together in New York, I had suggested to Janet that she take some exercise classes. I had always exercised and felt the need for it. That winter a friend of Janet's, George Hoyningen-Huene, the famous photographer of *Harper's Bazaar*, had told us about a special up-to-the-minute gym run by an ex-circus athlete, where he himself had built up his own muscular body. Fired by a vision of trapeze, ropes, ladders, *et al.*, I had convinced Janet that it would be good for our health to go there twice a week. We bought the equipment we needed and started our classes. Janet, who had never exercised in her entire life, was totally inept. I, on the other hand, was having the best time and felt in grand form. However, that was the year we caught the worst colds and flu of any of the winters we spent in New York.

"Dammit, give me a smoked-in bar and a good old martini anytime," exclaimed Janet, blowing her nose. And depression set in.

That had been the first and last attempt I ever made to get Janet interested in exercise of any kind, so I could well imagine her depression at Abano, where there was little else to do except sit in hot mud and eat good food. "I am still terribly melancholy," she wrote as soon as she returned to Paris at the end of May. "I can think of nothing except the errors in conduct or judgment I've made in my life, the crass actions or mistakes, the coarseness of youth. . . . Never have I appreciated Italian food as I did this time. Already French food displeases me beyond measure; no taste in it, no savour. And I miss the Colli Euganei, like enormous pine trees in shades of blue on the horizon. . . . I am back on yogurt for lunch after having reveled in artichokes in oil, fettuccine, calamaretti, prosciutto, good broth instead of French broths made from bouillon cubes and that darling little lettuce no bigger than your thumb, with oregano in the dressing which I discover to be Sweet Marjoram of Shakespeare's time. . . ."

While Janet was indulging in self-examination, I became involved once more with Anna Magnani. She had arrived in New York to do another film, one based on Tennessee Williams's *Orpheus Descending*, and had called on me to be of assistance during rehearsals, which were to be held in New York under the direction of Sidney Lumet, a new young director whose *Twelve Angry Men* had so captivated Anna that she had asked for him to be the director of her second film in America. She had also insisted on having Marlon Brando as her co-star. To entice him into accepting the part of Orpheus, she had written a twelve-page letter to Tennessee suggesting enlarging his part, making it more important than hers. I remember how astonished Audrey Wood had been when she saw that letter.

Anna admired Marlon. She felt she had finally met an actor of her own quality, and she had a soft spot for him in her heart.

I remember the evening they spent together during her first visit to New York in 1951, riding on the subway and on the ferry to Staten Island, because Brando had wanted to show Anna the skyline of New York. I, who had been asked by Anna to go along and had reluctantly accepted, felt somehow responsible for these two movie stars. The astonishing thing was that no one recognized them. People never see faces when they look, nor imagine that movie stars would ever ride on subways, which, of course, they almost never do.

What persuaded Brando to accept the role of Orpheus was neither Anna nor his enlarged part, but simply one million dollars, which in 1959 was quite a sum. Anna was overjoyed, but soon disappointment set in. Brando remained aloof, seemed uninterested, mumbled his lines, was always on the defensive. I could see that Anna was going to have trouble with this film. "Nat," said Anna, on leaving, "if I send you an SOS, please come." The location had been selected around Poughkeepsie, in upstate New York.

"That you are living under the reign of Anna the Great, as passionate and tyrannical as Catherine of Russia but more dramatic, gives you a new international standing, like an ambassadress, unpaid, alas, but freer that way," wrote Janet, when she received my news.

During this period, Mondadori arrived with his wife, Andreina. His presence liberated me from Anna's demands on my time. New York was a revelation to the Mondadoris. It was touching to see the Presidente's ecstatic expression as he looked at the majestic city and its buildings.

Strolling down Fifth Avenue one day, I pointed out a group of small buildings next to a church. "Why don't you buy one of them and open an international bookstore in New York?" I asked him. He shook his head as if to say that the stakes were beyond his wildest dreams. "I am only a publisher," he answered. A few years later, Angelo Rizzoli, his greatest competitor, would open the most elegant international bookstore in one of those buildings, and for eleven years I would occupy the equally elegant office above it as vice-president in charge. By that time, Mondadori had retired. On one of his trips to New York he came to see me at Rizzoli. Looking sad but smiling, friendly and, in appreciation, he said, "Cara Natalia, one makes mistakes in life."

A few weeks after the Mondadoris' departure, I was summoned by a frantic Anna, on location upstate. "I cannot arrive on a set all marked out. I cannot act worrying where I must stand or move to . . . Tell Lumet, explain to him I cannot work that way . . . He must allow me to act the way I feel and know. If he doesn't like it, I'll do it his way, but first he must give me freedom. . . ."

She was troubled by Brando's behavior, too. He never talked to her; he was sullen, distant. "What did I do to him? Why doesn't he talk to me? He avoids me. Why?"

Then there was the question of screen credits. Brando's agents had demanded first billing over Anna everywhere in the world. Anna was offended. "Not even in my own country, in Italy, my name can come first? And in South America where I am better known than Brando?" The atmosphere on that set was all gloom and doom, just as in Williams's play itself. Anna herself, in fact, was a Williams heroine.

"So now you are at Poughkeepsie with Anna," wrote Janet on June 23, "the best arrangement you could have made, I feel, for the exigencies of affection and help that she demands. I can well believe that with a combination of autocracy, nervousness, the loneliness of being a foreigner among indigènes who may well be illiterate or even mental thieves, an actress experienced in her technique and above all her own bitter disappointments, she feels that you and only you can fill the bill, as her honest, stalwart, intelligent, reliable friend. A pity you won't be paid for it, frankly."

Eventually Anna became less tense and I returned to my more peaceful, reasonable, pleasant job, now more appreciated than ever; I was looking forward to Janet's arrival in August. She herself had had misgivings. She was worried about the Magnani profile she had been considering as one of her next projects, while staying in the United States.

"I'm very frightened of this assignment, as I told you. I take interviews badly, become all mixed up, can't write fast enough, never ask the right, constructive, chronological questions, and so on. . . ."

At my suggestion she was planning to come to New York to start interviewing Anna at the end of the film. But Janet was convinced she would be too nervous, exhausted, without any notion of the routine work that interviews demanded. What she suggested to Shawn was a "character" profile of Anna's eccentricities, talent and nature, comparing her tragic genius in acting as related to her tragic, dramatic personal life.

In case the profile wouldn't work, she had other ideas in mind that would give her enough to do while in New York.

Meanwhile, Gypsy Rose Lee, one of our favorite and funniest friends, best known as the most successful stripteaser in history and the author of a murder mystery and several stories published by *The New Yorker*, was staying in Paris at her hotel, on her way to Yugoslavia via Rome. She told Janet she thought Anna was the most influential screen personality of the day, a woman who had, with her shabby hair and manner of dress, set a style for young people everywhere. This encouraged Janet.

[June 28, 1959]

Darling one,

This letter contains the carbon of a letter to Shawn about Buffet, Magnani and also a new idea for a profile, Mlle. Nadia Boulanger, the musician, as you will see. I am sending a carbon of this present letter to your New York flat in case you have left Poughkeepsie, trusting in that case that the Poughkeepsie Hotel will return its copy and also that of the Shawn letter. I hope I make clear that I am not in any way anything but honored at the idea of doing Anna, but the extreme trouble I had with Buffet has lowered my sense of surety on profiles generally that are difficult to get, as she will be. I don't really think even you could persuade Anna, any place, either New York or Rome, to give enough question and answer interviews with me to base a regular factual profile on, and furthermore I think it would be dull. Also unworthy. It is SHE, it is her character, her genius that counts. I imagine the profile I could do as being on those lines, for the reader a great relief from these promenades of facts, dates, events which have become our monotonous style (or so readers frankly complain).

As you see, I have asked Shawn to answer at once about the Boulanger so I can start material on that, to be needed in any case in New York after the Magnani piece is done, if he agrees to my suggested treatment of that, and if we can get enough for it; however, that I feel practically sure of. This new treatment idea interests me in any case, which will be an aid.

Gypsy is here (also dear Marc Blitzstein, seeing him and Miss Lee Thursday, also Virgil [Thomson], for drinks). She is funnier than ever, funnier stories, which she acts out, half-dressed in her room, with son Eric and some albino actor who seems to be chauffeur-handyman for her Rolls-Royce, en route to Rome, then Yugoslavia, because has never been there. She is always a burden, bless her heart. She has arrived with 15 millimeter films she took on voyage and France en route from Havre. Wants them developed in twenty-four hours, also sound track shifted to tape recorder, to send to NBC to Jack Paar. If good enough, she will send more, to be paid for, to be used in her absence on his program. All this she wanted done between Friday night and Tuesday night. She leaves Wednesday for Rome. Impossible, of course, though I had to make as many useless phone calls for her, to offices that didn't answer, as if there was a chance. Finally I have suggested she look up Franca in Rome who will, of course, adore her, for your sake as well. Ask Franca where to have film sound and tape printed or whatever, some in color naturally, to make it harder. This she has accepted. Is phoning Franca tomorrow, Monday night.

. . . You can imagine all the phoning I have done in the midst of a Paris letter. Also, Gypsy has ordered new corsets and shoes from her special corsetier and bottier, bringing back old shoes to be recopied, new shoes he made wrong last year—I cannot TELL you the complications, especially with her French! Last night she had a nightmare, dreamed her house was on fire, her animals burned, and also Eric her son. At one a.m. she phoned the desk downstairs, asking where the fire escape was. She had had a nightmare about her son and animals burning in New York. The man at the desk became alarmed, shouted, "Fire? Ees zis hotel en fire, mon dieu, ow much damages is your room burned?" It took an hour to make him understand she had only dreamed all this. Then he told her dreaming of fire was "verrreee verreee looky." Lucky—and she took a sleeping pill. My God, they will probably never let her in here again, though I had to use pressure this time. Hotels all packed, especially as this hotel has no fire escapes. Apparently she also told the desk man that the staircase (which she had inspected in her nightie) was made of wood. "Oh yes, madame, verreee fine wooood, ma'oganneee." It must have been a riot.

I must get back to work IF I can. I thought we were dining tonight, but as they didn't find me in the bar at six—it is closed on Sunday—they tootled out, had high tea, cheese, God knows what, so now after laughing an hour I shall dine alone. She is the funniest, drollest woman on earth, a wonderful friend, and I adore her. Next time she comes, I am going to hire an office staff, a hypnotizer, somebody from the Folies-Bergère to give corseting advice and a large French fireman with a bucket outside her door.

Love, kisses, love darlinghissima . . .

[July 10, 1959]

Darling Natalia,

It has been 110 in the sun, according to the kitchen thermometer on my floor at four this afternoon. There is, however, a breeze, unlike that oven of palisades and banks forming the Valley of the Hudson River where you must have suffered. Your pencil letter on yellow paper written in Poughkeepsie came last night. I cannot for the life of me recall any Declaration of Independence that I have written you lately which could have roused your admiration, as you recount, so give me a hint later. I have not felt uproariously independent in this heat and the slow waiting for an answer from Shawn, still not arrived. No answer to my letter about the psychological rather than factual profile of Anna, no answer about Mlle. Boulanger, certainly a less exciting personality than Anna, but as an intellectual more in my line and far easier to do, though he must give me time to collect some material here before leaving if he wants it. No answer about the Buffet nor proofs. After all these weeks of waiting, it is useless to cable an inquiry again to Botsford who will handle the Buffet profile. As for Anna, providing that Bill accepts the psychological angle, rather than the historical, and after changing our ideas of dates from August to September and now back to August, for my New York arrival, I think the obviously intelligent thing for me to do is to wait until her arrival in Rome, then go to talk to her, to find out what in her life interests HER to be recorded and above all to see and take notes on her wonderful apartment and what is in it, what it looks down on, what the building formerly was, whom it belonged to, etc. This is the kind of physical esthetic background I MUST have to work and see her on the sidewalk at Rosati's, with everyone stopping to stare at her at night.

These two elements will be like photographic material for me. I could do them both in three or four days in Rome. Then I would come to New York late in September. That the flat will be empty is a loss that will have to be carried, that's all, and I expected it, darling.

Lucky it did not happen before, owing to your energy in finding a lessee.

I have not been either pleased with my Paris Letters of late or filled with hope about New York, so these, coupled with the delay and lack of interest in the office in giving me any answers to my queries, have depressed me. I gathered from the parts of your postcard's last lines that something had made your situation with Mondadori much better so that is a relief. That you want to go to Rome and Sperlonga in May is all right with me, too. That you may be able to purchase the other property is, of course, encouraging to the highest degree.

I have a postal from Gypsy in Venice, so she has passed through Rome and out the other end of Italy for Yugoslavia. . . . I must get back to work on my Paris Letter. Am dining tonight with Peggy Bernier and Olivier, the son, after his first year at Harvard which should be a treat. God knows where George is. It must be a paralyzing experience to be present at making that film in which you know Brando receives a million dollars as his actor fee. We were born under different financial stars, you and I, my love.

[July 31, 1959]

Natalia cara,

The cable I received from Shawn of *The New Yorker* this morning, at last, clarifies the Magnani Profile idea as I expressed it in detail to him more than a month ago. He is enthusiastic about my idea of the treatment—a character Profile, one of the essence of her genius, personality (good and bad), her ways of work, mannerisms, moods, appetites, preferences, distastes—the physical, psychical and artistical Anna, an essence like something in not too big a bottle which through condensation is like the perfume or smell of her, as from a liqueur Magnani. Behind this must be only sufficient framework of a few important events in her life—a flash of childhood in the convent, where it was located, its importance lying in the education it gave her in French par example; then whatever references to her mature life in the early days she would choose to give, still only like a frame to enclose her in. Her marriage (since there is a son), her first theatrical experiences, what theater, when, what did she sing, when. These will be scattered around, these facts, like croutons in a broth made of real flesh, à l'Italienne. You spoke of two Profiles or explicit articles written about her in Italian, one by Barzini as I recall. Have you copies in Italian? Has Audrey? These will be invaluable frame material I should think. Then a summing up of her by Tennessee is of vital importance, obviously.

His notion of what acting talent consists of, how hers differs from that of anyone else, why she *satisfies* him, what she sums up that leads him back to her again and again, culminating at last in this present film. What he thinks her best films to date have been, why. Frank's chirpy opinions; he is as shrewd as a sparrow. Whatever Audrey can say about her as a business proposition would be invaluable. How do most actresses act about money and contracts? Is Anna anything like them? I rely on a great carefully illuminated and illuminating amount of comment from Audrey. Then the director's opinion, that of a couple of grips. Anyone's opinion that sheds light or darkness on her makeup, her entity. The son's illness and operation, as much of their family relation as can be told. And what she symbolizes today to the film public in the western hemisphere; how differing from the other two great European stars and their influences—Garbo, Dietrich.

I might add, with dry detachment, if such be possible where your knowledge of her is concerned, that your mind and observation, memory and interpretations will be of the most vital importance, because of your sense of almost fatalistic justice. I want to recall and picture Anna sitting there on the sidewalk at Rosati's, the sidewalk queen, receiving (with a kind of sense of burning sensibility on her part, part pleasure, part imprisonment) the gaze, the concentrated stares of the little crowd of Romans that collect to look, to whisper, to give her her due.

It is very difficult, especially on a character Profile of so difficult and emotional a female of Thespian genius as she, to say in advance what one wants, to write with, to work on. One wants all. I was bitterly disappointed that we could not hear each other on the transatlantic phone today. It must be the sun. By now it should be breaking out with its own spots, like fever. Bless you, darling, and thanks.

[July 31, 1959]

Darling,

For the first time I had nearly no pleasure in hearing your voice because I could understand nearly nothing of your words, except your opening ones that it is hot today in New York! For the rest, we sounded like a couple of old bassos, voices deepened to low G by cigarettes, shouting amiably at each other across the Atlantic. This

Magnani Profile seems to have had the gypsy curse put on it except
that Shawn is enthusiastic about my idea of the treatment. I shall now
repeat his cable received this morning so you may read what I could
not make you hear! "Janet dear, your Paris Letters have been full of
life and surprises lately. Despite the heat you have been going fine.
Buffet proofs were mailed to you today. Hope we can run Profile in
September. Do you think you might ask Buffet if he has any self-
portrait we might use as illustration for Profile? We would naturally
pay for right to reproduce the drawing, but the drawing itself would
remain his property. Yes, Magnani done as you outline would be
exactly right. We have been trying lately to get more Profiles done
just that way. It is one of my main objectives at present, and it is the
kind of profile you could do superbly. Boulanger is also okay as a
subject, love, Bill."

As this is literally the first communication on work or anything I
have had from the magazine in nine or ten months—which was why
I flew out to New York this spring, to find out how the Buffet really
stood—I am now greatly strengthened by this cable from him. I had
cabled twice to know where the proofs were, had explained why I
had to have them before the holidays, because Buffet has bought a
boat and might be fishing God knows where and he or his wife who
speaks excellent English, Marie-Louise Bousquet says, must read it
to check the facts.

Marie-Louise just heard from him that he is in residence at his
château, luckily for me, unluckily for him, poor man. He has rheu-
matism and is taking thermal baths near Aix in some little grotto. I
shall try to phone him again tonight. This morning at eleven the
servant said they were already out—I had been told he is never
awake until eleven—but would be in this evening. He phoned Marie-
Louise last night, but she was out.

I am dining with her tonight and shall ask her to phone him, to
plead my cause. I was not even sure they really were out, but that
out of nonchalance natural to him and perhaps pique that his Profile
has been delayed for a year and a half he did not choose to speak to
me. After dining with her and talking to him if possible, if he will
receive me this next week, I will fly to Marseilles and taxi to his
château with the proofs, providing they come Monday as they should.

Pardon my boring you and me with all this. I could have condensed
it, should have. But it has shaken me considerably which made me add
lost confidence to my worry about being able to do Anna. Anyhow, I
feel greatly refreshed on it as a possibility and shall start it with hope

and vigor. With Tennessee in Cuba, that is another snag! I think it absolutely vitally necessary to have his ideas on her as an artist and personality. It will sound almost like puffing his own film, I suppose, except we know he thought it before. This is an interview which, if he goes to Japan before I arrive, you will have to take for me, my darling, please. . . .

Also, Frank's sharp, observing mind should be heard from, very important. We would not necessarily name him because he is too well known as Tenn's Boy Friend, but could use his views. Also Audrey's, also the director's, gripmen, anybody in the cast whose sense of observation or blunt opinion could help. I don't mean this to sound like a series of interviews only, but they will be ESSENTIAL for me, knowing how little I understand or know her. Has she any pictures of her flat which would show its objects and setting? That would have to serve me as a reminder of it, as background, also essential. I must try to finish this letter and enclose the queries you asked for to give Audrey before the six o'clock collection of mail.

Janet decided to fly to New York on August 28, after Shawn had answered yes to the Magnani character Profile. The intervening correspondence was mostly about collecting the necessary information from Tennessee Williams, who was planning to fly to Japan as soon as the filming had ended. The movie by this time had been retitled *The Fugitive Kind.* Anna had immediately realized the importance of having a Profile in *The New Yorker,* written by Janet whom she had met before and liked, and was all set to collaborate.

[August 8, 1959]

Sunday. Grey, chill, yet promising warmer, perhaps through human optimism. Yes, do tell darling Anna how much Shawn wants the profile. You heard him. Knowing the magazine's standards, I doubt he would consider that newspaper or even movie magazine press releases on her life story in such fragments as they use would interfere with his interest in what he considered our complete, penetrating profile, in its superior form. A long life story on her run by the *Atlantic Monthly,* let's say, or even worse the *Satevpost* could, however, cancel my Profile I would think. I will come to New York late in August if you think that the right time to gather material just before she has finished the film. I cannot do it without you, and this will be unsatisfactory because hurried then, plus her fatigue. You and I might have to fly to Rome (my expense) for a fortnight for more leisurely flow of reminiscence.

Another thing which could make my Profile impoverished would be her deliberate withholding of interestingly intimate background material which she would wish to save for her memoirs which she will never write, or which few who are not professional writers ever do. Her life story by her serialized in *Epoca* and published in book form in Italy would be a big thing there, if and when, but could not be envisaged as aiding in giving attention to her within this next year, as my Profile would, in the U.S.A., which would count more and where her book, once translated, which would take a year, would not be a *fait accompli* until around 1965, I am willing to wager. These will doubtless be weak arguments against her egotism, her sense of struggle against all others, her emotional intimacy with herself in battle against the world. The most illuminating periods for me would be enough fragments on her childhood, education, grandmother who reared her, etc., and her debut in Rome as *chansonnière* or whatever she was, with types of songs, descriptions of theater and its conditions, and *Città Aperta* with Roberto, all her early film work and success.

Then, of course, the tragedy of her son. It was a pity she was given no prize at all at Cannes. Only once was her name mentioned in possible relation, as the best actress of the year. Have you any idea when *Orpheus* will be released in New York? Impossible surely for me to have profile finished until early spring . . . you know me.

Your outbreak, your rebellion in your last letter against Le Système de Mondadori broke my heart. You are like someone either in prison or, both better and worse, like a courtier of intelligence in some backward provincial duchy where needed reforms and vision are strangled by the other courtiers and the old duke is unavailable, so busy he cannot listen. It is not only the lack of comprehension and intelligence Milan and Verona show, not even the intrigues which I suppose are an inherited, highly appreciated factor in Italian life in business today since the Medicis and Borgias are dead, but the injustice which rankles, and, in you, as an intelligent worker female, it is poison, like putting a drop of poison on a worker bee. How can she fly? How hunt flowers efficiently? Let's say that flower hunting in your case would consist of trying to put some money by for your future. You mention considering looking very quietly for a job with some American New York firm of publishers.

You have talked of it before, though your loyalty paralyzes you. I believe if only to satisfy your curiosity you should now seriously make such queries.

I am very touched you went to the Academy party. They, unlike Mike, bombard me with official letters, inquiries, booklets, requests for votes on this and that, now a nomination for a gold medalist of 1959, on previous work. Well, I gladly nominated Mary McCarthy and listed five lines of the most cogent reasons. Glen [Glenway Wescott] is, alas, in his glory as president. (Damn it, it is going to rain.) What a time-wasting exploit of vanity.

Dined with Kenneth [Tynan] last night. Very elegant, fussy French costly food at Drouant which, frankly, I loathed. He loved it, with marvelous Maison Lafite-Rothschild, 1953, which was perfection. Then off to see old Josephine Baker at Olympia in her revival and review, a third-rate Folies, but she quite wondrous, cheered and bravoed. Why do aging actresses or dancers try to do feats of physical danger which they never bothered to attempt when young enough to give the audience no sense of danger? Garson Kanin and Ruth Gordon here, lunching at wonderful Hotel Berkeley on Friday. He will write next year a play on Lael Wertenbaker.* Love story with Charles and his death. In the meantime, am working on New York version of *La Bonne Soupe*. *You* are that to me.

[August 14, 1959]

Darlinghissima,

Your fine letter yesterday, filled with helpful reports of your helpfulness, it can't be put more completely, greeted me at cocktail hour last night. The tape recording of Tennessee's views on Anna and your managing to obtain it, by having Audrey make no engagements for him that second day, was sheer genius of management, and I thank you and indeed him, infinitely. I shall write to thank him from New York. The tape recording was a better idea, something I have heard of but do not know personally, in my old-fashioned way having had to resort only to costly stenotypists.

Rebecca West's review of Thurber's book on Ross** in the London *Sunday Times* I believe I sent to you. Her main deadly point was

---

* Based on her book about the death of her husband, *The Death of a Man*.
** *The Years with Ross.*

that the comicalness of Ross as a human might lie only in the eye of the beholder—i.e., Thurber in this case. She has written me twice on the subject. I have been very careful to give her no quotable quips (because she is a great gossip and repeater), to explain *why*, in my honest opinion, his blindness has led his friends to realize he is beyond reforming, like a man over the horizon on his own desert of remembrances, many of which are sterile, lack greenery and the natural urban communicating touch. Mind you, some of *her* ideas also are pretty odd and beyond correctives that are logical, such as in today's letter. She wonders if there is a plot on by denigrating Ross, dead, to rid the magazine of its Ross-man who is Shawn, as part of what she calls "this well-rehearsed maneuver, this unspontaneous business" of pretending that Ross had no social conscience, paid poorly, was an ignoramus, "but a great editor" though never giving any proof of that, otherwise than his hiring White, Gibbs, Mitchell, Thurber and Liebling.

I thought Liebling's piece, sent me holographed by Woodward, our London businessman for the magazine, was the worst. It was dialect *thinking*, not just writing. It was an account of finding out what the boys in the back room would have, now that Ross was dead and still paying for the drinks—and thinks. It was funny, too, as all the funeral pieces on Ross. Strange that both these staff writers and all the Left Wing critics who liked Thurber's books—Muggeridge in the *New Statesman*—are men of such strong political consciousness that they can hardly hold their pens straight for roaring with laughter. Au fond I think that your comment once is still right; that it is jealousy that has turned their wits, that put poor blind Thurber on a zigzagging destructive track, trying to find that it led more to his glory than Ross's. I know this bores you; it doesn't bore me.

I enclose Sam Behrman's letter, which Rebecca sent a copy of to me today. Read and save it for me. I never heard of *Commentary* magazine before. Now, don't say that I should attack Thurber to his face. I did, to his drunken face to boot, since that was the moment the scene came up.

Lunched with Ed Morgan today, just back from Siberia with Nixon. In some remote Siberian big city he with the others of the press went to see *Swan Lake* danced. He entered through the swarming Russian crowd with Jinx Falkenburg, who was wearing a leopard-patterned wrap-around garment that looked, he said, wonderful, fashionable, exotic, but was really a raincoat since she had not had time to dress. The Russians were so delighted that they applauded her, thinking it an evening garment. They were followed into the theater, in the other aisle a moment later, by a Negro who is the editor of the Negro magazine *Ebony*, and his much lighter Negress wife. They walked down the aisle in an absolute silence, a hush from the crowd as it observed them. Later, one local Russian who spoke English said to Ed, "We none of us have ever seen a Negro before. It was a wonderful, impressive sight to see a new kind of man. We noticed that his lady was much lighter in color. Are Negroes then like birds, perhaps? Is the female always less deeply colored than the male?"

What a charming, strange story, so true to an observer of nature. Ed said he used it in his broadcast. . . .

Janet arrived in New York on August 29. She panicked every time she took a plane. This time she had managed to twist her left foot a week earlier, so she arrived limping but spirited. She had been alarmed, too, that week by the electricity blackout in New York, which did not last long, but "demonstrated how dependent modern man is, whether in New York or Moscow; how much more wisdom is demanded to meet his helplessness in a crisis in civic life, as the editorial of the *New York Times* pointed out the next day," wrote Janet, thinking of us, Mother and myself, in it and the climbing of the seven flights of stairs to our flat.

We met early in the morning, Janet slightly drugged by her Dramamine, but looking well, elegant as usual, and relieved to have landed safely. Our meetings were always jolly because of the happiness they generated. This time was no exception. And there was work to do, besides.

Anna returned to New York at the end of the picture for a brief stay before going back to Italy. During this time, Janet had a chance to see her, following her in her activities and joining in the fun at night. But I could see that Janet was still in doubt about the profile. Her heart was not in it.

We planned to meet again in Rome or in Paris, where Anna visited often, for a more leisurely flow of reminiscences.

Before Janet left for the coast, and as soon as Anna had sailed for Italy, we took a vacation at our favorite place, the house on Fire Island.

In September the sun is still warm, though the air is cool. You can already smell the approaching autumn. The immense ocean is calm and warm. The sunsets over the Great South Bay, just in front of our deck, are bright red and the entire sky lights up in a variety of colors as the evening slowly descends. The birds fly low over the water;

the white sails turn for home. Lights begin to flicker along the distant shoreline. Soon it will be dark. It is then that you can sit in front of an early fire in the intimacy of the end of a day, and realize what happiness is, how happy you can be. But the hurricane season, with its winds, storms and rains, begins to threaten and blow. You must leave, close the shutters, board up the doors. The leisure and the dreams are over; the long winter months are around the corner.

We didn't spend Christmas together. This year Janet was spending it with her family in Altadena. We soon said good-bye again. It would be for a shorter period this time, perhaps for only two months or so. A special time to look forward to.

I looked at myself; I looked at Janet; at my extraordinary mother, aging so gently, writing poetry, participating in the life around her, kind, understanding, serene, without bitterness or complaints; I looked at Bill, struggling as a writer, happy, amusing and fun, his catchy resounding laughter his signature; at Doris, matching the humor, the fun, the handsomeness; at tottering, comic, curly-haired four-year-old Doodie; I felt content to have such riches in my life. I felt blessed. I almost could savor the intensity of the feeling.

The Sixties

1960

As we entered the sixties, our lives had acquired a rhythmic pattern. As a rule, we would be together twice a year. Janet had been coming more regularly to the States, and I would go to Italy once a year, partly on business and partly on vacation. We would meet either in Milan or Rome, or I would fly to Paris, pick up Janet and we would proceed to Italy together. But every year we would plan to spend some time alone, make side trips to some foreign land just to be refreshed by new sights and to find ourselves again, in terms of each other.

Work had been of paramount importance to Janet all her life. It had first call on her time, because writing for her was an overwhelming urge—a real, deep pleasure, like eating or drinking. I had resented it in the beginning, but as time went on and her superb health and energy slowly waned, so did her intensity and the demands she made on herself. In 1960 Janet would be sixty-eight. She became more ready to give up her Paris life and habits to be with me for longer periods. She became more relaxed, more conscious of my needs and wishes. By then, of course, she had become famous, a public personality.

On the other hand, I had become deeply involved in my own career, less demanding of Janet's time, more understanding of her special needs. I was also enjoying my work, pleased by its success and the appreciation it received. What had troubled me earlier—challenging the accepted social tenets of the day by living openly according to my beliefs, in honesty and truthfulness—had ceased to upset me. After all, Janet and I were two mature women when we had met; we had led full earlier lives, our experience and independence had given us the right to choose the kind of life we wanted to lead; our tastes, backgrounds, ideas, interests, if not always identical, could at least complement each other, and our careers ran on somewhat parallel lines.

Our lives, therefore, had become more pleasurable, more satisfactory. Our respective families had become very fond of both of us. Mine, the larger of the two, actually adopted Janet as one of its own. She had a deep admiration, a real fondness for my mother, and a genuine affection and appreciation of my son, Bill. If she had at times been impatient and critical of him as a teenager, she had watched his career as a writer with interest and approbation, and was proud that he had shown signs of wanting to follow in her footsteps by going to work for *The New Yorker* and writing for the magazine. She had also followed with keen interest the dramatic events in my sisters' lives during the war. She was particularly fond of Franca, just as I had become attached to Hildegarde, the youngest of Janet's two sisters. Maria, the older, a musician, never married, and often exuded unhappiness and loneliness. But not Hildegarde, the poet, who was gentle, warm, tender, humorous, with a superior intellect and in love with nature. She was very happy with her architect husband, who was equally cultured, a good artist and just as eccentric. Their company was a a treat for the mind. Their only son Jan was born late in their marriage. He was very handsome, a typical American teenager when I met him, perhaps a bit overwhelmed by his intellectual parents and aunt, who pinned such high hopes on him. Like many youngsters of the period, he sometimes rebeled against his elders and was panting to live his own life, an attitude that disturbed and occasionally shocked them.

The 1960s was mainly a period of family affairs—marriages, births and adjustments. Janet had been spending the holidays with her family in California, where she always enjoyed herself. This time, though, she found some tension in the air between father and son. Her nephew, Jan (who had been named after her), had, much to her bafflement, changed his name to John and acquired a teenage bride by eloping to a neighboring state where parental permission wasn't required. His father's understandable fury had taken the form of a disapproving silence. Despite her critical attitude of youth in general and of her nephew in particular, Janet, simply by her presence, had helped to ease a painful situation, one in which Hildegarde, caught in the middle, had been the main sufferer.

My sister Franca's son, Fritzy, who had been living with me in New York studying photography for his intended career in films, had moved to the Village, where he went around with a young crowd that included an attractive girl named Merrill, but who was better known by her very appropriate nickname of Pixie. They got married in June. He was twenty-two, she barely eighteen.

"*Santo Cielo!*" wrote Franca in distress from Rome, skeptical of this union's chance of success. "So soon . . . what are they going to live on? . . ." Relations between mother and son became strained; Franca couldn't come to the wedding. She was working. I went in her stead and then tried to pacify Franca, though I could see her point.

My housekeeper Maria's situation had also become a continuing worry. For years she had been hounded by the Immigration authorities. She had finally been summoned to appear before Senator McCarran's committee in Washington, D.C., which refused to grant her the green card of residency and decreed that, to remain in the States, she would have to have diplomatic immunity. A bachelor diplomat friend jumped at the opportunity to employ her. Sheltered under his diplomatic umbrella and passed on to each successor in the post for several more years, Maria was able to remain in the country. Her daughter, Gemma, born in the U.S., would be ready to go to college by the time Maria was finally granted her green card, but she was still frightened and worried.

In August, my second grandchild was born. She was given the pretty Roman name of Julia.

The truly sad news concerned Ester. She was slowly losing her sight. She would spend her long days of solitude listening to music and radio news. Sometimes I would find her bent over a large sheet of paper on her desk, writing poetry. She often spoke of Italy, with a tinge of nostalgia in her voice. This year she would be eighty-two. I hadn't thought of age until I saw it in my mother. My own hair was turning white, though Janet's had always been that way. It didn't matter; she didn't seem older to me. We did not *feel* older. Our loving tender feelings for each other had not grown dim with time; if anything, they had evolved, increased, deepened. For me, Janet was immutable, unique and eternal.

"We have been like two caryatids, carrying our burden but with the classic beauty of the post and carvings of love on our faces, as time proceeds, and we remain in our small way two of its most tender ornaments," wrote Janet on her birthday, March 13.

As we entered the new decade, the political atmosphere was one of peaceful détente, except for the still-unresolved Algerian situation. In the spring, a summit meeting had been scheduled in Paris between President Eisenhower and Soviet Premier Nikita Khrushchev.

Once more, hopes for a peaceful world flourished, only to be dispelled in May, when an American U-2 plane was shot down by the Russians over their territory and the pilot imprisoned. The summit was cancelled; tension returned.

In November we would have a new president, John F. Kennedy, who was to rekindle our hopes. At the beginning of the year, the omens had seemed fairly good.

Janet's letters from Altadena vividly described her visit to Hildegarde and Eric:

[February 4, 1960]

. . . Hildegarde and I leave at eight a.m. tomorrow, that is this morning, it is now running on toward two o'clock I see, for Santa Ynez, to lunch and spend the day with her friends, the Walter Thompsons, for whom Eric is building a magnificent house. They have 1,700 acres now, two peacocks, a cockatoo, had two of John's bantam chickens but the dear little old cock, named FDR—this shows his age—died last week . . . simply failed to get up for breakfast, pampered to the end. They also have a Dalmatian bitch, who is a fool I hear, and eleven cats whom Holly feeds personally, and usually about a dozen brood mares, as they have a stallion at stud. He is supposed to breed race horses. Well, the tragedy is that though he has only just arrived from England, where he was bought for thousands of dollars, the poor dear is impotent! My God, what a scandal. The vet is feeding him hormones, biotics, calcium, heaven knows what, probably orchids if he has a taste for them. It's a tragedy and a disgrace for their stable, but I burst into roars of laughter. All three of us did when Eric came back with the shameful news. (A dove in a cypress tree outside is singing to himself; he does almost every night at this hour.)

I adore my days with Hildegarde. She is such a charmer, has such fantasy and spirit. She is certainly an eccentric. The other day I asked if she had three pennies. I needed them so as not to break a large bill in paying for something. She said yes, she thought she had, emptied her change purse and out fell two small peach stones, three berries and a lovely little pebble she had picked up someplace and the three pennies. She bought me a stunning pair of black slacks. They look like basketweave, lined with silk, match my new sweater wonderfully. Bought for herself some tricot black ones. I also bought myself a pair of black suede pumps to wear with them, black stretch socks with a tiny scarlet pattern like a butterfly, and a watermelon satin shirt!! I look rather well in it all. . . .

I dined with Romain Gary and Lesley [Blanch], gave her your love. We had a divine evening. It seemed so sophisticated, cynical and gay, after my families' superior, unworldly intelligence. . . .

[February 18, 1960]

Darlinghissima,

Both your fine explicit letters, as full of good news as a fruit tree in spring blossom—with one tragic exception, Maria's news—are to hand, the second returned from you via Calistoga came yesterday. It had not arrived when I was there where we were marooned in the little ranch house on the property by a rainfall of five inches in thirty hours, which washed out our hill driveway, depositing much of it on the disaffected high road below and cutting crevasses in the road surface that were nearly a yard deep. Eric and I spent a day filling up the crevasses with boulders. Hildegarde worked with the hired man they keep there, fortunately an old Massachusetts chap, fired with morality and a zeal for truth and work, cleaning out the culvert at the hill top which had become clogged by an overflow from a little dam, belonging to neighbors absent in San Francisco, while the rain kept coming down, the valley vineyards being completely under water.

At Yosemite, Eric ran his car into a snowbank while admiring the tremendous view of the mountain peaks under fog—admiring at our insistence, instead of merely keeping his eye on the park road as he should have, fortunately utterly flat, and we were stuck there for two hours, most peaceful in the blazing sunshine, which began melting the snow from the giant tall pines, and it fell along with little avalanches from the mountaintops with the sound of soft Gatling guns, like a war between sun and snow. Yosemite is a tremendous physical experience of nature, left intact for millions of years for our scientific eyes, after the glaciers passed over what must have been the original terrain, reshaping it in terms of drama. In such a national park lies the amazing splendid, savage beauty of the country, a scene created only by nature as artist, whereas your land contains the report of sentient artistic man.

Your news of Maria's wicked Christian treatment by those coarse, phallic politicians rouses me to fury. That she was praying with her rosary in hand while they were talking adultery is horrifying. Again it brings too vividly my hatred of what males have done with the masculine foundation of the Christian faith, turned it into two sexual repositories in which morality lies. In the Old Testament, the necessity for having the male organ circumcised and nipped off for the good Jews from whom we receive our notion of the monolithic single God, for the New Testament Christians the necessity, on the contrary, of keeping the female hymen intact until legal marriage . . . I have always despised the depositing of ethic and social morality between the legs. I can only ardently hope and believe that some kind of nonreligious justice and common sense will give the final coming interpretation to that noble good woman's international standing and citizenship so she may stand vindicated as the ardent example of mother love; and that surely must be the true basis of our civilization that we rant so about.

I passed a motel the other day in the San Joaquin Valley, returning by car with Hildegarde from Calistoga. It was near one of the Franciscan Spanish missions, and the sign read, "Madonna Motel. Vacancy." Just room for Joseph, I suppose . . .

Drew [Dudley, a friend of Janet's in Paris,] phoned last night for a long gossip. Thanks for giving him my phone numbers. He said Ruth Gordon and Garson's *Good Soup* had cancellations by all Jewish charities because author [Félicien] Marceau had been Belgian collaborator. As both are passionate anti-Nazis and Garson is a Jew, it is another form of belated social reaction to anti-Germanness, so rarely found today in the U.S.A. which yearns only to help the Germans grow rich and strong again as usual, a reaction which punishes the wrong people, it seems to me. Better punish the cartel of New York and Wall Street and Washington that reestablished the Krupp syndicate.

Yes, ten days will be pitifully short for us, but we have some summer time to vision in advance, thank God. I want to hear Thelonious Monk play.

I saw a report in vivid, brilliant writing this week in *The New*

Yorker by [Whitney] Balliett. Ask Bill to ask Balliett if these concerts and jam sessions continue. I want ONE EVENING of the best jazz possible. I invite you and me, Bill and Doris, and Santha and Phobian* if they are there on a party. Let's be gay, let's fill our ears with the new musical sound that reverberates in the composition of savage, inspired tonal mathematics. NO theater, please, unless you want to see *The Good Soup.*

I am terribly excited at our reunion again, my beloved. Even minus two invisible molars it will be a passionate joy. Alas for you that your splendid, impressive, elegant teeth begin to waver. My single weak one is still in my jaw, thank God, though my New York dentist feared it might fall into my coffee any day.

Have bought a new suit at Bullocks, summer suit, a Davidow, costly but thin, fine stuff.

I adore you, my darling.

By April, Janet was back in Paris:

[April 6, 1960]

My darlinghissima,

What a charmed and charming sobriquet is this word for you, corrected and bettered by your spelling after my invention of it, lacking one "h" like a bird lacking one feather for flight. It is useless to declare I do not know where the time has gone these last days. I know by looking at my notations of it in rendezvous for work mostly, some exceptions for pleasure, though even a portion of them turned out to be labor, at least laborious, too, notations written down in my new carnet for which I thank you for the sending, with apologies that you were bothered by consulting the manufacturer in your search for a red copy, as I had asked, not dreaming of the trouble it could be. At any rate, what you did send and thought was blue, mistakenly I am glad to say, is really black, the next best thing to red always, in fact, usually my substitute much of my life. I have thought "red," felt it, too, while masquerading as it were in conscious black, in dresses; black looked black to others but was to me privately red, the

---

* Santha Rama Rau, the Indian writer, and Faubion Bowers, who was an expert on Oriental dance and drama.

next best thing so often that in their positiveness, their positive op-positeness, they *were* the same thing, like the two lines aimed at infinity which meet.

I have worked very hard at the two *New Yorker* Letters with little in print to show for it, though long in length. The work does not show because whatever gift I sometimes have has been tied down, deadened by repetitive overwork, paralyzed by the movement of the clock hands and the calendar numbers as the hours or days moved and crushed. The second letter was injured by a different circumstance, by my sending three different endings for poor Botsford to choose from. He chose the last, but cut it in spots very clumsily. It is always wrong, at least in dealing with what I've written, to cut a part of a thought or incident out. It should all be cut out. In cutting a part, he made what was left not worth using, like serving the chicken's neck, having cut off the rest of its roasted carcass. There must always be taste in carving. I can blame only myself. I shall be surer of what we both do in the Letter I am now working on by giving myself limits and him no choice, or little.

I have just finished reading the last of the [Max] Beerbohm series. I did not restrain my tears at the news of his death, as fresh as if we readers all watched him die, in print, on that particular page, and Behrman's obit, chiseled by his own talent, but relating to the dead, in a way combining them both, major and minor talent (to have had such direction as Behrman gives it has given it permanent stature and high size). ". . . The discrepancy between the man and the mask was always slighter in Max than in most people, and by that time the two had become indistinguishable. Under the Maxian mask was, ultimately, Max." This series is the magazine's undubitable connec-tion with literature just as Hersey's *Hiroshima* was our undeniable relation with current history, both our singular private property and unique, for us too, and which would have had no immediate home in a weekly but for us, but for Shawn, a kind of hebdomadal glory in a way nor will it fade over years.

I saw Ionesco's *Rhinoceros* last night. It must have seemed a fable with more reality—like a rough, more durable lining on the back of tawdry silk—in the German original première at Dusseldorf, repeated by the same company here last week in the international theater program at the Sarah Bernhardt. That was horrible, but wore well at least. Barrault's Frenchified antics and preposterous stage activities, jumping, hopping, were farcical. Ionesco and wife took me to the theater in their taxi, from Josette Lazar's cocktail party for literary editor Brown of the *New York Times*, here on a visit. I dislike Ionesco more each time I meet him, though not necessarily each time I see him in a new play, his talent being more bearable than he, perhaps because more intermittent for me. He is a whining Roumanian.

I am reading *Le Guépard** in French. Am enjoying it with excitement and with sympathy. At first I found its language too fancy, perhaps the fault of the French language, not the Italian thinking. I still miss any sense of history itself as taking place, except through the rococo limitations of the decorative brain of the Prince, with no vista really except one on him himself, as a portrait, complete and satisfying as a person in a time, though the time, were it not dated once or twice in the book, could almost escape the reader as background. I cannot imagine how anyone—several readers have—identifies it with Stendhal, except that both are romantics and foreign to us and in themselves in their relation to Italy. The Sicilian focus of *The Leopard* is fascinating, informing, exotic. It is a book of dust, flowers, of dialect in thinking, of extravagant provincialism, whetted, fired to tragedy, comedy, decoration, remorse, oblation and diffusion. The character of Tancredi is dazzling, attracting. He and the Prince sharing magnetism for the reader. I know my opinion must and should sound illiterate in its limitations, so do not pass them on to darling Ester, who might be offended as if these were marks of lack of appreciation, of active sympathy and aesthetic interest on my part, for they are not. There is a coldness in Stendhal which makes him easier for me to drink. In *The Leopard*, I am most reminded by the subject matter only of Conrad's *The Arrow of Gold* about the Carlist coup in Spain, which in Conrad's scene takes place entirely in Marseilles. Monica is reading it in Italian, though with great difficulty and constant use of her dictionary when she has the time from correcting and rewriting her Napoleon's mother book by hand for the FOURTH time. Her arm is now semi-paralyzed.

This gives her time for the dictionary, I gather. Her book is remarkable. It is positively scholarly. It has grasp and retention. She stands every chance of popularity with it. She is thinner than a mackerel's bones, takes saccharin in her coffee for fear of gaining an ounce, is nervous, wraithlike, very happy. Odette is acting in rhythm

* *The Leopard*, by Giuseppe di Lampedusa.

with the springtime, like a clucking, happy, setting hen with one egg, half hatched, half still shelled and warm under her feathery bosom, is dieting for ten weeks to lose a kilo a week by omitting starch and all alcohol. . . .

[April 14, 1960]

Darlinghissima,

. . . So the Italian government has fallen again, if it could have been called one. I enclose some articles to show you how carefully Italian affairs are followed here. . . . The Italian political situation is always identical with the French except at the moment we have a man who makes a one-man government instead of two, having in the past a thousand-man confusion of aspirants, tricksters, men of greed and even of some intelligence and of much practice, all climbing on top of each other like insects hatching in spring from some enormous egg cell, all trying to quickly dry off their wings and fly—to the Avenue Matignon where power dwells. Temporarily and repeatedly, till de Gaulle came in and sat down hard.

I was surprised by a note from Ernst who said politely he did not agree with me about de Gaulle whom he admires as a strong political personality. But so do I. How can Ernst suppose that when I *report*, as I did in my first Paris Letter, the unfavorable situation he finds himself in—the one hundred years' Algerian War, farmers' riots, etc.—that I am enjoying what I write because I do not like the man. Truth is factual truth, isn't it? Scold him, darling. He will be re-influenced by the obvious panegyric on de Gaulle in London in this week's Paris Letter. It was a great mysterious event. Napoleon was popular from the beginning and fairly well comprehended. De Gaulle remains mysterious because, though the most literate literary chief France perhaps ever had, by policy he does not speak clearly. The cartoon showing his upper half, legs and stomach, saying to a cross little Mr. K at his knee, "Stop asking to meet the French people, Monsieur Khrushchev. I AM the French people," was truest of all.

I enclose Rebecca West's very great and simple piece of reporting from South Africa for fear you may not have seen it in last Sunday's London *Times*. I am taking an extra copy until the series is finished to send you air mail. I would not have believed until she explained it, how the trap sense, *le sens du piège*, could have so overpowered a man's mind as that of Mr. Verwoerd. A pity he was not killed definitely, in the complicated invisible labyrinths of pass books, constrictions for living and working, for sex or for even walking about, that his ingenuity imposed on the Afrikaaners in an effort to shrink their size, as it were, compared with the whites and coloreds even, a real mania, a phobia, a fetish, which makes simpleminded American brutality or segregation toward Negroes seem comparatively less cruel, anyhow, healthier. The basis of the whole struggle is sex, of course, the old sex taboos, based originally on ocular instinct, that one people should not fornicate with another because their skins and sex organs didn't match in color, were black or yellow or plaid or speckled. Only birds perfectly manage their ethnological restrictions. The robin does *not* marry the lady blue bird and set up a nest in your country mail box, neither of them being interested in the other. How lucky. Their baby birds would be cunning, too, all mixed red and blue, like new flags.

Yesterday I was suddenly so tired, around five, that I simply *sat down* without reading or even thinking and snoozed for a half hour in consequence. Art Buchwald was giving a big cocktail for our Minister to Israel. I wanted to go because I like big cocktail parties, just as I don't like big dinners. Wanted also to go to see Pat Highsmith's movie [*Purple Noon*] afterwards, but literally could not face the thought of dressing, moving me from here to there, taxi hunting, etc., so went out alone. That's what I wanted most, to be alone, like you on the Island—and dined in a bistro, another thing I wanted. Very simple, excellent, humble food, no flafla sauces. Was asleep by eleven and today feel elegant again.

The vitamins I've been taking and the thyroid again, after having stopped it on Ernst's advice for two years, have picked me up like a new colt, somewhat *arrière* in developing because still so spry. I feel almost apologetic sometimes to have such strength, resistance and to look so well for my years. Even my hair has stopped falling with these pellets Dr. Coke gave me, which contain—oh, damn, what is it that is in bones? It begins with "C" I think.

It is very, very chilly here. Trust the Catholic Church—it is the end of holy week, and the Pope's magicians or weathermen always pick the worst days of spring to force the faithful to imagine again the dreadful fate of Jesus. What a horrible thing to have made a *religion* of such brutal civil government as that which casually used crucifixion for any intellectual rebel. It is more distressing than inspiring, the story of the Nazarene, all clouded with morbidity and racial antagonism instead of being clarified by his superior intelligence and advanced spirit, his forward, loving kindness even to those whose ideas he did not share. In this way, Buddha is far superior in his life as an illustration, merely a rich young man who voluntarily became poor and devoted to contemplative thoughtfulness and magic. Yes, magic too. Always there has to be that as man's protest against the normal, so tiring, so universal, so uninspiring. No, let's have a few miracles, let's have a rich youth who renounces riches. Let's have anything that we cannot do or would not. Then we can have faith in the exception that makes to sprout a religion.

Happy Easter. Happy every day until we meet and are happier.

On April 17, 1960, Janet had been the guest speaker on a CBS television program entitled "Paris in the Twenties" which was part of a special series called *The Twentieth Century*.

During her stay in New York those two weeks before returning to Paris, she had taped the program, which was to be televised the following April 17, and had promptly forgotten it until she received praise from colleagues and friends and the *New York Times* television reviewer.

[April 19, 1960]

Darlinghissima,

I had forgotten about having made that TV film. It seems to me I made it in Paris before going out to New York.

Interruption: Second letter just came, after seeing the TV program. I can simply hardly believe it that I was so good, although I used to talk well, that's true, but how I look at my age must have been a shock. Your letter is such a loving and amazing analysis of how I seemed to you that I have read it twice through, with open-mouthed astonishment. As a Mr. Kleinerman was supposed to arrive last Saturday, I see by looking at the big date calendar you gave me, where I had noted down his arrival, then forgot about it, and has not yet phoned me to show me his kinograms of me. (I have just learned that word.) I phoned CBS to ask. It seems I made the TV in New York!! Do you remember my saying anything about it? I could swear that I recall the looks of the studio perfectly AND FRENCH WORKMEN on the set. I must be a bit batty. It is clear I forgot the whole thing, because I feared I was making a fool of myself and wished to forget it that I lost it to mind in merely hoping it would be better than I feared. I certainly recall telling the director to cut it all and chuck it out if it wasn't any use or good. The mention and praise from Jack Gould in his TV column has simply added to my amazement.

Kris [Kritikos] wrote me also, enclosing Gould's column, saying that I had "plastered" the opposite program of CBS given at the same time. Well, I keep laughing and laughing with amazement, as if this were a kind of very jovial dream. Kris mentioned my wind-up, the finale, as fantastic; I do recall having said to the director, "I think that's all I can recall, that I can say in public at least," and saying after I was off the air that I was sorry I had run down hill at the end. I had no idea that I was supposed to be the annotator of the program. Didn't anybody else talk? Ernest or Dos* or anybody? Shawn and Cecille sent me a round-robin of congratulations with Hobey Weekes, Edith Oliver, and the Hamburgers, at whose house they were assembled. You say Ester watched it. Did Maria? Did you?

. . . My Lord, my mother was right, poor darling. She said I would be better as an actress or public entertainer. I am glad I never took her advice, poor lady. I am deeply satisfied I stuck to writing. Kris also said she was going to the island the following week, "command performance from Natalia. She wants the house moved bayward one foot!" I don't even remember being *paid* for this TV film, though I recall perfectly being paid for the record sleeves of *La Voix Humaine* and Josephine Baker.

Well, this is as close to aphasia as I have ever come, with delightful results, absolutely charming and surprising. I shall certainly be interested to hear and see the kinogram and find out what "the fishing bit, the Picasso bit, the Fitzgerald bit" were that you mention. Your praise and enjoyment mean more to me than anyone's, except Hildegarde's. Less critical and in no way professional, just loving and proud. Thank all the girls. I am sending Kris a note.

Spring has come and I hope to remain a resident. She came yesterday evening suddenly, no sun to aid but the night air was soft. Today sun, more green leaves and my happiness at having pleased you so much. Yes, it must have been as if I were there with you, my beloved. Well, metaphysically I *was*.

———

In May the Mondadoris—the Presidente, his wife, Andreina, his two daughters, Mimma and Pucci, and his children's book editor,

---

* Ernest Hemingway, John Dos Passos.

Nardini—arrived in New York for a second prolonged visit, including
a trip to California. Mondadori was the Italian publisher of the
popular Disney comics and had been invited by Walt Disney to
visit his Burbank Studios in California, and, of course, Disneyland. I
was to accompany them.

This time my trip to California was delightful. The Mondadoris
were royally received, given the run of the studios and, more important, of their rich film archives, which were open to Nardini's eager,
expert eye. The movie world, as seen from the outside of our deluxe
hotel, also seemed a fantasy land to my Italian guests, until we flew to
San Francisco, where our friend Stanley Eichelbaum, Janet's ex-chief
checker at *The New Yorker* and now a movie and theater critic for
the *San Francisco Examiner*, had reserved for us the presidential suite
at the Mark Hopkins Hotel. From there, Mondadori could see the
entire city, with its Golden Gate Bridge over the splendid Bay. Stanley
acted as our guide, until he, too, had to squire his own boss around
Europe.

Mondadori showed great interest in Ferlinghetti when I took him
to his bookstore, City Lights. I noticed a glint in his eye as he observed the young poet and his press. He had undoubtedly been reminded of the small stationery store in Verona, with its similar hand
press, where, in his youth, he had begun his career. He became
Ferlinghetti's Italian publisher then and there. The contrast between
the portly older publisher in his executive's dark suit, conservative
tie, with his golden chain dangling over his waistcoat, and the young
American sixties' intellectual, a member of the Beat Generation, was
striking, but they had understood each other.

[May 13, 1960]

My darling one,

Such pressure have I never known as this last ten days, something
like what you are experiencing now with your president. . . .

Stanley and I and his boss, an unexpectedly charming, handsome
giant with a German baronial name—that being what he is, a German
baron—went tonight to see *Oedipus* performed by Sadlers Wells in
the International Theater Season in the most eccentric set ever I saw,
with Oedipus like a terra cotta statue draped in red on top of a ladder,
a chorus with masks down to the mouth and made up to look like

fungus. And *Sacre*, both by Stravinsky, of course, with the music wonderfully played by the Monnaie of Brussels, danced by the ballet in leotards exactly like in Robbins's ballets, Stanley said. Well, it is easily the most fornicative, procreative choreography any of us ever saw, nothing but crawling up from the earth's mud and slime and hopping on top of a girl in Act II. The chief dancers got in that position first and held it longest as stars, the girl with her legs bent beneath her, lying on her back, the man on top, holding himself a little distant by leaning on his hands, an insemination that lasted for a quarter hour.

The summit begins Monday closer to earth and less high with hopes than anyone would have thought possible one month ago, until Ike lied, carrying hope as well as our puritan reputation for superior Christian intentions all straight down to Hades. De Gaulle will have the inside track and Mr. K the outside. That's all anyone can suppose. Otherwise, nothing except whatever K's mood will dictate. He has been working up to a proper fury the last few days, judging by Moscow reports. Now holds Ike responsible whereas at first he at least excused his recent friend and host from having known what was going on in the spy department, a poor, affectionate compliment. K's remark two days ago that if Ike came to Moscow, "I wouldn't like to be in his shoes," is the most brutally comic low-down on host and guest relationship in advance we have ever heard of in history. The truth is that the chief government heads, K, de Gaulle, Macmillan, Ike, Adenauer, are all in the position of monarchs today, all with the personal power of diplomacy resting in their own heads and hands, are in a position to call each other Cousin as the European monarchs used to, all royalty having a theoretical and often physical family relationship and all powerful enough to indulge in the family quarrelsomeness over money, marriages, land that led to war as in lower families they led and lead to lawsuits.

These heads of state have practically the same power and relationship, and the recent visits gave them all the real family intimate cousinly touch. Well, the cousins are quarreling now, the West ones against the East one, though de Gaulle will doubtless be the bridge. He and K are the only two very intelligent ones. The others are either the Anglo-Saxon dummies, stuck in the corner with a fool's cap on their heads, or so old, like Adenauer, that despite his shrewd brain, his voice is considered avuncularly faint with age, hardly heard. . . .

[May 19, 1960]

Dearest Voice,

. . . This has not been a summit, but the depths for our prestige and more important than that sort of foolish ranking for a country, often based mostly on its wealth or merchant marine, a depth for our standing in our own eyes and those of others where a national intelligence is measured—stupidity, blundering, silliness, gaffs, naïveté, and finally loyalty toward ourselves because we are we, a loyalty being given by those who should criticize, Lippmann being the only one who has really lifted the rod and chastized us until we have bled under his words this morning. *The New York Times* objects to breast-beating, it says. Well, I object to stupidity and the kind of egoism which forbids self-criticism, which says it's our country right or wrong, which nobody denies.

At this moment, it's our country wrong. [Douglas] Duncan, the photographer who took those marvelous photos of the Kremlin jewels, was here in my bar to see the Gunthers day before yesterday with a special copy of his magnificent book bound in orange leather with the Russian arms in gold, a special copy for Mr. K, there being one just like it for Ike, too, he said, but he won't give K his copy because how can you give a gift like that to a man who has called your president a liar? I said, well, wasn't he a liar? What's that got to do with the book? No, he says, it *has* to do with the book. I don't feel friendly to him because one must stand up for one's own. I said even for a president who has acted like an imbecile? Yes, he said, "He's like a loony old father who has lost his mind, but we have to take care of him." Et voilà.

The boos that greeted K as he walked in were terrific. He turned scarlet, then caught himself deftly and, on hearing some applause (from French communists), applauded his hands, too. This somewhat calmed down the crowd, but it repeatedly booed. The Khrushchev press conference yesterday from three exactly until 5:18 was the most worrying and indeed frightening experience I have had in listening to a chief of state since Hitler. K acted alternatively crazy with anger and fury, then like a clown, being cute, then like a great leader making decisions, then like a ritualist talking doctrine . . . he could have been killed any minute, and every minute of those two hours. We all had journalist's badges on, but anybody could borrow them. I myself wore one for two days that said on it Roberts, *Newsweek*, until they made me one in my own name at my insistence. There were many

Hungarians in the big hall where he spoke. Anybody could have assassinated him, and Duncan had his camera ready, saying if it happens, I shall picture it. K's energy, anger, endurance, riposte, vitality above all, were such that at the end he won a grudging respect for his physical qualities at least, though was despised too for his coarseness in pushing his *jeu* too far, though why not? He is like that just as Ike is like whatever it is he is, a baldheaded, elderly, brainless head of state with a reputation for honesty now besmirched by a foolish lie, not an intelligent one but a silly one. . . .

I am convinced that this has been the lowest point this last week in our national history, like a table filled with broken, dirty dishes, like a mixture of poverty of mind and remnants of wasted luxurious food, great gluttonous pieces of cake which, by wasting, give us the sense of power that comes with money and an arrogant belly, and with that the stink of vulgarity of mind as the party has closed, with the echo of the foolish babble and braggadocio, the uncertain drunken steps in the hall, the loud patriotic belches. I am sick at heart.

[June 9, 1960]

Darlinghissima,

Just a note to thank you with all my heart and head, what is left of it, for your full and entertaining and informative and also alarming letter received this afternoon late. Still laboring on yesterday's Paris Letter.

Yes, de Gaulle may have been to blame for delaying the summit talk, but whatever pressures in the Kremlin, IF, IF, IF they exist, which made K decide to wreck the meeting would still have pushed him to wreck it in a different manner, equally brutal doubtless. But de Gaulle and U-2 between them gave K his ideal platform for curses and insults. Considering the weakness of Washington and past weakness of France and de Gaulle's boundless mystic nose for Marianne,* it is probably native to him to have tried to put France further forward, considering how backward is the White House and torn with Labour Party troubles is England.

Yes, I think the Soviets will win in the long run. How soon that will be we do not know. Perhaps peaceably if they can catch us sitting like a duck with oranges, at a capitalist dinner party. Perhaps by annihilating us all, they, us, you, me, God, too. . . .

* The emblem of France.

[July 12, 1960]

Dearest,

. . . I have been undergoing melodramas here because of my poor friend Nancy Cunard who has been certified for lunacy and shut up in a very liberal lunatic asylum in England near Windsor. Over the past two months in London, she had been arrested several times, first for soliciting on the street which is an absurd policeman's error I feel sure. She was doubtless trying to pick up men merely to talk to them. Then in her drunkenness she attacked the police who tried to take her in charge after fights in bars. As for the magistrate who committed her to Holloway Jail for medical attention and treatment, she threw her shoes in the magistrate's face! It is all squalid, unbelievable, yet as I look back has been true for years. She has been wild with hatred and hostilities for years, her own semi-poverty has embittered and unbalanced her, and I feel she has taken over all the injustices meted out to her Spanish friends. Spain seems to be the first fly-wheel in her political reactions which have aided in unbalancing her and now America.

When Raymond Mortimer arrived last week to visit her, he wrote me that she said, "It is America which has unjustly confined me here." And when I tell you her Spanish friends are all anarchists, you may be sure they have had plenty of persecution, police cruelty and rank injustice as part of their protest and suffering. These sufferings and injustices she has taken over as her personal burden, I feel. I think they have inflamed her hates, hostilities and anti-Christian ethic until she is socially mad, mentally not always.

It is a very liberal lunatic asylum indeed. She is allowed to go walking alone which allowed her to phone long distance three times the day before yesterday to beg me to give ten pounds sterling to some Spanish youth arriving here to aid him to go on to London, "and to come to me," apparently at the asylum. Fortunately he arrived twice at my hotel while I was not here. I still have the ten one pound notes I bought at the bank. Her idea, Raymond just told me, is to ADOPT HIM! He is to pretend he is her cousin! He is a very young working man, the concierge here tells me, speaks no language but Spanish; was able to print his name as identification to leave for me adding, "de parte de Mis Nanci Cunart," which she probably finds adorable, such semi-illiteracy. Apparently she has been crazy about him for two years, but it all seemed so fantastic that the doctors thought it a delusion. Stupid. All her delusions are her own truths.

I made four phone calls to England yesterday. Raymond made two to me, to try to plan how to head off this youth from attempting to get to London and then to her asylum where it seems clear she plans to flee with him. However, the boy has not appeared since his first two calls in my absence. I think he got in only from someone else and is now being turned back by the English immigration authorities, I am sure.

Roger Senhouse, her publisher, had to appear before the court to certify her lunacy. She was perfectly clearheaded on the phone with me and said, "I am not allowed to sign checks, but you will be refunded." I think Senhouse manages her money by court order. Now she has quarreled with her own doctor, a brilliant medico and friend of thirty years, because he believed the Holloway Prison authorities' report of her conduct in the first ten days she was sentenced there, when they could not find any of her friends. This seems strange, indeed. Apparently she acted the true lunatic and rebel, tore off buttons from her clothes, raged with vile obscene insults, etc. She has always so tempered her wild violences in her relations with me that they have only been legends to me. Now they are truths, legally and indisputably. It has been a profoundly sunken period for everyone, these last three weeks, as one has seen the Communists move forward inexorably and on well-organized plans toward touching nearly all the colonies in trouble through their savage ignorance, which their former white masters must be blamed for, who left them in so helpless a state for this century of so-called democratic eruptions. Democracy for Lumumba and Bomboko. It is like a jungle sickness, not a political understanding, merely a delirium of liberation and revenge on the whites who since Leopold II have treated them as slaves, more useful better-herded slaves lately than formerly, better paid, too.

Monica, who went there five years ago on a reportorial job, said Belgian natives were paid six times the French Congo natives, but risked crossing to French side at night over river filled with alligators to work for less for the French—and they no great Christian colonizers either—because in Belgian Congo they were not allowed to learn to read. You, I, all liberals of the West, now pay for the stupidities of the Tories of the West who preceded us. And these crazed blacks pay, too.

The rain which has fallen for three weeks may have stopped, judging by the sky . . . no, clouds are already appearing. The followers of that loony messiah at Mont Blanc who says the end of the world is coming tomorrow, as Jehovah's Witnesses have been saying in

California, have seemed to have an item in their favor—this constant rain, supposed to become a deluge tomorrow. However, his French followers have now decided it will not come until Thursday, *after* the fête Republicaine du 14 Juillet which is wonderful. By jove, they are going to perish as Republicans anyhow.

Kisses. Love. Depression, but humor too for the Comédie Humaine is sometimes explosively comic. Even Nancy Cunard. Even Lumumba. He sounds like something from Edward Lear or Alice in Wonderland or some tragic black-skinned Gilbert & Sullivan piece with tomtom music and satire played as bloody reality. Yours ever, into the increasing communizing of our world. As the planner and doers and world shakers, they advance.

J.

P.S. Some of Nancy Cunard's letters are absolutely as of old, brilliant, sharp as well as sane, others are very unhinged, wild with furies as always, yet peculiar, a quality that is spread then in all directions, then upheaved, then hot, then cold— At this present time of life, she is sometimes mad, but with a home or husband or family to have controlled her—though who could?—she would have been spared a lunatic asylum no matter how liberal as hers is.

[August 12, 1960]

Darlingest Natalia,

We are both so preoccupied and busied readying to see each other and at peace that we seem to have no time for writing to say this. Also, I fancy you have a new grandchild by now; there are only two sexes at first at least, so it must be boy or girl, and I rather hope a boy, if only for variety. . . .

I am reading Simone de Beauvoir's continuation of her first book of autobiography, *Mémoires d'une Jeune Fille Rangée*, this including her relations with Sartre with which the other ended, her reasons, their reasons for not wishing to marry, anarchism, disapproval of bourgeois standards and inheritances. No desire by either for children. All extremely interesting. She is not brilliant as writer or thinker, curious but true, though she is logical, pursuant, analytical, truthful, so her report on herself especially is of greatest interest to me. No American woman could or anyhow has written so intimately with such dignity, yet candor, of herself in her early love life, also their travel life which is fascinating, on Spain, their first big trip, their passion for movement, for looking. Like me, she cares most about the sense of sight. Says if she could only save one feature of her face she would save her eyes which I remember as being very handsome, grey-blue.

I also red Tom Matthews' autobiography*; parts of it tip-top on American early life, parts too unemotional, too unfertile as Europeans would have been to hold my interest. He is almost silent about Luce, though slashing about *Time*. Then why did he stay? He's like Georgette Leblanc in her *Mémoires de ma Vie avec Maeterlinck*. She spoke of him with such contempt, although lived with him eighteen years. When I asked why the eighteen years, she said airily, "Ah ma chère, tu ne comprends pas le grand amour."

I have your room. Am starting a modest little group of welcoming presents and I have myself as the only great gift that can receive you as the greater gift.

When I arrived in Paris, I found Janet armed with road maps, a *Guide Bleu* and a small Peugeot for our motor trip through the châteaux country on the Loire, a part of France I did not know. We were both excited by this trip, especially me by the prospect of this new experience with Janet as my master guide. Janet was the most pleasurable and entertaining companion, interested in everything, observant of everything. Her knowledge and her delight in the beauty of the land, in its architecture, was a continuous astonishment to me. Her enthusiasm, so seldom found in Europeans, was like a cool spring. She was never blasé, seldom tired, almost always funny, witty, illuminating, loving. At the end of a long day, we would find the best eating place and celebrate with a good dinner and excellent wines. The next morning off we'd go to new discoveries.

In a completely different atmosphere from the elegance of the French châteaux, we ended our vacation at Sperlonga, where I had purchased the ruined huts I was slowly remodeling into our future vacation home. This was primitive stuff—simple, quaint, informal, intimate.

The small *piazzetta*, the center of the town, with its one and only bar serving delicious espresso, would become, in time, the place of her morning ritual. She would sit at one of three or four tables put out by Maria or Concettina for us foreigners, and over a good cappuccino

* Thomas Stanley Matthews, former associate editor of the *New Republic* and editor of *Time* magazine; *Name and Address* was published in 1960 by Simon & Schuster.

would read the morning paper, exchange the gossip of the day and eye the nearby market stands selling fresh fruit, vegetables, fish and so-called buffalo eggs—the special, soft mozzarella of the region. The inveterate, sophisticated dweller of big-city hotels would soon become a summer fixture of that *piazzetta* in Sperlonga.

I went back to Paris with Janet and returned home the first week in October. By the end of the month my sister Franca had announced her visit to meet her new daughter-in-law and her family. I was very fond of my sister Franca, so gay, so charming, so outgoing. I often stayed with her in her lovely apartment overlooking Campo dei Fiori, the colorful market piazza in old Rome, and we always had good times together, so I looked forward to her New York visit. The fall also promised to be exciting, with the hoped-for election of John F. Kennedy in November.

Janet returned to the great turmoil created by a Manifesto signed by 121 intellectuals against the Algerian War in its seventh year, "with no signs of its stopping and the French people increasingly impatient for peace." Her first Letter, therefore, was entirely dedicated to it. The Manifesto, called a "Declaration on the right of nonsubmission in the Algerian War," had been signed by "well known left-wing or belatedly humanistic-minded notable Paris figures." It created a sensation in the Paris press as well as in the major European papers, above all in French government circles, for "its three articles of faith: first, that the present war is one in the cause of all free men, being the Algerians' natural struggle for national independence; second, that fifteen years after the destruction of the Hitler regime, French militarism has restored torture as an institution and a tactic; and third, that refusal by any French soldier to bear arms in such a war is justified, as is also the giving of aid to the enemy, to Algerian oppressed in the name of the French people." It is to this letter, published October 29, that Janet referred in the following letter to me.

[October 19, 1960]

Beloved,

Better I had gone with you to the airfield and have seen your plane fly at a distance than have wasted any time in not seeing you, as I did in leaving you in your red coat in the bus for Orly. What a rich time in intimacy we had. I was conscious of you and your personality all the time we were together, even when absent—even when you were working or with your family or not in the same room, for the impact of you as an entity was more deep this time than ever before perhaps. I do not know why. You are changed in some ways. There is a territory you inhabit, that of your work and ambition, which is a new address in a way, but I admire it. It is an extension of you. It is a locality you have made your own, where I can find you.

Your intensity of work rises as mine goes down. I kept time with you as you flew on Sunday, conscious when you would reach New York at three in the morning, our European time. I was awake and with you. Thank you for your cable announcing the voyage made. One always waits for it.

I set to my labor feverishly after you left, tearing up writing, writing more to tear up, etc., my usual scheme today and even Tuesday, with the Letter completely finished. I tore up the last pages and extended them. What it will look like in print I can only wonder. Each time I swear I will compose slowly, carefully, balance this with that. Each time I end by being so dull that the explosion of haste is better. Please tell me with candor your opinion on this first Paris piece, entirely devoted to the déclaration des 121 intellectuels.

I dined last night with Mme. Nathalie Sarraute. Being born Russian, she will always seem to us Westerners loosened from our sense of reality, a kind of middle-aged child. She said only Marguerite Duras, who wrote the scenario of *Hiroshima* [*Mon Amour*], had any importance among the twenty-five now indicted who signed the manifesto, the others all being minor people no one ever heard of, so when tried in court they will be of no consequence or use to the cause. What snobbery exists even in martyrdom!

The weather has been wet and cold since the sun of Sunday when you left. I walked back to my room across the Tuileries, then to my room to look at the trees from my balcony and to grieve . . . I worked until five a.m. Tuesday morning, and have not yet caught up on sleep. . . . Thank you, my beloved, for visiting me here.

I embrace you again

[November 12, 1960]

Dearest darling,

Scusi. There is no excuse but work, mostly, for not having written sooner. Yours of this week with justified complaint came this morning. I dined with Anna last night and Johnny Nicholson* and Anthony

* Restaurateur and man-about-the-theater.

Perkins, a stage decorator named Martin (who once lived in my in-
elegant old hotel in the rue Bonaparte), a director named Ritt and
an American actor named Paul Newman, I think, whom I thought
smart alec, and his very sweet wife, Joanne Woodward, all at the
Escargot d'Or, and I think Newman paid the bill. As Anna ate only
a dozen snails and a peach Melba, it was fortunate she did not have
to feed the army, in which four of us, guided unerringly by me to the
best dish, also the costliest, took venison. She looked *very* beautiful,
seemed in grand form. The Newmans, Johnny and of course I then
got dragged to some amazingly dull fairy nightclub show. Third time
I've seen it. Always dull and I got to bed at two. The whole evening
cost around $150 I suppose, for we were nine at dinner. I felt politi-
cally sick afterward.

The main thing is her dozens of messages for you, "ees she well, ees
she 'appy, ees she working too moch like crazy?"

Perkins has charm but acts haughty and rather bitchlike. I thought
him amazing in *Psycho*, which scared the wits out of me. I shall never
go to a horror film again, never . . .

Last Friday's *Guardian* contained the first newspaper printing, as
far as we know, of one of the Lawrence Chatterley words repeatedly
spoken by the Queen's Prosecutor at the Penguin trial in London.
Spoken by a witness, a schoolmaster who said in admiration of Lawrence's Puritanism—that irony made me laugh—that the author
merely wrote truly, "his is a simple statement for us all. One fucks."
It was the British impersonal pronoun, too, the "one" that made us
Americans roar. It was almost as funny as the night Gypsy told you
and me about the stripteaser who had turned herself into a Russian
princess. Recall? Complete with boots and accent, and said bitterly,
"Nobody geeves a fook for ze Princesse Nadja." Then Kenneth Tynan
in the Sunday *Observer*, doubtless furious that the *Guardian* had
beaten him to it, reported the same schoolmaster's phrase in his
report on the trial, also referring to Rebecca West as "wandering but
persistent in her opinions," as I recall. She will shoot him.

We have had one or two half-bright, sunny, chill days like true
autumn which have helped us all to try to feel more optimistic about
the present Fifth Republic. Riots in Algiers again last night, Armistice
Day, with shouts of "de Gaulle to the gallows, de Gaulle au poteau."
I would like to shudder if I heard that, so foul, so brutish, so frivolous
with hate, so French.

[November 19, 1960]

Beloved,

Today is a dry, sunny, wintry day, encouraging to the eyes at least, with its brightness, if not to the flesh, with its chill. I am sure you will have read Rovere's Washington Letter in the current *New Yorker* of this week with appreciation, the best thought-out, best written, clear analysis and dissection of the narrow Kennedy arrival—one can hardly call it a victory—at the condition of being president-elect that I have read. It informed me more than aught else. I felt more involved emotionally with this election than with any since FDR's first and second campaigns, the third seeming a Greek and tragic tempting of fate, a drama of ambition or greed which, combined with advanced age, seemed sure to bring lightning down on his handsome head, to kill him as an act, since as a man he showed no discretion in withdrawing voluntarily from his Washington scene. . . .

. . . I think what most involved my feelings about this election was *seeing* the candidates, in two of their television debates, shown here as I may have told you at the cultural section of our embassy, without any announcement (except for the last) to the American public here, apparently for fear too many might come. So nearly no one came. What a policy. What a characteristic of the basic timidity, the basic lack of psychological intelligence in foreign relations especially—for we are practically foreigners here—this small incident shows, describing completely the Republican mind and regime which you and I amid other millions wanted so to be rid of. That is our real victory, no matter if it is short weight, no matter if the popular votes only barely affirmed what the electoral college votes had made automatic by their majority. NO MATTER, A DEMOCRAT WON and will change Washington, to certain degrees at least.

I am invariably and have been since adolescence inimical to the Republican mind which shows at the most inflated size the bad qualities of the bourgeoisie rather than the good qualities of the middle class which the Democrats call forth. To me they are utterly different classes and not to be regarded as synonymous. . . .

Johnny Nicholson and his present traveling companion Jim Martin and Anna and I all dined at a Spanish restaurant—or did I tell you?—with absolutely marvelous dancing and guitar playing and abominable food. . . .

She looks beautiful, wonderfully so. But how limited most theater people are mentally. They are really mummers, as Shakespeare said.

They are frivolities. They are literally actors, not thinkers, always acting someone else's thoughts.

Simone de Beauvoir's new book of mémoires [*La Force de l'Age*] just out is splendid as an opus of a mature woman's truthful life and love. Not easy reading as she has no sense either of humor or malice. Her sense is of la verité.

Bless you, my love. You have had a fortnight perhaps of the Roman family, which must have been exciting because experienced in a new setting, that of Manhattan. . . .

Je t'embrasse avec amour et fidelité et passion.

J.

P.S. Kiki the cat just made a visit. Sneering at a piece of veal I brought home for him from my dinner at my bistro last night—

[December 16, 1960]

Darling one,

This is to wish you a happy family Christmas, with your Mother, Bill, Doris, Doodie, the littlest newest rascal and I hope, too, Maria and Gemma. But at any rate your own flesh and blood and I pray in good health. I say "pray" because I have just come from an impressive Vigil of Prayer at Notre Dame tonight, which began at 9:30 and closed at past eleven, organized to pray for peace, with young people from forty different parts of the world assembled. Or so the announcement declared. I myself saw nothing but young and old French people. The Cathedral was packed, with people sitting on the stone floor in the aisles (catching their death of cold, I fancy, though I heard no sneezing), with the priests in the side chapels giving confessions by merely sitting in the open, facing the penitent who knelt behind the chair, three priests to a chapel, two inside the confessional booth and one in the open as I say. The busiest night for repentance I ever saw. It was announced on the program which was handed around that confessions were obtainable, so hundreds, perhaps thousands, took advantage of the opportunity. The service ended with fairly fine Gregorian singing, the only artistic portion of the long evening. The main interest for me was that Bidault, the ex-head of the Catholic MRP, the French Demo-Christian Party, and old Mauriac, among several other laymen, recited their "intentions for prayers," all for peace, of course. Mauriac who has only one vocal cord (the other operated for cancer, I fancy, many years ago) has a strange, rasping hollow voice which identified him at once and I wanted to hear him. He prayed for "an interruption of hatred" and the capacity to love Algerians as brothers. Bidault prayed that *les chefs au pouvoir en Alger* would have wisdom and strength and Christian hearts. It was a strange Christian night, utterly devoid of beauty unfortunately. But impressive.

Mario [Pennachio] was expected this morning from Brussels, full of gossip to be sure about the wedding.* I saw a half hour of the TV on it in my bar, the most stupid, dull marriage show imaginable, bad lighting, poor directing, dull old chromo pictures of the ancestors to fill in time, the dull Belgians lining the streets sparsely as it was frightfully cold and the only fine sight I missed because I got bored and left. The new Queen waving her arms with theatrical pretty gestures and throwing kisses. She and the King actually acted so tenderly in love, it was touching, smiling rapturously at each other. I fancy each has been alone and both unloved all their lives. I hope such tenderness, such a strangely *private* sense of their emotion as they disseminated, before those thousands of people who were staring at them, can last between these two isolated relics of royalty.

The Algerian outbreaks were a great shock to me and to all French with any political sensibilities. The newspapers always make the most of events, more than the citizens' reactions justify perhaps, but I think that their editorial duty. They merely estimate them as they should be weighed. I had my Paris Letter almost complete in advance by Sunday morning. I could have added the colons riots without cutting the rest of the Letter out, as prepared. But the Sunday riot of the Moslems changed the whole picture, made it dangerous, daring and in a way wonderful. The first time they had ever dared manifest their feeling for their own independence, except in the small FLN army. That aspect has really shaken the French ultras here. It gratified the liberals who accept that independence was inevitable and anyhow think it right and want PEACE. How inexplicably odd that no one except the Communists kept insisting in a hollow propaganda sing-song that naturally all Muslims would love to be free of their capitalist colons. How odd they should have been correct, TO THEIR SURPRISE, as *Humanité* made naïvely clear in its reports of the insurrection. They had merely been playing the Soviet tune, to help tear France apart as an old European element of bourgeois habits and aid the around-

---

* Of King Baudouin and Queen Fabiola of Belgium.

the-world-Communist victory. All the other newspapers with equal naïveté also made perfectly clear that they, too, had not known how the mass of Moslems, or a big majority, felt, doubtless egged on by Muslim extremists who in turn had been excited by the ultra complotteurs, whose maneuver was to excite the Arabs to demonstrate, then turn the troops on them since they thought they could rely on the paras as usual, thus allying the army to the colons cause once more, since already de Gaulle had succeded lately in detaching the army from politics, to a certain extent. And this the ultras resented. The fact that two white French youths were shot by the paras in Bône [Algeria] in a riot so shocked the Europeans there they have not yet recovered. And God knows the paras acted the murderous brutes as usual wherever they could, though in several streets in Algiers their officers held them in restraint, unwillingly, it is reported, but obedient to the higher orders, filtering down from de Gaulle.

His trip there was like the fuse on a bomb, his mere presence in the land, at a distance, was what caused the explosion, most people think, with sad conviction. And so do I. His chemistry as the symbol of France acted like nitroglycerin. As the more complete bad and bloody news began pouring in on Tuesday, I simply started my Letter all over again, wrote eight pages from eight a.m. to eight p.m., and cabled it, entirely new, telling Botsford to hold over the long review on de Beauvoir's book which had already been cabled on Monday. The Algerian news came in on Monday with such confusion it was difficult to know what was true, what false.

The Herald Tribune stuff was better than The New York Times, which is always so conservative, so impersonal, as to muffle a great and terrible human story such as that was. I still do not like Arabs, which has nothing to do with the fact that I love liberty and wish all to have it. It would be nice, though, to see some of the new amateur black democracies and colored republics being partially successful in their new freedom, poor devils, instead of being as selfish, greedy for power, treacherous and crafty as any whites. And now Haile Selassie driven from his throne by his son. Well, the old gentleman gained the throne as I recall by a couple of judicious family murders. It is awful to admit, but the cheapness of life or pain in the habitual Congo people's relation with each other gives us the privilege of relief in coarse laughter that the lost colonel of one of their regiments turns out to have been eaten somewhere in the jungle by rival officers. All we need now is a cannibal republic.

This snowstorm cannot be gay like ours was when we lived on

58th Street. Remember how we loved it, darling, the fun we had sliding down the streets that first night and how the buses lay in the streets like lost elephants.

A Christmas kiss, darling one.

———

As the year closed, I remembered the words Janet had written me on March 6, from the H.M.S. *Queen Mary* on her way home: "We embrace with such desperation on boats or at airports that I should stare at it with wonder and appreciation to see such obvious passion and love, were I a bystander. Being a participant is, of course, less of an astonishment and more of a drama. . . . You are my heartbeat of these twenty years."

1961

Since Janet's return to Paris our correspondence had been minimal, just a few cables back and forth for the holidays. Janet plunged once more into the confusion of the Algerian peace negotiations, "which only de Gaulle could bring to conclusion if only he would get down to peace negotiations instead of calling for referendums, confusing the people even more."

The reports of the violence and cruelties that seemed to mark each step toward independence and democracy had so appalled Janet as to make her sick with political nausea. She wrote, on January 19:

"The great difference between Victorian times or pre-First World War years is that now brutality is current among youth, new republics, the totalitarian regimes like the Fascists and Nazis (who really set the mold) so that torture in the French army, though denied by the government, is a daily method to obtain information, as you and I would go to a briefing for journalists. I used to deplore sex as the basis of morality in Christian civilizations; now brutality and cruelty seem a physical dialectic and sodomy is practiced on Arabs with electric pricks to disembowel them until they wildly tell all, including what is not true. Perhaps sex was a very simple refined standard. This is dull. . . ."

I went to Washington for the inauguration of President Kennedy.

I reported to Janet the hopes that people like us felt in having a young democratic Harvard man at the helm of the country and surrounded by Harvard professors, who had shaken the people from the immobility of the Eisenhower years into voting for a young democratic President. There was a new wind blowing in the country. The experience had been exhilarating, President Kennedy's inaugural speech promising, the enthusiasm of the people genuine. It was heartening to see such a young man, such a young couple, such an eager family taking over the reins of government.

[January 17, 1961]

Darling,

. . . I am glad you like the Modern Art Musée piece's writing. I worked very hard on it. Those big shows take hours to synthesize. I hope my little Profile in the Letter next week on Le Monde turns out all right. I spent this morning there in the Monde office with Nathalie Sarraute's daughter who is second on theater criticism, very nice young woman who gave me lots of stuff. I did not tell her this. Yesterday I went to L'Express's office archives to hunt up and buy the copy which had a big piece on Le Monde written several years back by Françoise Giroud, who had been Servan-Schrieber's lover, for whom he left his wife, then left her six months ago to marry a de Fouquières girl twenty years old. The woman in charge of les collections said, "It will be very difficult to find Mme. Giroud's piece because we no longer have her name on our file." I said, astounded, "But for years she wrote some of Express's major pieces."

She saw she had let the cat out of the bag, so said hastily, "Well, we have just started our morgue here this month. We are very far behind," and pointed to all the old Express copies in the corner on the floor which still awaited classifying. How shocking! Servan-Schreiber fired her from the paper, had a staff meeting to tell the staff she no longer belonged, and now her name is not on file as having written major articles. Well, sex is a wonderful force in strength at least.

Last week, I saw a citation from some English priest of the eighteenth century who worked in a leper colony and was so horrified to see those mutilated creatures still coupling that he remarked, "Sometimes I think that God was not in a serious mood when he invented sex!"

. . . My bar man had told me that last Sunday his pet tortoise had come out of hibernation from her box of leaves on his balcony where she sleeps all winter and that her emergence meant spring. Well, she is better than the meteo system* of *Figaro* for today is really hot almost. I asked him why on earth he happened to have a tortoise anyhow. He said, "Well, I have a little daughter, as you know, and children should have an animal pet to teach them about nature and kindness to dumb creatures. And we didn't want a dog because it barks or a cat because it has to have a box of cinders, and one is a slave to both dogs and cats, so it seemed to us that for the fifth floor, which is where our apartment is, a tortoise was ideal." I listened fascinated. Can you fancy a duller little creature for a child to play with than a tortoise? I said drily, "Yes, and it doesn't eat as much as a cat or dog, either." "Mais oui, mademoiselle. Elle mange peut-être deux grandes salades par jour, ah oui, ça mange comme un ogre." The French are often still capable of amazing me. . . .

I must get to work, darling, on my Letter for next week.

Bless you, my love.

P.S. Oh, here's a strange story. Told a friend of mine who thinks this man is a secret service French agent. He was also gossiping a lot about Vatican affairs and quoted the Pope as saying to some young Italian who had just visited the Vatican museum, "You must remember all the beauty you have seen there. Because it may happen in your life-time that it becomes a propaganda museum for Moscow. But do not lose heart or faith. For it will be ours again in turn. The church can never die."

––––––

On March 13, her birthday, Janet was once again at Abano for the mud baths. During her stay, she also went to Rome for forty-eight hours to see Alice B. Toklas, who was sitting out the Parisian winter in a convent of the Dorothean sisters on Monte Mario. She took her to lunch and drove her about in a taxi to look at the parks. Virgil Thomson, who had seen Toklas earlier, had reported to Janet in Paris that she was increasingly feeble.

"I went to Rome to see her with the feeling it might be for the last time," wrote Janet. "Her mind is still clear, though argumentative, but she can barely walk. She gave me a few pages, the beginning of her autobiography, which I should think she might never finish. She

* The Paris weather-reporting bureau.

can no longer see well enough to read her own difficult writing, so is dictating her manuscript. It has that jerky spoken rhythm. Saw nobody except Mary McCarthy, whom I ran into at Caffè Greco. She is marrying in April in Paris. Kirk Askew,* who was there, spoke highly of Bowden [Broadwater], said he had refused the divorce at first only because of her impetuous nature and his uncertainty as to whether her lover would be able to divorce, himself, and marry her. When he was sure, he complied, of course. I just read a piece in *Life* magazine dated March 13th (how on earth a European copy of today manages to arrive in Abano on the day of publication I don't know) by Tennessee, on Anna [Magnani], Taylor, Leigh and [Katharine] Hepburn. Interesting and ill-written. I was most of all, of course, interested in what he wrote of the Anna-Brando ill-fated movie, very bold and truthful of him. Most of the people on cure here are Germans: Marienbad is in the Russian Zone, but apparently even before the war the Nazis were here. The Germans have changed sartorially at least . . . dress well, act well, and, of course, eat like elephants. The first two days of baths tired me a little, but am feeling fine now, with the tension down, pills which I can take from time to time in the future. I miss you terribly. I felt your letter made my birthday bearable. Thine."

Early in April, Janet announced that she would sail on the *Flandre* in May to spend several months in the States, with, as usual, a visit to her sister Hildegarde in California.

Everything had been readied for her sojourn according to her wishes. Her flat had been vacated by young Alan Pakula, on his way to Hollywood and fame; air-conditioning had been installed in her living room, and a door erected between her working studio and the rest of the flat. A good spring and summer in New York and Fire Island were waiting for her. However, another damnable insurrection in Algiers, actually a planned military coup involving five high-ranking officers, and a general strike in France almost delayed or cancelled her trip. I was also worried about the situation. When would it end? The war had been going on for over six years.

At home, the Bay of Pigs fiasco, masterminded by our CIA and executed by Cuban exiles in Florida, had become a black mark on

* Kirk Askew was an art dealer.

President Kennedy's first year in office. It was a shock to us, a bad omen. It left us in doubt about his ability to handle the presidency at all.

The Algerian army coup failed and Janet sailed on schedule. The successful flight of Alan Shepard, Jr., in his space capsule, lifted our spirits and gave us a good excuse to forget muddled worldly affairs and rejoice.

[April 14, 1961]

Darling one,

. . . The weather has lifted everyone's morale, bright, with the white chestnuts in full bloom beneath my window in the garden, an annual refreshing sight for confidence and the habit of hope once a twelvemonth.

I have been rather gay, too, owing to Mary McCarthy's being married Saturday noon at the Mairie in the rue de Lisbonne, then a luncheon after with friends of Jim West, her fiancé of intimate standing, I should imagine. Her son Ruel by Wilson is here. Will also be in Crakow, where he has a scholarship in Slav[ic] languages. West is USIS as it was called in Moscow, a pure coincidence.

Last night the Berniers suddenly gave a soireé for her, from ten on, but at half after midnight the prospective bridegroom began murmuring with fatigue, "I'll never live to marry Mary if I can't have some sleep first," without Mary, perhaps. A nice man . . . I should think, worked here with Walter Goetz on that USIS French language magazine. Very good, too. . . .

Then tonight, Bill Cody, cultural attaché, also with a brand-new wife after a divorce or so, is giving a dinner. I shall wear my new Lanvin black frock which fits like wallpaper and is becoming, much like the other one and also with a jacket, but very low cut in back. The other has been recut, too. Fits tight and looks more up-to-date. I'll never lose weight drinking Mary's health in champagne. . . .

[April 28, 1961]

Darlinghissima,

. . . The French are peculiar people, certainly. The unanimity of the Monday afternoon hour strike from five to six, really simply leaving work an hour early, was followed all over France with extraordinary unity by Communists, socialists, the whole pack, except what-

ever ultras might be in clerk positions who probably took off at five
like everybody but with no loyalty in their heart. It was the biggest
general strike France had ever known, ten million strong. And they
meant business. Meant, I am sure, that if the paras had landed, there
would have been blood flowing at once on the streets, led by Communist commandos, naturally, but joined by myriad other Frenchmen
in fury against a military Putsch, even if supposedly activated by the
general fear of Communism taking over in Algeria if it is liberated.
Well, possibly, or certainly. How about Cuba, which demonstrates
more than that supposition, it being a fact? The rich and the con-
servatives in politics take a quarter century to comprehend what is
going on politically. A conservative Frenchwoman asked me the other
day what my partisanship would be if I were a Cuban. "With Castro,
against the Yanquis," I said. "I, too. And here in France, in this
insurrection?" "I would be for fighting in the streets against every
paratrooper." "I, too." Her sister then gave me a long lecture about
how wonderful the insurrectionist generals were, saving Algeria,
where they have cousins and nephews in government posts, all of
whom "feel kindly toward the poor, stupid, ignorant Algerian fel-
laghas," but believe God ordained that Algeria should belong to France
on some kind of sacred map that was apparently drawn up when God
created the world in the chapter of Genesis in the Bible.

Cuba has been lost for ten years at least. Revolution was inevitable.
Communism the natural second step. President Kennedy's error in the
Cuban counter-revolution, in assistance and connivance especially on
a scene utterly unripe for any possible counter-revolutionary success,
has been a disaster, both politically and emotionally in relation to our
high hopes, love and devotion to him, to his mind. His speech to the
press was one of the finest written American state papers I ever
read. Yet what he had just done was one of the most regrettable lapses
in presidential authority and selection. We must stick by him, of
course, and willingly, hoping for more wisdom, less silliness from his
college professor advisers. My heavens, are NO Americans adult in
their minds, even those who wrote powerfully critical books on our
social scene and have been graduated with highest scholarly honors,
continued by graduated studies, grants, travels and communications
with each other and foreign men of consequence? I begin to despair,
where with Kennedy I had renewed hope. I am so sure that you
know every corner of my mind, my darling, and feel the same as I
that I shall say I love you, instead, and interrupt this stale complaint.

It was a strange feeling to hear that fool [Michel] Debré say over the radio after midnight Sunday night that paratroopers were readied to fly over the Paris region and drop jumpers or land at any minute. I somehow didn't believe it possible, though if it had occurred the insurrectionists would have won—that night—but I do not believe the victory would have lasted the week out. The French had enough of being occupied by the military when there were Nazis, without standing for it from their own cousins.

Darling one, what do you want me to bring you as Paris gifts?

[September 29, 1961]

Darling one,

Your tender worried letter came last night just before I dressed to dine at the Finletters, newly come here, he as ambassador to NATO. I feared to be late and was, too, by fifteen minutes, and in my haste left my room without transferring my purse into my evening bag. Had promised the chauffeur a five franc tip if he would even take me as he was due to quit work. Got there, no money! So my initial introduction to the ambassador was to say, "I am so delighted to meet you, Mr. Ambassador. Will you be an angel and lend me a thousand-franc note?" He liked the whole incident. There was, of course, considerable table talk about the insurrection, though no one had read the fantastically alarming front page of *France-Soir*, as I had (which made me late), which simply printed the number of arrests for complicity (with, surely, more to come). General Gouraud with four other generals and five colonels taken to Santé Prison here. Two hundred officers charged, four regiments dissolved, including First Parachute of Foreign Legion, also fourteen and nineteen paratrooper regiments and one other Foreign Legion regiment. A general who is commander-in-chief of some service called E.M., a colonel who is chief of the Third Bureau (secret service). All those from Algeria. In Paris, two officers from military bureau of the Minister of the Anciens Combattants, arrested. One hundred functionaries arrested in Algiers, members of government's Organization of Secret Army.

That seems to be the bag. This depressed me more than did the insurrection itself, which seemed clearly localized in the four generals led by General [Maurice] Challe, though naturally one knew they had secret backing from the Right, from the lunatics who as a form of patriotism, from their viewpoint, and fear of Communism once the Arabs are liberated, were giving aid and would have helped had the paratroopers landed in France, which would have meant civil war and blood on the streets of Paris. But that there was such corruption of morale, or duty, such demented partisanship creeping through all the services like poison, here in Paris, in the state administration, in the very government—no, I had not thought of such treachery on so enormous a scale, nor had most Parisians, and we are aghast. It is true, all you write, that, of course, if France had been seized in the insurrection, the whole Western alliance would have been shaken and Europe changed, but during it we never thought of that. We didn't think of the Algerians, either. The peace problem, I mean. There was such normal life by day in Paris that one thought one was thinking of that, lunched and dined, etc., but we were really thinking only in terms of worry. I never heard anyone use the word "angoisse" nor felt it. The depth of the worry could be measured by the joyous relief on Wednesday morning when the breakfast papers announced the quartet of generals had collapsed and fled. We don't know where they went. We don't know whether Challe was arrested, or whether he surrendered, and now that one other of his generals was locked in prison here last night, we discover we don't know how he happened to come back into circulation either. The notion is that Challe, as ringleader and the best of the four not very bright minds, was chosen to represent them all when tried in court, since he could present their viewpoint better than all four could, bound to talk at cross purposes and repeat the confusions of the Barricades trial recently (in which everybody got off, in a way, including [Pierre] Lagaillarde with five years' prison I believe; only one, Ortiz, a bistro owner in Algiers, receiving the death penalty, which he will now get since the Spaniards turned him over to the French the other day). If this coming trial of the four generals is like that of the barricades, which ended in February or March, though the barricades insurrection was January of 1960, it will be an even greater scandal, also greater proof that Frenchmen think with greater difference from each other than in any other country today. That is probably a basic truth, anyhow.

It is said now that Challe will get the death penalty at his trial and de Gaulle will reprieve it as he did for Pétain after his trial, turning it in the same way to life imprisonment in a fortress. After all, de Gaulle came to power through the first of these insurrections, a rather awkward circumstance in which to let the leader of another, also a general, go before the firing squad. The moral and mental value between the two generals, Challe and de Gaulle, makes so great an historical gap between them that the logic of the conclusion I have just drawn fades away, though it should not, as crime is crime, whether rewarded by

salvation and change as France was in the first case, or not. She would
have been partly bled to death in the second, if Challe had won. I did
not believe France would fight well in 1939 when the war broke. All
the evidence was against that, but I do believe the people would this
time, would have put up a terrific street-fighting civil war. De Gaulle
is the only general they can stand even to think about now. He has
emerged as high as the clouds.

You think more internationally than I in your excellent letter. We
all thought locally here it was part of our worry and the fear of many.

It is a lovely, sunny Saturday, milky but sunny.

[May 5, 1961]

Darlinghissima,

. . . We Americans remain in a primate stage like earth man-monkeys
against the homo sapiens with the silk and satin mind, the brain of
books, the arrow of logic and the inner cranial climate of thought,
centuries after centuries and still going forth for further exploration
of opinion and knowledge.

I love and admire you. With kisses.

_____

Janet arrived as scheduled in mid-May, this time for a longer stay.
The plan was to spend some time in New York, where she intended
to finish her Ethel Merman Profile, which she said was going well, and
come to Fire Island for rest and relaxation.

In New York, she was immediately invited to parties by people who
wanted to entertain her, to meet her, to interview her. She enjoyed the
excitement, the friendly reception, the recognition, and especially her
New Yorker colleagues, who dropped in to greet her in her temporary
office, to chat and gossip. They gave her a true demonstration of affection and admiration. She was the senior member now.

This year she could also participate in the annual summer party
given by our beloved Shawns to celebrate the anniversaries of Ann and
Brendan Gill, Naomi and Bruce Bliven. Around them gathered the
faithful collaborators and old pals—Phil Hamburger, Hobey Weeks,
Edith Oliver, and others. The Shawns' sons, Wallace and Allen, with
their friends, would sometimes be there. The party, held, as it often
was, on the lawn of their summer house near New York, was jolly,
intimate, special. Cecille and Bill Shawn were perfect hosts, and the

food was delicious. This year it was enhanced by the presence of Janet, a rarity.

Janet was also a friend of Djuna Barnes, "the most important woman writer we had in Paris," as she wrote in her introduction to *Paris Was Yesterday*, published by the Viking Press in 1972. Djuna was then living in Greenwich Village. One afternoon she came to see Janet, and I met her. She was an impressive figure, not only because of her striking appearance—tall, wearing a cape and a turban, which allowed her pale face, still quite beautiful, to stand out, her eyes seeming to pierce through you—but also because of the severity of her stare, which struck me as hard and unkind. She looked me over, up and down, with curiosity, but without benevolence; quite harshly, in fact. I had, of course, read *Nightwood, Ryder* and *The Ladies Almanack* (the latter a spoof on a group of noted women who revolved around the notorious Natalie Barney in the Paris of those days), and I was curious to meet her. She represented too much of a past I did not share, and her unfriendliness made me feel uncomfortable. The meeting was not a success. She was living alone at the time, almost like a recluse, with very little money. Neighbors would supply a bottle of gin for her from time to time, leaving it outside her door. When we saw her again, a few years later and for the last time, she had been very ill. She hadn't left her room for days and it was dark and messy, strewn with papers. She was weak and frail, a sad parody of herself, unglamorous, old and terribly alone. A large bouquet of fresh roses stood on the floor beside her bed.

In that same introduction, Janet had described her character by remembering an episode: "Djuna wrote a play that she showed to T. S. Eliot; he told her that it contained the most splendid archaic language he had ever had the pleasure of reading, but that, frankly, he couldn't make head or tail of its drama. She gave it to me to read, and I told her, with equal candor, that it was the most sonorous vocabulary I had ever read but that I did not understand jot or tittle of what it was saying. With withering scorn, she said, 'I never expected to find that you were as stupid as Tom Eliot.' I thanked her for the only compliment she had ever given me."

In July we went to Fire Island, a wonderful haven from the pressures of the city. No cars were allowed to poison its air, fresh and cool; no noises disturbed our sleep, except for the lullaby-like rumble of the distant waves, or the fluty songs of the birds in their own special haven. It was a good place to rest, to read, to enjoy visits from friends, even to peep in occasionally at the local discothèque dancing, which Janet loved. A few of our best "islander" friends had been taken from us by then—Wolcott Gibbs, John Mosher, Tom and Bea Farrar—but there were still some old-timers around for drinks and good talk, like Irving Drutman, who later edited *Paris Was Yesterday*, and Michael de Lisio, the sculptor. Sometimes, out of the blue, Tennessee Williams would appear, with his friend Frank Merlo; they even stayed with us.

The days were pleasurable, the weather mild and clear with blue skies; time flew quickly by. In August, rested and ready, Janet left for the Coast to join Hildegarde and Eric in Calistoga, where their new house was being built. She was looking forward to her cross-country train ride. When she was a child, before deciding to become an author, she had wanted more than anything else to be a train conductor. From Chicago, where she stopped off to board the *California Zephyr*, with its so-called Vista-Dome, she wrote that she found the town very hot, "an unlovable city. I recall my university years here in the bitter winds of two winters, almost blown flat on the Michigan Boulevard by the lake as I fought to cross the street to go to the opera to hear Mary Garden in *Love for Three Oranges*, a favorite of my youth. I sat in the top gallery high in the air, more like a ship than an opera house." Then, on the *Zephyr*, she described the voyage through the Rockies:

> Friday, August 11, 1961
> In the midst of the Sierra
> Madre mountain tops

Darling one,

I have caught my breath at last by one whole day of silence and quiet, sitting alone in my roomette, reading an excellent history of the Civil War, a steadying paperback. For four hours yesterday we traveled cautiously through the heights of the Rocky Mountains in amazing intimacy with their jagged terrific surface only a few feet from window and five thousand feet above sea level. A fantastic useless *tour de force* of railroading construction created so that we travelers could go and *look* at this paleolithic rocky barrier like a spine with fir trees as flesh. Below in gullies were rotted wooden roads hung on precipices where miners had brought out lead and silver on donkey backs. Our route was not far from Aspen in Colorado. A miracle I can write this much. I almost *pray* now to be better in my hand, mind and memory, for I am alarmed. I will phone you Sunday at eleven. Sky grey. Mountains are like skeletons and the plains are the flesh of the globe.

———

Janet became nervous whenever driving through the unavoidable mountain passes of Italy. In airplanes, she actually trembled. She only liked *terra firma*.

She had recently been alarmed by the pain in her hand, and feared for her work. Every time she used it for typing or to use her pen, it burned. She hoped that her favorite, Dr. Coke, would be able to help her. The Abano mud baths evidently hadn't. In fact, her first letter from Altadena, on August 19, sounded more confident. On September 5, she wrote, "I am seeing Dr. Coke again today. My hand is better in a slow way, can type longer without pain or burning than a week ago. Coke thinks that by October first I shall be nearly normal. Maybe. The myography of the nerve injury, which none of the three doctors consulted advised, is the only way of really calculating the extent of the injury, the medial nerve being of larger radius, which affects principal three main fingers that were bruised." She was applying heat and regained hope.

By September 21, when Janet returned, we flew together to Paris. I had to go to Milan on business and wanted to see Sperlonga and the building situation there. Janet came with me.

When we finally reached Sperlonga, I found that the work on my house had been delayed by two unexpected events, both typically Italian: the architect had eloped with a new lover, abandoning his former mistress as well as my bewildered workers; and the rich landowner of the property below mine (a terraced slope of orange, lemon and pomegranate trees all the way to the beach) had threatened to call in the *carabinieri* to stop my builders from continuing their task. They had enlarged the existing small windows to provide me with a panoramic view. They worked at night so as not to arouse the ire of the landowner, knowing that he would have objected. The reason for all this was a centuries-old law that prohibited opening windows looking out on someone else's land. At this dramatic turn of events, much to Janet's amusement, I had to go to argue my case before a local judge in nearby Fondi. "This is the twentieth century, not the fifteenth," I said. "Is it possible you still are applying this law today? People don't throw things out of windows any more. People like to breathe, to have light, to receive the sun inside their walls." The judge showed no compassion or comprehension. "The law is the law, Signora. You must pay a fine for this infraction." He stated quite a high sum. "You're lucky. Your landowner could have asked anything he pleased." I had been defeated and had to pay the fine, but the windows were not touched.

We left, hoping that no more crises would interfere with the completion of our little house, and went together to Milan. By the first week in November, we were on our way back—I to New York by plane, and Janet to Paris by the Simplon Express.

"My taxi rolled by your bus so that in a last intimacy I saw your red coat with you in it, so upright, and leaning on the front seat your hat high on your intelligent head. My tears at parting were a relief to my feelings. We will *not* wait so long, time and distance are too short . . ." scribbled Janet before leaving.

Janet found Paris reeling from a series of OAS bombings, which forced her to write what she thought was a gloomy Letter, her first after her return. "An error," she wrote, "to have used no gay or complimentary material, but by God there is not any here nor does anyone pretend there is. They are merely so frivolous as to be indifferent to the bombs, sadism, violence and hate in the atmosphere, a sordid, sleazy semi-civil war of explosions in garbage pails," as Janet defined it. By the next letter, the political drama had shifted to a personal one concerning Alice B. Toklas. She had just returned to Paris from her long stay in Rome—"my first infidelity to Paris, and a big mistake"—to find that the collection of pictures Gertrude Stein had left to her upon her death in 1946, as a security for her old age, had been legally seized. Janet's *New Yorker* Letter of December fifth gave the first concise, complete account of this sad story. It said, in part:

"The collection was removed from the Stein-Toklas apartment, in the rue Christine, on the order of the Tribunal de Grand Instance de la Seine, and it is at present in the vault of a bank in Paris under the trusteeship of a court-appointed administrator. Today, the only trace of these masterpieces in the apartment is the faint, empty outlines left by the picture frames on the white walls. Miss Toklas—now eighty-four and fragile, though spirited—was fortunately not present for the shock of seeing Miss Stein's pictures borne away." According to Janet's report, the action had been instituted by "Mrs. Allan Stein, in the interests of her children, the ultimate heirs to the collection now worth several million dollars." "Miss Toklas's eyesight is, naturally, not what it was once," Janet concluded. "Of the disappearance of Miss Stein's familiar pictures from her salon and foyer, she only says, 'I am not unhappy about it. I remember them better than I could see them now.' "

At home, I found my mother more like her own self, a consolation shared with Janet, who remembered having gone through such ups and downs with her own mother. But the news that Bill and his family would be shortly moving to Europe came as a sad blow to me. He had left his editorial post at *The New Yorker* to become a full-time staff writer and had decided to move to Rome, from where he planned to write regularly for the magazine. It would be a lonely Christmas.

[December 25, 1961]

Mon petit coq en pâte,

... Your voice is semi-precious on the transatlantic phone. It has at least half its to me always moving melodic dark values, one of the finest vocal speech organs I have ever known. Privately, even publicly. . . . Never have I been so relieved to see the end of a year as of this one, filled with accidents so small in stature as to partially wreck a human body, like your instep, my hand, or Alice Toklas's third of the last two months. After the left wrist and left knee, she fell last week and dislocated her right hip. I called on her today. She is in bed and looking better than for years! Plump faced, her still lovely narrow quite youthful hands, after all her years of fine cooking, and cross as a Chinese tyrant, her devoted old maid Madeleine says. She loves to gossip, to recall quarrels and confusions back in Gertrude's days.

I am glad the piece in the Paris Letter on the immolation of Gertrude's collection seemed of interest. Alice says (I asked her) she will now not be permitted to sell another picture from it, though actually I should think a clever French lawyer could manage it. She also said she is not yet short of money. Gave me her word of honor she would tell me if she were, but added on her word of honor she would not accept any money if she needed it.

It is now raining after the coldest Christmas in Paris for ninety-two years. Dry, clear, a handsome American cold, now turned to French mist and wet. . . .

The biggest difficulty since my long trouble with my hand is organization and concentration. It takes me nearly a whole week to do a Paris Letter now. My dictionaries and reference books are still not unpacked from my boxes in the basement. Each day I promise myself to bring them up. Did yesterday with a signal effort, but no dictionaries appeared in the boxes we brought up. So I must hunt other boxes.

Have you seen the caddish piece on Hemingway in this month's *Encounter* by Dwight Macdonald? With much of what he said in literary criticism I agree. But as he sneers at Ernest's male manner, so I sneer at Macdonald's. For he, too, has a hairy face, with a long book-writer's beard.

Blanche Knopf is here, with a cane, after breaking her hip in a fall. De Gaulle speaks this week to his nation. The French are very calm in all their governmental undecisions and de Gaulle's uncertainties, because France is prosperous. It can afford the war and can even afford not knowing what the peace will consist of, a high luxury indeed.

My hand still jerks but hardly burns at all. I can only be grateful and swallow all my pills and stand with a bare bottom to take my injection each day.

My beloved, my dearest love. . . .

1962

The year started normally, for us anyway—Janet in Paris, I in New York, both working too hard, both longing to be together but still living apart. This time I didn't have the consolation of Bill's family near me, because they had just sailed back to Italy. Ester, however, was with me, and I rejoiced in her presence, always so comforting and understanding. My friends adored her. In fact, they supplied the merriment during the holidays, a period that can be depressing without the younger generation on hand. I missed them.

I had gone with Anita Loos to see a protegée of hers dance in *Nutcracker*, and wrote to Janet about it. In her next letter, she commented:

"Your last Sunday and Monday letter arrived Wednesday, a pleasure, also with material to laugh at, an extra nourishment these days. Poor Nit. Yes, she is politically floating; her intentions are good but her instincts are to side with money, which she gives generously, madly, for which she has worked since a little girl of fourteen in pigtails, whose terror was that she would die in the poorhouse. She is not like normal politically sentient people, sensibly developed, any more than physically. She is like others nearly half again her size. Her goodness, love and patience with her husband John are unforgettable to me. The patience came after the faith was gone. What a trickster he was; educated to be a Protestant parson, read Latin, and was a born adulterer, superior in mind to all around him in that early, mud-like movie world of Jo Schenck, which was just moving from illiteracy into the use of two-syllable words. But spiritually Nit is on a level superior to most people except saints, even today. Her kindness has in it the circus quality of the Freaks in the Sideshow and the little *négresse* is, as you intelligently comment, a plaything instead of a pet, like a baby tiger or lamb; but she feeds her pet on love and kindness."

Janet had been following doctor's orders and seemed more hopeful about her hand. I had been so worried about it that when we were in Rome I had taken her to see Professor Frugoni, a famous diagnostician. He immediately ordered her to stop smoking and gave her a prescription for her tension and incipient arteriosclerosis, which, he added, we start having when we are born; smoking simply speeds it up.

With her mind at rest, she turned to politics: "The mystery of de Gaulle, the lack of clear communication after he made up his mind on auto-determination on Algeria, which three years before he had been against—what led him to change his mind is unknown or never stated. I personally think he saw which way the wind blew, that more French civilians believed in Algerian liberty than he had supposed, so he followed them in a way so he could lead them afterward. . . . I like President Kennedy's speech to the nation. It seemed strong but fluid enough not to frighten the Republicans or the Democrats. . . ."

[January 3, 1962]

Darlingest,

. . . I had a comic message from Anita Loos (such an evening you must have had with her at Virgil's memorial concert and he alive to enjoy it, though I hear he blushed at the great honor), who says to come back to New York. The air raid shelters are DEEVINE.

I hear the Chagall show—if it is of his stained glass window designs —is superb. I care rather little for his fantasies in painting, agreeing more with Picasso who said, "What a fanciful man. He always has a donkey on a roof in his paintings and in his head."

I saw the reviews of Tennessee's Iguana play* and was very pleased for him, as they were really seriously excellent, selecting under the necessity of true appreciation of what he had done, those major, final elements. The strangest theater contributor of our time, anywhere. He makes the angry young men of London seem merely furious socialists

---

* *The Night of the Iguana.*

and Red Brick College (i.e., poor boys) graduates. This is their tragic warped payment, as just that, as poor born intelligent youths, that they are forced to make to the aristocratic England, once so rich, which biased their lives, and is no longer rich.

You will be greatly interested in the C. P. Snow article on American delusions which I enclose. It is of painful major importance. It was an article which demanded to be written, and no one could so clearly have edited it as he, an Englishman who was also born poor, but who has grown rich in work, honors, gifts and painful information from his island, which he tries to give to our untidy minded, conceited continent.

I must go visit an old Seattle woman, now eighty-two, whom I mostly keep alive, to wish her a good New Year and to assure her of my further affection and aid for as long as may be. She said something so sad to me. She said, "My friends are less afraid of me now that they know you take care of me. For they know they will not have to."

Bless you, my love, bless your body, mind and soul. We are happy, happier now than for some years.

[January 13, 1962]

Darling,

I saw returned newspaper pals from New York yesterday who said this is the latest: To defeat Kennedy in 1964 election, the Republicans will put up (guess)—Ike and Nixon. There is big Republican money behind this in New York, and Ike has said yes, he will accept. It could work, if anything could. Only way they could be sure Nixon could be president—by Ike dying in office. When I was told to "guess"—I said Harding—then Ike as Vice-President.

My Lord, the rain has begun again, so hard and fast falling I can barely see the Tuileries Gardens.

Kisses, darling. I had to tell you this. It is so comical—and even funnier being true!!

[January 22, 1962]

Darling,

It is now six o'clock. At four-twenty as I sat at my table writing the Malraux part of this week's Paris Letter, there was a terrific BOOOOOOOM close at hand. I thought it was on the Seine somewhere, rushed to the window which was open for air to the balcony, as the pompiers began rushing by and ambulances. I could tell by the direction of their sirens that they were crossing the Chamber's bridge. Soon my pal on the *New York Times Magazine*, Josette Lazar, rang me. It was the plastic bombing of the Tunisian diplomat's car behind the Quai d'Orsay. She had already talked to an American professor who came to her office, shaken, horrified. He had been going into the Quai d'Orsay to go up to its library when the bomb exploded. The smoke and fumes were strangling, he said, blood was on the staircase. He fled. All the three-story windows on the Cour Constantine were in crumbs on the stones below.

I entered that court only once when I lunched with Mme. Edgar Faure, whose husband was then Président du Conseil, i.e., head of the government in that Fourth Republic. Must mail this to give you news.

Cheryl phoned yesterday from Munich—arrives here Wednesday afternoon by air, at the Ritz. We dine that night. I ordered two tickets for *Flora* again on Thursday. She said so pitifully, I can't understand French. She knew the play had bad reviews, nevertheless wants to see Mercouri act—see if she CAN act. I think she can't, at least as long as [Jules] Dassin dominates. She comports herself on the stage as if she were making a movie, all the cinema exaggerations, screams, jumping up and down on a couch, throwing herself exactly on top, sex to sex, of poor Jean-Pierre Aumont as her husband as he lay there, then rushing off to travel round the world, maybe in purple satin pants and jacket in which her figure is absolutely wonderful, that I grant. I find her of incredible vulgarity, just like *Jamais le Dimanche*. Don't f— on Sunday, eh, what piety. The house was full when I was there Saturday—far better house than Sagan's piece pulls. I think the *Semaine de Paris* and advertisements for *Flora*, which mention "les plaisirs physiques," and the critiques, which said parts of it were as bad as *Dolce Vita*, were what drew the crowd—que c'est joli, eh?

Must get back to finish my Letter's next topic, the Russian ballet dancer Nureyev, before dinner. He is probably as great as Nijinski and also as ugly, but with better-proportioned body. It was one of the greatest ballet nights I ever saw, a dancing night really, because there were only two couples who danced, like a quartet of stars. . . .

———

Michael and Connie [Ernst] Bessie had been seeing Janet during their visits to Paris. Michael had been editor-in-chief at Harper & Row, and her particular editor on *Men and Monuments*, the collection of Janet's art profiles, published in 1957.

I had met Mike when the United States entered World War II and I was broadcasting at NBC. He came to our International Section as a censor on behalf of OWI. Later we met again in Algiers, waiting to go into Europe—Mike to France, I to Italy. Connie, too, was in OWI and had been sent to England; they were not yet married. So we were old friends.

Mike had just founded Atheneum, a new publishing house, with Pat Knopf and Hiram Haydn. They were three ambitious young men, eager to make their own way in publishing. Mike had been after Janet for a book. First, I think, he asked her to write her memoirs, an idea Janet simply abhorred. Then he suggested a collection of her "Letters." She had been so disappointed by the reception and sales of *Monuments* that she was not very receptive to this idea either, nor did she want to do the selection, editing and so forth herself.

I was much in favor of it, and told her so repeatedly. My main interest was to preserve her writings between hard covers and not watch them disappear into a wastebasket. I remembered a day I had spent incommunicado at an estate on Long Island, right after having been called for overseas duty. We had been sent there to be instructed and briefed. One of the most interesting and important lectures we attended had been on France, and it was based entirely on Janet's *The Old Man of France*, her Profile of Pétain. It had been published in *The New Yorker*, and then by Simon & Schuster in early 1944. In telling the story of his life, a long one, Janet provided a lucid, succinct, miniature portrait of France and of its sad, shameful Third Republic. People learned more about France from that brief, shrewd, psychological portrait of Pétain—"Who survived a hundred and seven French governments and then founded one of his own, the hundred and eighth, over whose end he now presides"—than if they had read textbooks on the period. It had been a real surprise and satisfaction.

"Mike Bessie has written me. I gather he envisages *Letters* only SINCE the war: I believe that may be a good restriction and idea. I shall write him tomorrow," Janet wrote to me on February 3.

I got hold of Mike as soon as I could, and we formed an alliance to see to it that the idea would be turned into a workable plan, with a splendid book as a result. When Janet came to the States, we could talk again. But a first step had been taken.

We didn't write to each other much in February. Janet had been very upset by sad news concerning dear friends: Vera, the wife of her oldest crony, Russell Page ("the gardener," as she called him), the most famous landscape architect in England, was mortally ill in

Switzerland; and Margaret Anderson was also reportedly very sick near Nice, "after having faithfully nursed and buried three that she loved, one after another, Georgette Leblanc, Dorothy Caruso, and old Monique Serrure, a few months ago, Georgette's *dame de compagnie*, a Belgian schoolteacher who left teaching on seeing Georgette as Mélisande at the Brussel's Monnaie, a true stage love."

Janet had begun to lose faith in her hero, de Gaulle, and looked upon President Kennedy with some misgivings:

"I am worried about President Kennedy's lack of ability to take advice from people outside his circle of advisers, who all seem unpractical. Twice lately a European-American banking congress or meeting in Switzerland or London have warned in a very polite hands-off manner that he should raise the interest rate on the dollar to protect it; but that means dearer money, even to save it, which is a Republican practice, not Democratic, so he has so far refused. He has a strength of obstinacy greater than a mental strength of broad planning, I fear. I do not think he has so far carried his office in a way to encourage the same kind of Democrats to vote for him again. Reston's pieces in*The New York Times* have been excellent in their criticism, especially yesterday, on how wasteful for him to have given his financial philosophy in his Harvard Commencement address and on the weak lack of organization in our Congress which EVADES rather than demands debates which would make such matters of national interest understandable to all."

[March 9, 1962]

Darlingest one,

. . . The cover story in *Time* this week on Tennessee is excellent, fascinating, exploratory. The new drama man who wrote it aimed to be truthful in both realms, the strangeness of the man's nature, of his plays, and their even stranger importance in the American theater and indeed, by report everywhere, although the material of the plays and of his life are so nearly unknown as a form of experience to the millions who know about him. The content of his work and its overwhelmingly abnormal sex-ridden homosexuality. I never knew anyone so one hundred and one percent homosexual as Tennessee . . .

. . . Jo Barry, a great friend of Miss Toklas, told me that Gertrude once said to him, "Normal is more interesting than abnormal. Abnormal is always the same." So true. She was not specifying sex, but not leaving it out either, he said.

. . . I have been greatly impressed by Mary McCarthy's book of essays, *On the Contrary* I think it is called. The most educated female mind of our time in both America and England, I believe, as biased as Rebecca West in some directions, but more truly literary, which to me is more truly interesting, for she is a more conscious writer than Rebecca who lashed out with words like someone swimming or skating. Mary, on the other hand, flew on them somehow. . . .

[March 17, 1962]

Beloved,

A warm-looking sunny Saturday when viewed from behind one's window, deceptive as a mirror except to a handsome woman, for the truth is that it is cold as I discovered on going to the modern art museum to view the extensive, indeed enormous, Arp show. How it brought back my youth! I wonder if any of the Venetians said that about Tiepolo later, or Florentines said it about da Vinci when late in their lives. If they traveled to Paris and knew the king, they had a peek at the Mona Lisa. The curious organic Arp shapes which he almost patented as art—inside organs such as the uterus, I should think, and outside ones such as not quite the phallus yet including some rounded shapes that could be thought testicular (also spectacular at that time) all date today, yet have such intense a sense of syle, of personal creation, as to leave the present artists dangling, hanged by their own work which in representing nothing became almost the enemy of the artist himself—not representing him either, one feels. . . .

Anothr tiring wait for the peace as it is now called, though it is only a cease fire and may well unleash more OAS violence and set more blood flowing in a city stream in Oran or Algiers. George Bernier said the other night that Americans (like Cy Sulzberger, especially, with his Gaullist cult which he still retains as I do not) show merely ignorance in their idealization of a loveable France with cultivated Frenchmen whom George declared have never existed either in such general wisdom or charm or influence as the Yankees think—and as the French think, too. Somehow the French have profiited by, have been profiteers really, in swelling their own national reputation which is somehow based on false goods as I see it now. When I first came here in 1921 to live, I swallowed the entire map of France and every French citizen on it, as I did its Gothic and Romanesque architecture. I still swallow the latter, but am poisoned by the people. They are like slightly spoiled crabs or lobsters and give mental food poisoning. This conversation was provoked, of course, by the events in Algeria where the acts of the French OAS and their devoted followers in the cities have been such an emetic for one's feelings for France as to make one think one can never do aught but regurgitate its very name. Its intelligence one has greatly enjoyed. I feel it has little today. It still has education, however. . . .

[March 27, 1962]

Tuesday, my darling,

Your splendidly indignant letters against the de Gaulle government's protection of the OAS have animated this dull, dreary day by my rereading them. France will obtain from its population what it deserves or deserved from past populations, here or in Algieria, as history is always an addition of conditions and the whole or temporary total makes up a coming decade or epoch or maybe century. The only way for any country to be rid of its extreme right wing conformist rich citizens is the Russian revolutionary way. Kill them. This discourages any illegitimate children they might have had. If such tastes or tendencies begin anew later, send them to the local Siberia, or its counterpart, as the Russians now are doing to some of their revived profiteers. Did you notice that for a Moscow tradesman who was stealing lipstick metal cases and filling them with some red salve, selling the whole as a good brand of Soviet Marxist lipstick that the Tribunal passed the death sentence? Surely the only man ever killed by *les bâtons de rouges*. Yet the hedonistic tendency cannot be prevented from sprouting again, like weeds or flowers, to show their arrogant pro-American tastes by their tight trousers and passions for our jazz have won their battle. There are now two or three jazz clubs (without liquor) for them in Moscow, where they can listen to Russian jazz at least, and perhaps even U.S.A. records. Ten years ago, this would have been unthinkable.

This is Mr. K, and one of the reasons why it seems to me he is a Democrat, fractionally at least. The only one since the revolution.

Hoffman, a reporter on *The New York Times*, whom we knew in Rome, . . . has had to return from Algiers this week. He had been there nearly six months, telephoned Paris last week and said he could not stand any more murder, blood, bombs, violence. Was on the edge of a nervous breakdown. I haven't seen him yet, but have heard some of the things he has said to others. He says Salan is there, could easily be captured, but possesses compromising papers on the de Gaulle government, especially on Debré and his earlier Algérie Française connection; also the bazooka murder case, which would break a terrible scandal in Paris. I doubt if this will prevent Salan from being captured and the dangerous papers also.

Josette Lazar of *The New York Times Sunday Magazine* here said she was offered a story by Mayor Lesserre, or perhaps his name is Leferre. Yes, socialist mayor of Marseilles, with highly compromising anti-Debré stuff. The *Times* has turned it down and also on Chaban Delmas, which would only be sheer libel. Well, every country seems to have its group of politicians who wear vicuna coats supplied by Mr. Goldfein, or who by ambition or even belief have involved themselves where the scandal would be even greater than that of Sherman Adams. I suppose his vicuna coat was in Ike's estimation clean as a hound's tooth, eh?

I am worried about Bill's difficulty with his first Rome Letter. Those long Letters, or even the short ones, are very tricky to do, and I am the one who knows it, having more or less invented the formula which Bill would not like to have to follow, he being very independent. But some similar formula which combined special writing and a treat-ment of news both illuminating yet with a certain mixed light and dark touch will have to be invented to replace mine. The only chap I know who has done it entirely differently than I ever did is the fellow who lately wrote the piece on Gibraltar.* He is actually a poet who sent in his piece on a mere chance. His mixture of old background and news was highly personal, a new foreign letter style. I have even met him. Can't recall his name or face; recall only giving him praise.

I am delighted you loved [*Last Year at*] *Marienbad*. I wish I had, totally or even a great deal more than I did. Photogenically it was ex-quisite. Its thesis that time is interchangeable is of scientific mystical importance. But it will not change or lessen the impact of really first-rate normal films. If you had to see ten *Marienbads* in a row, you'd go dotty, my darling. . . .

[April 14, 1962]

Darling,

This has been a difficult and painful week. The only pertinent continued pleasure in it has been the beautiful bracelet. You have bestowed on me wonderful ornaments, my darling, of taste, creation

* Alastair Reid, 1961.

and generosity. You overwhelm me; it seems to me I have never given
you anything that carried beauty with it at all. We must mend that
bad habit of mine. The fastening of the bracelet is brilliant as a secret
affair, so clever, surely so strong and firm, too. I have learned to do it
one-handed, with no difficulty. I heartly thank you, from my heart to
yours.

I wrote you a postcard, airmail, from Geneva Tuesday . . . no,
Wednesday . . . just before flying back early. Vera [Page] had died
Saturday. I could not participate in the three-day Russian *veille* in the
little Russian church, but wanted to attend the funeral, which was
beautiful and touching, and the chanted service gave Russell great
satisfaction. He looked amazing. He looked thinned by grief and also
made younger by sorrow, a strange result. He looked beautiful, like a
monk, as he stood by her bier. Two of the Vilmorins flew up also,
André and his wife, Andrée, so confusing, and they comforted him,
too. As he told the stuffy little old priest in presenting me, "She is my
oldest friend, not only in Europe, but on earth. We have been friends
since 1925." True. Today there is a memorial service at the Russian
Cathedral in the rue Daru in Paris, at noon, a brief one. He has just
phoned and will be here for a week or more. I was doing all I could
for him, phoning almost daily before and after her death to him in
Geneva, forwarding his book proofs, giving orders to the concierge,
etc., as his flat is to be closed and everything sent to Charterhouse in
England.

Darling, soon we will be in Sperlonga . . . HOORAY! I enclose two
hundred dollars for the dunes fund. You did the work of us both,
alas. You are a fine little sandpiper.

No spring here. NONE so far. Yours forever and my thanks forever
for the beautiful golden proofs of your love.

                                                          [April 27, 1962]
Beloved,

I enclose a copy of the note I wrote Bill on his *excellent* Rome Letter
so you may be sure I did write to him and on his book, too. I forgot to
tell him I loved his Magnani tag line in his Rome opus—strong, witty,
true. I also enclose a check for you. It is an Easter present if you choose,
or a love present or a work present or a Rome present. In any case, it
is a gift that will ease your preparations and a part of your burdens for
your coming journey, where I will join you as soon as you are settled

there, have seen every Mondadori ever born and most of the Traver-sari-Danesis, too. If the house is not yet finished at Sperlonga, Piero deserves a beating. It will be shocking if with all winter at his command he has not fulfilled his last summer's work.

Easter and the Saturday preceding gave us spring at last here, limitedly, for with Easter Monday, spring was withdrawn again, but at least the trees turned green and many tulips managed to bloom in the Louvre garden, between cold nights. Katie and the Nun* were at Orgeval and have now departed. Katie as tiresome a convert to Catholi-cism as she was to Gurdjiev, bless her simple, excitable heart. She is so emotional and without critical faculty. When she said she could not bear it if she were a Jew on Good Friday, I was enraged, said that Jesus was a Jew, that she as a Catholic was damned lucky he had filled his destiny by being crucified. Otherwise, where would Christianity be? And that I was sure He would disapprove of her narrow-minded anti-Semitism on any day of the year, all the years he had been dead. . . .

A gray day. My black cat that lives on the roof has been missing for two days. I am worried he fell off. . . .

[June 8, 1962]

Darlinghissima,

. . . I wonder how much you and I lost on the Monday crash in our mutual funds and what happened to your individual investment on what stock I have forgotten. Well, I didn't mention it earlier; it seemed inept and useless. We take what comes, as do others, except we must be grateful that the INCOME from our funds will not be affected in all likelihood. That is our gain, our preservation, composed of a mix-ture of stocks which have lost on the market in price. Their interest will not be affected this year at least. Perhaps next, of course, though doubtless the solidarity of the investments will save them even then. It is a wicked error psychologically that small investors so greedily suck at the Wall Street market until its very bosom becomes falsely swollen, really by irritation in a way, and it puffs beyond reasonable shape, and bang! explodes from gaseous hot air. I read only in *The New York Times*, nowhere else, that once more the protective Wall Street organization decrees on control of margin stocks had NOT been care-

---

* "The Nun" was Lou Abetz, the real-life heroine of Katie Hume's *The Nun's Story*.

fully enforced, so when the downward explosion started, panic started with as a necessity—selling which became panic, like looking in the bread basket when no more bread is there. . . .

I am working on my Letter in advance, as I do each other weekend, staying in town, and hope such difficult work as these last ones have been, with such careful combing of newspapers for facts and references, will cease when Algeria starts voting after its autodetermination referendum July first. God knows if blood will follow it. How Christian can the Muslims be in turning the other cheek to those whites who have continuously murdered them, like rats, like sacrificial dark goats, on sidewalks, on country roads, in dark casbah neighborhoods?

My darling one, please send that postcard to me NOW.

        Now,
        Now,
        Now.

———

This summer I was planning on bringing Ester with me to Rome, where she would be settled temporarily in a spacious, luminous, terraced flat belonging to an Italian journalist friend. It was located on top of the Aventine, quite near Bill, Doris and the children. It was going to be a kind of try-out, prior to a possible definitive move. My darling mother had been showing signs of wanting to return home. I could see the advantages.

Janet was to meet me in Milan, once I had freed myself of family responsibilities, then we would be able to go to Sperlonga to inaugurate the little house. An exciting event!

Unexpected news reached me before leaving: Doris was expecting another child. Would it be a boy this time? I was eager to see them, but they had made plans to spend the summer in Menton, on the French Riviera, after which they would return to New York, where Doris wanted to have the baby. They had given up the idea of living in Europe. Janet worried about Bill's seemingly capricious uprootings and his ability to make a living by his writing.

Our house did not disappoint Janet. It had a special flavor, as she said. We found a garden of geraniums and bougainvilleas on the terrace, partly roofed over so that Janet could read, work or relax in the shade, where we had our breakfast tea in the morning and cocktails at sundown.

This time we would *actually* inaugurate it. My sister Franca was

awaiting our arrival to celebrate the event with us, which we did with
a good bottle of wine.

My neighbor Concetta and her family became a devoted housekeeper and protectors. She would be assisted by her Franco and
Pinuccia, then ages eight and six, for errands; by her husband,
Pasqualino, who would provide baskets of vegetables and fruits from
their farm in the valley; by the old grandfather as the look-out against
intruders.

We became *"le signore americane"* and they would run to greet us
at every arrival.

In July the town teemed with summer vacationers. Everyone seemed
to gather in the tiny main piazza to shop, sip coffee, gossip. A sweet
smell of freshly baked bread filled the air. We had our first cappuccino
at the *caffè* and made friends with the two lady bartenders and with
the newsdealer down the main street, who would reserve the papers
for us. We discovered old friends and made new ones. Every morning
I would descend the hundred and fifty-five broad steps to the beach
and bathe in the friendly, trustworthy Mediterranean, then climb back
under the hot sun to lunch with Janet on *insalata caprese*, a favorite
of ours, made of fresh tomatoes and mozzarella. Sometimes we had
picnics on the beach and took long walks to the archaeological sites.

The atmosphere was pleasant, life quieter and less complicated than
in our beloved Capri. We had thought it would be difficult to find
another place suited to our taste, but Sperlonga did not disappoint us.
We were divinely happy and carefree there, making the feeling of
tenderness and love that had bound us for over twenty years seem only
a day.

At the end of August, Janet returned to Paris by train. I flew back
to New York alone, having left Mother in Rome.

                                                    [August 8, 1962]
Darling,
    . . . Mary McCarthy was the queen of the International Literary
Caucus at the Edinburgh Festival according to the London *Times*,
which photographed her with Angus Wilson. She said *Naked Lunch*
by a writer named [William S.] Burroughs of whom I never even
heard and *Lolita* are the focal works of our century. I shall ask Terry
to send me the nude luncheon affair. If I like it no better than *Lolita*
as a major work, I shall find myself démodée indeed.

. . . I can see you in my mind's eye at the Island in your purple blouse and green (or brown silk) pantaloons, a woman in a million in mature elegance, charm and sensuality.

My beloved—

———

Back from our idyllic vacation, we resumed our work routine with renewed energy. We didn't have much time for anything else, except on weekends when Janet would go to Orgeval and I to Fire Island. That was my relaxation. It was a far cry from Sperlonga, but it had its own special charm and both Janet and I were especially fond of it. It is there that we had met and become friends, where we spent almost every weekend during those early days of the forties until we both left for overseas. I felt at home in the familiarity of its surroundings, the typical charm of an American frame house—cozy, full of memories, like the familiar scene of a beloved. I caught a few of the last parties of the season, a speciality of its predominantly gay population, and managed to have a pleasant time.

Janet had to deal with various visitors, but, far more important, she resumed her *New Yorker* Letters, which she always began to research by reading all sorts of newspapers and magazines. Her room, in fact, usually looked like a battlefield, with publications strewn about and her desk drawers a mess of clippings. To escape the pressure she took a brief vacation in London, a city she was very fond of and where she had many friends. More than she had ever had in Paris, and more stimulating, she said. After Italy and France, she must have longed for a little Anglo-Saxon relaxation, if only because of the language, let alone the more peaceful character of the people—restrained, orderly and obliging. For four years, during the latter part of the thirties, Janet had written a series of pieces about London life and happenings which were quite as brilliant as her Paris ones. She knew she would have a good time. She did. She even had two sunny, blue days, she reported.

That October had prepared us very little for the so-called Cuban crisis that confronted President Kennedy in his second year in office, pitting him against Soviet Premier Nikita Khrushchev and the missiles the Russians had installed on that island. For thirteen days we—and the whole world—trembled; the unthinkable, a nuclear war, had become a possibility. Our young president's handling of that alarming situation and the restraint displayed on both sides convinced us that Kennedy had acted with courage, skill and political intelligence.

[August 31, 1962]

Beloved,

Thank you for your cablegram of safe arrival since speed in good news is always of highest importance. And with you in the airs flying above, the Atlantic always seems endless in its breadth. Modern mechanics change, but the heart remains old-fashioned and sensitive to rapid dangers.

... There was a very interesting *New Yorker* piece on the Formentor novel prize. Did you see it? It must have been in the early August issues. I had never heard of the German writer Uwe Johnson in my life. Had you? An extremely fascinating interview with Ezra Pound in last *Paris Review*. What a fool I was in the old days, never to try to KNOW important people, except those who through affection, like Ernst, thrust themselves into my existence, enclosed by timidities like a wall, a stone wall built earlier in Indiana. Pound was one. Also Ford Madox Ford, mentioned in the interview, whom I met and fled. Pound's ideas in this interview seem to me of amazing clarity and rationality. (He slides over the Mussolini broadcasts a little too smoothly.) But do read what his mind still says, if you have a moment.

Are you all right, sweetheart?

[September 8, 1962]

... I have declared each day this week I would write to you again, because I so desired to, but have been caught also by the infliction of visitors, not all of whom can be pushed aside. Another one just phoned from a room on my floor. I had forgotten she was due, worse luck. The worst luck, though, is that she forgot one suitcase which she left at the airport at midnight, containing her jewelry and nearly a thousand dollars in [American] Express checks. I have just given her the requisite advice as to what to do now. She is a fool I have known since prep school days at Tudor Hall, utterly devoted as a friend, a good creature and enough to drive one to drink.

My personal list of the lost friends of my generation was added to by the death of e.e. cummings this week. It saddened me greatly, because he and Marie, his wife, were so happy together, and who could not think he had practiced choosing badly long enough with two earlier wives, before finding this handsome jewel. . . .

My beloved, I am rushing to the Ritz to lunch with an old friend from Chicago! The one who said since she was going into a small apartment, she had saved only "a small Botticelli," from her dead husband's great collection. . . .

[September 11, 1962]

Darlingest,

. . . The relief from the pressure of fears of a weekend ago in Cuba is immense. The French were too interested in their referendum to worry about the two KK's power struggle. More than ever they were in love with their own hateful partisanship. How can they quarrel so about their Republicanism when it is nonexistent except for its difference in parties and too many of them? Whereas in Monarchy I suppose there is only one party and the King is it. De Gaulle has been of supreme use like the capsule on top of a bottle: he prevents it from leading in all directions . . .

I shall be in London at the Stafford Hotel, St. James's Place, behind Green Park. I am glad as a young man on his first voyage to take this week off, in a new scene.

Kisses—devotedly yours.

[September 15, 1962]

Darling one,

Another perfect, sunny Indian Summer day. This past week has been a physical pleasure in weather to look at and smell. A city smells cleaner the first days of autumn than any other time. Spring has a certain stench of rut, of birth, of the discard, of the afterbirth really.

Glenway [Westcott] sent me his new book of essays on Thomas Mann, [Katherine Anne] Porter, Baroness Blixen* (the elegant, elderly dear—she knew two days before that those were her last two days and saw the world with dimming interest for the last time) and [Thornton] Wilder, only the last excellent in my esteem. Wilder is peppery and true, much based on a conversation years ago. How Glenway holds the past as his present.

I finally got the first Paris Letter off, not easy, and it sounds rather sour if intelligent. Well, Paris is a bit sour. The General's [de Gaulle's] German triumph scandalized many here, yet friendliness between the

* Isak Dinesen

two countries three times drowned in blood in one hundred years is necessary.

I sent your mother a postal card yesterday. I hope she is well and her dear friend at least dying not in agony. Why are we so attached to the body when it tries to leave us in old age? Our home, the body is. That is why, and we can no longer live in it or rent it for immortality.

Have seen no one this past week except an old childhood friend in my hotel on my floor, confound her, rich enough never to make up her mind about anything: what to do, when to eat, where to go, etc. I bundled her off to *Tosca* last night, because she hadn't seen the opera since she went with Scott and Zelda Fitzgerald in 1930, and she said "they're playing that *Tosca*. Is it good?" I nearly exploded. She lives in Pasadena and is sweet, obstinate, and a fool. . . .

[October 1962]

Wednesday, darlinghissima,

Dearest one, your distressed blue note—paper and morale—came to my hands Monday morning, a blue day by nature since it always means work. The loss of your mother's presence there at night I can imagine, sight and gesture, as clearly as if I saw it. It is useless to recall now how great the burden was, too, that you felt tied, first to your office all day, then to your apartment all evening. When Bill arrives and you have him in your office, part of your family emotions will have an outlet which will be a relief, though it will not be the same pleasure nor responsibility, the latter being what you seem to miss more, which now you feel alone gave a reason for your labor and existence. What you say about family emotions, their durability and intimacy that lasts a lifetime for many Europeans and seems no more than the relation between birds for Americans—feed their little greedy, opened beaks, teach them to fly, then they do not recognize you nor you them in the tree tops a few weeks later—all this is too horribly true a criticism to dispute.

Don't forget that as much as Americans displease you now because of their changed characters, less and less tenderhearted or unselfish season after season, so that now they seem completely different as a race than they were, naïve, silly, hopeful, after the first war, so and even more do they displease your poor mother so that her constant tirade or criticism against any contact with them on the streets or bus or at the movies was an irritation and bitter disappointment to her, as a humanist and wise, elderly European woman. It is too soon now to evaluate whether she is happy enough in her beloved Rome, without her profoundly favorite Roman, yourself, to make up to her for the companionship with you she so exclusively enjoyed and which now nobody has quite the heart nor leisure to give her at night, as you did.

It is a tragedy to lose faith and sympathy for one's own people, and for you to have this loss twice, first for the Italians under Mussolini and now the Americans under no matter what president.

I lunched with Marquis Childs* and his charming wife today. He asked at once for your news. He said as he walked in the Crillon last night that the old concierge, a trifle in his cups, said, "But monsieur, what are you doing here? There is no trouble in France right now." I kept trying to avoid writing about de Gaulle in my Paris Letter, as you had begged and counseled, but could not avoid him. As a subject, he is as overpowering as his nose in size. The French are now worrying a lot about the Italian fridgidaire's superior sales appeal, so great that General Motors here in Paris, which had founded a factory, have closed it, throwing three thousand men out of work, and are moving to Holland. As there is a labor shortage here, the opposite of our unemployment, these men will find jobs instantly, but the incident has added to the French irritation with all of us Yankees, and they would like to freeze us to the marrow in our own ice boxes, I fancy.

Marquis seems worried about the extreme right-wing politicians in Washington who are so belligerent they want to attack Cuba, East Berlin, and God knows where else. China it may be. He thinks they talk like paranoiacs.

I saw the Antonioni *Eclipse* film last night and found it comprehensibly dull as many do, though some say it is a chef d'oeuvre of simplicity. Delon looks so much like a faggot that one cannot believe he could be in love with the Vitti girl and, indeed, the point of the plot is that they are unable to fall in love, both of them. The scenes on the floor where they roll about, laughing like darling little kiddies, biting each other's hands and necks and giggling as if tickling each other was to me imbecilic. Nursery sex play. *Divorce à l'Italienne* now still playing at SEVEN Paris movie houses. Romain Gary's new play opened to play once a week at the Comédie Champs-Elysées. The little theater will be lucky if it lasts for the next Monday night, its single night. It was more than panned. It was boiled, fried and roasted to a cinder by the critics. It's about the failure of ideals in a UNO character! ! . . .

* U.S. journalist. Awarded the first Pulitzer Prize in commentary, 1969.

[October 12, 1962]

Darlingest,

I had a sweet card from your mother, perfectly legible, thanking me for my belated birthday card to her; her tone seemed happy. By now all your dear family must be assembled, which means you will have blood company, so precious to you. . . .

She just had a marvelous post card from Lesley Blanch, Romain Gary's wretched wife, in Siberia saying, "Siberia is a snug, lovable country and I hope to see more of it." Oddest report on Siberia I ever heard.

The vote of censure against de Gaulle in the Chamber was exciting as an event and for endurance, though not for oratory or impressive parliamentary conduct; the usual mêlée, screams, yells, squabbles. I was there a couple of hours in the afternoon, returned about ten in the evenings, and remained until the end at five and walked home, the Concorde looking beautiful with its renewed, cleaned palaces illuminated even just before dawn. I wonder if the Latin mind, that is the Italian and French, which fancies itself Latin and had the same Latinic education, is not too varied, too faceted, too full of nature changed, already old, to be able to support a republic, or to make it function. After all, it is initially an English or Anglo-Saxon experiment, actually Swiss to begin with as an example, but behind them a development of the British check against its monarchs which is very different than a French or Roman parliament which exists to be a check on each of its own parties, thus paralyzing them all in quarrels and futilities and getting nothing done. The intolerance of the French party views is hideous, is like the Spanish inquisitional attitude toward a heretic, any heretic, for here anybody not a member of your own party IS a heretic to your mind. I feel apologetic toward you as a reader each time I give so much space in my letter to politics, but my beloved, how can I help it?

I have been reading for the first time William James's *Varieties of Religious Experience,* and have been greatly illuminated on my own psychology, very helpfully, too. Sorry this is so badly typed. I worked six days entirely on this last Letter. My hands are really tired.

I embrace you, I miss you terribly.

[October 26, 1962]

Dearest one,

Have to go to Versailles for trial of kidnappers of Peugeot little boy of two years ago. Recall? It will be a change from de Gaulle. I am disillusioned about him and France, too, as usual. He has simply proved that the only way to govern France is by ignoring its Republicanism and parliament with the result that the governor in the end is hated and suspected, as by this time he should be. A dictator should be more careful to be legal than he has been, and with powers to pass every kind of special law in his own favor and convenience. He has been abysmally careless, like a man running a bus over mountains, who forgot to equip it with good brakes, so everybody falls down into the valley below on the first wet, slippery day. I really wept bitterly last Monday for France, as if it were the end of a love affair I had thought long since extinct anyhow. They are unreliable and defective, even toward themselves.

Thank you, my darling, for your enjoying my political stuff as mysteries. Yes, that is how I try to focus on it. It is rather the truth, too. Odd, but fear inspired by Cuba will help the Oui votes for de Gaulle tomorrow. Who would have thought Castro would have aided him?

I love you darling, always, as ever.

[November 21, 1962]

My poor darling,

How a helpless, elderly, beloved parent complicates life, tearing the progeny apart with both worry and tenderness, and how essential money is at the end of life, the base of independence. I was always glad my mother died with her financial boots on at least, leaving nearly no money to "her three talented daughters" as she fondly and fatuously described us always, but at least able to pay for her own hired service. But that did not free Hildegarde of all she went through in all the earlier years with Mother across the garden and practically in Eric and Hildegarde's bed, with her dependence on them, her fears by night, her fear of ever being alone, so she went on their holidays with them. Poor Hildegarde. I was certainly too selfish to help.

My conscience weighs me down more than you can imagine for more things than you know about.

The week (six days) in London with Moura von Budberg, every day in some capacity was dreamy. Three whole days of wonderful blue skies and Indian summer, two days in the country, one at Mollie P.-Downs's exquisite Elizabethan brick cottage in Surrey, a fine, heartening, friendly day. . . .

I heard Mahler's Third Symphony for the first time. It runs for nearly two and a half hours, with choruses, at the new Festival Hall which looks like a railroad station, terrible. Looks like it on the inside, and you can see suburban trains whizzing by through its glass walls on the outside. Insanity of ugliness. Acoustics too brilliant for comfort. The symphony was poetic, profoundly moving, reverent, lyrical, great personal private music in the post-Wagnerian style by a smaller genius than Wagner. . . .

I went to Evreux, two hours motoring, to hear Mendès talk Friday night in his election campaign. Stayed the night, went with Bob Doty of *The New York Times* and Josette Lazar of the same paper. We had an interesting evening, but Mendès talks less well than he writes and, though he was cheered by the crowd and his princeling Gaullist opponent booed, Mendès lost on Sunday. He is, alas, really through politically, or so we all fear. Worked like a dog over the week on my Paris Letter on this fantastic Gaullist parliamentary election landslide. Who would have thought the old general could ride the country like that again after these four years? Almost inexplicable.

Must rush to coiffeur, darling one. Hair filthy, nails broken on three days of typing for Letter. Bless and keep you, handsome one, and darlinghissima sweetheart.

———

Bill, Doris and the children had returned to New York. The new baby was expected in January. With Ester in Rome, I would have more time to enjoy their presence—I was not exactly the baby-sitting kind, but would gladly offer my services in an emergency.

While re-establishing himself and his relationship with *The New Yorker*, Bill came to work in my office. I had entertained a secret hope that one day he could take my place. I clearly underestimated his fiercely independent spirit.

Janet was right. I was always trying to solve family problems, especially when they concerned my mother, whose age had turned her into a gentle, submissive person. She had just moved in with Franca in Rome, and I decided to fly there during Christmas week and see for myself what the situation was. I wouldn't have time to stop in Paris, or to see Janet in Rome, as she was sailing at the end of January on the *Queen Elizabeth*. We would meet with pleasure and at greater leisure in New York.

[December 7, 1962]

Darling one,

. . . Ingrid Bergman is *splendid* as Hedda Gabler. I wrote a critique of extreme enthusiasim and I think intelligence on her interpretation and performance, in which her own Scandinavian entity is basic to the characterization which must be the only one we have ever seen that is native, that includes almost the geographic northern influence, the chill instability and morbidity of that curious unmatronly female. What an interesting, unstable egotist Ibsen created in her, how close to fleshly reality in his psychology and without help from Freud, then undiscovered. Hedda's frigidity is only one part of her decadence. The other is her hyperesthesia, her insane and rather idiotic cult of beauty considering how little she contributed to it, except her longings that others perfect and produce it, not she. Tickets for her Hedda are already advertised in the papers as selling fourteen days in advance. She looked beautiful in black in the last act as she glides forth to shoot herself. Her laughter when she was shooting on stage at Judge Brack in the garden was wonderfully strange, a lovely, almost childish joy and viciousness.

I am lunching with her Thursday. Her French accent is very easy and not harsh like her American accent in English. Her husband* has a little office in Paris in the Avenue Vélasquez, with a bed and bath and kitchen behind where she has been living while rehearsing. Strange, the French do not at all know Ibsen, as the English, Germans and Americans do. I wonder why he was omitted for so long after the very early introductions to him.

In the Letter I sent this week, I end with a kind of essay on the French lack of talent for being Republican. I dared not write as strongly as I wished. Anyhow, this was clearly enough on a psychology which is so strained, so little democratic, that it would take deep analysis, far deeper than I would be able to plunge into or arrive at, to make clear where their lacks are.

---

* Lars Schmidt, Swedish producer.

Mother had been writing poetry throughout her lifetime, even after her sight had begun to weaken and she could hardly read any longer. She had left her poems neatly assembled on the top shelf of her bookcase in New York. I secretly took them with me to Rome that summer, with the idea of collecting them in a small volume to present to Mother as a surprise the following Christmas.

Diario Poetico, a delightful volume, in quality paperback, beautifully designed, with the Danesi imprint and our dedication to Mother, contained thirty-five poems and was ready when I arrived in December.

Mother was speechless. Her hands trembled as she held this small volume of her thoughts and feelings over the years. It was the best Christmas we could have given her.

1963

At the news of the birth of Billy, Jr., Janet wrote a brief note on the eve of sailing on the H.M.S. *Queen Elizabeth*:

"January 29

"I sail tomorrow and so I shall soon see you and the masculine new member of the family. I am delighted it is a boy. You girls have done well in consideration of the female difficulties in life, but after two daughters, a son is a psychological change you and I can appreciate, being part of a trio of daughters."

She arrived just in time to celebrate the event. Her arrival, in any case, was always an occasion. The entire staff of *The New Yorker*, it seemed to me, wanted to entertain her—the Shawns, the Truaxes, the Botsfords, the Hamburgers, and many others.

Finally, we flew to Puerto Rico for a week of relaxation at our friend Burt Martinson's place in the so-called Junca, an enchanting spot high on the edge of the rain forest.

Another brief note, postmarked March 19, said:

"Two hours late, owing to a wreck on a freight train, just after Salt Lake City. Poor Hildegarde will have been waiting at Sacramento one hour and will wait one more before I appear. On waking, I looked out on a Japanese painting. Snow-clad mountains reflected in an enormous lake in a desert. My porter said, 'I never laid my eyes on it before!' We had been rerouted. The lake is prehistoric and owned by Indians, so it is virgin. No hotels, no houses. They refuse to sell, and how right they are. Maybe they are the only U.S.A. inhabitants who, not being citizens, act like philosophers and moralists above the low cult of money. The Feather Canyon route today was exquisite in scenic beauty: snow, some deer and an eagle, and the little Trout River which once floated many pigeons' feathers far below. Getting off now. My heart is yours."

On March 22, she wrote her first letter from Calistoga, where she visited Hildegarde in her new house.

[March 22, 1963]

Darlinghissima,

The views from the new house over the Napa Valley and up onto the hills opposite and semi-mountains are superb, extending to a vista of perhaps sixty miles, with only one house in view in all that sweep. The house hugs the hilltop in a mixture of greys and dull green colors of painted wood, spread out like a fan with "butterfly" roofs, which means a lifted roof here and there as decoration, which I fail to find very decorative, and there are no trees immediately around the dwelling, nor will there be, as they fear fire like most experienced Californians. The setting nevertheless is elegant and lovely. . . .

From my bed, I see the length of the sixty mile view when the lovely pale greenish curtains of my room are drawn open. I am happy to be here. We drive through the countryside in the afternoon.

There is a sweet white and brown spotted lady cat named Peanuts, who adores us all, is a great mouse catcher in the garden, and officially brings her mice to the back door of the kitchen. . . .

Pardon typing—this machine is *terrible*.

Yours forever . . .

Janet always had a good time motoring through the countryside, and she always managed to send me postcards of places and vistas she had admired. She had planned to go to Lake Tahoe, where Ethel Merman was opening at Harrah's, a local casino. She was going with Stanley Eichelbaum, her ex-*New Yorker* checker, who later reported on the experience.

At one point, Merman asked Janet: "Don't you think my gams are holding up well?" Janet hadn't heard that word for legs in years; the question startled her. In turn, she startled Merman, who, when she heard that Janet had written a Profile of Picasso, confided to a friend: "Do you mean she wrote about Picasso and now she is going to write about me? She is a fine old broad . . ."

From Lake Tahoe, Janet sent me a postcard:

[April 12, 1963]

Darling,

Divine weather at last! Sun, warmth, snow in the mountains and a fine journey in Stanley's scarlet Volkswagen. We are in this great gambling establishment, an *incredible* sight. Slot machines on all sides. I thought the lunch counters were roulette tables at first. [Stanley added]: Janet, I'm afraid, will not permit me to gamble. She is fascinated, but disapproving.

———

This time, when Janet returned from Calistoga, I was alone in the apartment. I so wished that she could have remained with me a little longer before going back to Paris. As the day of her sailing approached, I became tense and unhappy and was a figure of doom when we said good-bye at the pier.

Janet sailed back to France at the end of May, with her friends Alethea and Hawley Truax. Her first day on board the Holland-America liner she wrote, "Of one thing I am already sure—the food is appalling, judging by lunch. It is old *matière*, old-frozen you know, so it has a dull, arctic taste, like frozen reindeer, I fancy."

In her last note before arriving, she wrote: "Perfect weather. Three days of calm sun, despite there being three priests first class, two Episcopalians and one Roman Catholic of St. Thomas Seminary, New York, who appeared at the dance floor last night wearing (only momentarily) a red Turkish paper fez. A German Countess snob, who sits near us, has finally deigned today to speak to me unintroduced because I have the Légion d'Honneur and so did her grandfather, an American from Poughkeepsie named Van Bergen who lived in Paris in 1890. Sister also on board, but less chic—married to a Black [or Papal] Roman nobility. However, my pickup is pro-Pope John XXIII. He thinks Montini of Milan will be the next Pope and equally liberal and anti-black aristocracy. God hope and help us that this will be true. The meals and drinks with the Truaxes have been as lush as an oasis in conversation. I bought the champagne last night of the very best quality, $8 for 1952 Dom Pérignon, and superb it was. I must work at once on the belated Sylvia Beach piece for the *Mercure* [*de France*]. I miss you, I miss you. Yes, we must arrange for no more work . . ."

When I read that last phrase, I had to smile, knowing all too well that this was pure fantasizing on Janet's part. She always *talked* about stopping, mainly because I was always so miserable at our partings.

[June 12, 1963]

Wednesday, my dearest creature,

Your nearly impenetrable airmail letter welcomed me on my arrival. We spent several hours in Southampton in the harbor and dock. Very interesting as any port always is, and I saw the Isle of Wight en passant, which I do not recall having viewed in my journeys. I recall when I first visited Mont-St.-Michel in 1922. The church was disaffected ever since about 1906 after a French quarrel between church and state, and there were no priests there, they having spent all those years on Wight and planning to return in a few days with a great pilgrimage of welcome, and I was then romantic enough to imagine it in medieval terms. I later heard it was like a Cook's tour.

Monday night I saw opening of Colette's company of U.S.A. players. *The Zoo Story* done EXCELLENTLY. *Death of Bessie Smith* atrocious in acting and directing. House semifull. Colette [de Jouvenel] in a gold tailleur, very plump. Dear Carlottina [del Pozzo] looking unrecognizable, no make-up, a "ladies dress" on. She looked like some provincial aristocrat growing into a spinster. A shock and a sad one.

I believe Alice Toklas will be able to keep her apartment. My cable to Malraux plus others like Monroe's* seem to have helped. Am lunching with her this noon. Will hear full story. Virgil will lunch, too, and he knows all as usual.

It will rain today prehaps. Fine weather, but with a terrific interrupting electric storm Monday afternoon. I thought the garden en face would blow up and my hotel and room, too. Terrible lightning and thunder like war.

Must work to finish my Sylvia Beach piece. . . .

I send you one dozen kisses, as sweet as little fruit cakes.

* Monroe Wheeler.

[June 1963]

Darlinghissima,

Tenere e appassionata!!! All true whether grammatical or not. It was difficult to hear your voice on the phone at the Manin, so the pleasure was vague but gratifying. I shall go to Notre Dame Friday night to see the son et lumière, given here for the first time, so odd. Why not earlier? Why start with Napoleon as they did? Jesus also had a dramatic life, as did this cathedral. The central front entry door has been cleaned and scraped so one can see its legends in stone more clearly.

Rain, rain, chill wind, no summer except one day, Monday, which was a pleasure. This is the kind of weather I always had when in Bavaria, outside Munich. I recall the two months spent there in a big hotel with my family, Hildegarde a little girl of eight with long, black curls. Such damp chill winds from the Starnberger See, the huge lake there, that the very grass harbored all sorts of horrible snails and creatures without shells, like red rubber tubes, that crawled around, with tall heads like prehistoric tiny monsters and eyes on branches.

Hawley and Alethea came yesterday from Vienna. They will be here several weeks. I spoke frankly, if daringly, last night to him. We dined together, we three, and I said I thought the magazine was now faced because of its very liberality and its Negro article by James Baldwin, also its recent Talk piece, on the same subject, quoted in part by Joe Alsop, by the necessity to have some Negro employees. He admits it, but sees less clearly than I feel I see the urgent necessity. I quoted Reston, who said this week, "Do what you can; march in a parade or write your senator or congressman, but do something." Well, we must do something whether we need more workers or not. As I said, there are plenty of people on those New Yorker floors who do not work enough to be there in justification, so why declare against a dozen more of a darker color? I shall talk further with him on this subject. This prospect of giving work at ONCE is necessary, I think. He talked about "token" work. I said, well, why not? Token employment would be something, at least, instead of nothing. . . .

This summer I wanted to give Mother a few weeks in the country, and in my rented car I drove her through the picturesque Castelli Romani, a series of small towns in the Alban Hills a few miles south of Rome, perched around two lakes that were once active volcanos.

Mother's youth and part of my early childhood had been spent at

Rocca di Papa, the so-called Papal Rock. It sits on the slopes of Monte
Cavo, an ex-volcano two thousand feet above sea level. Here my
grandfather, Augusto, had built a charming villa for his beautiful wife
and family.

The hills were covered with lovely chestnut trees and cyclamen, with
tiny strawberries in the summer and delicious mushrooms in the fall.
The area is famous for its *porcini*, the large-capped mushrooms sold by
peasant girls at the roadside. They are exquisite broiled with garlic and
parsley.

I returned just in time to see the great Washington Freedom March
on television, on August 28. Janet saw nothing, she wrote disap-
pointedly the next day. The TV Telstar II failed to function in Paris.

Janet's father had been concerned about the injustices toward blacks.
He had founded Flanner House in Indianapolis to help black women;
Janet herself in her youth had worked for a year in a reform school for
black girls, and as a child she remembered having sat on Booker T.
Washington's knees. The great educator asked her, "You are not afraid
of me, are you?" "Why should I be?" she had answered.

In my early days in New York, I had met many black writers and
musicians. It seemed natural. We often went up to Harlem to see their
shows and hear their jazz. My husband and I even took Arturo Toscanini one night, after a Carnegie Hall concert. He had never been to
Harlem, or heard any jazz bands. When we entered the night club,
Louis Armstrong was playing. Toscanini stopped to listen, and sat
down only when Armstrong had finished. "What a breath, what a
breath," he said. We stayed until four a.m.

[August 26, 1963]

Darling,

It seemed supremely important that I see you, that you see me,
when you were in the plane and I was on top of the tribune [observa-
tion deck], so my relief was acute, my satisfaction swelled, senselessly
in a way, for what could it really amount to, one more glance at that
distance? Yet that is how it seemed. I knew it was you waving, for
though another woman in a red suit had appeared there a few minutes before, I could tell it was not you by the clumsy way she waved,
and you waved like Tosca and threw kisses. That was the identification. I walked from the Invalides station, as we had after Versailles,
to my fifth floor, via the Tuileries Gardens, stopping to rest at the
pond, as we did, where you remarked the fat fish, today gluttonous on

bits of bread thrown by children. I heard singing and the phrase, in American, "five hundred miles from home," and walked over to watch and listen to a half-dozen compatriots, some with young beards, two with mandolins and guitars, singing in a lovable, manly way and with excellent harmonies about being that distance from home, a long ballad story. The French listened politely, liked it, applauded cautiously for fear they might have to contribute if the hat were passed. The singers said "Merci beaucoup," as if they had given a free concert as indeed they had, even more for their pleasure than for the listeners', all except me. I love street singing, and thy sang deliciously. Then I came to my room and read my papers, in readying for work.

I had an ice cream at nine downstairs with Pierre, the waiter, and now I know you must have landed. I watched your plane down the runway and into the sky. It was to it I spoke saying, "Fly, birdie, fly." I could see it a long, long way into the distance after it soared off. It was so enormous. Every tear is like a drop of acid now. I shall go to bed and try to sleep, No wonder you admired the Tour Eiffel last night. It was especially illuminated, all over, the liftman said. A moment ago, there was an orange slice of the moon by it, like a slice of melon. I love you; that is sure and true at least.

Thine, such as I am.

[August 29, 1963]
Thursday, the day after the Washington Freedom March

My darling,

Your pained letter did not quite cross mine, since yours came only this morning with tea, so often my hemlock these days, being the beginning of another day. The figure you made and your gestures on the platform of the plane still remain and will in my memory, like a tableau en permanence.

I am deaf still from our plane ride and lost a couple of pounds in anguish and sadness while you were here, suffering at your suffering.

I shall arrange with Shawn to work only six months a year, autumn and winter, for *The New Yorker* if he will accept me on those terms in the Paris post. He will, I dare say. The rest of the year I shall spend with you. The other six months I shall spend in Fance. That is my homeland of my imagination and habit after all these years.

I love you and am only now conscious of how often I sigh as if bringing up my soul from its depths. It is my depths where I live, where I really live.

It rained in the morning two days after you left. Today is bright, sunny all morning, but now clouds gather in melancholy. I could not find enough material to do a Paris Letter this Tuesday past; there has never been so emptied an August month. I am cabling my first Letter on September 3, this coming Tuesday. I shall work hard and try to make these last fifty or so of them count as better than any others, in diligence and wisdom and knowledge and facts of French life. . . .

[September 16, 1963]

Darling,

No, by Jove, it's Friday the thirteenth. A fairly lucky day here because as yet it has not rained. I thought today of how inept you found me with anything mechanical this summer in the Sperlonga kitchen where my limitations showed up worse (except at peeling tomatoes with those darling little sawteeth knives). The reason I thought of it today was that I had bought in New York, or Terry bought for me, a fat roll of that new kind of misty-looking Scotch tape that doesn't tear, and a kind of cage to enclose it in. Well, I couldn't get it open at first, until my waiter showed me how to do it. Then I couldn't insert the roll of tape inside, so I had to dress and go to Smith's bookshop on two corners down the Rivoli, and there a kindly English lady clerk inserted the roll, snapped the celluloid cage shut and wished me good-day with a smile. Not even a contemptuous smile.

Today has been wonderfully sunny, bright, summery. The first in two months, I am told. Everyone in Paris is out and on foot. I am glad my morale is better again, better than in the last year since being in Italy and since, at least most of the time, the other days of the week when it is low I am prostrate with melancholy and memories. If I believed in heaven and hell, I would be really desperate at the eternal punishment awaiting me. Fear is a great guide, but a shameful weakening influence. But so is the weakness of the ego, like mine.

Poor Kay Boyle and poorer, doomed Joseph. Had you heard that after the brain operation, the cancer went to his spine? She is taking him to California by plane where he will die, as she teaches in San Francisco or perhaps it is Berkeley, at the state university. She dare not refuse the job just offered. After poor Joseph perishes, then she will have the children as usual, and their husbands. What a sad family novel from such a brilliant, broadminded mother and two intellectual fathers, Laurence Vail and Joseph.

Your own devoted . . .

[September 19, 1963]

My darling one,

It is warm, misty and semi-autumnal, and lovely to look at, lovely to feel. Feel, smell, look at—one can do all three with this kind of day. It literally touches all one's senses. One becomes both a painter and a *collectionneur*, buying the picture nature holds up, but feeling one has had a hand in it, an eye in selecting it, the flash of genius in the joy of creating it. Send another longish typed letter like the last. I am impatient, always, to read what you say.

I lunched with Moura von Budberg here in my bar. Moura has been seeing French friends, with money, even without money, but at any rate with an education which would be the same, if only slightly in imitation of the other, since money is educational, too, I suppose. They are all rather chilled toward de Gaulle. They think he has bitten off more than he can chew, they told her. This evidently did not refer to the anti-inflation plan, but his international diplomacy. They are now worried Washington and Moscow will become too intimate, get on too well. Then as the pair of great powers will so move together that "there will be no more Europe." To my astonishment, she added, "It could be true, of course."

She lunched with the Italian ambassador yesterday, of whom she is very fond. She said, an old friend. He told her Italy was in a certain difficulty financially and industrially. The Communist strength in Italy either in manifesting its existence with the new government or by the last elections has frightened off foreign investors which Italy needs, the ambassador said. They do not want to put money in a country which the reds could dominate, is the way Wall Street would put it, I suppose. I find the idea itself nonsensical, except that of course strikes and factory troubles can indeed make troubled industries as a result. That can ruffle the hope of a good five percent interest, I dare say. As for her first French theory, that there will be no more Europe, it cannot be true in our lifetime, at least. She has a tenderer heart than I. She feels the entities of countries which I feel as their strengths rather than their human values which do not change, so much at least, from border to border on the continent. I will bet on Europe for another three-quarters of a century. Then gigantism may win. It is bound to win in the end because global money will stretch its power and performance in an increasingly mechanized world (this may all be rot). You will put the nickel in the slot in Holland, and it will come out a chocolate bar in India, or something of that sort.

Peter Brook wants to meet me, Moura said. He is here, working on *Sergeant Musgrave's Dance.** I had met him earlier in London and here once, and liked him.

I must write to Kay Boyle, too. Her daughter Bobby phoned last night to give news of someone else. She hadn't heard if Kay had arrived in San Francisco or not with poor Joseph.

This is too dull a letter to continue with, yet were we merely chatting in the flesh, you would forgive. Please forgive it in ink, my dearly beloved friend.

[October 19, 1963]

Darling one,

A letter from you first greeted me, the one that was not forwarded, then a new one in the blue note formula, this time intact even after opened. I am in no way tired by my baths in Abano, feel tremendously well, despite the serious shock I underwent when the doctor rather recklessly (I think) cut down my blood pressure from 20 to 14 in two days, so I was able to start at once on the new Paris Letter for Tuesday. I must apologize for the amazing dullness of my Letter on French books, which I only got around to reading today. It seemed so curiously dull, I was unable to read it for the first time last night. I now discover why: there are ELEVEN CUTS in it, for no reason on earth that I can discover. They drained personal comment out of it, also occasional bits of spice such as the fact that Julian Green became conscious of his "sexual bias" at an adolescent age by poring over the Doré illustrations, showing beauteous seminude young men, in the Protestant Bible which was the Green family's pride and his Sunday reading material. Why cut that, I ask you? I am writing to Botsford and very strictly as soon as this upcoming Letter is cabled.

Mary McCarthy went to Madrid yesterday to the Annual Writers Conference with Nathalie Sarraute—even my comment on her being

---

* John Arden's *Sergeant Musgrave's Dance: An Unhistorical Parable* was first performed in London in 1959.

a Russian and that her book thus "reflected anxiety" was cut. So I have not seen her, talked to Jim, and may see both this week or next. Will ask her New York address. Katherine Anne [Porter] is seeing no one, is living incognito or without relations with anyone in some obscure hotel near the Observatoire, finishing her selection of a book of her favorite short stories from her own pen for which publishers offer twenty thousand dollars advance on which she will buy a house to die in, she says. She has still to finish a few payments on her emerald ring! Monroe said. I shall write to her.

Giancarlo Menotti, to whom I sent a telegram asking for a ticket Tuesday night for the opening of his new opéra bouffe,* kindly had one sent to me, so that can be included in this Letter, thank heaven. Little enough new of genuine esthetic importance, except Cocteau's death and Piaf's, too, but they have been buried several times by the American press, so that now not a bone shows above the funeral flowers. Difficult to make fresh again.

Here is beauteous weather, today warm as summer, the summer that did not arrive during its season, but now comes as an out-of-season treat. It is better to have good than bad skies for all your Italian contingent of visitors, welcome as they are and slightly burdensome as large companies also always are. That any of them determine to eat American seems insanity. May they soon get their fill of hamburgers.

Poor Frank [Merlo] the sparrow. Yes, he served Tennessee well and faithfully as a truthful voice, as the only voice of truth he ever heard or anyhow listened to. How rapidly cancer can kill nowadays, as if with practice it has speeded up its fatal action, perhaps kindly. . . .

[October 28, 1963]

Darlinghissima,

What charming letters from you Saturday. How I enjoyed them. I enclose the three major damning musical reviews of Paris on Giancarlo's opéra bouffe. You will see my report of it in this week's *New Yorker* Letter of Thursday, gentle on the musical production, for it is, alas, not musically meritorious, impossible to think so or say so. It lacks any kind of personal style, such as he had in *Consul* or even *Medium*, such as Bernstein had to such brilliant high degree in *Candide*, that great loss as the only bouffe New York ever produced, allowed to sink underfoot, like a musical comedy that failed to earn cash.

* *Le Dernier Sauvage.*

Now back to Giancarlo. The audience in general LIKED it, applauded, had a good time, but as Doda Conrad said that first night (he liked it more in loyalty than aught else, for there was no other basis), "the critics will spit on it." They did. I lunched with Giancarlo Thursday here in my bar. It has now a nice prix fixe lunch for three dollars, very delicious. I gave him a vodka cocktail which he needed, and by chance, Katherine Anne Porter was there alone, also lunching. "Was meanin' to phone you, honey, to see if you could come down an' lunch with me, honey." So I said we three will have coffee as I want to talk to him alone a little. He was an object of misery. I must say, he left laughing, kissing me twice, said we had both saved his life for that day at least. Said he had never received such brutality even here in Paris as from Clarendon in *Figaro*.

Mary McCarthy sent me her book before leaving. Now really darling, did young ladies in college talk of sex organs and relations so constantly in 1933? True, Freud and scientific eroticism as a commonplace had been discovered but, by Jove, my dear, though I am a hardened old expatriate, I wonder if I can get on with her book after chapters two and three. Chapter one, the wedding, is sharp, truthful, realistic in its social gradations in the minds of those same girls, not satire but of a type called satire because it is intelligently, lightly stated TRUTH. Your comment that it was sex, not fiction the buyers were buying *The Group* for is, I would suppose, only too obvious, now that I see it in print.

Am suddenly invited to dine tonight at Ambassador Finletter's (UNESCO ambassador) with Lippmanns, unexpected here. I am so pleased and looking forward to good listening and friendliness. I fancy the international situation is irksome, but why more than usual? Nobody wants to accept the fact that Russians are now being perforce well intentioned to us—for these months, perhaps these years, because of China. Here the Communists report the Moscovites call them the Trotskyites—The Chink Trotskyites. It's too comic. Good Lord, what sillinesses ideology leads men into, and how they fail to laugh at themselves!

Yes, I cabled Botsford demanding an explanation "instanter repeat instanter" of what had happened to that book Letter, telling him I was sure he had not carved it up with a knife like that, but the result in any case was "the removal of the white meat with nothing left but the Pope's nose." Glenway found a terrible typo recently in the magazine head over poetry critique, which said "everse" instead of "verse." I hope Ross is cursing loudly in his grave, bless him. . .

[November 6, 1963]

Darlinghissima,

Thank you extremely for the two copies of the *New York Review of Books*. My word, how officially literate and authoritative we Americans have become, how many heavily minded critics appear like mushrooms, poisonous or nourishing, in a new periodical, easily the only one of consequence we have now, and I hope it doesn't take to jazz records, politics and other forms of intellectual salesmanship like the *Saturday Review*. I thought Mailer's review of McCarthy's *Group* was pretty revolting in its pomposity and scabrous point of view. He is a fine one to be shocked by sexual realism. He, who realistically stabbed his wife's abdomen. It was his pomposity as a know-it-all I found the worst, just like that day at the Diamonds' cocktail when he interrupted Dr. Rosen, and I said, "Young man, keep quiet. You are interrupting an intelligent, older man."

Jim West told me that Mailer's latest notion for himself was to run for mayor of New York and settle the gang wars by having the rival gangs assemble in Central Park and joust to death. The only really spirited truthful, accurate and illuminating review on Mary McCarthy's book I have seen I here enclose from the *Observer* this last Sunday. There is nothing [Francis] Wyndham says—or not miss, I suppose, but am not sure—to which I do not agree, though would not have been able to think of it all with such lucidity. Cyril Connolly's in the London *Sunday Times* was ludicrous, loose thinking, sloppy. Jim said it was something hashed up from a luncheon with her at Véfour, in which she told him in advance her ideas. I see she must have used Zola as a reference, which I, too, thought of. Her realism has the same rights as his had.

The strike today has been bothersome. No electric light; a candle is an oddity for reading by, but late this afternoon the sun shone faintly which helped the gloom of the rooms. I hope you like the *Feu Follet* film piece in my Paris Letter. It is one of the finest films I ever saw for making, for clarity and subtlety combined, and the acting is perfected by Malle's directing. Put on the screen with no *générique* [credits], it was refreshing, stimulating, to be plunged right into the film without having to read what musician had played the bits of Satie whom I forgot to mention. It was his *Gymnopédies*, isn't that it, a piano piece of elegant, thin discord. I have always loved it. What Jewish gent had supplied the décors, what script girl had held the book, etc.? It is a film not to miss.

Sartre's autobiography, whose opening I reviewed also, will not be published as a book, complete, until the end of 1964!!! Hasn't finished it, I dare say. But de Beauvoir's,* now out this week, is having splendid serious painful reviews, like reports on a woman's belated childbirth. *Express* has the best, so far, as usual.

Botsford has never answered my request for an explanation of the mutilation of my book letter. Tell Bill that Roger Angell was here with his pretty and very, very nice new wife on their honeymoon, and I took them out to dinner Saturday night, delightful evening, good talk. He said *Group* was essentially a badly written book. I said I doubted if I could wade through chapter three on pessary fitting after chapter two on defloration. He said there was no change in editors or readers of copy at *New Yorker*, so didn't understand what had happened to my book Letter, nor why Gardner hadn't answered me, but would "put a rocket under him," the latest space slang I gathered for getting something moving that has been inert.

Tomorrow I am going to see Beriosova, the new Russian dancer, acclaimed as great with the London ballet here in ten performances of nothing but *Swan Lake*. How delightful. Then see Fonteyn and Nureyev in it Friday, their second and last appearance. Then comes the Finland ballet in *Mlle. Julie*, after that the Hungarian with Bartók's *Mandarin* ballet, which was suppressed years ago because it contains a suicide, as I recall. How death's values change, almost socially.

Lunched with Schiaparelli at the Ritz recently, my treat. She asked many questions about your Sperlonga house. She is portlier than before. Who is not? But always truthful, energetic of mind, a likable woman, a good friend.

So, Elsa Maxwell died. I saw her at the Ritz Bar (those are only two times I had been there in years!), walking with stick, Dicky Gordon with her. Saw Dicky later about to take her to boat to New York to die. When I said to Dicky, are you going with her? She said in her quick Scottish snarl, what on earth would she do without me? A strange fascinating woman, Dicky, another favorite of mine. Elsa was a marvel. She took care of the rich unemployed, she gave them something to do with their idleness.

Must go to bed. Russell [Page] arrived tonight. His mother just died at eighty-four, furious that she could not go to parties as before or play as much bridge. His father is the same age. When Russell took his tea

* *La Force des Choses.*

in the morning after she had died at dawn and had not waked his father, the old gent said, "Anything happen?" Yes, said Russell, it did, sir. Ah, said the old man. Now I am at liberty at last. Yes, said Russell. Two lumps of sugar or three with your tea, Papa? I forget. At ten a.m. the widower went to his law office in Lincolnshire as usual. His own grandfather—i.e., Russell's great-grandfather—lived to be ninety-seven. Russell is alarmed at their longevity. The English are great oddities. . . .

My beloved, you are a great treasure.

[November 23, 1963]

My darling,

I was delighted to hear your voice. About eight o'clock the phone rang at Josette Lazar's flat where I was dining with her, and Vladimir Vogey, a Petrograd artist—the one who did that Cubist drawing in the Shawn's flat, which I gave them—I heard Josette say, "Kennedy shot. Oh, no. Not *dead*—it can't be true." Someone had just phoned her from the *Times* where she works—shock produces a kind of paralysis on everyone always.

I began being able to believe the dreadful, shocking insane truth when finally I got you and you gave brief reports on yourself how you had heard it, what Fifth Avenue looked like with knots of people simply standing, talking, trying to understand together. The fact that the stock market had shut down. Oh, trust money to smell danger in the cruelty of assassination of its Chief of State. I received the communication with you very easily, to my astonishment within forty minutes, because the transatlantic lines were loaded, as you can imagine after such a horrifyingly dangerous event.

First the operator said quite casually, in French, Madame Murray is out, but will be back in half an hour. Then I heard Maria saying as usual, "Good afternoon, Mondadori's office." Then you. Kennedy was too young and not enough of a reckless leader, and nothing like a great political genius for one to know how much better he might have grown to be. But he was alive and working, laboring, a young Democrat of as much good will as he could summon for his task, which means as much as his opponents and his own party would let him use. If a racket killed him, this is the first melodramatic payment on slavery since Lincoln's assassination. If (as the rumor has it here) it was a pro-Russian, pro-Castro type, it is a crime of the contemporary world.

It helped me and strengthened me to hear your voice. Poor Kennedy. How alive he was at the Smith graduation. Recall?

[November 29, 1963]

My darling,

Knowing your loyalty to President Kennedy and knowing your heart and mind, I can well imagine to myself your reactions of grief and fury, can even imagine some of the storm and gestures—pantomimes in my imagination like those in the air you make when talking over the phone, which cannot be seen by the listener, yet which help measure your speech and emphasis. But I wish also to be the listener, or rather the reader, of your grief and expression of it, because it will have a quality superior in expression, in your acute democracy and command of language, to that voiced or written by anyone else, so do write. You are probably doing it tonight or will tomorrow morning. This has been almost a speechless time, it is true, for what can one say except to cry out loud at our loss, to cry out against all the impacted ignorances which let an energetic, addled oaf like Oswald loose on the western world and travel, so that from the folly of Civil War southern sentiments in New Orleans over to Russia and the hopes he had invested in it, which it refused to pay, then back to lawless Texas and its gallon hats and empty hearted hatreds and gun-toting curbstone civilization he was able to make his tour of destruction which exploded in Dallas. A little learning hath made thee mad, the Bible says (I think), and he had learned enough Marx to be crazed on it.

I said to Edmund Wilson on Thursday—he and his intelligent present and final wife (I should think) live in a little hotel near me; he had phoned up from my bar and said, "Do come down"—that I wondered if the dissatisfactions and angers of those who earliest settled in America were not partly responsible for the infuriated hatreds we manifest now. All the emigrants who left Europe and England with a chip on their shoulders against government, the kin or community or church or bishop—anyhow, haters of the society they were brought up in, a hatred sufficient to leave it, plunging across the Atlantic and once on shore, pushing across the continent. What they soon became searchers for was not whatever it was they had singly wanted back in Europe, but money. For though men, hungry for liberty, for freedom from war, from oppression, starved for a chance to earn a little, to be a little Mr. somebody, the smallness of their legitimate hopes which led them on their original journey was lost in the bewildering possibility of not earning a little, but earning a fortune, which was also a confused part of their new liberty which they had not even dreamed of. But the thwarted antagonistic spirit which had led them to emigrate perhaps stayed in them; otherwise, how can it be that such millions of Americans are now so filled with hatreds, violence and the desire to exterminate those who do not agree with them on how wide the new road should be, on how guilty is guilt when it is innocent even in association or a new form of hope? No other people I know, with such prosperity and satisfactions, are so evil-hearted, so angry-minded on a whole. Good Americans like Cheryl or you or Bill or me are rarer than hen's teeth, with solid gold fillings.

Take Tennessee. His imagination is a dire dramatic cesspool which fortunately spills onto the stage where it still shocks me, instead of into murders or destructions in bars or motels. But he is a real hater, seeing as an idealist (true? I wonder) only the hateful side of life and love, in a continual fury and filter too of dissatisfaction. Maybe mass emigration and the further loss of a shapely religion such as Catholicism in the wild fantasies of Protestant cults as peculiar as peep shows is more than the genes of humble, ignorant people can stand and after early 1800, most of those we got were humble to a painful degree.

I am troubled and tortured by what has happened, the tragic loss, the sullying shame. The French have been really humane, have come to the sound of an American voice even to express their sorrow, in a shop or bar or taxicab. Had de Gaulle's neck been less stiff, Franco-American amity could have been restored by Kennedy remaining alive rather than benefiting to an extent by his tragic death. . . .

[December 7, 1963]

Darlinghissima,

It happened two weeks ago yesterday. The mind and memory know it is true, yet the waking instinct in the early morning is to slip back into that irreality of recovery of peace which marks the human emerging from a nightmare, a load of unbelievable, horrible dreams, and in that waking moment, for a fraction of time, it is NOT true. The nightmare will, for a second, seem only that, and will disappear, if one can only get one's eyes open.

Your letter was the most informing account of you and your work there, and also of the technique of news communication I ever read, with details I never even heard of in their association, as well as complication. As the *Life* man said with admiration, "Mrs. Murray, I should hate to have to race with you." Meaning, he would likely be beaten. That your photos were, at the last lap of their journey, fogged, sealed out of Milan and sent to Rome was of the same piece of mis-adventure which marked the whole tragedy, except that yours was resolved, since your pictures did appear in *Europeo-Match* of this week with that same series; yours—*Der Stern* and *Life*'s to begin with —is sensational as a document, at once sold out and the French are keeping it intact as a document for their children or their own old age, to show how history happened. It is almost with disappointment that this morning in the *Herald Tribune* there was a photo of Jacque-line Kennedy smiling. Must she ever change from that Persephone-like face and situation of grief which has made her our legend, the world's legend, and in her way of beauty immortal? . . .

Your letter I shall ever keep. Je suis un peu exténuée, écris moi pour me dire quand tu veux me voir à Rome.

One dozen kisses, more to come.

[December 15, 1963]

My darling one,

. . . It is snowing. It looks pretty in the garden, like a living Christmas. Poor President Kennedy. He will miss the greatest annual gift of all—life.

Je t'aime—

[December 26, 1963]

Beloved sprite,

. . . Last night I went to Mary McCarthy and Jim West's eggnog party and had a couple of whiskies between eight-thirty and there-after was home in bed by eleven-thirty. She was delightful, but had to talk to other people. Few were still there when I arrived, to con-sume a few slices of most excellent ham she had baked in the Virginia manner, which one turned into a sandwich with fresh French bread of the kind you love.

Sonia Orwell, her most intimate friend whom I very much like now, was there, and one or two State Department couples. Mary was herself vital as usual, and, at the last, slumming about in her stockinged feet beneath rose wool, long, loose skirt of the shapeless type I have seen advertised as the new "interior" look for home parties, and which is as ugly as I was sure it would be, for whatever else could it be, so loose and shapeless and sagging. . . . Several things have happened to clothes since Chanel modernized them, and those changes she made remain permanent. Women like short skirts. They like skirts that fit and show their buttocks behind, and nearly show their little cunts in front. Everytime someone invents something different, like Dior, it runs like a wild fire, perhaps as his New Look did, and then women settle down again inside the clothes Chanel created and are happy again. I haven't seen any NEW winter clothes in Paris, all the same. A tunic frock, whether it costs a million or $50.

Thank you for recalling to me what I had written to you about President Kennedy's death. I had forgotten, of course. And now I must announce a more normal death, but still very intimate and sad for us, that of dear, darling Marguerite [Caetani di] Bassiano, in Rome. It was announced in *Figaro*, but no obit given in *Le Monde* at all, and only a brief one in *Figaro*. George Bernier is giving me some information from his marvelous memory so I can do an obit in my upcoming Letter, because *Commerce* was the most important avant garde magazine of all France, and hers. Also, [Tristan] Tzara died yesterday and if Dadaism is never heard of again, I shall not mourn. It always seemed mad to me.

Kay Boyle has settled down in "the Negro district" in San Francisco, "which we preferred," and the vast output of her womb, with their husbands and offspring, have all sought refuge there. She will be keeping them all, except those in Florida. She drudges at her teaching, which seems little pleasure, and writes of poor Joseph with utter devotion. He merited it. . . .

1964

An important event inaugurated the New Year: Janet was giving what she endearingly called a *fête* in my honor—a party for me! I was arriving for a brief stay in Paris from Milan and Rome, where I had gone after the New Year on business and to see Mother at Franca's. It had become apparent by then that she needed constant attention. By sheer luck, Franca had found a small apartment under hers to sublet. We jumped at the opportunity. Mother and her housekeeper were soon installed in what she typically termed "my own personal republic." Franca supervised it from above. I could now leave Rome with a light heart, and arrive in Paris in time for the *fête*. One side of the grand old Oak Room bar of the Continental had been set aside for the events, with George, the bartender, in charge of the best martinis in town. Janet had invited a carefully selected list of French and Italian friends, as well as a group of Italian Paris correspondents. To top it, she had reserved a small box all our own for the hottest hit in Paris—*The Vicar*, by Rolf Hochhuth—and a good time was had by all, especially by our closest friends, the writer Monica Stirling and Odette Arnaud the literary agent. Janet had never been so proud of herself. I was overcome by this bold social initiative!

[February 3, 1964]

My Darling,

Everything seems altered by your departure, by the lack of your presence, I should say. What I liked when you were here and I was with you now has no meaning, except material, such as swallowing the dinner at Louis XIV where you and I alone filled the upper room with talk and our charms and appetite for food. How many analyses of love, how many different appreciations of it, not even imaginary or poetic, but real, verifiable, come to view in separation—as also in reunion. Passionate love must surely be one of the most acute methods for perception and observant human knowledge that exists. By the French method as of the 18th and above all 19th centuries, one would think that money and conventions were the most methodical informers and one sees by the results what low information they bring to mind. Better, by far, the English with their various centuries of passionate, lyric love, or Shakespearean drama, so clear in its organic shape of tenderness that Ulanova and the Bolshoi Ballet danced *Romeo and Juliet* as clearly and textually by their bodies' motions as if they were silently speaking, muscularly, Shakespeare's own words. Speech can be other than vocal surely.

It is warm today, foggy but soft. I give you news of the climate since you were so recently witness to it and part of it, in our embrace, heated like summer. Goodnight, my darling. I am wearing the scarlet bathrobe, doubly warm by reminiscence.

[February 18, 1964]

My beloved one,

. . . A grey winter here, a mild one, thank heaven, but for ten days the only sun has been the midnight brightness of the Eiffel Tower, turning and whirling. It has been declared a monument historique, which seems redundant. . . .

My new Lanvin suit, tried on this morning, is lovely, bluish grey stuff, with a few faint long hairs, lighter, woven in. Have ordered two new blouses, my usual, with cuffs and scarf. One of off-white, the other of pale grey, to match the suit but much lighter, as a change. Also ordered today a new black silk dress and jacket, for cocktails, theater, etc. A straight dress of tunic and straight skirt, a shortish jacket with a few froncs [gathers] at throat and round collar, very smart, simple, of some sort of black silk, rather like rep, which won't turn shiny, they say. It sounds odd for me to be writing about clothes to you, eh?, but I am so sick of my two old suits I could perish, except the black alpaca, my favorite of all time, after all. . . .

[April 10, 1964]

Oh, who do you think phoned the other night? Pat Highsmith, about ten p.m. Had been here a few days, lives in London, and will perhaps buy a house in England to live. When I told her how much we admired her talent, she was so touched she could hardly speak. She's a very gifted writer and what she has made of her own personality and life is quite extraordinary, a gift of growth which only Americans could offer. It is a joy to see the exceptions still appear in its monotony of the gold rush, the hurry for cash only, with honesty gone down the drain as of no value. It is the MAIN value in a country and, when it is lost, the country starts towards its decline and eventual fall. Such simple pontification seems pompous and not filled with the grief which gives it its validity to me, from me . . .

Dearest one, my treasure, please send me a line.

[May 14, 1964]

Darlinghissima,

Brava, the *Epoca* Fair number is superlative! The color photos . . . of the Globe in reflection . . . I thought especially handsome . . . The photo of the real New York of skyscrapers . . . is actually terrifying. What a way to live. How falsified, how depended upon steel and height and getting off the earth, but no nearer heaven you can be sure. No wonder Americans are psychologically less stable than Europeans.

I was very interested in your *équipe's* White House visit to the President, the lack of security measures, the forgotten passport left in the taxi (there is always at least one in every traveling group) and the reaction—that it seems to your European group quite possible that Oswald did indeed shoot our Kennedy. The lack of real caution underneath all the often brutal interference of our police, the basic presumption in *Dr. Strangelove* (here excellently translated as *Dr. Folamour*) and a hit with the intelligentsia, though I hope de Gaulle never sees it. It will be the complete end of NATO in his eyes. All these childish, clumsy, amateur attitudes and practices, the lack of what is *sérieux* in our country—all these make the heart sick. We are not a nation which seemed to mature on the plains and mountains as pioneers, but a nation that has become utterly hothouse in mind and habit in the past twenty-five years, a new nation, a different one, a weak drooping one like a flower on a weak stem or a vegetable with short roots that fades in the sun and is not worth eating. I don't think any sensible cannibal even would want to eat us Americans today. They would have enjoyed chewing on my grandmother. She was a tough old Quaker.

You say Rome about June 15th or so. . . . It is difficult to make tentative plans, because they must always be opened like a raw egg and then sealed up again, shell included, to be opened later for a new pattern of yolk and white.

Yes, age is dreadful, my darling. It is neither satisfying nor avoidable. No wonder the Bible is so full of consolations for its wisdom which we see so few examples of in our country. Your mother is wise, yes, and so are many old French peasant women. But I think the young French of today will not ripen much better than the American youth they imitate. "None of the White House pens ever write" is now my axiom. A historic statement! . . . .*

———

In May we had been greatly distressed by the news that a very dear friend had been drinking heavily and had attempted suicide, and another had recently died from a lifetime of excessive drinking. In her letter of May 22, Janet comments:

"How much beter had American Puritans cultivated the grape and made wine or hops and made beer in those early days of wild turkey and corn pudding and stern laws against any pleasure. Perhaps we descendants would not have become so easily alcoholic as a delayed reaction in the middle of this century. We are a curious, strange nation and mixed race without religious faith or glory to God anymore, or not much of it, and nothing to fall back upon as salvation except pride of money it seems. Forgive me if I say at least that much!! I wish I could compare us to some other mixed race, though is there one so blended as ours, to draw some more comforting illuminating conclusions?"

That spring, too, Mondadori decided to move out of the Scribner

* President Johnson's phrase upon signing copies of *Epoca* magazine for our group.

Building into a more modern suite of offices on Madison Avenue. How I was going to miss my dear old one, with the lovely bookstore downstairs and a feeling of publishing tradition all around! Things were certainly changing in the old Mondadori firm, now that the youngest son, a commercially minded businessman, had been named to head the company . . .

"Your new office sounds fine, though your dear, old one I have loved," echoed Janet. In this same letter, she sent me the review by Morley Callaghan in *The Spectator* of Ernest Hemingway's memoirs, *A Moveable Feast*, just published. She added:

"The Callaghan review of Hemingway's last book, enclosed, is the most equable I have seen, I think. He says much I felt, including the sad, bitter taste, also, above all, the peculiar weakness of Ernest's complaint against the rich coming to his hideaway in Austria to ruin his private life with Hadley, as if he had helplessly become a public attraction at a fair, which was true, but he did not have to perform like one, like a carousel or a fire-eater or a juggler. Strange. He had the irrational faults of a genius of our time, and I loved him loyally then as I do now."

While I was making plans for the early summer, Bill and Doris had made theirs for the fall. They would go to the milder and easier climate of California for several months, as an experiment in living outside New York. I did not have a particularly enthusiastic memory of Southern California and looked upon their decision with some misgivings. So did Janet, because, when I informed her, she commented in her April 16 letter:

"I cannot comprehend why Bill wants to live in California, despite its occasional geographic beauties like a park that has become half-urban in most cases except in the deep ranch country, where, except for Hildegarde in her valley, there is deep moaning this spring because of lack of rain. They are several vital inches short of their normal . . ."

And again:

"It is no help in the way of something new to have Bill go to California in a covered wagon to live for a year, depriving you of the children and certainly overfilling the magazine with lengthy reports about a civilization so-called which is appalling and tragic and only less violent and cow-minded than Texas . . ."

Janet felt she had better not come to Rome this time, when I would be visiting my mother. She did not wish to interfere with my filial duties, or to be a burden. We would see each other later on in

New York, she said. I became so upset on the telephone that I cried
with disappointment. We finally reached a compromise. All three of
us—Ester, Janet and myself—would go to Sperlonga. I knew Mother
would love the place, and we would be together. At first Janet was
reluctant, full of misgivings and worries—about the stones, steps,
lack of space and so on. Wouldn't it be too daring for an old lady like
Ester? Look at what happened to poor Alice Toklas, who had fallen
and broken a hip right in her apartment, she wrote apprehensively. I
pleaded, and she gave in. Though I felt guilty toward Janet, I was
glad I had insisted on taking Mother with us, for she spent happy
days, like old times in New York, in cozy "Sperlonghina" and in our
company. It was going to be her last time outside her home. I, too,
had had my premonitions. At the end of our stay, we said good-bye
until September in New York.

I was fed up with politics and politicians, here and in Italy. Furthermore, I had been thinking seriously about moving to Rome, a thought
that was keeping my attention focused entirely on my own life, not
only because of Ester, who had become frailer and older, but because
the Mondadori office in New York was slowly losing its character,
with more changes in the company and more commercialism invading
the publishing field. I was not happy in it any longer.

It was a hard decision to make, but one that, with my own American
family preparing eventually to move permanently to California, left
me with less of a choice. I set about finding out what Mondadori
might offer me if I should leave New York, a thought that frightened
and saddened me.

Janet came back from California in time to watch the election returns in *The New Yorker* office, "late at night when the returns
would be more indicative and where we could gossip with colleagues,"
she said. She was full of tales, too, about the great fire not far away
from her sister's house in the Napa Valley. It could be seen in the
red glow of the skies and smelled in the air. All night Hildegarde and
Eric had been watering their own land around the new house, fearing
the winds might spread the fire. Janet also talked about the Democratic campaign going on among the wine growers—"men with grey
Johnson's hats, rather becoming, not too wild or western," she said,
"a crowd very high-class and middle-class, the BEST of the valley
for brains and political hopes." They had been going to fund-raising
parties, where Eric gave speeches; he and Hildegarde were both
always so active in the affairs of their county and state, in defending

the encroachments of interests dangerous for the preservation of their trees and soil. Hildegarde found them all against Goldwater, because California had helped his candidacy at the Republican Convention at the Cow Palace, a place that Janet wrote "she hoped to heaven that heaven forgave the State for that grave error in that appallingly named stadium . . ."

Well, Johnson was elected; at Thanksgiving, we could go for a last swing into the rain forest at Burt Martinson's home in Puerto Rico, before returning to our respective jobs.

Janet was complaining about my having to stay in Milan before our vacation: "I would follow you there in a couple of days, taking time merely to give you time for the first two or three days of settling into the Mondadori offices and arms," she wrote on June 12. "My Lord, they are cannibals. They eat you alive. That is the truth, and it is a tiring, wearying process, being consumed as they consume you. You serve them as nourishment in every way. . . ."

[June 19, 1964]

My darlinghissima,

Please cable me if I shall really have the pleasure of seeing you first here in Paris on June 23rd or 24th, because rooms are difficult to get in my hotel which now takes American tours, Amurricans who have never been tu Yurrup before, of an appalling type for the most part, who yap like poodles, sit in the halls all day and on their paid-in-advance tour do two things—go to the Folies-Bergère or some substitute and to the Lido. Maybe they have an hour in the Louvre, but I doubt it. I HOPE you cable YES, but CABLE, my pet, so I can get a bed some place on this floor. . . .

[June 23, 1964]

Darlinghissima,

. . . I am now trying to get a copy of Gertrude Stein's will in Baltimore to see if her will is invalidated by the sequestration of her pictures when Alice abandoned them for nine months in Rome. If still valid, Alice can have one or two pictures withdrawn from the Seine Tribunal vaults and sell them and relieve her friends of this financial worry of seeing her trying to live on $400 a month with two maids and self to feed, social insurance, etc. Her major maid had not been paid her wages for six months. This can't go on.

Old age is a hideous experience. I know it now, if only through her and my poor mother, too, and yours. I pray you and I are struck by lightning and die in bliss in a burst of heavenly flame. Thine . . .

[August 27, 1964]

Darling,

The hottest day in Paris since 1889, or something or other! It is 95 degrees, and yesterday felt even hotter. I hope this heat wave has not enveloped New York and you, too, with your re-entry into your office in a marsh of Manhattan humidity and sweating citizens. I shall probably have a card from you tomorrow, or so I hope, giving a fact or two in your so awaited handwriting. But don't give it a thought, darling one, for you have enough on your hands and shoulders.

Yesterday I went to see the movie *Becket.* The speech is too witty, too droll, too Shavian. One laughs too often for such serious drama. But the gravity, the admirable solemnity of the direction, the color, the scenes themselves furnish a strangely effective corrective, like a punch made of many wines and fruits, with a mixed taste of sweet and of bitter, intoxicating and thirst-inspiring rather than thirst-quenching.

O'Toole was the better actor by far, I thought, his being the anguished role, but Burton looked sublime and the great Primate Lover. Certainly there was cause for the London critics saying it is a homosexual love story. How curiously tawdry O'Toole made himself look as King Henry, that disreputable amoralist, yet fascinating in his tormented love, power and loneliness.

Paris is deserted, restaurants closed, pharmacies shut up, yet a million or more Parisians in town, many dining expensively at the costly restaurants that never close!

I have been reading a lot and pleasurably. Have been rereading Conrad, especially enjoyed rereading *Typhoon,* surely the most literal storm in words ever written in any tongue. I regret his preface to it. In it, Conrad says he never went through a typhoon but knows bad and terrible weather as a sailor so has extended it. That the strange, stupid but almost witlessly honest captain who divided all the silver dollars among all the Chinamen locked in the hold whose pitiful little fortunes had burst loose in the tempest from their Chinese chests (less handsome than yours)—that Conrad says this captain is merely a summation of a type of master once known on the China run took

much of the spirit away from the captain's character, for me. I dislike
the prefaces of Henry James, too, that accompany his last edition.
He so intricately and vaingloriously explains his "donnée" and with
such pride, as something he thought up like a sleight of hand in the
head that the reader, who has anguished over his characters in the
novel itself, feels alien to their sufferings—for they are rarely happy
heroes or heroines. James brags so much about those damnable
"données" that he sounds like a pimp for his own genius.

The sweat is pouring down between my breasts. It is six p.m. I
shall go down and post this and have a lemonade in the bar, perhaps
with a shade of gin. There is not a lemon sherbet available in my
hotel, maybe at the Ritz but certainly in none of the cafés. How I
would LOVE one from the Café des Notables at Sperlonga. I am
trying to become used to French food again. I am never tired of
Italian dishes and wine. Nor of you, dearest one.

I think Nancy Cunard is slowly dying now from her emphysema.
Her letters are pitiful. Her fury all pain and helplessness and disgust
with food. And she is seven years younger than I am.

                                                    [December 24, 1964]
Darlinghissima,

I just heard your voice and news. You do sound fatigued and worn
as events had made you. This year can be regarded as containing at
least one paradisiacal omission of any troubles or pressures: our
Thanksgiving in the tropics, where, if there were few birds, we were
the rare larks, high flying in our spirits. . . .

It does not feel like Christmas to me, and probably not to you,
though you have much to thank heaven and fate for this December
25th, that your mother is spared as an ornament to your life and
happiness—and now for a happier New Year!

                                        Kisses like candy . . .

1965

Several major developments dominated our lives in the New Year. For one thing, Janet's eyes were better. She no longer had to write through a "veil of tears." She had reduced her smoking to a few cigarettes a day, in the belief that she had been suffering from "fireman's affliction"—eyes inflamed by smoke. "I explained that to my oculist twice," she wrote on January 28, "and he still solemnly said he had never heard of firemen complaining of any such effect, the humorless fool!" A letter dated February 11 tried to make some sense of my worries about my mother's health:

"News of your darling mother is both good and, of course, bad. I feel it is my duty, since you are so emotionally knitted with your insistence that your mother live forever because you love her beyond the limits of rational relations, that I point out what I have already known—that the heart may go on beating like an engine producing no work, except the extension of life itself, but which can be an extension of existence without full faculties. The antibiotic which saved her from double pneumonia cannot have saved her from the destruction of her faculties or may even have contributed to it, as you now report. That she sends word to you daily that she is waiting for you to fetch her to go away and that she is ready, with her fur coat! She is old and magnificent in her resistance, but for God's sake do not once again insist upon keeping her alive as a memento of your love for her, in your youth, and in your sense of what you have owed her so that as a result she lives on in the humiliation of a beating heart and lost faculties. The Aesculapian oath of doctors, once simple and primitive, has today merged into experimental science which to a doctor brings its own satisfaction for his technical brilliance or mere cleverness, in having an entity of age beyond its competences, upon which he congratulates himself professionally without relation to the law of actuary reason. . . ."

I had moved into the new Mondadori offices on upper Madison Avenue. Gone was the cozy atmosphere of the shabbier office in the Scribner Building, where every wall spoke of writers and words, where on every floor you came across people working with them. I remember the excitement of seeing through a crack in a door what looked like trunks full of Ernest Hemingway's papers and notes, probably retrieved from Cuba, over which editors worked with concentrated attention. I remember the lovely, old-fashioned bookstore downstairs, where the salesladies not only knew authors' names, but had actually read their books! All that was gone. Now it was like a dentist's office, nothing but cubicles and white walls smelling of fresh paint. I felt trapped; I felt menaced. I knew I would have to leave sooner or later. I was anxious to know what Mondadori would offer me in Rome.

Janet had read my letter twice and had its contents and problems well in mind, she wrote, though one was unsolvable: "Your patent grief at leaving New York. Europe is not in solid condition, and your beautiful Italy least of all. This lack of surety and its attendant lack of consecutive prosperity is one of the non-joys of living on this continent . . .

"I think you should seriously consider and talk with Bill about not coming over to live, because you will not be so happy in Rome as a citizen at work as in New York."

With her innate generosity, Janet offered to share the expenses of a flat, food, maid, etc., so that I would not feel uneasy financially. "I can rearrange my work with *The New Yorker*," she went on to say, "spending half the year in each capital city, as God knows as long as I am strong in health I do not want to give up my work entirely. As you will be torn on leaving New York, I will be torn on leaving Paris forever. The brevity of the flight to Rome makes commuting several times a year possible, with work. The financial details of Rome living are all right—with my help will be even better. That is not the point. The point is, will you mourn for the rest of your days, beloved, for Manhattan?"

The decision was hard, indeed. Besides the work I so enjoyed doing, I would be leaving my own family behind, except for a one-month yearly visit. I took my time. Then curious circumstances made up my mind for me—later.

A major loss in Janet's life had been Nancy Cunard's death in March.

Nancy had been very much a part of Parisian life since she had first appeared on the scene—young, beautiful, rebellious, literary and scandalous.

Janet had always had a soft spot for Nancy in her heart, admired her talent and eccentric personality, though she was often critical of how she lived her life. Her death, not so unexpected, was nevertheless a shock, but her distress was not devoid of Janet's typically analytical humorous observations of the circumstances surrounding it.

[March 20, 1965]

Darling,

Nancy died Tuesday noon in the ward of the city Hôpital Cochin. As she was being carried by the taxi driver across the garden at Lib and Solita's* house where she had spent the night, sitting in a chair, refusing to go to bed like a Christian, she said to Solita, "Good-bye, darling. I don't suppose I shall ever see you again."

I waited four hours for her at the doctor's where she had a noon appointment. None of us ever saw her again, but others did, to their regret, poor woman. She phoned Laurence Vail, Kay Boyle's husband, father of those three girls, to come see her Friday late at a dingy little hotel near the Panthéon where she holed up that night. She was in bed with a bottle of rum and told him she wanted to come spend some time in his flat. He refused because Bobby, Kay's oldest daughter, had just been operated on. I gathered he was taking care of her. Nancy was determined NOT to go into a hospital or clinic, scream-

---

* Solita Solano described herself as "Genêt's friend, amateur secretary, and guardian of the thesaurus: birth to retirement." (Letter July 20, 1966, to Chief Manuscript Division of Library of Congress, Dr. John C. Broderick.) Janet met Solita, a journalist-publicist, in New York in 1921. Soon thereafter they left together for Europe and eventually settled in Paris as aspiring young writers. Solita died in 1975 at Orgeval, where she had been living with a friend since her return to France after World War II.

ing, "Damn you, you're trying to take my liberty away from me!" She was thrown out of the hotel the next morning for burning her private papers she carried with her on the carpet, doubtless the carpet, too, because when Laurence phoned in the morning, the patrone screamed, "She nearly set us on fire. I hope we never see her again," after which she must have phoned Aragon, who phoned me Wednesday to say she had made a rendezvous for that day with him, too late of course, poor woman, and then sometime on Saturday she had been carried, always by a taxi driver since she was unable to walk. She had broken her hip in January and had been operated on. The taxi driver carried her into the apartment of Georges Sadoul, the cinema critic on the Com. weekly literary paper, where a former lover named Michelet (one I missed) had come to tea with his wife. Nancy tried to tear the poor woman's hair out, removed her own clothes, was dressed by force and carried down by Michelet, an ex-concentration camp man, in ill health, and he dislocated a vertebra doing it, Aragon told me.

Then silence until on Wednesday the British Embassy phoned me to say she had died the previous noon and they had only just been informed. I phoned the Embassy from the doctor's on Friday with his approval, to say I had an English friend *en fugue* who seemed mad (his wife had seen her early on Thursday, before she drove to Orgeval, and thought her mad and alcoholized) and, after sketching in the situation, then candidly told the intellignt woman at the Embassy her name and the fact that several years ago she had been confined a year or so in the Virginia Water's asylum as a certified lunatic, that she was carrying her British passport and, if the police reported her, please to phone me. So I was the first to know, which was a relief, only from Friday to Wednesday with no news, constant worrying and then the only news that of death.

She had been taken to the Cochin Saturday night. What she died of (it must have been emphysema plus drink) or where she was picked up, the Embassy does not know and cannot ask because only an official demand from the Cunard family for such information could lead to its being given by the hospital or the police. I suppose we never will know, though what difference does it make. Better a void than knowing details and that she must have fought off the police whom she hated at sight. Surely she left life struggling against it to the end. Hers was the longest suicide I know. It took her years, months, days and nights finally to kill herself by dissipation. Also, she poisoned herself by hate, by hating so much and so violently— hating people, nations, etc. Yet two weeks ago, she sent S. some more of the long poem she had been writing, utterly logical, often poetic, rather strange, but far less so than much poetry of today. . . .

On top of it all, a darling Chilean, Tony Gandanlios, happened to be in town about to go to England to visit the famous David Kinross on his estate. Well, the castle burned down three days ago, so I had to hear about all that. Tony had been with her mother, Lady Cunard, to her death . . . and he phones constantly to know when the cremation will be and what is the latest news since he knows several Cunards in England. One, Lady Something, he phoned said, "Dead? Oh, the poor thing. Did she leave a will, do you know?" She had been Philippe de Rothschild's mistress years back, Peggy Bernier told me, as did others, and he never gave her a penny. Now she, too, is poor. Such drama and revelations as make Proust's *Temps Retrouvé* a mild saga. Tony did tell me one thing that made me roar hysterically with laughter. Lady Cunard had been cremated at her request, but no one knew where to deposit her ashes, as she had not specified her wish on the matter, so her few best friends (Tony refused to take part) carried her ashes to Grosvenor Square, the heart of fashionable Mayfair, and threw them in the air in front of the great mansion where she had lived and entertained so many years. One of the funniest disposals of a former great hostess I ever heard of. Horrible, but funny just the same.

I tell you, the English are strange people. I am doing an obit of Nancy in my *New Yorker* Letter this week. She was a famous Paris character. I shall follow the line taken by the London *Times* in its obit, the interest in her Surrealist connection and the books she printed. It is all so strange. Her sudden loss of her intelligence and reason. I had a letter from her three weeks ago, completely rational. She had a persecution mania. Nobody persecuted her as much as she tortured herself, alas. A greatly admired and loved character when first I knew her has now gone into peace at last. Hers has been the most dreadful, frightening decline imaginable.

Wet, gloomy day, and I must work. This is an ill-written letter. Sorry.

Love, darling; keep strong!

[April 14, 1965]

Darling,

Perhaps this admirable, comfortable and legible new typewriter, a Royal with white keys and pale greyish body, will encourage me to write more easily, and thus more often. Thank you for letting me hear your early morning voice, always the most touching for unexpected communications. I have in the past two years slumped in social relations with people not my intimates, like Célia Bertin whom I had not seen since 1964, she said, who wrote me so sympathetically after Nancy's death that I emerged and answered. It did me good socially to speak to a friend who had the patina both of longish years of communication and of fresh experiences I knew nothing of, such as the fact that while she wished to write a book on Mme. de Staël, her editors preferred Mayerling* with the old, old, exaggerated love interest which, according to most recent documentation, never was true anyhow, the prince being a frigid man who had invited three earlier mistresses to commit suicide with him, almost as a way of merely breaking off relations.

I must have been even more beaten down by Nancy's death than I had known, yet the final news coming very belatedly was consolatory. I don't know if I told you. She was picked up on the sidewalk, we don't know where in Paris, unconscious, and taken to the hospital by the police secours to die, still unconscious after three days, so she knew nothing of her final flight from this world. It was the destructions involved that was such a shock, the tearing into bits the shape of her life and gifts, talents, and charms, too, charms which were like a natural gold mine, or emerald mine, a depot of natural treasures that others could not purchase, which nature had given to her free. There was such a sense of mystery in it all. Was she in part destroyed by mere world politics, mere human burning fury at the selfishness of the rich and helpless desire by the poor to be as well off as the rich and therefore soon as selfish too? Was it what I feel—that the nature of mankind is so recalcitrant to goodness that if it is not rigorously, cruelly held in check by some strict religious ideology like puritanism or Catholicism in a monastery, or communism when it was Stalinist and fear-motivated and effective, that to hope with the hopes one once had for a better society seems naïve? . . .

As for the ten thousand words on de Gaulle, I will try it. If it does not "gel," well, I shall merely renounce it without much pain. It would be good for my so-called standing to do something new, some-

---

* *Mayerling or the False Destiny of the Mittelsbach* is the romantic history of the double suicide of Crown Prince Rudolf, heir to the Austro-Hungarian Empire, and Baroness Maria Vetsera in the hunting pavilion of Mayerling, near Vienna, in 1889; the book was published in Paris in 1967.

thing not an eternal Paris Letter, though not far from it either since the General is the obelisk of Paris on the Concorde, a city that has only one, not dozens as yours in Rome. . . . I think the treatment of him should, in a way, follow that I gave Pétain, should be against a background of the failure of the French, once more, to accept the thesis of the revolution of applying its republicanisms voluntarily so that the working class and the poor had a chance to move upward. They have moved, but it has been perhaps largely because of the drive and pressure of the syndicates and strikes which have forced the industrialists to give the workers a better life—better through pressure, not by extension of political imagination in the upper classes.

This made France spiritually démodé, made it easier for de Gaulle to take over, and made it almost a necessity. He had made France more COMPACT than it was before. The French seem to have no gift for revolutionary ideas, only for the brutality of street fighting in repeated small revolutions. . . .

The *Time* magazine piece on Shawn* and the fight against the Wolfe writer on the *Tribune*—he looks like a regular British cad, flamboyant, cheap, energetic, and not unintelligent—shocked me. How curious. There is a real campaign against *The New Yorker*, isn't there?

Nasty weather as always during holy week here, cold, grey. The church calendar for moveable feasts was worked out in Rome and for its early spring, not for a Paris Easter. . . .

I hope this Easter fête brings some kind of peace on earth and resurrection of hopes in the heart of man. I wish I believed in something. Or do I? No, the decisions of conscience are all a good man needs. The rest is architecture (for the church) and politics and police (for communism). Probably a good sunny day would heal many of us.

I know how you felt at my not writing. Twice I phoned you in New York, recall, because you had not written to me. Forgive me. I was spiritually emptied. But not emptied of love.

I am not drinking, except wine at dinner. I weigh 130 pounds and seem unable to lose even by avoiding whiskey! . . .

The excitement of the next events curtailed our correspondence. Janet had been absorbed by the arrival of the proofs of her first col-

---

* Tom Wolfe's celebrated attack on *The New Yorker*.

lection of Paris Letters, edited by William Shawn, which Mike
Bessie of Harper was bringing out in the fall, under the title *Paris
Journal, 1944–1965*, signed by her own name, with her pseudonym,
Genêt, following in parentheses.

I had finally signed the new contract with Mondadori for a new
job in Rome, to begin the following year, which ended indecisions,
palpitations, frustrations, even though it created other uncertainties.
At least I was assured of a yearly visit to the States to visit family,
friends and Manhattan. I would also be nearer Janet, after fourteen
years of living across an ocean from her, and to my mother during the
last days of her life.

In May, as I was going through the reorganization of the new
Mondadori office, Janet, who had closely followed the latest developments that would also affect her own working plans, and who understood my predicament, wrote charmingly:

"I only wanted to send this note to say that you deserve a BIG GOLD
medal for all you have done for Italy, including lately—you should
be able to obtain one in Rome, my pet, what fun—and that I deserve
the Pulitzer Prize and will never get it, so that settles our destinies.
We better just wear Cartier jewels in our buttonholes, like ladies."

                                                    [May 7, 1965]

Darlinghissima,

Not yet raining, but it will in a minute, I am ready to wager. My
two eight-pound packages of proofs from Mike Bessie were brought
to me by a kind air-traveling friend of his. I have already done perhaps
250 out of the close to 2000 pages. Since I have feared turning my
cut Letters into a book, I should tell you and do with unexpected
pleasure for me that, especially in the political parts, I find I have
written with spirit, clarity, often charm that aids to carry the reader's
interest and even humor. Have on the whole written with authority,
style and personality that makes me suddenly all the more indignant
that with all the prizes that float about in New York, I was never
awarded one for writing, as well as information, and record to you
that I deserve it. An unbecoming moment to mention it now with
the campaign on against *The New Yorker*. Of all the replies favoring
Wolfe, the only one that carried weight with me was one which said
that Luce and *Time* had never complained when Gibbs did that
merciless Profile on them both, nor had the *Reader's Digest*.

I think Shawn's cutting of the Letters has been splendid, fine, of unforgettable patience and persistence. I think far too much Gaullist stuff remains . . . My God, how in love with him I sound. I regret that now, but it was true then. Too much of the art references has been cut, too much music (though Boulez was left in twice)—too much of the face of France and Paris has been surgically lifted away to preserve the General's phiz and accomplishments. But in that I cover with the best detail and applications the real explanation of why he came to exist—because France is incapable of governing itself, but must be governed by a non-republican outsider.

I THINK I can do the de Gaulle booklet, but I have written so much and with such emotionally, well-chosen vocabulary that could I hit so high again? I am very, very tempted to try it, would stop my Paris Letter for six weeks this summer to do it. It's the only way. I cannot do two things at once. . . .

I must stop, my angel. You have my love as ever and grateful I am to give it to you . . .

[May 25, 1965]

. . . I keep saying this is the last year I am likely to be able to earn, but surely this is NEARLY the last year. I feel everyone on earth must be as tired as Wolfe said he was of reading my Letters or reports made from looking out the window of a second-best Paris or London hotel . . .

This is a period of strange confusion and uncertainties and changes for many of us Americans, in the large national senses of the words. Leaderless, as so many of us feel, with that Lone Ranger thinking through his cowboy hat in the remoteness of the White House, where Dante is certainly not a familiar political name to him, regardless of Alberto's hopes of a special visit there. What folly and egotism seize men who are the heads of big business—or governments. De Gaulle's recent whistle-stop tour through the center countryside drew from him larger conceits than usual—"The French genius which all the world recognizes," etc., and now in tonight's paper the report that once again, for the third time, an attempt was planned to interrupt his constant speeches by assassinating him—a plan by one of the same men who plotted on the murder plan Number TWO. What would be GAINED by killing him now? I am baffled by men's insanity at times.

I saw the play *White America* tonight. Done by semi-amateurs, better than most professionals, Negroes and whites mixed. Really most arresting and tragic. Thank God I was not born black. It takes all my courage to have been born white!

My darling one, it is past midnight. I have a hard day tomorrow; I must sleep which I am grateful to say I do well and easily. My darling, sleep well yourself!

With the prospect of my settling in Rome, I had written Anna Magnani, who owned several apartments, asking if any would be suitable and free for us. She was arriving in Paris for the International Festival to star in *La Lupa* by Giovanni Verga, a dramatization of a Sicilian story of passion and jealousy, directed by Franco Zeffirelli . . .

On June 12 came the offer of one of Anna's apartments in the magnificent Renaissance Palazzo Altieri. She lived on the top floor, surrounded by terraces, with her pets, her piano, her paintings, awards, flowers, scripts and a series of scared secretaries and maids, and used to call for champagne or *caffè espresso* as if she were going into battle. Janet reported on *La Lupa* on June 12 and 18:

"Anna was splendid in a way and in part. She was inaudible in Act I as you will see by the enclosed critics unless she absorbs them from me this afternoon. She's coming to say good-bye. I only saw her after the premiere. She invited me to a party at Pierre Cardin's, the dressmaker, for her and Jeanne Moreau, but it was already past midnight, a big crowd was still waiting backstage to greet her. I loathe to go to such a house reception when I know no one, so I excused myself on fatigue, which was as true as gospel. When I told her that I had not been able to hear her in Act I, she said, 'That was the correct technique—to play it sotto voce.' I said that when a woman plans to seduce her prospective son-in-law, she should take the entire audience into her confidence and not keep it a village secret. The Verga play was heavily criticized as old hat which, God knows, it is. On the phone last night, she said she had played it PERFECTLY, AT LAST. HOW TRAGIC . . .'"

From Janet's letter of June 18:

"Anna Magnani has left. I enclose the only severe yet accurate critique of her performance and play. The axe murder seemed shocking, awful. She came to see me the other day, and it was a shock, too. Gay, loving, etc., but her appearance in the center of Paris caused people to stop on the sidewalk and stare when I took her to get a taxi. Tight, checked trousers, and she is fat, a tight gray silk sweater, a black one tossed on her shoulders, and poor, blind Lily, the dachshund. But it was her dark hair that caused the crowd to stare, so magnificent it is, and she kept combing it with her fingers like a lunatic until it stood up like a bush. Wild, crazed she looked, a freak. I was so humiliated for her. She wants you to take extra flat for next year for you and me and Ester. It would come to about $343 monthly. I enclose her estimate. She would be making a great reduction just to have you in it. You might prefer living with the POPE as quieter. Write to Anna instanter, she says, to say yes or no . . .”

In the interim, Janet had been taking care of Alice Toklas, who needed a cataract operation: “I am taking Alice Toklas to the American Hospital in an ambulance to have one eye operated on. She is eighty-nine. If it succeeds, the other will be operated on later. This is a worry and responsibility. Her affairs are in such a mess, I can’t tell you, but her rich friends keep sending checks. Thornton Wilder just sent $1,000 . . .”

July and August passed very quickly, both of us busy with our new plans, Janet working like a beaver correcting the proofs of her book and contemplating her new projects—the de Gaulle pamphlet for Frank Taylor at Avon and the new offer from Times Books to write the text for a richly illustrated volume on Picasso. I was overburdened by office-moving—clearing out papers after fourteen years on the job, receiving my non-English-speaking replacement, introducing him around and preparing to go to Rome. We were both so tired out that we were unable to write to each other as often as usual.

Janet went to Toulouse to see the Picasso show, which included ballet curtains and sketches—the only new aesthetic material she would have for her book on him. On her return she wrote (August 21, 1965) that she was stopping “. . . en route at the château of Douglas Cooper near Avignon, who bossed the Toulouse show and will give me the main gossip before I see the material. His collection of Braques is supreme. It was he who wrote Stanley that if he knew how many Braques he owned, he would not tell him any more than how many suits of clothes he had. We are now quick friends since Nancy named him her literary executor, poor man, and he attended her funeral, sitting in front of me—we making three out of the six who attended.

“I enclose the most important Paris press appreciation of Anna—really splendid publicity, if somewhat personal, about her former private life. Her affair with Rossellini will never die in reporters’ memories simply because nothing equally important has happened since. I well understand that (a) you did not want to live as Anna's sub-renter in her palazzo and that (b) it was much too costly. But you will have to tell her, darling. Write her, I mean.

"I had to laugh at Hawley's having lately written me: 'Milton wants to know what your Paris expenses are. Could I help in any way?' The darling old fox. It was to him that I wrote early this year, sending the figures of annually raised Paris salaries for all employees in UNESCO and also *The New York Times*. I've forgotten the percentage now. I wanted the magazine to raise my compensatory annual allowance, which has not gone up one penny since I arrived in November of 1944 . . . with Paris the most costly capital in Europe for three years now. . . ."

[August 21, 1965]

Darlinghissima,

. . . It is raining again. We have had a midget summer of six days of continuous pleasant weather. The Los Angeles riots were horrifying to read about and think of, horrifying to think, too, that political squabbles between Washington and Los Angeles had prevented millions of dollars being properly used in Watts, which might have mollified the Negroes to begin with, horrible to think that since the Civil War its major premise for the color people, who had been slaves before, did not release them from the serfdom of poverty and social ghettos.

Hawley, who is here with Alethea, tells me the very long Talk of the Town piece on Stevenson, as an obit, was written by Lillian Ross, who was writing a profile on him and in it used some of her material. What a disappointment for her, like me with Blum and his death, which cut my profile short, like his life.

[August 31, 1965]

Darlinghissima,

Are you living on the moon? Have you become illiterate, no longer knowing how to write? Are you in trouble, my poor darling? I hope not. Or are you so pinned down under work that you cannot free yourself even to write a post card or cable? It is close to three weeks now since I have had news of you and from you. PLEASE COMMUNI-

CATE, Natalia my darling, for I shall continue to be troubled and worried until I hear from you, even briefly. Love, ever and ever. This is no moment to change, nor have we changed . . .

Thursday: Had hoped for a note today in response to my cable. I spent yesterday afternoon at a police station, called for in state by two nice young detectives in a police car (private, not the big Black Maria), because I had been lightly robbed over the weekend, and the intruder had been caught. Eighteen years old, father works for gas and electricity state company; mother long ago abandoned the family. A silly-faced boy, a liar and polite. He had stolen my key three weeks ago, finding it in my door one day. NEVER AGAIN. Unable to figure out system of control button by which all the lights in my room are turned on with that one button, he had found a candle in my drawer, given a month ago during an electricity breakdown, and burned it in an ash receiver, to see to rob. . . .

I had spent the weekend at Orgeval—and the valet found him standing there, with my key in his hand, which he showed. Thought he was a member of the reception department because he also had a big bunch of passkeys. He did NOT sleep in my bed nor doze on my chairs, because they were not flattened, but plumped up as valets fix them always. BUT, he spent part of Sunday night in my room with a candle, robbing, with considerable inconvenience. It was a nasty shock. Luckily when I walked in at three Monday afternoon, my valet had reentered at two, and the thief took the hint and departed with him, for the elevator, like a gent. . . .

Bill has made his career; it is organized in success. As I look back, I can see how uncourageous and lazy I was, with my good critical mind unused, my inventive critical faculties all dribbled away on the Paris Letter, of no consequence really until the end of 1944. I am delighted Glenway likes the new book. His statement, it is better than he thought it would be, is my reaction, too. I am seriously considering your suggestion to come to New York for the book and your return voyage which would be a great détente for us both. Don't you think I would be in the way of all your last minute labors? Above all, I couldn't bear to be in America without seeing Hildegarde. Could I have her in New York for a fortnight, too? Be frank with me, darling.

The storms in Italy are terrifying. How could our lovely Via del Sole be washed away like that in sections, so magnificently built? I suppose the mud on the hills had not settled yet and slid under pressure from the rains. A disastrous year.

Yes, Reston is the only man who makes sense in his Saigon report.

This is a dull letter, my darling, full of relief, projects, hopes and plans and courage, which is part of my hopes. Thine, Natalia, make no doubt of it. We will be happy together even with my ineffectual nature and lack of Italian. I shall try with desperation to learn it this time. It frightens me, of course. I have been so inert, so stupidly lazy. I look forward to doing the de Gaulle pamphlet with great eagerness. Believe me. My memory is terrible now, I warn you darling. But my heart is young, my senses alert, and that will reknit us. Love.

On August 28, Janet announced that she had refused the Picasso book because she couldn't "face the work of it all," and also that Frank Taylor had resigned at Avon, because "publishers wanted *sex* paperbacks in greater numbers, so there goes my de Gaulle pamphlet."

During this time, I had been spending my weekends with Bill and Doris in Princeton, where they had settled into a charming old house, and it was then that an unexpected event solved all my problems. It must have been early in June that, at one of the Italian diplomatic receptions, I met an old friend I hadn't seen in a long time. He had just returned from Rome. Eager to know how things were, I asked him questions and announced that I was moving there in the near future. "You mean, you are going to live and work there for good? You will not like it. I went there with the same idea and came right back. I mean, you are foolish to leave your position here. You are too used to working in New York."

Then, in early October, I received a phone call from Mr. Andrea Rizzoli, asking me for an appointment. Would I see him right away, that afternoon?

Rizzoli had just opened its international bookstore and offices at 712 Fifth Avenue, in the elegant, five-story French-style building that had once housed Cartier. Except for the original mirrored entrance to the building, the rest of the interior had been transformed by Milanese architects—wood paneling, marble floors, oak shelves, handwrought chandeliers, leather seats, antique furniture, and the like. They had imparted to the place, in the middle of the most modern city in the world, a feeling of past elegance that drew praise from press and public alike.

"I will open in New York—not just a bookstore, but the most beautiful bookstore in America, an oasis of Italy right in the heart of Manhattan," Angelo Rizzoli had told an interviewer in 1961.

It was there that I went that afternoon to meet his son, Andrea

Rizzoli. He was sitting at a large desk in a grand-looking office—a corpulent, middle-aged man, who greeted me with a soft voice as I entered.

"We would like to offer you a position as head of our company here," he said, without ceremony. "My father was told that you are not happy with the set-up at Mondadori, New York, and that you were contemplating moving to Rome. We would be interested to know your answer before I leave New York. Possibly by tomorrow." With that, he got up and left.

I was startled. This was something I had not dreamed of.

I couldn't wait to tell Giorgio Mondadori, who happened to be in town. I did so, and instantly resigned. Then I called Andrea Rizzoli and accepted the offer, after which I wrote Janet and phoned Bill the news. Finally, I wrote to Arnoldo Mondadori, the powerless Presidente.

A few years later, during his last trip to New York, the now-retired Presidente came to see me in my luxurious office, a far cry from the first one I had occupied for him, but which I had dearly loved.

"Cara Natalia," he said, admiring the surroundings with his great, friendly smile, "cara Natalia, one makes mistakes in life!" I loved the old man. No one could replace him in my affections.

When Janet received my news, she sent me a special delivery note.

[October 10, 1965]

My darling one,

You emerge from this confusion and dastardly amorality on G's part in a position of triumph and morality and dignity. I would never have been able to think you would have acted in any other way than the *superior* way your fine head, your decent, clean conscience, and your clear, warm brain functioning with the pulse of your body and heart to protect you, to ally you with other good sources and relations, all these elements within you making you the victor.

My heart and love are yours. I will meet you in Rome. I will come to New York. This is a shock for you, but it will bring you the appreciation of all friends and admirers and from your new employer the compliment the other failed to give you and so lost you. You have won.

Your adoring . . .

Several notes from Janet followed, expressing satisfaction at my news.

In October, she announced her annual trip to Abano.

[October 14, 1965]

Darlinghissima,

. . . The more I see of so-called contemporary art, the more foolish it seems. DO LOOK AT LAST Sunday's *London Times* magazine. It has an attack on Picasso as over the past twenty years, in which he has been "impotent" artistically, the writer alleges, that is very interesting. I think justified in many ways. All those silly drawings of young girl models with a nasty little old naked satyr with his genitals hanging like old leaves. Remember them? All of them, all three of them—the girl, the old man and his cock. What is happening is that somebody has arrived at a calm decision to deprive him of his godhead, which will be a relief to many. . . .

I had planned to go to Rome as soon as Janet's book came out in Novmber. I wanted to break the news of my changed plans to my dear mother, though arteriosclerosis had so weakened her memory, her sense of time and place and recognition, that it wouldn't have made much difference to her at this point. During my last visit, it had broken my heart to see the ravages of longevity and illness on her brilliant mind, to see a being so attractive, so rich in nature, always so active, now reduced to helplessness—so miserable, so detached, so lost. All we could do was to pray and hope, what humans keep on doing to the last breath. I wanted to be with her, as if my presence could miraculously help. I felt guilty at not being able to stay beside her to the end.

It came with a telephone call from my son in Princeton. "It is necessary to go," said Bill, who had talked to Franca in Rome, I knew. The ultimate spark of life had been exhausted. Mammina Ester lay stretched out on the bed in her room, resting. Her lovely face was serene, pale, spent. She was almost smiling. I bent over and kissed her. She was terribly cold. Outside, a pale autumnal sun was shining; life was going on in the ancient piazza below. Bill, at a window in the next room, was sobbing. The funeral was simple. A small procession of relatives and friends walked behind the coffin carried by four men across the bustling market to a church nearby. It was placed before the altar and a simple mass for the dead followed. A few words and some incense. Mother would have liked that modest good-bye. When the coffin was lowered into our family tomb at Campo Verano, the Rome cemetery, and the marble top closed over it, only then did I realize I would never see her again.

I will always remember Mother, seated at her desk, elegantly attired—a pretty hat, white gloves—editing the first woman's magazine in Italy. Or, with a veil floating in the wind, standing on the trenches to visit the front during World War I. Or bending over her three daughters to make sure that we were happily asleep, like any other good mother at night. Widowed so young, she had not been as successful in her own private life, because she had never found a companion worthy of her. But she had earned her daughters' devotion, and she had been loved and admired by many.

With her disappearance, a whole epoch came to an end. She had studied by candlelight and traveled by jet. It was November 8, 1965, and she was eighty-seven years old.

[November 9, 1965]

My darlinghissima Natalia,

This has certainly been the saddest day of your life. There can be no loss like that of the mother, if she is still loved and was so meriting of devotion as yours. And there is no loss in life like that of death or losing a body and spirit to the grave. You arrived too late to have her speak to you, yet it may be that was your phase of good fortune in the tragedy. Sometimes I recall my mother in the night as so little coherent, looking so lost and devastated by merely living longer, by breathing more, by taking longer for her final preparation for leaving, sadder for Hildegarde and me than if she could have been spared those last efforts and thus spared us. Nobody knows because nobody can control those slight or great movements of mortality at the last, nobody but the doctors, and they seem like racers against time and death, setting up records when they can without regard to emotions or what is suitable.

I was glad to hear darling Bill's voice. He sounded so young and masculine and loving and rational about his Mammina Ester. I hope you flew over together. That would have made the journey and the denouement easier for you. I had a big candle with a picture on it burned in Padua in Sant'Antonio for her. It will burn for days, the monk said.

You didn't sound like yourself on the phone. How could you? It was the first time I ever heard your voice since you had become an orphan.

Your devoted, loving one . . .

[November 11, 1965]

Darlinghissima,

I just recived your tender letter of love and grief for your beloved mother. I shall save it for you, for later it will touch you to read how clearly you appreciated both her great qualities and your great tenderness for her, making two sides of an intaglio which made a portrait of her. . . .

Try to meet me at the station alone. I always like looking out and seeing you like the only individual among all the travelers on the platform. Be so kind as to take a room at my dear hotel near Piazza Navona, where you can perhaps spend some time with me. It is better and easier for all if I stop in a hotel. . . .

I met Janet at Rome's Termini Station on November 19. When I sighted her small, white-haired figure smiling and waving that afternoon on the railway platform, I felt as if manna had fallen from the skies to lift my spirits. We embraced tenderly. Those few days she remained in Rome were restoring for everyone, Bill and my sisters included. She looked wonderfully well, rested and in good form. I shall never forget the effort she made to be with me in those sad days.

Janet went back to Paris on Thanksgiving, and I joined her two weeks later.

After three days in Paris, which were a solace, I returned to New York to prepare for my new job and the move to a new apartment, looking forward to spending Christmas with my family in Princeton. It would be cheerful to be with the children, ready to give their interpretation of the Beatles to their one and only appreciative audience. It would be the last Christmas together at this end, for Bill and Doris were soon to move back to California and the sun.

1966

In New York, I had to confront a new set of changes—the move to Rizzoli and to a new apartment as well. With mother's death, other things, too, had come to an end: my working relationship of fourteen years with Mondadori and the tearing away of established friendships, old habits and familiar faces—my own quarter, with its small shops, friendly neighbors, and those rooms we had lived in together so happily.

Janet's arrival, and her unbounded belief in my strength—Oh, how it had been wavering!—couldn't have been more propitious. Her presence, as usual, steadied my nerve. I walked with confidence into the elegant Rizzoli building, up to that second floor where only a few months before I had met Andrea Rizzoli.

First of all, I had to organize work routines and an open-door policy for consultation and collaboration with my co-workers. At Mondadori I had had to deal with at most a handful of people; here there were at least forty employees, with varying responsibilities. I soon discovered jealousies and distrust, especially among the correspondents for the Rizzoli publications, all of whom came around to establish their turf and rights—even Oriana Fallaci, the star of them all. I decided to ignore the intramural rivalries and concentrate on my job.

Janet stayed three months in New York, her longest visit since the early forties. I was delighted. It was then that we decided to move into a new apartment more suited to our needs. And it was there that Janet was to live permanently for three years, the last ones of her life, and where I still reside, among her books and memories.

Time flew, what with my two moves and Janet's popularity. This year the celebrations were many. In March, on her seventy-fourth birthday, Janet's *Paris Journal, 1944–1965* won the National Book Award for "the most distinguished work in the field of Arts and Letters." "It seems I have won some sort of prize," she said when she heard the news. She was naturally delighted and quite amused to notice that the award had given her some kind of "status" in the literary world, after forty years of writing! "Magazine journalism is something to be thrown away, I guess," she said, ironically. We were dining in Mr. Shawn's favorite corner in the Oak Room of the Plaza Hotel. She was most grateful to him for his masterful editing of the book. He had performed a "beauty operation," she told an interviewer. "He took out the wrinkles. For three months, including a vacation, Shawn whittled this mass of material into an historical narrative. The words unchanged are Genêt's; the words omitted, in effect, are Shawn's."

We were both pretty exhausted when we left on April 7 for Calistoga. I had been invited, too, so I took a week off and left with Janet.

[May 6, 1966]

Darlinghissimassima,

That means doubled darlingest. Thanks for very interesting clippings on Old Wormwood [Lady Diana Manners' smart set sobriquet for de Gaulle], and especially for Reston's comments. Today is Thursday, May 5. I shall leave here one week from today by car with Hildegarde and Eric to spend four days en route in the Olympia Valley Rain Forests . . .

This trip is not my plan, you may be sure, but is a dream Hildegarde and Eric have had for years to see these glorious forests and mountain views, and I am the animator part of it—my departure, I mean. Have not the heart to refuse, especially since they insist I continue being their guest en route. They have spent a fortune already on me, it seems to me, considering how little they usually spend on themselves. I stuff $5 bills in Hildegarde's handbag, but she has caught on to that, alas. Stuffs them back into mine.

. . . *The New Yorker* has been amazingly improved of late it seems to me, . . . better talk than in years (vide this current week's). The big article on oranges which is fascinating and last week's in Books, an enchanting piece by M. F. K. Fisher, from Mary Frances Kennedy, and one-time wife of Covici Friede, then later someone named Fisher. She writes on food, I suppose, but this includes fantastic animals. Her last week's piece began with the diet of a mouse she was fond of. Hildegarde and I are having cocktails with her today in St. Helen's where she lives, a strange, highly civilized, elegant woman, not rich except mentally and emotionally, not impoverished, but less golden, I fancy, than in the brain—she is coming to France this summer.

I am greatly impressed by the state university quarterlies Hildegarde takes, such as the *Southern Review* (Tulane, Miss.) with the most complete illuminating long piece on Faulkner by Robert Penn Warren I ever read. The current *Hudson Review* contains an article and analyses by Sir Kenneth Clark that I found really illuminating —the interview with Stravinsky in the current *New York Review of Books* is *not to be missed*. I am very impressed by the general high modernity of the intellectual comprehension of the U.S.A. writing crowd—not a specialization as in France, but an overall knowledge here.

Your own.

P.S. Your visit here was like that of a foreign angel from Rome and Fifth Avenue—you made a date of history in their lives. The iris in Hildegarde's garden are like a rainbow—there are six white amaryllis (with red stripes) in bloom in the big porch garden room and one dozen red and cerise epiphyllum in one inner plant room—such a glory of bloom I have never seen. Flowers as large as giant chrysanthemums.

———

That spring the Rizzolis arrived *en masse* for the inauguration of the adjacent building, which added a new wing to the bookstore, a gallery above, and a pretty preview theater below. Janet missed that inauguration day, but arrived from Calistoga in time for a last weekend at the Island. Then back to work until our next meeting, planned for September in Rome.

Her first letter from Paris of June 12 expressed confusion and concern about resuming her regular *New Yorker* pieces, after a hiatus of so many months: "I am in a state of confusion, still partly mental, also financial. I can't recall what French money is worth and so over-tipped twice as handsomely. . . .

"Everyone here is anti-Johnson as you and I. Everybody here or everywhere thinks this is a bad period to be still alive after the worst period of Germany's murdering six million Jews. It is strange to be a woman and so little part of the male rule of the world."

The war in Vietnam was worrying us. By this time we had com-mitted over a hundred and eighty-four thousand men to that war and had begun the bombing of North Vietnam. Twelve days later, a less gloomy letter cheered me up.

[June 24, 1966]

Darlinghissima,

. . . Your diary-letter was a *pleasure*, so complete, such a record of love and the work that drives you like a motor. It is true it is the best form, and I must treat it as such and copy it. As for my future activities, all I have to report is that yesterday, Thursday, came a wire from Mary Hemingway from Porto Ercole saying, "Happiest if you could dine with me Tuesday night," which I shall do with real pleasure. She has courage, and she has had a hard life, a bloody brutal one, killing animals and then seeing Ernest like a self-slaughtered creature, head-less like a primate in the jungle shot by a vicious hunter. How males kill, kill other men, other animals, birds, beasts, to eat and merely for the fun of being a good shot. An expert technician at killing on the wing. . . .

Tuesday last I lunched with Mary McCarthy, Kenneth Tynan and Jim West over behind Ste. Clothilde church in the Avenue Matignon, where de Gaulle should occasionally be, and I gather never is even when not in Siberia as today. Only the *Guardian*'s female reporter reported that the peasants greeting him on the muddy roadside carried lilac branches to wave and the Siberian flag which has a blue band on the outer edge of its red surface. . . .

P.S. Weather has been so foul I have not worn my nice new red suit as yet!

[July 14, 1966]

My darling,

This has been a hard five-day task for me to finish my first Paris Letter, of which I had lost the habit of discipline and necessary concentration, so the writing came with greater difficulty than normal, if normal it was before, I always being a slow producer. Twice the electricity was blown out of this Paris sector by intense electric storms and pelting rain. So far, the habit for this summer's weather seems to be established—rainy and uncertain. Yesterday the enclosed letter from me to you was returned, misdirected. That is the worst black mark against me in all our years—that I cannot remember numbers any more and have twice sent you letters to the wrong digits. Now I consult my address book each time, like a dunce, alarmed by my own confusion. It is no time for forgetting them with an increased mathematic involved in every step of relatively old-fashioned communication such as the telephone, which here, as in New York, has lost or is losing its bureau names of Balzac or Oxford, they being translated into more numbers by the dial. Plus the French code areas instead of town names and zip codes for cross-country post, here as in the U.S.A. Sometimes I become utterly addled, please forgive me.

I dined with Alfred Kazin and his wife tonight, whom I had invited, then forgot about until they turned up, also phoned up, as I was giving a brief interview to the Canadian Broadcasting Company for a TV half-hour this week. That will be the last of my career, I have decided. I like the Kazins; he has had a rich life of learning, teaching and critical faculties behind him, a scholar in his way.

I went alone to the new Ionesco play.* For such a play I find I can concentrate better without comment from a companion, even though it might be a good guide. I wrote about it too extensively in my Paris Letter, but found it fascinating, certainly richer than surface sex or spiritual desperation in its attic or front porch school forms that we have had enough of the past two years. My God, but sex really *is* the star in the publishing and theater business, isn't it? That powerful little crotched corner of the body which religion, the Christian religion at least, had so long tried to keep covered up and quieted down, has suddenly swollen to a clitoris or penis the size of a mountain from whose height the view is extended all over the western world.

---

* *Le Soif et la faim.*

Your report of little Julia's vocabulary in dirty words was touching. How confiding for her to speak so openly, how unabashed and therefore pure. You must be the only Nonna on the whole continent to have received the confidence so calmly and humorously. You have great wisdom, darling. There is no question but what the dichotomy of education in politeness or even dignity which so early makes parents teach children (or civilization teaches them) to leave their little parts alone for the first fifteen years, let's say, of their lives, during which sex is socially taboo, and thus is always a great shock in children's lives, as we may both recall, when it turns out later that one's parents indulged in it, often without the females enjoying it much. Maybe the progressive "sex play" theory by which some kids are now brought up is a better idea. I should think it would lead to an unusual amount of incest though! . . .

Violette Leduc has just sent me a pale pink pamphlet which turned out to be *Thérèse et Isabelle*, which was, I believe, cut from *La Bâtarde* as too explicit an exposé, apparently written with the same impassioned accuracy and lack of lewdness that marked the book's girl-and-girl scenes in the convent dormitory. I haven't tried reading *Thérèse* yet; it is published by Gallimard, but surely not on general sale.

The Jeanne Moreau film, *Mademoiselle*, which I shall mention next time, [based] on a script by Genet, was called simply *Merde*, exactly that, by the *Canard Enchaîné* critic, usually a good and accurate man. Of the dozen best critics in town, ten voted openly for its not being worth seeing, though, as usual, she is excellent in a bitch role. Had anyone else written the scenario, it would not have been accepted, such is the snobbery today about patronizing a writer more famous for his licentiousness than for the amazing fine style of his French language when he is not writing pornography, which is not often.

I have not as yet unpacked my books even, but am doing so this week, and so really settle to try to start the opening page of the de Gaulle book. Don't think I am not still set on it. I am now utterly convinced that my basic notion as I explained it briefly to Frank Taylor and you that afternoon at the St. Regis bar is what I want and indeed the only one of interest I would be competent to do—why the French fail to be Republican enough in their republics to avoid a Pétain or a de Gaulle. . . .

From my window, I can see the sandbox in the Tuileries across from me, with little citizens aged two or three digging away under the patient maternal eye, so the real drama of begetting and educating, washing and drying and feeding goes on, with women in command only of infancy.

My darling, how often day and night my heart and mind turn to you. . . .

———

Early in August I flew to California to visit Bill and his family, newly established in Malibu; then, on my return, I went to Italy, where Janet and I would spend our vacation.

[August 5, 1966]

My darlinghissima.

. . . I am not a sheep so I do not move more slowly in CONSTANT rain because my wool is wet. Yesterday at six p.m. suddenly there was a lovely clear sky of pink at the horizon till advancing blue in the vault, the first clear evening since late June, followed by a clear night that is. It did not start raining again until seven a.m. I woke at six; it was still lovely, with rain for my breakfast an hour later and pouring all day.

In this month's *Encounter* I found an article which enormously interested me on pornography, can you beat it? It is an analysis of what it consists of—hallucination, mostly—that the orgasm can satisfy, which it cannot, since desire begins immediately even if impossible to fulfill and existing only in the sickened imagination. It is the only article on this subject I ever read and was interested in, with my full attention, and I actually commend it to you as *worth your time*, with so much pornography rampant today, and so much of it so bogus, so thin and unvoluptuous. The author of whom I have barely heard is Steven Marcus, among those who was present at Indiana University recently when the pornographia which Glenway spoke of in the Kinsey collection there was opened for study, to a limited few.

There is a mysterious story Truman told here about a wonderful watch he had from Cartier, unique it was, which ceased functioning. He was going to bring it back here for repair, told a certain friend of his (name unknown by me—he did not tell me this story), who is one of the boys and seemed covetous to have a watch like it. In any case, when Truman went to his safety vault in his apartment house, I gather he found it completely smashed. What a strange tale. . . .

Malraux's first wife, Clara, has published the second book of her marital recollections of her youth with him, especially out in Cambodia, including the incident of the stolen Khmer statues. I feel strangely disgusted by it all. Either he lied to me when he told me his tale (I rather thought so at the time), or she lies now, since her story of today does not match with hers as told when she returned to Paris to rouse the NRF literary stars to plead for him, to get him out of prison—neither of them, man or wife, seem what the French call *sérieux* in their recollections. She writes of him quite lovingly so apparently it is not sheer bitchery, but her book has done him a lot of harm in literary circles. He is suffering from a nervous breakdown, I hear, also claustrophobia, which cannot be a great help as a government minister on whom le grand Charlie leans. . . .

[August 19, 1966]

Bellissima, tenderissima, darlinghissima,

Two weeks from last night we shall meet in your natal city, that of the Roman Empire, a great many fine Latin writers of two thousand years ago. I can barely contain my anticipations. . . .

When Truman was here, he invited us—or did I tell you?—to his Plaza Hotel ball, in black and white for November 28. We shall be in Glenway's pre-dinner group, he says. Either black or white frock, white mask and a fan. What a mark to look forward to. You will dance like a queen of the Juju Isles, unpainted by Gauguin.

Thanks for your California postcard. I made out "dood" on the side, so darling Doodie was at *your* side and you used the word "groovy" in a way which defines it as "delightfully," I gather. . . .

The moon Orbiter pictures were a disappointment. Not even a sign stuck up saying "Keep off the moon. This means you," including photographers. I hope you liked the doubtless too-longish piece in this week's cabled Letter on the Grand Trianon. It interested me to do. Always a bad sign, for then I wrote too long in it. Also wrote lengthily because there was nearly no new news here that was interesting.

Paris looks like a shambles, like a *chantier* or a mine head, with red and white barricades above and under ground everywhere, all over town, with a new Métro track being built to go some place or other and new undercut UNDER the Concorde for the curse of motor cars which make flesh and blood unnecessary except to own them. I can't tell you how sick I am of the French Leftists, always squealing against anyone who does not dirty his hands at work.

The only reform of real utility, indeed necessity, that I am interested in is profit-sharing, so the U.S.A. and France don't have these constant strikes from the dirty handed—or the white collared in offices, ill paid, more ill paid than those with grubby fingernails in factories. Man talks of justice as he used to talk of God, forgiveness of sins, charity to others, and heaven after death, but he does not really WANT justice any more than he wants to go to heaven, which would necessitate dying first, just as justice would necessitate the rich dividing up their earnings and the workers not punishing the rich for having been rich so long, too long, unbearably long.

CABLE me when and where exactly, name of hotel too, please, and our dinner engagement that night. I adore this expectation. It is an amative drug nibbled in advance.

I didn't write often to Janet after we waved good-bye to each other at the Rome airport, from where she flew back to Paris. Too tired after the Frankfurt Book Fair, and too busy with a new winter ahead, I had to reserve as much health and strength as possible, but I did write a few lines from Milan to tell her I had been well received at Rizzoli. "Well, I hope to heaven so. You are their most brilliant acquisition!" Janet commented. Sentiments such as those from her were my pillars of strength. But on the phone from New York she sounded fatigued. "No," she said, she was merely very sad. "The heart was beating slowly without joy, except in your spoken words." Luckily a letter from Raymond Mortimer from London cheered her up. "Raymond Mortimer of the London *Times* will do a review of the English edition of *Paris Journal.* 'That book of yours has every virtue, every grace.' Breathtaking. I did not even know it was being published in London now. By whom? Do you know?" And she added, "Truman's invitation to the ball just came!"

The news was going the rounds in so-called smart circles in New York and everywhere: Truman Capote's black-and-white masked ball was to be held in the ballroom of New York's Hotel Plaza at the end of November. Everyone was asking, "Have you been invited? Will you go? What will you wear?" Truman Capote's name was on every jet-setter's tongue and in every society type's hopes. "Depending on which masked and bejeweled guest was talking, it was the party of the decade. It was the party of the century, or, plainly, it was the biggest and most glorious bash ever," *Life* magazine reported later on the event.

[October 20, 1966]

Darling,

. . . I have ordered a new eight-hundred-dollar Castillo long black gown for the ball. I needed one for embassy dinners, etc. I hope it comes off well—doubleface crepe, black one side, white the other, the black being the outside, but a rear panel, etc., showing the white beneath, in movement, plus a tiny white collar. Long sleeved of course, with a turnback cuff which will show a little white, like a schoolboy's cuff. Am ordering a five-strand string of white pearls which are needed below the collar to set off the whole affair. It is belted behind, I forgot to say, like a reefer. Frightfully, frightfully smart, so you will be proud of me.

I am tired. Going out to dine alone at Hôtel Lotti, steak and spinach, I hope. Have sent eight pages on this week's Letter by cable, with one more . . . to go tomorrow.

Love and love and weariness but satisfaction.

[November 14, 1966]

Darling,

How inexplicable that Truman's invitation to you has not arrived. What shall we do? Yes, he is a snob, but that should prove the legitimacy of your being present that night. Were he a naïve country boy, I could comprehend his failing to treat us as un couple charmant et dévoué. I confess I have had too little experience in such high social matters to have any idea what to do—except let him know through Glenway, perhaps, since he would be our dinner host, that without you I do not come. I do not know if that is putting the peak value on you or me. In any case, it sounds like both devotion and blackmail. . . .

No, I have no long black evening dress, but have ordered one. Have just been invited FOR THE FIRST TIME to Ambassador Bohlen's to dine November 9. The invitation specifies "long dress," just as simply as that. I went to my old vendeuse Jane, from Lanvin, now with Castillo. She at least knows what I can and cannot wear. I dread the experience. One hates to look an elderly fool. My back is still good, but my front has to be hidden under a jacket rather like the portcullis of a fortress hung with a Gobelin tapestry on a fête day. Monica has been lent a fine necklace for the ball, gold, flecked with quite sizable diamonds, offered by her devoted friend Lisette. Truman owes Odette

[Arnaud] tremendous thanks and gratitude. She fought like a tiger—loving every claw-stroke—with Gallimard to make him pay high for his book and advertise it . . .

So Monica is invited. Truman (I think I told you) told Odette she would only get five percent commission because he was going to make so much money on the French rights that ten percent would be too much. An illogical statement—rather mean also.

The obit I did for this last week's Letter on André Breton and surrealism was very, very difficult, but I think I did it well, giving information on him and what surrealism was founded on and meant to its members that surely is unknown to most New Yorkers. A strange cult, I suppose a necessary, natural revolution against family, church, the nineteen cent. French novel and patriotism.

I am going to tea this afternoon at five to see old Natalie Barney, Remy de Gourmont's Amazon, in her old house and garden in the rue Jacob. Germaine Beaumont will be there too, and one or two academicians still able to walk with canes. She has grown very, very thin, Germaine told me. I lunched with her. First time in two years, but her mind at the age of ninety is as alert as ever, wonderful. As I said to Germain, lesbians lead such healthy lives, no childbirths, abortions or miscarriages.

———

On November 5, in a brief note announcing her arrival on Thanksgiving, Janet wrote, "I enclose the London *Times* on the Italian floods. Perhaps the sad Grosseto picture is new to you. What a catastrophe it has been and is!"

The rains Janet had been complaining about in her letters from Paris had begun falling on central Italy until, toward the end of October, the Arno, Florence's famous river, began rising and finally flooded the city after the engineers of the hydroelectric dam about thirty-eight miles upstream decided to open it in order to keep it from bursting. The flood was recorded as the worst in more than a century.

On November 7, Janet cabled from Paris:

"*Je pleure la beauté d'Italie noyée. J*"

On the 11th, she exclaimed: "Poor *mamma mia*, she it will be who cleans up the mud on central Italy from all the houses! *Papà mio* will be no help at all."

Our Rizzoli preview theater had been transformed into a busy shop selling objects donated for the Florence relief fund.

Oriana Fallaci brought me back from her city a tarnished little antique salt cellar, its cracked blue-glass lining still in place, which had been retrieved from the mud near Ponte Vecchio. With its daintily chiseled wolf-handle top, it sits proudly today among my most cherished mementos.

On November 11 Janet announced her arrival for Thanksgiving.

[November 11, 1966]

Darlinghissima,

. . . My new dress which I wore to dine at Ambassador Bohlen's the other night is chic and strict. I hope it pleases you, darling. We will have much to be thankful for on the day of my arrival—that we are together. Cold turkey will be merely a leftover from the Indian Puritan days. We can eat eggs instead, wren's eggs, pigeon's eggs, lark's eggs, nightingale's eggs . . .

My striking black-and-white striped gown, fashioned by Maria Antonelli, had arrived from Rome, complete with mask and fan, so I was set for the season's biggest social event. Our friend Monica Stirling had also arrived a few days earlier, looking pretty, thin, but relaxed. She hadn't been in New York for years. Her latest book, a biography of Hans Christian Andersen, had received good reviews and was a success. She was in good spirits; we had much to talk about.

The best part, in fact, of Truman's ball was the reunion of old friends at the dinner given by Glenway Wescott and Monroe Wheeler beforehand—Janet, Monica, Anita Loos, Virgil Thomson and myself. Once in the Plaza ballroom, with five hundred guests, the occasion became a *grande mêlée* of the beautiful, the famous and the infamous, ogling one another, dancing and greeting one another under spotlights. Truman had reached the height of social success with that ball. It had cost him a fortune, too—one he had just made with his book *In Cold Blood*. It later cost him some of those "friends" as well, when he committed the unpardonable sin of publishing some indiscretions about them. But that night had been historical and fun.

"It was worth it," wrote Janet, back in Paris. "I thank Truman with all my heart for the evening and part of the days spent with you."

She had barely returned when she received another invitation, from Pauline de Rothschild for a New Year's weekend at their château, sixty miles from Bordeaux.

"I try not to fear this visit as being like a goldfish pond for a small, old, wise freshwater trout like me, though obviously Glen and Monroe will be great comfort. I hope I act delicately and gentle while there," she wrote on December 19.

I went to Malibu, where the family was having its first Christmas in its new home. The air was balmy, filled with shrieks of excitement and laughter. It was pleasing and lively, and I certainly felt comfortable and at ease.

[December 23, 1966]

. . . The year ends bitterly, with our country hated more than ever, not for its prosperity but for its evil doings. Only Lippmann spoke the simple truth yesterday which none of us had thought to find. In Vietnam is being fought one more war by the Asiatics to throw the White Man out of the East where once more he tries to dominate, if only in a new anti-colonial manner. But it is one more attempt to throw the Whites out of the Yellow East.

It is so warm today that it is an abnormal spring. I am almost resigned to the possible pleasure of going to the Rothschilds over New Year's with Glenway. In the little sweater shop next to my hotel is a skirt fitter who worked at Balenciaga who is shortening and tightening my new skirt you gave me. My suède jacket looks wonderful on me. I tried it on again so I will have one perfect costume at least and shall hope not to break any museum cup my tea will be served in. I have slept later in the mornings than at any time since my girlhood, probably because I can never get to sleep except at about three on the New York schedule.

You will come for a week in Paris this spring. Don't avoid it. Love to all your dear family, including the new generation, though I wonder what the world's future will be for them. It has turned out publicly badly for mine, but privately producing great joy with you since the beginning of the last war, which did NOT make us unpopular in Europe, for once.

My blessings on you and us.

1967

[January 6, 1967]

My darling,

. . . The letter of wisdom and command you sent me on us, on our lives and deprivations, and even on its riches of love I have read three times and save to read again. It is a privilege to have a friend who can write and think with such wide philosophy and knowledge. You might indeed be a philosophy professor at Princeton with a long beard, and thank God you are not.

Glenway brought the beautiful silver suit which fits *perfectly*. I had bought a white silver dickey with turned-down collar and tie like a man's dinner shirt and as I walked into the Mouton drawing room New Year's Eve there was a cry of "Sensationnelle!" from the other guests. The double-breasted jacket was the perfect solution, and I thank you for this grandeur present.

I have been too tired to write more on the house party at the Rothschilds, one of the nicest, most stimulating I ever heard or talked to in my life and NO château life even building [life] except for food which was exquisite and not heavy, and wines which were, i.e., Lucullan. Glenway and Monroe were here, too, and left for Holland today, and Raymond Mortimer is staying longer, not well—alas.

I embrace you, I cannot say how often. How often have I in twenty-six years do you suppose? Not enough.

Janet had been very much in demand from book publishers and magazines for articles and prefaces, and I had asked her if she wanted me to act as her agent, since she didn't much like discussing business and fees.

"YES," she wrote on January 20, "but I *insist* you take an agent's commission of ten percent if that is the regular non-Truman Capote's figure. YES is my answer to the Roger Straus arrangements for the Colette preface to *The Pure and the Impure*, and YES also to the *Life* piece of 1200 words on *Les Halles* to be sent by middle March at perhaps $1500 or even $1200 whatever you bargain for. That shall not be too difficult, though all I write is always more work than my optimism foresees. . . . I always seem to be a little late on everything including breathing."

So I became Janet's agent.

On January 20, I received a wonderful letter of praise from Janet to a summing up I had given her of my first year at Rizzoli. Rizzoli had become not only the most-admired bookstore in town, but also an international center, a meeting place, where books and art shows were launched and enjoyed. American authors had been added to the Rizzoli list, and some of its Italian authors' books had been sold to American publishers.

My relations with the company employees were good, especially with Oriana Fallaci, who was then covering the Vietnam War for *L'Europeo*. Bold, sharp, fearless and daring, it was difficult to imagine a more feminine-looking woman—so delicate of feature, so small and slender, like one of the three Graces in Botticelli's painting, but with such a strong character and with nerves of steel. She was passionately committed to her work, as much so as Janet, perhaps even more. She would go without sleep or food, consuming packs of cigarettes, to finish a story, to type up her interviews, famous everywhere. Janet, in fact, liked her, admired her. I opened my home to her; we became friends. In effect, I became her agent, too.

Janet often asked, "How is Oriana?" or, "And your mad little Florentine writer, what happened to her in the Far East?" She knew that sooner or later Oriana would find herself in dramatic situations. Whenever Oriana was in town, she absorbed my attention and kept the office busy and jumping.

Both my sisters came to visit during the winter. Lea had, since the fifties, become a play agent, and together we followed the openings on Broadway. With Franca, who was a film editor, I went to see every important film. Janet was delighted that I had their company to keep me from "lonely dinners."

[January 26, 1967]

. . . Your description of what a literary agent looks like in your imagination made me shout with laughter—fat, elderly, ill dressed. No, in those ways you are no agent, my darling, but had you mentioned intelligence and office experience in dealing with publishers, adding that an agent is handsome, well-dressed in Roman clothes, and my sweetheart, that would have been the perfect description!

Poor England—I hope that hard, stony de Gaulle permits them to enter the Common Market. How ferocious his devotion to France makes him. He is like a double parent, both male and female, with both their jealousies and ambitions combined where la Belle France is concerned.

[February 14, 1967]

My darling,

I cabled you to thank you for the delay granted on the Colette piece. I am lunching with young Colette [de Jouvenel] Thursday, dined with her and [Robert] Phelps (who did the Colette biography) last week, and am lunching with Germain Beaumont Wednesday, to revive further physical souvenirs of Colette's own Lesbic period (which I shall treat only historically), but needed, I believe, to bring some kind of warming, picturesque aspect to Le Pur et l'impur, which after re-reading five times I now comprehend as an important analysis, pre-Kinsey and therefore startlingly original and clear, of sexual duality. I now understand why she herself thought it might eventually be considered her most important work, which was clearly her opinion.

Unfortunately for me, it contains not one phrase of her gifted, entrancing, physical writing from which I could be inspired to the kind of writing which I also do best. I was astonished at the great good sense and weight in values evidenced in young Colette's talk the other night and especially for a half hour on the telephone the next day. With critical faculty and real thoughtfulness, she analyzed her reaction to *Le Pur et l'impur* in terms of what she knew of her mother's character, which she knew in so strange a distant way, by observation rather than by intimacy. She referred to her mother as Colette, never as Maman, and only once or twice as Ma Mère, as if she, the daughter, were a literary critic of first-rate observation, though no great gifts, making a report to a colleague to be respected for a mutual interest in the subject. It was a curious experience; I took notes.

She has already been extremely useful. I must confess that had I known in advance how difficult and at first how unsympathetic *The Pure and the Impure* seemed to me, I would probably not have accepted to do the preface. Now I am very interested in managing the difficulties and presenting her mother's ideas, rather like incunabula then. This will help save me the commonplace transvestism of today. With long-haired male boys and short-haired, breeched, very female girls, as against the cautious "smokings" worn by Colette's admirers, in private parties, and her own devilish recklessness in wearing a shirt with a man's collar and scarf. What contortions has Christianity put on sex, already considered a dubious activity unless for procreation (because pagans had employed it for more pleasure). I think about the Colette essay a dozen times a day between work on my Letter, etc. I believe I shall do something intelligent and of interest, though it will not, cannot, equal in writing charm the obit I did of Colette in *The New Yorker*, where I had her whole sensuous past to draw from like flowers if only on her funeral wreaths.

Like everyone in Paris, I have had a wretched grippish cold, and I wonder how on earth you have weathered your snowfall and blizzard in New York. It sounds handsome in its way, but nothing like so gay or such physical fun for one's body as well as one's eyes, as our blizzard when we lived in the 58th Street roof house and went romping over to Park Avenue in trousers that night, to meet others whom we did not even know but talked to in a geniality of companionship created by the snow itself which isolated our social conventions but liberated our animal relation. And the look of 58th Street, with the buses lying at angles like enormous winter green caterpillars paralyzed by the cold. What a spectacle. I loved that little house. I was happy there; it was one of our best epochs. . . .

No, nothing has been reported on the Mozart manuscript theft. You will see in this week's Paris Letter how I followed up the story, giving more information and of complete accuracy, from the Bibliothèque itself, than even *The New York Times*. . . .

The weekend weather has looked divine from my window, sunny, icy cold. It is nearly one a.m. I must go to bed; I have worked for three days on my Letter, hardly leaving the house. I do not write so quickly, but perhaps better for style than in the old days. I thought of you in writing about the Mozart manuscript and how Rossini had kissed it.

———

In sending me the first agent's commission for the Colette preface, Janet wrote, "Spend some of it right away on you and Franca for Easter champagne." The preface had been much praised by Roger Straus and Hal Vursel at Farrar, Straus & Giroux, as was the piece on Les Halles for *Life*. That delighted her, and she took a brief holiday in London with her friend Noël Murphy. However, she couldn't help following the political electoral campaign going on in France, with several political factions antagonistic to the so-called Gaullists, and she was shocked at de Gaulle's decision to speak alone on TV, after the legal end of the campaign. She wrote from London on March 2, "It had been a terrific shock here, to Gaullists and even to me. It is shifty, egotistical and immoral. I am forced to remember his statement in his book dedicated to Pétain, 'the Fil de l'Epée,' in which de Gaulle stated what a great leader had to have, to lead. Machiavellianism, complete and total. Well, his Saturday night illegal broadcast is exctly that, except that Machiavelli also believed that amorality should be semi-hidden or at least managed with civilized superior gestures like those of a prestidigitateur, which would prevent its nakedness of necessity being observable while the tricks are being done . . ." And when, later, the Gaullists received a very low percentage of the vote, she wrote, "It is a great and merited setback for him as he cannot ever be quite the same, I now believe. . . . The election fiasco by the Gaullists was the most healthy political blow France could have suffered—like a terrible shaking given physically to someone in a semi-coma of conceit and satisfaction. . . ." Janet was obviously losing some of her admiration for the General! Sad news awaited her when she returned from London. She wrote a few lines at the end of her letter of March 9:

". . . Alice Toklas is to be buried tomorrow. Her Spanish maid called me Monday to say she would not last the week, so I went out at once with flowers but she was in a coma. I asked the maid to telephone me at any hour of the night which she did at one-thirty Tuesday morning to announce the end. Am glad for her, as all still alive say they are whose life has worn out and who has been able to leave life behind at last. It has been a shock."

[April 6, 1967]

Beloved,

What welcome, wonderful, joyous news. We shall have at least two days together here in Paris after you finish your Rizzoli stint, three maybe if you can cheat a trifle. On the strength of it, I shall try to have a new suit made at Chanel to change my appearance, but shall carry a large pancarte in my hand saying, "THIS IS YOURS," as identification of my person.

I wrote a *good* Paris Letter this week, one of my best in a long time, and have had Wallace Shawn here for two days, intelligent, gentle, logical, unpressed, unkempt, but a darling youth, with a voice with a note or two something like his father's and a remote shape here or there in his homely face of his mother's perennial prettiness. I walked two hours on the Paris Quais with him yesterday, took two meals with him and this morning am a fraction weary, but shall lunch again to carry it off all well.

Yesterday, the wretched Vice-President Humphrey received riot treatment down the street from my balcony while Wallace and I watched. Three or four thousand Communist students, French—not Americans—demonstrated before the embassy with placards and shouts of "Johnson Assassin, Go home Hooomphrey." Very difficult to make out at first and "paix aux Vietnam" and "USA Assassins" for good measure. It is painful and I admit it to be the member of so unceasingly unpopular a country. Often you and I as demi-Europeans both have discussed it. We, the Americans, seem to take too long to mature, being shut off by the Atlantic from our education in Europe, scholars who would have to swim for two hundred years to have participated, since in 1776 we were moving with splendid force and scholastic ignorance toward another direction and shore, toward the West, with its appeal of prosperity. Liberty plus the pleasure men find in slaughtering a young, minor race, those noble Indians, and eventually the discovery of yet one more Protestant faith, Mormonism, in a desert, and finally the discovery of blessed black oil, to take the place of Prometheus' more antique flame.

Am going to drive Wallace up to see the statue of George Washington, painted red by the students who yesterday burned an American flag near it, taken from the American cathedral church near by. He is so sickened when he sees a reference in the papers to Vietnam that he refuses to read any papers at all except at Oxford.

I don't at all understand the huge Snow White piece by [Donald]

Barthelme, Bill's new favorite I understand, in the magazine two weeks ago. Did your Bill like it? Ask him, please. I did NOT understand one thing at all in it; its humor, satire and meaning escaped my eyes and mind.

Am reading the first volume on Proust by [George] Painter. Enjoying it in a middling fashion; what a distorted youth Proust was. Am glad I read Lord Russell's memoirs—how uneven, how intimate physically, yet how far from intimacy with the reader today, a question of mind and of taste. His candor about his sexual relations is bracing in so old and so famed a philosopher. The great thing was his mental hunger, his tremendous searching, his sense of decision on the world and man, so unlike the shapeless youth of today Wallace tried to explain to me, those who say, "well, it doesn't really make much difference what you do; it is not important since nothing is of consequence and we don't believe in history. It bores us."

. . . Strikes are already in full force against the class patronal and de Gaulle's government. Well, the French don't thank us for saving them. They will never thank the Grand Charles either, an ungrateful race by nature because themselves ungenerous and inhospitable. One does not develop good qualities without other good ones to bolster them up. Our good qualities are bolstered by ease and money, usually bad bolsters.

The sun is growing pale, clouds are gathering, the spring has arrived but without its proper luggage of steady warmth. I look forward with GLEE, with Laughter and Joy to our meeting, my handsome sweet.

[April 21, 1967]

My precious,

. . . A bad, chilly hailstorm this morning at seven and now this afternoon untrustworthy sunshine, with dark clouds over Montmartre I can see by the corridor windows over the court.

I don't know if you ever see the London *Times Sunday Magazine*; this last Sunday it contained a profile written by Miss Brody on Colette that treats her nearly exclusively as a lesbian (so named) and incestuously in love with her mother (so phrased). Quite brilliantly written but excessively sexual I find. After all, she had another organ too, did Colette—her writer's brain, and it was not between her legs but in her *skull*. . . .

Did you admire Mary McCarthy's piece on Vietnam in the *New York Review of Books*? I thought the last two-thirds were splendid, with extraordinary unity she dealt with the utter, total, elaborate and enormous confusion of vocabulary, ideas, aims, acts, reports and evaluations which the Americans there have put on what they are doing. What she made was like a No-Man's Land mental map; the phrases used by the soldiery, officers, by the wretched natives who pick them up, in complete ignorance of what selection or taste or intelligent definition has FAILED to offer them, instruction which is inevitable with an occupying foreign race, it is sickening. Come see my sister; she number one fuck was the perfect obscene example of lack of grammar and decency. What a record we are leaving instead of history . . .

. . . I have been reading Nabokov's *Speak, Memory*, reminiscences with great fascination. Also read Lord Russell's memoirs. Very uneven, but illuminating. How wonderful to have had his privileges, an aristocrat of great descendance and family inheritances, a genius intellectually by birth and one of the great mathematical minds of this century. What good fortune. He makes an American like me feel like a root vegetable, a turnip; or, if on the human level, of such coarse misbreeding and ancestry that one is ashamed of having been born. I have been profoundly discouraged at the America scene lately, as have you and our friends. To be so disliked, even hated, so despised as frauds who talk of peace and generosity and yet wage war, leave our own poor in ghettos of poverty and despair and with all our cant about democracy are faced with the most difficult demonstration—the acceptance of black skins (and foreskins).

I long to see you, talk with you, to be redressed in my mind by you. Your energies have been spread in so many directions of late with all you have had to do that you have at least had the satisfaction of success as with your Toscanini anniversary, but you have had the fatigue too of creating and organizing. I feel I need organizing, too. My beloved, what are your summer plans as well as your May plans??? I embrace you with a great love and admiration.

[May 10, 1967]

Darlinghissima,

. . . I think Mary McCarthy's Vietnam pieces are the most acute analyses anyone has written of our national mentality and shameless euphemisms of our do-good vocabulary, and what the doing turns out to be in the way of wretchedness, defoliation, crops ruined, children burned by napalm bombs, and a new form of concentration refugee camp, with occasional PC rations and no plumbing as usual. I read parts two and three today and have been sunk in a most profound miasma of shock and humiliation for our country, pride in her work and discernment and clear analytical brain. She told me she had a letter from Walter Lippmann saying her pieces were "superb." Praise from him and to her runs on the highest possible communication level.

I keep wondering how Stalin's daughter happened to promise her book to Harper's. Had she a literary agent already before leaving Moscow? I wonder how you have come out in this highway robber competition for the foreign rights. There is something disloyal to the whole theses in what she has done and doubly—her defection from her own land of which her father was the tyrant and leader, then her selling her memoirs like a movie star, and she from a country which forbade Pasternak to enjoy the Nobel Prize money. I know this may sound strict, applied by my Mid-western ignorant sense of political logic, but put in another way it sounds better. I feel that you would never have done what she has done. There is proof that Communism was right perhaps, that capitalism has its dingy, crass, glittering, mean spirit when money alone so clearly and triumphantly tempts her, with her past, to join in the investor's future. . . .

I had made a brief surprise visit to Janet, thanks to a tour of Venice and of the Palladian villas along the Brenta with a group of American magazine writers sponsored by the chain of CIGA hotels. For me, two of the delights of that deluxe trip had been the presence of Marina Chaliapin, daughter of the famous Russian singer, who functioned as hostess, and of Wally Toscanini Castelbarco, the daughter of the maestro—two dear friends and stunning-looking women—attending a party in the Grand Hotel Excelsior on the Lido in their elegant European gowns.

I don't know why my visit to Janet, after this voyage, had been so unhappy, the unhappiest of our long experience. Perhaps it had been the result of that successful trip, which emphasized my longing for companionship at least, and of how alone I continued to be; the sense of impotence and frustration at the status quo with Janet was making me restless, demanding decisions about our life together. We were getting old. Would we ever stop working? I knew all the good reasons, and yet . . .

Poor Janet was dismayed. When I arrived in New York, she wrote,

"My darling, you were at Fire Island without wind and without extreme sadness, the bad weather of the heart. I have slept only a few
hours the two nights since you left. I was glad to wake at five-thirty
this morning and read and started to work at eight. Do you truly want
me to come to you or not? I want to, violently want to. The evening is
opaline and fair after storms all day including hail which is agreeable.
It is noisy in its staccato way. If you will write me, I shall be glad.
Please. You know I adore you."

                                                            [May 31, 1967]
My darling one,
    A lovely day for once which helps lift my spirits, so lightened by
your telephone call and your saying, "anyhow, I love you," to me. You
and God both know *I love you*. Not mere words but truth, costly with
emotion, often with pain as well as joy. It is my selfishness, my egotism,
my constantly accumulated sense of guilt and of guilts that has made
me so unsatisfactory to you and to me, but mostly my professional
deformation—my devotion to my writing that Paris Letter as if it were
one of the important communications of mankind instead of merely the
rather disgraceful means to an end—my livelihood—which when
handed to me I stuck to in my laziness. I am heartbroken but lazy—
rather than using my literary talent—the one good thing I have to say
of myself and that merely a gift—to write articles, books, to have really
developed myself as Mary McCarthy has and as is normal to any fairly
good intelligence, I have let mine run fallow. I merely copy myself year
after year in *The New Yorker*, getting better with practice in copying
me, but not expanding. I have learned this year to understand why my
Paris Journal getting the prize gave me status which so puzzled and
insulted me at first. A book is positive and even a book of reprints gave
me more size than the appearance of fortnightly letters, I now know
and agree to. I thought that writing in the first place was more important than a book publisher's focus: wrong. I have deformed my life
and yours. I am the assassin of our happiness and our middle-aged love,
when we started. My constant unfaithfulness has been to my love of
writing, my instinct for preserving my small but precious career and
my love for Paris. I think I love it in part because I am a stranger, a
foreigner, who still speaks bad French as a form of sloth. In geography
it is the only place I have ever loved, and Fire Island. Yes, I was indeed
dismayed.
    I shall come in three weeks, so I must tell Shawn. How could I

NOT come to be with you again and be happier than we were here? To wipe out the last pain with a fresher joy. Yours, still in pain but not in the agony that I was; your voice helped heal me.

At the end of June, when Janet arrived, the skies had cleared in my heart. I had been ashamed of my childishness, my egotism. July was spent in our usual fashion—work, friends, weekends. I tried my best to make Janet's visit enjoyable, serene, to erase from her memory my recent burst of dissatisfaction and irritability.

In August, we escaped to visit Katie Hume and her friend Lou Abetz in Kauai. We had never been in those semitropical Pacific islands of Hawaii, and Katie and Lou, who had settled there, were an extra attraction. Katie had arranged a perfect scenario: an intimate cottage among a forest of huge palm trees, pink and white lilies floating on a green canal at our doorstep, a luscious nature and flowering bushes. Silence and beauty around us. Kauai is a garden island, and the high mountains surrounding extinct dead volcanic craters become red as fire at sunset. On top of one of them was the Quonset hut they had transformed into their home—a reminder of where Katie and Lou had met, in the aftermath of World War II, while working in refugee camps in Germany. Katie the writer, Lou the teacher, now together, enjoying their middle years. Katie the American, outgoing and full of life and laughter; Lou the European, quieter, emanating inner strength and kindness. After a week, we left enriched and happier.

Janet was at work again by mid-October. Before leaving, we had a painful experience. Our friend Carson McCullers had another stroke, this time paralyzing her good side, so that she became inert and bedridden at her house in Nyack. She looked so pathetic when she smiled at us, trying to reach our hands, pleased to see us. Faithful Ida was at her side. Also attending her was a tall, spinsterish-looking Englishwoman who had been Edith Sitwell's nurse, a strange choice for Carson. You could tell that she wouldn't get along with her or Ida. It was a sad sight to see Carson in that large bed, so alone and so miserable!

Janet didn't find much to write about in Paris, but came across a "grand piece" on Oriana Fallaci in a London paper, "very spirited and fairly accurate, too," she wrote. "She should be pleased but probably will find something to anger her; she has a magnificent fund of dissatisfaction in her nature like the volcanic earths from which eventually diamonds, big or little, are cooked over time, over a kind of ceaseless

Hell fire. She is less human than geological and chemical; her brain is like a modern extra feature, like the corporation head that makes them function and pay."

[November 12, 1967]

My darling one,

. . . I am ear-deep in my second Paris Letter with both too much and too little that is really fascinating to write about. I hope you liked the first one about Malraux's interviews with Nehru and Mao. I thought they were extremely interesting per se, and that my selection of them, exclusively, out of that enormous and VERY confusing volume showed judgment on my part, especially with literally nothing consequential to find in the rest of Paris news that week. This time there is a bit too much, including color TV which costs one thousand dollars to install so that nobody one knows has installed it.

Today Dali was to give and I suppose did not fail a kind of free-for-all painting brawl at Issy-les-Moulineaux where Matisse used to live, now a Communist suburb, forty minutes by train from Paris where there is a color TV studio. It might have been fun and good copy, but it would have been so vulgar because of his insanities and inanities that out of modesty for his sake and what he once represented as a remarkable painter technically, I refused to go. Maybe he did, too.

Pauline de Rothschild sent me her book on her trip to Russia called *The Irrational Journey*, published by Harcourt, Brace. It is a contribution of rare, fine writing and acuity in phrase and faculty as part of the rare travel anthology to that country, and I remain dazed at her talent, as when I first read it at night at Mouton, in manuscript. We writers work all our lives for style and special faculties of expression; she has them as an amateur and out they flow as if part of her fortunate wealth, though this time being uninherited through marriage and instead earned with her head bowed over her pen . . .

She mentions at length Elsa Triolet, her sister in Moscow who was the lover of Mayakovski and Louis Aragon, Elsa's husband (or whatever). We adult intellectuals should, I think, cease being poisoned by the hippies and their mad dirtiness, though not relieved from worry by the extending use of drugs in the States, and take our satisfaction in the fact that in the general lowering of staid, dull, social, bourgeois morality, such as we knew as girls and our mothers either clung to (or splendidly tossed overboard like Ester), there is now a liberalism about sex in emotional relations which lets people who are not married live together without any particular scorn being attached, in even bourgeois levels at least in New York. I admit that hippies are a terrible price for serious lovers to have to pay for their improved position.

How can we suppose that the young Russians with their serious studious habits and determinations will not grow into a flourishing, well-educated male society which loves its own country and will beat us and everybody in Europe, while we fritter with hippies and drugs and rebellious youths who aren't worth correcting and are patrons of ignorance and drop-out groups in our colleges? I am so appalled by what I see and suspect that I am glad I am as old as I am, for I will not live long enough to see the worst of it all, including the tentative civil war which breaks out between whites and blacks because we will not face the blacks' poverty intelligently or generously. They being good servants and dirty, squalid house owners and housekeepers of their own property. In other words, Negroes might have to be paid to keep themselves as clean as they can keep us, by the day or by the hour, at the rate of perhaps fifteen dollars a day in wages.

There is an uproariously witty, humorous, brilliantly critical long piece in this week's *New Yorker* called "New York Diary" [in "Reporter at Large," Nov. 11, 1967], I think, by a Polish writer [Leopold Tyrmand]. He is so witty and glibly clever, one finally hardly believes what he says; it is too good to be true. . . .

I am suddenly tired. It is one-thirty. I started working at ten this morning. My God, I miss you more than ever before . . .

[December 8, 1967]
My darling,
    Your splendid, intelligent, informative letter was like an essay to be read in the midst of relaxation at last after ten days of severe sciatica. . . .

Like a miracle, the end of my sciatica attack was almost synchronized with your voice on the phone. I was stricken at the question put to Shirley,* "What has *The New Yorker* not contributed to American literature?" because I had to sit and think to find out if I agreed. I do, in a way. It has contributed writing, such as [E.B.] White's, and his pieces which are pure Americana. We have published enough short stories by that man I dislike and can't recall his name who writes about Pennsylvania, writes too well, too, and how about Thurber as part of American literature, also Wilson, the dullard? Too little of McCarthy,

* Shirley Hazzard, the novelist.

but Salinger counts, doesn't he? We haven't had the great Jewish novelists like Bellow and Irwin Shaw, the Merde School, etc. I suppose there we have failed. But the shock of reading that query and knowing I was not sure of the answer when all these decades I have been so proud of writing for *The New Yorker*, as if for THE BEST, that I almost fell to pieces morally. It was a helpful shock. It has made me stop and think and be more modest than ever. I told Joe Wechsberg about it. He turned up yesterday with the amazing news that Shawn WANTS a profile on Rizzoli, as Joe said, "dese condittiori Italian types are all de rage, ja? More fascinating dan de Amurrican go getters." Joe said he had to have great help from you, of course, and said you had spoken of coming to Italy in the late winter. . . . WOULD YOU? I could come and sit at home in the hotel or in the Brera museum till Joe was finished with you at night. It does my spirits good even to think of our meeting in Milan.

[December 30, 1967]

My darling,

. . . It is a sad New Year for humanity, my beloved. This is deep in my heart and yours like a worm in the heart of any flower. I saw the most conclusive demonstration theatrically I have seen here—this being the new [Fernando] Arrabal show, made up of three of which we have seen two before. It takes place in a garage of broken down old cars—called La Cimetière des Voitures—in which the Passion of Christ is somehow worked in and He is crucified on the handlebars of an old motorcycle. The cars were made so that the doors worked and could be banged like gunshots all the time, flagellation in front of a woman who screamed like bloody murder—theater??? Isolated evil passions, shown without analysis nor philosophy, all naked like a turkey before being roasted, but with rivals pulling at the wishbone. What in the devil does it do to the audience already deprived of its own possibility to analyze itself and even more incompetent to analyze the cruder, muscular passions and acts of garage hands who are at the same time infernal gods (perhaps), such a mixture of what had been creation and now is merely the middle which comes from no physical or verbal modesty and is now vocabulary composed with the aim of shock like small sound bombs—words but without any more meaning.

If you keep screaming merde, the act of defecation loses its importance or urgency. The maître-en-scene Garcia, in his little page of self-advertisement in the program, signed himself Merde . . . Why?

How do these things happen? We were not so sure before that we must have this delirium of unbuttoned trousers today. . . .

My beloved and only one, I hope I have a nice time at the Rothschilds, very few guests, Monroe, Raymond Mortimer and the Spenders and me. Small Beer as the trade says.

And my heart will be with you in that strange, barren-looking vintage country, of small, short, ugly vines, not lovely and draped as those I always looked forward to near Naples . . . en route to Capri, remember? . . .

1968

Nineteen sixty-eight turned out to be a bad year, even a shameful one. The war in Vietnam escalated and spread to Cambodia.

The Russians invaded Czechoslovakia to subdue its rebellion. There were endless strikes, bloody riots, demonstrations at home and abroad.

Two more assassinations shocked us: Martin Luther King was shot in Memphis, Tennessee; Senator Robert F. Kennedy was shot in California.

In the spring, President Johnson announced he would not run for a second term. People were perplexed and had become angry. And what was worse, at the end of the year, Richard Nixon finally succeeded in seizing the presidency.

Our private calendar wasn't as dismal, with the exception of Janet's painful attacks of sciatica, which distressed her; she was not used to being ill or feeling impeded in her movements. "I am doing all I can to remake my health and energy; I walk slowly with care, which humiliates me as I always enjoyed scooting down the hotel corridors like a lively cricket, proud of my quick steps and neat ankles," she wrote.

By the end of December, she was well enough to accept Pauline de Rothschild's New Year's invitation for the second time.

"Pauline looked fantastic, in velvet or leather breeches like Shakespeare's Rosalind, very elegant. I spent two days and three nights here in the pouring rain, but with two huge libraries and splendid companions, including Stephen Spender and darling Monroe Wheeler. The food is really divine, of extreme delicacy. I drank with great restriction as the wines are so fine here, one is given three or four sorts, one-fourth a glass or less in each! They are so generous, as if they knew all people are not as rich as they, which means they are imaginative . . ." said Janet, in a brief note conveying her New Year's greetings.

[January 14, 1968]

Darling one,

I am so glad I am not a centipede. Two legs are sufficient trouble since if one is affected, one limps with one or the other. Imagine having to limp with 98 legs in an attack of sciatica. . . .

Last night . . . I bought a paperback of Fitzgerald's *Great Gatsby* to read in bed. My God, his superiority as an artist over Ernest Hemingway is incomparable. Ernest was a recorder; Scott a novelist. Little seems being written by novelists now to make one respect the literary formula, yet isn't life novelistic? Isn't it fictional in shape or realistic, anyhow, treated by literary artifice as a painter treats landscapes by colors from a palette? I enormously enjoyed writing and liked my Ingres Paris Letter I wrote. Did you? I hope so. I wrote it during the fortnight I never left my room.

Oh, I hope this year will bring an end to war, an end to being angry with our president, to people being angry against us, too, as a nation. I am sick of our position in world affairs as if we were white pirates attacking yellow natives in their own islands. . . .

I am too tired by sciatica to be lively socially, but my heart beats, it beats for you; otherwise, why should it move?

[January 17, 1968]

My darling one,

The front page of the newspapers is like a trump of doom these days. The horrible earthquake in Sicily has made a second contortion of the earth's surface for those unhappy people, with Wilson's cut from England's power over the East. In cutting national spending, there is little left of Queen Victoria's power and Disraeli's policy of control of the East via the Suez canal, so all the great former nations come to their small size if the acid of time starts to shrink them. Beware of an empire; it gives the habit of greatness until it turns ino a mere remnant of what it once was. Our turn will come later. At least by the *Herald Tribune* it looks as if the bombing in Vietnam might cease for a brief moment of no-death while questions are asked and let us hope answered by Washington, with the possibility of ceasing the war. Wars cannot go on forever; even the Thirty Years' War had its limit.

It is pouring as usual in the mixture of warm days and freezing that is Europe's fare today. I feel nearly WELL, left leg still unreliable, but osteopath says in a month it should be solid. He warns me to be careful in walking, not to sprain my ankle. Dieu me garde. . . .

I must put on my boots again and go to my osteopath. I wanted to talk to you if only by letter. I shall see you sometime early in the year for some weeks, for hope and love for the soul.

[February 11, 1968]

My darling one,

What a terrible day yesterday was, merely to be conscious of its blood, fright, pain, noise, horror, all that the inhabitants of Hue and Saigon suffered. It seems incomprehensible that General Westmoreland could consider it "a costly military defeat for the enemy" when it looks like a costly military defeat for the U.S.A. Marines, poor devils.

. . . Naturally, the French, who went through Dien Bien Phu (and out the other side into defeat and the end of their Vietnam War) would not grieve except in a purely semi-political nervousness if the same fate overtook the U.S.A. in our Vietnam guerilla war, too.

. . . After a thorough investigation yesterday, [Dr. Cotlenko] dismissed me as once more in perfect order, though with a somewhat weakened left thigh. It measures a little smaller than the right one, but I walk PERFECTLY at last and in comfort. Actually, I don't walk at all except to a cab.

What a comfort to hear your voice and even your breathing on the telephone from New York. . . .

I was enormously surprised at your more generous attitude toward de Gaulle. I agree with what you say. He has been right almost always —except psychologically. Turning the Americans against the French and himself was a major stupidity. Actually, the American tourists here now (only a few) seem very patient with the loss of intimacy they used to be so proud of when les Yanquis were popular.

Poor de Beauvoir's last book, *La Femme rompue* received the most candidly appalling critiques I think I ever saw a major writer suffer. Her three women characters are all selfish horrors, aged fifty and

screaming for their youth again. How dare she? She has not had even
ONE complimentary review that I have seen. . . .

. . . Big melee between police and pro-Vietnam students in Latin
Quarter. Usual results, boys' brains cracked open by matraque [trun-
cheon] assaults. I wonder what life would be like without any males at
all? Quieter, sillier, but not crazier . . .

———

I often told Janet what was happening at Rizzoli. I had been running
some special events in the gallery—art shows or publication parties,
much as I had done when I ran the Special Projects division of the
USIS in Rome after the war. I enjoyed that aspect of the work, even
if it overtaxed my time and effort. Janet didn't look upon such activities
with sympathy; she thought they were below me. At one point she
wrote that "running art shows and cocktail parties for the publishing
of everybody else's important book in New York is below your mentality . . . your job at Mondadori's did not include sandwiches and
whiskies. . . ." But when I described the showing of the Rizzoli publication of a limited, numbered, deluxe edition of the Bible—illustrated
by Dali, signed by him—Janet commented as if I had published it
myself: "What a triumph you made of the Dali Bible! . . . What a
strange combination Dali and Holy Scriptures make, though heaven
knows there is much that is mad and super-realistic in the Old Testament and the prophecies in the New Testament written by what could
be taken today for drug addicts. The drug vogue in our country worries
me more than the Negro-white civil war whose bias is logical; but I
could strike with my own hand or a stone any man or woman I caught
giving drugs to your Doodie. . . . If only we could understand how or
why they so resent what has been a civilizing basis for ordinary life in
ordinary lands for the ordinary centuries of progressive time. . . ." And
in the next letter she asked: "Did your Bible sell well? What luxury
for the word of God and Jesus, He so poor, the carpenter's Son, coming
out in de-luxe edition. . . ."

[February 22, 1968]

Darling one,

. . . I enclose the openers on Oriana's two pieces here in *Figaro
Littéraire* to give you an idea of the top treatment they are giving her.
I only read the second piece; I cannot read both. It makes me too sick.
Where I can't stand to read, she can stand to hear, see, smell and face

constant danger. She is like a man, maybe only some men, but to have the bravery of the other sex while not having lost the gift she has as a female writer is doubly remarkable. She is a very important human being because of her bravery and her eyes and ears which can look and see for those who ARE there but have not the gift of observation and recollection, and she looks and reports for all those who are NOT there, like you and me. I would go crazy if you were out there doing what she is doing and, indeed, she makes me feel sick with worry for her, too. My God, I hope nothing happens to her, that she comes out without a wound or loss of an eyelash.

. . . Did you see the last Sunday London *Observer* with the last chapter of [Michael] Holroyd's biography of Lytton Strachey, and the one before? I never saw the word homosexual repeated so often in print as in that next-to-the-last chapter. EVERYONE at Cambridge with any brains or lineage was a homo, even Keynes. He and Lytton were in love with the same yellow-haired boy. Strachey's final comment was fantastic: "If this is death," he whispered, "I don't think very much of it," and shortly after drew his last breath.

I must go and dine, alone as usual, and then work on my Paris Letter tonight. I can only thank God I can still work. Or should I say I am sorry?

I am reading a life of Flaubert. It is very dull, poor man. I think geniuses often have such confusing existences that joy escapes them except in its wilder forms. We have known that, too, without being burdened by genius either, so we are fortunate, my own.

[February 23, 1968]

Mon amour,

. . . I am going to see [Professor] Frugoni in Rome. . . . He is old; I am not young. I think he may well be one of the greatest living diagnosticians for nerve conditions. I am of two ways of thinking about modern medicine. I flee their alternation of heavy drugs . . . and tranquilizers which daze me so I am comatose like a mouse in the sun.

The ration they use is geared higher than I am accustomed to like language today—the four-letter words everywhere like explosions in the brain or senses, a lift in excitement. I note that in this week's *Paris Review* which I at once threw away its fiction contained nothing but the four letters as if the rest of the alphabet of 26 letters did not count. At a cocktail party at Mary McCarthy's the Plimpton sister [Sara] was there, a nice girl and someone said she objected to the new style in vocabulary but some female who has power in the magazine has persuaded [George] Plimpton himself this is the new formula or you are dead. Better be that. Never has there been within my lifetime such a shift and change in styles and values and vocabulary. With my background and self-training, it is easy for me to see in writing what has been lost. What has been gained, though, in other media of life? More sensitivity to truth? By these coarser words to act like explosions that obviate other explanations? I think I live too much alone, am too much of a hermit to be in the manner of this decade; for instance, the [Arthur] Kopit play I wrote of in a recent Paris Letter was really silly, the Arrabal was really demented; Christ being crucified on the handlebars of a motorcycle and hoisted to heaven has no meaning except of sheer invasion of all its previous meanings and values. They may well be *de trop* now, but surely there is something beside motorcycles and the Angel of Death as a means of transportation to eternity.

I went to the farewell cocktail party given by Ambassador Bohlen, and we kissed good-bye. I wish he were IN government not merely representing it. Talk here is that he will not be replaced, relations between the two capitals are too strained to bring in another functionary to do nothing which is what Bohlen did. But he fed his mind by observations; those could count. But with whom in Washington? Yesterday (I see by the *Monde*) there was another series of big anti-Vietnam war demonstrations in the Latin Quarter, professors as well as students. The propaganda against it and American distribution of death on the great scale is unceasing in the papers here. The photographs are horrible, though no worse, if perhaps the same even, than in the U.S.A. papers, where the poll says more than half of the citizens are behind the President. I wish to God they would bunt him into the Pacific, out of his raw Texan state which I dislike through association with him.

I hope you approve of my arranged visit with Frugoni, my darling. I believe it rational and of high utility. I know no one else I trust. I want someone and only he with his wisdom can supply it, who can give me drugs which will aid not whip, not dominate, not *disorganize* into giving me a norm again. . . .

[March 14, 1968]

Darlinghissima,

. . . I had a cable last night on coming in after the Boulez concert from Phonm Penh where Malraux was supposedly arrested after steal-

ing that statue of Banda Serai. It said, "Good birthday, dear, Mary."
From Mary McCarthy. I don't know how she knew it was my fête
day, but it lifted my spirits at midnight. I so rarely see her and she is
always so loyal, as I feel toward her. I shall worry until she returns
(from Cambodia). The Schell piece this week in *The New Yorker*
gives little confidence that danger is not constant. In a French piece
here by a correspondent, he said, "If you stay long enough, you will
be killed." This makes me fearful for Oriana, as she is bolder than Mary
could ever be. She is a born reporter; Mary is not, so why did she
determine to go where she will not write anything of a weight to
balance the danger she will be running. Oriana will always give the
weight of her body danger to the copy she writes. This is her proportion
as a great professional.

I enjoyed one of Boulez's pieces, the latest. It began with a terrific
piano contribution of such rich cacophony as to be breathtaking. It was
like a tempest, useless to complain that wind, rain and thunder should
be so mixed. That was the condition and it had to be accepted or leave
the concert hall and the earth.

Before the concert I saw a magnificent movie yesterday, a long
series of Cartier-Bresson photographs taken all over the world of all
kinds of people, never explained or placed, but edited by Depire, his
publisher, so that they seemed a stream of international humanity, not
fraternity, but of human differences. I was never more moved because
it was a MOVING picture, not just stills. The film and his book have
been bought by the Museum of Modern Art in New York. It will be
shown there certainly. I HOPE you do not miss it. It moved me more
than anything I have seen for months, years. It was human and
humane beauty showing ordinary, mostly ugly people, ordinary people.
I kept wondering who they were, from what country. No clue.

There is no pity, of course, from the French that the dollar may
collapse and the entire financial mechanism of the western world fall
apart with our leaving the gold standard and gold covering of our
money. We were too arrogant with our dollar, and they too sly in
collecting our gold. If there is an international panic, which seems
possible, who will be the richest country and on top, as the most solid?
La belle France, ma chère. She has the most gold. Johnson seems to
have been a poor steward of our wealth, with those unpaid balances of
payment running on over years, putting us in debt and jeopardy. The
Tribune here, our only American source, seems to take it as natural
that he would risk escalating the war, risk doing anything, so as not to

interfere with his chances of being re-elected president. This is more than vanity; it is a kind of colossal self-participation in the political movement of history which could go on without him, better than with. Is it devotion to the Democratic Party, now so smirched and dispirited with all its late errors brought by him? I would see the Democratic Party drowned like a kitten in a bucket rather than risk his being elected again.

If you will pardon me, may I say I love you and have to eat my dinner, downstairs, it being now ten p.m.? I have no appetite these days. I am sorry for you that you have loved me. You might have been spared that at least, with better luck, my poor Natalia.

[April 11, 1968]

My darling one,

What a destructive, agonizing, shameful week we have known with another political assassination, of our leader of Negro intelligentsia and Christian spirit. The black anger resulting in fires, looting and menaces in a half-dozen cities over our countryside surely must carry some information to the white segregationists beyond that of their decision that the only answer to the problem is to shut the niggrahs off in an apartheid compound where they can do no harm to the whites except by mere hope of murdering them all. Our blasphemous, uneducated American violence is so great a shame, this time practiced by our most uneducated, violent, racial elements, but basically there is little difference between the brutality of millions of our whites and of our blacks. Your mother at the end was so offended, shocked and sickened by American brutality which she felt was growing like skyscrapers of cement-like cruelty and indifference in a new race she had formerly had some confidence in.

I had thought my Paris Letter on LBJ's renunciation was fairly good but, on seeing it in print this morning, it seems clumsy, weak, unimportant, almost uninformative. Whereas our Washington Letter this week is BRILLIANT. Don't miss it. It is a consolation for what I don't excel in when I see a colleague touch his height of excellence.

You can imagine how my imagination hurried through the New York streets, calculating distances away from you, when the newspaper here carried news of Harlem rioting, after the other cities. What can NOT be settled is the instinctive physical emotion behind racism, the feeling of repulsion on the part of most whites at the idea of intimate physical contacts with Negroes; none of us feels that way entirely about Red Indians or Chinamen or Japs. At the American church service Monday for Dr. King, it was packed, very touching too—I sat next to an American Negress, rather a pretty, roundheaded girl, but as black as licorice candy. I could only think again what I have often said to you. I would never have had the courage to be a Negress and maybe not even a Jewess.

Do you like those interminable movie analyses by Pauline Kael in *The New Yorker*? I find them boring.

I wish for your mind talking in my ears during the painful tragic news of [Martin Luther] King's slaughter. You would have spoken with wisdom and intelligence which could have informed and quieted me. I could say nothing to me that calmed me. I felt outraged and damaged.

. . . Write me when you have an instant, my darling, one. Darling enough for two, really.

[April 20, 1968]

Beloved,

What an adorable pink checkered handkerchief, of such grace and delicacy. Your taste is always supreme, and I thank you for it as an Easter gift. What a cruel season it has been for us Americans, the Vietnam War not really bloodless yet, and then the horrible assassination of Dr. King. A complot? The French always see a plot in everything. They doubtless teach in their first communion lessons for French children that Jesus was crucified in a Roman plot and it may well be the truth, though doctrinally weak. I never felt so ashamed of America and the stupidity of the American populo reaction as I do this spring. It is OUR fault, of course, that the Negroes loot and steal. They have never owned property and have no respect for it, merely an itch to possess it, if possible free.

As the *Time* article said, "They have killed what's-his-name," one looter said, so he stole an armful of shirts from a broken shop window. Not only social justice but social education is the imperative necessity for our Negroes. They must be taught the meaning of property by POSSESSING property; otherwise, as soon as they enter a decent new apartment house, they sully it by the boys urinating behind the front door and the mother who works down in the Village as a maid by day cleaning apartments fails to clean her own. Cleanliness also is a class affair in their minds. Another lesson they will have to be given so that cleanliness may belong by energy to them, too, not just to you and me as a privilege.

This is ill written but clearly felt. Also, I am serious in my notion that we should have perhaps four vice-presidents. One for the New York East Coast industrial area, one for the South, one for the Middle West farm areas, and one for the West and California and cattle states. These vice-presidents should act as information collectors for the presidential office in Washington, to keep the White House informed of the way the wind blows.

Josette Lazar passed on my idea to a couple of political writers on *Le Monde*, and they thought it excellent. After all, it is exactly what the Prefects for each department do here, and their creation was one of Napoleon's most brilliant inventions in organizing modern France on the basis it still uses.

Will it be June when you come and for how long, beloved? . . . It will be *gorgeous* to be in Rome with you even for this opening visit in June. Do you want to come to Paris first for a few days? You would be most, most welcome, and Paris should be seen before it is too late and too ruined. Skyscrapers everywhere and streets torn up like Pompei.

Today is warmish and spring-like, almost the first we have had this chilly vernal time. Bless you, soon and soon thine.

[April 28, 1968]

My darling,

De Gaulle fell yesterday and I felt as if he had died and was sad, very sad. With the dangers he projects, you felt Fascism which was far from his notion of controls—he has given France a unity such as it never had in my life here with its multiple parties rising and falling like black tides. The unity was formed by the French being exclusively interested in being for him or against him. I have been working on my new Paris Letter to be cabled this week yesterday and today. I have done, though not perfected yet, four pages. Much still to do to enrich and make a fuller, stranger picture, the strangest election anyone here ever saw.

Your character study of your colleague from Milan was like something written by Molière, the perfect competent managerial borrower, arranger, thief of ideas, underground mole, surface fox and wolf and lion in his own estimation. An amazing portrait you drew, terrifying and beyond supporting, I can well believe. All business as you describe it is corrupt, a power snare and money trap. You must know by now and to your own disillusion and sorrow.

. . . Forgive my necessity to sleep. Thine till the end of life.

[May 12, 1968]

My darling one,

What a week Paris has had with the students' riots, with a violence and sense of explosion that seized the whole city, for everyone knew what was transpiring, since everyone's sons or daughters were involved, or the neighbors! The violence and brutality of the police was not so astonishing as the fury of the students, amateurs in fighting in the streets and on the sidewalks. Had the young French fought like that against the young Germans in 1940, France would not have fallen in thirteen weeks, in weak disgrace. I did not personally "attend" these riots, as I did the last one of students against Minister of Education Fouchet, perhaps four years ago, he now being minister of something else and still no good at it, but then I took a vow never to humiliate my eyes by seeing the police club hitting a student's head supposed to be filled with information and modern brains. My former colleague on *The New Yorker*, Jordan, who checked my Pétain with me, an odd chap who has become a Frenchman and lives here behind the Panthéon, in the midst of the students' barricades Friday night, gave me invaluable personal information of what he saw and smelled. Even Saturday noon, going to drive in a taxi near the rue Gay-Lussac, where perhaps forty cars were piled in a barricade and set fire to, the smell of tear gas so inflamed my eyes that I was soon weeping. Doda Conrad probably said the most subtle truth, "The citizens are with the students but not quite against the police since destruction of property shocks the French citizen who probably owns a jalopy himself and cringes as he thinks of its having been possibly burned, had he left it sleeping in the Quartier Latin by the curb to avoid paying garage fees."

The whole city was roused by the riots. For the first time, the students shouted, "de Gaulle assassin," because of the police brutalities. The charming woman, Mme. Ferbos, who gives me my *piqûres* [injections] and has high-class French friends, had one living in the rue Gay-Lussac, gone south with her husband on museum business for the week, when the students occupied her street, with her three children in the fourth floor flat, a girl of fourteen, boy of sixteen, and girl of twenty. She flew back from the south in fright, found them doing very well, with seven unknown students sleeping on the floor who climbed down over the roof. They had all eaten everything in sight, cleaned up, bathed as much as possible, and were all sleeping on floors and corners. Madame Ferbos' oldest daughter, second year Sorbonne, has of course missed two exams like everybody, but they will be offered later. She says that the real base of the students' anger is not revolution or politics, but dissatisfaction since late last year with the school programs, changes in everything, named as if they were butchers or valets, not looking down on them, but not giving them any meaning as humans . . .

I enclose Doodie's drawings. . . . They are extraordinarily stimulating. She is clearly very talented. How strange is the material in the brain. One child is merely normal, and another has the makings of an artist as Picasso had the makings of a genius, and he must have worried his father, devoted to painting pigeons . . .

It is a beautiful evening, the first in three weeks, lovely sky, no clouds, no high wind, no cruel weather, no brutalities in the streets. . . .

[May 25, 1968]

My darlingest and handsome Natalia,

This has been a week like a public nightmare, not a private one. If one stays at home or in bed without news, since there are no newspapers easily available, it is not a personal nightmare. It is a French-crazed visitation in which one has to decide at once who is the crazy one, oneself or the Parisians. I repeatedly said at first to myself, "I cannot be mad; they are the mad ones," because what they do seems so idly destructive, taking energy and even forethought to bring tools for destruction with them when they go out at night to fight the police such as axes to cut trees down. In one's childhood, Mother always said, "Have you a clean handkerchief?" when we went some place. It is as if some parental watchfulness makes sure these devilish youths think before their nightly sortie what they need to do harm on a bigger scale and remember to bring it, like our childish handkerchiefs. Paris has become filthy all over, clots of wet paper turning to a kind of cement in gutters, and in the Latin Quarter turning into a war-torn devastation. In the crunch Friday night (it is now Sunday morning that I am writing), parts of St. Germain and the Latin Quarter were really destroyed by the students. The fine tall iron fence around the Cluny museum is now a twisted snake, used as a barricade, half a dozen fine trees on the St.-Germain were SAWED and CHOPPED down and put across the boulevard as a barrage, the stone railing around the Métro

Cluny station was torn down so there is nothing but a hole and stair-case left.

I have not had a bath for a week, washing all the corners and bathing all over with toilette water, costly process, but no hot water at all, not a cupful. This hotel is served by the municipal hot water system, now on strike, instead of its own hotel boilers. Shawn in his cable to me this week said you had tried to phone me but without success. I was probably walking some place, the legs being the only transport means and slow at that.

My garde-malade aristo who gives me my daily Frugoni *piqûres* just came in with her oldest daughter, Dominique, aged twenty-one, at the Sorbonne. Tall as a young tree, handsome, too, who talked about the riots, etc. Her mother lets her go. She was out until three a.m. Thursday morning, a very bad night of terrible tear gas, etc., and destruction. When the boys started cutting down the fine trees on the Boulevard St.-Germain, she said she screamed, "Don't you have any poetry in your souls, that you kill a tree?" She supposes there will be exams, now being suppressed, or no longer scheduled, in September; otherwise, it is a lost year financially which her mother has to pay for. . . .

For a moment I feel relaxed. Boys of all ages are playing ball in the Tuileries Gardens. It gives struggle which the male likes and health which riots do not. It is a pleasure to watch ball players for a moment, idly. The strictness of Pompidou's warning yesterday, that the police would instantly put down any manifestation no matter where or for what, sounded fierce and forceful, as if he meant it. No more insanity will start this next week, we all feel. Not a shot has been fired, not a person has been killed. Peculiar, miraculous, in this terrific week of repeated rioting, by professional fighters which the CRS* police are, well-trained, perfectly armed with plastic shields which cover their torsos (or heads, whichever they choose as most valuable to protect), and the students in espadrilles or tennis shoes, with no shields, nothing really except guts and youth and hate. Now the two forces are begin-ning to fraternize, the cops and the kids. Can you beat it? They talk their fights over the next day over a beer. It has been chilly, too, which has added to everyone's depression. No hot baths, no hot rooms, not very warm weather outside except a pleasant dry day here and there.

On one of them, I heard myself saying cheerfully to Marie, my maid, "Belle journée pour la révolution." She was shocked, of course.

---

* *Compagnie Républicaine de Sécurité.*

I shall be sending you in all a half-dozen letters and postals which you will receive in a batch, I suppose, all at once, when the postal strike is over. I see nearly no one, though dined at Ben Holt's as I said for the de Gaulle broadcast. I grow so tired of imitation U.S.A. food here in Paris now—grilled this, grilled that, hamburgers, steaks, etc., or else veal which I grow tired of eventually, that I enjoyed the odd pasta at Ben's, the only kind he could get. It looks like a curlicue of white, like hair almost, but coarser and he made really delicious bolognese sauce, full of tomatoes and ground steak and NO garlic, for my sake. I ate two plates with pleasure, not touching the delicious roast lamb Josette L. had had cooked by her butcher. I haven't been hungry for a month.

Violence is so burdensome to write about, one should not mention it without doing it justice in writing, good, fierce writing. I shall expect a basketful of post from you, too.

Thine, rather tired too.

[June 9, 1968]

My darling one,

I am back in my hotel this afternoon, arriving by taxi from Orgeval, where I spent five days of much-needed rest since I had done three extra half letters in ten days, because one of them was done twice over to keep up with strange news. As a European and newscaster, you know what has been happening better than anyone I know, including me. You have been through this kind of semi-civil war before, except yours became a true one. This has remained more fright than reality, yet a week ago Wednesday was close to turning into an outbreak of blood. The whole revolutionary attitude disappeared so quickly when the workers were offered more pay, decent pay at last, that one had the impression that mere meanness on the part of the French patronat, famous for its stingy attitude, was basic to the near commencement of a civil war, when coupled by a dramatic accident of coincidence with a youth revolution which was *genuine*, and hateful. The third factor was an old-fogey university system. And meanness again in not building sparkling beautiful new universities with fine, big classrooms. The U. at Nanterre is a disgrace, Nanterre being a Poor Man's zone town so that students hate their environment to begin with.

Surely this must have been one of the worst periods for European and American solidarity since the final part of the war, with political emotions so shaken, so lacerated, such grief, such despair. The three

assassinations in our country—John Kennedy's, then Dr. King's and
now the youthful Bobby—are like three major battles for democracy
that American has lost. When I refer in the sentence above to "solidarity" I do not mean European and American solidarity; I mean individual solid political bases for each continent, in its different countries
or states (with us). Perhaps democracy seems wearing out because it
has never been fully used or even fractionally except in its mere
systemizations which are undeniably democratic since everybody has
a ballot in his hand to vote with. But what happens after he casts his
ballot? Is society made more democratic by each new election in the
U.S.A.? It should be.

I have not read any great or fine statements here or from the U.S.A.
of late. Even the murder of that youthful Bobby, so great a breeder and
general charmer, even his death did not inspire any great thoughts,
nothing but the tragic photo of his wife with her two fingers lifted like
a Pope's as she gave his coffin and gave him her farewell distant kiss.
What a strange curse seems on that family, too many children and too
easily dead, as if unstable by birth in their fate.

My darling one, I shall phone you this week, probably Tuesday, for
a brief chat and rendezvous for further talk in your flat. . . .

[June 21, 1968]

My darling one,

Thank you for your last letter with its serious, intelligent analyses
of youth everywhere, moral sickness, murder, Kennedys dead, cata-
clysms abounding. Is it because in the western hemisphere this is the
first time that Christianity has truly lost authority over the majority
of Christians? God and Jesus and the Church are the first lost links
in the life of the young; the Protestant God went first into New
England theology and the Catholic God of Europe has lost much of the
gilt from his throne that sparkled in belief.

This past month has been the most shocking I have known in my
long years in France. The callous destruction of property, so unlike
the sou-conscious French, made the students seem like barbarians; only
the peasants in the countryside seem as shocked as I by the burning
of people's cars left on the streets, as careless as that economy was;
three or four more cars were burned two nights ago, long after the
riots had been forbidden. The car owners now threaten to sue the city;
a fine chance they have of winning since nobody knows even who

burned them. It is a good thing there is to be the first leg of an election on Sunday. It props up public interest a little, though nobody ardently believes in party governments any more, and I note with sadness that in Rome the government is having trouble and in Venice the students are rioting against the Biennale which I don't blame them for as the art shown is no better than of late years.

What has happened to the students' organisms is something like nausea and colic; they vomit up everything, they lose it through their bowels into the toilets of the cities, museums. Nothing seems to nourish them; everything is roughage except the early classic arts in Greece or Italy and those they are too out of touch with to reach and consume again, through the eyes at least if not the spirit. The people, including little children three years old, and the physical rubbish that came out of the Odéon when it was "cleaned" were appalling. It was like the Sorbonne, a kind of a flop-house for tramps, foreigners, syphilitic mothers and cheap prostitutes, all infected. The photo of these girls with scrubbing brushes and brooms washing the Odéon classic porch were strange. They looked ashamed to be there, though had never shown shame before while living there like tramps, at whose invitation? The students. And they think they can run education and theaters and governments even, no doubt, with their ignorance of technique, discipline and exactitude.

Ils ne sont que des clochards, like the men lying under the Paris bridges on sunny days, delousing themselves. Violence has become an international portion of entertainment on stage and screen, and two Kennedys have paid with their lives for being shot In Cold Blood, like a male pair of Bonnies and Clydes who at least were bank robbers in a good cause. . . . .

I have been, like you, sick with civic pain; I went to my osteopath two days ago saying I felt pained all over. He said I was not the only one, but was certainly in a bad state such as he never knew me to be in the thirty years he has known my body by memory. He could not give me a proper treatment, was afraid of injuring me, I was so stiff, so tense. I am going again today for a long treatment. I feel more relaxed because I have been going to bed at about ten and without riots have slept better. Even in Cologne, when I slept there under gunfire at first, I slept better than I have here under the riots. . . .

This is a letter filled with anger. It is like your anger, my darling. Please don't fail to come to Italy next month, please, please.

At the end of June, we formalized our plans for the summer. Janet's sciatica seemed to have miraculously disappeared. She could travel, she said, so we decided to go to Portugal, a country we didn't know.

The moment we entered the Ritz in Lisbon, we knew we had made a good choice. It was old-fashioned in décor, with impeccable service.

The bellboys wore white spats and gloves, small caps coquettishly tilted to one side, and double-breasted boleros, with shining brass buttons. They looked as if they belonged on a stage, in the *Nutcracker* ballet. Janet would have loved to have taken at least one of them to the Continental to bring her papers!

Every morning a limousine picked us up and drove us around the city and out into the country. We felt like royalty, exiled like other deposed monarchs such as Umberto of Savoy, who lived in Cascais. I didn't pay homage to him, as many Italians would have in my place. Intellectually, with my anti-monarchical feelings, I didn't want to; in my heart I would have liked to, I think. He later came to pay a visit to the Rizzoli bookstore and Gallery in New York. I escorted him around, and he admired the store, especially the art books. I could see that he was moved to find himself in that small corner of Italy; I felt sorry for him, because he would never be able to go back there.

Portugal is not famous for its food, but we loved the oversized sardines in a humble restaurant across the river Tagus, and the Porto wines, white as an aperitif, red for the sardines. It was in Lisbon that we saw the delicately woven open-patterned straw carpets Janet later found in Paris for our house in Sperlonga. It was in this part of the world, whose riches and empire had long vanished, that we still found gracious people, devoted to family, devoted to their religion, with their processions of flowers and banners and their sad *fados*—the nostalgic, harsh, sometimes savage songs expressing the longings of women for their men, who had sailed across the oceans to discover Brazil or India.

We ended our vacation at the fishing port of Sesimbra, where I could swim and stretch out in the sun while Janet relaxed on the balcony of our suite, reading. In the afternoons we watched the arrival of the fishing boats, with their rich catch of the day.

Another attack of sciatica, just as we were leaving, made our flight back to Paris painful for Janet and very difficult for both of us. I remained in Paris until the pain subsided and she felt better. I flew back to New York on August 3, determined to find Janet a good specialist for when she came in late October.

[August 3, 1968]

My darling,

You are in the American scene now. You have left behind you a half-dozen new admirers. I have never seen you so *correctly* appreciated, with spontaneity. Libouché* phoned to say she had had *pleasure* in meeting you, Une femme intelligente, pénétrante dans ses idées, la vraie base d'une éducation permanente sociale and politique, as Europeans she and I have much in common; she mentioned the exactitude of your opinions and decisions. I have never heard her praise any friend of mine as she praised you. Josette talks of you with delight: "She is so lovely to look at and listen to, that Italian voice and accent, what pleasure she gives." She was warmed with the other pleasure of amity, of feeling that your friendship for me was reflected in you both by sympathy and friendliness for each other, like a third mirror representing another version. She talked about you laughing and smiling all the time with sheer delight in a new acquaintance of quality. What good sense, what balance, what surety, what devotion to you (meaning me, JF) she shows, what a fine woman, how she makes us all laugh and smile. . . . Even Henri [Cartier-Bresson], who is usually rather reserved, said you were a real charmer. They all appreciated you for the right, the big reasons. My heart swelled with pride. Never have you had a circle of more admiring, friendly appreciators. Elle est fameuse, ta Natalia, Henri said.

. . . Thank you for your cable, mon amour. Did you find mine? This was a lovely holiday of freedom at least, and luxury.

I love you more than ever.

————

On August 20, I was back from a week in Malibu and on the twenty-first Janet sent me a scribbled note quoting the headlines of the French evening papers. In huge letters, *France-Soir* had proclaimed: "Russian tanks are firing on Prague," and *Le Monde*: "Czecho is occupied." She was heartsick.

"For the first time, they have been occupied and this time by the East *Germans* again which is what the East German troops are, Russified on top of that. This is a wicked world run by men as greedy for power

* Libouché Novak, pianist who had escaped from her native Czechoslovakia, whom Noël Murphy met during WWII in France and later lived with at Orgeval until her death.

as if drinking blood, thirsty for it again, thirsty once more. Does none of them stop to think of the *pleasures* of liberty and the pain for the loss of it? I am still not well, my darling. I feel uncertain in mind and body. I feel desperate. For your love I thank you with every beat of my heart."

I became alarmed and cabled Noël Murphy. Noël wrote back immediately. She and Josette had convinced Janet to enter the American Hospital for observation and tests. On the twenty-third, Janet wrote that "she had probably suffered a *minor* nervous breakdown," but that she felt "solid in organs if patchy in mind and soul. This is my diagnosis of what is wrong and God knows it is upsetting but does not throw the patient flat on his (or her) back, though his balance is troubled."

On the twenty-ninth, from the American Hospital at Neuilly, she wrote:

"I entered here yesterday at ten a.m. and I am leaving today at two-thirty infinitely better than I had been tho' my recovery certainly has nothing to do with anything that occurred here. I simply emerged from my fit of desperate depression as mysteriously and inexplicably as I had sunk into it."

It was not like Janet to be depressed to the point of feeling desperate. I had been frightened. This news relieved my anxiety.

In the meantime, Mike Bessie had been writing to Janet, proposing a second volume of her "Letters" from 1965 to 1968. On September 7, as a sign of her well-being, she wrote:

"Please tell Mike what I have told you here. YES on the book if he will give me into November to write extra stuff which, as collected, looks rather fascinating. I am interested at last. . . ."

[October 8, 1968]

My darling,

Your blue Aérogramme letter came this afternoon for my pleasure . . . The hotel is in such a state of confusion in this, its last week, that there is nearly no service. When I asked if I might stay over the weekend, I was told NO. Both light and water will be turned off on Saturday, which is the official closing day, at noon. I go to the Hôtel Regina, 2 Place des Pyramides, Paris I, on Friday. I see the corner of the Tuileries and also the side of the Louvre.

What a drama with Oriana, wounded as she was. Her pictures are in

Newsweek* this week, but nothing so far in Paris papers. She is courageous, but what suffering and for you in your office what overwork. Was Mexico a Fascist government when you and I were there, in our innocence and pleasure? Having been through some of the students' riots here, I can suppose that any government tries to stop their destruction of everything in sight. Their real joy is in smashing, breaking, destroying, so the essential liberties they are fighting for are in part lost by the confusion of issues, perhaps like many wars in history in their beginnings. Never have we lived through such epics of violence among the male young. Here when the CRS brutal but well-trained police were lined up before the Stock Exchange, they stood motionless in line for a half hour while the yelling students spat on them until their faces dripped spit. A man who saw it told me. Every evil or brutal gesture is paid for later, by half an hour or half a week, by the revenge of further brutality. Yet after the riots had formally ended in the square behind the Panthéon, someone with intelligence persuaded some students and some of the CRS police to start talking and in half an hour they were jovially telling confessional stories to each other of things that had happened during the riots which were against the narrators, not for his glory nor to vaunt his courage. But nothing has been as bad as the Mexico City students' riots and treatment and in the face of the coming Olympic Games, which from year to year have increased nationalism and partisanship, all the bad elements of competition.

We all thought the Second War and the Nazis had reached the zenith of vile misconduct. We now find they merely were the first to exploit and enjoy it, alas. . . .

I went to the Parliament this afternoon to hear Minister of Education [Edgar] Faure defend his educational reform bill, a very great intellectual performance in his high, barking voice, so tiresome for one's ears after he had talked two hours. For his throat, too, at the last he was drinking water like a thirsty animal.

How much patience Mary Reynolds must have had to love Marcel Duchamp, who has just died. He was always doing something exaggeratedly useless or absurd, like sending a urinal, called by him, "Une Fontaine," to the Salon des Indépendants. It would be enough to make me explode with irritation!! . . .

---

* Ms. Fallaci was wounded when military planes swooped down on a student demonstration in Mexico City.

The only piece of "new" theater I have seen was the Polish Laboratory players. I thought it nonsense, but, there again, my patience does not include watching actors plod around as noisy as horses in their wooden shoes with stove pipes in their hands, putting them together, taking them apart, hanging them onto strings on the ceiling, etc. One can understand that Zeffirelli's film *Romeo and Juliet*, which is really not very good, I am told, gave great pleasure here because it was a recognizable version of young tragic love.

Yes, the Kael woman is too long-winded. She seems not to care if a film is good or bad. All she wants is to ANALYZE it at length, a process which has made her famous. I wonder what Bill thought of [Winthrop] Sargent's saying symphonic music was dead, that Rock was the new music of the future? . . .

This was Janet's last letter before sailing for New York.

She would not be going to California this time, but had asked Hildegarde to come to New York, where she arrived on November 5.

1969

We had three months of perfect bliss, dividing our time between work and play, running to our respective offices during the day—Janet seeing her pals, discussing her book, her future projects; I at Rizzoli tackling Oriana, the various co-productions in the making, the books, the visitors, the works—to meet home later in the day for a "cocktail-lino" or two and then off to some special party or entertainment. Janet might have met everyone in Paris during her lifetime there, but everyone in New York wanted to meet her here, until finally the time had come to go back to serious work.

She returned to Paris, on March 2, not to her room on top of the Continental, with its familiar view of the Tuileries she so loved and her devoted maid Marie, where she had lived and worked for nineteen years, nor to the Regina ("too noisy and inconvenient"), but to the Ritz. A young Scotsman on the staff took her under his wing. She was given the room over the garden she wanted, with a fine view of trees, rooftops and the dome of the Polish church. "No one can see me in it, nor can I see anyone; a perfect situation," she wrote. She sounded pleased.Having immediately settled down, after an especially good first meal in Montmartre with her friend Doda Conrad (sweetbreads "in a little cream sauce"), she started to work on her first Paris Letter, postmarked March 9.

Miss Flanner at the Ritz! It seemed almost an anomaly for Janet to be there, among the moneyed grandees of the world. In looks, she belonged, as she was always the most distinguished and best-dressed woman living there, in her well-cut suits from the great couturiers in town. But despite her reputation in the world of letters, she was innately modest, though she later referred to her quarters at the Ritz as that lovely, old-fashioned "shabby" room which, indeed, it was.

[March 15, 1969]

Beloved,

. . . I fear it is preparing to rain again after two dullish days after an early part of the week with radiant unParisian sun. In the midst of getting my Paris Letter off, Marie my maid came and unpacked me into my new elegant room on the garden, which is very large, has many good roofs to look at, two fine old buildings and the dome of the Polish church in the rue Cambon behind which the Eiffel Tower shines bright at night, though how on earth it can be there on the Paris horizon is a mystery. I have no sense of direction any more. There are blackbirds in my garden singing at dawn and rooks in the church dome rooking about with their strange, cracked voices. They are very Christian, since they always inhabit churches.

Last night I went to the old Bobino music hall in Montparnasse with Josette to hear Reggiani who sings the whole last part of the program. He has become very melodramatic, which delighted the crowd—makes gestures and waves his arms, wears a superb short white linen tailored jacket, very informal, like a garden jacket and unbuttoned, and he sang "The woman in my bed no longer has twenty years of age for a long time," your favorite and mine and several others we loved. I plan to write briefly about him in an upcoming Paris Letter. He has been such a hit that his engagement has been prolonged, and he has been singing for two months I think. You will anyhow enjoy what I wrote about Le Concile d'Amour* and Leonor Fini's wondrous cloth-of-gold dresses and huge swollen hats like golden puddings for the Borgia ladies' heads. There were more scandalous things in the play than I mentioned in my report. At one point, a seated virgin, not a very respectable virgin I should think, began caressing the head and throat of

---

* This was a translation of a short work written in 1895 by a Bavarian doctor, Oscar Panizza, who later died in a madhouse. The piece was discovered by the Surrealist André Breton.

a Negro prizefighter seated at her feet. At one moment the poor old figure of God was amorously attacked for an instant by a naughty angel, who knelt to kiss him, or was that just the Borgia pope who was thus treated—perhaps.

There is a new short novel by Marguerite Duras, *Détruire dit-elle*, strange title, published by Minuit. I have bought it to read over the weekend at Orgeval, the first time I have been out. My new room is very large, without the imposition of the built-in closets about as large as your bedroom. Only one window, nice little balcony. It is on the fifth floor and, except for the birds at dawn, not a sound all night. It faces south, so I have sun all day. It will cost me just half of what I earn in a month with my Letter, but tant pis. . . .

Janet sounded in good form and peppy; her health seemed to have held up quite well. She was careful about drinking her martinis and eating sparingly. No sooner had she arrived in Paris than she found herself in the middle of a political uproar over the General's unconstitutional maneuvers and a semi-political scandal involving his dauphin, [Georges] Pompidou and his wife. As Janet started gathering her material for her first Paris Letter, another strike blacked out the city. The Ritz had its own generators, which provided enough light to keep going.

Tired of de Gaulle's dictatorial behavior, I had urged Janet in New York to write more about life in the city, leaving out the political squabbles everywhere, which had become sickening and depressing. We had had enough for a while. So her first letter to me of March 12 described the story which had just broken in the press, but had been talked about for some time, ever since the strange murder of a Yugoslav photographer:

". . . The Pompidou scandal is now out in the open, mentioned in *Express* only obliquely by their running a long profile-interview with the movie star Delon, in whose entourage figured the gangsters from Yugoslavia of whom one was murdered by another, the dead one being found a year or so ago in a dump heap rolled in a plastic bag, like garbage. By now all the papers have mentioned that the live Yugoslavia of whom one was murdered by another, the dead one that they dined a year or so ago with Delon, which they have denied, saying they knew nothing of the entire faits divers. The dead Yugo was a photographer who specialized in pictures of people making love, then sold for ransom money to the wretches thus photographed.

Madame Pompidou's photo is in *Express* this week with her husband, but the main article is about Delon and Parisians will catch the clever makeshift and its submerged meaning as news. A nasty story and political scandal which may well cost Pompidou as de Gaulle's follower in power and add only to the disgrace of such political passions which have not concentrated on La Belle France."

March had been a busy month. Maurice Grosser, the painter, brought Janet the news that Virgil Thomson's new opera, *Lord Byron*,* was being accepted by the Met, which pleased her, but also word that Jane Bowles was very ill, which upset both of us. We had been very fond of Jane and admired her talent. We had lost touch when she went to live in Tangier, where Maurice was now going to paint. Janet liked to see such old friends. Her social life had been busy. A large dinner at the Sargent Shrivers', for instance: ". . . I have not had a decent meal since Thursday when the Shrivers gave excellent spring lamb, etc., to about forty. Feared to know no one, but took a fancy to the [Henry] Cabot Lodges and Mrs. Shriver herself, unaffected, kindly, very slender and tall in a turquoise blue very cutaway classic evening gown. When I asked her if I could invite her to lunch some day, she said NO, I always lunch with my best young man, now age three, but ask me for a drink at your hotel room. He is kindness and beaming hospitality itself. The first course was jellied bouillon with a great wallop of caviar on top, an odd combination. Bordeaux wine 1959 and splendid . . ."

[April 12, 1969]

My beloved,

. . . His highness de Gaulle spoke in a questions and answers TV dialogue Thursday night, too late for me to hear and analyze, but he received such a slashing reproof from *Le Monde*'s editor signed Sirius, the Dog Star, which he uses only when he has risen in wrath to denounce something, as I think I have never seen. He referred to the coming referendum as a cross between a fight and a seduction. Above all, he asked if the citizen approved of de Gaulle simply choosing a dauphin Pompidou without consulting either the nation or the Parliament and says, "Do you want to inherit a country (after his departure????) which is anti-constitutional, probably worse than the political

---

* *Lord Byron* was commissioned jointly by the Koussevitzky and Ford Foundations in 1966–67, for the Metropolitan Opera. A studio performance was given in April 1969, and the production premièred at Juilliard in April 1972.

chaos of the old days?" My opinion is that he has become absolutely anarchistic, the old man has, is so illegal that he should be jailed. . . .

I have just heaved into my wastebasket *Evergreen* and *Playboy*. I cannot force them to stop sending them and am ASHAMED to have the servants find them, even thrown out. Today's indecency is unbearable.

I can't read Philip Roth's *Portnoy's Complaint*. Read some and laughed, and then got sick of it. Semen splashed as high as the electric light bulb I found a little excessive. . . .

I miss you simply inhumanly. I didn't think I could suffer so at my age or at *any* age from longing.

In May, without waiting for the results of a special referendum, General de Gaulle resigned from the presidency. "[It was] unexpected by the French people, and nearly as great a shock, as if he had suddenly and almost voluntarily died at that hour," wrote Janet, in her Paris Letter of May 1. The referendum had been called for two "marginal reforms"—the regionalization and renovation of the Senate, which he had backed and was defeated by the voters. He had said on television a few weeks earlier that "if they failed to be passed, he himself ought not to continue as Chief of State." Sensing defeat, he had resigned and exiled himself at his home at Colombey-les-Deux-Eglises, "mystifying the country."

[May 3, 1969]

Beloved,

I wrote you during the week. I cannot remember which day because after I started this last de Gaulle letter on Sunday afternoon; one day was like another until I cabled it Thursday. Shawn sent me an astonishing cablegram which I could hardly believe, it was so formal. "Janet dear, we thank you for your remarkable letter. It is the letter called for by these large events, and we are fortunate to have it in the magazine." Did the *New York Times* use the extraordinary interpretation of *Le Monde*, also Camus' little old fighting paper *Combat* and *France-Soir* that, as *Le Monde* said the most simply— "Was it not a theatrical sortie, an act of political suicide?" *Combat* said, "He fell because he wished to fall," and *France-Soir* said, "General de Gaulle was defeated by General de Gaulle." You can imagine how hard I worked condensing and including and choosing.

Reston's *Times* "Regret and Relief" was superb. The best of anything published here in Europe. Well, he saved France once or twice, but chose not to save himself.

Yesterday was the first fine, spring day, interrupted in the afternoon by a terrific electric storm, but today is *lovely*, and I am glad for I shall go to Orgeval and rest and look at Noël's flowers, which are splendid this year. God knows why, as it has been a late and chill spring. She has huge beds of mixed pale lemon and white tulips and some pink and red ones scattered in side beds. It is childish how I love flowers in bloom. It is not difficult to understand how I am in love with you, as if you were a flower I wore in my arms and on my breast.

[May 14, 1969]

Dear one,

. . . I am having difficulty writing my present Paris Letter; the Boulez concert has sunk me as I don't understand his music, but I cannot write nothing but election politics. Shawn's cable to me about my de Gaulle resignation Paris Letter astounded and overwhelmed me . . . He never wrote me like that in my forty-three years of work. It is now past one o'clock, and I must go to bed. I hope [Alain] Poher, the ordinary man, wins against Pompidou who is acting like a rooster now that de Gaulle has disappeared, like a fighting cock, vulgar, brash, noisy.

A great emptiness has seized France since Le Vieux went to Ireland. What tragic photos of the old pair wending their way down the hill roads in County Kerry. Do you want to go to Ireland for your holiday? That's an idea, a wonderful idea. I fear the water would be cold for swimming though. What do you think????? Do please write me to help decide, what you want my darling one, please. We MUST have at least a month by the ocean and two if you dare to take them. Do you want to go to Ireland? The de Gaulle hotel is on the Gulf Stream and has tropical verdure. He and Tante Yvonne will be gone in a few weeks. We might go to their little inn. What fun that might be, no?

[May 17, 1969]

My love,

Your voice always stirs me—almost more on the long-distance phone than elsewhere, except your evening greeting at the door of your apartment, home from your office. YES. Then, Ireland!! We will rent a car and see the country and hear their speech and eat their fine bacon. Now don't let Rizzoli interfere and whatever you choose will be perfect for me.

I had cocktails at the Hôtel Meurice with the Lippmanns yesterday. Gave them your telephonic love. Walter understands no more than you or I as to why the young are all gone mad. He is as disgusted as we. Twice he turned his head toward the light in such a way that I cried, "Walter, you look just like your *Herald Tribune* photograph," and I wish I saw it thrice weekly as over years.

This morning bad news from Berkeley University with rioting and the guards firing salt at the students. . . .

Yesterday it rained nearly all day in floods. The rain came down like solid strings of water from the sky. The world is gone awry.

I love you. Yours beyond life.

By early June I could write Janet that I would come to Paris to collect her and proceed to Milan, where we would meet Joe Wechsberg. Old Angelo Rizzoli had recovered and could be interviewed by him for a possible *New Yorker* profile. We would then proceed to Rome and Sperlonga for two weeks' vacation. As Janet had suggested, we would return to the States together and visit our respective families in California. Then, on her return trip to Paris, we could steal a few days or a weekend at least on Fire Island.

In a letter of May 20 she commented on our preparations to dispatch an astronaut team to the moon:

"I know your heart is in your throat during this flight to the moon, and I read with fear and trembling what those eagle men plan to do. Naming everything after the cartoon characters of Peanuts seems to me a little more Amurrican than necessary, but it, of course, pleases the U.S.A. public. It seems a little as if when the apple dropped down from the tree, Galileo had cried 'hi-ya poppins' instead of coming to a conclusion about gravity, stated with gravity. (It was not Galileo. Who was it? Newton?) . . ."

Everything went well that summer. The hotel had a royal aura, a feeling of great privilege, a world in which neither I nor Janet belonged. But I have to admit that we enjoyed the Ritz. It was more agreeable than the Continental, even cozier, though I felt Janet missed that hotel, especially the view from her balcony. She was hoping to move back on her return. She kept peering inside every time she passed by.

The food was good in Milan, especially the *risotto* with saffron, and my favorite veal *alla milanese*, with mushrooms. It wasn't the season for truffles or even *ovuli*, the exquisite egg-shaped mushrooms generally eaten as salad. Once, years before, on my way from Milan to see Janet, I had bought a handful of precious white truffles from Piedmont, as a treat for her, and packed them in rice for the train trip to Paris. They smelled very strongly right through the rice and pretty soon the whole wagon-lit reeked of truffles. Fearing the customs at the frontier, I poured my Guerlain perfume all over the compartment. When the customs agents opened the door, sniffling, they examined nothing and disappeared. After the train had left, I realized that my passport had not been returned, a serious thing in those days. Finally, and against Janet's advice, I had to turn to the Paris *sécurité* agents, the secret police so feared by the French. Janet thought I would be arrested on the spot. Those Corsican officers couldn't have been more efficient, once they realized they had to deal with the historically hated Italian police. My passport was retrieved in no time, and the truffles became a grand occasion for a triumphant feast.

By the end of August, we were again together, after our California family visits, and we had time to spend a few days at the island all by ourselves. Then back to our respective jobs. Janet had hoped that her work would be easier. "No politics, or little at any rate, with de Gaulle becoming an author and a country gentleman again, no longer head of state." As usual, she was eager to start writing. She felt fresher in mind and rested in body.

On her return to France, Janet went directly from the airport to her old hotel, now called the Inter-Continental, and sat down at ten-thirty p.m. to sip a gin and tonic in the courtyard. She had wanted to get back there, in part because she had found the Ritz too expensive, a fact that lay heavily on her social conscience and on her sense of balance as well. "It disgusts me with myself," she had written six months earlier, in April. But in her first letter she described her arrival at the modernized Continental.

[September 14, 1969]

. . . I have had the first shock of a day and night in this ultra-modern hotel, so damnably modern that I can't even dial on the phone: it contains a dial of such complexities as I never dreamed of. I don't know if I shall remain or not. I am seeing the manager Tuesday to discuss the price of my room by the month. Paris looked lovely in the skies, a beautiful day like yesterday for the flight, and as a city it is clean. But it is more torn up by workmen than ever. It is like a city that has been quietly bombed. There is a railroad strike on!!! I miss you.

And again:

[September 18, 1969]

Darling,
    . . . Today returning to my room I saw a young woman sitting on the floor in front of her room—English and fit to be tied. She had tried for half an hour to unlock her door with a fancy, complicated lock, had vainly hunted for a chambermaid or valet. The lifts are automatic, so no elevator boy, no *anybody*. I phoned at once from my room and told the concierge to send help to her.

    I was unable to get out of my own room this morning. I could not unlock my door until I phoned for my coffee and the waiter liberated me. Already I am beginning to think I may go to the Hôtel Vendôme, which is not so damnably modern and mechanized. The livery of red and grey mixed makes all the personnel look like gypsy band masters out of a job with no orchestra.

    I feel too empty to say more. The Tuileries trees look fine. The only familiar natural sight. . . .

But a brief note the same day announced that she was back at the Ritz: ". . . I moved over here this afternoon into the room you occupied with me. The shabbiness of the Ritz is a great comfort after the garish modernism of the Inter-Continental. . . ."

[October 18, 1969]

My darling one,
    There is a strange exotic bird which whistles in the garden my room faces on, in the court I share with the Ministry of Justice. He just this moment whistled again—with a passionate, deep, penetrating sonority, like the song of a nightingale in spring. He is doubtless caged, poor creature, but whistles from five in the morning till sunset, which is now. He whistles every five or ten minutes and is my delight, as you can imagine. His song is so transcendent in tone. I can't place the spot where he lives in the court. He just whistled again; sometimes he

whistles in ascendant tones, sometimes descending. I think perhaps it is a mynah bird, an Indian bird that can also be taught to talk. I heard one once give a performance with his trainer at Macy's, in the ladies' tea room, years ago. I thought him lovely. . . .

. . . I eagerly await Milton's sending me the new Alliluyeva book on Stalin and Russia.* Suddenly I am so angry as to be in a ferment against the Russians and their manner of having tricked their own vast population by promising liberty with the revolution back in 1917.

I was only a girl and can remember how shocked I was at the *Indianapolis News* (owned by old Vice-President Fairbanks, a rigid Republican) when it spoke of the "nationalization" of Russian women —distributed freely among the men. Where did they get so strange a notion? Even if afterward it became true! And voluntary! What a period we have lived through. I in great ignorance, but with ever deeper conviction that the Russians are the new enemies of Europe, determined to conquer it eventually, just as the Germans were.

Poor Libouché. Already her family wrote that in Prague there is little coal and staple food is already short; they will be let to freeze this winter and go nearly starving, you will see. How wicked the male instinct is for conquest, beginning first with a wife, then your neighboring country. . . .

Never have I seen such a beauteous, sunny autumn in Paris as this year, each day brilliant, enviable, poetic, physically inspiring. Because of the great difference in temperature between the warmish days and the increasingly chilly nights, the early morning fogs are frightful. Yesterday four motorists collided on the south autoroute and ran into each other, all killed and two cars set on fire and a child badly burned.

Shawn asked me to lunch yesterday here at the Ritz and I was very touched. So few of my old friends or acquaintances bother to look me up—or I them, to be truthful. I lunched last week at Natalie Barney's. She looks her age, which is 93, but is bright as a button, though walks with difficulty. . . .

(The whistling bird has gone to sleep, I fear. The sun is down.)

Mary McCarthy is going to New York next week—dentistry, poor woman. She was giving a small literary cocktail for a French girl writer named Monique Wittig, whom she and Nathalie Sarraute think very gifted. She is sending me her novel. I shall report on it to you. . . .

---

* Svetlana Alliluyeva, *Only One Year*.

On the first of November, Janet asked: "Would you like it if Shawn would let me come to New York for New Year's week, say ten days???? I would adore."

Of course, I would adore it, too.

Janet felt better, was in high spirits, once she had made up her mind—"resolutely," she wrote—to return to the Ritz, despite its cost ("not too easy to swallow") and her social conscience.

I had just had a moving experience with my old friend and publisher, Arnoldo Mondadori, in New York. I hadn't seen him since I had left the company for Rizzoli, his major competitor, and our relations had cooled. This time, he came to see me.

There had been no need for explanations. We both knew what had brought about my separation from his company. We just embraced, as if four years hadn't gone by, as if we had seen each other only yesterday. I loved him. I bore him no grudges, no recriminations. He was impressed by my office. He sat in front of my desk and remembered how I had asked him, as we walked together during one of his earlier visits to the city he so admired, why he didn't open a bookstore in New York. He shook his head. "I am only a publisher," he had answered, in a tone of regret or envy.

Janet remarked:

"How pleasing your meeting and with such affection with Mondadori there in New York, and yes, had he done what you so early suggested he would be in Rizzoli's place today, without doubt, and you too and happier. With the Mondadori you felt a family relation. Nancy [Cunard] used to talk about the 'circles' by which people who had known each other knew others who also later knew the first circles through outside figures, one tying up to another so that in the recollections of one with her memory they were like concentrics in a modern graphic drawing."

[November 2, 1969]

The new Anouilh play, *Cher Antoine*, was so involved and Pirandellian with a play within a play, then with the dramatist who was dear Antoine and dead when the curtain rose, coming back to life again to direct all his mourning friends into one more last, lengthy concentration on him, as a character and wearing the most lovely green plaid silk dressing gown with full skirt, that the audience grew very puzzled. The house was packed, and it has had good, if guarded, reviews. The clothes of the women were a delight, all from just before the first war, of an elegance in long clinging skirts and high hand-made shoes that were a treat. Old Françoise Rosay played the drama-tist's first wife (divorced,) and made of it a kind of imitation caricature of [Sarah] Bernhardt that was screamingly witty. She is coarser than Madeleine Renaud, but of the same training, actresses who even when they are not speaking watch the other speaking, as they would with good manners in real life . . .

Darling, are you well? I feel wonderful. I am seeing Dr. Hewes in ten days, just for a check on medicines he gave me. He is so busy that really ill people might be dead before he would have time to take their temperatures. Write me if it is convenient for me to come on Decem-ber 28. Please say yes, my beloved.

[November 2, 1969]

My darling,

And whom do you think I took to lunch today? LEA! We had a pleasant time. She looked handsome and smart with a large fur hat à la Russe . . .

The breakdown in the color camera which cut off the TV pictures here of the astronauts was a great disappointment from which I suppose you, too, suffered, for, after all, there is only one moon and only three men were on it, and only one colored camera was there to break down. I thought the astronaut who said, "So I just hit it with a hammer," made a very bad impression by such a brutal state-ment . . .

Dearest, do you expect me or not on December 28? You have not written me to express ANY interest in my arrival. I am worried. Are you ill, indifferent, or running for president? . . .

Friday morning, my darling. Letter from you at last. For breakfast, like caviar. Yes, yes and yes again to all your anticipated pleasures as stated by you, and by me, to me a dozen times a day in anticipation. Inge and Arthur's book* which they generously sent me, autographed, is great ocular and mental reporting, a *rare* book, I think. The plung-ing troika horses, the plunging observing, political social mind not only of him but of her, too, show vitality carried through her lens. A remarkable and happy couple. Oh, Inge wrote in her dedicace, "and from Podsybrokie" or little Rebecca . . . touching, yes?

* Arthur Miller and Inge Morath, *In Russia.*

I must bathe and get money from bank. I spend it like water-in-summer, so much more a spending time than winter for bathing at least. I am hurrying to dress—my darling, yes, meet me at the airport . . .

Joy and joy and joy—
et la voix répond—

[November 7, 1969]

Darling,
     . . . I went to the new Arrabal play with Tom Curtiss the other night. It is lovely to look at; Delphine Seyrig looks like a goddess, and the man who played Man, the Bad Monkey, suspended from a cage overhead, was very appealing. The play is based on Bosch's *Garden of Delights*, the picture in the Prado museum . . . It is charming to look at, except when the hero, who becomes the villain (it's one of those change-about roles), cracks his whip which is as loud as a revolver shot. . . .
     In one scene, Marpessa Dawn says to Seyrig, as blonde as a boiled egg, "Kiss me again. Kiss me more lovingly." Tom heard her say (I didn't, of course), "Fous-moi." Well, she is quite dark you know. I don't think even integrated New York will swallow a Negress and a blonde kissing on the mouth repeatedly, and if Marpessa says, "Fuck me," I think there might be a riot. Then we went to a night club for supper up on the Ave. Franklin Roos called by the name of some drink, but not brandy. It's Calvados. And a chap played the piano very softly which I enjoyed, and we had lobster cocktail and then shared a big spaghetti dish as we had had no supper. All this was very unusual in my life, which is quiet and tame. . . .

[November 28, 1969]

Darling one,
     This week's *New Yorker* has a very fine Washington Letter by [Richard] Rovere, of large intelligence on the administration, Nixon, et al., another proof of what fine reporting we turn in quite often. The "Casualties of War" of course, by Dan Lang, has made history. I am proud for him and for Shawn who must have suffered to accept and to print so brutal and painful a report on Army conduct. It seems to me that never has the country been so low in its morality as practiced by people who actually know better. On top, money is the most

desirable commodity, and at the bottom pornography and lewdness make the solid base on which entertainment and humor function. I worry about the U.S.A., because it is, it seems to me, obviously headed for some kind of self-treachery in which it will betray itself beyond redemption, which will take more time than we would ever give to restoring morality, taste or honesty. Your descriptive phrase in your letter about the astronauts marching around in the moon dust like *Petrushka* figures, costing us all a million dollars a step, seemed to me memorable. The astronauts are highly educated in their technique and self-control, but are uncultivated in every way, those voices, those slang, meager, cheap phrases, not a word of historic simplicity or worth or poetry, nothing except variants of "Oh boy, did we hit it good." I was ashamed of them, of their poverty of appreciation. Christians they may be, but not familiar with the verbiage of the Bible, or they would have had more words and phrases of noble recollection to cover their own poverty of thought. . . .

———

In a postscript to her letter, Janet referred to the death of our friend, the sculptor Mirko, in Cambridge, Massachusetts:

"A little notice in the *Herald Tribune* this morning announced the death of Mirko. He was fifty-eight years old, so young to die. It mentioned his great gates in the Ardeatine Caves. God rest him. Pat his little Apollo on the shoulders for me, in farewell."

This was sad news for us. The artists Mirko and Afro, the two Basaldella brothers who had come to be known by their first names, had been close friends of ours since we had first met them in Rome, in the forties. Afro became a well-known international abstract painter; he had a one-man show at the Guggenheim Museum; Mirko, a most gifted sculptor, was the younger brother, and a charmer. He, too, came to the States, as a resident professor at Harvard University, with a superb studio in the only modern building on campus, or in America, designed by the French architect Le Corbusier. We visited him and Serena, his wife, the sister of the painter Corrado Cagli. I had arranged for an exhibition of Corrado Cagli's recent *Siciliane*— a series of colorful prints in abstract designs reminiscent of Sicilian folk art—in our Rizolli art gallery. Mirko had volunteered to help hang the show, and had stayed on for the opening; it had been like the return of a lost friend. (Cagli, too, had lived and worked in America before the war.) Mirko was very fond of sculpting small bronzes in the classical manner, typical of Cellini. We fell in love with a delightful one—Apollo, the sun god—on the first day we visited his studio in Rome, and bought it. It rests over my fireplace, a most beloved possession.

[December 5, 1969]

Darling,

It is cold today in a pleasant, physical way; the cold makes one's skin burn, so one is dually warmed and chilled, like baked Alaska pudding. Your letter was splendid in its report of your soul and experiences, apropos of the magazine. Soon we shall have talks in New York in the living room at night or at the breakfast table Saturday mornings. I see your geographic position as an emigrée in America, a normal civic situation in which you have ripened; there seems no normalcy for me, born there but despising my locality. Perhaps had I been born a New Yorker with privileges of seeing beauty I would not have turned into a geographic rebel.

Ernest [Hemingway] was not one to begin with, but became one. Italians long to return to their "paese" because they recall it as lovely. He did not yearn for the beauties of Michigan in the autumn, the only season the Middle West is handsome, with its Signac-like stripes of colored leaves of different shades of yellow, red and brown, with forests as gay as flags. That motor trip you and I took on the tops of the mountains en route from Washington to New York was a palette revelation, a journey for a painter, not a citizen necessarily.

I am very confused in my likes and dislikes now, upset by my own ignorance of what I truly feel. All you say about your own people, the Italians, I feel too. They would not murder children and old people. Do you recall that I said they remained civilized by Love and the passion for beauty during their dark ages when education was only for priests or occasionally princes? Do you recall the scene that night you and I were walking back down to Capri from the Roman emperor's ruin and we came to an inn lighted for wine on the second floor, where a young father came in holding his firstborn, "a beautiful little girl. Think of the pleasure she will later give others in her life." That is the civilization of love. I hope my imagination will be active and my mind recollective in our three weeks together in New York, where you will animate me but will I stir you in the same rich way? Yes, Rome as a future sounds reasonable if you wish it, better than Paris surely. Better than New York. . . .

I took Josette with me to see the Bolshoi Ballet last night, whose

opening ballet was like a fresco in movement of slender males and
females in suntanned tights and GREY wigs, as if prematurely wise,
and was very beautiful, poetic, calm, with stretching muscles and a
complete absence of physical passion in evidence, a mood and manner
I never saw before which I shall have to analyze to understand or
write about. The Leningrad group were provincial and vulgar in
comparison. There was one from Bakou too, dressed as oil workers, a
real workman's ballet, but no more interesting for that fact. Probably
less so, for it was esthetically so provincial, with the ballerinas popping
around on their toes, dressed in pale blue with a waving scarf tied to
their wrists, pretty awful. The new Russian film* of which I wrote
lengthily in the last Paris Letter is not to be missed. It is in the old
golden style of history, being poured out of a horn for the crowd, like
Potemkin, though not so good for that long public staircase *Potemkin*
scene with the people fleeing down it under bullets and finally the
deserted baby carriage bouncing down alone with the screaming child
remains a historic personal horror of great cinematic significance.
History furnishes so few small anecdotes. One of the reasons why the
chemin de la croix, as told in the New Testament about Jesus, is so
moving is that it contains several small incidents which are lighted by
history forever—like that dreadful moment at dinner when Jesus gives
the sop to Judas, to him who will betray Him. I wonder if it really
happened, or if it was inserted later to prove Jesus had the gift of
prophecy. Men always undergo such alterations when being changed
into gods.

My darling, this is from one who loves you from the depth of mind
and heart and memory.

[December 16, 1969]

Darlingest,

In twelve days, if I am counting correctly, we will be together. Do
NOT come to meet me at the airport except for your own pleasure
(and mine) for Pan Am will send a car. However, we can ride back
to 73rd Street in it in state. . . .

The photos here in *Figaro* of the crowd in Milan in front of the
cathedral and the hearses winding their path through the public
mourners was anguishing. I don't know why exactly. With the
Vietnam War and our own dead and our own disgrace with the Mai

---

* *Andrei Rublev*, directed by Andrei Tarkovsky.

Lai massacre, merely eight dead is a small toll by anarchist bombs, but it was the bitterness that lay behind the violence—the desire to kill in a panic that seemed so painful because so devilish and so naive, too. I am unable to believe easily that on the recognition of a taxi driver who saw a young man hurry into the bank with a satchel and come out a little later without one that the police are honestly sure they have caught one of the terrorists. Anarchy cannot be a form of government. It can only be a temporary dynamiting dream. There are too many millions of humans in the Western world to fancy we can all live without any government at all, which is what in desperation perhaps drives the anarchists to their bloody fancies and impraticalities. And their horrors. The little boy in Rome who lost his leg, what a panic the bank must have been in, and also the Piazza Venezia (where at least there is room for it). I sent you a cable I was so distressed for your natal city and for Milan and for your country on the whole. . . .

Eleanor Packard sent me the most lovely Christmas card I ever saw in my whole unChristian life, one of the UNICEF ones, a huge globe in squares of green and blues floating in a red and purple squared sky. The colors make me want to weep with delight. So far, I have NO gift for you, so will peer around to see what is to be seen. I also must take something impressive to the Shawns to whom I have given nothing for several years. I never know what they might like, they are so odd in their tastes. Or so conservative, which? It is late, nearly one a.m.; I must go to bed in the rain. I have not even sent Hildegarde a card yet, but will send a fine big silk handkerchief for her head and throat, useful in California. I had a charming letter from Mary Frances Fisher, who simply got tired and bored with her family and capered off to New York. I have not yet even seen any book I yearn for. . . .

I hope we are happy in New York. I hope I don't fail you for one instant, my darling.

La tua . . .

The Seventies

1970

In the early seventies, our correspondence decreased somewhat, because we were more often together. During the winter, Janet began coming to the States for longer periods; in the summer we met abroad as usual.

I was overjoyed by this development, charmed by her presence, warmed by her affection, stimulated by her mind, and—yes—worried by our separation. The demands of her work, the pressure of deadlines, events to follow, people to see—all were starting to take their toll on her. Her health, which had been so resilient all her life, now showed signs of weakening. She would be seventy-eight years old in March. During her stay in New York, I realized for the first time that she was taking pills for a mild angina, slight, but nevertheless worrying. I worried, too, about her living alone in a hotel, her lifelong habit of always eating out in restaurants, smoking countless cigarettes, drinking martinis (which she was trying to cut down on), of always doing too much. That was her life, her pleasure, her choice, her reward. Yet she enjoyed home life, too. I could see it when she spent the weekends at Orgeval, or stayed with me in New York or Sperlonga or Fire Island, or when visiting her sister in Calistoga. She relaxed, felt at ease, rested better, looked better. Together, we laughed a lot. We were rejuvenated and reinvigorated by each other. I was pleased that she wanted to come oftener and stay longer.

"The pen you gave me in gold writes it and truly—you are that to me: my source of pleasure and of decisive political acumen," she wrote, in her first letter, dated January 28, after her return to Paris from New York. "This seems to be an epoch without talent for fiction or for great reality, which may be why you and I derive such vigor and dreamlike passion from our love. It is always in its climax, like a novel, and in its realism like the great *fact* of our lives' joy and experience—our truth, our body's government. . . . I shall come over again before long; the strain is otherwise too great. . . ."

With her next letter of January 31 she assured me that "I take my two pills to reduce my pressure twice daily and only three times this week have I had to resort to the midget doses of nitroglycerine. I feel quite well except that I sleep badly or not at all. The medicine that makes me sleep no chemist can prescribe. . . ." In a week, she had taken up her routine.

She was still fussing about the Foreword to *Salute to the Thirties*, a book of splendid photos by Horst of famous characters from that famous period, and she thanked me copiously for some modest advice I had given her, which she termed "a judicious *stimulating* presentation of the thirties of any that we talked of." And she asked: "Did you notice that one of my thirties characters died yesterday—Marie-Laure de Noailles? Her obituary was strict and flat compared to that of Loulou de Vilmorin. I saw also that Caresse Crosby had suddenly died, a year or so my junior: her invention of the *soutien-gorge* [brassiere] was mentioned in the Paris *Herald* obituary!"

Of the Vicomtesse de Noailles, Janet wrote:* "She was the most intellectual of the Paris mansions' social figures, eccentric and vigorous, who suddenly died, aged sixty-seven, and who will be irreplaceable.

"Her ancestry included three famous figures from widely differing literary legends. She was descended from Laura de Novalis, Petrarch's beloved Laura—for whom she was named. She was also descended from the Marquis de Sade, of the infamously famous memoirs. And her maternal grandmother Chévigné was the model of elegance on whom Proust shaped his Duchesse de Guermantes. Her father was the *richissime* Alsatian banker Bischoffsheim. She said of herself that

* In her Foreword to *Salute to the Thirties*, by Horst (Viking Studio Book, 1971).

she looked like Louis XIV." She was a painter and a novelist, backed artists and made films with her husband.

Louise de Vilmorin, nicknamed Loulou, was another of the great hostesses of the thirties. She was a poet, singer, jewelry designer, and, in later years, also a novelist—"one of the most beautiful young Frenchwomen of her day," wrote Valentine Lawford, in his notes to the Horst photographs. "One of those women only France can produce: an enchantress," said Horst.

Marie Crosby, known as Caresse, was an American who died in Rome at the same time, at the age of seventy-eight. More than merely a hostess and backer of modern artists, she had been, with her husband, Harry, who was a nephew of J. P. Morgan, the founder of one of the most active and famous of the small Paris publishers, The Black Sun Press. When they arrived in Paris in 1928, young, beautiful, eager and rich, they were both poets and in love. They had decided that the best way to get their poems published was to have their own press. Their first books were their own. Later they published D. H. Lawrence, Laurence Sterne, Kay Boyle, Hart Crane, Archibald MacLeish, even James Joyce. The Black Sun Press books were carefully handprinted in limited editions of a few hundred copies, sometimes no more than a dozen in all, on delicate vellum paper. They were illustrated by the rising young artists of that time.

I had met Caresse, already a widow by then, in New York in the mid-thirties. The occasion had been the costume party she gave in honor of Salvador Dali's first New York exhibition. "Come as a dream," said the invitation, and the party made the society-column headlines.

As I recall, it was much more amusing than the later Capote ball. Caresse had taken over an entire nightclub and had it decorated as a labyrinth of myrtle in the grand manner of Renaissance gardens, out of which protruded skeletal limbs—feet, hands, legs, arms—as if to grab you. Somewhere else, in a corner, a whole calf in bridal veils lay inanimate in a bathtub, a flower in its mouth.

The costumes were imaginative and less gruesome. I recall a group who came as the Four Saints in Three Acts, from Virgil Thomson's new opera, with a libretto by Gertrude Stein, which had just opened in New York at the 44th Street Theatre, on February 20, 1934.

I saw Caresse again years later in her medieval castle a few miles from Rome. It looked like a large transatlantic liner stuck on top of a peak dominating the valley below. She had established her residence there and called it the capital of "One World," an idea she was propagating with the same missionary spirit she had devoted to her Black Sun Press days.

She had even had a specially designed banner hoisted above the ramparts to proclaim to the winds her message of universal peace. There, in the overhanging garden, sat Caresse under her parasol, entertaining the notables of her village town: the mayor-poet, the parish priest, the local doctor, and a number of young artists, to whom she allotted space in the stables—actually within the castle itself, where the soldiers had once quartered their horses and which had been transformed into spacious studios. At night we all met around a large table for a simple, lively dinner served by a local peasant. When Janet and I visited her, the artist-in-residence was the Chilean painter Matta, with his Sicilian wife Angela. The villagers remember Caresse today as the lady who brought water to their town and had wooden benches built at the bus station along their sun-baked country road.

In 1914, on the eve of her debutante ball, she had rebelled against having to wear the tight, heavily boned corset customary at the time. She tore off the lower part of it, leaving only the top, and so gave birth to the brassiere! Typically, she sold her idea for a pittance to buy a work of art.

After the disappearance from the French scene of "Le Grand Charles," events in Paris semed to have lost momentum, and Janet occasionally found difficulty in finding topics of importance to report on.

"Events here are calmer, but there is such an 'intox' as the French call it, an intoxication of sensitivity, nerves, etc., leaning in an exaggeration on the public nerves, a phrase that developed in the war when the French exaggerated from fear and lack of courage with the German occupation. . . ."

We began talking about where to move. "So where do you want to settle? Which continent and city? I love Rome, as you know, but do you? Are you SURE you do not prefer to live in New York with all its hideous drawbacks, since your friends are there?" And we began discussing our plans for the summer.

This year I would begin my vacation in late August, because I was going to the Frankfurt Book Fair. I had suggested to Janet that she come with me; she might have been interested in the experience, at least once in her lifetime. Mike Bessie's plan for a second volume of her *Paris Journals*, from 1965 to 1971, had been finalized. Her appearance at Frankfurt would be beneficial as well, since Mike might be announcing it for his forthcoming 1971 list.

While we were planning our meeting, I received the following letter, written on postcards, from Belley, in France.

[June 2, 1971]

Saturday. Darling, am here with Virgil from New York, Maurice Grosser from North Africa, our woman director from the Educational Film Company for whom we three are to do a piece for the BBC on Gertrude Stein. We motored here from Geneva this afternoon, where we had our rendezvous this morning. We were only told last week the date for this little intellectual TV show. We will speak it tomorrow, Sunday, at Bilignin, forty kilometers from here, in the garden of the house where Gertrude and Alice lived down here. We have five movie men (French), with whom I have talked Left politics. Virgil is more fabulous than ever for intelligence and memory. The food has been so remarkably gastronomic that I was rather sick after our Geneva lunch—*truite au bleu* and guinea hen with *morels* in cream and very fine white Burgundy wines chosen by Virgil. We are all on expense accounts and living high since we get no pay for the show.

Tonight we are in a country hotel in this modest town: it is heaven, bath, etc., lovely old country furniture and for dinner local green asparagus with a heavenly sauce and new quails, poor things, and wonderful conversation after. I am *enjoying* myself, the first journey I have made in the French countryside for seven years. We drove down from Geneva this afternoon, about two hundred miles through high hills and modest farms; it was heavenly. It is fairly warm, can go out with a suit and scarf and no top coat. Geneva is very pleasing, the little I saw. I arrived at ten a.m., and Virgil and I sat in a café terrace and *talked*. He said he had spoken to you on the phone and you sent *love*, which I enjoy having. I return Monday afternoon to Paris by train, alas. There is to be a Monday strike at Orly of the air traffic directors, and I will not risk flying around overhead for hours waiting to get a chance to come down, too boring. We also have a postal strike on in France so this letter may be late. The Wednesday students' riot was bad in St.-Germain-des-Prés, mostly beastly destruction. What a world we live in. Je t'adore. Virgil and Maurice talk of you with love.

I saw that "little intellectual TV show," where Virgil monopolized the conversation. Considering Janet's own verbal ability, it was quite a feat. She did manage to get in a few phrases describing Gertrude Stein's head as looking like a Roman emperor's, and the full, infectious laughter so characteristic of her. I don't recall Janet having been able to say anything about Alice B. Toklas, her favorite. Nevertheless, it was an unexpected pleasure, an offbeat historical documentary by three important personalities about two extraordinary ones.

Janet was in good form when we met in Paris on August 21. After a few days there and in Rome, we arrived in Sperlonga on September 1, a perfect time for pleasant relaxing. The weather is always good then, the air is cooler, but the sea is warm and the beaches are empty. The vacationing families have gone home, and the children are back in school. Only adults are around, and friends at home. Franca was in residence, too. We had a car, we motored, we ate good, simple food—fresh fruits and vegetables, fish, good wine—and had fine talks. We enjoyed our nest.

Frankfurt was a bit of an ordeal, as always, but it was an experience for Janet. The Bad Homburg Hotel where we stayed was old-fashioned and cozy, across from a lovely park and a small Russian Orthodox chapel with a multicolored cupola that entranced Janet.

By October we were back in our respective cities.

Janet's first letter expressed satisfaction at our summer:

"I am deeply grateful for our quiet, happy days and dinners at Sperlonga for we *were* happy and joyous and confident of our joy. So we had a holiday of our bodies and tender hearts. . . . You are in your posh Rizzoli office directing all that depends upon you, and I am between reality and remembrance, in a daze. . . . The death of President Nasser last night seems not even to be as useful as major demises are sometimes, pushing events further forward like outriders of history, too few out front. In my ignorance and poor memory, I simply rejoiced that our leading anti-Jew was dead, still my major consolation."

In her letter of October 7, she remarked on the news that *Life* magazine might cease to publish:

"We are in for a clean-up of extravagance that will lead to less extravagance and swollen notion of American know-how, success and commercial grandeur. Then the country may start on a new basis. Every so often we swell up like a peacock and then comes a recession. We are not a sensible nation and not intelligent psychologically. . . ."

Janet was already making plans to come over, starting with her usual visit to Hildegarde in Calistoga, where "nothing ever happens, thanks be to God!" She planned to stop in New York on her way, a very pleasant prospect. She was arriving on October 26, she said, and looking forward to it, since she found the bad weather, disorders, strikes, and even her room at the Ritz unsatisfactory, with a bad lock on her door that had "incarcerated" her, she said, and had forced her to call for help. She had stormed down to the reception desk and said to her friend David Campbell, "This hotel is too damned picturesque!" and walked away. She was promised a better room!

The peace and quiet of the Napa Valley that Janet had been enjoying was interrupted by the news of General de Gaulle's death, in his French village of Colombey-les-Deux-Eglises. I phoned her, because I wasn't sure she had heard it on the radio, and she wrote the obituary that was published by *The New Yorker* on November 11, which began:

"Upon the death of General de Gaulle in his rural retreat last week, President Pompidou stated, 'France is a widow,' thus announcing the country's new historical condition with the loss of the single elderly citizen who had husbanded the nation's failing strength in the war in 1940 and from then on had given himself, in devoted obstinancy, to saving France whether in war or in peace, whether in office as its President or in retirement as its critic."

And she ended:

"The foremost man of Europe and a great French eccentric for more than a decade of personal power, he remained a profound believer in a better, civilizing world. His voice on the air was that of the French leader of his epoch, reciting his convictions."

This obit ended the second volume of her *Paris Journals*, which would be published in 1971.

In the summer, while talking about what was going on in the world, she had been astonished that France had gotten along so peacefully and prosperously without de Gaulle: "I miss him, I must be truthful. Look at his beaked face and recall his words and then look at Pompidou's moustache, eyebrows, and think how common-place his words are!"

A few days later, on Thanksgiving, Janet wrote:

"We have great things to be thankful for: our love, our fidelity, our devotion, our good health, our jobs and our friends' admiration and affection. So thanks be to God. Thanks, too, for accommodating me in this return plan in giving me more free time with you in New York, where I plan on our precious time together. I am writing

Bill Shawn today that I would like to start work again in Paris the first fortnight of the New Year—*my last labor of my life.*

"Your praise of my de Gaulle obit excited me. Eric called it a very Gothic appreciation of the great man . . .

"We will have a wonderful Christmas and New Year's together." And for the first time in our long relationship.

1971

The holidays passed with the usual number of parties, but, with Janet in New York, there were more of them this time. The best part was that we were together, no matter what was happening in the outside world. Not that we didn't care; we just wanted to set aside worries for a while and concentrate on ourselves. We got along famously together—not one recrimination. Older and riper, with a lifetime of experience behind us, we had mellowed. We had such an entertaining time together that, yes, I thought we could easily live happily in New York. The city was becoming more internationalized; it had become the center of our modern world. "Even Paris didn't have the opening night social excitement of the Picasso-Stein show," acknowledged Janet. Perhaps, one day, she might even think of settling down here: so many friends, her beloved *New Yorker*, a recognition she enjoyed everywhere, and our families nearby. It was only a thought, for the moment. In summing up her writing for the past year, Janet thought that she had done some of her best work, "an exceptional satisfaction to me, frankly, and my use of it in which I have produced the best writing stuff the magazine has printed as a steady diet."

Just before leaving for Paris, she had a pleasant surprise. She was honored by the Department of Journalism of New York University

and by Theta Sigma Phi, in recognition of her work as Paris correspondent for *The New Yorker*, and a lively reception was held for her
at La Maison Française. It pleased her to have been honored by young,
aspiring journalists and by the women students who one day hoped
to follow in her footsteps.

It was not the Pulitzer, which she had hoped to receive, but just
the same it was a recognition of her performance that she appreciated.

After two months of New York I expected she would feel a letdown
in Paris; physical changes were confusing to Janet, and her first letter,
of February 8, confirmed my suspicions:

"It was fortunate that my grief at our parting was like a blow to
the body as well as the heart inside it. I slept until the hostess gently
touched my arm and said: 'It is one o'clock—do you want some
luncheon?' I drank a vodka and ate a delicious rib of fresh broiled
lamb with false green asparagus (from a tin). . . . I missed your
presence violently. . . . I am still like a lost animal. I was never more
happy with you this time, more strengthened by your wisdom, intelligence and sense of decision and choice. All I know of New York is
what *you* think and experience; what other people said ran through
me like rain through an open window. . . . It's a pleasure to eat
(French) restaurant food instead of the horrors of the Algonquin. But
there is no cheekie here that can touch yours, à la romana adorée . . .

"I am emptied of pleasure. My mind works like a broken mechanism.
But my head is alert and intelligent in tender passion, believe me my
beloved. Yours forever, J."

"I have never seen Paris so provincial, so empty of entertainment,"
she lamented on March 12. "There is literally NO theatre to go to
see worthwhile here. Fellini's new *Clowns* is the newest movie of
magnitude. Strange, a capital city that lets its Opéra and Comique
[theatre] stay closed for half a year and not even any notion of
reopening before next autumn loses its pace, its style of hospitality.
Regular opera gives a capital city its proper touch of grandeur
apparently."

Then she added:

"I have just been told by the chambermaid that two little windows
without curtains across from me in the narrow building that houses
the Cambon side of the Ritz were Chanel's tiny suite, two little rooms.
She kept her clothes across the street in her suite in her shop. Odd
woman, rich as Croeseus and mean with money AND unpopular with
her workers, whereas Schiap [Elsa Schiaparelli] was very popular

because she was humane and likeable. . . . Tomorrow is my birthday and I wish it were not! I went to a new oculist this week, very good I think. He said my sight could not grow worse but could not be aided by different glasses as my vision has been extended to its limits. Cheerful news! . . ."

Janet had barely started working when she slipped and broke two ribs. I had called her, worried not to have received her news.

[March 31, 1971]

Darling one,

I had to cancel my Paris Letter. I was in too much pain from those damned two broken ribs. I couldn't concentrate or think straight. Bad luck. It's only the second time in my *New Yorker* career that I was so ill I had to cut a Letter. I now am taking a suppository each night and capsules each day of pain killers. I feel better today than I have for almost four days, so don't worry, beloved. The ribs take thirty days to heal. I have only borne with them about ten days, so each day now should be easier. How accidents like that destroy the unity of one's pattern of work. Yes, "Avoid Accidents!" How we laughed, you and I, at the wise Red Cross. My American Hospital doctor who saved Josette's life when she had her first heart trouble last year was in the hospital when I turned up the morning after my accident to have a radio photo of my ribs, and he didn't even call on me to find out if I was alive or dead until ten that night. He probably had intensive care duty on his hand, and I didn't deserve that, but it was hard-hearted of him and I don't forgive him.

We still have no spring! Two days of chill, fine, bright weather.

Yes, I do NOT intend to work next year. This is my farewell year AND YOURS! Your collaborators are horrid and mine are angels, but time is now of the essential. We must be together, so I shall come out in the autumn for our first year, my own. I shall cook your dinner at night and you will be *well taken care of* by ME.

Coughing, which broken ribs promote, has been so painful that twice I have sat on the edge of my bed and cried like a child. But after I called Dr. Cotlenko [Monique's husband], who gave me drugs, the pains have been eliminated almost entirely.

I shall hope to do a brilliant Paris Letter on the Malraux–de Gaulle conversation at Colombey, which is the end of their relations, for shortly after it at Colombey the grand old gentleman died. Malraux

looks awful on the program, jerking, ticking, almost slobbering. He
has suffered too many losses and tragedies. The most talented of any
French writers of our time, I believe.

Bless you—write me at the hotel—Your warmth would heal me.

Yours til eternity.

[April 19, 1971]

Darling,

Eliot called April the cruelest month for poetic and amatory reasons,
but for me it has been the unluckiest month in years. No sooner had
my ribs healed than I dined at La Quetsch to celebrate with a decent
dinner and ordered a lamb curry which poisoned me. Fortunately, I
spit up with ease, but after all night and the next day I was exhausted.
Dr. Cotlenko was busy marrying off his oldest daughter, but called on
me with medicine and a strict diet including tea, quince jelly and
mashed carrot soup which I lived on for four days after coming out
here [Orgeval] where I could have someone close at hand. The attack
left me very weak and shaky, but now all is well, though I still have
had nothing to eat until today when I had mashed potatoes and a tiny
sliver of steak for lunch while everyone also was eating capretto and
asparagus. I lost a couple of pounds and feel fine now but weak. The
doctor said I was in a very rundown, nervous state and ordered me
NOT to work for a fortnight. I could not have. You will be disgusted
with me as an old crock.

I am cancelling the upcoming Paris Letter—the second one this
month, and I think *the third in my entire career*. I have almost
stopped smoking, a few cigarettes a day, and do NOT inhale. Please
do not be disgusted with me, my beloved. It is a lovely sunny and
rather cool day. Noël's garden is full of hyacinths and tulips in bloom
as my heart is full of you and longing for you. I do not know how that
long Malraux–de Gaulle conversation at Colombey will have passed
in the magazine. Maybe they found it dull and cut it.

My morale is shaken and I don't feel sure of my judgments. I shall
go back to Paris Tuesday. I feel greatly reposed now. I am so rarely ill
that sickness has been a moral shock. Summer is coming in and I have
no light clothes to wear as usual. I implore you to write me, dear one.
I shall phone you Tuesday during the day at your office just to hear
your voice.

Yours till the end of life.

Irving Drutman, a witty and sophisticated friend, who had been an avid reader of Janet's for years, had been working on an idea for another collection of her writings, this time to be drawn from her earlier "Letters" from the very beginning of her career.

Irving's idea was to select a series of miniature portraits, "which would result in a continuous, brilliant, illuminating record of an epoch with its social, artistic, political highlights," in the manner of *Brief Lives* by John Aubrey. It would cover the years from 1925 to 1939, culminating with the rise of Hitler. *Paris Was Yesterday* was published by the Viking Press in 1972, and became a best seller.

That spring, Irving and his friend Michael de Lisio would be arriving in Paris, and Janet was planning a good welcome. In the meantime, she had received the proofs of the second volume of her *Paris Journal, 1965–1971*, which Atheneum was publishing in the fall.

"It is six a.m., and I am up and getting my corrected proofs off to Atheneum," she wrote on May 8. "They read very, very well. I love rereading them. I have a weakness for my kind of writing on these varied new subjects. I have forgotten them since writing them, and they are interesting as if they were brand new to my mind. A blank memory is a good assistance to pleasure sometimes. . . .

"I did not think very highly of the Paris Letter I sent off this week, except for the *Chagrin et la pitié* [*The Sorrow and the Pity*] documentary which is really fascinating and a good contribution to the history of our time, in terms of the cursed Nazis. Mendès-France as the chief speaker is brilliant and impressive as Jew and politician and memorialist. That the French state TV was forbidden by the Prime Minister himself to show the film on the state time is a great disgrace to France—four and a half hours to sit through the film and crowds stand in queues first to wait to get into the Champs-Elysées movie where it is now showing commercially. . . ."

[May 15, 1971]

Darling,
. . . Last night with Josette and Ben Holt who invited us we went to see Nureyev dance in the Palais des Sports in *La Belle au bois dormant*, whose Tchaikovsky music I dearly love and many of whose dances I am familiar with in memory. Nureyev has grown heavy in the thighs, but has developed stranger perversities and individualisms in his dancing that are fetching and gay and beyond the prowess or

even the interest of another dancer, I should think. His walk is incredible, like a rather portly, hipped, forty-year-old Russian female, with incredible self-satisfaction in each step and sway of his bottom, a very strange and rather touching cartoon of himself and his mother perhaps. No dash as when young, and he has great style in hand-kissing and bowing like a middle-aged courtier at a provincial court. He almost waddles when he walks, especially when viewed from behind, leaving the stage. The new girl dancer from Marseilles, Noallee Poitiers* or something, is exquisite. She floats like an apple-blossom petal.

It is raining again; good heavens, we have had enough of it, I think.

I am not surprised that Roger Straus turned down the second Flanner reader. Really, the second journal is quite enough to come out under my pen this autumn. It is *good*, at least, and useful.

A note from Irving says he and Mike will be here next week. Goodie.

It is thundering now, damn it, the third day of electrical storms. Am starting to read Troyat's life of Gogol; his Tolstoi was the best biography written in our time, I think. Mary McCarthy sent me her new novel which looks painfully harmless, called *Birds of America*, and she dedicated it to me handwritten, "To Janet, an eagle." Very sweet indeed. Her head is beautifully shaped, isn't it? A beauty of a photo of her on the dustcover of the new book.

Goodnight, my own beautiful Italian, my favorite of all. Soon now, yes?

La tua.

"Never have we been at such sixes and sevens for our holidays," wrote Janet, on June 8. "Mexico was an absurd idea on my part. Now you decide. I am at your disposal, that you know, for whatever you choose. I shall be glad to leave the Ritz. It is still being refurbished and every day is a racket of wall tapping and hammering in all the corridors. Who could have thought it could not have been done in the winter season rather than the full summertime with windows open for every noise to reverberate? No matter where you say to go will suit me, but PLEASE choose some place somewhere, my dearest one."

The choice fell on Dubrovnik, and we could go by way of our

* Noëlla Pontois.

beloved Venice. Janet was delighted, and set the wheels in motion for hotel reservations and tickets for the various entertainments Dubrovnik had to offer. So I phoned her and set the date of my arrival in July. ·

A brief note included a clipping on the death of Arnoldo Mondadori, the Presidente. It was sad news—for his family, for the many Italian and foreign authors he had introduced to a vast public and for the people who had worked for him with dedication and affection, in a company he had created and built into one of the major publishing houses of Europe. Personally, I felt I had lost an older friend, the best.

[June 9, 1971]

My darling,

I know you have had news of the death of your old boss of whom you were fond—Mondadori—but I thought you might be interested that he was recalled here, too, and his demise noted, as you see by the enclosed. Allen Shawn called on me this afternoon and we talked music!! We both like the same Grand music such as Verdi. He does not know *Rosenkavalier* at all, but I enthused him over wanting to hear it, and we agreed on Stravinsky as the great genius of our own time. Allen is like his mother, so intelligent, well mannered, so appreciative of both his parents, especially Dad as he called Bill, admires him greatly, a rare sentiment for a son for a father these days. . . .

[June 18, 1971]

Dearest darling,

What a surprise that Irving's selection is sold to Viking. How happy he will be and how delighted you and I are! And what a grand down payment! Really, this news coming from you via telephone makes it a red letter day, embroidered in silk. I am happier for Irving or almost than for me, except we will take our holiday on that advance payment. The plans for our holiday seem magnificent and highly interesting. We will rent a car and you will NOT drive fast as the Yugoslav roads are bordered by precipices. Your idea of a brief visit to Monica in Lausanne is too kind of you to have thought of. Poor girl, she will faint with joy.

A very slim *New Yorker* came out today with absolutely nothing interesting to read in my opinion. What has happened to our writers or to Shawn?

I am so excited I can hardly type! A friend is going to give me the names of the most picturesque towns outside of Dubrovnik to visit for a day or so, so as to see the country a little bit. I must hurry out to mail this and eat; have not eaten since breakfast as usual, but feel empty. Nothing but cold and rain here, a dreadful summer so far as its first days go and spring utterly *pourri* [rotten].

The *New York Times* squabble_with the government on what it has printed from the presidential pasts seems to me very important and hooray for the freedom of the press, though it is sad to see one more fragile god, Jack Kennedy, tainted along with the others, but ambition is always a corruption. God love you my darling; I do.

[June 25, 1971]

Beloved traveler,

What an exciting conversational, informational interruption yesterday to my elegant luncheon under the blue tent in the Ritz garden with Josette given for Punch Sulzberger's wife, so nice, and wife of another *Times* chap. Your long schedule letter arrived this morning; everything is perfect. Four days in Dubrovnik is quite enough as the countryside is filled with precipices, I am told, which you would love to drive out to see and would also drive me mad with nerves, and for which, thank God, we will not have time but will stay in town, in a loving way, and roam about locally.

Botsford admired my Proust letter, cabled this morning: "It is a jewel in the crown of journalism," the old diplomat—what a pity I remain only a journalist, but that is my limit, which I love. Yes, let's go SEE Monica, poor creature, in Lausanne. So morbid, she longs only for the grave beside Odette's. . . .

———

We liked Dubrovnik, a small, medieval town on the Adriatic sea, where Venetian influences could be seen in the architectural details of its old palazzi lining the main street of the walled town, where vehicular traffic was forbidden. That entire Dalmatian coast had been influenced by Venice, when she dominated the trade routes to the Middle East, in the halcyon days of the Republic. Our hotel was further down the coast, modern and comfortable, but the nicest thing was the clear water for swimming, for the food was poor and the atmosphere dreary, like all places under communist rule, even in Yugoslavia.

The best part of our vacation had been our stay in Venice after the visit to Monica in Lausanne—a few hours' pleasant train ride from Milan. It was worth the effort, for the pleasure our visit gave her; she was living alone in a hotel with only her memories of Odette.

I returned in time to spend a few days of my vacation with my grandchildren in Malibu. They were growing so fast it was a surprise every time I saw them. Janet then joined me to go to Bar Harbor to see the Walter Lippmanns. A beautiful house, and gardens full of blossoms. Lovely walks on the rugged coast; friends for dinner. Helen was a perfect hostess; Walter a pundit to listen to. I wish I had had a tape recorder. By Labor Day we were at the Island; the summer had ended. In just a few weeks we had done a lot of traveling, and, so far, Janet had stood it well. The fall was busy in New York. Janet was again much in demand and loved it. Her first Dick Cavett TV show put her on the New York map, as if she had materialized suddenly as a fullblown public personality! In fact, she made history that December broadcast, when she intervened in a vitriolic exchange between Norman Mailer and Gore Vidal, Cavett's other literary guests on the program. Janet, who had tried in vain to stop the nasty quarrel between the two men, finally exploded. "I've had enough of you!" she said, putting an end to it. Delighted, the public applauded her!

Janet was savoring her success. The second *Paris Journal* had appeared, and she had now become a well-known, much-appreciated figure on the New York literary and artistic scene. She was surprised, but appreciative. Later that month, we left for California.

1972

Janet stayed all of January and February with Hildegarde and Eric in their Calistoga home, sharing their happy country life, taking long scenic drives, occasionally seeing old friends.

"It has been very chilly here," she wrote. "Water left for the dog outside freezes solid. But a humming bird who remembered that Hildegarde had hung out honey for him on the back porch returned to refresh himself and within the hour had even brought along his girlfriend. . . . Hildegarde and Eric did the *Saturday Review* double acrostic yesterday until two a.m., when they finished in triumph. . . ."

A little later, on January 18, she reported:

"Today we are smothered again in fog which has hidden the lower part of the property and we also have another visitation of robins and *starlings*, another variety of city marauders in the country to feed. Already Hildegarde worries about the starlings, for if they return here in October when the grapes are ripe, they will eat them all and ruin the wine-making of the year. I like hearing about the rural problems. I am still a country-jake at heart. . . .

"Hildegarde and I are lunching tomorrow in a new house forty miles distant that was built for Mary Frances K. Fisher, the food writer, on the property of Mr. Bovary, a rich rancher, and I hope we have a jolly time—I shall enjoy the drive across country.

"I finished that Maurice Grosser book review [*Painter's Progress*] and posted it today to Gardner Botsford. It was like trying to condense fifty years of art talk into some sort of report that had validity. It reads very well. Spent three days writing it. Hildegarde typed it for me while I dictated it to her. We get along wonderfully and last night with Eric away at a Council meeting, she and I sat in the kitchen, telling affectionate tales of our old Irish cook we both loved. I cried more at her funeral than at the funeral of my father."

In her next brief note, thanking me for my phone call, she recounted the luncheon given for M. F. K. Fisher by Hildegarde:

"We had a fine spinach soup, salad of tomato and avocado and grilled mushrooms on toast, all delicious. M. F. K. Fisher writes for *The New Yorker*, or did; food is her specialty. Her translation of Brillat-Savarin is masterly."

Commenting later upon reading the proofs of her *Paris Was Yesterday*, just received from Irving Drutman, she wrote:

"I am very confused about the *opening* Paris Letter in Irving's book; it is NOT as he and I re-edited and rewrote it, and what he has NOT used is a loss. I worked on it very carefully. I found in doing the proofs (148 full-length pages) that many of the entries are very funny and the Wharton Profile is excellent. I insist that some of the brutal crime reports be omitted. They are vulgar and ruin the tone of the volume, which is, of course, a kind of rag bag at best, with its violent mixture of time and topics."

[February 14, 1972]

My darling,

It is now six a.m. Dawn has come and gone; it is day. I have fed the cat, who had been prancing before my window, staring at me with special curiosity and hunger. The day looks clear.

I could not help laughing at you on the phone, you sounded so angry, like a Shakespearean comic character of exaggeration . . . I am flying back the twenty-fourth. I have torn up three dedications for Ross and will do a fourth today. They were all dull and meaningless— and pompous.

I feel like a vinter who has treaded the grapes underfoot so repeatedly that there is no fresh juice left to make new wine of. We three took a long drive today to Clear Lake, the largest natural lake in the state, about seventy miles distant, and very beautiful in its long, elaborate curves among the hills of the landscape where God placed it, for once. We surprised a herd of wild deer, the first I have seen this time—so graceful, foolish. Then in one of the residential sections of the town above, Hildegarde gave a sudden shout of "Stop. I never saw an oak leaf like that before." She leapt from the car to pluck one from the tree overhead, consulted her botany book in her hand, and read aloud that there was ONE example of this species in the State of California, at *Clear Lake*, and she had spotted it driving by. It was a miraculous identification. She gathered many acorns to plant here on her property, with Eric cheering her on.

They are a wondrous team to drive with. They see *everything* with identical and identifying eyes, and he is a wonderful character, never dull, always scholarly and kind and patient. There was little traffic on the road, so the trip was highly enjoyable.

I just asked Eric the name of the oak tree Hildegarde discovered at Clear Lake. It is called the Oracle Oak, perhaps so named by the Indians who used it ceremoniously. There is a certain red-barked tree called the *Madrone*, of which one ancient specimen is so gigantic, not far from here, that the Indians called it the Council Tree and met beneath it to hold their tribal councils. It is the largest of its species in the state, and must date before the arrival of the white man in this region. (My God, but *I shall be glad to be in your flat* with you again, *alone.*)

I have read three times the complete material on Scott Fitzgerald in the small Kazin-edited pocket book, of all the obits, etc., on the poor man, a genius in his way at least twice, in *The Great Gatsby* and in *The Crack-Up*—the whole juvenile hedonist frame of *Tender Is the Night* and his short stories are so little nourishing that to read them is like sucking candy by the hour. . . .

––––––

Janet returned to New York on February 24. She looked rested and felt fine. On March 13, we celebrated her eighty years with a grand party at which Eustace Tilley played a prominent role; he was reproduced to perfection on her birthday cake. Janet had not changed much with time. She looked almost the same as she had at our first meeting, thirty-two years ago—perhaps a bit more rugged, the lines more pronounced, but her expression had not been cruelly altered by age. Her hair had always been silvery white; her eyes, despite her complaints, still had that penetrating, observant, reflective look so characteristic of her. Her smile did seem mellower and she was a bit heavier, but her figure, in her smart French suits, had retained its so-often-admired elegance.

She was glad to be here. And this year she would receive much praise for the upcoming new collection of her writings, *Paris Was Yesterday*. The date of publication had been set for Bastille Day, July 14, but by then Janet was back at work.

"Write, write, write, that's what I wanted to do; that's always what I wanted to do," she told the reporters who interviewed her. She had been moving from cocktails to dinner parties, going to the opera, seeing a musical or two, listening to jazz bands, her favorite music. In between, she managed to appear on radio and TV, which she really disliked. "I think it is drivel, a waste of time and brain. It is merely a way to entertain people who don't buy books, so far as I am concerned!!!" But she was so good at it—witty, informative, erudite, a delight to listen to—that Dick Cavett once more asked her to appear on his program that spring. She was a born actress and she enjoyed it thoroughly.

Personally, I tried to anticipate her wishes, to make her feel at home, welcome and beloved. I cherished her long visits. I began to be accustomed to them, and so I missed her even more when she left to go back to her favorite city—Paris.

She was barely back when Mike Wallace and his crew descended on her to film a segment of a "60 Minutes" TV program on Paris in the twenties, with Janet as commentator. That fifteen-minute documentary was part of a special series called *The Twentieth Century*.

[June 29, 1972]

My beloved Natalia,

I have worked all day every day since I arrived Monday night. Tuesday, Wallace arrived at my room at nine-thirty a.m. He gave me an interview of more psychological import for his own curiosities than of factual questions. We struck it off together like a pair of lighted pinwheels, both whirling with strength and pleasure. At one-thirty the crew of one British cameraman, Wallace, an elderly English light expert, a French camera assistant, Christine Ockrent, who is a handsome Polish girl assistant and secretary, and I all went to the Louis XIV restaurant, where arrangements had been made for filming me and Wallace in conversation all afternoon until six p.m. I had lunched lightly (fish), had had ONE Scotch highball, one glass of white wine.

We all separated at six; Wallace started for Orly and caught a plane
for New York with his crew, except for Christine, who lives in Paris
mostly, I think. She sent me with Wallace's compliments a *huge*
bouquet of snapdragon flowers: "With our compliments for your
splendid performance." She is a fine young serious woman, good
looking and in no way theatrical or cinematographic. Wallace's crew
all work like *perfect* professionals.

[July 7, 1972]

My dearest darling,

The writer Hugh Ford, who has compiled the volume for Macmillan on the private publishers of their own writings* here in the
post-*Ulysses* epoch, returned back to New Jersey two days ago, after
I had worked with him for three days, since I must do its brief introduction. To begin with, I polished up his brief manuscript a little to
make it more tempting to read. He left with a most touching note of
gratitude to me and an exquisite silk scarf, fortunately small and only
for the throat, of orange, blue and white, as a gift—a highly civilized
man. . . .

I talked of you so much, he felt he knew you, he told me. Then
yesterday I gave an interview to an American journalist preparing a
book on "writers of communications," a large project and he really
drained me. So today I did *not* start my Preface for Ford's little book;
it has to be very good. It is the last contribution I have to make to
that epoch. I have it all in my head but was too fatigued to start
pulling it out onto paper, in words. Tomorrow I shall write the first
paragraph for which I have a very good opening idea.

It is chilly here, but the sunset evenings are lovely, of pale colors
in the Paris sky over the Ritz garden and flushing the final sunset
around the Eiffel Tower, dominant in my window view. I am glad:
it is cheerful during the night when I miss you, if possible, more
than the days. I am *glad* your poor toe has recovered, glad you bought
opera tickets for October. . . .

I take my pills and have eaten my light lunch of tomatoes with
olive oil and a small slice of ham at four p.m. and shall have an ice

* Hugh Ford's *Published in Paris: American and British Writers, Printers,
and Publishers in Paris, 1920–1939,* published by Macmillan in 1975, is the
story of the small presses in Paris.

cream at the bar downstairs at nine. I have not once mixed wine and whiskey at night (or noon). I have been most obedient.

A dull letter, but as alive as my heart is, *for you*—I shall send you a post card tomorrow.

Goodnight, my dearest treasure.

[July 12, 1972]

My darling,

I enclose the Medicare sheet signed by Dr. Stock. Thank you for preparing it so I knew what to do, *and* to omit. Illness and medicines are invariably as costly as champagne and gaiety at a party. Both are portions of life and I have had little of the melancholy costs of illness in my existence till now, so I can still count myself lucky. My champagne bill has not been high either, alas. I suppose my tobacco bill has been highest of any, alas!

The preface for Hugh Ford will be brief, and I shall be paid for it. I asked him last week before he flew to Scranton University where he teaches. What he has written for Macmillan is a small book on the private publishers that followed on *Ulysses* because they were all authors who could not get their books published by regular publishers, so were forced to publish for themselves, all being ambitious writers. How odd a wind so-called fame is, and who can guess how long it will blow when it suddenly starts?

That was an odd inquiry about identifying me as a Paris reporter on that talk program. You were right; only TV programs make an American hum identifiable. I must go out and try to eat something. *I take my pills conscientiously.* . . .

[July 12, 1972]

Dearest darling,

Your generous enthusiastic cable came this morning at breakfast, announcing the *New York Times Book Review* to come, the *Washington Post* ditto which I have just seen and what *fantastic* photos of me, so true to life, so caricatural and so frighteningly expressive. I look like an agreeable but unreliable lunatic! Tonight I am going to see the film Virgil (and I, only a little) made at Bilignin where Gertrude Stein and Alice summered during the war until ejected with kind words by one French army family to whom the place belonged and who wanted Alice *out* and themselves back in their own home. It will be the second time I see it. Ned [Rorem] has not seen it at all and will be furious that I hardly speak in it—bowing to Virgil's vigor in relating all about *Four Saints in 3 Acts.*

Weather very uncertain here, threatened rain each day and sometimes arriving, *hard,* for a half-hour. I take my pills regularly and sleep well and eat only at lunch, not at night (or very slightly).

The interview in the *Washington Post* by my old friend Benjamin Bradlee was excellent, I thought. Never have I known such populous popularity! So much of it due to you and your choosing of talk shows on TV. . . .

[August 11, 1972]

My darling,

Well, the film work was finished today, just before noon. This is sooner than I expected from the way they talked yesterday, but it may be that this afternoon their British photographer will get some of the shots in Paris they tried for yesterday, but the weather was murky and it rained a little. They act like gypsies, the most amazing disregard for throwing money around. Bill McClure spent nearly a whole day hunting an old-fashioned open auto from which they could photograph Paris spots, with a recording machine stuck on behind me, as I sat there. None of this worked because he could not find the old-fashioned open touring car. It seems London is full of them; they thought Paris would be, too. So there was all yesterday afternoon *wasted* (except I took the sound man to my room where he played me my tapes which are *excellent,* amusing, informative and well-spoken). At least I got something done.

McClure even talks of returning to Paris in September to take more pictures of places I mention. Why he has not taken them this week is a mystery to me. . . .

They tired me yesterday; I had to go into the new Opéra subway station. I thought I would never get up those moving staircases. Then today we began at nine-thirty, rather early. I am more exigeant than they are about the job and the scheduled events, but that is because I am an amateur!! My "talks" interested me to listen to; they are really interesting reports of the changes in Paris, some of them quite dramatic, especially the old market where we used to go to eat and dance while the vegetables were being laid in rows on the pavement.

It was picturesque with the little shops all around. It has ALL BEEN
TORN OUT!! Nothing but a barren *hole* remains. I could not believe
my eyes and said so. I said only in Germany where whole sections of a
street had been bombed to dust in the war had I ever seen such total
destruction of a site. . . .

I don't know if I told you what I shall do for my first Paris Letter:
it will be all on Colombey-les-Deux-Eglises where de Gaulle lived (and
died) and it has turned into a *pilgrimage center*, with a huge croix de
Lorraine, visible for a mile it is so tall. I will motor down there with
Josette to help me, taking extra notes and picking up oddments to
report on. I am enthusiastic about the idea of doing this piece, because
it has not been written about in New York. It is just what de Gaulle
did NOT want to happen there. In his wisdom and cynicism, he
seemed to have feared it in advance. Shops are full of little china
statues of him, ashtrays with his face on them, cigarette boxes with
his 18th of June speech printed on the lid—every ceramic horror of
hagiography, as at Lourdes. Don't talk of it, please, or somebody else
will steal the idea!! . . . .

My summer plans had been hectic that year. Bill had been living
in Italy for some time and was having his children over for the
summer months. I joined them in August, in Castellina in Chianti,
where we stayed in a delightful old Tuscan villa among the delicate,
picturesque hills and vineyards of the Sienese countryside. There my
nine-year-old grandson Billy got acquainted with Sambuca Romana,
a sweet liqueur served with coffee beans that became his nightcap.
"Only the beans," he assured me, though one evening I thought some
liqueur must have found its way down his little throat, as he wavered
slightly when bending for his goodnight kiss.

I enjoyed the children, now nine, thirteen, and sixteen years old,
and watched them take in the sights—the museums, the churches,
the cities themselves. It was the first time they could really appreciate
what they were seeing in Italy.

After the children had left, I went to visit a very dear friend in
Provence, and then on to Milan. There was no question of meeting
Janet this time; we were each too busy with our own affairs. I had
barely returned to New York when a letter from her friend Noël gave
me bad news. Janet was back in the American Hospital with an infection of some sort. Then came her own letter.

[September 24, 1972]

Darling one,

At last I have a private moment to speak to you. Illness takes so much time with this pill to be swallowed or that potion to be added to normal liquid. I feel much, much better than when I arrived here on Thursday. I felt so peculiar as to be crazy and this alarmed me and frightened me. I thought I was going mad; in fact, I was a little off my right mind and only mild talk was all I could stand or understand. I had no way of knowing I was ill with an infection and thank God my doctor ordered a general series of tests that localized the trouble. My general health has improved, also my memory, and my common sense, at first badly affected. I am not at my best when ill, my beloved! My memory was affected; I could not remember what I had been talking about. As for trying to collect ideas for *The New Yorker* piece on Colombey, it was impossible.

I have no appetite, can eat pasta and melon and boiled eggs with home-made mayonnaise, but meat disgusts me. Noël is an angel and takes perfect care of me medically and at table for food, but I am not rational. It is hard for me to read anything. I don't see the sense in this last *New Yorker* piece on early plant life we are now publishing. I thought Bill's Rome Letter was quite good, but rather dull, but so is everything in the magazine except the violent talk pieces against the American stupidity in killing the Vietnamese to ward off the Russians.

Today has been a lovely sunny autumn day with the last flowers of the summer still holding their pink of roses or scarlet of other blossoms. The three days with the kind nurse they gave me to look after me at night almost drove me crazy. Josette Lazar came to lunch today here. She makes sense and that helped. Also, the suicide of Montherlant, the philosopher, gave a special intellectual finality to the editorial page, devoted to his death alone. It is only ten p.m., but I must go to bed. I am tired.

Oh, I miss you like *breath*, my darling one; please don't stop loving me. I am glad Cheryl [Crawford] had a nice birthday party—I hope I don't live forever.

My arms embrace you with tenderness and love. Yours till the last breath.

———

Janet was at Orgeval, where she remained all that fall to recoup her strength, when my letter arrived announcing a reception in her honor to be given by the French consul-general and his wife in New York, on November 14.

On October 13, she wrote:

"That our book (yours and mine and Irving's!) is selling at around seventh or eighth on the first-place list is already astonishing. There are no copies for sale in Paris at any bookshop. . . . I hope Irving is happy with the success of his book, only in part mine. When I read in *Time* magazine of the several *million* dollars that will accrue to the book of memoirs and photographs of Tallulah Bankhead, I realize that I am only a small scribbler!"

Her health restored, Janet announced her arrival by November 13.

Noël added a few lines to say that all was in order for the great departure, that Janet's health was "solid," and that she was bringing the doctor's report and X-rays with her. They were flying together to New York, Noël on her way to visit her own sister in California.

I met both of them at the airport and took Janet home with me. I held her in my arms for a while, as if to transmit to her some of my energy. She looked frail but happy, as if she had reached a haven.

The house was warm, all lit up to receive her. Bouquets of flowers were spread around from friends; a bottle of champagne was ready to toast her arrival.

Janet came home to celebrations and honors. In fact, by December, when Noël Murphy stopped for forty-eight hours in New York, she found that not one but two women had been honored by a foreign government: at the reception by the French consul-general, Henri Claudel, on November 28, Janet had received the highest honor a civilian could earn in France; she was made Grand Maître de l'Ordre National de la Légion d'Honneur by the President of the French Republic, one grade higher than the Legion of Honor she had already been awarded. I received the decoration of Cavaliere dell'Ordine al Merito della Repubblica Italiana, bestowed on me by the President of the Italian Republic. Both decrees were signed in December 1972.

We congratulated each other. Such recognition, especially for me, was unexpected. We felt proud and pleased. All in all, it was a good ending to the year 1972.

1973

Janet stayed in New York all winter and into the spring; we left together for Europe on June 4. Noël met her at the airport in Paris and took her to Orgeval. I planned to meet her again on June 29, in London, for the publication of the English edition of *Paris Was Yesterday*. At the insistence of her publisher, she was to appear on television and be available for a week of interviews. After I had left her in safe hands, I proceeded to Milan and Rome.

Anna Magnani was in town when I called her, which I always did on arrival. By this time of year she was usually at her place at Circeo, a few miles from Sperlonga, but at the moment she was finishing the last episode of a series of films for television, and I found her in Rome.

"Come to Circeo," she said, when I called her. "Here I'm working all day. At night I am *kaput*. I'll be through in a week or so; call me then." But we were unable to get together. The film took longer than expected and I had to leave for Milan. When I called her to say good-bye, she said: "Give my love to Tennessee [Williams]; tell him I owe him a play on Broadway." Anna had many offers, but accepted none. Only to Tennessee had she promised that some day she would do a play of his on the American stage. But she was too afraid to try it. "If you make a mistake on a film, it doesn't matter; you can stop and do the scene over again—but on stage?" she would say, when the topic came up.

I was sorry not to have seen her. "*Ciao, ciao,* come back soon," she said.

In the early spring, Picasso died. In the fall, another old friend of Janet's from the twenties in Paris, Margaret Anderson, died in the south of France. Janet's obituary of Picasso was published by *The New Yorker* in April 1973. Often, when talking about the past, Janet remembered episodes that she would recount with her usual wit and perception. It made her company a continuing delight.

She had never met Picasso during the years she used to see him, night after night, sitting with his Spanish friends at the Café Flore, on the Left Bank—a regular meeting place for writers and artists.

"One of the things that marked one's pleasure," said Janet, "was that you found the place you liked and you turned up there once a day, after dinner, for an extra coffee, or an extra brandy." Janet sat there every night and stared at Picasso, "fascinated by his mobile face, his watchful eyes," but never spoke to him. A photographer friend, who was driving to Picasso's villa on the coast, in the south of France, asked her to go along with him. She accepted, on the understanding that she would not get out of her seat. But after they had arrived, on learning that she was in the car outside, Picasso came out and invited her in. "You!" he shouted, recognizing her. "Why didn't you speak to me at the Flore? No one spoke to me then!" And he embraced her. "You don't look older," he added, looking her over. "You and I, we don't get older, we get riper! Tell me, do you still love love?" And when Janet answered, "I do," he exclaimed, "We are great ones for that, you and I! Isn't love the greatest refreshment of life?"

In remembering Picasso, Janet wrote: "Pablo Picasso was born and died a phenomenon. 'What is a painter?' he once asked, in front of others, while talking to himself. Having asked his question, he then answered it: 'He is someone who founds his art collection by painting it himself.'"

Janet also recalled an episode in the friendship between the painter and Gertrude Stein. It had to do with a small still-life, "The Apples," by Cézanne, which she had sold, leaving a void on her wall. Every time she looked at the space where it had hung, she complained about its absence. Finally, one day, Picasso lost his patience: "I'll paint you one like it!" he exclaimed, and did so, thus shutting Miss Stein up permanently.

Our stay in London turned out to be successful and pleasant. We were both very fond of London and had many friends there. Dotty and John Bainbridge of *The New Yorker* took us in hand and made our stay cheerful and delightful. When I arrived, Janet had almost completed her publicity stint, so we could enjoy the London season then in full swing. The Londoners were in the city, visitors abounded, and, with Irving and Mike, we made a lively foursome around town.

Janet stood up well under the ordeal of publicity and all the festivities. The London reception of *Paris Was Yesterday* had given her morale a boost; it had been low recently because of her difficulty in gathering material for her Letters while living in the country. Yet both Noël and I had been worried about her being alone in a hotel, eating at irregular hours, forgetting her medicines, trying to get around town in her casual way. So, for the time being, she returned to Orgeval and I could leave with confidence, knowing that Noël would watch over her, even go to Paris with her if need be.

When I returned to New York, the war in Vietnam had come to an end. It had taken twelve years to get out of that quagmire! But we were now in the middle of the Watergate investigation, the disgraceful, scandalous event that justified the distrust I had had of Nixon ever since the shameful Joe McCarthy years. My outbursts against Nixon had sometimes amused Janet. They were too theatrical, she said, but the degrading spectacle of the goings-on inside the White House and the revelation of the tapes were too upsetting. Mary McCarthy told her that *The Observer* magazine had commissioned her to write the cover-up story. "Well, she wins! She beats me now, as I used to beat her; that's all. And I must face the truth . . ." she wrote.

In August, Janet mentioned plans to come to New York by the end of September. The house at Orgeval needed major repairs and would not be habitable. She would wait for my return from Frankfurt at Hildegarde's, where Noël, who was visiting her sister near San Francisco, could take her.

To cheer Janet up, I suggested that we could take a cruise during the holidays. The blue, calm sea, the small islands of the Caribbean, with their green hills, tropical vegetation, flowers and spices, might divert her. She had always been so keen on nature, so sensitive to its beauty and variety. She responded enthusiastically, even though she said she was a bad sailor.

"Yes, the Christmas voyage sounds delightful, with isolation and I hope calm seas, as I am a poor sailor, who wisely lives on Dramamine once the captain waves me aboard. To see new islands sounds like magic . . ." she wrote, approvingly.

On September 3, Janet wrote from Orgeval:

"The garden is a miracle of mixed colors of all kinds, with some huge bright-red begonias with multiple flowers of solid shape and huge French pale lemon marigolds like pincushions. I am tired of seeing people; we had had lunch guests, and I have had enough of their appetite for good food and chatter. I have just raided the Vichy bottle in the ice chest. How good icy, clean water tastes. . . . I didn't think my Chinese art piece was super—good, yes, but not gleaming! I thought it a dull show, better to read about than to look at. The Flying Horse is fine, but very sentimental; his popularity will be sickening to us all in a year or so. He is too handsome. There was nothing in the Chinese art that took my breath away into eternity, like the early Greek things. I have been reading *The Other de Gaulle* by Mauriac: *very* good, and also not monotonous because de Gaulle himself is so lively, so filled with his own rebellion even against himself, let alone against the French. . . . The boat trip entrances me. I look forward to it . . . *Je t'aime pour toujours.*"

Janet had to remain in Calistoga longer than expected, because I couldn't get back to New York before the middle of October.

At the end of the Frankfurt Book Fair, I flew to Rome. I had never regretted anything more than not having seen Anna Magnani in June. It had been the last chance I had had to see her alive. She had been struck down suddenly by a mortal illness and died on September 28. She had just finished the last episode of the film series "1870" and died the very day it was being telecast all over Italy! A TV had been brought to her hospital room for her to see it, but she expired at six p.m., just as her dramatic face and talent was gracing screens all over the country.

I couldn't be in Rome in time for the funeral, which was attended by thousands of people, who came from all over the city and from every walk of life. The crowd overflowed from the church of the Minerva down the steps into the square and the side streets. Many people wept and, when the casket was raised high over their heads as it was carried out of the church, the mourners burst into loud, spontaneous applause. It was a last tribute to a great star, to a woman they thought of as their friend and who had been my friend—Nannarella.

I wanted to say my good-bye to her, too. I went to pay my respects at the Rossellini family tomb in the Campo Verano. where her ornate casket lay, in the small, round chapel through whose iron gates I could read her name in bold, golden letters. It seemed right to me that she would some day rest beside her Roberto, who had been with her through to the very end, and who would follow her a few years later.

In the silence around me I could hear her voice, the many voices of her many characters, but, above all, I could hear the Anna I knew—at work and at play, with her sudden rich laughter, her bursts of anger, all the emotions she expressed that reflected her suffering and her joys, her deepest feelings. I could hear her husky voice, her songs, her picturesque Roman slang. Memories tumbled over one another. A thousand Annas made themselves heard in that silence, none more clearly than in the lacerating scream at the end of *Rome—Open City*. That was the Anna of the drama, as well as of her real life.

I walked slowly through the aisle of cypresses in a Rome that seemed empty of its soul without her.

When I returned to New York, Janet was in California. A letter begun October 18 and left unfinished on October 25 was the last one I received before she rejoined me in New York.

[October 25, 1973]

My darling,

You phoned me yesterday from New York, so already the ocean is between us. I shall fly over in a couple of weeks. I'll give you the date as soon as I have a flight confirmation. The Kitty is weaving around my feet on the floor and demanding that I pet her, so I must.

This has been a delightful familial visit here with my darling Hildegarde and darling Eric, one of the gentlest of men who never says anything foolish and often says what is wise and is an *artist* in his engravings. Hildegarde is a fine cook and I have perhaps gained a few pounds, certainly not lost any while eating her fare, and the talk is always refined and scholarly, especially from Hildegarde.

———

We did not go on a cruise after all. We decided to spend the holidays in California, with my family. Bill and Doris had been living apart, and the children were unhappy. I had come back from abroad with a very bad cold, tired out by the Book Fair in a Frankfurt drenched by rain, and emotionally upset.

The trip to California turned out badly. In the middle of the holidays, I suddenly fell quite ill. Janet, who was with me, immediately and quickwittedly summoned help in the form of a couple of giant firemen, who arrived in no time in their red uniforms and who entranced Janet with their expert attentions. They gave me oxygen and took me immediately to a hospital, leaving her alone on New Year's Day at our motel on the Malibu coast, until Doris arrived. Bill found me later in the hospital emergency room, coughing my life away, or so it seemed at the time, and scaring everybody. Whenever Janet recalled that famous day—a lovely, sunny, mild winter day, which we had spent looking at the surf riders—she couldn't imagine what had happened. Neither could I. I found myself covered with blood and I couldn't stop coughing. What everyone thought, including the doctors, was that I had been struck by a terminal illness; it turned out to be only a case of some ruptured blood vessels in my lungs caused by an infection. I recovered fairly quickly and we moved to the Beverly Wilshire Hotel for my convalescence, where we lived in luxury until our return to New York at the end of January 1974.

1974

Janet had been a wonderful companion and a great solace during my convalescence. She astonished me by how well she had handled herself in the emergency, and I was moved by her devotion, surprised at her patience. She never once complained about being stuck in Beverly Hills, a place she did not care for, despite the balmy weather and our comfortable circumstances. I became the center of attention, and reveled in it.

At the end of January, we returned—I fully recovered and both of us well rested. After the calm rhythms of California life, New York seemed even more hectic.

Janet wrote several excellent pieces, long articles, while in New York, which kept her busy and happy. She had a studio equipped with a desk full of drawers for her clippings, where she could work undisturbed. In the evening, intimate friends came by for drinks or dinner. Irving Drutman always brought along his cookies or an apple pie, which were much appreciated. Janet was, as usual, stimulated by good company and witty conversation.

The Watergate scandal kept us glued to the news. If it hadn't had to do with the President of the United States and his entourage, it would have been like reading a cheap mystery story. As it turned out, the spectacle was disgraceful, to the presidency and the country. In

August, Nixon was threatened with impeachment and resigned, the first president in the history of the Republic to do so. At least the people were vindicated, though a great many of them had voted for him.

Janet had been in good form all through the winter; her angina had been kept in check. In the spring, she was ready to go back. She left in June with the David Schoenbruns and went directly to Orgeval. I followed later.

She had kept quite busy during those winter months, writing a memoir of Margaret Anderson, who had died in the south of France in the autumn of 1973. "Her demise," wrote Janet in the opening paragraph of "A Life on a Cloud: Margaret Anderson" (published by *The New Yorker* in June 1974), "removed the last standing figure from the small early circle of amateur American publishers—oddly enough, all female—whose avant-garde output a half century ago unexpectedly became a new kind of important international literature. Her most remarkable labor was the serialization—over three years, in the famous vanguard magazine *The Little Review*, which she had founded in 1914—of James Joyce's "Ulysses," that masterpiece of verbal shock and emotional repletion which slowly turned into what it immutably remains today: a literary classic and the guidepost marking the new territory of the twentieth-century English-language novel."

It was during this period that her first effort at a novel, *The Cubical City*, was reprinted as part of The Lost American Fiction series, edited by Matthew Bruccoli for the Southern Illinois University Press. It had been originally published by Putnam in 1926. For the new edition, she wrote an afterword which began:

"It was on my fifth birthday that I stated I wanted to be a writer when I grew up. It was my mother who in a semihumorous adult joke had asked me at the breakfast table, with its disorder of my various modest birthday gifts and their discarded gay paper wrappings, what my choice of a future profession was going to be—'to assure for me an interesting fairly prosperous adult life.' Apparently my answer to my mother was immediate, unequivocal, and surprising, even to me. I said that when I grew up I was going to write books. 'You are going to be an author, darling,' my mother cried with pride. 'Do you know how to spell it?' I made a bad job of it, leaving out the *u*, the diphthong being beyond me. . . ." Writing fiction was not her gift, she said, but writing is. "For a writer of stature, the great need is to have been born gifted. Talent is the supreme surprise furnished by nature. . . . It is the richest of all possessions. . . ."

To celebrate its publication, I gave a smashing party at Rizzoli.

[August 13, 1974]

My darling,

Thank you for phoning—almost impossible to get New York here from Orgeval. Am air mailing today my only Paris Letter this week, featuring Françoise Giroud and Giscard. It is pretty good, but was exhausting to do; Shawn will use and like it, I am sure.

The weather is superb. The garden is so full of fresh peas and beans we cannot eat them all. Both Noël and Libouché in good health; the roses and flowers in the garden are like prizes. Paris is more expensive than ever seen before. Hamburgers at butcher at $1.00 per pound, and a good hotel (*not* the Ritz) room is $90 a day. I shall be ready to return to New York with you after little Natalia's visit there, in late October.

The big Cézanne exhibition here will give me material for Cézanne profile which Shawn wants, and I will do it in the autumn in New York with you as opener of work. Thank God I can still write, so am not yet desperate. Giroud as new minister of feminine affairs is most important Paris figure. . . .

Noël is kindness itself to me, never cross. I miss you each day, my treasure—each day, each night—

Thine forever.

[August 22, 1974]

My darling,

. . . I sent a Paris Letter off to Shawn by air mail yesterday and hope he likes it. I had it copied on a typewriter by a nice girl saleswoman at the Ritz. I cannot type decently anymore and so pay her to type it for me.

My physical competencies have dwindled sadly this year. I doubt if I will try to write another Paris Letter. The news is scant and of nearly no interest. My health is very good. I am looking forward to the Cézanne profile that Shawn has asked for, and I shall write it in New York. I've read nothing very good in *The New Yorker* of late, nor in any other magazine either.

With a sigh of relief, the French feel Nixon is as good as buried now. However, there was one strange lachrymose Nixon piece in the *Manchester Guardian*. Rockefeller is an experienced man, and people trust him as the new Vice-President.

Noël's flowers are still blooming gorgeously, the red begonias are superb and the garden of mixed blooms is like a jewel case of mixed jewels. Nature is the best artist a home can have out of doors.

I have a new Rex Stout mystery story to read which will be fun. Technically he is always the best.

Send me another sweet note, my darling one. I miss you *more than you can believe*.

Send me a note, my beloved one, telling me you miss me, too.

[September 17, 1974]

My darlingest,

Another letter from you and thank you and thank God, too, came yesterday. You will be here Friday, October 4, then out here at Orgeval to lunch on Sunday the sixth of October. My joy will be unconfined. We (you and I) will put up at the Ritz till we leave for New York on TWA on Monday, October 7th, leaving the airport at twelve noon. Then we will be at peace again with Audrey. I hope my brain and memory work better than they do now. . . .

The weather has been fine, which is a blessing that refreshed all the French. I am to do an interview with Françoise Giroud, I suppose on the air, and hope I am equal to her brains and intelligence, but am worried in advance as I have been living in a rural distant manner.

Noël has been of a patience and kindness that cannot be exaggerated. I shall be relieved to be back in New York again and shall normalize myself at the *New Yorker* office. I sleep rather badly but that will regularize itself with you at my side.

. . . Today I am wearing the plaid trousers and yellow jacket you gave me and feel protected by your gift. You must have had a fine July 4th at Fire Island. Irving's post card was very welcome!

The Cézanne profile is beginning to take a shape in my imagination, but will demand work. I shall be glad to work again, my darling—glad to live in your fine apartment among your things. Hildegarde sent me a darling photo of herself standing by the new yellow car I gave her, both looking handsome.

I must give this letter to Libouché to mail, as she is going down to the village.

I am less dull than I seem in this letter!! But I am not much stimulated here.

With my heart at your feet, my darling love. . . .

We had barely returned to New York when a request came from CBC-TV of Toronto to film an interview with Janet for use in a series called "Gallery." A small crew, headed by the director Sam Levene, would film the interview in our flat in New York and shoot various sections of Paris on location. Sam Levene came to New York, met Janet, who agreed to do the program, and the date was set up for the end of October. It took three days of work. The apartment was turned into a studio, and Janet held forth brilliantly. I had asked Irving, who knew the material well, to be there to help Janet reminisce and to supply her, once in a while, with a light Scotch. I managed to come home early and all went smoothly.

The documentary, entitled "Paris Letter," was ready to be shown on March 13, 1975, as part of a surprise party on Janet's eighty-third birthday. She had no idea what she was going to see when we all marched into the Rizzoli preview theater that day, and she was utterly astonished to see so many familiar faces, friends from all over. Brendan Gill opened the proceedings with a gay and moving speech; Janet was applauded and the film began. When she appeared on the screen, Janet looked at herself with utter surprise. As the *bateaux mouches* sailed down the Seine past Notre Dame, and her wonderful voice, with its clear, elegant diction, described her Paris, over a Ravel score, there were very few dry eyes in the audience. There was an ovation at the end.

1975

Our correspondence was interrupted by the presence of Janet in New York and resumed in May, when we went abroad together—Janet to Orgeval and I to Italy, with a stopover at a health spa in Switzerland.

In February, a small crew of filmmakers—a cameraman, a sound man, producer-director Richard Moore—took over our apartment for another film documentary on Janet. This time, not only on the twenties and the famous people Janet had known, but also on the role of the writer as artist and journalist.

The film was part of a PBS/Channel Thirteen series in ten episodes on the life and work of contemporary American writers entitled *The Originals: The Writer in America.*

Again I summoned Irving Drutman to assist with a ready cigarette and a Scotch. Janet was a born actress, a first-class performer, completely at ease in front of the camera. I didn't have to worry on that score, but she did need to relax and to refresh her memory occasionally. Irving was just ideal for that. The shooting went smoothly and well. The crew had been so attentive and adroit, and Richard Moore was so captivated and amused by Janet that, after screening the film, he wrote to tell her how good it was, especially the last few days of shooting; he only regretted not having gotten her harmonica concert on film. The series opened with Janet Flanner and closed with Eudora Welty; it has been shown several times on TV since then.

On February 25, *The New Yorker* celebrated its fiftieth anniversary with a grand party in the ballroom of the Plaza hotel. Everyone connected with the magazine was there, from the earliest backer to the youngest administrator, all celebrating their magazine in full-dress regalia. Even William Shawn, the editor, put in an appearance, though he came late and remained almost hidden in an outer room. Janet, who always enjoyed parties, had the time of her life and was made a fuss over.

Her colleagues, in turn, threw a party for her at the Century Club during this period, and my diary lists numerous social engagements that took us into the spring. Her health stood up fairly well under the strain, but she had to keep to her regimen, which was carefully supervised.

When I returned to my office, after having been away for a month, I began to be aware of changes, some of which at first I took for granted as being part of a normal process of evolution, with a younger generation of Rizzolis taking over the firm. New faces appeared on the scene; trusted and experienced ones vanished. Eventually, these developments would lead to the ruin of the company, but I had no way of knowing that then.

I soon realized that my own time was up. I was part of the old guard, an uncomfortable presence to the young brood, and highly critical of them. In a reorganization of the Rizzoli International Publishing Corporation, I was given the new and meaningless title of director. By the time I left in 1977, everyone of the old guard in both Milan and New York had been replaced, except for the elevator man, Jo, and a couple of old hands in distribution. A few years later the company was bankrupt, and both Bruno Tassan Din, the general director, and Angelo Rizzoli, the head of the company, were arrested, accused of having illegally exported funds abroad. It has been a tragic story of greed and power politics, which involved a once-flourishing publishing house as well.

I had no way of knowing all this at the time. I simply stood my ground and put up with much unpleasantness, as a point of honor.

In talking to Oriana Fallaci one day, after Tassan Din's first visit to New York, I remarked that I didn't trust him or like him. He had a thin, bladelike profile, with pointed vulpine features. "You don't understand power, Natalia," Fallaci said, disapprovingly. "No, I don't," I answered. "Power corrupts." Oriana liked power, and she used it.

Visiting firemen succeeded each other in New York, keeping me busy until the end of April. My great consolation and nourishment was Janet, so close and so loving. We were able to spend some time alone, to cherish each other's presence. For how many more years? June would mark the thirty-fifth year of our friendship. We celebrated it with a glass of champagne before leaving for our vacation. This year it would start earlier. I would have to get back in time for the arrival of another set of big brass in the autumn.

[May 26, 1975]

Darling,

I don't know which of us is the worse correspondent. I wrote you in Rome, but perhaps too late to catch you at Gina's, and so this goes to our dear nest in New York. I wish I were in it with you.

This has been a comfortable country exile, but not stimulating for work if a Paris Letter is to emerge. You gave little Rome news of your family, by which absence I gather the clan has been peaceful of late, which is not always the case. No news is in its way good news. That is a description of my life, empty of any activity except admiring the remains of Noël's flower garden, of which borders of yellow pansies still flourish. The summer has been chilly; Paris is more costly than we have ever known it to be, and with less entertainment than normal. Shakespeare in little theaters and without stars and with the feeling prevalent even without Shakespeare's talent noticeably present. The only event has been the strike of cigarette distributors so that purchasing them is difficult and, during the first week of the strike, impossible. Strikes seem nothing more than wind-ups to lift prices.

I find Brendan Gill's volume on *The New Yorker** is regarded as an unpopular opus by all the magazine's employees; however, the last chapter in it, written about Ross by Shawn himself, is a remarkable character analysis, the most intimate I ever read, and the most valuable as an explanation of why the magazine has had the popularity and importance that has always saved and magnified it. If by chance you happen to see the book, read that chapter. . . .

The purple wisteria flowers over the doorway of Noël's house are

* *Here at The New Yorker.*

beautiful this year. Maybe Japan is a moist island to make the blossoms there so famous. I love and miss you with real appetite for the sight of your darling face and person.

Yours forever.

[June 17, 1975]

Darling,

You phoned me yesterday from New York, so I had the pleasure of hearing your rich Italian voice in my ear, as intimate as if you spoke to me in the same room. There is no news to report because the country produces no events, which is one reason I hate coming out here. I am isolated like a vegetable in a patch of garden earth. I have read almost all of Edmund Wilson's book on his own early collegiate days and recollections. I do not agree when his editor refers to him as the "leading young American writer of talent," though talent he did have. But his reports are but little more than adolescent gossip. He mentions seeing Edna [St. Vincent] Millay and I envy him that intimacy, and I admire the energy of his appetite for experience, more penetrating and observing than any I recorded at that time of my New York life. But then, I was married, and so at sea in my disappointment in not being in love as I had been with women that I had no sense of recording any veracity of any sorts, my emotional push toward my lesbic approach to all of life being so dominant that if I did not have it so vibrant a permanent problem in my daily life, I had nothing at all to replace it. How strange that I was turned in that direction, the way the branch of a young tree is turned and twisted without pressure from anything outside of its own inclination, acting like a rope or a chain though none exists—no constraint, no pressure from any element except the shaping of my erotic emotions within me which were like an emotional nearness, constantly pressing me into the company of some woman who excited and charmed me and when her influence waned, another took her place. But it was always a woman, never a male.

I found in my papers a Kodak picture of you in a white long skirt on the back porch of the Fire Island house. It must have been taken by me, I suppose, in the first week of our new love for each other. How we burned and so publicly. I could report on each motion of our bodies. I recall them all so vividly. Poor John [Mosher] so choked at the waste of oil in the lamp that I let burn all night when we lay awake.

There was a strong rain today, but now at the pre-sunset hour the sky is clear and the horizon empty of clouds. Fortunately, the rain did not injure the roses, still in full bloom, two great displays. One of enormous pink roses with redundant petals falling on each other; the other an opulent enormous display made by a huge old rose vine that I have known for a quarter-century now, clinging to the side of the barn with a flower which emerges at first as white, but that is only a masquerade for its center soon lifts up in a mild orange color. The vine stretches over the whole side of the barn, from the roof to the ground and perhaps twenty feet across in its occupation of all free space which it has taken over the years for its territory. The vine was planted by old Mme. Chartier when she was youngish and must today be more than fifty years old, more than sixty perhaps. I can't recall what her face looked like exactly, though if I saw a photo of her I could supply her name to her body. But I have lost her face now.

I don't yet know if I can write a Paris Letter for Shawn as he requested. I seem not to have the knack of collecting salient news, as I used to. The most important feature to report on is the extreme costliness of Paris and everything in it of use to visitors. Hotels that were ranked as nice but modest seem now less nice because so costly that they have altered their personality. Prices in Paris used to be part of the pleasure of spending time there because one could afford it. Now, hotel prices have reached an extremity which demands a pencil and piece of paper for one to discover if one can stay two more days or not, probably not. High prices hurry one, somehow, and inevitably even if one can afford them. Thirty-four percent des voix recently gained in Italy were won by communists. This changes the picture as if it were now painted by a different artist.

Our maid is very nice, lives in the next village and arrives on her motorcycle, bringing asparagus from her garden. We have eaten it for two weeks daily, with pleasure. It is a present she bring us, very nice it tastes, too. Many presents are tasteless.

One of our white cats (this year's) had an odd tail when she matured. Her body is normal, short hair, but the tail is fancy, with long hair branching out on either side of it, very arbitrary and eccentric.

It is nearly ten o'clock and I am tired and I hope sleepy. I don't always sleep easily until late. Noël is shouting musically for the cats by name—Brio, Tempo (with the odd fancy tail) and Polka, who has feet like a dachshund because her feet were injured when she stepped in a trap as a kitten.

I so wish I had made you come here with me the night I arrived and shown you the garden. It is really beautiful.

Forgive my lack of letters to you. I love you with all my organs and sensibilities and mind.

———

On June 22, Noël wrote that Janet, after a long respite, had had a bad angina attack, was in great pain, and had called an ambulance to take her to the American Hospital in Neuilly. She stayed there for two days and nights, and, after tests and rest, went back home. "She is now rested, resistant, and rambunctious!" Noël wrote. "She drinks little, but is now worried enough to try and smoke less."

On June 24, Janet followed with her news:

"Two days ago, I had a rather disquieting heart attack at Noël's house and decided I should consult a doctor, did so, and phoned the American Hospital at Neuilly outside Paris, and called an ambulance here in our village to take me there with Noël going as attendant! I had phoned my Paris doctor, who arrived at eight a.m. with the hospital doctor, Dr. Peacock! I give his name, which is famous in British fiction, and both agreed I had shown good sense in hospitalizing myself. I only stayed two days and nights and took a taxi back to Orgeval. I probably will try to write a Paris Letter for Shawn; if too difficult, I'll simply cancel the idea. You can imagine how angry I will be if I cannot write that Paris Letter. It has been a rainy summer with only a fortnight of sunny weather, sufficient for Noël's roses to hang in white or red festoons on the big rose vines that decorate her house walls on the garden side. You see how limited my imagination is when I am confined to nature alone. It is lamentable that the new so-called secretary is such a cheap egotist as to be no aid to you in your work. Helen [Brann] must be as disgusted with her as you are, for both of you know what work is in your profession. Give Helen my love and say that I miss her. *I miss you constantly.* Your devoted, grateful darling of those early Fire Island summers."

"Janet is very well, only huffs and puffs," wrote Noël on July 5. "I try not to nag her, but I do raise hell over smoking," to which Janet added a few words:

"A rainy and chilly summer so far, with beautiful flowers, as if proving nature herself has been a fool. It has rained for two or three days, though not hard, so the roses were not battered to bits. Your photo of your rose vine at SPQR [the name of my Fire Island house] looks splendid; you never had such a flower display. I miss the Island very much; it will always be a special region in my memory and life."

On the nineteenth, Noël was formulating plans to take Janet to New York, when and if she could finish her Paris Letter: "Janet has suffered no angina attacks, so far." To which Janet added:

"No one is in hospital now anywhere, a great vacation and economy. No one can afford to be ill except fatally, which might be cheap! I have not yet started my Paris Letter, not out of laziness, but from too much past experience, I think. I shall start tomorrow. . . . I think of you darling. . . ."

I had planned a brief trip to Malibu to see the children and Bill at the end of July, expecting to return in time to receive Janet.

I left on August 13 and came back a week later. Shortly afterwards I developed a fever and a bad infection, apparently caught on the plane, which attacked the back retinas of both my eyes, impairing my vision. The world around me suddenly became a dark shadow; I thought I was going blind. "You could have," my eye specialist said cheerfully, after weeks of treatment, and I was terrified.

During those hours in darkness my memory went back to my school-days in Rome. In my fourth year I was assigned a classmate, awkward in her movements. She was blind, one of three blind girls in our class who came to school, accompanied by a nun. They lived in a convent. We went through two years of school together. She studied in Braille; took down lessons in Braille; even taught me Braille. She used to touch my face, my hair, to get some idea of me, she who had never seen the light since birth. I remembered too the sadness of those blind soldiers in World War I, to whom we read aloud.

It was perhaps from these early experiences that I began to hate war that robs young men of one of nature's greatest gifts—the ability to see, to look at the beautiful things around us, such as the roses of Orgeval, which were a wonder to Janet's sight.

                                                        [August 21, 1975]
Darling Natalia,

A very wet day, but invigorating because the garden flowers are in such glorious bloom. I never saw such a magnificent muddle of colors— yellow marigolds as big as apples, so big indeed that they split their stems holding them up. I am grateful to God himself for inventing flowers after he had invented vegetables to eat, of which we have beets so sweet you would think we added sugar to them. I am muddling through my Paris Letter for Shawn, principally on roses which are odd enough in their new inventions to be worth recording: one variety has petals *white* on one side but *scarlet* on the other. How can botanists breed so strange an arrangement?

We eat buttered beets and also beet greens, more delicious than spinach. We live on veal chops and hamburgers, both good country meat. Noël is an excellent cook, very tasty in her flavoring. She works hard, on her hands and knees, often scrubbing the kitchen floor. She is NOT afraid of work; Libouché has baked a couple of pies that were very tender in crust and with rhubarb as fruit, from the garden. No plums this year, a very omission of nature, so delicious when eaten with cheese as dessert. We eat what God sends and are thankful. There are hardly any pears on our trees, usually loaded with sweet, juicy little pears . . . but as our *femme de ménage* moans, "C'est pas une année à fruit," a great loss in money for the farmers here.

It has been a greater rose year than any I ever saw in this valley. The tallest pink ones in the garden are as tall as a hedge, with enormous blossoms and named Elizabeth for the Queen.

I think my friend Russell Page stole them from the royal garden outside London. All gardeners are born burglars, which is a good thing and spreads beauty. A few years ago an old British gardener invented a new breed of multicolored lupins and, if you didn't have any in your garden, you might as well have planted dandelions, which this year are a perfect plague.

France is most interested in Portugal, that spiteful little land. Whoever thought it could stir up Europe?

I hear thunder. A storm is coming up and will ruin the last of our rose blooms.

Darling, please don't use that fine-pointed pen. It writes so thin, I can't read what you say, which is a loss.

The storm is finished, without any destruction in beauty. This is a dull letter, and I am hungry for my lunch which we are having at the new small house of our friend Barbara, mistress of Clemenceau, the Tiger's grandson. She was a former drunkard and her tales of her self-redemption are fantastic, comic, also rather noble. She has a will of iron now where self-control is concerned. Her new little house is a small, quiet dream: she also knows how to work and to help others to their salvation. She is part of a new selection of friends all local to our village now. I appreciate them, different characters than any I ever knew before.

Do write me, darling, with a pen I can read!! I can hear the *femme de ménage* ironing in the kitchen with great thumps of the iron. I must give this letter to be posted today, Thursday. Best greetings from Noël and Libouché.

Yours forever.

[End of August 1975]

My darling,

What a geographical mix-up that a Spanish infection should afflict your beautiful eyes in New York! Germs, like humans, should stay where they belong and originate. Thank you for your cable, which reassured me somewhat, though your oculist doctor did not seem any too satisfied, less than Gerald [Dr. Brill] himself.

We are having the summer's end here—autumn flowers if no fruits. I shall miss those tasty little pears that grew in our trees in the valley. Noël takes minor disasters like that with spartan calm. At least we still have beans in quantity and delicious tomatoes, both of which we eat daily. The farmer's wife eats like the farmer himself, just what grows on the family earth. Already the evenings are cool and the dahlia flowers (of rare beauty and color) announce the changing season. Nature regulates us, though we think it is the stock exchange and the dollar.

Polka, my favorite cat—all have musical names; Gavotte is Noël's choice as a friend, I think—and the others all try to push into the kitchen at dusk to profit by the kitchen stove's warmth, and we are already baking some potatoes in the stove. The seasons have more meaning than when one simply buys the result.

A wonderful letter from you this morning, so full of energy and activity. You are a great, great human, my darling. I appreciate you more than I can say or show.

I finished my Paris Letter for *The New Yorker* and cabled it yesterday to Shawn. Have not had his reaction as yet, but think it will be enthusiastic. I thought it a very good letter, full of news and good writing about the flowers in our valley, mostly roses. Never did I see so many; it has been a great rose year and thus a pleasure to the eyes. Also, the wheat crop is good, which means that the delicious French bread will not go up in price this winter for the poor. The unemployment is terrible, Giscard cannot solve it as a problem; nobody in Europe can this year. There is not enough work for men's hands and brains. There is too much mechanization everywhere. Machines do the thinking and the theorizing.

Noël hung an empty white sack on a stick above the red raspberries
to keep the birds away, but it has not been effective. They swoop
down and eat their fill each day. Nothing frightens them. They act
like members of the family.

Thine.

[September 12, 1975]

My darling one,

I hope to God that your eyes are better and that you are not alarmed
by their condition. What a strange visitation—a bug from Spain in
your Manhattan eyes. I am sure Dr. Brill is taking proper care of you,
my dearest. You have such handsome eyes. It's grief to think of them
as a source of dissatisfaction for you.

I had a long gossipy letter from Irving. I have already answered it
with as much gossip as I can collect, that being what he most appre-
ciates. I cabled my Paris Letter to *The New Yorker* the day before
yesterday and hope the letter will please and satisfy Shawn. I thought
it excellent myself—frankly! Also, both Noël and I thought it was
charmingly written, so I hope Shawn agrees in part at least with our
self-satisfaction.

I tried to read Henry James's book on the Initiates, but I find it
obscure and dull, and I will remain uninitiated, which shames me. I
have not read anything that interests me for months, I fear.

It is chilly today. The autumn is approaching and it is *not* welcome.
We had great food from our garden behind the house—lettuce, red
raspberries, new potatoes which are still small and delicious when
boiled with their skins on and eaten with butter. We also have
zucchini, which Noël cooks deliciously, baked with a tomato on top
and cheese, plus red raspberries or at least as many as the birds have
left to us, the greedy pigs! For flowers we now have superb dahlias of
bright colors, which make superb bouquets. I so regret I did not bring
you in to see the garden and house on my entry from the airport. The
house is adorable and furnished with fine furniture and exquisite taste.
Noël recently purchased a really great carpet of cross-stitched squares
with alternate black squares included, a really stunning floor covering.

I have not seen any new styles for tailored suits. Lanvin has nothing
smart. Their suits might as well have been made two years ago and
look like it. I want to order a new tailleur, but have seen none I thought
new and smart. Noël says Bergdorf in New York is better than Paris
this year. If she flies out to New York, we have planned to go to some

musical comedy, you, she and I, to have a big gala evening, yes? It sounds fun.

It is really chilly today. I am wearing one of my purple sweaters to keep warm.

Send me a line, my beloved. I miss you so deeply and constantly. There is no one like you to charm and stimulate me.

Thine,
Janet

In her struggle and difficulty at starting her Paris Letter, those magnificent roses Janet so charmingly described in her last written words to me became the main subject of her piece for *The New Yorker*. It was published in the issue of September 16, 1975—her last tribute to a lifetime of work.

From then on, beginning October 10 of that year, Janet lived with me in New York. Our correspondence of thirty-five years ceased.

For the last three years of her life, Janet lived with me in New York. They were happy years, though the ravages of time were taking their toll as her memory was slowly fading. She was especially outgoing then, demonstrative and affectionate. She felt protected, cared for and beloved.

In the morning, while I would prepare breakfast, she would appear in her red robe, smiling cheerfully. She would say, hailing the day, "Good morning, darling," and sit down, looking forward to her tea and toast. Breakfast was her favorite meal. It was our most intimate meal, certainly. We would look at the papers, comment on the headlines, talk about the day ahead, as we sipped our tea. Then, as was her habit, she would sit at her desk and begin the day. As she had done all her life, she would spread the papers before her, carefully read and mark them with a large red-and-blue pencil. Some especially interesting items would be cut out or torn off the page and stored in her desk drawer, which was cluttered and messy, as always.

With her first cigarette (she smoked less now), held as usual between her third and fourth finger, and surrounded by papers, books and ashes, she would spend the morning until summoned to get dressed. Sometimes, out of the bathroom, a chorus would be heard—a deep contralto from Janet, and an alto from her Jamaican maid—singing spirituals or the Methodist hymns she was so fond of. I would then dash off to the office, confident that Janet was feeling well that day. Upon my return in the afternoon, I would find her at her desk again. "What have you been doing, darling?" I'd ask her. "Working. And you?" she would answer. "Working too," I'd say. She would smile, pleased.

A great tenderness would overwhelm me as I'd bend to kiss her. "Bravo! Let's have a cocktailino." Holding hands, we'd march together into the living room.

On a sunny day she would be convinced, with great effort, to go out for a walk; she hated it so. She eventually agreed to use a wheelchair. "My feet are too small," she would say, as an excuse for not walking.

I don't think she missed Paris. At least, if she did, she never mentioned it. She missed writing—of that, yes, I am certain by the way she went through the motions every day. Often I would find her rereading her *Paris Journals*. She would underline words or phrases she particularly liked, even making corrections in the margins. At times she would laugh heartily. "I am enjoying my own writing best of all!" she would exclaim.

Several new projects had been in the making during this period. She followed them with interest, but also with a kind of detachment. She liked the idea of a new collection of her writings, to be assembled from work other than her Letters from Paris, and including Profiles never collected before.

I had asked Irving Drutman to do the editing, as he had for *Paris Was Yesterday*. Even though he was feeling ill, he was delighted and immediately went to work. He kept at it all through what proved to be a terminal illness, and with such dedication that he finished the paste-up on his hospital bed.

Neither he nor Janet lived long enough to see the stunning volume, entitled *Janet Flanner's World*, published by Harcourt, Brace, Jovanovich in November 1979.

Janet had, of course, approved the selections. She was pleased to see that the volume included her profile of Hitler, written in 1936, the first such piece ever written about him. She recalled, with a certain irony, that when she had told *The New Yorker* that she wanted to do it, the magazine had inquired "Are you sure it is worthwhile?" Evidently *Mein Kampf* hadn't yet been taken seriously.

She was more cynical about the one-woman show entitled *Paris Was Yesterday* that playwright Paul Shyre had been working on for some time. At the first reading, given by Marian Seldes before a small invited audience, she occasionally commented loudly, as if the text were not her own. She did it again the evening it was given its first tryout onstage, at the George Street Theatre in New Brunswick, New Jersey, a year later. The occasion was the climax of a three-day conference on Women of the Twenties, held at Rutgers University. That day, April 8, was in honor of a quartet of remarkable women: Lillian Hellman, the dramatist; Kay Boyle, the novelist; Berenice Abbott, the photographer; and Janet Flanner, the journalist.

It was quite an experience, because Janet hadn't expected to see herself being impersonated by someone else—in this case by Celeste Holm, whom she had met before, when the actress came to see her in order to study her voice and personal mannerisms. Janet didn't remember any of it; she was astonished and confused. She kept asking loudly, "Is she me? Did I say that?" A great deal of diplomacy had to be used to keep her quiet. At the end, to Janet's surprise, both she and Celeste were given a standing ovation.

The show opened for a limited time at the Harold Clurman Theatre in New York, on December 20, 1979. But Janet could not be present.

The summer of 1978 was spent at Watermill, in Long Island. I had chosen the place for its proximity to Southampton, just in case. It was a very hot summer, not an easy one. Janet didn't want to meet people or be entertained. Occasionally, friends dropped in for a brief visit, adding some variety to quiet days, while I commuted to New York. She sat most of the time on the patio or in the house in the company of an unfriendly Siamese cat, reading or just staring at the flowers and the beautiful lawn. She did enjoy the drives we took at sunset. And she favored the charming old town of Sag Harbor. From its pier she would admire the sunset, look at the white sails on the bay, at the color of the sky. We both wished we could have been at our house on Fire Island, but it wouldn't have been wise, considering the frightening experience of the previous summer. Janet had to be taken off the island in the middle of the night by a Coast Guard speedboat and rushed to a hospital in Bay Shore.

Hildegarde came to visit her in July, a pleasant treat for Janet, and I went for the Fourth to see my family in California. We returned to the city after Labor Day.

Except for her angina, Janet had been feeling fairly well that early fall. She was in such good spirits that I was able to dash off to Italy on business, leaving her in the care of Maria and Audrey. Cecille Shawn, Bill Maxwell and a few others came to call, but most of the time she was alone with her books and papers.

When I came back, to my utter surprise, I found her watching baseball on television, and with some interest, too. Our Maria, who had become a fanatic for the game, had persuaded her to watch it with her. It brought back her school days, Janet said. We both laughed heartily.

That October there was going to be a concert of Ned Rorem's music at the Library of Congress in Washington, D.C. We were looking forward to it, because Ned, a long-time friend from Paris, where he had spent most of his youth studying music, had composed nine settings for chorus and orchestra based on descriptions of Paris taken from Janet's Letters. In fact, they were entitled "Letters from Paris," and dedicated to her. It was a special occasion, too, because some of Janet's earliest papers had been given to the Library of Congress. Janet was very fond of Ned; they both came from Quaker stock and admired each other. By October 29, however, it was clear that the trip to Washington would have been too tiring for her, and we didn't go.

The weather was glorious that Tuesday, the seventh of November, 1978—sunny, mild, a true Indian summer. In the early afternoon, Janet had been wheeled into the park. I joined her later and took her around the pond, where children were playing with sailboats in the mild wind. We stopped and watched them. It seemed as if every child and every older person in the city had been out in the sun that day. Soon winter would be setting in. On a side path, several youngsters were playing guitars. Children on roller skates and bicycles dashed by. Ice cream vendors were doing a good business. On our way home, around a corner, Janet noticed a bush full of red berries. We stopped and she picked a small branch.

At home, we had tea and later a light Scotch. I was in my last few days at Rizzoli, and I gossiped to entertain her. An intimate, quiet dinner crowned a delightfully pleasant day. A day almost like any other. At ten o'clock, I tucked her in bed. When I bent to kiss her good night, she held on to me for a while and, looking deep into my eyes, she murmured, "I love you, Natalia. I love you so much."

Nothing could have prepared me for the cry of pain that woke me at midnight. I found Janet in the hall, holding on to a chair and moaning. She looked terribly ill and in great pain. "I am dying, Natalia. I am dying," she whispered. I held her in my arms, "No, no, darling, no, no." I couldn't say anything else.

Events followed in frantic succession: I called the doctor, I called Maria, I called the ambulance. The police arrived, Maria arrived with Gemma, her daughter, then the ambulance. We rushed my darling Janet to the emergency room of a nearby hospital. A couple of young internists took her away. I tried to follow her. "Who are you?" asked a nurse. "A friend, the only person she has in New York . . . she lives with me," I said, pleading. "Wait in the entrance," she retorted.

A young doctor appeared. "Aneurism," she said. "We must operate, with only a ten percent chance of survival." Our doctor agreed to the operation. I had nothing to say. I was not even allowed to wait on the operating floor. I waited with Maria in an empty hall downstairs in the main entrance for interminable hours, without any information; two women alone in the silence of the night. We didn't speak. We just waited.

At daybreak, a man began to wash the floors. Then the day nurses began to appear. At six a.m. a man approached us. It was the anesthetist. "The heart failed," he announced as a matter of fact. Without further words, he handed me a bundle: pyjamas and the red robe; all that was left of my Janet.

Maria took my arm and gently pushed me out of the hospital. Around me people were rushing by. The day had begun, like any other ordinary day. But the apartment was silent.

Perhaps Janet would be arriving from Paris at any moment, I thought, through my tears. I still think so. One day she will appear at the door and say, "Darlinghissima, here I am!"

Sperlonga, June 1984

INDEX

ABOUT THE AUTHORS

JANET FLANNER was born in Indianapolis. Under the pen name Genêt she was *The New Yorker*'s Paris correspondent from shortly after the magazine's founding in 1925 until her retirement fifty years later. Her reportage on European political and cultural life set a new standard for journalism and brought her many awards, including membership in the American Institute of Arts and Letters and the French Legion of Honor. Her books include *The Cubical City*, a novel (1926); *An American in Paris* (1940); *Men and Monuments* (1957); *Paris Journal 1944–1965* (1966); which won the National Book Award; *Paris Journal 1965–1971* (1971); *Paris Was Yesterday* (1972); and *Janet Flanner's World* (1979). She died in New York in 1978.

NATALIA DANESI MURRAY was born in Rome and came to New York in the 1920s to marry an American. Her friendship with Janet Flanner began in 1940. Mrs. Murray has had a distinguished career as a broadcast journalist and in book publishing, and after the Liberation worked in Italy for the Office of War Information, which later became the U.S. Information Service. She was the American representative for two of Italy's major publishers, Mondadori and Rizzoli. At present she is consultant to the firm of Sperling & Kupfer of Milan. Mrs. Murray received the Italian Republic's Order of Merit. She lives in New York.

The Cubical City: A Novel (1926)

An American in Paris (1940)

Pétain: The Old Man of France (1944)

Men and Monuments (1957)

Paris Journal: 1944–1965 (1965)

Paris Journal: 1965–1971 (1971)

Paris Was Yesterday (1972)

London Was Yesterday (1975)

Janet Flanner's World:
Uncollected Writings, 1932–1975 (1979)